KU-531-245

The Economics of Tramp Shipping

The Economics
of Tramp Shipping

B. N. METAXAS

THE ATHLONE PRESS *of the University of London*
1971

SCHOOL OF NAVIGATION
WARSASH, NEAR SOUTHAMPTON

Published by
THE ATHLONE PRESS
UNIVERSITY OF LONDON
at 2 Gower Street London WC1

Distributed by
Tiptree Book Services Ltd, Tiptree, Essex

U.S.A.
Oxford University Press Inc
New York

© B. N. Metaxas 1971

0 485 11127 6

Made and printed in Great Britain by
WILLIAM CLOWES & SONS, LIMITED
LONDON, BECCLES AND COLCHESTER

Preface

During the last twenty years or so transport economics, including the more specialized field of maritime economics, has been developing rapidly. But such progress has taken place mainly in men's minds and such published material that has appeared can be found in the form of scattered papers and articles.

This does not deny the importance of such major works as Dr S. G. Sturmey's *British Shipping and World Competition* (1962) and Mr R. O. Goss's *Studies in Maritime Economics* (1969). Everybody would agree however, that much more needs to be done.

There is very little current literature on the present state of the tramp shipping industry. Indeed, contrary to existing realities some observers of maritime affairs take the view that tramp shipping is a declining industry. The purpose of this book is to put the record right in this respect and to apply some tools of analysis with a view to explaining the most significant economic phenomena of the industry. It is hoped that this will assist both the reader whose interests are academic, and those who are more closely involved in the working of the industry.

I am indebted to so many people in writing this book that I cannot hope to mention them all. I would like, however, specially to thank Mr G. J. Ponsonby, formerly Reader in the Economics of Transport at the London School of Economics, who has assisted me throughout. Many serious mistakes and omissions were corrected thanks to his advice and his influence has been invaluable in the final shaping of the book. I also want to express my gratitude to the Staff of the Athlone Press for their handling of a difficult manuscript.

London, December 1970   B. N. M.

Contents

List of Figures

List of Tables

Appendix

Introduction

The aim of this book is to give the reader an insight into the working of the tramp shipping industry. The first task is to describe what a tramp ship is and does and how it differs from other types of ships such as the cargo liner, the tanker, and the big bulk carrier. Certain basic measurements of cargo-carrying capacity are required for comparison between ships to be possible so there is a section on tonnage. Then the nature of the tramp freight market is discussed together with the characteristics of shipping firms engaging in this market. There is a small section on the economic effects of flag discrimination.

Firms or governments, or their agents, wishing to ship commodities are the sources of demand for the services of tramps and agreements of different kinds—voyage charter, time charter, and bareboat charter—are made with the shipping firm. The magnitude of this demand, the factors affecting it and its incremental nature, the relationship of demand to costs, and its elasticity lead on to considerations of the nature of demand in the short and long run.

Having discussed demand we turn to supply, and here the influence of other types of ships is felt. The opportunity is taken to give details of the structure of the liners' market with its conferences and methods of maintaining rates and discouraging competition from new entrants. A similar survey is made of the tanker and bulk carrier markets, together with the effects of imaginable but unpredictable factors such as technical progress. The economic effects of these both in the short and long run complete the account.

Having established the nature of these different shipping markets the book turns to the interaction between the markets which causes tramp ships to serve as cargo liners on fixed schedules, tankers to carry grains, and bulk carriers to operate on routes which had previously been the preserve of tramps.

The next chapter gives a detailed account of the cost of operation of tramp ships. Included here are many little-known facts about capital and operating costs, and depreciation, labour costs, and the relationship of these to size and scale of operation. The mention of labour costs leads on to consideration of flags of convenience and the special influence they have through labour costs, tax concessions, and freight rates.

All this forms a basis of established fact used in the remainder of the book to examine the most important economic feature of the tramp shipping industry—the wide fluctuations in freight rates. The concept of equilibrium in both the short and the long run is considered and then the nature of fluctuations examined in detail. Possible reasons are given, not least the endemic tendency on the part of shipowners to over-invest during the comparatively few but highly profitable good times.

A final chapter deals with attempts that have been suggested to organize tramp shipping through tonnage stabilization schemes so that fluctuations could be controlled. This is shown to be largely unworkable because of conflicting interests and to result in a generally higher cost to the shipper with consequently negative effects on world seaborne trade. Finally, some concluding remarks regarding the future of the industry are attempted.

Chapter 1

The Tramp Shipping Industry

1. The tramp shipping industry and its neighbours

Students of maritime economics may be attracted to the subject either because they have a purely theoretical interest in this special field of the economics of transport or because they are directly concerned with the actual problems of the shipping world and wish to know how far a study of economics can help them to understand these problems. The purpose of this book is to apply some of the tools of economic analysis to the realities of just one of the maritime industries, namely 'tramp shipping', and it is hoped that it will be useful to those whose interests are academic and those whose interests are of a more professional nature.

As a start it is necessary to define precisely what is meant by such terms as the 'tramp shipping industry', cargo liners, bulk carriers, tankers, and so on.

The merchant fleets of various maritime nations are classified into different categories or branches to which their productive units, the ships, are assigned. Thus, we have tramp ships, tankers, bulk carriers, passenger vessels, trawlers, coasters, tugboats, and so on. A similar classification of vessels is applied on a world scale if necessary.

No maritime economist would dispute the fact that these distinctions are of capital importance both from a theoretical and a practical point of view. It is encouraging to note that the shipping world has begun to become fully aware of the need to classify ships on the basis of the particular kind of transport service that they perform.[1]

---

[1] 'Passenger liners, cargo liners, bulk carriers, tankers, coasters, and so on, all have

3

It will become clear at a later stage that tramps, bulk carriers, cargo liners, and tankers are closely related types of ships so far as substitution at the margin is concerned. On the other hand it must be stressed at this point that the main productive service of each type of ship is to satisfy a different kind of demand for transport of commodities by sea. Consequently, these types of ships are productive units that belong to different markets. Briefly speaking, the position is as follows:

Demand for spot transit of bulk commodities	The tramp	The tramp freight market
Demand for regular transit	The liner	The liners' market
Demand for bulk material on regular route	The bulk carrier	The bulk carriers' market
Demand for bulk oil on regular route and controlled transit	The tanker	The tanker market

In the circumstances, it may be assumed for analytical purposes that all firms that own and operate tramp shipping tonnage constitute a separate industry.[1] Similarly—even though the 'gap' is not marked very clearly—we will assume that all firms that own and operate cargo liners constitute another industry, and so on. As already indicated, the respective markets for these industries, i.e. the tramp freight market, the liner market, the tanker market, and so on, are distinct and function under different conditions.

To put 'all your eggs in one basket' is not regarded by shipowners as a sound business policy. Thus, there are many ship-

their separate difficulties and problems and will have to be studied separately.'
Extract from a speech delivered by Sir Nicholas Cayzer after the launching of the *Clan Grant* at Greenock Dockyard on 22 December 1961 as quoted in the *Shipbuilding and Shipping Record*, 4 January 1962.

[1] 'An industry is any group of firms producing a single commodity. The correspondence of such an industry to the industries of the real world is not perhaps very close. But in some cases where a commodity [or service: B.N.M.] in the real world is bounded on all sides by a marked gap between itself and its closest substitutes, the real-world firms producing this real-world commodity will conform to the definition of an industry sufficiently closely to make the discussion of industries in this technical sense of some interest.' See *The Economics of Imperfect Competition*, p. 17, by Mrs Joan Robinson.

ping firms which, in addition to tramp shipping tonnage, own and operate at a given period of time cargo liners or bulk carriers or tankers or passenger vessels, and so on. In other words they participate in more than one market.

The rather common phenomenon of the multi-service shipping firm is an important factor so far as substitution at the margin is concerned. For example, shipping firms that own and operate, let us say, tramps, liners, and tankers, depending on market conditions may use substantial percentages of their tonnage—irrespective of the main function of the vessels concerned—as tramps or as liners or grain carriers (tankers). The management of such firms possesses the necessary 'know how' and, therefore, is sufficiently equipped to face both the technical and economic problems that may arise from the utilization of the firm's resources in each one of these 'trades'.

The importance of substitution with regard to the level of prices or freight rates will be discussed in a separate chapter. Thus, what should be stressed at this point is that the existence of the multi-service shipping firm does not alter the fact that world merchant shipping consists of several sectors or industries each performing quite different functions.

Also, shipping firms participate in the first and second-hand tonnage markets both as buyers and sellers. The demand for tonnage at a given period of time is not satisfied only by the output of the world's shipyards but also by shipping firms who are anxious or willing to sell at a price. Moreover, shipping firms constitute a basic source of supply as far as scrap-iron yards are concerned.

We have assumed that tramps, cargo liners, tankers, and bulk carriers are productive units which belong to different but closely neighbouring industries. The main differences of these units, both from an economic and a technical point of view, are as follows.

(a) *The tramp*

It may not be advisable to attempt a sharp and rigorous definition of the phrase 'tramp ship'. However, having regard to the kind of demand that this type of vessel is intended to satisfy it can be stated that:

Any vessel with a tonnage of 4000 d.w. or above which in the long run does not have a fixed itinerary and which carries mainly dry cargoes in bulk over relatively long distances and from one or more ports to one or more ports is an ocean or a deep-sea tramp.

nb

Some further comments are necessary regarding this definition:

(1) In the short run a traditional tramp ship may be employed by such charterers as for example a liner company, a government, or a big industrial firm for the purpose of carrying general cargoes on a more or less regular route. This type of employment is not different from that of the traditional cargo liner. Thus, in the short run the tramp ship can function as a cargo liner satisfying tonnage demand for regular transit. In fact this kind of demand should be considered as part of the overall demand for tramp shipping services.

(2) The lower tonnage limit indicated in the definition, that is to say, 4000 t.d.w., is based on the contemporary scene of the industry and is therefore a relative one. There do not seem to be at the present many ships below 4000 t.d.w. that are wanted to perform transoceanic voyages. Moreover, the small tramps of 4000–6000 t.d.w. that are carrying bulk cargoes over long distances are doing so at a price which is between 15 and 12 per cent higher than the one prevailing in the market for the old conventional tramp of 10 000 t.d.w. The number of small tramps below 7000 t.d.w. is presently decreasing.

There are many small tramps mostly from 1000 to 5000 t.d.w. which are trading in various regions such as the Mediterranean Sea, the Far East, the Carribean Sea, and so on. In several regions these small tramps are now trading in competition with the modern 'mini-bulk carrier' and other specialized types of ships. Price fluctuations in these local markets do not synchronize with those in the world tramp freight market.

Highly specialized fleets, such as for example ore carriers limited by capacity and construction to cargoes of ore, should not be included in the world tramp shipping fleet which is by definition a general-purpose fleet.

6

In the circumstances, the statistical data published by various institutions in the shipping world regarding national and world dry-cargo and tramp shipping fleets and which includes all dry-cargo vessels or only tramps above 100 G.R.T. or above 500 G.R.T. can hardly form a basis for estimating the actual magnitude of the world tramp shipping industry at a given period of time.

(3) With regard to the upper tonnage limit of the industry, the 36 000 t.d.w. mark seems to be realistic provided that we take into consideration the fact that both bigger bulk carriers and tankers compete in the tramp freight market from time to time. There are many vessels of bulk carrier specification in the range of 31 000–36 000 t.d.w. that are employed on voyage charter over relatively prolonged periods of time.

Technical innovations and developments in the tramp freight market, including fluctuations, affect shipping firms that own and operate small tramps as they affect those firms that own and operate modern and larger ones. For obvious reasons this book will mainly centre on the ocean tramps, that is to say, those with a cargo-carrying capacity of 8000–36 000 t.d.w., which from now on we shall call tramps. We now examine the basic differences between the tramps and the productive units that belong to the neighbouring industries.

(b) *The cargo liner*

The main function of the cargo liner is to satisfy the demand for regular transit. Thus, cargo liners are vessels with a fixed itinerary calling at predetermined ports at more or less fixed and advertised dates. Cargo liners transport mostly semi-finished or finished goods which are usually packed. They may also carry a limited number of passengers.

Since they perform in the main a different kind of transport service, cargo liners and tramps also differ with regard to their construction. For example, cargo liners are usually vessels able to develop higher speeds than the average tramp, their holds are separated into compartments suitable for the stevedoring mainly of semi-finished and finished goods and of 'sensitive cargoes', such as butter, sugar, coffee, cocoa, etc., which are usually packed in parcels or boxes. Their accommodation is larger with usually more facilities and comforts than that of the tramps.

Modern conventional cargo liners are even more 'highly specialized' ships possessing electric winches, air-conditioning systems, special tanks for the transportation of expensive oils, such as coconut oil, castor oil, and so on. On the other hand, in order to facilitate stevedoring of cargoes in bulk, such as coals, minerals, grains, sugar, salt, and so on, tramp ships are built with fewer decks and larger holds.

Cargo liners are, as a rule, more 'expensive' vessels than tramps, for their building and operating costs are usually higher. The various cargoes transported by liners belong to many shippers and not to one shipper only as in the case of tramps. The administrative apparatus of the cargo liner firm is far more extensive and complex than that of the tramp shipping firm. It does not require the establishment of only one or two offices, as in the case of tramps, but of many (or at least the appointment of trusted representatives on a permanent basis) that are located at the main ports of call.

The advent of the container ship is a significant development that will influence primarily the 'liner trade'. Several container ships, most of them under U.S.A. flag, have been sailing successfully as far as is known for some time. According to a study made recently by the Research Department of Lambert Brothers, Ltd., London, by 1973/74 thirteen trading routes will be served by 212 container ships.[1] A number of container ships are now under construction for the account of liner firms.

The basic idea in this type of ship has been to combine the cargo (i.e. mostly finished goods) into larger units and to improve accessibility of the hold. Containers are dropped in vertically between a system of container guides and are stacked six high in the holds. A further three or four tiers can be carried on top of the hatch covers. It is expected that the 'container traffic' and 'through transport' will reduce costs on goods in transit substantially in spite of the heavy capital cost for tonnage capacity.

[1] *Container Ships*, Lambert Bros. (Shipping) Ltd., London, 1970.

(c) The tanker

The demand for the transport of oil by sea is satisfied in the main by productive units that belong to the tanker industry. In addition to various oils, tankers also transport other liquid cargoes such as creosote, molasses, asphalt, and water.

The tanker industry began to develop during the early years of this century.[1] Transportation of liquid cargoes in barrels or in tin boxes, which was carried out by dry-cargo vessels including tramps, was more costly and less safe.

The differences in construction between the tankers and the tramps which are a direct result of their different productive function are obvious. For example, the means of loading and discharging of the tankers consist of pumps and pipes instead of winches; the main engine of the tanker is fitted, for reasons of safety, aft and not amidships, etc.

Needless to say, one of the basic distinguishing characteristics from an economic as well as a technical standpoint is the difference in the average size between the tanker and the tramp.

Long practical experience has shown that up to a point the larger the ship employed in the transport of cargoes in bulk, liquid or dry, the lower the cost per ton-mile. So far as the contemporary scene is concerned it would appear that, for various reasons, the entrepreneurs of the tanker industry were the first to make use of this important economic fact on a really large scale. Thus, during the 1950s and 1960s the average size of tankers increased dramatically and the 100 000 tonner is now considered as nothing extraordinary. For example, during October 1967 the total tanker tonnage on order at the various shipyards of the world was 40 000 000 t.d.w.; 157 of the tankers on order were above 100 000 t.d.w. and 69 of them above 200 000. The average d.w. tonnage of all the tankers on order at the same period was 175 000 approximately. It has already been established that the construction of 500 000 and 1 000 000 t.d.w. tankers is technically feasible.

Owing to their large cargo-carrying capacity and smaller costs per ton-mile, tankers, as we shall see later in some detail,

---

[1] 'The prototype of the modern tanker, the Glückauf of 300 ft in length with a carrying capacity of 3000 tons, was launched in 1886.' See Our Industry, p. 178, by British Petroleum Company Ltd.

have been able to compete rather successfully in recent years, i.e. from 1957 onwards, with tramps in the transportation of grain cargoes.

(d) The bulk carrier

The entry of the tanker into the dry-cargo market helped to make it even more obvious that the newly created demand for regular transit of large quantities of bulk commodities could be satisfied at a smaller cost by a larger ship than the tramp, i.e. by the modern bulk carrier. Thus, as will be seen later, bulk carriers of 50 000 and 80 000 t.d.w. are not now uncommon and some in the neighbourhood of 300 000 t.d.w. are either under construction or have been completed and delivered to the owning firms. During 1963 there were only about five million d.w. tons of bulk carriers employed on long-term time charter.[1] The position of the firm in the 'market' of this new industry has been described as follows:

Ships built for such employments are not ordered haphazardly, but are the fruits of a close partnership between the charterer and owner, which commences long before the laying of the first keel-plate. The result is that after prolonged study of the prospective customer's trading pattern he gets a vessel 'tailor-made' to meet his needs. For a period as long as 20 years she will carry his goods at a stable freight. Cargoes will be of the size desired and be shipped and delivered at intervals most convenient to the scale of his operations. And as he has to pay for the hire of the ship he will want the kind of carrier which can most cheaply lift his goods, this involving very profound consideration on hull design, propelling machinery and cargo-handling gear.[2]

It has been pointed out that the 'three-island single-decker', a common type of tramp ship during the first three decades of this century, was in effect a small bulk carrier well suited for coal, grain, and other bulk cargoes. It is not necessary to com-

[1] According to the survey of Messrs. Fearnley and Egers Chartering Co. Ltd., Oslo, during July 1966 the world bulk carrier fleet was 30 616 000 t.d.w. and another 18 576 000 t.d.w. were on order. It should be stated that in this survey some vessels with a d.w. tonnage of 10–14 000 are included in the fleet. Since July 1966 several orders for relatively large bulk carriers have been given to various shipyards.

[2] See 'Trends in the Bulk Trade', by C.F.H.Cufley, in The Syren and Shipping, 3 July 1963.

ment in detail on the technical similarities and differences between the modern bulk carrier and its predecessors. What is new and significant so far as economists and shipping experts are concerned is the size and the cargo-carrying capacity of the modern bulk carrier.

The fact that some of the bulk carriers may be more suitable than others for the loading, carrying, and discharging of special cargoes in bulk, for instance iron-ore carriers, grain carriers, and so on, should not be taken to mean that they cannot transport full cargoes of other bulk commodities.

It will be seen that the original or building cost of a bulk carrier represents a sizeable investment by any criteria. On the other hand, the longevity of demand for a particular service to be offered by a bulk carrier is an unknown factor at the time of investment. Thus, the shipowner is unlikely to follow the policy of putting all his eggs in one basket. This point is, we think, well demonstrated by relatively recent investment decisions made by the American shipowner and builder J.K.Ludwig:

J.K.Ludwig never fails to astonish us. Following upon his 60 000 t.d.w. ore-carriers, 85 000 t.d.w. tankers and then 100 000 tonners, his National Bulk Carriers shipyard has delivered its fortieth ship... The latest is the 50 090 t.d.w. ARGYLL... This ship has been designed specially for carrying salt between Mexico and the Pacific Coast to the U.S.A. and Canada, but can also carry other bulk cargo, minerals, coals, or grains, as well as oil in the ballast tanks.[1]

Oil/ore carriers are relatively large vessels suitably constructed for the carriage of both dry and liquid cargoes in bulk. It has been maintained that what had become known in the shipping world as the 'marriage of the tanker with the bulk carrier' had produced a relatively costly type of vessel which originally had certain technical disadvantages. However, according to more recent reports it would appear that the oil/ore carrier fleet, particularly the Swedish one, has been expanding. For example, the annual report for 1964 of the Grangesberg Company shows that over half the tonnage of the company's shipowning divisions consisted of ore/oil carriers. In a fleet of 33 ships totalling 717 285 t.d.w., ore/oil carriers repre-

[1] See *The Marine Engineer*, April 1962.

sented 451 525 tons, bulk carriers 220 950 tons, and shelter deckers 44 810 tons.[1] The comparatively small number of large pure bulk carriers on order in the late sixties compared with the big number of large combined carriers suggests that owners preferred to pay a premium for combined carriers in order to make them suitable for carrying oil and thus increasing the flexibility of their investment. During 1969 only 28 pure bulk carriers above 60 000 t.d.w. were ordered. The largest number of pure bulk carriers on order were in the range of 25 000–40 000 t.d.w., but these vessels can participate in the tramp freight market as any other tramp.[2]

The magnitude of the supply of tramp shipping and of the supply of sea transport services generally will be discussed in chapter 3. However, it should be pointed out at this stage that according to the International Tonnage Stabilisation Association, the total supply of tramp shipping tonnage during 1964 was 30 214 000 t.d.w.[3]

This figure would indicate that the total number of tramps available at the time was about 3000. These vessels were owned and operated by hundreds of shipping firms originating from many maritime nations such as Great Britain, Greece, Japan, Norway, Italy, and so on. Many of these vessels have been or are still registered under 'flags of convenience'.

A considerable proportion of the above tonnage, about 40 per cent in the early sixties, consisted of relatively old vessels mostly of the Liberty type which were approaching the end of their physical and economic life. It is expected that practically all these units will be withdrawn from the tramp freight market during the early seventies. On the other hand many larger and speedier tramps, i.e. the 'Liberty replacements' as well as bulk carriers, are now under construction in Japanese, British, German, Spanish, Greek, and other shipyards.

There is very little current publication on tramp shipping. Some observers of maritime affairs have the feeling that tramp shipping is a declining industry. However, this belief cannot be

[1] See *Fairplay*, 26 August 1965, p. 8.
[2] See Fearnsley and Egers Chartering Co. Ltd., Review 1969.
[3] See Circular no. 1121 of the Greek Shipping Co-operation Committee London, dated 13 May 1964. Tramps belonging to the U.S.A. government-owned reserve fleet, mostly of the Liberty type, are not included in this figure.

substantiated by the facts. At the end of 1967 the world tramp fleet consisted of 3470 vessels, 54 730 000 d.w.t.[1]

The magnitude of the supply of tramp shipping services in the long run will of course be determined primarily by the estimated magnitude and the longevity of demand for spot transit of cargoes in bulk. It will be seen later why the relatively rapid growth of demand for transport of large quantities of bulk commodities over regular routes and the development of the bulk carrier industry should not be taken to imply the end of the tramp shipping industry.

Before discussing the structure of the tramp freight market itself, a word must be said in connection with the measurement of maritime transport capacity.

2. The tonnage of ships

For various reasons that will become clear shortly, the productive capacity of a ship or a group of ships should be estimated by transport economists and shipping experts in terms of ton-miles (i.e. nautical miles). In practice, since the distance of a voyage is known the cargo-carrying capacity of vessels is measured in terms of tons. Thus, it is necessary for the student of the economic problems of the maritime industries to have a broad understanding of the concepts used in measuring the productive capacity of vessels.

The deadweight capacity, or the carrying capacity, of a vessel is the total weight of cargo, bunkers, water, and extra weights[2] expressed in tons of 2240 lb which it can lift when loaded in salt water to maximum draught, either winter, summer, or tropical

---

[1] See Westinform *Shipping Report*, no. 280, published September 1968.

[2] The following is an example of the extra weights that are usually carried by a modern 15 000 t.d.w. tramp ship:

Main engine spares and stores	50.69 tons
Water and oils in tanks	43.00 tons
Water and oils in system	68.00 tons
Deck spares and stores	25.00 tons
Provisions	12.00 tons
Crew and effects	7.00 tons
Total of extra weights	205.69 tons

loadline, whichever is the case. The deadweight capacity is equal to the difference between the vessel's displacement on her loaded draught and the displacement on her light draught. The draught of a vessel is the vertical distance between the waterline and the keel.

If from the deadweight capacity of a vessel we deduct the total amount of bunkers, fresh water, and extra weights onboard, we find what we might term its deadweight cargo-carrying capacity.

It may be safely assumed that any efficient management and any competent Master will endeavour to maximize the cargo-carrying capacity of their vessel by having onboard at loading port the minimum required of bunkers, fresh water, and extra weights.

The amount of cargo that a vessel may take onboard does not depend only on its deadweight tonnage but it also depends on the space available for the stowage of cargo.

It has already been indicated that for economic reasons such a ship as the 'perfect tramp' for a particular trade, for instance the minerals or the grains trade, does not exist. The 'general-purpose' tramps differ in respect of their construction. Some of them have been built with a view to carrying mainly 'heavy' cargoes such as minerals, whilst others have been built for the purpose of carrying relatively light and bulkier cargoes, such as grains. The latter have more cargo space available than the former.

There is no space problem in the case of heavy cargoes. In the case of light cargoes the position is different. Light cargoes are those which have a coefficient of loading above 66. The coefficient of loading of a ship indicates the relationship between its deadweight cargo-carrying capacity and its cargo space.

As is well known, the deadweight tonnage of a ship and its grain space are, in the first place, calculated by the builders. Subsequently, final measurements are made by a surveyor of a recognized international agency, such as Lloyd's Register of Shipping or the American Bureau of Shipping. These agencies act on behalf of the State in which the new vessel is to be registered.

The deadweight tonnage of a ship and its grain space are

known and constant quantities. Consequently, as soon as the weight of bunkers, fresh water, and extra weights which a vessel will have onboard on the loaded part of a contemplated voyage is known, it is possible to determine the coefficient of loading or stowage factor.

The following simple example shows the coefficient of loading of tramp ship X for a special kind of grain:

Deadweight of vessel X at summer draught marks		14 505 tons
Bunkers	300 tons	
Fresh water	200 tons	
Extra weights	200 tons	700 tons
Deadweight cargo-carrying capacity		13 805 tons
Grain space		775 660 cubic feet
Average per ton $= 775\ 660 \div 13\ 805 = 56$ (Stowage factor)		

In other words, 56 cu. ft of the cargo space of tramp ship X hold 1 ton cargo of the special kind of grain under consideration. Thus, on this voyage grain stowing at 56 cu. ft per ton will fill vessel X's cargo space to capacity and put her 'down to her marks'.[1]

Several simplifying assumptions have been made in this example.

The relationship between deadweight cargo-carrying capacity and cargo space available is not identical for every voyage, as the deadweight cargo-carrying capacity may differ depending on whether the ship will be loaded to her winter, summer, or tropical loadline. Also, the number of tons to be deducted for bunkers, water, and, to some extent, extra weights is subject to change.

Furthermore, the stowage factor is not the same for all types of light cargoes and it may be different even for the same kind of cargo. For instance, the stowage factor for wheat depends upon its moisture content. The moisture content of wheat and therefore its weight depend upon the country of origin and its age.

When two kinds of grain have to be loaded on one voyage, the

[1] For other examples and a more detailed but not highly technical discussion on the subject see J. Bes, *Chartering and Shipping Terms*, pp. 153–5.

stowage factors of both kinds have to be taken into account. Moreover, in the case of light cargoes, various considerations affecting the stability of vessels are taken into account before the maximum amount of cargo to be loaded is finally determined.

The cargo space of a ship is measured in tons and each ton is equivalent to 100 cu. ft of the underdeck tonnage. Thus, the gross registered tonnage of a ship is a measure of the internal volume of all enclosed spaces in the ship and is equal to the tonnage below the tonnage deck[1] plus the tonnage of all enclosed spaces above that deck.

The gross register tonnage (G.R.T.) of a vessel is a figure of commercial significance for it constitutes the basis for the payment by shipping firms of such items as calls (premiums) to Shipowners Protection and Indemnity Associations (Clubs), port dues (in some cases), and so on.

The net register tonnage (N.R.T.) of a ship is the residual tonnage after the various allowances for propelling power, crew spaces, navigation spaces, etc., have been deducted from the gross tonnage.[2]

The net register tonnage is the figure on the basis of which most of the terminal costs of a ship (i.e. port dues, cargo dues, light dues, pilotage, towage, etc.) are assessed in various ports. This is so because the N.R.T. of a ship indicates the cubic space available for cargo. However, in certain cases, when vessels may be loaded, let us say with a cargo of timber or other goods, in any uncovered space upon deck not included in the cubical

[1] The tonnage deck is the upper deck in ships which have less than three decks and is the second deck from the bottom in all. For more details see Cole, *Shipmaster's Handbook to the Merchant Shipping Acts* (6th edn.).

[2] More specifically the net register tonnage of a cargo ship is ascertained by making the following deductions from the gross register tonnage:

(a) Space occupied by propelling power. (It should be noted that this is not the actual space but is an artificial figure arrived at by calculation according to certain rules laid down.)

(b) Spaces, certified for the accommodation of the Master, officers, and crew.

(c) Space used exclusively for the working of the helm, the capstan, the anchor gear, and for the keeping of the various instruments of navigation and boatswain's stores.

(d) Space adopted only for water ballast (other than the doublebottom).

(e) Space occupied by the donkey engine and boiler, if connected with the main pumps of the ship.

16

space forming the gross tonnage, additional dues may be paid on the space occupied by those goods after a relative estimate has been made by representatives of the port authority.

The light weight of a ship is the actual weight of the steel and wood of which it consists. This figure is also of commercial importance, for it constitutes the basis of determining the price per light weight ton at which old tonnage is sold for scrap.

The rules for ascertaining the tonnage of ships are laid down by national governments. However, unfortunately, there is no internationally accepted standard of measurement of ships, and this fact results in the placing of some of the productive units of the maritime industries which may be registered under one flag at a comparative advantage or disadvantage over others of more or less the same specification which are registered under different national flags.

There exist three basic systems of measuring ships, the British, American, and International (Oslo) systems. However, each country's ships are regulated by its internal laws. This gives rise to variety and diversity in the measurement of vessels. Furthermore, national rules for the measurement of vessels are subject to different interpretations as can be seen from the following:

We have in mind the case of a 22 000 d.w.t. bulk carrier which measured according to British rules is found to have a gross tonnage of 14 700 and a nett tonnage of 8500, if measured by Lloyd's Register and 15 100 G.R.T. and 8500 N.R.T. if measured also by British rules, by the American Bureau. The same vessel measured according to American rules works out at 12 000 G.R.T. and 8400 N.R.T.[1]

Following the failure of the Oslo rules to gain unanimous approval, attempts are being made by the representatives of the various maritime nations at the I.M.C.O. (International Maritime Consultative Organization) to agree on a system of rules which would become internationally accepted.

It is unfortunate that reports in this connection do not seem to be optimistic. A body of rules for the measurement of vessels that is internationally accepted would enable their cargo-carrying capacity to be measured more accurately.

[1] See *Naftica Chronica* (Nautical Chronicles), 1 June 1962.

3. The tramp freight market

During the course of a century (1869–1969) tramp freight rates have tended to fluctuate sharply. In 1873, 1888, 1900, 1920, 1926, 1937, 1951, 1956–7, 1965, 1968–9, freight rates were abnormally high. However, these relatively short peaks of prosperity were followed by prolonged periods of depression and low freight rates or periods during the course of which entrepreneurs were making normal profits.

Statistical evidence shows that although prices in the tramp freight market do fluctuate with general fluctuations in international trade they do not follow them absolutely. For example the downward trend in tramp freight rates usually begins earlier and is more sudden and sharp than in many other industries. Thus, the popular conception of tramp shipping being 'the barometer of international economic activity', which in a way expresses the feeling of uncertainty for future economic developments by many of those working in the industry, is without doubt based on economic reality.

In fact the sudden and sharp fluctuations in the tramp freight market constitute the most important economic problem of the industry. In order to understand the nature of this problem, i.e. the mechanics of price formation, the demand and supply relationships in the market will have to be analysed in detail. However, before proceeding with this task a bird's-eye view of the main characteristics of the market will be given.

Prices for the services offered by tramps, liners, bulk carriers, and tankers are determined in four contrasting markets. It will be seen in chapter 3 that in these markets the shipping firm functions under different conditions.

Tramp shipping services are bought and sold in the main commercial centres of the world such as London and New York, etc. As is well known, the greatest number of fixtures takes place in the 'Baltic Exchange' of London. Nevertheless, the fact that employment for tramps is secured at relatively few commercial centres should not be taken to mean that the freight market for tramps is limited to certain geographical areas.

The type of service that a tramp ship is capable of providing is in universal demand and can be easily specified. Consequently, it can be bought and sold by persons at a distance from one another and at a distance from the ship itself. Tramp shipping firms as well as the users of tramp shipping services, i.e. the exporting merchants or 'shippers' the world over, are in close communication with their offices or representatives at one or more of the main commercial centres by telephone, telex, or telegraph. Thus, a ship which is fixed, for example, in London may be in any port or ocean whilst the main office of the firm to which it belongs may be located in London, Oslo, Piraeus, Monte Carlo, and so on.

The productive units of the industry are characterized by their physical durability as well as by the fact that as a rule they are capable of carrying cargoes to any part of the globe. The chartering departments or representatives of the firms and the shippers' representatives are, to a certain extent, acquainted with one another's affairs; also, they are fairly well acquainted with the level of freight rates for the various voyages. From time to time there may be a small number of secret fixtures of which there are no means of ascertaining the rates that have been paid.

Although, as we shall see later, there are imperfections to be noted in the functioning of the tramp freight market, there exists a strong and dominant tendency for the same rate to be paid for the same voyage within a given and relatively brief period of time. Furthermore, a change in the level of freight rates for a given geographical area always influences the average price level of the market taken as a whole.

4. The shipping firm and the tramp freight market

Tramp shipping is an industry that has a market which functions under conditions that are not dissimilar to the theoretical model of perfect competition.

As already indicated there are hundreds of firms owning tramp ships which are capable of producing identical services. All potential entrants have free access to all resources needed for producing the transport service under consideration, since there is virtually no monopolization of ownership by established firms. Moreover, there are no artificial impediments to entry, and new entrants can produce services identical to those of established firms.

The increment to the industry's output resulting from the entry of one additional firm is so small as to have no perceptible effect on freight rates. Thus, the potential entrant is not deterred by fear of changing the existing situation so far as price levels are concerned. Nor are there any artificial obstacles to free exit from the market for the tramp shipping firms. Needless to say that the exit of a firm from the freight market does not necessarily mean a corresponding decrease in the supply of tonnage, since a firm leaving the market may decide to sell its tonnage to another firm and the new owners may continue operating this tonnage until the end of its economic life.

Advertisement for the services offered by the tramp shipping firm is not necessary and information regarding freight rates and other business matters is freely obtainable.

As will be seen shortly, with the exception of the periods of the two major world wars, prices in the market are determined by the free interplay of supply and demand.

Thus it may be said that, on the whole, the tramp shipping firm participates in a world-wide market functioning under conditions closely reflecting the theoretical model of perfect competition.

During the course of our discussion on fluctuations it will become apparent that this real-world competitive system has its imperfections. For example:

(a) The investment that is required to establish a tramp shipping firm that owns even one productive unit is nowadays relatively large. Table 1 gives a general idea of the sums necessary to build a 'representative' tramp ship during the period 1939–62.

During the late fifties and early sixties prices of relatively old tramp ships which were approaching the end of their economic life, i.e. the 'Liberties', even during periods of low freights, were in the neighbourhood of £75 000–£55 000, whilst in the late sixties the price of a tramp ship built in the early fifties was in the neighbourhood of £250 000. On the other hand the building cost of a Liberty replacement in terms of 1967 prices

Table 1. Cost of a 9500 t.d.w. tramp ship

Date		BUILDING COST			READY SHIP		
		Price	Per ton d.w.		Price	Per ton d.w.	
		£	£	s	£	£	s
August	1939	145 000					
31 December	1945	265 000	28	0	240 000	25	5
30 June	1946	290 000	30	10	290 000	30	10
31 December	1946	300 000	31	10	310 000	32	15
30 June	1947	330 000	34	15	370 000	39	0
31 December	1947	350 000	37	0	420 000	44	5
30 June	1948	360 000	38	0	420 000	44	5
31 December	1948	380 000	40	0	425 000	44	15
30 June	1949	400 000	42	0	395 000	41	10
31 December	1949	400 000	42	0	320 000	33	15
30 June	1950	400 000	42	0	300 000	31	10
31 December	1950	440 000	46	5	450 000	47	10
30 June	1951	480 000	50	10	550 000	58	0
31 December	1951	550 000	58	0	675 000	71	0
30 June	1952	580 000	61	0	610 000	64	5
31 December	1952	620 000	65	5	600 000	63	0
30 June	1953	620 000	65	5	600 000	63	0
31 December	1953	620 000	65	5	580 000	61	0
30 June	1954	630 000	66	5	580 000	61	0
31 December	1954	625 000	65	15	650 000	68	10
30 June	1955	665 000	70	0	710 000	74	15
31 December	1955	690 000	72	10	775 000	81	10
30 June	1956	730 000	76	15	865 000	91	0
31 December	1956	750 000	79	0	920 000	96	15
30 June	1957	775 000	81	10	900 000	94	15
31 December	1957	795 000	83	15	750 000	79	0
30 June	1958	800 000	84	5	650 000	68	10
31 December	1958	800 000	84	5	675 000	71	0
30 June	1959	780 000	82	0	635 000	67	0
31 December	1959	745 000	78	10	635 000	67	0
30 June	1960	755 000	79	10	620 000	65	5
31 December	1960	730 000	76	15	650 000	68	10
30 June	1961	730 000	76	15	650 000	68	10
31 December	1961	730 000	76	15	650 000	68	10
30 June	1962	735 000	77	10	625 000	65	15

was $2 550 000 or more. More specifically, the basic building cost of a 'Freedom' type modern tramp (13 600 t.d.w., 14 knots, 21 ton/day fuel-oil consumption) was $2 550 000 in terms of 1967 prices; the basic building cost of the 'Conqueror' type of modern tramp (14 000 t.d.w., 14.5 knots, 19 ton/day fuel oil consumption) was $2 600 000, and so on. Needless to say, a firm must have additional capital funds available with a view to meeting such costs as 'commissioning' or 'recommissioning expenses' and other operating costs that occur at the beginning of the economic life of the newly acquired capital asset.

The following comment may be of interest in this connection:

I frequently remember the past with some nostalgia when I think of my activities during my youth, that is to say, in the thirties. It was then possible for persons with average economic means to enter the shipowning profession and, little by little, to advance themselves to a sound economic position. The prices of old vessels and the values of the ones ready for scrapping are now so high that it makes it impossible for a Master with his savings to cover the 10% deposit... I would, therefore, like to see cooperation established either as far as joint ownership of tonnage is concerned or as far as chartering is concerned. This would enable a total of small shipowners to negotiate business on a large scale.[1]

Thus, it may be concluded that the investment required to establish a tramp shipping firm limits to a certain extent freedom of entry.

(b) Taking into consideration the large number and the relative smallness of tramp shipping firms, it will be logical to assume that they are price-takers. Although this assumption is quite realistic, it must be pointed out that under certain circumstances the impact of a firm on prices on a given trading route is tangible in the short run.

This point may be demonstrated by the following example: Let us assume that during a brief period of time there was tonnage shortage in the South African area. Thus, charterers

[1] See *Naftica Chronica*, January 1957, 'Reviewing a Quarter of a Century 1931–1956' by M. Kulukuntis, chairman of the Greek Shipowners' Association in New York, pp. 9–11 (transl., B.N.M.).

were making their inquiries in the market rather anxiously with a view to securing tonnage for the carriage of their cargoes to the U.K.-Continent area at the earliest possible date. In the circumstances, the management of firm X was not in a hurry to secure employment for its vessel named Y, which was completing the unloading of her cargo at the port of Calcutta, West India. Consequently, instructions were given to the Master to proceed towards South Africa as soon as discharging of cargo at Calcutta was completed. Vessel Y was not fixed until she became 'prompt', that is to say, until she arrived near the port of Durban. No other vessel was available in the same area at the same period of time, and in these special circumstances the demand for the services of firm X was less than perfectly elastic. Thus, a relatively higher rate was agreed between the management of firm X and the charterers for a full cargo of grain to be carried by vessel Y from Durban to the U.K. Therefore it may be concluded that proximity in space and time is a factor which in special circumstances (mainly tonnage shortage and high average freight rates) causes the price decisions of the shipping firm to have a tangible effect on rates in given trading routes. On the whole, however, this situation is exceptional and the statement that the tramp shipping firm participates in a world-wide market functioning under conditions closely resembling the theoretical model of perfect competition is reasonable, the firm is thus a price taker.

The source of the data contained in Table 1 (p. 21) is *Fairplay* (4 July 1962, no. 4115). Although the tramp ships presently under construction are larger and faster than the 9500 tonner, this type of tramp still remains a 'representative unit' of the industry, and as *Fairplay* points out it 'is still a useful type and one which may increase in popularity in future'.[1]

The price of this vessel is estimated on the assumption that it has the following particulars: Moulded dimensions 425 ft by 58 ft by 29 ft to second and 38 ft to upper deck; draught 25 ft 8 ins. deadweight with open shelter deck 9500 tons; machinery, diesel engine of 3300 b.h.p. to give a speed of 12 knots at sea;

[1] See *Fairplay*, 5 July 1962, p. 99.

steam auxiliaries; Lloyd's Register's highest class and Ministry of Transport requirements.

The table gives, in the first place, a general idea of the magnitude of the original cost required in order to build a 'modern' tramp ship. The data contained in the table is also of significance from the point of view of the fluctuations in shipping values. As will be seen later, the differences in price between the 'ready ship', i.e. a ship the construction of which has been completed and is ready for trading, and the one to be constructed are primarily due to the fluctuations in the tramp freight rates. When freight rates are at a high level, for instance 1956, entrepreneurs want to acquire tonnage immediately, and therefore the price of the ready ship is higher than the one to be ordered for construction, but when the freight market is at a relatively low level, for instance 1957–8, entrepreneurs are not interested in obtaining tonnage immediately and, consequently, the price of the ready ship is lower than the one that will be ordered for construction.

5. Flag discrimination

Flags of convenience, subsidies, and flag discrimination are usually discussed together in the reports and periodical publications of the shipping world. The significance of flags of convenience and of subsidies from an economic point of view will be discussed later in this book. However, a few comments should be made at this stage in relation to flag discrimination because the application of such policies by national governments has a direct effect on the free functioning of the tramp freight market mechanism.

During the 1950s and 1960s more than forty governments of countries, both industrially advanced and relatively underdeveloped, have been actively seeking to divert to ships of their own flag cargoes which, in the normal course, would find their way into ships of all flags, depending on their availability and market conditions. This objective is achieved by the application of flag discrimination.

For example, the U.S.A. government applies cargo preference legislation in respect of International Cooperation Administration and generally aid cargoes. Certain loans made by the United States are subject to a condition that all the goods moving under such loans should be carried in American ships. Normally, U.S.A. insists only on 50 per cent, leaving the remainder of the cargo to the ships of the loan-receiving country. Where such a country has discriminated against American ships, however, 100 per cent American carriage is insisted on.

Other typical examples of flag discrimination are those of Brazil and Guatemala. The Brazilian government has issued a decree designed to ensure that 70 per cent of Brazilian imports are carried in Brazilian-flag ships or in ships chartered by Brazilian companies under government authority. The Guatemalan government is waiving a 100 per cent customs surcharge levied on imports into Guatemala provided they are shipped in vessels of the national flag, and so on.

On the whole the pattern of bilateral trade treaties, which include provisions designed to direct the goods moving to the ships of the two flags concerned, is spreading, as is the tendency of state organizations to impose a trading policy of selling c.i.f. and buying f.o.b. in order to ensure the movement of cargoes in ships of their own flags. Generally speaking, the trend of discriminating between vessels on the grounds of their flag, including tramps, has been an upward one during recent years.[1]

One of the reasons given by some of the countries with relatively developing national economies which are applying flag discrimination is that they do so for the purpose of saving foreign exchange. Indeed, it may be easier to obtain a loan for the purpose of purchasing a ship than to solve problems arising out of short-term balance-of-payments deficits. Thus, even if the cost of transport of the goods of these countries if they are carried on their own vessels is higher, the fact remains that in doing so they avoid payments of freights to shipping firms of foreign nationalities. Thus, it may be stated that countries with developing national economies, such as, for instance, some Latin American countries, have a case for the conclusion of bilateral agreements in respect of the carriage of their goods on vessels registered under their own national flags.

[1] See *Annual Report 1959–60* of the Chamber of Shipping of the United Kingdom, pp. 27–29.

Our purpose in this section has been to examine the effects of flag discrimination on the tramp freight market mechanism. In this connection it should be concluded that wherever policies of flag discrimination are applied, price is not determined as a result of the free interaction of supply and demand for shipping services. Consequently, additional increments are added to the cost of transporting commodities by sea.

Thus, in those areas where flag discrimination is applied in respect of the carriage of commodities in bulk, the free functioning of the world tramp freight market mechanism is limited.

6. Concluding remarks

In this introductory chapter the main economic problem of the industry, the fluctuations in the average level of freight rates, has been sketched. The nature of the causes of these fluctuations cannot be understood unless some of the basic properties of the demand for and the supply of tramp shipping services are examined. These properties and their effects on tramp freight rates are discussed in chapters 2 and 3.

Chapter 2

The Demand for Tramp Shipping Services

1. Sources of demand

As in the case of other forms of transport the demand for tramp shipping services is a collective and derived one stemming from many sources. Chartering agreements, that is to say agreements between shipowners, or their representatives, and exporting merchants, or their representatives, in respect of the use or employment of tramp ships, vary and the main economic reason for such differences is that the demand for tramp shipping services does not arise from one and the same source. Thus, before describing the sources of demand it seems appropriate to outline the basic characteristics of the main charterparty forms, viz: (*a*) Voyage charter, (*b*) Time charter, (*c*) Bareboat or demise charter.

(a) *Voyage charter*

Under a voyage charter a shipping firm undertakes to put a vessel at the charterer's disposal for the carriage of a full cargo or part cargo (usually the first) from one or more ports to one or more ports within a certain range, at rates and conditions mutually agreed in advance.

The freight or revenue to be earned depends upon the quantity of cargo actually loaded, unless the vessel has been fixed on deadweight charter, in which case the freight earnings are based upon the deadweight placed at the charterer's disposal.

Under voyage charter the shipowner has to pay for all operating and terminal costs, such as crew wages, stores, provisions, insurance, bunkers, loading and discharging expenses (if not otherwise agreed), agency fees, commissions, brokerage, etc.

(b) Time charter

A time charterparty contains the terms and conditions mutually agreed upon between a shipping firm which has let and charterers who have hired a vessel for a stated period of time. Such a period may last for several months or for a year or more. Also, a ship may be let on time charter for one or more consecutive voyages.

The time charter hire per ton per month is based upon the deadweight capacity of the ship's summer loadline, irrespective as to whether the ship may be loaded down to her winter or summer loading marks during the course of the fixture. In fact, the quantity of cargo carried has no bearing whatever upon the charter hire. It is entirely up to the charterers to provide, or not, for a full cargo in order to utilize fully the vessel's cargo-carrying capacity.

As a rule time charter hire is payable in advance. Time charterparties usually stipulate that the shipping firm shall provide for the vessel's operating costs, such as crew expenses, insurance, provisions, spare parts, stores (including galley fuel and drinking water), and so on, except those which, under the terms of the charter, are expressly payable by the charterers. Maintenance costs are also paid by the shipping firm, for during the period of hire it must exercise due diligence to maintain the vessel in a seaworthy condition as well as keep her in a thoroughly efficient state as regards hull, machinery, and equipment. If repairs necessitate a temporary stoppage in trading for drydocking, etc., the vessel is put 'off hire'.

Whilst the vessel is on hire the charterers usually provide and pay for such operating and terminal costs as fuel (except galley fuel), water for boilers, pilotage, towage, port charges, dues or state taxes other than those of the nationality of the vessel's registry. Overtime is paid to members of crew by charterers in lieu of employing additional shore labour.

(c) Bareboat or demise charter

When a ship is fixed on bareboat charter terms, the shipowning firm is placing it at the charterers' disposal at a certain rate per t.d.w. on summer freeboard per calendar month. The fact that in certain periods the vessel may only be loaded to her winter loadline does not affect the charter hire. As a rule, charter hire is settled per calendar month and is payable in advance.

Under a bareboat charter, charterers obtain the complete control of the vessel which they are operating as if it belonged to their own fleet. They are responsible for all crew matters including the appointment of the Master and the chief engineer (although the owners retain the right to require their removal if they have reason to be dissatisfied). All costs incidental to the use and operation of the vessel are for charterers' account. Charterers are also responsible for keeping the vessel in good condition and running order, and this requires them to overhaul and repair it whenever necessary.

Charterers accept and pay for all fuel and consumable stores on board at the time of the vessel's delivery and, in turn, owners accept and pay for all such fuel and stores left on board on re-delivery at the current market prices at the respective ports of delivery and redelivery. As a rule, the vessel is insured for or-dinary risks, and war risks if necessary, by the office of the shipowning firm. In other words, most variable costs are paid by the charterers.

The three different forms of chartering agreements outlined above reflect the varying nature of the sources of demand for tramp shipping services.

The largest source of demand stems from the many small or big exporting merchants of cargoes in bulk the world over. These exporting merchants and commercial houses are interested at any point of time in the carriage of relatively small quantities of bulk cargoes (8000, 10 000, or 14 000 metric tons) from one or more ports to one or more ports. Thus, they charter trampships on a single-voyage basis.

Exporting merchants act independently of one another. During periods of tonnage availability exporting merchants and their representatives in some geographical areas have dis-cussed the possibility of agreeing not to charter ships above certain rates.[1] However, such discussions have never reached the stage of formal agreement.

Thus, it is clear that the demand for tramp shipping services which stems from the activity of the many exporting merchants and commercial houses who are acting independently of one another complies with one of the conditions of perfect competition, i.e. many buyers to work with many sellers.

Another important source of demand for tramp shipping services stems from the cargo liner companies. When their own tonnage is not considered adequate to meet their requirements, liner companies supplement their fleets by chartering tramp ships temporarily.

For technical reasons some tramps are more suitable than others for this type of employment. For example, a relatively modern tweendecker, 9000–11 000 t.d.w., capable of a speed of 14 knots and equipped with heavy lifts, may be considered by a liner company as more suitable for employment than a Liberty or a more modern or larger tramp with the same or even higher speed but without heavy lifts. Thus, in circumstances of relative tonnage shortage of this type of tramps in a given area at a given point of time the demand for the services offered by the shipping firm owning a tramp of the above specification may become less than perfectly elastic. Consequently, assuming that there is a demand stemming from the liner companies, proximity in space plus certain technical advantages may cause the price decisions of the shipping firm to have a noticeable effect on freight rates and more specifically on time charter rates. However, it should be emphasized that as a rule the tramp shipping firm *vis-à-vis* the liner market is a price taker.

The tonnage requirements of the cargo liner companies, although of a temporary nature, are as a rule of longer duration than those of the independent merchants. Thus, tramp ships are usually employed by the liner companies on a time charter or consecutive voyage charter basis.

Bareboat or demise charter is used in rather exceptional cases. For instance, during periods where building costs are at a high

[1] According to information given to us by members of the Baltic Exchange of London, such discussions have been held amongst London representatives of grain-exporting merchants and amongst Japanese exporters.

level cargo liner firms resort to chartering suitable tonnage on a barerboat charter basis in order to meet their long-run commitments. Also, casualties to their own ships may necessitate the chartering of suitable units on bareboat basis.

Bareboat charter has been used at the transitional period by tramp shipping firms intending to transform themselves to cargo liner firms. In order to minimize the risks of uncertainty and to avoid possible mistakes in the important investment decisions presupposed for such a transformation, these firms have employed suitable tramp tonnage on a bareboat charter basis.

Demand for tramp shipping services in peacetime stems also from two other sources, that is to say various national governments and relatively large industrial enterprises. In fact the quantitative importance of the latter source has been growing rapidly both in respect of the bulk carrier and the relatively large tramp.

Chartering of tramp ships by governments has at times assumed considerable proportions. One may mention as examples the government of the U.S.S.R. in the 1930s and the U.S.A., U.S.S.R., Chinese, and Cuban governments from the late 1950s onwards.

Tonnage requirements of governments and of industrial enterprises are usually of greater time-length than the ones of the independent merchants. Consequently, most fixtures are concluded on a time or consecutive voyage charter basis, i.e. two, three, or more voyages under the same charter.

During periods of wars of a world-wide nature, and for reasons that we shall point out when examining the effects of war on the demand and supply of tonnage, the tramp freight market mechanism does not function freely. Tramp ships as well as other types of merchant ships are 'requisitioned' by allied governments and the terms and conditions of such types of employment of vessels do not differ basically from those of the bareboat or demise charter.

2. The magnitude of demand

It may be assumed that the magnitude of demand for tramp shipping services depends mainly upon the following factors:

(a) The volume and structure of international trade.

(b) The geographical pattern of world production and consumption of raw materials, agricultural and industrial commodities.

(c) The level of demand for the commodities transported by tramp ships at the countries of origin and destination.

A rough indication of the magnitude of demand for sea transport facilities in general is given by the annual figures for world seaborne trade. Table 2 gives an idea of world seaborne trade

Table 2. World seaborne trade 1937–67 (weight of cargo carried)★

| | MILLION METRIC TONS | | |
Year	Dry cargo	Tanker cargo	Total
1937	375	105	480
1950	300	225	525
1951	360	255	615
1952	350	285	635
1953	360	295	655
1954	390	320	710
1955	450	350	800
1956	490	390	880
1957	500	420	930
1958	470	440	910
1959	490	470	960
1960	540	540	1080
1961	570	580	1150
1962	600	650	1250
1963	640	710	1350
1964	720	790	1510
1965	760	870	1630
1966	800	960	1760
1967	810	1050	1860

★ The figures of this table which originate from the *U.N. Bulletin of Statistics* have been obtained from the Chamber of Shipping of the U.K. *Annual Reports* for 1959–60, 1962–3, 1964–5, and 1968–9. The figures for the period 1960–6 are the amended ones as given to us by the Statistical Department of the U.K. Chamber of Shipping.

and its development during the period after the second world war. The figures in the table indicate cargo carried—excluding trade within the Great Lakes—in terms of millions of metric tons (2204.62 lb per ton). For example, the figure of 540 million metric tons may be taken as a broad indication of the magnitude of demand for transport by sea of dry cargoes as a whole during 1960. However, the figures for dry cargoes in Table 2 include finished and semi-finished products which are shipped in the main by liners as well as bulk cargoes that are mainly carried by tramps and bulk carriers. Tables 3 and 4 below give an approximate idea of the total volume of demand for tramp shipping services during the years 1951–61 and 1966–7 in terms of weight (metric tons).

Table 3. Demand for tonnage (dry cargo) 1957–61 (unit 1 000 000 metric tons)

Commodity	1957	1958	YEARS 1959	1960 (9 months)	1961 (9 months)
Coal and Coke	38 523	9 755	7 755	6 733	5 381
Grains	14 115	20 823	28 554	20 723	21 135
Scrap Iron	3 174	878	3 011	2 958	4 048
Minerals	9 322	4 943	6 713	4 884	4 035
Sugar	2 766	2 861	3 019	3 699	3 912
Chemicals and fertilizers	3 134	3 242	3 180	2 836	2 692
Timber	1 170	1 303	1 274	1 417	1 175
Various	3 530	3 219	4 104	2 464	3 039
Total	75 734	47 024	57 610	45 714	45 417
Consecutive voyages	28 705	2 840	6 504	4 544	4 544
Single voyages	47 029	44 184	51 106	40 900	40 863

Source: *Naftica Chronica*, 1 January 1962, p. 82.

The data contained in Tables 3 and 4 were obtained from the magazine *Naftica Chronica* of Piraeus, that is to say the *Fairplay* of the Greek shipping world. However, the original source of the figures is the Westinform reports for the periods under consideration.

There are several technical points of relevance to the figures

Table 4. Demand for tonnage (dry cargo) 1966–7 (unit 1 000 000 metric tons)

| Commodity | 1967 | | 1966 (11 *months*) | |
	Volume of cargoes	Percentage of total	Volume of cargoes	Percentage of total
Grains (incl. seeds)	38 140	48.27	35 009	46.87
Grains (incl. seeds carried in tankers)	4 093	5.18	8 966	12.00
Ores	8 892	11.26	8 308	11.12
Coals	7 919	10.02	5 398	7.23
Sugar	2 855	3.61	3 158	4.23
Scrap iron	4 958	6.27	3 629	4.86
Timber and wood products	741	0.94	906	1.21
Fertilizers	4 268	5.40	3 097	4.15
Phosphates	3 201	4.05	2 321	3.11
Pyrites	117	0.15	84	0.11
Sulphur	2 173	2.75	1 633	2.19
Copra	524	0.67	583	0.78
Cement	365	0.46	394	0.53
Esparto	25	0.03	82	0.11
Sundries	743	0.94	1 122	1.50
Totals	79 014	100.00	74 690	100.00

Source: *Naftica Chronica*, 15 January 1968, p. 181.

quoted in Tables 3 and 4. For example, it could be argued that the tables tend to minimize the actual magnitude of demand for sea transport of dry bulk cargoes during the time periods under consideration. Considerable quantities of bulk commodities were transported during the fifties and the sixties by vessels fixed on a long-duration basis and time charter employments do not seem to be taken into account fully in the figures. Moreover, bulk commodities are carried also by ships owned by the steel companies, and the employment of such units is not subject to business transactions in the open market.

One further point must be taken into consideration when studying the figures of Tables 3 and 4, or any other figures of a similar nature, namely that the quantities mentioned are representative, up to a point, in respect of the magnitude of demand for transport facilities as a whole and not only in respect of the demand for tramp shipping services in particular. We shall turn to this point at a later stage.

Thus, Tables 3 and 4 may be considered as a broad indication of the volume of demand for sea transport facilities for dry cargoes in bulk. What is really needed in this connection is dis-aggregated data showing effective demand (actual fixtures) for tramp shipping services in as many trading routes as possible. Such a study would have made possible some accurate fore-casting regarding future demand trends. In the absence of such a study one can not do better than comment on the basis of aggregates. From Tables 2, 3, and 4 it can be seen that the de-mand for sea transport facilities in respect of dry cargoes in general, and therefore the demand for tramp shipping services in particular, in addition to being subject to quantitative changes is also subject to significant qualitative changes in the long run.

From the data contained in these three tables it can be seen that during recent years the dependence of the tramp freight market on the grain trade has become overwhelming. This, of course, means that the type of tramp ship most wanted at the present time is the one characterized by a high ratio of cubic capacity to deadweight in order to cope with the increasing proportion of lighter seeds and cereals now being shipped. On the other hand, as already explained (see chapter 1, section 2), this high ratio of cubic capacity in relation to deadweight is not required for shipment of such cargoes as iron ore, minerals, scrap iron, etc. In other words, as in the case of other transport industries, the demand for tramp shipping services is not homogeneous.

The quantities of cargoes transported within a given period of time offer a broad indication of the volume of demand with regard to the time period in question. However, any estimate of the magnitude of demand for sea transport services or facili-ties cannot be indicative of the true position unless the distance factor is taken into consideration.

A relatively recent development may illustrate the capital importance of the distance factor so far as the magnitude of demand for sea transport facilities is concerned. During the early

1960s the volume of Cuban sugar exports declined. However, owing to political reasons, the trade pattern for Cuban sugar changed—and this has resulted in a sharp increase in the demand for tramp shipping facilities that could only be accounted for in terms of ton-miles, i.e. ton-nautical miles. (One nautical mile or Admiralty measured mile equals 6080 ft. One statute land mile equals 5280 ft.)

The big sugar movement between Cuba and the United States, involving a relatively short voyage, has practically disappeared. Instead of this flow there are now shipments to the U.S.A. from the Philippines, Brazil, and Peru, offering employment for tramp ships. In addition, the trading arrangements between Cuba, Russia, and Socialist-oriented countries, including Jugoslavia and China, have opened up new trading routes for tramp ships. Such changes in demand for tramp shipping facilities cannot be measured unless the ton-mile unit is used.

In the *Maritime Transport* report of the Organization for Economic Cooperation and Development, the following attempt has been made to measure the demand for tonnage in terms of ton-miles in three of the most important grain trade routes— covering about one-third of the total world grain trade—for 1959–60, 1960–1.[1]

	Thousand million of ton-miles	
	1959–60	1960–1
U.S.A. (Atlantic and Gulf)–Europe	46.7	55.0
U.S.A. (Atlantic and Gulf)–India/Pakistan (via Suez)	41.2	45.9
U.S.A. (Atlantic and Gulf)–Japan (via Panama)	11.1	16.4

A 10 000 t.d.w. tramp, carrying 9000 tons of grain, with a service speed of 11 knots, is taken as the standard ship. Assuming that she makes round trips—carrying grain and returning in

[1] See *Maritime Transport*, 1961, published by the Organization for Economic Cooperation and Development, pp. 13–14.

ballast to the loading area—and that she spends 280 days at sea annually, the following figures emerge:

	Number of standard vessels required	
	1959–60	1960–1
U.S.A. (Atlantic and Gulf)–Europe	140	165
U.S.A. (Atlantic and Gulf)–India/Pakistan (via Suez)	124	138
U.S.A. (Atlantic and Gulf)–Japan (via Panama)	33	49

Some of the assumptions on which this particular example is based may not be wholly realistic at the present time. However, there is no doubt that it shows quite clearly that for any estimate in respect of tonnage requirements the distance factor must be taken into account.

3. Factors affecting the magnitude of demand

The main factors that determine the magnitude of demand for tramp shipping services were given at the beginning of section 2 of this chapter. However, it should be pointed out that the volume and structure of international trade changes all the time, and that such changes may be due to a variety of reasons of a physical, social, political, or economic nature. For instance, a bad harvest in country X owing to adverse climatic conditions may cause a sharp increase in the volume of her grain imports and, thus, an increase in demand for tramp shipping services. A change of government in country Y may cause shifts in her foreign policy, as a result of which her foreign trade may be re-oriented. Such re-orientation may result in an increase or decrease in the demand for tramp shipping facilities, and so on. In other words, in the last analysis the magnitude of demand depends upon exogenous or external factors, that is to say, factors existing outside the tramp freight market mechanism. The influence of some of these external factors is of a seasonal nature. Generally speaking, statistical evidence proves that the level of demand for tramp shipping facilities increases with the general increase in international seaborne trade and world prosperity.

It is unnecessary for our purpose to deal any further with the relation between international trade and the magnitude of demand for tramp shipping services. However, it is worth while commenting on the degree that demand may be affected by even a minor disruption of or change in the structure of international trade, as shown for instance by the figures in Table 5.

Table 5. Transport of grain

Year	Tons of grain Melbourne– Shanghai	No. of ships	Tons of grain Vancouver– Shanghai	No. of ships	Total no. of ships
1961–2	566 000	4	2 000 000	15	19
1962–3	566 000	4	2 000 000	15	19
1963–4	566 000	4	2 000 000	15	19

During the late fifties, a period of low freight rates, chartering of tramp ships by the Chinese Government assumed considerable proportions. This development continued in the early 1960s. As is well known, during 1960 the government of the People's Republic of China signed important contracts for supplies of bread grains principally from Canada and Australia. It was reported that Canada was to supply about 5 million tons of wheat and 1 million tons of barley between mid-1961 and the end of 1963, and Australia 1.7 million tons of wheat at the least. Further purchases were reported later.

For the sake of simplicity we will assume that the above quantities were actually purchased by the Chinese and that it was agreed that their delivery from Vancouver to Shanghai and from Melbourne to Shanghai would be evenly apportioned within a three-year period (mid-1961 to mid-1964). Thus, as can be seen from Table 5 the total quantity of grains to be shipped each year from Vancouver to Shanghai would have been 2 000 000 metric tons and from Melbourne to Shanghai 566 000 metric tons.

The distance Vancouver–Shanghai–Vancouver, including a minor deviation at Yokohama for bunkers, is about 10 260 miles, and the distance Melbourne–Shanghai–Melbourne, including a minor deviation at Tarakan for bunkers, is about 10 375 miles.

Let us assume now that, in view of the low level of average freight rates and tonnage availability that characterized the period under consideration the desire of the Chinese government for employing modern tramp tonnage was satisfied fully. Thus, only ships with a d.w. tonnage of 15 000, 15 m.p.h. service speed, and able to carry 14 000 tons of grain per voyage were chartered on a consecutive voyage basis. Allowing six days per voyage for loading and discharging and twelve days per annum for repairs, a vessel of the above specification will need approximately 36 days to complete each round voyage and she will be able to carry about 138 100 tons of cargo each year to the port of destination.

On the same assumptions, the round voyage Melbourne–Shanghai–Melbourne will take approximately 35 days and each vessel will be able to carry approximately 141 200 tons per year. Thus, as shown in Table 5, four vessels of the same specification must be kept in continuous employment (allowing only 12 days for repairs per annum) in order to carry the quantity of 566 000 tons of grain each year to the port of destination.

Now suppose that whilst the nineteen vessels under consideration had just completed satisfactorily their second year of trading, i.e. mid-1963, a sudden minor cold-war episode of short duration took place in the Formosa Straits between the U.S.A. and the Chinese People's Republic. Consequently, Chinese imports of grain from Canada and Australia were interrupted. It follows that, as a result of such an episode, tramp ships with a d.w. tonnage of 285 000 (i.e. 19 vessels × 15 000 t.d.w.) would suddenly become available in the Far East and Pacific 'markets'. It will become clearer at a later stage that such a fall of demand brought about by a relatively minor episode would have had serious repercussions in the short run, not only on local freight rates, but also on the average level of tramp freight rates as a whole.

As may be gathered from the data contained in Tables 2, 3,

and 4, the magnitude of demand for tramp shipping services has been increasing in the long run. However, on the basis of the foregoing it can also be safely stated that the demand for these services depends upon many external factors of a varying nature, and for this reason its magnitude over a given period of time tends to fluctuate sharply.

4. The incremental nature of demand

Industries depending on foreign trade, such as tramp shipping, are more sensitive than others to fluctuations in international economic activity. An expansion or a contraction of international trade leads to an increase or decrease in the volume of seaborne trade, and consequently to an increase or decrease in the demand for transport of dry cargoes in bulk.

It could be argued therefore that, as shown in Fig. 1, the demand for tramp shipping services shifts to the right, i.e. from DD to $D_I D_I$ as international trade expands and to the left, i.e. from DD to $D_{II} D_{II}$ when it contracts.

Fig. 1. Shifts of the demand curve for tramp shipping services

One of the reasons for the relatively sudden and sharp shifts in the demand for tramp shipping facilities is what may be termed the incremental nature of demand for the bulk commodities transported by tramps. Broadly speaking, the various countries importing bulk commodities that are shipped on tramps are producers or potential producers either of the same commodities or of close substitutes. In other words, the total of commodity X transported from country or countries A to country or countries B in the same geographical area is as a rule aimed at satisfying what may be termed the incremental demand requirements of B for commodity X. It follows that when such marginal requirements are satisfied partially or entirely by an increase of domestic production in country B of commodity X (or close substitutes) the demand for tramp shipping services is either minimized or it tends to become zero. On the other hand, when for one reason or the other domestic production of bulk commodity X in country B decreases, the demand for tramp shipping facilities increases. In other words, from a long-run point of view, it may be stated that most of the commodities transported by tramps aim at satisfying temporary excess demand at the importing country. This is even more so at the present time when the demand for sea transport of bulk material on regular route over regular time intervals is satisfied by the big bulk carrier.

The significance of the incremental nature of demand to the industry may be demonstrated by the following example given by M. S. Seland, Director of Economic Research of the Norwegian Shipowners Association.[1] During the beginning of 1956 economists were forecasting that the energy requirements of Western Europe would be 20 per cent higher in 1960 than they were in 1955. For other purposes this forecast would have been considered as reasonably accurate even if this increase proved to be 15 per cent or 25 per cent instead of 20 per cent. However, in the case of shipping, the 5 per cent difference which would have been the result either of an erroneous estimate by the economists, or of a corresponding change in domestic production, would have meant that 40 million tons of coal (and or oil) would or would not have been shipped to Western Europe. If we assume momentarily that coal was the only raw material available to meet Western European energy requirements and that the only supply source was via the North Atlantic sea route then we would have found that a difference of 40 million tons of coal for a period of one year, let us say 1960,

[1] See John Seland, 'On Forecasts and Forecasters. Pitfalls of predicting Tonnage Demand' in *Shipping World*, 13 January 1960.

would have caused an increase or decrease in Western European tonnage requirements equal to 500 tramp ships of the Liberty type. This total is equal to the total of tramp shipping tonnage laid up during 1959, a period of low freight rates and relative unemployment of factors of production in the industry.[1] Thus, a 5 per cent difference in Western European energy requirements could have caused a sharp increase or decrease in the magnitude of demand for tramp shipping services. Furthermore, a change in demand for the bulk commodities transported by tramps of these dimensions would have been sufficiently large to cause a sharp rise or fall in the level of tramp freight rates on a world-wide basis.

Another example which demonstrates the significance of the incremental nature of demand for the bulk commodities transported by tramps is the increase in tonnage requirements for the transport of grain from the U.S.A. and Canada to the U.S.S.R. during 1963–4. As a result of a fall in domestic production during the period under consideration, the U.S.S.R. imported from the U.S.A. and Canada 12 000 000 metric tons of grains. As is well known, grain shipments to the U.S.S.R. were the main reason for the relatively high level of the tramp freight market during 1963–4.

We may therefore, safely conclude that the incremental nature of demand for bulk commodities transported by tramps is another factor which makes the demand for tramp shipping services capable of fluctuating sharply in a given period of time.

5. Demand in relation to costs

At any point of time it is possible to distinguish between commodities which are and commodities which are not traded internationally.

All commodities which are regularly exported or imported, even if only in small quantities, should be classified as international goods;

---

[1] It has been estimated that due mainly to a rise in domestic production U.S.A. coal shipments to Western Europe amounted to 116.0 thousand million ton-miles in 1956, 143.7 in 1957, 91.9 in 1958, 50 in 1959, and 42.2 in 1960. (See *Maritime Transport* report of O.E.C.D., 1961.) This was one of the main reasons for the depression in the industry during the late 1950s, i.e. after the re-opening of the Suez Canal.

but it is perfectly conceivable that a commodity which is exported from country A to country B may be produced in countries C and D for the home market and neither imported nor exported. Moreover, the list of international goods is continually changing. Whether at any particular moment a given commodity is 'international' or not depends on whether the cost of transport is smaller or greater than the difference between the marginal costs of production in the countries concerned.[1]

It will be seen later that during the course of the last hundred years the cost of sea transport per ton-mile has been reduced substantially. As a result of this significant development, different commodities which were internationally traded only between countries A and B are now internationally traded between countries C and D and so on. Consequently, tonnage demand has been created in areas actually unknown to the industry at the beginning of this century.

This point is discussed in chapter 5. Thus, all that needs to be emphasized at this stage is that there exists a direct relationship between the process of reduction of sea-transport costs and the growth of tonnage demand. As the cost of transport per ton-mile decreases it becomes smaller than the difference in the marginal costs of production between countries that are more and more distant to each other. Thus, new tonnage demand is created for longer and longer voyages. Hence the present complex structure and world-wide dimensions of the tramp freight market is, to a large extent, a consequence of the gradual decrease in the cost of sea transport.

6. The elasticity of demand

The importance of the concept of elasticity so far as tramp shipping is concerned, lies in the fact that it gives an indication of the reaction of the industry's gross revenue and output to changes in freight rates.

One of the most significant characteristics of the demand for transport is that it is a derived demand. Tramp shipping services are wanted to bridge the main gap, either between dif-

[1] See G. Haberler, *The Theory of International Trade*, p. 34. For simplicity's sake throughout this section we assume that trade barriers are non-existent.

ferent stages of production of commodities at different geographical points, or between the point of production and the points where commodities will be eventually consumed.

Most of the cargoes carried by tramps consist of bulk materials. Thus, the demand for tramp shipping services depends upon the demand for these bulk materials at the importing country. However, the demand for the bulk materials under consideration depends upon the consumer demand for the final products or services that go to make it. In the case of finished products that are carried by tramps, mostly when they are functioning as substitutes for liners, the demand for shipping services depends upon the demand for the finished goods at the importing country.

Having in mind its derived nature, we may now consider how the demand for tramp shipping services will change as freight rates change. Will demand fall greatly if freight rates rise or will it hardly fall at all? As in the case of other forms of transport, three factors must be taken into consideration:

(i) The elasticity of consumer demand for the final product that the bulk commodity is used for at the importing country (or the elasticity of demand for the finished goods at the importing country).

(ii) The quantitative importance of the freight rate in the market price of the final product.

(iii) The availability of substitutes, that is to say, alternative means of transport.

(i) Let us assume, momentarily, that in the short run, tramps carry only bulk commodities which are used at the importing country for the production of different goods and services. It can then be stated that the elasticity of demand for tramp shipping services varies directly with the elasticity of consumer demand for the final goods that the bulk commodity is needed for. More specifically, the position is as follows: (*a*) A rise in freight rates causes a rise in the price of bulk commodities and consequently a rise in the price of the final goods. (*b*) The rise in the price of the final goods (or service) causes a reduction in the quantity demanded, the amount of the reduction depending on the elasticity of demand for the final goods. (*c*) The reduction

44

in demand, and hence in production, causes a reduction in the demand for the bulk commodity and consequently a reduction in demand for transport facilities, the relative amounts depending on the amount of the reduction in demand for the final goods.

Thus, the more elastic is the demand for the final product, the more elastic will be the demand for sea-transport for the bulk commodities that go to make it, and vice-versa the more inelastic is the demand for the final goods the more inelastic will be the demand for sea transport for the bulk commodities that go to make them.

We are already aware that the demand for tramp shipping services is a collective demand consisting of the individual demands of the various commodities that are transportable by dry-cargo vessels. Consequently, the demand elasticities for the final products (for example, bread, electricity, machines, furniture) that the bulk commodities (grains, coal, iron ore, timber) are needed for may differ. However, it has been maintained that, with the possible exception of timber (used for furniture, etc.), consumer demand elasticities for the final goods for which the bulk materials transported are needed tend to be inelastic. It follows that the demand for the trans-oceanic transport of the bulk materials under consideration will also tend to be inelastic.

Needless to say, the elasticity of demand for transport of the final products that are carried by tramps (sugar, fertilizers, general cargoes, etc.) depends upon the elasticity of consumer demands for these products at the importing country.

(ii) The smaller the cost of sea transport as a proportion of the total cost of the final goods, the more inelastic will be the demand for transport of the bulk material that is needed for the production of the final goods. And in the case of final goods carried by tramps, the smaller the cost of transport as a proportion of the final goods, the more inelastic will be the demand for transport of the final goods in question.

Let us consider two bulk commodities A and B that are transported by tramps. The sea transport of bulk commodity A makes up to 50 per cent of the total cost of production of the final good X, while the sea transport of commodity B makes up only 10 per cent of the cost of production of final good Y. Now a

45

10 per cent increase in the sea transport cost of bulk commodity *A* would raise the cost of producing *X* by 5 per cent, while a 10 per cent increase in the sea transport cost of bulk commodity *B* would raise the cost of *Y* by only 1 per cent. Consequently, a 10 per cent increase in the sea transport cost of bulk commodity *A* would occasion a larger increase in the price of final good *X*, and hence a larger reduction in demand first for *X* and then for the transport of *A* than would a 10 per cent increase in the cost of transport of bulk commodity *B*. In general, the smaller the proportion of total costs of producing *X* or *Y* that are made up by sea transport costs, the more inelastic will be the demand for sea transport services in respect of bulk commodities *A* and *B* (or final products *X* and *Y*.)

In March 1960 a study of *Maritime Freights and Commodity Prices* was completed by a group of Dutch economists. This study was prepared at the request of the Royal Netherlands Shipowners Association.[1] The data of the relationship between maritime freights and commodity prices assembled in the study proves that the view widely held in industrial and commercial circles, that maritime freights are 'prohibitive' and that they form a serious obstacle to overseas trade transactions, cannot be considered as substantially correct. At the same time, the data contained in the study is extremely useful for our purpose because it gives a rough indication of the proportion of freight rates to the market prices of various commodities transported by sea, including some shipped on tramps.

Raw sugar from Cuba to German North Sea ports is taken as the first example in the study. The data given is as indicated in the table below.

It should be pointed out that although there is a conference quotation, sugar shipments are in fact made at fluctuating open market freight rates. The table above shows that the share of the open market freight in the approximate market prices at the West German ports of destination fluctuates between 4.9 per cent and 17 per cent.

[1] Only a restricted English translation of the above study has been made for the benefit of the Maritime Transport Committee of the O.E.C.D. The writer is most grateful to the Commercial Attaché of the London Embassy of the Royal Netherlands Government for having seen a copy of this translation.

Table 6. Freights: raw sugar from Cuba to German North Sea ports

		f.a.s. Cuba $	c.i.f. German North Sea ports (approx) $	Maritime freight f.i.o. $	Percentage freight of price at German port
June	1955	30.19	36.5	4.68	12.8
October	1955	30.38	38.3	5.85	15.3
August	1956	30.93	39.4	6.73	17.1
November	1956	36.20	45.9	7.75	16.9
February	1957	53.71	63.7	7.90	12.4
September	1957	42.13	47.3	2.34	4.9
November	1958	31.58	35.7	2.11	5.9

f.a.s. (free alongside): where goods are sold f.a.s. the ship, the buyer is responsible for payment of the costs of putting the goods into the ship and for all subsequent transport, insurance, and unloading expenses.

c.i.f. (cost, insurance, freight): under c.i.f. terms, the cost of product sold, the insurance during transit, and the relevant freight are included in the agreed price; the costs of loading and unloading the goods are included in the freight.

f.i.o. (free in and out): loading and discharging expenses (terminal costs) are the responsibility of the seller or the buyer of the cargo, but not of the vessel.

Data of the same nature is given in the study for other commodities, some of which are carried by tramps. For grains, maize, and barley from La Plata to Continental ports have been taken as an example, and also wheat and barley from North America to Europe. With these grains the relation of the maritime freight to the c.i.f. quotations varies between 12 and 29 per cent respectively in the first case, and 6 and 21 per cent in the second.

For coal, the Atlantic trade from Hampton Roads to Western European ports has been taken as an example. In comparing the maritime freight, i.e. the sea-transport cost, with the market price in the port of shipment which, in this particular case is in fact the f.o.b.[1] price, it was found that at the very high level of the freight market at the end of 1956, the single voyage charter

[1] f.o.b. (free on board): under f.o.b. terms, the goods are placed on board the ship at an agreed point of loading by the seller and the costs of this operation are included in the price; the payment of the cost of transport, insurance, and unloading is the responsibility of the buyer.

freight rate was almost one and a half times as high as the f.o.b. quotation at Hampton Roads and about twice the price of U.S.A. coal ex mine.

An evaluation of the above data must take into account the following two basic points:

(a) that, in the case of sugar and grains, the proportion of maritime freights to their c.i.f. price is not inconsiderable, whilst in the case of coal the quantitative share of the maritime freight in the price at the port of destination is high indeed;

(b) that there are very wide margins of movement of the maritime freight component within the c.i.f. prices.

The c.i.f. price of a commodity should be considered only as a broad indication of the selling price which the buyer, i.e. the industrial firm that produces the final product, pays for its service. Between arrival at the port of destination and the final place of disposal further cost price factors emerge, viz. inland transport, distribution costs, storage, etc.

For example, during January 1963 the f.a.s. price of 1 ton of cocoa at a Ghanaian port was £112. The cost of freight per ton from Ghana to Northern European ports was 135s, and the cost of cargo insurance ½ per cent of freight or less. The wholesale price of cocoa per ton at the port of destination was roughly about £130, but the retail price at the same time varied between £160 and £200 per ton. Thus, whilst freight constituted 5.2 per cent of the wholesale price of cocoa at the port of destination, it was only 4.02–3.04 per cent of the selling price.

Furthermore, the transport cost of a commodity from the point of production to the point of consumption, and the maritime freight in particular, constitutes only one of the supply and demand conditions that determine the market price of the commodity which tends to be considerably higher than the c.i.f. price. Consequently, we may broadly conclude that as a rule freights for commodities transported by tramps do not constitute a substantial component of the final market price at the importing country. It follows, that the proportion of maritime freight in the total cost of the final goods that the bulk commodity goes to make is even smaller and, as we are aware, the smaller the proportion of total cost of producing goods or service X that is made up by the cost of transport, the more inelastic will be the demand for the relative transport service.

According to the data given in the economists' study, the only definite exception to the above was coals via the North Atlantic route. Fluctuations in freight rates for coals were exercising a demonstrable influence on market prices and on the cost of fuel; in fact, during 1950–60 increases in freight rates, and consequently in the substantial quantitative share of freight in the price of coal on the Continent, were determining how far American coal could compete in the West European market.

(iii) The demand for the services offered by a particular form of transport will be more elastic the easier it is to substitute these services by those of another form of transport. When the cost of a particular transport service rises, that transport service becomes more costly in relation to the services offered by other forms of transport if these are available.

In the present stage of technological development the services produced by tramp ships can also be produced by productive units belonging to the neighbouring industries of dry-cargo liners, bulk carriers, and tankers—so far as carriage of grains is concerned.

The fact that there may exist in the short run alternative means of transport on some trading routes, gives a wider choice to the user, and it may be assumed that in such routes the elasticity of demand tends to be greater than unity over limited periods of time. However, as will be seen later, tramp shipping is a moderately substitutable industry. Substitution of the tramp by productive units of the neighbouring industries is a marginal process.

Up to this point the aim of the analysis in this section has been to give some idea of the determinants of the elasticity of demand for the services offered by the tramp shipping industry as a whole. On the basis of such data that has been assembled, and taking into consideration the present overwhelming dependence of the tramp freight market on the grain trade, it may be concluded that as a rule the overall demand for tramp shipping services tends to be inelastic in the short run.

In this connection some of the conclusions reached in the Dutch economists' study are of extreme interest:

... fluctuations in maritime freights cannot be shown to have any immediate and lasting influence on the fluctuations in c.i.f. prices

and:

It is clear... that there are periods when grain prices follow the trend of freights directly and that sometimes price changes even correspond exactly with the changes in the freights' figures. On the other hand there are periods in which there seems to be no interrelation, or even an opposite movement.

Thus, a higher average level of freight rates applied to the services offered by the industry, which has an inelastic demand curve as shown in Fig. 2a, will up to a point result in an increase in gross revenue, what is lost by way of a reduction in traffic volume being more than offset by what is gained by the rise of the level of freight rates.

Fig. 2a. An inelastic demand curve

Fig. 2b. An infinitely elastic demand curve

The position does not seem to be the same so far as the long run is concerned. The elasticity of demand for the final products for which the bulk commodities carried by tramps may tend to become greater than unity owing to the availability of substitutes. Moreover, the substitutability of the tramp by alternative means of sea transport is definitely greater in the long run than in the short. Consequently, it may be assumed that the elasticity of demand for tramp shipping services in the long run tends to be greater than unity.

If we were to assume for the moment that a monopolist was to gain control of the world tramp fleet, we could then have concluded that in the short run the demand for the services of his firm would be—like the industry's demand—relatively inelastic. Thus, the monopolist would be in a position to make large profits by putting up freight rates. However, the freight market mechanism functions under competitive conditions and consequently—as in any other competitive trades—the demand for the services of the individual tramp shipping firm tends to be infinitely elastic.

One shipping firm may charter at about the same time two or three or more of its tramps for the same or for different kinds of voyages. Under normal conditions the effect of such fixtures on the rates prevailing will be negligible. If the managers of the firm demand for a certain voyage a rate which is higher than the one prevailing in the market, potential charterers will go elsewhere asking for the services of other firms at current market prices. In other words, the demand curve for the services of the individual shipping firm tends to be infinitely elastic, as shown in Fig. 2b. As a rule the tramp shipping firm is a price taker.

It has already been pointed out (chapter 1, section 4) that in periods of tonnage shortage and relatively high freight rates the impact of a firm on prices in a given trading route is measurable. In these special circumstances the demand for the services of the shipping firm that may have a prompt ship in a given geographical area will tend to be less elastic than under normal conditions.

7. The short run

It may be assumed that the short-run period in tramp shipping lasts only for a few months during the course of which the user, i.e. the exporting merchant, may bargain and carry out the shipment of his cargoes, whilst the long-run period is of far greater duration and refers to the time required by the market forces to readjust themselves towards the direction of equilibrium. This process of readjustment may take years to complete.

As we are aware, the demand for tramp shipping services finds its expression through the many charterers of tramp ships, that is to say the shippers of bulk commodities. The charterer of a ship is not always the relatively small exporting merchant who has founded his business at the exporting country. His representatives at the main chartering centres, such as London and New York, may act on his behalf. On many occasions, depending on the kind of commercial agreement, the charterer may be the buyer of the commodity or his representatives or another commercial enterprise located neither at the exporting nor at the importing country. Nevertheless, whoever and wherever the charterer may be, he has to face problems of the same nature with regard to the employment of tonnage for the carriage of his goods.

In the circumstances, we propose to examine the demand for tonnage in the short run in a given trading route (let us say Canada–U.K./Western Europe) for a given bulk commodity, commodity X, on the assumption that the location of the charterer is immaterial. Furthermore, we will assume that all fixtures are concluded on a single voyage basis and that the behaviour of governments and industrial enterprises as charterers is in the short run the same as that of the relatively small merchant. In addition it will be assumed that in the short run the shipper has already purchased the normal quantity of commodity X which he anticipates he will be selling abroad.

In the short run the exporting merchant, i.e. the shipper, is interested in one or more tramp ships that are located in port or nearby and are suitable in every respect to take his cargo or cargoes. In other words, exporting merchants are primarily interested for what has been termed 'spot ships' which will enable them to carry their cargo or cargoes to the port of destination without delay. Whether or not there will be spot ships at a particular area at a given period of time depends primarily upon the state of the tramp freight market. If the freight market is at a high level spot ships will tend to be scarce, whereas if it is low there may tend to be an over-sufficiency of tonnage in

the area. Thus, the short-run questions that the exporting
merchant has to face with regard to the shipment of his cargoes
stem from the following two sources: (a) the time limits within
which he must carry out the shipment of his cargo; (b) tonnage
availability at the geographical area of interest.

There are three possible short-run alternatives for the exporting merchant: (i) the shipment of his cargo or cargoes;
(ii) storage of the commodity in order to be shipped at a later
period; (iii) sale of the commodity in the home market.

It is obvious, however, that the entrepreneur, i.e. the exporting
merchant, does not have to take into consideration developments in the tramp freight market only because, in the first
place, he will have to consider the price of his commodity X at
the importing country or countries. In other words, before an
agreement for the transport of commodity X is concluded with a
shipping firm, each shipper has to consider the price of commodity X at the importing country as well as the level of freight
rates and tonnage availability at his trading area within the
necessary time limits.

For the sake of simplicity we shall assume that tariffs and
other barriers to international trade are non-existent. Also
let us disregard momentarily transport costs!

Fig 3a shows the conditions of supply and demand for a bulk
commodity, i.e. commodity X, in two countries, country E the
exporting country and country I the importing country, before
trade takes place between the two countries. As we know the
shipper has already purchased the normal quantity of commodity X at a price P_e. Country I produces a certain quantity of
commodity X (or close substitutes) but she must import a
certain amount to meet marginal requirements. P_i the price of
commodity X at the prospective country of import is considerably higher than P_e. In the circumstances it can be safely stated
that conditions are favourable for trade to take place between
countries E and I and that the exporting merchant will endeavour to sell and ship his cargo to country I.

We can now drop the assumption of the non-existence of
transport costs. Fig 3b shows that $P_e = P_i$. Conditions are not
favourable for trade to take place between E and I and the

Fig. 3a. Conditions of demand and supply for a commodity in two countries (short run)

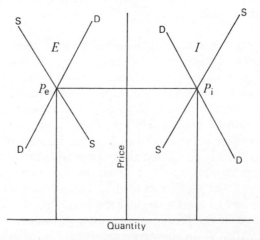

Fig. 3b. Conditions of demand and supply for a commodity in two countries (short run)

shipper will endeavour to avoid selling his cargo to country I and will look for alternatives for its disposal. In addition to the price of commodity X at the importing country, the shipper, before concluding a fixture with a shipping firm in respect of the carriage of his cargo to country I, will have to take into account transport costs, that is to say, freight plus insurance on cargo plus miscellaneous expenses. This is shown in Fig. 3c where t indicates transport costs. In this figure $P_e + t$ is smaller than P_I. by an amount m (the margin). It follows that conditions are favourable for trade to take place between country E and country I.

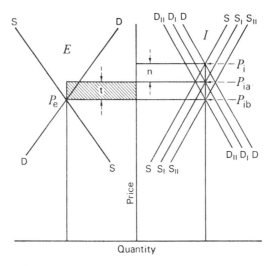

Fig. 3c. Conditions of demand and supply for a commodity in two countries and transport costs

Taking into consideration transport costs, there are two other possibilities that the shipper may have to face in the short run. The conditions of supply and demand for commodity X in country I may be such $(D_I D_I S_I S_I,\ D_{II} D_{II} S_{II} S_{II})$ that its price in the exporting country plus transport costs is either equal or greater than its price in the importing country $(P_e + t \geqq P_I$ as shown in Fig. 3c where $P_e + t = P_{I_a}$ and $P_e + t > P_{I_b})$.

When there is sufficient tonnage available at a given geographical area or when shippers expect that there will be enough tonnage to meet their short-run requirements, estimates are made with regard to the difference between the export price and import price of bulk commodities and the cost of transport of the commodity (i.e. the difference between

55

$P_e + t$ and P_i). If the shipper finds this margin, $[P_i - (P_e + t) = m]$ in Fig 3c, satisfactory from the point of view of maximizing his profit, it only remains for him to conclude a c.i.f. agreement with the buyer and charter a vessel for the carriage of his cargo within the time limits agreed.

However, m may not be large enough to induce the shipper to conclude a fixture for the shipment of his cargo to country I. Furthermore, as we have already seen, the price of commodity X at the exporting country plus costs of transport may be either equal to or greater than the price of the same commodity at country I. In such cases the shipper usually decides to charter a vessel and ship his cargo 'for orders'. The term 'for orders' means that the shipowners or their representatives have agreed that their vessel must proceed from loading port to a certain position not far from a number of possible ports of discharge (let us say in the case of our example Churchill/Manitoba–Land's End) where the Master will receive orders from the charterers about the actual port or ports of discharge. During the period of time, starting from the date of the vessel's fixture and terminating when the vessel is near the position agreed, the shipper endeavours to sell his commodity in one or more ports at a price that may be higher than the one prevailing at country I on the date of the fixture. Needless to say, the alternative markets where the shipper may sell his cargo are limited, for it must be discharged in ports located in a certain geographical area not far from the point where the Master will receive the orders.

Prices of bulk commodities at the importing countries may vary considerably in the short run. It is therefore possible for the original shipper to sell his cargo to a buyer long before the vessel's arrival at the position where orders must be sent to the Master, thus enabling the original buyer to resell the same cargo, and so on. In the words of the U.K. Chamber of Shipping:

The advantages of this system [i.e. tramp shipping, B.N.M.] to these charterers is, of course, that they have long periods at their disposal in which to watch market tendencies before they need sell their cargoes. In fact, it is by no means uncommon for the same cargo to be sold and resold several times before the original charterers need be called upon to give the owner his discharging port orders.[1]

[1] See U.K. Chamber of Shipping Report, 7 December 1938, p. 9.

Another possibility in the short run is that the margin $P_1 - (P_e + t)$ is rather wide. In such a case it can be expected that the shipper will endeavour to secure additional quantities of commodity X for sale abroad. However, such quantities are usually scarce in the short run, particularly if commodity X originates at a mine or if it must be harvested. Home supply of bulk commodities tends, as a rule, to be inelastic. Nevertheless, it has been proved possible in the past for shippers to secure additional quantities of bulk commodities that have been available in the home market because of surplus production during previous seasons. In such circumstances shippers will be in need of additional tonnage. Thus, tonnage will tend to become scarce in the area and, consequently, tramp shipping firms will be in a more favourable bargaining position. However, before we examine developments under conditions of tonnage shortage, it may be worthwhile to make a few concluding remarks in respect of the exporting merchants' behaviour when there is sufficient tonnage in their trading route.

From the foregoing it should have become clear that when there is tonnage available the factor which determines entrepreneurial decisions as to whether, when, and in what way cargoes will be shipped is the price of bulk commodities in the export markets.

Furthermore, under conditions of tonnage availability the exporting merchant or his representative is in a position to follow a 'wait and see' policy *vis-à-vis* the shipowners' representatives with a view to obtaining the minimum possible freight rate.

Under such conditions exporting merchants of a given area may even endeavour to come to an understanding amongst themselves not to pay freight rates that are above a certain level.

However, even under conditions of tonnage availability, the shipper is as a rule a price taker because he must ship his cargoes within definite time limits.

Relative insufficiency of tonnage in a given geographical area creates rather favourable conditions for tramp shipping firms. All efforts made by the chartering departments of shipping firms—in the event of tonnage availability—for securing a fixture that will enable their vessel to cover operating costs are now made for the purpose of securing the maximum possible freight rate.

It is well known that during the stages of revival and prosperity in the industry, when prices of bulk commodities in the export markets also tend to be at high levels, exporting merchants conclude sale agreements for their cargoes with fixed time of delivery. Thus, their requirements for tonnage become rather urgent. In the circumstances exporting merchants have no alternative but to conclude fixtures at high rates.

Moreover, there are short-run periods of relative tonnage insufficiency when the exporting merchant anticipates that the price of commodity X at a given importing country will increase. Other exporting merchants in the area may have already concluded fixtures for their tonnage requirements. In such cases, instead of having to face serious transport problems the exporting merchant proceeds with the conclusion of fixtures at rates that may be higher than the 'last done' (i.e. the rate paid for the last charter for the same voyage). Such charters are concluded usually well in advance of a vessel's arrival at the loading port. Thus, relative tonnage shortage at a trading route is a rather favourable state of affairs for the shipping firm.

Another situation that the exporting merchant may have to face in the short run is the following. The position in respect of prices in the exporting country and the foreign markets may originally be as shown in Fig 3a, which indicates that there exist favourable conditions for trade to take place between countries E and I. However, in the event of tonnage shortage, freight rates may reach such a high level that transport costs may become equal to or greater than the difference between prices in the exporting country and foreign markets. In this situation it is natural to expect that the exporting merchant will study the advisability of following one of the two alternatives indicated at the beginning of this paragraph, namely, either to store his cargo in order to be shipped at a later date or to dispose of it in the home market. It should not be difficult to see the disadvantages of these two alternatives. On the one hand, the cost of storage of bulk commodities, as a rule, tends to be high and on the other, home demand tends to be inelastic. As a result, on many occasions, particularly during the period between the two world wars, such commodities as grains have been sold in the home market to be used as animal food. Needless to say, that this resulted in the shippers making considerable losses. Thus, when shippers face situations such as the one described above, in order to avoid heavy losses they usually decide to ship their cargoes either for orders or after having sold them at prices which do not guarantee that a profit will be made. It may therefore be safely concluded that in the short run the main transport problem of the shipper stems from the fact that freight rates tend to be either at high or at low levels. Periods of high freight rates are characterized by shortage of tonnage. During periods of low freight rates tonnage available is more than adequate to meet shippers' requirements.

8. The long run

If the quantity of tonnage available for trading in a particular route is greater than the quantity required by users, freight rates will fall to non-remunerative levels. Consequently, tonnage will be withdrawn from the route in order, either to lay up (in the event of low freight rates the world over), or to be chartered for different voyages which may be more remunerative. Thus, in the long run, freight rates will again tend to rise in the same route.

On the other hand, if the tonnage available in a particular route is not sufficient to satisfy shippers' requirements, freight rates will rise. The rise in freight rates will invite further tonnage for trading in the same route. This tonnage will come either from the withdrawal of vessels from less remunerative trading routes or from the laying-up berth. It is also possible that newly built vessels may begin their economic life by trading in this particular route. As a result of the increase in the number of productive units trading in the area, freight rates will again tend to fall.

Thus, it may be said that in every trading route taken separately, there is a long-run tendency towards tonnage equilibrium, i.e. a tendency of supply to adjust itself to demand requirements. It will be seen later that this long-run tendency towards equilibrium characterizes the functioning of the world tramp freight market as a whole.

Nevertheless, it can be argued, quite correctly, that the tendency towards equilibrium in a trading route is not apparent. New developments caused by the influence of both external and internal factors intervene all along the way, changing the average level of freight rates both on a local and a world-wide basis. As we are aware, the structure of international seaborne trade is subject to frequent changes; the patterns of consumers' demand do not remain constant; the quantity and composition of supply of tramp shipping services is also changing. As already indicated, such changes are due to various factors of an economic, social, and political nature.

Thus, adjustments towards equilibrium may begin in a given area at a given period of time under a given set of conditions. A change in these conditions may bring a reversal of these adjustments. Indeed, there is very little in the shipping world that may remain fixed for a long period of time. On the contrary, it can be safely assumed that all relevant factors would never remain constant long enough for the processes involved to work themselves out completely towards a permanent long-run equilibrium position.

Moreover, even if we assume that all productive units were of the same specification and age, it still would not have been possible to determine accurately the equilibrium price for the transport of a bulk commodity in a given trading route between, let us say, points A and B. Traffic of bulk commodities in the traditional routes for tramps tends as a rule to be unbalanced, i.e. the volume of traffic passing from A to B is not the same as that passing from B to A. Consequently, vessels trading in the route will have to perform part of the voyage in ballast. Furthermore, the in-ballast part of the voyage of tramp ships trading in the same route at a given point of time is not the same. However, given the competitive structure of the market and the fact that each one of the shipowners will endeavour to obtain at least approximately as small an in-ballast voyage as his competitors, an average equilibrium price for a given trading route at a given period of time could be assumed.

All we can conclude, therefore, at this point is that in every trading route there exists a long-run tendency towards equilibrium.

It could be maintained that in the long run the exporting merchant faces a series of short-run periods were it not for the following two basic differences:

(a) The exporting merchant has sufficient time margins to decide whether he must buy commodity X, and if so what quantity should be purchased.

(b) Prices of bulk commodities vary in the exporting as well as in the importing countries.

In order to discuss how the demand for tramp shipping services fluctuates in the long run in a given trading route we must assume *ceteris paribus* and more specifically that the average level of tramp freight rates remains the same for a certain period of time. Furthermore, it will be assumed that as a result of a development in the trading route under consideration (let us say a bad harvest, a prolonged miners' strike, or even a local war) there is a deferred demand for bulk commodity X in the importing country. Thus, immediately after the event, supply and demand conditions for commodity X in the importing country I and the exporting country E will be as shown in Fig. 4,

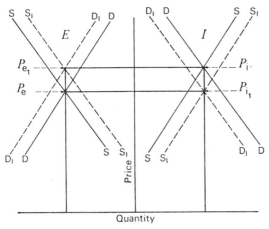

Fig. 4. Conditions of demand and supply for a commodity in two countries (long run)

i.e. DD and SS and I and DD and SS in E. P_e, the price of commodity X in country E is considerably less than P_i the price of commodity X in the importing country. Consequently, conditions are favourable for trade to take place between E and I. Experience has shown that most probably the following developments will occur:

(a) The price of commodity X in country I, P_i, will tend to remain at a high level and profitable trade will continue for as long as there is a deferred demand.

(b) Owing to the increase in the magnitude of tonnage demand in the area and the considerable margin between P_i and P_e freight rates will rise. If the greater part of tramp shipping tonnage is employed at the time and the level of the world tramp freight market is relatively high, freight rates in the trading route will rise rapidly and sharply. If on the other hand a substantial part of the industry's resources is idle at the time and the average level of the tramp freight market is relatively low, freight rates in the trading route will rise slowly at a level approximating equilibrium point. Thus, tramp shipping firms will be able to make normal profits if they employ their tonnage in the route. Consequently, in either case in view of the increase in the demand for tramp shipping services, sea transport costs will tend to rise.

(c) As a result of the increase in foreign demand for commodity X, supply and demand conditions in country E will be changing (and from DDSS will tend to become $D_lD_lS_lS_l$). Hence the price of X will tend to rise from P_e to P_{e_l}.

(d) When deferred demand at country I is satisfied and home production (or regular supplies from abroad) of commodity X (or of close substitutes) eventually increases, supply and demand conditions will also be changing (and from DDSS will tend to become $D_lD_lS_lS_l$). Hence the price of X will tend to decrease from P_i to P_{i_l}.

On the basis of the above discussion it could be concluded that the demand for tramp shipping tonnage in a given trading route may rise sharply owing to the influence of an external factor, but that, in the long run, it is bound to fall as soon as the marginal requirements of the importing country or countries for commodity X may be partially or entirely satisfied.

This is not an unusual pattern of demand fluctuations in different trading routes. However, the structure of international seaborne trade does not depend only on economic factors, and hence reality is much more complex than our simple model. Even under our original assumption that demand for tonnage in a trading route depends upon one bulk commodity only, commodity X, the previous analysis may not always reflect real world developments. More specifically, there are cases when the originally high demand requirements of the importing country (or countries) for a bulk commodity are satisfied, but the demand for tonnage in the same route for the transport of the same commodity continues to remain at a high level. This may be due to various causes.

For political reasons a bulk commodity may be imported from country E and then re-exported by country I to another. For example, it has been stated that in the early sixties Cuban sugar was re-exported by Jugoslavia to other Mediterranean countries, and so on. Furthermore, the same commodity that may be imported in one part of a country may be exported by another. For example, prior to the second world war when there was a single German state, wheat was imported into Western Germany but was exported from Eastern Germany. Further, owing to seasonal fluctuations, a given bulk commodity may be imported and exported by the same country at different intervals of time. Also, the imported commodity may differ slightly in quality from the domestically produced and exported commodity.

Therefore, all that may be concluded with certainty is that in the long-run demand for tonnage and freight rates in a given trading route tend to fluctuate continually.

When the supply and demand conditions for commodity X in countries E and I are as originally indicated in Fig. 4, shippers' expectations tend to be high. Consequently, the maximum possible quantities of commodity X are obtained and stored for shipment. At the same time shippers' requirements for tonnage increase. Experience has shown that changes in the quantities of bulk commodities stored and shipped tend to synchronize with changes in their prices. When such quantities increase, the home prices of the commodities in question also increase. At the same time in view of the higher tonnage demand, freight rates also rise. In the circumstances shippers' expectations tend in the long run to become low and their entrepreneurial decisions depend basically upon whether they have purchased and stored their cargoes for shipment or not. If they have done so, the alternatives open to them are those described in our discussion for the short-run period. If they have not purchased and stored their cargoes, they will bargain with producers with a view to obtaining the lower possible price.

In the long run as in the short, shippers are endeavouring to conclude chartering agreements at the cheapest possible rate. As already indicated, in periods of low freight rates and substantial unemployment of the industry's resources, the influence of shippers at given areas has some effect in keeping freight rates at a relatively low level. This is particularly so in present-day conditions when the grain merchants in certain areas are few. On the other hand, shippers are in an unfavourable position in periods of high freight rates and high utilization of the industry's resources. However, as we have already pointed out, on the whole the level of freight rates is determined by the world demand for and supply of tonnage.

We have discussed in some detail the behaviour of shippers at this point with a view to obtaining a broad understanding of the mechanics of price formation in the world market for tramps. We think that such an understanding must be considered as a basic pre-supposition for the examination of the sharp fluctuations in the average level of tramp freight rates which will be undertaken at a later stage of this book.

Throughout this discussion we have assumed that the behaviour of all charterers of tramp tonnage is the same as that of the relatively small merchant. It is now time to drop this assumption by stating the basic difference in chartering policy between the relatively small merchant on the one hand and the liner firms, governments, industrial and other large commercial enterprises on the other.

When the tonnage requirements of those institutions are of a short-term nature, in other words when, let us say, one or two tramp ships are wanted at a given point of time to carry 10 000 or 20 000 metric tons of cargo from one port to another, then their chartering policy is actually the same as that of the individual shipper. However, as a rule, the tonnage requirements of these institutions are of a long-term nature. Thus, to avoid the market problems created by the sudden fluctuations of demand, liner firms, industrial, and other commercial enterprises and governments follow the policy of concluding time charter agreements with shipping firms which are of greater duration than the single voyage charter.

9. Conclusions

Our aim in this chapter has been to discuss some of the basic properties of the demand for tramp shipping services which are of significance so far as price or rate fluctuations in the tramp freight market are concerned. In this connection the following points should be borne in mind:

(a) That the magnitude of demand for sea transport of dry cargoes in general and for tramp shipping services in particular is increasing in the long run.

(b) That owing to external factors, the demand for tramp shipping services is capable of varying sharply at a given point of time.

(c) The demand for the industry's services tends to be price inelastic in the short run. On the other hand the demand for the services offered by the individual shipping firm tends as a rule to be infinitely price elastic.

Chapter 3

The Supply of Tramp Shipping Services

1. The supply of tonnage

Our aim in this chapter is to describe some of the economic realities of the industry and at the same time to pinpoint the factors affecting the supply of tramp shipping services.

The main source of supply of tramp shipping services is the relatively small and independent shipping firm. There are hundreds of shipping firms owning and operating tramp shipping tonnage, but in spite of the growing size of some, none of them is large enough to influence the world tramp freight market mechanism. A large number of shipping firms that own and operate tramp ships are also owners and managers of vessels that belong to one or more of the neighbouring industries of cargo liners, bulk carriers, and tankers.

Another source of tramp shipping tonnage is the various national governments. The American reserve fleet, which includes many tramp ships of the Liberty-type, is state property. The merchant fleets, including the tramps of the U.S.S.R., China, Jugoslavia, Poland, East Germany, etc., constitute state monopolies, i.e. they belong to state-owned enterprises. During 1939 the government of the U.S.S.R. owned 1.91 per cent of world shipping (in terms of G.R.T.). This percentage was increased to 2.46 during 1957, to 2.51 during 1958 to 2.53 during 1959, and to 5.83 during 1967. There is no reason to question the assumption that the percentage of government-owned tonnage, including tramp ships, will go on gradually increasing and that eventually some appreciable influence may be exercised by state oligopolies on the world's freight markets, including the tramp freight market.

The year of construction of a tramp ship and its tonnage give a general idea of its specification and offer a broad criterion for estimating roughly the magnitude of supply at a given period of time.

During the period between the two world wars it was assumed, not without justification, that modern ships were mostly owned by British, Scandinavian, and German shipowners, whilst old tonnage and particularly old tramp ships were owned mostly by Greek, Italian, Jugoslav, and Esthonian shipowners. In fact, during 1937, when 'modern tonnage', i.e. vessels 1–5 years old, constituted 9.9 per cent of the world's merchant fleet, 14.5 per cent of the modern tonnage was registered under the British flag, 18.3 per cent under the Japanese, 17.9 per cent under the Norwegian flag, 12 per cent under the German, and so on. The present position is somewhat different, i.e. considerable percentages of the world's modern tonnage, including tramp tonnage, are also registered under such flags as the Liberian, Panamanian, Greek, Swedish, Danish, and so on.

It should be borne in mind that tramp ships differ in the separation of their holds; in their loading and discharging equipment; in their draft and suitability for loading in ports with shallow waters; in the type of engine and its horsepower; in their auxiliary machinery; in the conduct and ability of their officers and crew, and so on. In short, apart from their age and tonnage, tramp ships differ in many ways that effect their cargo-carrying capacity, speed, and suitability for a given employment. However, in spite of these technical differences, as already indicated tramps are in an economic sense capable of performing the same function, i.e. they are by-and-large perfect substitutes. The only exception is of course the modern bulk carrier, which cannot be used as a substitute of the liner ship—a function which is performed by the traditional tramp.

Taking into consideration the realities already mentioned in section 1 of chapter 1, and especially the hypothesis on the tonnage limits of the industry, it would appear that the data given in the Westinform *Shipping Report*, no. 280, with regard to the magnitude of the world tramp shipping fleet may be a close approximation of the actual position. The figures for the early sixties are similar to those of the International Tonnage Stabilization Association. Tables 7, 8, and 9 are based on this report.

Table 7. World tramp shipping fleet (December 1967)

Type of vessel	No. of vessels	d.w.t. (000)	Average size	Percentage of total
Single deck	1325	31 443	23 731	57.4
Two decks or more	1483	15 895	10 718	29.0
Liberties	662	7 392	11 166	13.6
Totals	3470	54 730	15 772	100.0

Source: Westinform *Shipping Report*, no. 280, September 1968.

Table 8. World tramp fleet 1961–7

	1961	1962	1963	1964	1965	1967
Number of vessels	2447	2634	3027	3053	3090	3470
Total d.w.t. tonnage (in million tons)	26.2	28.6	35.9	38.0	39.0	54.7
Percentage increase annual rate		9.2	23.6	5.8	2.9	14.6
Average d.w.t. (in million tons)	10 722	10 870	11 860	12 422	12 628	15 772
Average speed (knots)	12.0	12.5	12.6	12.9	12.6	13.7

Source: Westinform *Shipping Report*, no. 280, September 1968.

Table 9. Changes in the composition of the world tramp fleet 1960–7

Year	1960	1961	1962	1963	1964	1965		1967
d.w.t. previous year (000 tons)	24 789	25 091	26 238	28 639	35 900	37 925		41 853
New buildings	1 510	1 094	2 470	2 796	2 964	2 081	} 16 076	
Ex-liners	385	779	336	479	492	1 387		
Conv. tankers	219	285	114	967	315	96	176	
Gross total	26 912	27 249	29 158	36 680	39 671	41 489		56 105
Less scrappings	1 152	570	405	528	1 038	1 065		1 300
Losses	114	54	14	132	113	162	} 75	
Transfers out of fleet	555	387	109	120	595	1 241		
Net totals	25 091	26 239	28 630	35 900	37 925	39 021		54 730
Number	2 391	2 447	2 634	3 027	3 053	3 090		3 470

Source: Westinform *Shipping Report*, no. 280, September 1968

An explanation of some of the terms used, particularly in Table 7, may be of some assistance. The term single-deckers should be taken to mean that a large number of ships that are now trading as tramps are of a bulk-carrier specification. The massive permanent entry of the modern bulk carrier in the tramp freight market—the relatively large vessel that cannot be used as a substitute for the liner ship—is a recent development.

The second category of ships in Table 7, with two decks or more, refers mainly to modern tramps which are gradually replacing the Liberties, the representative units of the industry during the last twenty-five years. More specifically it refers to such Liberty replacements as the S.D.14 and the Freedom type of general-purpose ship. These modern tramps, having a d.w. cargo-carrying capacity of about 14 000 tons and an average service speed of 14 knots, are larger and speedier than the Liberties. As may be seen from Table 9, the second category of ships in Table 7 includes also a number of cargo liners that have as a rule more than two decks and are trading in the tramp freight market.

Table 8 shows quite clearly that, contrary to the prevailing opinion in some circles of the shipping world, the supply of tramp shipping services has been increasing steadily during the period 1961–7. The figures for 1961–5 are at the end of March in those years. The last column shows the changes since then to December 1967.

As shown in Table 9, the additions to the fleet from new buildings have been at a very high rate, whilst conversions from tankers and liners have been minimal. Scrapping and losses have been proportionately small in quantity so that the rate of increase in total d.w. has been at a high average level. It is not possible to establish how many of the liners and converted tankers included in Table 9 are trading permanently in the tramp freight market.

The significance of Tables 7, 8, and 9 is that they show that the supply of tramp shipping services has been increasing during the last decade. At the end of 1967 the total supply of tramp shipping tonnage was in the neighbourhood of 54.7 million d.w.t. In this connection it should be taken into account that, as it appears from Table 8, the average speed of tramps has increased by 1.7 knots during the period 1961–7. According to later reports in the shipping world this expansionary trend is still continuing. The new building programmes of shipping firms, of various hypothetical or real nationalities with an interest in the tramp freight market, centre on bulk carriers and Liberty replacements.

2. Definitions

As we know, the term 'supply of tonnage' refers to the available capacity for carrying cargoes in bulk from one or more ports to one or more ports.

All tramp ships, and their substitutes, that are trading at a given period of time constitute the *active supply*. All productive units of the industry that are not trading at the same period of time, either because of the state of the market (i.e. the laid-up tonnage) or because they are under repairs, or because they are detained, and so on, constitute the *available* supply. All tramp ships that are suitable for trading within a given period of time constitute part of the *total supply* of tramp shipping tonnage.

As we are aware, in addition to tramp ships there are other vessels that, under certain circumstances, may enter the tramp freight market. The following types of ships are included in what may be termed *potential supply*:

(*a*) Cargo liners, big bulk carriers, and tankers.

(*b*) Vessels under construction (tramp, cargo liners, bulk carriers, and tankers) that are to be delivered to their owners in the not too distant future.

(*c*) Tramp ships or substitutes that are not trading but are capable of doing so within a given period of time. (For example, the U.S.A. government's reserve fleet or vessels that are used temporarily as warehouses in ports for the storage of such commodities as grains, etc.)

The unit employed for estimating the quantity of tramp shipping services produced or available is the capacity-ton-mile per unit of time. Thus, for any estimate referring to the *supply of tramp shipping services*, both the cargo-carrying capacity and the average service speed of vessels must be taken into account. The deadweight tonnage and average speed of vessels give an indication of their productive capacity.

In view of the substitution relationships between tramps, liners, bulk carriers, and tankers (which are discussed in some detail in chapter 4), it is advisable to comment briefly at this point on the characteristics of these units and their separate markets.

3. The structure of the liners' market

It has already been stated that the main services performed by the tramp ship and the cargo liner are essentially different. This fact has a profound effect on the structure of the market for cargo liners and, thus, on the conditions under which the cargo liner firms function.

The requirements of a high degree of specialization, regularity of service, and a comparatively large original investment as well as the need to minimize risks and reduce the overheads of a large administrative apparatus, which is required for the marketing of liner services, has resulted in a small number of liner firms growing to considerable size and in the emergence of an oligopolistic market structure.

The comparatively large but small number of liner companies of the maritime nations of the world associate together in conferences, the operation of each conference being confined to certain ports or geographical areas. The participating companies in each conference limit price competition from within by fixing a mutually agreed tariff of freight rates. Over-supply of tonnage within the area of a conference can, to a certain extent, be avoided by allocating a certain number of sailings from specified ports to each member, or by restricting members' shares on a percentage basis. Large liner companies spread their interests and make composite voyages feasible by operating in a number of conferences simultaneously.

Competition from without is restricted or eliminated by the following measures which may be applied by the members of a conference whenever it is thought necessary:

Rebate system. The conference lines periodically pay a certain rebate on freights, paid by shippers in the preceding year or half year, provided shippers have confined all their shipments to the lines which are members of the conference.

Contract–non-contract system. Under this system, contract rates and non-contract rates are introduced. Shippers who enter into contracts within the conference lines, confining all their shipments to these lines, have the benefit of lower contract rates. The higher non-contract rates are charged to shippers who, for some reason or another, prefer to retain freedom of action to ship by non-conference lines or tramp ships.

The fighting ship. In the event of outside competition, the conference may resort to berthing one of their vessels, loading simultaneously with the outside vessel. For shipments by such a 'fighting ship', drastic reductions will be made temporarily in the normal conference rates. The rates are restored to their normal level as soon as the outside vessel has been withdrawn, or has sailed. The loss incurred to the firm owning the fighting ship is borne by all lines participating in the conference.

The considerable concentration of economic power that characterizes the supply side of the cargo liner freight market is not, as a rule, matched by an analogous degree of concentration among shippers who tend to be numerous at the various ports.

In spite of the fact that competition in freight rates is officially eliminated, it would seem that competitive elements which are to be found in other directions are still strong enough to necessitate improvements by individual firms. Each member of a conference aims at reducing the cross-elasticity of demand between his own service and that of his competitors by advertising and, indeed, trying to promote special qualities for his own fleet, such as superior speed, facilities for special cargoes, reliability so far as handling of cargo is concerned, and so on.

Competition is not always limited to these officially accepted quality aspects but, from time to time, expresses itself in open or concealed rate-cutting and collapse of conference agreements. Intra-conference competition and breakdowns of conference agreements are, at times, due to the existence in one conference of firms belonging to different nationalities or to technical innovation adopted only by one or some, but not by all members of the conference. For example, it is anticipated that in some cases the container ship may lead to a breakdown of present conference structures.

The oligopolistic structure of the cargo liner industry is a serious limiting factor to free entry in its market. In the first place, it is difficult for an entirely new firm to start a shipping line as the cost of acquiring even a small fleet and building its own business and administrative apparatus in most ports of call, with a view to selling its services to the large number of users required to make the enterprise profitable, would amount to at least several million pounds. Secondly, conferences are, under normal circumstances, unwilling to accept new members and for this reason they employ the methods indicated in previous pages to discourage entry. Restricted entry in the liners' market affects seriously the substitution of the liner by the tramp. In view of the nature of the liner trade the effects of such barriers to free trade as flag discrimination and subsidies are much more pronounced in the case of the liners' market than in the case of the tramp freight market.

Many criticisms have been expressed against conferences, but no alternative system has been proposed. It would seem that in the long run the viability of the system would depend either on cost based negotiation between shipowners and shippers (long-run demand for the services of the liner firm may not have zero elasticity as is commonly assumed) or on regulation.[1]

4. The structure of the tanker market

The demand for oil transport stems mainly from the big oil producing companies and their subsidiaries which also own a considerable percentage of the world supply of tanker tonnage. Thus, the tanker market is characterized by the existence of both oligopsonies and oligopolies, that is to say, by few buyers and a few sellers owning the greatest part of tanker tonnage.

It is of interest to note that, so far as the big oil companies are concerned, the degree of concentration in the ownership of

[1] For a theoretical discussion of this important problem see R.O. Goss, *Some Financial Aspects of Shipping Conferences.* See also (a) S.G. Sturmey, *Economics of Liner Services;* (b) K. Trace, *Underdeveloped Countries: Shipping Problems and Policies,* and cf. pp. 116–22 of *Report of Committee of Inquiry into Shipping.*

tonnage has remained rather static during the last thirty years or so. During the last pre-war years the big oil companies and their subsidiaries owned 36 per cent of the world tanker tonnage. In 1939 the total supply of tanker tonnage was 17 000 000 t.d.w.

In 1957 the position was as follows: 'Apart from government-owned tankers absorbing about 10 per cent of total world tanker tonnage, about 40 per cent is owned and operated by the oil companies or through their subsidiary and associated companies, and 50 per cent by independent owners.'[1] In the meantime, the world tanker fleet had grown to 2860 ships totalling approximately 44 000 000 t.d.w. During 1958, the world tanker fleet expanded considerably, but the degree of concentration of ownership by the big oil companies remained approximately the same:[2]

	No. of vessels	d.w.t.	Percentage of d.w.t.
Oil companies	1263	20 310 000	36
Independent shipping firms	1683	32 011 300	58
State-owned	250	2 996 500	5
Various firms	35	406 900	1
Total	3231	55 724 700	100

On 30 June 1962 the position had changed little:[3]

	No. of vessels	d.w.t.	Percentage of d.w.t.
Oil companies	1340	26 092 856	37.5
Independent shipping firms	1718	38 138 152	57
State-owned	232	2 831 624	5
Various firms	31	371 138	0.5
Total	3321	68 433 770	100.0

During periods of full employment about 40 per cent of the tonnage available, which belongs to independent firms, is

[1] See *Our Industry*, published by the British Petroleum Company Ltd. (3rd edn.), 1958, p. 178.

[2] Data obtained from *Naftica Chronica*, 15 April 1959.

[3] Data obtained from *Naftica Chronica*, 15 September 1962.

time chartered or fixed for consecutive voyages mostly by the oil companies, and also by governments who may have national-ized their oil industry. The remaining tonnage that belongs to independent owners is available in the market for what has been termed the 'marginal sea transport requirements' of the oil industry.

It would appear that the big oil companies do not aim at expanding their ownership much beyond the 40 per cent limit. Their policy of chartering for long periods an almost equally large percentage of tonnage belonging to independent firms has certain obvious advantages. It enables them to supplement their fleets on the basis of their tonnage requirements without additional heavy capital expenditure. At the same time, serious and costly managerial and crew questions are avoided.

On the other hand, the specialized nature of the industry, its oligopolistic structure, and the existence of fluctuations in the market increases the risk of unemployment so far as indepen-dent firms are concerned. For obvious reasons, when the mar-ginal sea transport requirements of the oil companies are at a low level it is, in the main, the relatively small tanker tonnage belonging to the independent firms that will remain idle. To minimize this risk independent firms follow, as a rule, the policy of fixing a large percentage of their fleets, in many cases not less than 40 per cent of their total tanker tonnage, on time charter or for consecutive voyages, accepting rates which may be lower than those prevailing in the single-voyage market at the time. The remaining tonnage of such firms is left free for the risky alternative of securing employment on voyage charter at current market rates. Recently, oil companies have concluded time chartering agreements with independent firms of up to twenty years' duration. Entry in the market is not restricted. In fact, the basic factor limiting entry is the large initial capital expenditure required to establish a firm owning even one unit.

5. Bulk carriers

A bulk carrier is a relatively large ocean-going single deck vessel. The shipping firms that own and operate bulk carriers are heavily dependent on the demand for sea transport of large

Table 10. World bulk carrier fleet 1967

Flag of registry	Number of vessels	Total t.d.w. in millions	Percentage of total t.d.w.
Liberia	273	8361	24.0
Norway	241	5698	16.4
Japan	173	4854	14.0
U.K.	148	3322	9.5
Italy	83	1884	5.4
Sweden	68	1751	5.0
Greece	57	1419	4.1
W. Germany	44	1195	3.4
U.S.A.	54	1031	3.0
India	26	800	2.3
Netherlands	29	667	1.9
France	29	559	1.6
Denmark	15	404	1.2
Panama	22	388	1.1
Israel	10	338	1.0
Other countries (20)	108	2115	6.1
World	1380	34 786	100.0

Table 11. Size distribution of fleet

Size of vessels in t.d.w.	Number	Total t.d.w. in millions
10–14 000	143	1676
14–18 000	344	5442
18–25 000	425	9139
25–30 000	122	3300
30–40 000	188	6450
40–50 000	52	2374
50–60 000	66	3566
60–80 000	36	2453
80 000	4	386
Total	1380	34 786

quantities of grains, iron ore, and coals over relatively regular periods of time.

Table 10 shows the size of the world bulk carrier fleet during January 1967, while Table 11 shows the size distribution of the fleet. Data for both tables have been obtained from the January 1967 survey on *World Bulk Carriers* by Messrs. Fearnley and Egers Chartering Co. Ltd., Oslo.

In 1968 the biggest bulk carrier afloat was the *San Juan Exporter* belonging to San Juan Carriers Ltd., a subsidiary of Marcoma Corp. of San Francisco. This vessel, 106 000 t.d.w. with a service speed of 15.5 knots, was built at the Nippon Kokan Tsurumi Shipyard, near Tokyo. The *San Juan Exporter* is specifically designed for the ore trade between the Marcoma Mines in Peru and the Fukuyama Iron Works at Hiroshima. Bigger bulk carriers up to 300 000 t.d.w. are now in operation.

The magnitude of the world bulk carrier fleet continued to grow during the late sixties and, according to *Fairplay* (supplement 23 May 69), the number of bulk carriers on order by the major maritime nations was 307, their total d.w. tonnage being above 12 700 000 t.d.w. It remains to be seen whether the increase in demand for transport of big quantities of bulk commodities is large enough to justify such a substantial growth in the world's bulk carrier fleet.

According to the survey *World Bulk Carrier*, the greater part of the bulk carrier fleet consists of modern ships. About 72 per cent of the tonnage has been built in the sixties. The average age of the fleet for the years 1965 and 1966 has been estimated at 5.6 years per ton deadweight. It is not clear whether the age of ships converted into bulk carriers is estimated from the date of completion or the conversion.

In this connection it should be pointed out that during the late fifties and early sixties a considerable number of tankers had been converted into bulk carriers. Table 9 gives an indication of the size of the 'cheap bulk carrier fleet'. Owing to the growth of the modern bulk carrier fleet, the quantitative importance of the cheap bulk carrier fleet in relation to the total bulk carrier tonnage declined in the late sixties. For example, in 1966 the bulk carrier fleet had a net increase of 212 vessels, totalling 7.2

million t.d.w. The gross addition to the fleet comprised new buildings, conversions of tankers, and tonnage adjustments, and amounted to 7.3. million t.d.w. Of this, new buildings accounted for 6.8 million t.d.w., whilst conversions of tankers and tonnage adjustments made up the balance. About 0.15 million t.d.w. were scrapped or lost during 1966.

In the annual surveys by Messrs. Fearnley & Egers Chartering Co. Ltd., as well as in other literature on the subject, attempts are made to separate bulk carriers in two different categories of ships, the 'Ore Carriers' and 'The Other Bulk Carriers'. Although some of the bulk carriers may be more suitably constructed than others for the carriage of ores, it cannot be considered that, in an economic sense, this distinction is of any basic significance for, as we are aware, all bulk carriers satisfy the same kind of demand for sea transport. In fact, as a result of improvements in construction, the difference between the two categories of bulk carriers has been minimized considerably in a technical sense. To put it in the words of the survey:

However, the technical and commercial difference between these two main categories is not so large today as a few years ago. By making Ore Carriers more suited for other commodities, and other Bulk Carriers more suited for ore cargoes, more flexibility has been introduced in both fleets. Consequently, a division of the Bulk Carrier fleet into these two main groups must be less precise than previously.

Large bulk carriers are a field of specialized investment, but, in an economic sense, it is practically impossible to differentiate between a relatively small bulk carrier below 36 000 t.d.w. and a relatively large tramp. The average size of bulk carriers is increasing constantly. The average size of new buildings delivered during 1963, 1964, 1965 and 1966 was 27 100, 31 200, 32 000, and 35 000 t.d.w. respectively.

It may be argued that there are still cargo ships today which function as bulk carriers with a d.w. tonnage even smaller than 10 000. For example, the British Iron and Steel Corporation have in their employment vessels carrying iron-ore over regular routes over regular periods of time which are smaller than the above limit. In fact, taking into consideration the examples of South Korea and the Philippines, it may be said that this small bulk carrier fleet is growing. However, such vessels are, to a very considerable extent, functioning as permanent substitutes of the barge and the old coaster in their areas and they do not trade on a world-wide basis.

The demand for sea transport of relatively large quantities of bulk commodities over regular routes over regular periods of time is growing. This demand, which is satisfied in the main by the modern bulk carrier, stems from relatively large industrial and commercial enterprises which are located in large industrial centres. Thus, at the end of 1963, there were about 5 million tons of bulk carriers on long-term time charter and, with the growth of the fleet, time chartering kept on increasing.

In many cases the terms of the charter and the price for carrying such commodities in bulk, as iron ore or grain, is agreed between charterers and the shipowner even before the bulk carrier has been ordered for construction.[1] Thus, in such cases as these, the function of the shipping firm is merely to fulfil partially or entirely the transport requirements of the charterer.

In view of the long duration of these charters, i.e. from several months to twenty years, shipping firms endeavour to obtain from charterers guarantees with regard to future increases in the operating costs of their vessel or vessels by the insertion in the charter parties of an escalation clause. Such escalation clauses provide for a readjustment of freight rates in the event of increases in the costs of operation. However, this is by no means usual and, on the basis of the experience of the tanker freight market, it would appear that charterers have agreed to such clauses only during periods of tonnage shortage and very high freight rates.

There are cases when relatively large shipping firms owning a number of bulk carriers enter into long-term chartering contracts for the transportation of big quantities of iron-ore measured in millions of tons. In fixtures of this kind several big iron-ore carriers are employed. Each vessel performing the same voyage follows the same route and arrives at the ports of loading and discharging only a short time after the departure

[1] Charters of this nature had been concluded between large oil companies and shipping firms for relatively big tankers before the development of the modern bulk carrier, i.e. in the early fifties

of the previous one. This type of employment of several bulk carriers by one big charterer demonstrates quite clearly the nature of demand which has led to the creation of this new fleet.

As already indicated, liners, tankers, and bulk carriers can function as tramps and consequently they form part of the potential supply and at any point of time they may constitute part of the active supply tramp shipping tonnage. The substitution relationships of the tramp with its neighbours will be examined in some detail in chapter 4. Our discussion in the remaining sections of this chapter will centre mainly on the tramp ship.

6. The 'unpredictable factors'

The magnitude of supply in the long run depends upon several factors such as the level of demand for tramp shipping services; shipowners' expectations of future profits; progress in technical methods applicable to the construction and operation of vessels; port development; and the productive capacity and level of employment of the world shipbuilding industry.

The significance of these factors will be assessed later in this chapter. Also, the nature of other factors which may cause the magnitude of total and active supply to increase or decrease in a given period of time will be analysed in the course of our discussion for the short run. Our main purpose in this section is to point out that, in addition to all other factors that will be discussed later, there are also some unpredictable factors which cause the productive capacity of tramp ships to vary. At first let us assume two short-run periods of the same duration. Furthermore, let us assume that during the course of these two short-run periods:

(a) the quantity of factors of production employed in the industry was exactly the same;

(b) there was full employment of the industry's resources;

(c) all other known things 'remained equal' and prices remained at a level which ensured that tonnage demand matched supply.

Even under such conditions it would have been erroneous to conclude that the industry's output would have been the same in these two time periods. Such differences in output which may have existed would have been the result of one or more factors that were unpredictable, or impossible to take into account precisely; these are given below in order of importance and frequency:

(a) Unusually adverse weather conditions for the trade route or the period of the year. It often happens that the prevailing average conditions for a passage or for a voyage are considerably more severe than can be anticipated for the period of the year. If, for example, persistently heavy head winds and seas are met with during a passage the vessel's speed will drop, or the Master may even have to order the engines to develop less power and speed in order to avoid damage to the vessel's structure or to her machinery which may be caused by the considerably higher forces imposed on the structure by the heavy pitching, bearing, or rolling in heavy seas. Thus, it happens that a vessel which was expected to complete a passage at, say, 12 knots average speed under the usual sea conditions for the season, probably will do no more than 10.5 knots average, which means an increase of running time of more than 10 per cent.

(b) Although proper measures and precautions may be taken by the Master and the crew to avoid damage by heavy seas by easing the extra forces to which the structure may be subjected under such conditions, damage, sometimes serious, cannot be ruled out by any means. This damage may refer to parts of the vessel on the exposed decks, cracking and/or deformation of plates, frames or other structural members, slackening of rivets or splitting of welded connections, damage to machinery, shafting, etc. due, for example, to the racing of the propeller when proceeding in ballast, etc. In some instances repairs to the damage sustained are absolutely essential at the end of the passage in order to restore the vessel's seaworthiness. This may involve delay in port. Instances when a vessel has to be dry-docked after a passage in rough seas in order to repair damage to her underwater parts, rudder, or propeller shaft etc., are rather numerous.

(c) Accidents, such as groundings, collisions, contacts with quays, outbreak of fire, unexpected failure or trouble with machinery parts, etc., are other factors which may cause reduction of a vessel's speed, or delays in port in order to have the damage repaired, or the cause of the trouble eliminated for seaworthiness reasons. Into this category of unforeseeable factors we may classify damage caused by negligence or incompetence of the engineers, deck officers, and the rest of the crew.

(d) In this fourth group of unpredictable factors we may include labour disputes and strikes at the port of loading and/or discharging, delays in cargo operations due to bad weather conditions, delays in inland transport services from which the availability of cargo or its removal from the discharging berth may depend and which may cause delay of several days in port.

(e) Fouling of the vessel's underwater parts by seaweeds or barnacles resulting in an increased resistance and reduction of speed. It may be said that, as a rule, this factor is not unpredictable and is under the management's control, since they can arrange for periodical dry-dockings for cleaning and repainting the vessel's underwater parts. Occasionally, however, premature fouling occurs due either to sea water conditions or to unexpected failure of the paints used. Reduction of speed is more pronounced in ships not having any margin of power for coping with the increased resistance to maintain the vessel's service speed. Loss of speed of 1 knot or even more due to fouling is not unusual.

Moreover, at times it is not possible to put the vessel in dock as arranged because the dock is not available owing to unexpected repairs found necessary on the ship that entered the dock previously.

(f) In this last group we may include serious illness of crew members or injuries which may necessitate deviation from the normal course in order to land them at the nearest port for medical attention and which will make the duration of the voyage longer. Difficulties with crew members whilst in port is another factor which may cause delay in departure. However, the unpredictable factors mentioned in this paragraph and those of similar nature are rather infrequent.

It has been estimated that in the case of modern tramp ships, that are efficiently managed and are not defective in their construction, delays due to unpredictable factors, together with normal repairs, amount on average to about fifteen days per annum.

7. Technical progress

Technical progress and innovations in the construction and operation of vessels has resulted in the more economically efficient production of sea transport services, including tramp shipping services.

As a result of technical progress, bigger, speedier, more highly specialized, and safer units can now be built which are capable of producing the same services as older ships at a lower cost per ton-mile. Consequently, average freight rates in the long run are maintained at lower levels, thereby making possible the opening of new trading routes and the widening of the world tramp freight market.

However, before we discuss the economic effects of technical progress, we survey important developments in this field with particular reference to tramp shipping and its neighbours.

R.H. Thornton, in his well-known book, *British Shipping*, points out:

A thorough investigation of all letters patent relating to improvements in ships between the years 1618 and 1810 discloses no improvement worth recording.

And further:

Throughout the whole of the eighteenth century the average size of British merchant ships increased only from 80 to 100 tons.[1]

It would seem that the position changed drastically during the last hundred and fifty years or so. During the course of the present century technical progress in respect of the construction of vessels, their machinery, their radio and radar equipment, and their repairs has been rapid. The same is true so far as the

[1] See R.H. Thornton, *British Shipping*, pp. 3–4.

development of ports is concerned. Thus, in one of its issues *Fairplay* finds it necessary to suggest to shipping firms that future demand requirements must be carefully studied before new investments are made, because: 'The rate of technical progress in industry is now such that no company can plan effectively ten years ahead unless it knows something of the plans of others upon which it depends.'[1]

(a) Construction

During the period before the first world war the tonnage of the representative tramp ship was about 5500 d.w. and its average service speed amounted to about 200 nautical miles per 24 hours. During the course of the first world war, the 'standard' type tramp ships were built. Their tonnage was from 8000 to 9000 d.w. and their average speed about 225 miles per 24 hours. During the after-war period the size of the average tramp ship was further increased to 10 000 t.d.w. and its service speed reached 250 nautical miles per 24 hours.

During this period improvements in the diesel type of engines were made, and their use became more and more widespread. More attention was paid to the coefficient of fineness in the design of vessels and, as a result, they became streamlined. Thus resistance to propulsion was further decreased.

During the second world war the Liberty type of tramp ship was developed as well as the similar types of Empire and Park ships. The tonnage of these types of tramp ships is on or about 10 600 d.w. and their speed about 11 knots. Also during the same period the T2 type of tanker was developed. The tonnage of this type of tanker was about 17 000 d.w.

The trend for bigger and faster ships, including tramps, continued in the post-war period. A considerable number of tramp ships with a deadweight tonnage of 14 000–15 000 and above and average service speeds of 14–16 knots are now in operation. As we pointed out, the bulk carriers industry which consists of big ocean-going, single-deck vessels is a post war development.

The application of many innovations has resulted, directly or indirectly, in the increase of the cargo-carrying capacity and

[1] See 'Unorthodox Shipping' in *Fairplay*, 12 November 1964, p. 11.

speed of vessels. For instance, on many large tramps patented metal hatch covers are fitted, which can be easily opened, thus saving time and labour before and after loading and discharging. Some of the bulk carriers are equipped with conveyor belts. As a result of the use of conveyor belts, iron ore comes up from the holds automatically. Also, some bulk carriers are equipped with self-discharge booms and thus the processes of loading and discharging are further accelerated. The time required for the loading and discharging of these modern big ships can now be measured not in terms of days but in terms of hours.

(b) Marine engineering

Steam engines originally consumed 1.35 to 1.6 kg (i.e. from 3 to 3½ lb) of coal per i.h.p. hour (indicated horse power). This high consumption necessitated large supplies of coal bunkers. Thus bunkers occupied space which otherwise would have been utilized for cargo stowage and in the case of long voyages intermediate bunkering was necessary.

Technical progress was rapid in this respect. During 1860 coal consumption for steam reciprocating engines was decreased to 1 kg (i.e. 2.2 lb) per i.h.p. hour. In 1882 coal consumption was further decreased to 0.65–0.75 kg (1.42–1.65 lb) per i.h.p. per hour. Finally, for coal-burners, during the period before the second world war, consumption was lowered to the point of 0.6 kg (1.32 lb) per i.h.p. per hour. Moreover, in addition to the economies derived from saving space for cargo, time, etc., the cost of fuel was further decreased by the use of oil instead of coal.

As a result of the use of the steam turbine and the diesel engine, further decreases in the cost of fuel were achieved. The medium-power steam turbines which are used for tankers and bulk carriers of about 30 000 t.d.w. with a service speed of 16 knots consume 0.25 kg per shaft h.p. per hour, whilst consumption for diesel engines was lowered to the point of 0.16 kg per shaft h.p. per hour.

Another significant technical achievement has been the discovery that heavier and cheaper fuels could be used for diesel engines. Thus, diesel engines became much more popular with shipowners, and they are now successfully competing with the steam turbines which still seem to dominate the picture where-ever production of great power is necessary.

An important step forward, so far as the cost of fuel is concerned, has been the big increase in steam pressure. Progress can be seen from the following table:[1]

Table 12. Increases in steam pressure

Year	Pressure (lb/in^2)
1820	5
1850	25
1870	50
1880	100
1890	200
1900	250

For technical reasons no further large-scale increases, i.e. beyond 250 lb per square inch, were attempted after 1900 for merchant vessels with steam reciprocating engines and smoke tubes. However, in large passenger vessels and tankers with turbines and water tube boilers there exist installations with pressures of 1000 lb per square inch and above.

Another significant development was the use of superheated steam both for reciprocating and turbine engines. For turbine engines, temperatures of superheated steam are developed of 800–900° F. Considerable increase in efficiency was brought about as a result of improvements at the other corner of the steam circuits, i.e. the condenser vacuum, and also because of improvements at the intermediate points of pre-heating feed water and the re-heating of steam.

In the field of diesel engines the development of pressure charging (or super-charging or turbo-charging) resulted in a considerable increase in the horsepower which could be obtained from an engine of given principal dimensions and rotational speed or, conversely, in the decrease of the dimensions of the engine and consequently of its weight for a given horsepower.

[1] See *Marine Engineers Handbook* by Labbecton and Marks (1st ed.), p. 1055.

Research is going on at the present time for increasing temperature and pressure in steam turbines and turbo-charged diesel engines still further, with a view to minimizing the weight and the space occupied and to increase efficiency, i.e. to reduce consumption per horsepower-hour, particularly in the steam turbine installations.

Needless to say that progress in marine engineering should not be judged only in terms of economies in consumption, but also from the point of view of economizing cubic capacity and weights on board.

To make this point clear let us consider the case of two ships of the same dimensions, form, and speed. If the structure has the same scantlings, i.e. the same strength for both ships, the Freeboard and Classification rules will allow them to float, when fully loaded at the same draught. Their displacements will be the same, which means that the total weight (i.e. weight of ship and her permanent fittings, cargo, fuel, water, and extra weights) will be the same for both. In order to have the same speed their machinery must develop the same power which we assume is 4000 B.H.P. (this power will drive an 11 000 d.w. tons normal tramp ship at 13–13.5 knots). The first ship, ship A, is driven by steam reciprocating machinery using superheated steam produced by Scotch Boilers. The second ship, ship B, is driven by a modern super-charged diesel engine, say, a 7 cylinder SAD60 Sulzer engine turning at 130 r.p.m.

The weight of machinery of ship A (including boilers together with their water, auxiliaries, piping, shafting, propeller, etc.) will be about 900 tons.[1] The corresponding weight for ship B (including, as for ship A, exhaust and donkey boilers) will be about 580 tons.[2] Thus, we have a difference of weight of 320 tons in favour of the motor ship. Ship A will be consuming 46 tons of fuel per day, while ship B only about 16—taking into consideration for both ships the fuel consumed for auxiliary purposes at sea. Consequently, the consumption for a 15 day passage will be 690 tons for ship A and 240 tons for ship B. Thus, the difference in fuel consumption is 450 tons in favour of the motor ship. Consequently, at the commencement of the 15 day loaded

[1] See W.P.A. Van Lammeren, *Ships and Marine Engines*, vol. IV (2nd edn.), pp. 32–6.
[2] Ibid., and Sulzer Bros. Booklet no. e/22, 02, 7–1—Dec. 5.

passage the motor vessel B will be able to carry $320 + 450 = 770$ tons more cargo than steam ship A, since, as stated previously, both vessels have the same displacement (i.e. total weight) when loaded. The use of special light weight materials such as aluminium alloys which are used for the construction of super-structures, etc., instead of steel, results in a lighter construction, i.e. decrease of the light weight of the ship and, therefore, increased cargo carrying capacity.

It is rather premature to make any definite statements on the importance of the use of atomic energy in merchant shipping (i.e. the use of atomic reactors instead of boilers). Nevertheless, it would seem that neither the turbines nor the diesels are the last word. It has already been established that nuclear engines yield an enormous range of action, as they can run a distance of about 300 000 sea miles—i.e. several times around the world—on the same charge of fissional material. However, the building costs are still very high and there are difficulties to be overcome so far as the safety factor is concerned.

Automation, that is to say the installation of extensive systems of remote and automatic controls on modern ships, is well under way. For obvious reasons automation has been applied more widely in the liner industry. For example. the British liner *Clan Macgillivray*, built 1962, 9039 G.R.T. and 4904 N.R.T., has an extensive system of remote and automatic controls which has resulted in a saving in engine-room manpower of 20 per cent. It has been reported that this figure may even be improved on when further operating experience has been gained.

The United States Lines' vessel, *American Challenger*, built 1962, 11 185 G.R.T., 6633 N.R.T., has been described 'as having entered the automation age', both in the engine room and in cargo-handling facilities. All-weather deck hatch covers are hydraulically operated by lever controls for opening or closing in less than two minutes. 'Tween deck covers are mechanically operated by windle wire, using ship's gear and, like all covers below the weather deck, are flush fitting to the surrounding deck. Covers on the weather deck are quickly 'dogged' by an ingenious device operated by one man. The light convertible cargo oil tanks designed for the carriage of no fewer than 21 different liquid cargoes, are completely smooth-sided, and have heating coils located in a hot well at the bottom of each tank. The heating system provides perfect control of temperatures and each tank is a completely independent unit in all respects, having independent filling, discharge, heating, and cleaning pipes. *When required, the deep tanks can be used for grain cargoes* and all have a single leaf cover operated by ship's gear. Fork-lift trucks, of 2 to 6 tons capacity, can operate throughout the ship's underdecks since they are absolutely flush and the modern method of shoring by steel mesh instead of wood battens greatly reduces shoring time and minimizes 'chafing' damage to cargo. Deck-head heights ranging from 8 ft to 16½ ft give maximum flexibility in handling all sizes of cargo, particularly the substantial container traffic now being handled by liners of the U.S. Lines. Refrigerated containers are carried on the weather deck. All winches and derricks are manipulated by ten electric winch consoles *from which the whole operation of swinging, spotting, raising, and lowering of cargo can be controlled by one man,* the console being sited on the winch house overlooking the hatch. A heavy lift derrick, 70 tons, placed between holds 3 and 4, can serve either without re-rigging.

Systems of remote and automatic controls have and are being installed on bulk carriers, tankers, and tramps. Soviet schemes with regard to a greater degree of automation are impressive.

(c) Port development

The period 1950–70 has been marked by great improvements all around the world in port facilities and cargo handling equipment, thus making possible loading and discharging of cargoes in greater quantities within shorter time limits. Space precludes mentioning more than a few examples:

Nothing has happened in the history of the U.S.A. that has done more to enhance the economy of the middle west than the completion of the St. Lawrence seaway. Cleveland in the operating year of this tremendous progress enjoyed a taste of what is to come. General cargo tonnage imports and exports handled by Cleveland's facilities increased from 68 000 in 1958 to 225 000 tons in 1959. A survey made by the Department of Port Control suggests an estimate of 500 000 tons by 1965.[1]

[1] See 'Cargo Handling in the World's Ports' in *Syren and Shipping*, 2 January 1963.

During the late 1960s major schemes of expansion and cargo handling were under way in many of the World's ports, such as Port Talbot, Belfast, New Orleans, Toledo, Toronto, Rotterdam, Los Angeles, Hamburg, Glasgow, New York, Bristol, U.S.S.R., Japanese, Rumanian ports, etc.

The significance of improvements in port facilities lies in the fact that the processes of loading and discharging are accelerated, congestion in ports may be avoided or minimized and, consequently, the speed with which ocean-going vessels, including tramps, are able to carry out their productive function is further increased. As a result, operating costs of vessels for performing a given service are reduced.

Moreover, satisfaction of the demand for regular transit of big quantities of bulk cargoes, dry or liquid, would not have been possible without the development of port facilities necessary for this purpose.

Even one technical innovation may constitute in itself a factor for profound changes on the nature of supply of tonnage. As R. H. Thornton points out in connection with the submarine telegraph:

But the culminating factor in this cheapening process was the installation throughout the world of the submarine telegraph. If the Great Eastern achieved nothing else, she did at least contribute to that and by 1887 no less than 100 000 miles of cable has been laid. Upon the economics of transport its effect was profound, for it enabled every moment of a ship's life to be usefully employed. When she arrived in port, not only had arrangements been made to discharge and dispose of her cargo, but her subsequent movements had already been discussed with and approved by her Owners. With no more delay than what is required to take in fuel and provisions, she could proceed to carry out her next engagement. The galvanising effect upon the whole mechanism of commerce was immense. Not only did it facilitate the mobilisation of carrying power and its concentration wherever wanted, it revolutionised the whole technique of buying and selling and by rendering 'forward' business possible it both steadied and regulated the flow of international commerce. *And finally, it completed the evolution of the modern 'tramp' steamer, the cheapest commercial vehicle in the world.*[1]

[1] R. H. Thornton, *British Shipping*, p. 73.

8. Economic effects of technical progress

As a result of technical progress and innovations, bigger, speedier, safer, more highly specialized units can now be built which are capable of producing the same service at a lower cost per ton-mile. Consequently, average freight rates in the long run are maintained at lower level, thus making possible the development of new trading routes. The present expectation of entrepreneurs that the bulk carrier rate should be considered as the 'standard rate' on many trading routes seems to be correct. It may be advisable to elaborate a little further at this point on the increase in economic efficiency as a result of technical progress with particular reference to tramp shipping.

A pre-war standard type of tramp ship of 8000 t.d.w. with an average service speed of 9 knots could perform, within a year, eight consecutive round voyages Hampton Roads–Continent (32 days at sea and 11 days in port for loading and discharging, i.e. 43 days per voyage 43 × 8 = 344 days plus 21 days per annum for repairs and delays due to unforeseeable factors).

Thus, the pre-war average tramp was capable of transporting about 58 400 tons of coal per year over a distance of 3500 useful nautical miles (i.e. 7300 tons of coal per voyage, plus 700 tons of bunkers and other weights. 7300 × 8 = 58 400 tons, distance Newport News–Rotterdam about 3500 nautical miles). Consequently, the annual output of the pre-war average tramp was 204 400 000 ton-miles (58 400 tons × 3500 useful miles).

A modern tramp ship of 14 000 t.d.w. with an average service speed of about 14 knots, is able to perform about 11 consecutive round voyages per year over the same route (21 days at sea and 10 days in port per voyage—since the time required for loading and discharging is now shorter because of better port facilities— i.e. 31 days voyage and 341 days for 11 round voyages, plus 24 days annually for repairs and delays due to unforeseeable factors.)

Thus, the modern tramp ship can transport about 148 500 tons of coal annually (13 500 tons per voyage plus 500 tons bunkers and other weights. 13 500 × 11 = 148 500 tons, distance Newport News–Rotterdam about 3500 nautical miles). Consequently, the annual output of the modern tramp would be 519 750 000 ton-miles (148 500 tons × 3500 useful miles).

This comparison between the 'old' and the 'modern' tramp indicates that:

(a) An increase in the tonnage of the world tramp shipping fleet (or of a national tramp shipping fleet, etc.) at a given period of time offers a rough but not an accurate indication of the actual increase of total supply. For an accurate estimate of the magnitude of total supply at a given period of time, average service speed must also be taken into account. Supply is a function of size and speed.

(b) Modern tramps are capable of producing more ton-miles in a given period of time than the old ones. The significance of this fact in relation to costs will be examined in chapter 5.

Progress in naval architecture and marine engineering has made possible the construction of new types of ships which can satisfy better, and at a lower cost, the demand for transport by sea of various commodities. Thus, apart from the tramp ship and its neighbours, i.e. cargo liners, bulk carriers, and tankers, there are today other relatively new branches of merchant shipping, such as, for instance, refrigerating ships, wine ships, gas tankers, tankers for chemicals, and so on.

The transport of oils which were carried in barrels by tramps, or of meats which were carried by old cargo liners, and so on, was always problematical and dearer before the construction of specialized ships.

Thus, the higher degree of specialization brought about by technical progress has caused the permanent substitution of the tramp in some of its marginal functions—such as, for instance, the transport of oils in barrels—by more efficient productive units which now constitute separate branches of merchant shipping. Also, as we shall shortly see in some detail, technical progress has brought about the temporary or permanent substitution of the tramp ship in some of its main functions by bulk carriers, tankers, and cargo liners.

We do not think that it will be necessary for us to comment on the benefits of the division of labour and specialization in particular industrial sectors. The advantages of specialization in sea transport were propounded by Sir William Petty who, in 1676, wrote the following:

Those who have command of the Sea Trade, may work at easier Freight with more profit, than others at greater: for as cloth must be cheaper made when one Cards, another Spins, another Weaves, another Draws, another Dresses, another Presses and packs; than when all the operations above-mentioned were clumsily performed by the same hand; so those in command of the Trade of Shipping can build long slight ships for carrying Masts, Fir Timbers, Boards, Balks, etc. And short ones for lead, iron, stones, etc. One sort of vessel to trade at ports where they need never lie aground, others where they must jump upon the sand twice every twelve hours... And this I take to be the chief of several reasons why the Hollanders can go at less Freight than their neighbours, viz, because they can afford a particular sort of vessel for each particular trade.[1]

9. The short run

No definite time limits can be set so far as the short-run period is concerned. However, it could be said that the short-run lasts only a few months and is a slightly longer period than the time required by the average tramp ship to complete the lengthiest round voyage. Furthermore, for analytical purposes, the following assumptions should be made in respect of the short run:

(*a*) Vessels under construction or conversion and vessels that are under repairs of long duration should not be considered as part of total supply.

(*b*) Vessels that in view of their age, etc., will shortly be proceeding to the scrap-iron yard for breaking should be considered as part of total supply.

It follows that, in the short run, there cannot possibly be any expansion or contraction of tonnage. However, this should not be taken to mean that, in the short run, the magnitude of active supply remains the same.

If freight rates are above equilibrium for one or more trading routes and if shipowners anticipate that such rates are an indication of an upward trend in the freight market, active supply will increase as a result of the following developments:

(i) (*a*) Total or partial postponement of periodic surveys and repairs.

[1] Sir William Petty, *Political Arithmetick*, London, 1676.

93

    (b) Development of the maximum possible service speed whilst at sea.

    (c) Acceleration of the processes of loading and discharging mostly by overtime work.

(ii) Recommissioning of laid-up tramp shipping tonnage.

(iii) Entry into the tramp freight market of productive units belonging to the neighbouring industries—if freight rates in their respective markets are less remunerative.

If freight rates are at equilibrium or above equilibrium for some trading routes, but because of various developments shipowners anticipate a general fall in the level of the tramp freight market, then shipping firms will endeavour to keep their vessels trading 'whilst the going is good'. Under such circumstances active supply may increase, but only by the means indicated under (i) a, b, c.

If freight rates are at equilibrium or below equilibrium point for most trading routes and shipowners do not anticipate an early improvement in the state of the market, active supply will decrease as a result of the following developments:

(i) (a) Decrease of the average speed of vessels whilst at sea.

    (b) Conclusion of fixtures for the carriage of quantities of cargo which are less than the maximum cargo-carrying capacity of vessels.

    (c) Longer voyages in ballast for the purpose of making tramps 'spot ships' at areas where rates are at a more satisfactory level.

    (d) Retardation of the processes of loading and discharging.

(ii) Entry of tramp tonnage to the liner market.

(iii) Laying up of vessels on termination of their voyage.

Thus, depending on the level of freight rates and their expectations in this respect, shipping firms adjust their output in the short run with a view to maximizing their profits or minimizing their losses. Consequently, in the short run, there may be changes in the magnitude of active supply, but total supply cannot expand or contract in a given point of time. In other words, in the short run, supply tends to be inelastic.

10. The long run

The duration of the long-run period should be considered as slightly longer than the average economic life of a tramp ship.[1] It is obvious that during such a period of time—let us say about twenty-five years—the supply of tonnage can expand substantially because entrepreneurs may follow one or more of the following courses:

(i) The ordering of new vessels.

(ii) The conversion of productive units belonging to the neighbouring industries of tankers, cargo liners, and even passenger vessels into tramps.

(iii) Long-term repairs by which vessels out of use are once more transformed into tramp ships suitable for employment.

The supply of tonnage may contract in the long run substantially because the following alternatives are open to entrepreneurs:

(i) Disposal of old tonnage for breaking up.

(ii) Conversion of tramp ships to productive units that are suitable for employment in the markets of the neighbouring industries. (Mostly into cargo liners and very rarely in the past into tankers.)

The construction of new ships is of course the basic source for the increase of supply and the breaking up of old ships for the reduction of supply.

It has already been indicated that the magnitude of supply in the long run depends upon the following factors:

(a) The level of demand for tramp shipping facilities.

(b) Shipowners' expectations regarding the level of the tramp freight market.

(c) Technical progress.

(d) The productive capacity and the level of employment of the world ship-building industry.

[1] When defining the long-run period in shipping it should be taken into account that the element of indivisibility remains present during the entire period of the investment. Furthermore, any calculations of net present value or discounted cash flow requires an imputed economic life for the object of investment.

95

We have already discussed the significance of factor (c) in some detail. For analytical purposes in the remaining part of this study—unless otherwise specified—a static technological level will be assumed.

Shipowners' expectations have tended to be high when the freight market was at a high level. On the other hand, a spirit of entrepreneurial pessimism has prevailed in the shipping world whenever the freight market has been, for some months, at a low level.

There exist ample data to support the argument that most orders to the shipyards have been given during periods of high freight rates, whereas during periods when freight rates were below equilibrium point, orders for the construction of new ships were either few, or at times, non-existent.

During periods of high freight rates when there is an increase in the demand for tonnage by shipping firms the price of ships also increases, and vice versa; during period of low freight rates when the demand for new tonnage is at extremely low levels the price of ships is at its lowest.

For instance, during December 1951 and December 1956, tramp freight rates were at a very high level. The index of tramp shipping freights of the U.K. Chamber of Shipping was at 168.5 (1948 = 100) for December 1951 and at 189.4 (1952 = 100) for December 1956. The price of a tramp ship of the Liberty type was £590 000 during 1951 and £670 000 during December 1956. On the other hand when freight rates were at a low level, for example during June 1952 when the index was down to 73.8 and during June 1958 when the same index reached 66.5, the price of the same ships was £315 000 and £145 000 respectively.

During periods of prosperity the demand for new tonnage tends to exceed the capacity of the world's shipyards to supply, and on the other hand shipping firms want to obtain delivery of new vessels as soon as possible, i.e. 'whilst the going is good'. One of the consequences of these important facts is that, during the prosperity stage, the price of ready ships tends to be higher than the price of the ship which is ordered from the shipyard for construction for a shipping firm after all details concerning its specification have been agreed. For instance, as can be seen in

Table 1, whilst in December 1956 the price of a 9500 t.d.w. tramp ship to be ordered from a shipyard was about £750 000, the price of a new vessel of the same specification ready for delivery was £920 000. The position is the opposite during low freight periods. Thus, during June 1960 the price of the same tramp ship was £755 000 if ordered, but only £620 000 if it was ready for delivery.

As we have already mentioned, shipping firms also act as tonnage suppliers by participating in the 'second-hand market' for the sale of used tonnage. Price trends in the second-hand market follow those of the market for new ships. Thus, the price of a Liberty ship during the period of the Suez crisis was above $1 000 000, but during 1960 some Liberties were sold at prices of £40 000–£50 000, i.e. not much in excess of their scrap value.

One of the most significant characteristics of expansion periods is that there is a time-lag between shipowners' decisions to expand their fleets and the date of delivery of the new ships to the firms. Apart from the technical factor, this time-lag is due to the productive capacity and the level of employment of the world's shipyards.

Before the first world war, a period of 12–15 months was required for the construction of a standard ship of 6000–7000 t.d.w., with relatively small reciprocating engines of comparatively high consumption. During the inter-war period the construction of a standard tramp ship of 8000–10 000 t.d.w. with more powerful reciprocating engines and more economical consumption required about one year. During the 1950s and after, the construction of a modern tramp of 11 000–14 000 t.d.w., with diesel or turbine steam engines, required 10–12 months.

It should be emphasized that the time periods indicated above represent amounts of time actually needed for *the building of* tramp ships. If there is a time interval between the signing of the building contract and the actual date of commencing to build the ship, it is possible to begin the construction of its engine and machinery earlier. Indeed, such a possibility is not rare. One of the effects of periods of prosperity and expansion in the tramp shipping industry and its neighbours is that the factors of production employed in the shipbuilding industry are fully utilized.

If a shipyard accepts more orders for the construction of new vessels than its productive capacity allows it to take in the short run—'forward commitments'[1] is not an unusual phenomenon at times of prosperity and expansion—then such orders are delayed either until completion of work on previous orders or until construction of additional facilities in the same shipyard has been completed. For instance, during the period of high freight rates of 1956-7, contracts were signed between shipping firms and shipyards' managements for the delivery of vessels after three or four years—which, of course, meant that the actual building of vessels would not have started earlier than two or three years after the signing of the contract.

The most important factor which hampers the contraction process is the shipowners' reluctance to decide to break up their old tonnage, even during the recession and depression stages. This reluctance is based upon the expectation that so long as the vessel remains seaworthy a few fixtures during a future rise in demand and freight rates will once more result in profitable trading. Furthermore, the old vessel can always be sold when tramp freight rates are high at a price which will be considerably higher than its scrap iron value or the one to be obtained during the depression stage.

Another factor which hampers the contraction of the supply of tonnage at periods of low freight rates is the policy followed by the shipyard enterprises. The shipbuilding industry is largely dependent for its livelihood on the demand for the construction of large merchant ships. Owing to the rather sharp fluctuations in the demand for new tonnage the shipbuilding industry itself is also subject to violent fluctuations. Thus, shipbuilding firms, in order to maintain a minimum level of employment during

[1] The term 'forward commitments' refers to formal agreements between builders and shipping firms in respect of the construction of ships and their delivery at some future date. It is different from the term 'builders' over-commitments'. During periods of expansion some shipyards have obtained orders for new ships which have proved to be beyond their productive capacity. Such over-commitments have resulted in breach of contracts so far as dates of delivery, etc., are concerned, and consequently, on the submission of claims for damages on the part of shipowners.

the stages of recession and depression, offer to shipping firms unusually attractive terms for new orders, such as low prices or mortgages of up to 90 per cent of the building cost. In the event of total absence of new orders some shipyards proceed with the construction of their own vessels which are either sold as ready ships or they are operated and managed by shipping firms for the shipyards' account.

In the course of our discussion of the various factors that affect the magnitude of supply in the long run, it has been pointed out that there is a time-lag between the entrepreneurs' decision to expand their fleet and the date of delivery of new vessels. We have also stated that entrepreneurs are reluctant to decide to sell their tonnage for breaking. Such decisions are usually taken during the depression stage when it is anticipated that the period of low freights may be rather prolonged. The following table may assist in clarifying this important point:

Table 13. Changes in freight rates and the world supply of tonnage 1956–8

Year	Freight index 1952 = 100	Tonnage of new vessels t.d.w.	Tonnage breaking t.d.w.
1956	157.0	4 400 000	438 000
1957	112.7	4 650 000	599 000
1958	66.3	4 490 000	1 152 000

The source of the data for the above table is the Chamber of Shipping of the U.K. *Annual Report* 1959. Tankers are not included, but cargo liners are included in the figures shown with regard to the deadweight tonnage of new and broken vessels. The fact that cargo liners are included does not make them less representative of the position in respect of the tramp shipping industry.

As is well known, tramp freight rates began to fall sharply at the end of summer 1957. However, as can be seen from Table 13, the supply of tonnage continued to expand even during 1958 when the tramp freight market reached its lowest level. This was due of course to the fact that tonnage which had been ordered in the previous years (1955, 1956, 1957) began to be delivered to shipping firms during 1958. On the other hand, breaking up of old tonnage did not begin to assume larger dimensions until 1958, when there was large unemployment of the industry's resources and expectations in respect of future market developments had become rather low.

The inflexible nature of supply also becomes apparent during the course of upward movements in the tramp freight market. In view of the time-lag between entrepreneurs' decisions to expand their fleet and the actual time of delivery of the new productive units, sudden increases of demand cannot be satisfied by total supply in the short run. Thus, freight rates rise sharply.

The competition to the tramp from productive units of the neighbouring industries as well as the entry of the tramp in the markets of these industries affects considerably the magnitude of supply over given periods of time. However, the substitution of the tramp, and vice-versa, does not depend only on the level of the tramp freight market. For this reason we propose to discuss the question of substitution in the next chapter.

Figure 5 may be of assistance in describing the position in relation to the supply of ton-miles during periods of demand and price fluctuations:

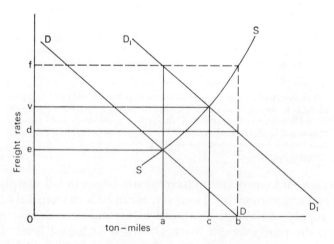

Fig. 5 Supply during demand and price fluctuations

The rise in demand for tramp shipping services raises the equilibrium freight rate from Oe to Ov and the equilibrium quantity bought and sold from Oa to Oc. In view of what has been pointed out in the last two sections we can expect supply to respond to the increase in the level of freight rates only after a period of several months. When the original increase in demand occurs, it will not be possible to produce a substantially larger amount of tramp shipping services until the building of new units has been completed. Thus, in the intervening period, the whole effect of the rise in demand will have to be taken out in a freight-rate increase. If supply continues to come on the tramp freight market at level Oa while demand rises from DD to D_1D_1, then average freight rate will rise to Of; this is the average freight rate that equates the new demand to the unchanged supply. Freights usually react quickly and may rise to Of within a few weeks after the rise in demand and stay there for a few months, that is to say, until the building of new ships has been completed. When new units enter the market, production of services expands to Ob, then freight rates fall drastically at Od level.[1]

11. Conclusion

As indicated at the beginning, our aim in this chapter has been to outline some of the economic realities of the industry and its neighbours and, at the same time, to pinpoint those properties of the supply of tramp shipping facilities which are of significance so far as fluctuations in freight rates are concerned.

It should be particularly remembered in this connection that the supply of tramp shipping facilities cannot expand or contract in the short run. Also, that in the long run there is a time-lag between entrepreneurs' decision to expand their fleets and the actual time of delivery of the new vessels. Furthermore, shipowners are, as a rule, rather reluctant to dispose of their old and uneconomic tonnage for breaking. Thus, supply is inelastic and not capable of responding to demand and price changes at a given period of time.

[1] See S.G.Sturmey, 'On the pricing of tramp ship freight services,' *Occasional Papers Series*, University of Lancaster.

Chapter 4

The Tramp Ship and its Neighbours

In this chapter we propose to examine the substitution relationships of the tramp with the tanker, the bulk carrier, and the liner, and the entry of the tramp into the markets for these vessels.

1. The tramp ship and the tanker

The tramp

The old method of transporting oil in barrels over long distances by dry-cargo ships, including tramps, is now obsolete and gone for ever. This source of employment for the deep-sea tramp is practically non-existent at the present time.

It has been reported that even as late as after the Korean War, i.e. 1952–3, when on the one hand the tramp freight market was at a relatively low level and on the other there was a growing demand for oil transport, there were a few conversions of large tramps into tankers. However, this kind of entry of the tramp into the tanker market proved to be costly both in terms of money and time. Consequently, it was not widely followed by shipping firms.

The development of the modern big and fast super tankers and mammoth tankers, which are capable of producing the same service at a considerably lower cost per ton-mile than the T2 tankers and the converted tramp, has eliminated this kind of long-run substitution of the tanker by the tramp.

The tanker: Short-run entry

The time and costs involved in the process of preparing a tanker

to be used as a grain carrier are relatively small.[1] Assuming
that this work is carried out with the assistance of crew members,
its actual cost will depend upon the nature of the previous
cargo carried by the tanker and its size. The cost of preparing a
tanker under the Greek flag with a d.w. tonnage in the neighbourhood of 20 000, the previous employment of which was
in the 'dirty trade', i.e. transportation of crude oil, is about
£5000 (i.e. cost of chemicals, fuel, timber, and payments to
crew for extra work), but the cost of preparing a tanker with the
same d.w. tonnage under the same flag, the previous employment of which was in the 'clean trade' (i.e. transportation of
refined oils) is below £1000 (i.e. fuel, timber, and labour
costs).

Big tankers are not, as a rule, employed for the carriage of
refined oils.[2] The cost of preparing a tanker under the Greek
flag for the transport of grain with d.w. tonnage in the neighbourhood of 30 000 is about £7000. Needless to say, that if the
tanker remains trading in the dry-cargo market for more than
one voyage, the above sums may be taken to constitute the
initial cost of entry. However, if the tanker re-enters its own
market after completion of one grain voyage the cost of preparation for its re-entry to the dry-cargo market will depend on
the time that the tanker will remain trading as an oil carrier.
If such a tanker is fixed for, let us say, one or two voyages for the
carriage of oil before it re-enters the dry-cargo market, the process of tank cleaning will be considerably easier and, consequently, the cost of preparation will be smaller than the figures
given above.

The larger cargo-carrying capacity of the tankers (and their
higher speed in comparison with the old tramps) made them
capable of: (a) competing successfully with tramps both 'old'
and 'modern' in the carriage of grains; (b) of replacing permanently (together with the bulk carrier and the modern large
tramp) the 10 000 ton tramps in the carriage of grain on those

[1] Such preparation consists of thoroughly cleaning the cargo-oil-tanks, encasing
with wood the cargo oil-pipe suctions in the tanks, closing off the cargo oil pipes in
the pump room, closing off the steam smothering and cargo heating oil-pipe lines.
[2] Up to early 1966 only a few relatively large tankers of about 30 000 t.d.w. were
employed for the carriage of refined oil.

trading routes where the necessary loading and discharging facilities exist.

The entry of the tanker into the tramp freight market is a relatively new economic phenomenon. There were several developments which led entrepreneurs owning tanker tonnage to the conclusion that this type of employment for their ships represented a positive alternative.

During the 1950s and particularly after the Suez affair, the world supply of tanker tonnage kept increasing at a faster rate than demand requirements. This rapid increase in the magnitude of supply was primarily due to the fact that the newly built 'general purpose' tankers were larger than the T2 type.

As a result of the creation of tanker tonnage capacity in excess of demand requirements, tanker freight rates fell sharply and by August 1959 idle tanker tonnage—excluding about 1 000 000 tons of the U.S. Reserve Fleet—was 'a little over 7 600 000 t.d.w.' During late August laid-up tanker tonnage reached the maximum figure of 7 717 468 t.d.w.[1]

Under the circumstances, tankers originally of the T2 type began to enter the tramp freight market as grain carriers. This form of substitution of the tramp by the tanker reached significant dimensions after 1959, when super-tankers (i.e. tankers of 30 000 t.d.w. or above) began to enter the tramp freight market. In this connection it may be worth while repeating the comments of the *Financial Times* concerning the effects of the entry of the first supertanker into the tramp freight market in 1959.[2] These concern the s.t. *Hadrian*, 44 000 t.d.w., 30 344 G.R.T. and 17 564 N.R.T., built in 1959. During early May 1959 this vessel was fixed to take a cargo of grain from U.S.A. Gulf to Antwerp/Hamburg range. A lump sum of $123 750 was paid for freight. This, in fact, meant that the management of the supertanker agreed to fix their vessel at the rate of $3.10 per ton, that is to say, a rate which was lower by $1.40 per ton than the one prevailing in the market at the time. As pointed out in the *Financial Times*, this fixture meant that the s.t. *Hadrian* substituted $4\frac{1}{2}$ tramp ships of the Liberty type which could have carried the

[1] See *Market Summary* circular issued by the Chartering Department of John I. Jacobs & Company Ltd., London, and dated 21 August 1959 and 4 September 1959.
[2] See: 'Supertankers in Grain Trade' in the *Financial Times*, May 13 1959.

same quantity of the same cargo over the same distance at a considerably higher cost per ton-mile.

During 1961 open-market voyage charterings reached the figure of 72 531 000 tons of dry cargoes. Out of this total 8 781 000 tons of grain were shipped on tankers.[1]

Subsequent favourable developments for shipping firms in the tanker market and the continuation of the growth of demand for transport of bulk commodities caused the temporary decrease in the size of the substitution margin. On the other hand, original hesitations by many shipping firms about the wear and tear that may be caused as a result of the use of the tanker as a grain carrier seem to have been removed.

Thus, many shipping firms are now using some of their tankers as grain carriers for relatively long periods of time, and in order to minimize the relatively long ballast part of these voyages such tankers whenever possible re-enter their market. For instance, the round voyage U.S. Gulf–Bombay grain and thence Persian Gulf–East Coast U.S.A. crude oil has been proved a rather profitable one. Briefly it may be stated that the short-run entry of the tanker into the dry-cargo market constitutes a well-known feature of this market. The margin of such substitution depends on the level of freight rates. Thus during 1963, when the level of freight rates in the tanker market was relatively low, the margin of substitution of the dry-cargo ship by the tanker reached the figure of 900 103 tons.

Although a little more single voyage activity was evident at the beginning of this week there is still insufficient substance in the business quoting to bring about any real change in the current low freighting levels. The number of tankers employed in the grain trade at the 15th July was 44 vessels of 900 103 tons d.w. with a further three of 62 036 tons fixed for forward loading.[2]

During summer 1965, when again the level of tanker freight rates was relatively low, the margin of substitution of the dry-cargo ship by the tanker assumed considerable dimensions:

The continued falling off in demand in the Caribbean Sea area has brought a further decline in Black Oil freight rates. At the same time

[1] See 'Economic Research as an aid to Planned Shipowning' by C.F.H.Cufley in *The Syren*, July 1962.

[2] See *Market Summary* by John I. Jacobs & Co., 19 July 1963.

demand from the Persian Gulf remains sufficient at least to maintain present levels. Tanker tonnage in the Grain Trade as at 31st August comprised 219 vessels of 5 103 183 tons d.w. whilst a further 28 ships of 682 071 tons d.w. were fixed for loading ahead.[1]

Long-run entry

The long-run entry of the tanker into the dry-cargo markets, in other words the conversion of the T2 tankers into dry-cargo vessels (see the 'cheap bulk carriers fleet', chapter 3), is also a relatively recent development.

The 'green light' for investing in this kind of enterprise was given to shipowners by the following two significant facts. On the one hand by the end of the 1950s it had become clear that the T2 type of tankers were becoming obsolete so far as the tanker market was concerned, and on the other the demand for transport of dry cargoes in bulk continued to grow. Thus, by the end of 1959 tramp freight rates were at a reasonably high level.

Under these circumstances a number of shipping firms were able to take advantage of the low order book of various ship-yards in Japan and other countries. In the case of Japanese ship-yards sums of $1 308 000[2] were paid for each conversion which lasted from 3 to 6 months.

As has already been pointed out, the T2 tankers were vessels with a d.w. tonnage in the neighbourhood of 16 500. However, their tonnage after conversion increased by 4000–5000 d.w. on the average, whilst their average service speed did not de-crease more than half a knot.

Owing to their low depreciation cost converted tankers could compete with bulk carriers rather successfully and shipping firms could offer them for employment at rates which were even lower than 'bulk carrier rates'. Also, some of these vessels, like other bulk carriers, were especially converted for long-term contract business (Australian coal to Japan). Furthermore, shipping firms owning or managing converted tankers obtained long-term contract employment at freight rates which were

[1] Ibid., 10 September 1965.
[2] See Westinform *Shipping Report*, no. 223, February 1963.

not considered remunerative so far as modern dry-cargo vessels were concerned. For instance, during late 1961 three 19 000 t.d.w. Danish tankers were scheduled for conversion into 26 000 ton bulk carriers for the carriage of pig-iron from South Africa to Japan.

In addition, for many of the converted tankers employment was normally secured in the 'open market' on a single voyage basis.

However, in late 1962 when 'bulk carrier' and tramp freight rates fell to lower levels than the previous two years, new schemes for conversion were halted. Consequently, some of the remaining T2 tankers are now more likely either to be used for employment in the 'clean trade' or as depot ships, or to go to the scrap-iron yard or to be converted into floating workshops instead of into cheap bulk carriers.

From the factual material contained in this section it may be gathered that the use of tankers as dry-cargo vessels must have had some marginal effect on the level of tramp freight rates. We now attempt to reach some broad conclusions about price effects of the short run and long run use of tankers as dry-cargo vessels.

The entry of tankers and old tankers converted into bulk carriers in the dry-cargo market assumed significant dimensions during the early sixties owing to lack of remunerative employment of these productive units in their own market. As will be seen in the next chapter, tankers were able to compete successfully with tramps because they were capable of producing services of the same nature, at a lower cost per ton-mile.

Consequently, in all those routes where the tanker could be used as a grain carrier and the converted tanker as a bulk carrier, that is to say, in all those trading routes where there was a demand for transport of relatively large quantities of grain and other bulk commodities and the necessary loading and discharging facilities for this purpose, freight rates tended to remain at a lower level than that which would have prevailed if the tanker had not entered the dry-cargo market.

Undoubtedly, the substitution of the tramp by the tanker was one of the contributory factors that caused the magnitude of available supply (i.e. unused capacity consisting mostly of pre-war and Liberty tramps) to remain relatively large in the early sixties in spite of the growth of demand for transport of bulk commodities. As will be seen later, the existence of a sizeable quantity of laid-up tramp shipping tonnage was one of the factors that prevented a sharp rise in the level of freight rates.

The relative decrease in the supply of tanker tonnage caused by the entry of tankers into dry-cargo market did not have any appreciable effect on the level of tanker rates. Most of the tankers used as grain carriers were unable to operate as tankers at the prevailing rates. Thus, their dry-cargo activity had little effect so far as the tanker market was concerned.

Moderate increases in the level of tanker freight rates, which were due either to cyclical or seasonal factors, have caused the exit of most of the non-converted relatively large tankers from the dry-cargo markets and the return to their own market.

2. The bulk carrier and the tramp

A brief description of the modern bulk carrier has been given in chapter 3. As has already been pointed out, the main function of the bulk carrier is to satisfy the demand for transport of relatively large quantities of bulk commodities over regular routes and over regular time periods. For example, during February 1963 there were 310 ships which could be considered as bulk carriers. Out of these 122, mostly of the larger size, were employed on long-term coal, grain, or ore contracts. The other 188 were fixed in the open market like other tramp ships. On all those trading routes where the necessary loading and discharging facilities were available bulk carriers, owing to their larger size and greater speed, proved capable of producing the the same services as the average tramp at a lower cost per ton-mile. Thus, on all those routes where demand requirements could be satisfied by the available supply of bulk carrier and modern large tramp tonnage freight rates tended to remain at a relatively low level. In the circumstances there can hardly be any doubt about the correctness of the view commonly held by entrepreneurs to the effect that the 'bulk carrier rate' should, from now on, be considered as the 'standard rate' in respect of these particular routes.

It has already been indicated that, in an economic sense, there is no basic difference between a relatively small sized bulk carrier and a modern large tramp. Consequently, one can see the basis of shipowners' expectations that the 18 000–24 000, and to some extent the 24 000–36 000 t.d.w., categories of bulk carriers, which appeared to be most popular in the sixties, will—together with the S.D.14 and Freedom types of tramp—replace the Liberties which have practically ended their economic life.

At the present period of prosperity in the shipping world it would appear that the only factor which prevents an even more rapid growth of the world bulk carrier fleet is the question of port facilities, i.e. the lack of deep-water berths and loading and discharging facilities.

Owing to lack of potential contract business during early 1963, a rather considerable proportion of modern bulk carrier tonnage entered the tramp freight market. The position was no different in the late sixties. Shipping firms managing bulk carriers up to 32 000 t.d.w. in size, trade these ships in a more or less similar manner to their tramps—the nature of their employment depending on the current level of freight rates in the open and time charter markets as well as on the shipowners' expectations in this respect.

As already indicated, the substitution of the tramp by the bulk carrier has resulted in keeping freight rates on a number of routes at a lower level than the one which would have prevailed had this development not occurred. Thus, it is not now possible for the 9000–10 000 t.d.w. tramp to compete with the bulk carrier in these routes. One may mention as an example the U.S. Gulf–Continent route which, until a decade ago, was one of the most significant so far as tramps were concerned. As is well known, bulk commodities over this route are now almost entirely carried by bulk carriers.

It may be logical to expect that the bulk carrier will replace permanently the present average-size tramp ship on all those routes where there is a demand for transport of relatively large quantities of bulk commodities. However, the over optimistic assumption that the modern bulk carrier will replace the 10 000 t.d.w. tramp ship on practically all routes where the latter is trading at present (and that, therefore, deep-water berths must be constructed on practically every route) does not seem to take into serious consideration the incremental nature of demand for tramp shipping services. In this connection it may be recalled that no more than two decades ago it was predicted that the 10 000 t.d.w. tramp would replace the 4500–6000 tonners on all trading routes. However, these small tramps are still in high demand. There is no economic reason to suggest that the demand for spot transit of bulk cargoes of 8000–12 000 metric tons will disappear!

3. The bulk carrier and the tanker

It is obvious that when—owing to reasons already given—the tanker is trading as a grain carrier it must also be considered as a substitute for bulk carriers.

Grain fixtures for tankers are usually concluded at rates which are a little lower than those obtained for bulk carriers. The reason for this difference is that, in the case of tankers, the discharging and loading processes are more costly to charterers because tankers do not possess the necessary equipment for the loading and discharging of grain cargoes. Also, at the initial stages of the tankers' entry into the dry-cargo market, the risk of damage to cargo (contamination, etc.) was thought to be of considerable proportions.

The short-run entry of the tanker into the dry-cargo markets as a grain carrier made it clear for entrepreneurs that the in-ballast part of the voyage could be minimized permanently by building ships suitable for carrying both liquid and dry cargoes. The 'marriage of the tanker with the bulk carrier' could produce a more economically efficient type of ship. It would appear that in the late sixties technical difficulties along this direction were overcome and the ore/oil carriers and bulk/oil carriers were becoming gradually more and more popular. During early 1967 there were 19 ore/oil carriers on order, totalling 1 562 000 t.d.w., and 38 bulk/oil carriers, totalling 2 675 000 t.d.w. As to the size of these bulk/oil carriers on order the majority were between 60 000 and 80 000 t.d.w. totalling 25 vessels and 1.8 million t.d.w. The remaining 0.9 million t.d.w. were spread out in the size group between 45 000 and 105 000 t.d.w.

The creation of the ore/oil and bulk/oil fleet indicated that another type of ship could be built, the 'three purpose ship' or the ore/bulk/oil carrier, that could be suitable for the loading of practically all bulk commodities as well as oils. This is a more economically efficient type of ship, because, in view of its suitability for the carrying of different kinds of bulk cargoes, the in-ballast part of the voyage is further minimized. Several of these new ships with d.w. tonnages between 50 000–75 000 were in existence in the late sixties. There is every indication that when the initial technical difficulties for the building of these ships have been overcome they will become more and more popular amongst the large shipping firms. In the long run no competitor will be able to remain in the market if his tonnage is not suitable for trading with as little in-ballast as the tonnage of the others.

4. The tramp ship and the cargo liner

During the after-war period, cargo liner firms have followed a cautious policy of expansion. Consequently, at periods of high demand in the liner market, a considerable percentage of general cargoes is shipped on tramps. Such tramps either belong to the liner companies or to other shipping firms and are chartered by the liner firms, usually on a time charter basis.

Freight rates for single voyages (or in the 'single voyage market') and time charter rates (or rates in the 'time charter market') tend to move in the same direction. When single voyage rates are at a high level, time charter rates (including liner charter rates) also tend to be on a high level. Usually, when the demand for tramp shipping facilities is at a high level, time charter rates—although on a high level—tend to be a little less remunerative than those of the single voyage market. This is due to the fact that, as we know, time charters, including liner charters, are of longer duration than the single voyage charter. Thus, the entrepreneur who concludes a time charter fixture for a relatively long period avoids the risks of the sudden fluctuations of the tramp freight market. However, this is not always the case. There are instances during periods of prosperity when liner charters are even more remunerative than those of the single voyage market. This is due to a variety of reasons. Most tramp owners, when they agree to a specification for their new tramps, have in mind the liner market. However, this does not necessarily mean that all tramps are suitable for the specific trade that may be wanted by a liner company in a given period of time. For instance, a liner company may want a tramp ship of 11 000–11 500 t.d.w. with a speed of 14.5 knots. There are not many of these at the present. Consequently, in order to secure the services of such relatively high speed tramps, liner companies may be compelled to offer time charter rates which are more remunerative than those of the single voyage market. Needless to say, there are other specific reasons as a result of which relatively high freight rates may have to be paid by liner companies, one of them being the 'spot ship' (see chapter 1, section 6).

When single voyage rates are at a low level, time charter rates also tend to be low too. Usually, during the stages of recession and depression, when single voyage rates are not at a remunerative level so far as the relatively small tramp is concerned, time charter and liner charter rates may tend to be a little higher in the short run than those of the single voyage market. However, this is by no means certain and it depends on the level of demand in the liners' market. Therefore, the only thing that can be stated with certainty is that freight rates in the single voyage and time charter 'markets' tend to move in the same direction.

As we have already pointed out, many existing tramp ships were constructed with a view to being 'attractive' to the liner companies whenever necessary. There are several reasons that make the temporary entry of the tramp ship in the liners' market a positive alternative.

During periods of low freight rates a liner charter may be the only means of avoiding having to send a tramp ship to the lay-up berth. During periods of revival in the industry, when the upward trend in freight rates is fairly uncertain and owners' expectations not very high at the beginning, tramp shipping firms prefer to recommission their tonnage by securing a liner charter or time charter until the single voyage market 'becomes firm'. On the other hand, during the prosperity stage, it is not considered wise by many of the industry's entrepreneurs to have their firms exposed to the sudden fluctuations in the level of tramp freight rates by trading all their tonnage on single voyage charter. Consequently, during periods of high freight rates, many entrepreneurs prefer to have some of their tonnage fixed on liner or time charter—even though this may mean a loss of revenue in the short run.

Moreover, there are several other short- as well as long-run considerations that make a liner charter a positive alternative so far as tramp shipping firms are concerned. For instance, entrepreneurs may wish to avoid the uncertainties of the tramp freight market because their firms are under heavy commitments. A liner charter may be the best type of fixture for the purpose of bringing back to the Continent a tramp ship that has been trading for a long time in the Far East so that repairs and new changes may be carried out. The degree to which a vessel depreciates depends, to a considerable extent, on the way it is used. Thus, a liner charter during a period of heavy winter, let us say, for a West African round voyage may allow the shipping firm to avoid fixing a tramp ship continually for transatlantic single voyages, and so on.

In view of the above, the temporary substitution of the cargo liner by the tramp has, over various intervals of time, assumed considerable proportions. For instance, it has been estimated that during the early years after the end of the second world war, owing to the relative shortage of liner tonnage on the one hand, and the recession that occurred in the tramp freight market on the other, about 20 per cent of the tramp shipping fleet was engaged in the transportation of general cargoes on liner charter.

The oligopolistic market structure of liners constitutes a serious barrier for the long-run entry of the tramp into the liners' market. This kind of entry is costly and difficult in the case of shipping firms which have not been previously connected with the liner trade and are, therefore, not members of any conference.

However, even as late as the period after the Suez affair, when tramp freight rates were at extremely low levels, there were attempts by shipping firms owning tramp tonnage for a permanent entry in the liners' market. It is said that only a few of them have been successful. Tramp ships were used as liners at the initial stages of the firms' transformation. Some of these ships, due to oligopolistic competition from liner companies and their higher running costs per ton-mile, were trading at a loss. However, during the same period of time new liners were ordered by the shipping firms in question and the necessary apparatuses of offices and agents at the various ports of call were built up.

On the basis of the experience of such attempts, and assuming that there is a demand in the trading routes selected, and also capital funds available to meet the cost of purchasing second-hand or new liners as well as the additional overhead costs that are presupposed for the formation of a liner firm and the probable initial losses (which will be due to the inability of the firm to provide the same services at a cost equal to that of the established liner firms at the beginning), it may be concluded that there is no other serious economic reason to prevent a shipping firm from entering permanently into the liner market.

There are no barriers preventing liner firms during periods of limited demand for their services and relatively high tramp freight rates from fixing their vessels in the tramp freight market. In fact, this policy is widely followed by shipping firms who own and manage both liner and tramp tonnage and, therefore, possess the necessary know-how.

Liners are, as a rule, vessels with higher fixed and variable costs than the average tramp. However, during periods of relatively high freight rates they can be fixed for one or more single voyages like the ordinary tramp. Also, during periods where the demand for the services of liner companies is at a low level, bulk cargoes are carried on their vessels for part of the round voyage. Such cargoes, otherwise called 'base cargoes', form part of the total cargo onboard and are carried at relatively low freight rates. Moreover, a liner may be transformed into a 'tramp' for part of the voyage, by loading bulk commodities, if the necessary deviations are not extensive and if the other alternative is to return to the home port in ballast.

In addition, there are other considerations which make the long-run entry of the liner in the tramp freight market a positive alternative so far as liner firms are concerned.

It has already been pointed out that one of the characteristics of the liners' market is the existence of quality competition and the speed by which vessels can carry general cargoes to their destinations is one of the most important elements so far as quality of service is concerned. One of the solutions that liner firms give to this problem, is to have all their vessels working at approximately the same speed. However, such an average speed cannot be different from the maximum working speed of the oldest and slowest units of the fleet. Apart from the question of costs, a low average speed may result in the loss of business to other liner firms. When the increase in the average speed of the firm's fleet becomes vitally necessary, one of the solutions is the permanent entry of the slowest units of the fleet in the tramp freight market.

The long-run effects of containerization are bound to be felt shortly in the tramp freight market. According to the study of Lambert Bros., mentioned in section 1 of chapter 1, by 1973/74 thirteen trading routes will be served by 212 container ships. It is estimated in the study that each modern container ship will replace 3.6 traditional cargo liners.[1] Thus, the estimated conventional cargo vessels to be displaced by container ships in the next four years will be 847. Assuming that the average size of each traditional cargo liner is about 10 000 d.w.t. we can conclude that there will be about 8.5 million tons of cargo liners available in an industry which is already characterized by excess capacity. There are additional schemes for container services still at the planning stage which, naturally, are not taken into account in the calculations of the study. Also, the study does

[1] The replacement ratio is calculated on the basis of the following formula:

$$r = (a \times b \times c \times k) \div (A \times D)$$

where: a = number of voyages per annum/container ship,
  b = number of containers/container ship,
  c = capacity of containers/container ship,
  k = constant ($= 0.95$) to all for a 5 per cent loss of stowage in containers compared with general cargo ships,
  A = number of voyages per annum/conventional liners,
  D = capacity of conventional liner in cubic feet.

not take into consideration the fact that due to the greater capital requirements of containerization the liner market assumes more and more of an oligopolistic structure on a world-wide basis, which may enable it, in the long run, to minimize excess capacity. In addition, it should be mentioned that several conventional cargo liners are presently under construction.

Thus, it would appear that in the next four years or so there will be about 10 million tons of conventional liner tonnage available either in the tramp freight market or in the liner market to replace tramps functioning as liners in the short run. This amount of tonnage represents an increase of approximately 18 per cent of the existing supply of tramp shipping tonnage, and it is bound to have a serious marginal effect on the level of tramp freight rates.

5. Substitution

We have seen in this chapter that, in the present stage of technological development, the services produced by tramp ships can also be produced by vessels belonging to the neighbouring industries of dry-cargo liners, bulk carriers, and tankers—as far as grain cargoes are concerned.

As is well known, industries producing goods or services with a number of close substitutes usually have elastic demands, whilst industries producing goods or services with no close substitutes have inelastic demands. The tramp ship is substitutable only by productive units of the neighbouring industries of cargo liners, bulk carriers, and tankers. All data available proves that the substitution of the tramp is a marginal process and that there are definite limitations so far as the margin of substitution is concerned. Moreover, the means of substitution in question, although close in many respects, cannot be considered as perfect. Consequently, it may be stated that the services offered by the tramp shipping industry are *moderately substitutable*.

The existence of alternative means of transport in some areas under certain circumstances may give a wider choice to the consumer, i.e. the shipper. It may be stated, therefore, that the fact that the industry's services are moderately substitutable is one of the factors which led to the hypothesis that the elasticity of demand for tramp shipping services in the long run, tends to be greater than unity (see chapter 2, section 6).

For analytical purposes we have examined the substitution relationships of the tramp ship with each one of its neighbours separately. As indicated, substitution in merchant shipping is determined by demand, price, and cost relationships. For example, when the magnitude and intensity of demand for tramp shipping services are high, whilst the tanker market is at a comparatively lower level, relatively small tankers enter the tramp freight market as grain carriers. Assuming *ceteris paribus* it could be stated that with the entry of the tanker, available supply in the tramp market increases and therefore average freight rates fall. On the other hand, so long as the entry of the tanker continues, available supply in the tanker market is reduced and consequently freight rates rise. Eventually an equilibrium point is reached and employment of the small tanker is not more or less, remunerative in the tramps' market than in the tankers' market. Thus, there is no inducement for the entrepreneur to transfer his tankers from the one market to the other. Although it is realistic to assume that once the entry of the tanker in the tramp freight market commences, such a tendency towards an equilibrium price is created, we would run the risk of over-simplification if we omitted to stress the point that the entry of the units of one of the neighbouring industries in the tramp freight market may create a chain reaction which can affect, to a greater or lesser degree, many branches of merchant shipping as well as the shipbuilding industry.

Let us say, for the sake of the example, that the tramp shipping and the liners' industries are passing through a period of relative prosperity, but that the tanker market is not on a satisfactory level particularly in so far as the smaller tankers are concerned. In the circumstances, it can be expected that in addition to other developments in the tanker industry (some of the smaller tankers may enter into the 'clean trade', i.e. carrying refined oil products, others may be converted or scrapped) more tankers will enter the tramp freight market as grain carriers. Such an expectation may lead entrepreneurs of the tramp shipping industry to charter more of their tonnage to liner firms. In view of the availability of suitable tramp tonnage some of the liner companies may, in turn, decide to transform the slowest units of their fleets into tramps by fixing them on a single voyage basis in those trading routes where the problem of bulk carrier and tanker competition is not present, and so on. In the long run orders for conversions and bigger and faster ships will follow.

As is already apparent, the substitution relationships of the tramp shipping industry with its neighbours have an obvious marginal effect on the average level of tramp freights. However, there is no evidence to suggest that these relationships have ever constituted the basic reasons for the sharp fluctuations in the level of freight rates that form the main characteristic of the tramp market during the course of about a century.

Chapter 5

The Costs of Operation in Tramp Shipping

A shipowner combining factors of production in various ways is seeking to ensure that in the long run revenue will exceed costs to a maximum extent. Thus, a brief examination of the nature of the costs of operation is essential for the understanding of the functioning of shipping firms as well as for the understanding of developments in the tramp freight market.

The theoretical basis of the concept of economic costs is that something must be forgone as a result of the use of a certain resource for the purpose of producing a particular kind of output If nothing is forgone, no economic cost has been incurred. Broadly speaking, as in the case of other forms of transport, the costs of operation of the shipping firm may be classified into:

1. Capital costs
2. Fuel and other material inputs
3. Labour costs
4. Land use

1. Capital costs

Production of tramp shipping services presupposes the use of capital structures and equipment such as, for instance, the ships, their engines, their auxiliary machinery and electronic equipment, canals, lighthouses, cranes, tugboats, and so on. Such assets differ amongst themselves for they are specialized in relation to the output which they can produce, but what they have in common is the need for physical and periodic replacement.

Shipping firms do not need to own all the above-mentioned assets. So far as they are concerned payments of such items as canal dues, light dues, dues etc. for the use of cranes, towage, are short-run costs. However, one way or the other, shipping firms in order to function as such must pay for their use and in the long run must contribute to their maintenance and replacement.

A distinction must be made at this point so far as capital structures and equipment are concerned. It is necessary to distinguish between the situation existing prior to their construction and the situation created once they are operationally available. The sums to be paid by a shipping firm for the utilization of the resources necessary to construct and equip a ship will indicate the anticipated alternative value of these resources. The sums spent by the firm in order to purchase the ship constitute the original cost which no longer features in the economic costs of producing the service for which the ship was constructed. Thus, once a ship has been delivered to its owners its purchase must be taken as a matter of fact. What represents a cost after a vessel has been delivered to its new owners is the interest lost on its saleable value, the cost of hanging on to the ship. The interest on money funds that may have been borrowed by the firm for the purpose of purchasing a ship constitute an opportunity cost.

If we take a look at the various assets that are indispensable for the normal functioning of a shipping firm, it will come to our notice that some of them are short lived whilst others are characterized by their longevity.

Such assets as various parts of the engine room (rings, springs, packings, etc.); various parts of the deck and the bridge (lifeboats', equipment, insulating material for pipes, etc.); various parts of the officers' and crew accommodation (curtains, bedsheets, crockery, etc.); and various parts of the office's equipment, are short lived and therefore their replacement becomes necessary. Such replacement costs of relatively short-lived assets—like maintenance costs—depend to a great extent upon the different conditions under which vessels are trading. For instance, if we assume that during the course of a heavy winter period two tramp ships of the same age and specification belonging to the same firm were trading continually, the first one on the route U.K.–Canada–U.K. and the second U.K.–West

African coast–U.K., we could safely state that the maintenance and replacement costs of the first vessel for the same period would—other factors being equal—have proved to be considerably higher. The cost of replacement of short-lived assets is not an overhead or a fixed cost to the shipping firm, but it is a short-run cost highly variable and allocatable to the provision of various stores, spare parts, etc., which may be required.

On the other hand some of the assets of the shipping firm are characterized by their longevity. Looking at a well maintained dry-cargo ship as a whole, we may say with some degree of certainty that its economic and physical life may last as long as twenty-five years or even more. However, apart from the short-run maintenance expenses, and depending on the kind of use of the ship, on the maintenance policy followed by the firm, on the efficiency of its officers and crew, as well as on time, in the mid run, that is to say, normally after the second special survey (each special survey is carried out every four years), it will be noted that even some of the assets of the ship that are characterized by their longevity (such as plates, pipes, valves, and so on) will be in need of replacement. It is vitally necessary, therefore, for the firm that provision should be made for these rather heavy and variable mid-run costs. It will be seen shortly that such expensive replacements are included in the 'operating costs' of some firms under the heading of maintenance and repairs. Just what items of expenditure should be referred to as maintenance, repairs, or replacement is ultimately a matter of convention, of choice, or opinion.

In the long run if a firm is going to continue in existence even such assets that are characterized by their longevity such as the hulls and engines of ships, that is to say, the ships themselves, depreciate and must therefore be replaced. Thus in the long run it is vitally necessary for the shipping firm that provision should be made for these expensive replacements. In the circumstances, it is necessary to comment on the depreciation of ships.

Depreciation and obsolescence

In order to be able to discuss depreciation as a cost we must assume that, as a rule, entrepreneurs want to keep their firms in existence for time periods that are longer than the average life of ships. 'Depreciation as a cost cannot be measured in terms of money apart from some defined objective.'[1] Depreciation of tramp ships is caused by two different and distinct factors:

(a) Wear and tear resulting from use and the way of use.
(b) Wear and tear due to exposure to the elements.

(a) Wear and tear resulting from use and the way of use

In order to appreciate the importance of this factor we may take as an example the main engine of a ship.

If we assume that a ship immediately after delivery to its owners proceeded to the lay-up berth—on account of the existing state of the market—and remained there over a long period of time; and if we further assume that the necessary measures for protecting the main engine from exposure to the elements had been perfectly applied, then on the basis of existing information we could safely state that the degree of wear and tear of this engine would be practically zero on termination of the lay-up period. The excellent condition of the machinery of various T2 tankers after a prolonged lay-up period supports this view.

However, if another ship of the same age and specification was trading whilst the first remained laid up, there would have been symptoms of wear and tear on its machinery. The degree of wear and tear of the hull and machinery of a ship is fully observed during the course of special surveys.

The gradual wear and tear of a ship is due to use, but it also depends on the *way of use*, that is to say, the different conditions under which the ship is producing its output.

In order to demonstrate this significant point we elaborate further on our example with the two ships of the same age and specification under the same management with the two different itineraries during a period of heavy winter. It will be recalled that vessel A was supposed to be trading continually on

[1] See G.J.Ponsonby 'Depreciation with Special Reference to Transport', *Economic Journal*, March 1956.

the route U.K.–Canada–U.K. and vessel B on the route U.K.–West African coast–U.K.

Under the circumstances, it may be safely assumed that vessel A would have been exposed for the greatest part of the winter period to heavy or stormy seas and winds with a force of from 6 to 9 (Beaufort scale). Such heavy-weather conditions would have caused heavy labour of its hull and engine over relatively prolonged periods of time. Engine and hull would have vibrated violently and racing of the engine would have occurred not infrequently. Furthermore, officers and other members of the crew would inevitably have had to neglect maintenance work both on deck and in the engine room because of the heavy-weather conditions.

As the deck-log extracts of any tramp ship performing continual voyages under heavy-weather conditions will show, the wear and tear—as well as the damage—caused on vessel A as a result of its employment would have been greater than those of vessel B, which most probably would have encountered heavy weather only during the crossing of the Bay of Biscay. Some of the rivets of vessel A would have become loose, leakages in the double-bottom tanks and bilges would have occurred, plates would have become rusty, the wear and tear on some of the bearings and white metals of the main engine would have become noticeable, and so on. In addition, part of such short-lived assets as the various protective covers on deck, life safety equipment, catering department equipment, etc., would have been wasted, and therefore in need of immediate replacement.

We may therefore conclude, that one of the factors that cause useful life of ships to be taken out of them is use and the way of use. In the short run user depreciation merges into maintenance.

(b) *Wear and tear due to exposure to the elements*

This is essentially a function of time and thus a time cost. We may mention in this connection the wear and tear of various parts of the hull, the deck and the bridge structure of vessels. Exposure to the elements causes corrosion, wastage and gradual decay of the plates, winches, pipes, electrical equipment on deck, and so on. Needless to say that wear and tear due to exposure to the elements occurs particularly on the hulls of tramp ships even when they are laid up.

Changes in future demand

One of the factors which affect the value of ships and the length of their economic lives is the future level of demand for their services. If the demand for tramp shipping facilities, the level of ships' prices, the level of freight rates, and the level of productive techniques remained static in the long run, a vessel could have been placed out of use at the moment its productive capacity was exhausted due to physical reasons[1] and replaced by another one of the same specification at a price equal to the original cost of the old vessel.

However, the economic realities of the industry are quite different. We already know from the preceding chapters that the demand for tramp shipping facilities is subject to big changes, that the money values of ships and tramp freight rates tend to fluctuate sharply, and that productive techniques do not remain static.

The longevity of demand for the service offered by a particular type of ship is an unknown factor to the entrepreneur at the time he decides to purchase the ship and, consequently, it constitutes a commercial risk. For instance, it would have been impossible to forecast during 1945-7, when most of the Liberty ships and T2 tankers were purchased by private entrepreneurs, that there would be a demand for the Liberty's services even as late as 1969, but that starting from the late fifties the demand for the T2 tanker in its own market would be periodically non-existent.

Changes in future demand for a particular type of ship may or may not cause the end of its economic life before its physical deterioration. Consequently such changes constitute a factor which, in the case of the tramp shipping industry, make the accurate estimate of obsolescence as a cost practically impossible

---

[1] The end of the physical life of a vessel must be taken to mean that point of time when the cost of repairing is assumed to be higher than its net present value.

and at the same time lend emphasis to the view that the tramp shipping business is a highly speculative profession.[1]

2. Fuel and other material inputs

In order to operate a ship the use of oil and of such other material inputs as, for instance, water for boiler consumption, or drinking water, provisions, stores, and spare parts is indispensable.

Fuel and the other material inputs necessary for the operation of a ship represent an economic cost which is characterized by its versatility. For example, some of the stores, provisions, or water consumed in a ship could be utilized for exactly the same purposes by trains, aircraft, and so on. The payments (less taxes and/or other fiscal obligations) that would have had to be made to obtain the fuel and other material inputs necessary for the operation of a ship for alternative uses are a measure of the economic cost incurred by the shipping firm for their use.

3. Labour cost

The use of labour, whether as ship's crew or as members of the office staff, or as dock workers, riggers, etc., is indispensable for the production of tramp shipping services. Labour can also be regarded as a versatile resource. The estimated payments which would have to be made for securing the labour employed by a shipping firm for alternative uses are a broad measure of the economic cost to the tramp shipping firm for using this scarce resource. However, in view of the nature of the nautical profession, some additional opportunity costs are incurred by the crew (long periods away from home life, less security and safety) which are (or should be) paid by the shipping firm.

4. Land use

Shipping firms owning vessels or cargo liners lease or purchase land for the purpose of constructing suitable loading and dis-

---

[1] For further analysis on the cost of depreciation in industry see J.L.Meij, *Depreciation and Replacement Policy*

charging berths at various ports for the use of their tonnage or for the use of tonnage which has been chartered by them. Similarly, oil companies have purchased land near their refineries for the purpose of building suitable berths to be used either by their own tonnage or by tankers that are chartered by these companies. Also, shipbuilding and ship repairing firms purchase or lease land near ports in order to install their factories, yards, dry docks, etc.

The land acquired permanently or temporarily by firms connected with merchant shipping may be of some value for purposes other than those for which it is used by such firms. The same land could be used, for instance, for open spaces, cultivation, hospitals, houses, sanatoriums, hotels, warehouses, railway stations, fishing ports, factories, yacht clubs, and so on. Once purchased and adapted the sums for which such land or property could, at any time, be let, sold, or leased to others for the use of such purposes as the ones indicated above are a measure of the economic cost for retaining or using the land in question.

In the case of independent shipping firms owning tramps, bulk carriers, and tankers, land or space use is a current cost. Owing to the fact that the area of trading of these productive units is world-wide and the time period that the same space is made use of by them is relatively small, independent shipping firms mostly pay port dues to the government or port authority at which their vessels are to call or have called. Consequently, such payments as port dues, dry-docking dues, and so on are considered in the shipping world as part of the current costs of the shipping firm.

In an economic sense, port dues are partly a form of rent. However, part of these payments is also a return on capital, for when a vessel enters in port, in addition to space, it uses various capital structures such as canals, berths, mooring posts, shore equipment, etc.

A shipping firm through its agents, makes payments to the port authority in the form of dues or otherwise, in respect of labour costs that are incurred as a result of a vessel's entry, stay, and exit from port.

Dues are, as a rule, changed on the basis of the vessels' N.R.T.

In some cases the time that a vessel remains in port (whether one, two, or ten days or more) is not taken into account and the same amount of dues is paid to the port authority by the Owners through their agents.

The pricing policies of many port authorities have created an unfavourable state of affairs for the tramp shipping industry and its users.

As already indicated, liner ships carry more expensive cargoes than tramp ships, and consequently, liner firms obtain higher rates per ton than tramp shipping firms. However, these firms pay the same amount of dues per N.R.T. for their vessels as tramp shipping firms. Moreover, on the average, conventional liner ships remain longer in port than tramp ships. In the circumstances it could be argued that in a sense the tramp shipping industry and its users (as well as the bulk carrier and tanker industries and their users) subsidize the liner industry so far as terminal costs are concerned. The criteria used for port pricing (if any) ought to be studied and revised.

It should be pointed out that a shipping firm makes use of more space that does not have any value for alternative uses. Sailing on the high seas (but not through canals) or carrying out of emergency repairs with the assistance of crew at relatively safe anchorages outside ports may be considered as two important examples of this.

Table 1 of the Appendix contains the average monthly expenses of a laid-up vessel in 1958. It will be noted that the usual cost of port dues is not included in the table. This is so because the vessel under consideration was laid up at an uninhabitable area at Taranto, Italy, which was unwanted at the time. With the exception of the mooring posts which were purchased and installed at the firm's expense, nothing else was forgone because of this temporary use of space and, therefore, no other economic cost was involved.

5. Measuring the costs of operation of the tramp shipping firm

The money prices of the scarce resources which a shipping firm employs in order to produce its services give us the general level of its costs of production in terms of money. The general level of money costs and its relation to freights determine whether or not these services will be produced. We examine first the position with regard to costs by taking as an example a hypothetical tramp shipping firm.

(a) The 'operating costs'[1]

For the sake of simplicity let us suppose that one or more entrepreneurs decided early in 1955 'to get into the shipping business' and that, as a result of this decision, a new shipping firm—Firm A—was established during the same year. The management employed by the entrepreneurs under consideration was just as efficient as those of older tramp shipping firms with long experience in the industry. During the course of the same year a new tramp ship, to be called X, was ordered by Firm A to be built by a Glasgow shipyard.

The new shipowners and their management agreed that vessel X should be of the representative type of tramps at the time. Thus, the main features of the specification agreed with the shipyard were the following: G.R.T. 9722, N.R.T. 5477, d.w.t. 12 500. Diesel engines. Consumption 17 tons fuel oil per day. Average working speed 15 knots.

Vessel X was delivered to Firm A without undue delay, i.e. during summer 1957, and its original or building cost amounted in all to £1 000 000.

Vessel X was fixed during trials to take a full cargo of grain from Montreal to London. Subsequently, several fixtures for Atlantic voyages were concluded. On termination of one year of service the average daily running expenses of vessel X, which was registered under the British flag, were estimated as hereunder.

It is obvious that the daily running expenses were not the only costs incurred by Firm A for the performance of voyage no. 1 Glasgow–Montreal–London of vessel X, part of which had to be done in ballast. The following additional payments were made by Firm A in respect of voyage 1 of vessel X.

As it appears rather clearly from the above simple calculations

[1] The term 'operating costs' as commonly used in the shipping world means all short-run and mid-run costs, but not depreciation and interest.

Table 14. The daily running expenses of a tramp ship—daily running
expenses of vessel *X* for voyage no. 1

Crew expenses				
Wages	£75	0	0	
Sunday and leave pay, national health insurance and merchant navy officer's pension fund	12	18	0	
Bonus	5	10	0	
Overtime	4	0	0	
Allowance for stand-by wages and sick pay whilst in the U.K.	1	10	0	
Repatriations	1	10	0	
Victualling	18	0	0	
			£118 8 0	
Stores:				
Deck, engine, and cabin			21 0 0	
Insurance:				
Marine insurance on hull and machinery, etc.	35	15	0	
Club calls and unrecoverables	7	0	0	
			42 15 0	
Management:				
Office	1	15	0	
Superintendent engineers and/or port captains, etc.	3	0	0	
			4 15 0	
Maintenance and repairs:				
Including allowance for spare parts and for annual and special survey			25 0 0	
Incidentals:			1 0 0	
Total running expenses per day			£212 18 0	

Bunkers	£1325	0	0
Loading expenses	4000	0	0
Discharging expenses	4500	0	0
Shifting boards	250	0	0
	£10 075	0	0
Total of 'running expenses' for voyage no. 1: 22 days @ £212 18s per day	4683	16	0
Operating costs re: voyage no. 1 *	£14 758	16	0

* For simplicity's sake commissions on freight are not included. We assume that
these were deducted from freight prior to its payment.

we have assumed that voyage no. 1 was a 'good and safe' one—not unduly affected by any of the unpredictable factors already mentioned (see chapter 3, section 6). Thus it lasted for 22 days and vessel X—not having experienced any trouble in the engine room or elsewhere—was proved to be a 'sound ship' in every respect.

The figures mentioned in respect of expenses incurred at the loading and discharging ports represent actual payments for disbursements made by Firm A. The figure of £1325 represents the cost of bunkers consumed during the round voyage. The £250 is an average of the total expenses incurred for the purchase, erection, and dismantling of shifting boards (less the sale price of wood). It is assumed that they were used for four voyages continuously. In other words, we estimate that the total cost of the shifting boards to firm A was £1000, a figure that may be thought to be rather conservative. This is so, for it is assumed that most of the work for the erection and dismantling of the shifting boards was done with the assistance of the crew.

The various daily running expenses are averages based upon the first year of the economic life of vessel X. The average for maintenance and repairs is also based on past experience of the management of Firm A and it may be considered a representative one.

All the above mentioned costs amounting to £14 758 16s constitute *the operating costs*, or working expenses of vessel X for voyage no. 1.

(b) *The cost of depreciation*

The decision of the entrepreneurs who founded Firm A to order a new ship and not to purchase one or two units from the second-hand market may be taken to mean that it was not their intention to enter the tramp freight market temporarily.

In the circumstances it could be safely stated that the long-run objective of Firm A would be to replace vessel X in due course. It is highly unlikely that the records of Firm A in respect of the cost of depreciation of vessel X, which would have been made in accordance with existing legal provisions, could serve our purpose which is to estimate the cost of depreciation of vessel X during the short-run period of voyage no. 1 on a historical basis.

In order to attempt such an estimate the following assumptions become necessary:

(a) That the total cost of replacement of vessel X will be equal to its original cost.

(b) That the life of vessel X (both economic and physical) was going to be equal to the one of many other well constructed tramp ships, that is, in the neighbourhood of 30 years. Consequently, it could be further assumed that vessel X was sold during 1987 to a yard for scrapping. The net revenue realized by Firm A from this transaction was £100 000.

(c) Out of the 30 years of its economic life vessel X was part of available supply over various intervals of time amounting totally to five years. During this period of time vessel X was not trading, either because of the depressed state of the freight market or because of repairs, etc.

On the basis of the above assumptions, Firm A had actually a period of 25 years to recover the original cost of its investment or the cost of replacement of vessel X. Thus, the cost of depreciation (including obsolescence) during the course of voyage no. 1 could be estimated as follows:[1]

Total original cost	£1 000 000
Less estimated scrap iron value	100 000
	£900 000

£900 000 ÷ 25 years of trading = £36 000 per annum or £98 12s per day

£98 12s × 22 days, i.e. duration of voyage no. 1 = £2169

Therefore, the total cost of voyage no. 1 of vessel X would have been:

Operating costs	£14 758 16 0
Depreciation	£2169 4 0
	£16 928 0 0

[1] It will be noted that this estimate is made in terms of constant prices and the 'cost of inflation' of the currency (which is said to be 3 per cent per annum approximately) is not taken into account.

131

Needless to say that, in the shipping world, costs are viewed in a somewhat different way. If the freight collected from voyage no. 1 was higher than the operating costs for that voyage, let us say £18 000, the difference or surplus, i.e. £3241 4s, would have been considered as the profit made by Firm A on 'current account'. Most probably the owners of vessel X would not have remained satisfied from such voyage results. This would have been so because, in view of the highly speculative nature of the profession, shipowners want to recover the original cost of their investment at the earliest possible stage of the economic life of the ship. We shall comment further on the attitude, of entrepreneurs towards costs and profits at a later stage. However, it must be stated at this point that the figures given in this paragraph reflect rather closely the true position so far as the costs of the British and Continental tramp ships in the late fifties are concerned. Thus, they form a good basis for making an estimate of the approximate cost per ton-mile for the carriage of bulk commodities by relatively modern tramp ships at the time.

(c) The cost per ton-mile

We assume that, as is usually the case, vessel X took a full cargo of grain (equal to its cargo-carrying capacity, see chapter 1, section 2), i.e. 11 900 tons. The distance of the round voyage Glasgow–Montreal–London is approximately 6000 miles. Thus, the cost per ton-mile to Firm A during the loaded passage was:

$$\text{Cost per ton-mile} = \frac{\text{Total cost}}{\text{tons miles}} = \frac{£16\,928}{11\,900 \times 3000}$$

$$= 0.144d/\text{ton-mile},$$

i.e. about $\frac{1}{9}d$ per ton-mile (or 0.05p).

It should be pointed out that the total costs of our example are those of the producer which, of course, are not the same as those of the user of tramp shipping services, i.e. the shipper who, as we are aware, has to pay the freight plus cargo insurance. However, as shown by the figures below, which are based on

user costs, on the whole sea-transport costs and par'
tramp shipping costs are amongst the lowest of all internatᵢ.
transport modes.

	Cents per tonne-kilometre available	Cents per ton-mile available
International scheduled air services: passengers, mail, and cargo	25.2	36.8
All cargo aircraft (e.g. CL-44, DC-8F) expected in the range	5–10	7–15
Road freight transport according to quantities, distances, and loading requirements, typically in the range	3–8	4–12
Rail freight transport according to quantities, distances, and loading requirements, typically in the range	0.75–5	0.1–7
Sea freight transport according to quantities, distances, and loading requirements, typically in the range	0.1–2	0.1–3

The above figures have been obtained from the study *Trends and Developments in the World Air Freight Industry* published by the International Civil Aviation Organization in 1961. As pointed out in the study it is exceedingly difficult to compare operating costs of various transport forms because the types of commodity transported by air and sea vary considerably. Consequently, these averages should be accepted only as a rough indication of the actual position during the period 1960-1.

The term 'sea freight transport' used in the study is a general term and, as we are aware, it refers to a sum total of closely interconnected but basically separate industries and markets. It can be safely assumed that liner costs are at the top of the range whilst tanker, bulk carrier, and tramp shipping costs are at the lowest point.

6. Is tramp shipping a remunerative transport service?

It was pointed out at the beginning of this chapter that some relatively small costs, mainly the cost of insurance on the cargo transported, are not paid by the shipping firms but by the cargo shippers. Moreover, as it appears from our hypothetical example of Firm A, the various shipping firms estimate their operating costs on the basis of actual payments made by them. Properly, Firm A, as well as all other shipping firms, should also include in their costs not only the payments made by them for goods and services, but also the imputed value or opportunity price of the productive factors which they use but do not directly pay for, Such costs would include the imputed but unpaid fees of a director of a young ship-broking firm, the imputed but unpaid salary of an owner-manager, the unpaid fees of a director who, because of his educational background and/or training, may be in a position to act occasionally or regularly—in addition to his managerial duties—as a port captain, or a superintendent engineer, or as a claims expert, or as a translator; the unpaid cost of repatriation of an officer or member of crew of vessel X by another vessel belonging or managed by the same company; the unpaid freight for spare parts, stores, and/or provisions brought over to vessel X—which may be trading at great distances from the home port—by another vessel belonging to or managed by the same company, and so on. In other words, in order to be able to determine whether the transport services offered by a shipping firm are remunerative or unremunerative, the accounting costs of the shipping firm should be considered as appropriately rectified to register the full opportunity prices of all productive factors employed plus those small costs that are paid by the shipper for the purpose of carrying a bulk commodity from loading to discharging port. If the resulting revenues are known or definitely expected to be sufficient to cover all these costs, it may then be concluded that the services offered by the shipping firm are remunerative.[1] Although the necessary information for estimating the economic costs of the industry as a whole is not available, it will be seen from the data contained in later chapters that tramp shipping has been a remunerative transport service. Moreover, there is no reason

---

[1] It is suggested that an unremunerative service can be defined as follows: 'A service, or part of a service, the resulting revenues from which are known (or definitely expected) to be insufficient to cover those costs which, but for its provision would not have been incurred, either directly or indirectly, in the short—or long run.' See G. J. Ponsonby, *What is an Unremunerative Transport Service?*

to lead us to the presupposition that the position will change in the foreseeable future.

7. The fixed, variable, and marginal costs of the shipping firm

The short-period relation of cost to output is a kind of operational period of such length that the hull and machinery of a tramp ship and the office building, or the part of the office building that the ship-owning firm occupies, remain unchanged in quantity, but the materials and labour used may be variable in quantity. As in the case of other transport industries—and industries in general—it is not advisable to endeavour to determine precisely the limits of the short-run period, but it can be assumed that it may last for some months. The longer the time period we contemplate, the more factors are potentially variable and the fewer are fixed. The long-run period during the course of which all production factors used vary in quantity may last as long as the average life of a tramp ship.

In the short-run period the shipping firm has certain fixed factors and certain variable factors that it uses. Correspondingly, the shipping firm in the short-run finds that its costs fall into two general categories—fixed costs and variable costs.

On the basis of the above one could feel tempted to classify all the operating costs of a tramp shipping firm into the short-run category of variable costs. Nevertheless, the actual position is somewhat different and in view of the fact that, for reasons that may shortly become obvious, the distinction between the short-run fixed and variable costs must be made as accurately as possible, some further comments become necessary.

Fixed costs are those costs which in the short run are absolutely invariant to changes in output, in other words, they are the total amount of costs that our hypothetical Firm *A*, or any other shipping firm, would incur when the output measured in ton-miles is zero. The variable costs in the short run are those costs which vary with output or in effect any costs added as a result of any increase of output above zero.

Thus, fixed costs for any given short period of time will include:

135

(*a*) Costs that are incurred as a result of commercial trans-actions carried out in the past, that is to say before the short run period under consideration, and allocated to the period.

(*b*) Outlays made during the same period which will, in any event, be made at zero output.

It should be noted that fixed costs that can be classified under (*b*), though fixed for the short-run period, are made in anticipation of operations in a future period.

From our example of Firm *A* we remember that the depreciation cost of vessel *X*—allocated on a daily basis—was £98 12s. If we assume that vessel *X* remained laid up for a short period at a small U.K. port and that its lay-up expenses during this period (port expenses, management, port risks insurance, watchmen, basic maintenance, etc.) averaged £30 daily, then we can say that the fixed costs of Firm *A* which owned and managed only vessel *X* were averaging (£98 12s + £30) £128 12s daily.

If we now suppose that when vessel *X* was eventually re-commissioned and performed the same voyage, i.e. U.K.–Montreal–U.K., then we can conclude that its variable costs during this voyage were averaging £230 per day (i.e. £212 running expenses, plus £48 being daily average, re cost of bunkers, loading and discharging expenses necessary for the performance of the voyage, *less* £30 being average daily payments if vessel remained laid up).

The marginal cost is defined as the cost per additional unit of output. In the case of the tramp shipping industry production of one additional unit of output, that is to say the transport of a bulk cargo from loading to discharging ports, presupposes the performance of one voyage. Therefore, all variable costs that are incurred because of the performance of the voyage including the cost of the in-ballast part and normal profit—or all those costs that would not have been incurred if the voyage had not been performed—constitute the marginal cost. It follows that in the case of vessel *X* the marginal cost in respect of the voyage U.K.–Montreal–U.K. was £5600 plus a normal profit which would not make entrepreneurs withdraw from the market or induce them to invest in another unit (230 × 22 days for the round voyage is 5060).

Having defined the fixed and variable costs of the tramp shipping firm as well as the cost per additional unit of output, i.e. the marginal cost, we may now comment on the entrepreneurs' behaviour in respect of costs and prices.

It has already been mentioned that a shipowner or a group of shipowners owning a shipping firm in combining productive factors in various ways are seeking in the long run, and under competitive conditions to obtain as large a surplus or revenue over costs as possible, i.e. to maximize profits.

On the other hand, owing to the fact that the demand for tramp shipping facilities is subject to big changes and, therefore, varies in magnitude over different periods of time, there are short periods during the course of which average freight rates tend to yield a higher or lower revenue than the one required to cover marginal cost.

More specifically, the position is as follows. Given the existence of changes in the magnitude of demand there will be forthcoming at any level of freight rates different volumes of bulk cargoes. The existence of tonnage idleness leads shipping firms which are functioning under competitive conditions to accept, in the short run, freights which yield revenues that are lower than average total costs and marginal cost. Thus, there emerges a level of freight rates on a world-wide scale which is lower, during the stages of recession and depression, than the level of freight rates prevailing during the stages of revival and prosperity.

During the course of the short-run period, when total supply does not expand or contract, the degree to which the level of freights will vary depends upon the degree to which the demand varies in magnitude. It has been, and still remains, the general practice of shipowners and their managements to conclude fixtures during periods of low freight rates, which yield freights that are below the amount that must be earned to cover marginal cost. So long as freight rates are estimated as being sufficient to cover the variable costs of a vessel (i.e. so long as the cost of idleness remains higher than the loss incurred if the vessel is kept trading), no experienced shipowner will miss such opportunities as the market offers to conclude fixtures and avoid idleness incurred by laying-up his vessel. In view of this policy, which is widely applied during periods of low freight rates, shipping firms have imposed upon them the necessity of earning more in future when freight rates will tend to yield marginal revenues which are higher than marginal costs.

8. Costs and the size of tramps and other cargo ships

Up to this point it has been assumed implicitly that during the course of different periods of time all existing tramp ships were more or less of the same specification and, consequently the average total costs of all the units of the industry tended to be on the same level. Thus, we have assumed further that, given the competitive structure of the market, they were, on average, expected to earn similar amounts. These two assumptions are helpful for analytical purposes but nevertheless quite pragmatic. Indeed such a thing as the 'representative tramp ship' of the industry has been a reality over various periods of time, for example the standard type of tramp, the Liberty ship, the SD14 and so on. However, it is a fact that not all tramp ships trading at the same period of time are of the same specification. Moreover, as already indicated in chapter 3, the supply of tramp shipping services like the supply of any other commodity or service depends, amongst other factors, upon technology. Over a period of time scientific and technical knowledge changes and so do the supplies of individual commodities and services including shipping services. As we are already aware (see chapter 3, section 7), as a result of technical progress the building of bigger and faster tramps and other cargo ships has become possible. Thus, we propose to drop the above two assumptions on this point, with a view to examining the size of tramps and other cargo ships in relation to costs and revenues.

Unlike productive units that belong to other forms of transport—such as passenger ships, cargo liners, or units of the road haulage industry—tramp ships, bulk carriers, and tankers take as a rule full cargoes, that is to say they usually load to capacity. This makes it easier to discuss the effects of their growing size on their costs and revenues, for it can be assumed that their cargo-carrying capacity is always utilized fully.

On the basis of the experience of the above three neighbouring maritime industries of tramp-ships, bulk carriers, and tankers, it can be assumed safely that with the operation of larger vessels virtually all costs rise, but at a smaller rate than that at which their cargo-carrying capacity rises. This significant point can be demonstrated by the following two examples:

(a) Tables 2 and 3 in the Appendix show that the average daily running expenses of a tramp ship of 8200 t.d.w. were (in 1952) £180 0s 4d and the average daily running expenses of a tramp ship which is 2000 t.d.w. larger, i.e. 10 200 t.d.w. were (in 1957) £221 7s 0d. Assuming constant prices and that both ships had the same speed and were loaded 'full cargoes' of the same kind for the same voyage (i.e. that the first ship had taken 7800 metric tons and the second ship about 9700 metric tons) we would have found that the average running expenses per ton per 24 hours of the first ship were $5\frac{3}{4}$d approximately and the average running expenses per ton per 24 hours of the second ship were $5\frac{1}{2}$d approximately.

(b) Table 15 is based on the data given in the *Syren and Shipping* 3 July 1963 issue[1], which refers to building and operating costs of bulk carriers of different sizes. This table, and particularly the two columns which show the differences in building and daily operating costs as the size of bulk carriers increases,

Table 15. Costs and the size of cargo ships

Total deadweight capacity	Building cost per ton d.w. £	Difference in building cost per ton d.w.	Cost of operation per day	Difference in daily operating costs
15 000	65		290	
		15		85
30 000	50		375	
		5		125
50 000	45		500	
		3		100
80 000	42		600	

[1] See C.F.H.Cufley, 'Trends in the Bulk Trades: their Effect on Ships, Ports, and Location of Industry' in *Syren and Shipping*, 3 July 1963.

offer a broad indication that as the size of vessels increase, costs are reduced, but such reductions become progressively smaller.[1]

9. Costs in relation to the speed and size of ships

In order to discuss speed it will be necessary to disregard for the time being such costs as fuel consumption, repairs, maintenance, and spare parts. Furthermore, for simplicity's sake, throughout this section unless otherwise specified we will assume a static technological level.

From the data contained in chapter 3, as well as from information that is freely circulating in the shipping world, it may be concluded that in the long run the speed of tramps and other cargo ships has increased within reasonable economic limits and therefore not in proportion to their size. For example, the average service speed of Liberty ships (which had a d.w. tonnage of about 10 000) was 11 knots, but the average service speed of the present bulk carriers with a d.w. tonnage in the neighbourhood of 20 000 or more is not 22 knots.

To increase the speed of a ship its power must also increase. However, power and speed do not increase in the same proportion. The horsepower required increases as the cube of the speed. For example, if we had a tramp ship with a speed of 10 knots for which, let us say, 2000 horsepower was needed, in order to double its speed, i.e. to make it 20 knots, we should need $2^3 \sim (2 \times 2 \times 2 = 8)$ of the horsepower which corresponds to the 10 knots, i.e. $8 \times 2000 = 16\ 000$ horsepower. Needless to say that no entrepreneur would see any purpose in considering such a costly conversion! Let us now assume that we wanted to increase the speed of a relatively small tramp of 10 knots (with horsepower 2000) by 10 per cent, i.e. from 10 knots to 11 knots. In such case we should need an increase in horsepower of 33 per cent, that is to say, horsepower would have to be increased to 2600. This is one of the basic reasons why small tramp ships have engines which produce smaller speeds. Apart from the

[1] In this connection it should be remembered that a static technological level has been assumed. For a later study on the subject in which bigger sizes are taken into consideration, see R. O. Goss 'The Size of Ships', papers presented at the Transport Economists Seminar, at Ealing Technical College, 29 May 1970.

higher building costs involved, more powerful engines are heavier and, also, they require more space which otherwise can be used for the stowage of cargo, that is to say, the only or the basic source of revenue for all cargo ships. As is well known, the problem of the space occupied by the engines is a real one in the case of passenger liners where high speeds are required. In the case of tramps, speeds which are considerably higher than the prevailing average do not represent an economically efficient alternative for entrepreneurs.

The building costs of engines do not increase in proportion with the power of the engine provided the type of the engine is not changed. The building cost of a more powerful engine per horsepower is smaller than the cost per horsepower of a less powerful engine of the same type.

The increase in the size and speed of a vessel (within limits) do not have such negative effects regarding costs as the increase in speed alone. For example, the T2 type of tankers had a deadweight tonnage of 16 700 tons and a service speed of 15 knots with 6000 S.H.P. Larger tankers now in existence with roughly the same type of engine and with a deadweight tonnage of 34 000 have a service speed of about 16 knots with 15 000 S.H.P. Actually the tankers we have in mind for this comparison are the *Rokos V*, steam turbines, Liberian, built 1956, G.R.T. 21 028, N.R.T. 13 060, and *Savina*, steam turbines, built 1956, G.R.T. 21 081, N.R.T. 12 842.

Let us now take one specific example which demonstrates quite clearly how costly is the increase of speed in the case of relatively small ships. For the s.t. *Apollonia* a passenger ship, with a displacement of 55 000 tons, 12 000 S.H.P. is required in order to develop a speed of 22 knots. In other words, the horsepower needed in the case of the s.t. *Apollonia* in order to develop 22 knots is approximately the same as that needed for tankers with a displacement of about 43 000 tons for their service speed of about 16 knots.

On the basis of the foregoing it may be concluded that large speeds are not an economically efficient alternative in the case of relatively small ships, including tramps. The larger a ship of a given economical shape the faster the ship can travel. For all practical purposes it is an established fact that the smaller ships cannot go as fast. Thus, the speed of cargo ships increases within reasonable limits as their size increases.

Let us now give a bird's-eye view of labour, maintenance, spare parts, and consumption costs in relation to the increase in the size and speed (within reasonable limits) of tramps and other cargo vessels. The data contained in the Appendix, and more specifically in Tables 2, 4, 5, show that labour, repair, maintenance, and spare part costs increase as the size and speed of cargo vessels increase, but at a smaller rate than that at which their cargo-carrying capacity rises. Consequently, up to a certain point we get average costs falling as the size and speed of vessels increases. For example, Table 4 shows that the number of engine room personnel employed by shipping firms operating cargo ships under the Greek flag rises as their cargo-carrying capacity and speed rise, but that such rises become progressively smaller.[1] Tables 5 and 2 show the running expenses of two vessels under the Greek flag with steam reciprocating engines. As can be seen from the tables, the deadweight tonnage of the first tramp is 6400 and its average service speed 7 knots. The d.w. tonnage of the second tramp is 8200 and its average service speed is 10 knots approximately. The cost of repairs and maintenance of the first ship average £16 per day and for the second £17 per day. The cost of stores and spare parts for the first tramp average £15 per day and for the second £19 per day.

The position with regard to fuel consumption costs is not the same. Two vessels with similar technical characteristics have been compared. Vessel A has a d.w. tonnage 9400, average service speed 10.5 knots with a fuel consumption 10 tons per 24 hours. Vessel B has a d.w. tonnage 11 200, average service speed 14 knots with a fuel consumption 16 tons.

---

[1] In discussing the data contained in this table the following points should be borne in mind:

(a) The figures under consideration are realistic so far as steam reciprocating and steam turbine engines are concerned and, therefore, they may be used as a rough guide for our purpose.

(b) On the basis of the information given in chapters 1 and 3 it may be safely assumed that as the size of vessels increases their speed also increases within reasonable limits. Thus, it can be assumed that the larger vessels of Table 4 are of higher speed.

The cost of fuel consumption per ton-mile for vessels A and B is as follows:

$$\frac{\text{Consumption per 24 hours}}{\text{Tons (d.w.)} \times \text{miles per 24 hours}} = \frac{10.0}{9400 \times 10.5 \times 24}$$

or in pounds:

$$= \frac{10 \times 2240}{9400 \times 252} = \frac{22\ 400}{9400 \times 252} = \text{about 0.0094 lb fuel per ton-mile.}$$

$$\text{Vessel } B \text{ consumption per ton-mile} = \frac{16 \times 2240}{11\ 200 \times 14 \times 24} = \frac{35\ 840}{3\ 763\ 200}$$

$$= 0.0095 \text{ lb fuel per ton-mile.}$$

Tramps A and B are comparable because they have the same type of engines (i.e. diesel engines). In fact, the engines of both ships that we have in mind were built by Doxford and Sons Ltd., U.K. If two tramps with different types of engines were compared, or in other words, if we were assuming that vessel A had steam reciprocating engines, then our calculations would have shown that fuel consumption costs per ton-mile would have been more in the case of vessel A. However, such a comparison would have only demonstrated the effects of technical progress on the supply of tonnage (see chapter 3) and not the effects of the increasing size and speed of cargo ships with regard to the costs of fuel consumption.[1]

It is risky to generalize on the basis of one example. However, if we also take into consideration the information available in this respect, we can state that the pattern followed by fuel consumption costs as the size and speed of vessels increases is not the same as that for building, labour, repair, spare parts, and maintenance costs. As the size and speed of vessels increases, fuel consumption costs tend to become higher.

Having made these comments on the size and speed of vessels in relation to their costs we can now discuss economies of scale and the benefits of larger and faster ships.

---

[1] For a technical discussion regarding the relation of speed, horsepower, and consumption, see Reed's *Practical Mathematics for Marine Engineers* (8th ed.), particularly pp. 447 and 947.

10. Economies of scale

We have already pointed out that up to a certain point as the cargo-carrying capacity and speed of ships increase, costs go up, but not proportionately. In the case of tramps, bulk carriers, and tankers, economies of scale are due to the following reasons:

(i) Reduced building costs per ton deadweight (see Table 14).

(ii) The number of officers and crew increases slightly with the increase of the ship's size and speed and certainly far less than in proportion (see for example Table 4 in the Appendix).[1]

(iii) Costs of stores, provisions, spare parts, repairs, and maintenance increase as the size and speed of vessels increase, but far less than in proportion (compare for example Tables 2 and 5 in the Appendix).

(iv) Lower port expenses per N.R.T. or G.R.T. (see for example Table 7 in the Appendix).

(v) Lower management and insurance costs (compare tables on costs in the Appendix).

Data on operating costs are not freely available in the shipping world, and thus the discussion of the serious question of economies of scale in specific terms is not possible. C.F.H. Cufley in his article on the 'Trends in Bulk Trades' makes an attempt to demonstrate the significance of the increase in the cargo-carrying capacity of vessels so far as costs and revenues are concerned. Some of the points made in the article are important to the student of the economics of transport.

The figures that follow (which are taken from the above article) illustrate the extent to which sea transport costs can be reduced by increasing the deadweight tonnage of ships. In each case, the examples chosen are motor vessels of 14–14½ knots average working speed. The building costs represent a rough average of current prices at the time (1963) 'leaving aside the extremes of £160 per ton d.w. recently paid for a 100-ton dry-

---

[1] The number of officers and crew serving in large bulk carriers and the mammoth tankers of the present is about the same as the crew of the average modern tramp. However, this is due to automation and to the fact that the scope of the duties of the seamen serving on the big tankers is limited. Moreover, there are symptoms of a social and psychological nature which indicate quite clearly that the number of persons on board these big ships cannot be reduced further.

cargo ship and a reported price of less than £38 a ton for a 130 000 ton tanker'. It is assumed, quite realistically, that the operational costs would show little variation between tankers and dry-cargo bulk carriers. In addition to crew expenses, stores, spare parts, provisions, and insurance the figures below are 'based on operation under traditional European maritime flags' and include an adequate allowance for management and proper reserves for maintenance and repairs including classification surveys:

Total deadweight capacity	Building cost per ton d.w.	Operational cost per day
15 000	£65	£290
30 000	50	375
50 000	45	500
80 000	42	600

As the author of the article points out, the benefits that accrue from the lower capital and operational costs of larger vessels can be most easily shown by time-charter comparisons which eliminate the complications arising from voyage expenses (i.e. loading and discharging expenses, bunkers, time spent in port, etc.). The break-even hire rate, indicated below, per ton of total d.w. per month allows fully for operational expenses and for each vessel to be 'off hire' for repairs, survey, etc., for a rather generous average period of 30 days in the year:

Deadweight tonnage	Hire rates break-even		Required to provide for:			
			+3% p.a.		+10% p.a.	
	s	d	s	d	s	d
15 000	12	10	18	9	24	8
30 000	8	3½	12	10	17	4½
50 000	6	8	10	9	14	10
80 000	5	0	8	10	12	8

It goes without saying that no shipping firm owning units below 14 000 t.d.w. which follows the policy of maintaining its tonnage in good condition can possibly agree to conclude time-charter agreements, even at the maximum rate indicated above.

The cost of fuel is not included in the above figures. The reason for this, according to Cufley, is that unlike the advantages which

145

derive from lower capital and other operating costs, 'the reduction in fuel bills' which accompanies increased ship tonnage only applies while the vessel is at sea. Maximum benefit from this factor can only be obtained if loading and discharging facilities are speeded up proportionately to the growth in the ships' size. The figures below assume this to be the case. However, the hypothesis that an 80 000 t.d.w. bulk carrier can be turned round in the same time as a 15 000 t.d.w. tramp does not seem to be entirely realistic, at least as far as present working is concerned. It is quite safe to assume that the 15 000 t.d.w. tramp can be turned round at 65 days per annum and that the length of time in port for the 80 000 tonner will be greater, but not in proportion to its size.

Allowance is made for 65 days per annum in port, loading and discharging, 270 days at sea and 30 days out of service. Diesel propulsion is again chosen (steam turbine fuel costs would have been 80–100 per cent higher) and an optimum service speed of 14 knots. It is assumed further that the engines burn ordinary heavy fuel oil which is priced at an average of £5 per ton. Each ship carries nine full cargoes yearly and allowance has been made for carrying capacity lost by reason of the weight of bunkers and extra weights:

Ship tonnage (total d.w.)	Daily fuel consumption (tons)	Annual lifting (tons)	Fuel cost per ton cargo s d
15 000	23	120 000	5 5
30 000	41	242 000	4 8
50 000	55	412 000	3 8
80 000	75	663 000	3 1

The figures are of significance so far as the student of transport is concerned because they demonstrate quite clearly the reduction in transport costs that is brought about as a result of the increase in the size of dry-cargo vessels.

11. The benefits of larger and faster ships

The benefits resulting from the operation of larger and faster ships are not different from those that are derived from the

construction of more and better roads.[1] More and b
roads lead to cheaper and faster transport of goods by
larger and faster ships lead to cheaper and faster transpo
sea.

Owing to the fact that modern, larger, and faster cargo ships
produce their service at a lower cost, such ships are able to carry
bulk commodities at lower freight rates. As a result of lower
costs the price of bulk commodities in the countries of consumption is lowered and all buyers benefit accordingly. In
addition, as a consequence of the fall in price at the importing
countries, more of the bulk commodity is bought in the long
run. Not only will previous buyers at the importing countries
buy more, but in the long run new buyers, at the same or different geographical locations, who previously did not buy the
commodity at all owing to its high price or unavailability, will
now come to enjoy its purchase and consumption. Thus, assuming that no other factor interferes to offset the effects of the
reduction of sea transport cost in the long run, the foundations
are laid for the opening up of new markets and for the extension
of the world freight markets (see chapter 2, section 5).

Another important consequence of reduced sea transport
costs is to stimulate and encourage production, possibly at a
lower cost at the country of export. Thus, larger and faster ships
reduce the real cost of production of commodities, and,
through prices, the cost of living too.

The chain of events does not end at the exporting country.
Tramp ships and bulk carriers transport mostly raw materials.
The factory or group of factories at the importing country that
may use these raw materials, whether ore, coal, or grain, will
produce more—up to the point of diminishing returns—and the
manufacturer will be able to realize more fully the benefits of
large-scale production. Thus, the cost of production of the various finished products for which the commodity in bulk is used
as well as their ultimate price to the consumer will tend to fall.
At the end even the location of factories and ports may be
questioned. This secondary benefit in the case of larger ships is,

[1] See G.J.Ponsonby, 'Pinpointing the Benefits of more and better Roads' in
Road International, Winter 1956–7.

we think, well demonstrated by the following hypothetical example given by C. F. H. Cufley.[1]

Assuming that a country has an annual import programme for a particular commodity, e.g. grain or ore, to the order of 10m tons and that the average length of voyage is 10 000 miles, of which one-half is ballast steaming, the net carrying costs, allowing for 5 per cent depreciation per annum, bunkers (diesel) and despatch at the rates presently given to such cargoes in major ports, will work out to something like the following overall amounts:

Shipment in cargoes of 10 000 tons	£20m
Shipment in cargoes of 30 000 tons	£11½m
Shipment in cargoes of 80 000 tons	£7½m

As the author of the article points out (*and assuming that there exists a growing demand in the long run*), it would seem that the economies made possible by the advent of the medium and large sized bulk carriers are of a considerable magnitude, and that the sums involved are large enough to warrant the construction of new dry-cargo bulk terminals and a rationalization of distribution methods similar to that carried out by the petroleum industry in recent years.

Indeed there are definite signs to the effect that since the large bulk carrier was put in operation the cost of transport of bulk materials has been reduced considerably. For example, since 1958 the price of iron ore throughout the world has tended to fall. The average value of Swedish exports in 1958 was $11.98 per ton, and in 1965 $8.78 per ton. During the same period Brazilian exports fell in value from $13.93 to $8.09 per ton (f.o.b.). Delivered prices fell even faster. The average value of Chilean ore delivered to Japan in 1957 was $30.69 per ton, in 1965 it was $14.89, the comparable figures for Brazilian shipments to the same country were $34.07 to $15.93 per ton (c.i.f.). The explanation of these price changes lies partly in the growing glut of ore-mining capacity and partly in the falling transport costs made possible as a result of the use of the large bulk carrier on these routes.

It can be argued that in many cases the bigger and faster

---

[1] It should be stated that the figures under consideration should be taken as a rough guide. For any detailed study regarding this important point the extra costs on shore and/or transhipment costs in the case of larger cargoes must be taken into account.

ships of the present may even call for the re-siting of industrial plants on the seaboard, to the detriment of established enterprises in the hinterland. This point is brought out very well by the French shipping financier Andre Verneuil.[1] Verneuil takes as his illustration the steel industry in the U.K. tracing its origin from the iron-masters who set up their forges in forests where they could obtain charcoal and water power for their hammers, as in the 'Devil' country of Surrey. After explaining how they were driven out of business after the eighteenth century by the use of coke in the furnace charge and the discovery of ore deposits close to the coalfields he suggests that the next step, as far as Europe is concerned, is the abandonment of the present steelworks in favour of new plants adjacent to deep water. Verneuil stresses how the advantages of the big bulk carrier can be dissipated by excessive cargo handling and inland transport charges, points to the cheap freights at which high-grade foreign ores can be imported and suggests that in many cases it is cheaper to use foreign (American) coals rather than pay high haulage costs involved in bringing domestic fuel to the seaboard. His article, which calls for serious attention by the student of the economics of transport, ends with a list of new steelworks designed to operate on imported raw materials in France, Holland, Germany, and Italy, and also singles out for praise the Richard Thomas & Baldwin project in the Bristol Channel.

The process of re-siting some industrial plants at the break-of-bulk point is an economic reality in some Western European countries. However, it should be noted that in the event of such serious changes other economic factors must be taken into account, one of them being the cost of inland transport of finished or semi-finished products.

For simplicity's sake, throughout this discussion we have assumed that no other factors interfere in the long run to offset the effects of the reduction of transoceanic transport costs. In other words, the benefits of larger and faster ships have been analysed in terms of constant prices.

The world freight markets offer many examples which prove

[1] See Andre Verneuil, 'Seaboard Steel Industry and Shipping' in *Journal de la Marine Marchande et de la Navigation Aerienne*, 1963.

beyond any doubt that in the long run on many trading routes where the tramp is substitutable by larger and faster ships the chain of events that have been described above is well under way.

During the late fifties and the sixties the bulk carrier became the permanent substitute of the tramp ship on many trading routes. For example, one may mention the Vancouver–Far East (grains) route, the South African–Japan (grains and ore) route, and the Australia–Japan or Australia–China route. In these routes freights are, as a rule, on a remunerative level only for large tramps and bulk carriers. Thus, it may be concluded that wherever the flow of traffic justifies the use of larger and faster ships we get in the long run (in terms of constant prices) a fall in sea-transport costs and costs of production.

However, it should be emphasized that—as already indicated —tramp shipping is a moderately substitutable service. Thus, there exists (and there will continue to exist) routes and geo-graphical areas generally where the flow of traffic is insufficient to justify the heavy capital costs that are required for the con-struction of bulk carriers and the necessary terminal facilities. It is on these routes that the tramp is and will remain the most economic alternative. In the circumstances, what calls for serious attention by the maritime economist is not so much the size but the optimal design of the tramp.[1]

12. The size of the shipping firm in relation to its operating costs

A survey of the various shipping firms of the world operating tramps and other ships belonging to the neighbouring industries will reveal a wide range of scales. Usually, shipowners owning more than two tramp ships find it more economical to establish their own offices and management. It appears that when a firm owns more than two ships the cost of maintaining a small managerial apparatus is less than the commissions to be paid to the shipbroking firm in respect of chartering, insurance, and other managerial functions. There are shipping firms that may

[1] See R. O. Goss, 'Economic Criteria for Optimal Ship Designs' in *Studies in Maritime Economics.*

manage from as few as two to three ships to as many as sixty or more, many of which happen to be tramps.

The difference in the size of shipping firms owning tramps can be partly explained by variations in location and managerial talent and experience which could cause even their optimum scales to be different. Shipping firms also vary in scale because, for various reasons, some of them have not yet arrived at their optimum and some have expanded beyond it. These reasons can be summarized as follows:

(1) *The level of demand.* There are periods when the level of demand is not sufficient to justify the expansion of a firm to the optimum scale. For instance, there may be small shipping firms sound financially who own four or five tramp ships with a managerial apparatus ready in every respect to operate two or three more vessels. This state of affairs, which is not unusual, could hardly be taken to indicate that the firms under consideration are approaching the least cost combination. Nevertheless, the entrepreneurs owning these small firms who, as a rule, are their managing directors, may not think it correct to expand further for as long as the level of demand remains at relatively low levels.

(2) *Lags in adjustments of scale enterprise.* In making long-run plans the shipowner has before him a wide range of choices. At the same time, however, there are many concrete practical difficulties involved in making adjustments of the scale of the enterprise. Most of these difficulties are due to the rigidity of many costs. Moreover, it is rarely possible to finance at the start, an enterprise of optimum scale, since the investment required is very large and the risks involved greater than those in many other industries. In many cases, therefore, shipping enterprises, if successful, grow gradually and to a certain extent they may approach the optimum of efficiency.

(3) *Errors in entrepreneurial judgment.* Shipowning is not an easy profession. There are many factors that a shipping entrepreneur has to take into consideration when deciding about the expansion of his firm. The shipowner has to decide on the size and speed and design of his new ships, on the effects of the application of new (known) technological methods in the industry, on the

availability of efficient personnel, and so on. Moreover, at a certain point of growth, let us say at the point where the shipping firm is operating about twenty/twenty-five vessels, the shipowner is called on to evaluate his qualifications as a manager in a relatively small and intimate organization or an executive in a large concern who may be absent from his office desk for most of the time. That all these questions will be answered objectively and with precision is most unlikely.

Tramp shipping is a highly competitive industry, and therefore, shipowners, as a rule, do not tend to over-expand their enterprises with a view to obtaining a position of dominance. Nevertheless, quite apart from profit-maximization, there have been examples over the years of shipowners with dreams of shipping empires who have over-expanded their organizations beyond the optimum point. Naturally, such attempts, most common in the period after the end of the first world war, have resulted in the disappearance of such firms from the market.

There are no comprehensive data available regarding the costs of operation of shipping firms. However, it seems to be maintained generally in the shipping world that larger investments on the part of the owners of small firms would have brought about economies of scale of the enterprise since their optimum scale has not yet been realized.

'Medium' shipping firms, amongst those that are owning or operating mostly cargo ships, are considered to be those with twenty to thirty vessels under their management whilst the 'big ones' are the few firms which own and operate more than fifty vessels.

In the absence of relative data, it is practically impossible to determine the optimum point (so far as the magnitude of investment on fixed factors is concerned) where a shipping firm may produce its services at the lowest average cost.

However, it may be stated with some degree of certainty that in the case of big firms the least cost combination involves higher and higher average costs of production. Managing and supervising more than, let us say, forty ships gradually becomes more and more impersonal. The diminution of individual responsibility and its substitution by committee decision invites as a rule higher managerial and general operating costs. Moreover, personnel problems in the case of the big firm are just as serious and acute as those of the relatively small firm. Broadly speaking, it may be stated that the least cost combination involves the lower average costs in the case of the medium-sized shipping firms who may tend to reach their optimum point so far as economies of scale of enterprise are concerned.

Chapter 6

Flags of Convenience

It is usually assumed that flags of convenience are the national flags of those states with whom some shipowners register their vessels in order to avoid (*a*) the fiscal obligations and (*b*) the conditions and terms of employment of factors of production (mainly labour) that would have been applicable if their tonnage was entered in the register of their own countries.

The following passage from a speech made by the Chairman of the Union of Greek Shipowners, Athens, may be of interest in this connection:

Since no criticism or polemics are made against those entrepreneurs who look for fields of action everywhere on this planet where conditions are thought to be profitable we do not see any reason why the shift of maritime activity to flags which guarantee efficiency and profitability should be considered as something illegal and worthy of persecutions and penalties.[1]

If we accept the above hypothesis to start with, putting aside the question of tax avoidance, it may be stated that the reason that has led many shipowners to choose the alternative of flags of convenience lies in the fact that the costs of operation of vessels under such national flags as the Liberian, Panamanian, Lebanese, and so on, have been and still are lower than those of vessels under flags of traditional maritime nations. On the other hand, the statement of the Chairman of the Union of Greek Shipowners suggests that in addition to 'efficiency', that is to say cost minimization, considerations of revenue-maximization also constitute a determinant in the choice of the flag that the vessel will be registered under.

[1] See Union of Greek Shipowners, Athens, *Report of Executive Council for 1960* (translation B.N.M.).

Table 16. Vessels owned and managed by Greek shipping firms

Flag	1960		1961	
	No. of vessels	G.R.T.	No. of vessels	G.R.T.
Greek	817	5 574 621	959	6 519 185
Liberian	414	4 773 032	358	4 903 567
Panamanian	177	1 247 642	169	732 789
U.S.A.	91	857 852	77	802 310
Lebanese	81	376 068	128	720 660
Honduras	16	180 980	15	174 729
Canadian	9	105 632	6	72 168
South Africa	6	45 093	4	30 704
Argentina	2	18 770	3	29 412
Italian	2	24 920	2	24 920
	15	48 421	10	24 626
Ethiopian	2	3 123	2	3 123
French	1	2 895	1	2 895
Uruguay	1	1 833	1	833
Egyptian	1	415	1	415

Table 17. Tonnage owned and managed by Greek shipping firms

Year	FLAG				
	Greek	Liberia	Panama	Lebanon	Cyprus
1949	1 301 512	50 016	1 025 726	—	—
1950	1 264 977	133 655	1 147 680	—	—
1951	1 238 868	396 116	1 668 025	—	—
1952	1 175 996	696 212	1 769 687	—	—
1953	1 139 609	1 309 620	1 847 601	—	—
1954	1 242 075	2 397 896	1 756 413	—	—
1955	1 270 221	3 236 550	1 729 236	—	—
1956	1 444 904	4 678 244	1 722 549	—	—
1957	1 575 899	6 414 910	1 903 253	—	—
1958	2 274 925	7 224 562	1 805 054	36 112	—
1959	3 892 392	6 366 303	1 691 779	202 808	—
1960	5 574 621	4 773 032	1 247 642	376 068	—
1961	6 519 185	4 903 567	732 789	720 660	—
1962	7 008 726	4 753 619	616 552	894 031	—
1963	7 503 563	6 033 505	661 491	799 905	—
1964	7 266 723	7 735 596	646 648	755 706	31 578
1965	7 198 394	9 663 181	784 440	704 587	159 062
1966	7 517 807	10 407 220	803 689	611 717	317 409
1967	7 665 297	12 382 836	827 440	353 995	536 223

The source of the data contained in Tables 16 and 17 is the Greek magazine *Naftica Chronica* (i.e. *Nautical Chronicle* issues of 1 January 1962 and 15 January 1968). Table 16 shows tonnage under various flags, owned and basically operated by Greek shipping firms during 1960 and 1961. It will be noted that the flags used by Greek shipping firms are not confined to those that are commonly thought to be flags of convenience.

Table 17 shows the growth of Greek tonnage under the main flags of registration from 1949 to 1967 as well as the shifts that are taking place from one flag to the other. For example, it will be noted that the Greek flag became rather popular during the late fifties and early sixties owing to the fact that a 'tax holiday' period was granted by the government to all those entrepreneurs who agreed to register their tonnage under the Greek flag. On the other hand, during the late sixties the Lebanese flag lost its popularity amongst Greek entrepreneurs when some restrictions were imposed by the Lebanese government so far as voyages to Vietnam were concerned, and so on. Furthermore, it should be pointed out that during the periods covered in the tables, firms of Greek origin owned considerable tonnage under the British flag. (Such tonnage was mainly registered under U.K. ports, but also in Bermuda, Gibraltar, and Nigeria.) Needless to say that the terms of employment for seamen under the British flag (U.K. ports) are more favourable and consequently more costly to entrepreneurs than those under the Greek flag or other national flags of convenience.

It would appear, therefore, that in addition to straightforward cost considerations and pecuniary economies other criteria are applied by entrepreneurs in deciding on the flag under which the vessel will be registered. In fact such criteria may, at times, be related more to revenue maximization than to cost minimization. The device of flags of convenience presupposes the existence of a certain business organization form. Therefore, before any further comment is made in respect of the criteria applied by entrepreneurs using these flags, a few words must be said in connection with the nature of their business organizations.

1. The firm and the ship's flag

In discussing the form of the business organization of shipping concerns operating tonnage under flags of convenience a distinction will have to be made between such national flags as the Panamanian, Honduras, Lebanese etc. on the one hand and the national flags of other states such as the U.K., U.S.A., Canada, Argentina, etc., on the other.

The position in respect of the business organization of shipping firms operating tonnage under the first group of flags is as follows.

The entrepreneur (whether one or more persons) creates a Panamanian Company usually for each one of his vessels. The Panamanian Company is legally represented in Panama at a certain fee per annum. The Panamanian Company applies to the Panamanian, Costa Rican, Liberian, or Honduras Government (whichever is the case) for the registration of the vessel in question under its national flag. Needless to say that all these formalities can be and are, completed by correspondence from London, New York, Piraeus, or Athens. The fiscal obligations of the firm towards the country of registration of the ship (i.e. registration fees, tonnage taxes, cost of other formalities) are relatively small. Once a vessel is purchased it can be operated by one or two or more ship-broking offices that act as agencies of the Owners and are located in the above-mentioned cities or in the South of France, East Coast U.S.A., and so on.

Therefore, in an economic sense, the firms that own vessels under flags of convenience of the first group do not, as a rule, have a direct relationship with the country of registration of the ship. The factors of production employed by the firm, i.e. capital and labour, seldom originate from the country of registration of the ship.

The position with regard to factors of production employed by the shipping firm may become clearer if we give some examples.

It is generally known that American oil companies such as Gulf Oil, Texaco, Esso, etc., own tanker tonnage that is registered under flags of convenience and mainly under the Liberian flag. Gulf Oil employs Italian crews on the basis of Italian terms of employment, which are virtually the lowest in western

157

Europe. Texaco and Esso employ Latin-American crews on their tankers at wage rates which are in between American and Continental scales. The well-known American shipowner Mr Ludwig owns tonnage, mostly ore carriers and tankers, registered under the Liberian flag. The terms of employment offered by his companies are more favourable than the Continental but less favourable than the American ones.

However, the labour employed on vessels under flags of convenience may originate from the labour market of the entrepreneur's country of origin. For example, as a result of the experience acquired during the period after the second world war, Greek shipowners tend to think, at the present, that the efficiency of Greek seamen is higher than those of other nationalities. Hence they prefer to engage Greek crews.

The position with regard to capital and enterprise is not basically different from the labour factor. The volumes *Panama and the Greek Ships*, published by Gunnar M. Gronvold at Oslo, Norway, the *Greek Shipping Directory* as well as the volumes published by Lloyd's Register of Shipping annually list the various Panamanian companies, the tonnage that is owned by them, and the offices and ship-broking firms that act as managers or representatives or agents of these companies at the main centres of maritime economic activity such as London and New York.

The economist who will read the above references regarding the business organization forms of shipping concerns that own and operate tonnage under flags of convenience—but who has has not sufficient background on the subject—will not find it easy to determine where these firms are actually domiciled or where the Owners are. In fact the organizational structure of the enterprise and its legal framework cannot be used as a guide in determining clearly the actual firm, that is to say, the decision-making body that hires and combines factors of production in various ways with a view to profit maximization.

The 'captain of industry', the entrepreneur, may appear on paper simply as one of the directors of the Panamanian companies and/or as one of the directors or managers of the London or the New York or the Piraeus ship-broking offices, and so on. Moreover, there can be cases where the actual firm (i.e. the names of one or more owners) do not appear at all in the various legal documents that refer to the ownership of the firm. This is possible when ownership can be transferred so far as legal requirements are concerned to the names of trusted relatives and friends. In other words, the actual firm in an economic sense, i.e. the decision-making body, may be within or without the legal framework of the shipping concern.

In the case of the second group of flags of convenience, i.e. the U.K., U.S.A., Canadian, Italian, or other national flags, there tends to exist, up to a point, a true relationship between the flag of the ship and the factors of production employed by the firm. Needless to say that there can be exceptions to this (for example the U.K. flag in relation to vessels that are registered at the port of Gibraltar or Hong Kong, etc.).

In parenthesis one must state that the practice of using national flags of other countries is not new so far as merchant shipping is concerned. In the case of Greek shipping the practice of using 'foreign' flags was known before the creation of the modern Hellenic state. By the treaty of Kioutsouk–Kainartzi, signed on 21 July 1774, Greek shipping was authorized to use the Russian flag. Moreover, there exists historical evidence to prove that during the 1770s shipping interests from the island of Hydra were getting and using a double set of ships papers, that is to say Turkish and Russian, which were used as the occasion demanded. Nevertheless it cannot be claimed that this device has been invented by Greek enterprise. During the course of the first decades of the last century the Ionian state and basically the islands of Cephalonia and Ithaca constituted small centres of commercial and maritime activity. In this connection the historian of the seven islands of the Ionian sea, P. Xiotis, points out the following:

The prestige of the commercial flag of this small state (i.e. the Ionian State) was high. The King of Naples, the State of Genoa and the Court of Rome had asked the Senate to use the flag of the State for the purpose of safeguarding their commerce from piracy. However, the Senate, acting quite correctly, refused to grant this request.[1]

[1] See B. N. Metaxas, 'The Maritime Development of the Ionian island of Cephalonia', part I, in *Hellenic Shipping International*, January 1970.

159

Ever since, many national flags have been used by shipping entrepreneurs of Greek origin. Purely commercial criteria are applied so far as the choice of flag is concerned. There are many primary and secondary advantages and disadvantages of an economic and, in some cases, of a political nature that have to be taken into account before a vessel is registered under a given national flag.

The use of the British flag since the beginning of this century, just as the use of the U.S.A. and Canadian flags that are mentioned in Table 16, have—so far as Greek shipping interests are concerned—offered positive elements of convenience over relatively prolonged periods of time. In the case of the British flag the elements of convenience were credit facilities, economies so far as time costs are concerned, and a good legislation defining quite clearly the obligations of the entrepreneur *vis-à-vis* the labour factor and the state.

During the late 1940s and the 1950s the U.S.A. flag was used by shipping interests of Greek origin because of low capital costs in respect of second-hand tonnage and because of the availability of subsidies. The Italian flag and/or Italian crews (under Panamanian flag vessels) have been used primarily because of the relatively low labour costs. The aim of the relatively few attempts made to use national flags of South American countries was to penetrate the walls erected by flag discrimination with a view to obtaining high freight rates and so on.

From the foregoing it may be safely concluded that cost minimization and pecuniary economies (i.e. low operating costs resulting from the exploitation of existing imperfections in the factor markets and basically the labour markets) do not constitute the only criteria for the choice of flag. The criteria applied by the firm in deciding on the question of the ships' flag are related both to revenue maximization and cost minimization.

Nevertheless, before we analyse in some detail the question of flags of convenience in relation to costs we must first discuss subsidies, grants, and other facilities that are given by governments of maritime nations to shipping enterprises. The reason for this is the following. One of the main justifications for the use of the device of flags of convenience—or as the Chairman of the Greek Shipowners Union in Athens, Professor Andreadis puts it, 'the shift of maritime activity to flags which guarantee efficiency and profitability'—is that such flags are used in order to protect the 'competitiveness of Greek enterprise' from existing market imperfections that are caused by flag discrimination and subsidies. Furthermore, it is pointed out in Greek shipping circles that entrepreneurs of other maritime nations enjoy the benefits of grants, credit, and other facilities which the Greek state is not in a position to offer.[1]

The fact that freight rates are not determined by supply and demand wherever flag discrimination is applied by national governments has already been discussed (see chapter 1, section 5). Table 18 gives a general idea of the kind of grants, tariff protection, and other facilities offered by governments of major maritime nations with a view to assisting their national shipbuilding and shipping interests. The source of this table is the *Economist* (2 March 1968). It should be stated in this connection that in a later issue of the *Economist* Norwegian sources pointed out that their government does not grant subsidies as such to the shipowners of the country for scrapping or any other reason.

The question of subsidization of shipping firms is a very important subject in itself. As is well known, the practice of external subsidization is widely applied by various governments with respect to domestic lines for passengers and freight. As in the case of inland transport forms, subsidies for sea transport facilities may be justified on the grounds of regional economic development or other socio-economic reasons. Subsidies are also advanced to big liner firms in order to build and/or maintain large luxury liners.

We do not propose to tackle this very important subject in detail. For our purpose it will be sufficient to point out that the kind of subsidy which affects the world tramp industry most is the so-called differential subsidy.

Differential subsidies are advanced by governments, for

[1] It should be stated that in the late sixties with the development of a shipbuilding industry in Greece some of these facilities (long-term loans at low interest rates etc.) were made available to Greek shipowners by local financial institutions on a limited scale.

Table 18. Grants, assistance, tariff protection

Country	DIRECT GRANT			INDIRECT ASSISTANCE				TARIFF PROTECTION		
	Ship-builders	Ship-owners	Credits/loans	Export credits	Export credit insurance	Tax relief	Special depreciation allowance	Duty waived on imported components	Other	Research grants
Britain	£37¼ m for ration-alization	Investment grants for U.K. shipowners	Up to £200 m credit at 5½%	Yes	Yes	Export rebates Investment rebates	Yes	Yes	—	Yes
Japan	—	Subsidies for scrapping	Japan Dev. Bank 5-6 yr loans for up to 60% of price at 8.7%	Two kinds: Ex-IM bank gives 8 yr covering 50% of price. Government gives 10 yr credits for 70-100%	Yes	Partial exemption on exports	Yes	For export ships only	Tariff on imported ships	Yes
France	11% of contract price	Compensa-tion for high operating costs	20 yr modern-ization loans at 5%	Yes	Yes	Investment rebates	—	Certain goods only	Import licences	—
Italy	12-15% of price	Subsidies for scrapping	15 yr loans for up to 60% of price. Govern-ment paying first 3¼% of interest	Yes	Yes	Turnover tax exemption	Yes	Partial	Import licences	Yes

Country	DIRECT GRANT			INDIRECT ASSISTANCE				TARIFF PROTECTION		
	Ship-builders	Ship-owners	Credits/loans	Export credits	Export credit insurance	Tax relief	Special depreciation allowance	Duty waived on imported components	Other	Research grants
Germany	—	Investment grants	12 yr modernization loans at 5–6% shorter term at 5½%	Yes up to 80% of price	Yes	Investment rebates	—	Yes	—	Yes
Netherlands	—	—	Subsidized credit	—	Yes	Turnover tax exemption relief on replacement and scrapping	Yes	Yes	—	—
Sweden	Special subsidy to 1 yard	—	Credit guarantees	Yes	Yes	Turnover tax exemption. Investment rebates	Yes	Yes	—	—
Norway	—	Investment grant subsidies for scrapping	Credit guarantees loans for 50–60% of price at 5½–6%	—	Yes	—	Yes	Duty re-imbursed	—	—

Table 18 (cont.)

Country	DIRECT GRANT			INDIRECT ASSISTANCE				TARIFF PROTECTION		
	Ship-builders	Ship-owners	Credits/loans	Export credits	Export credit insurance	Tax relief	Special depreciation allowance	Duty waived on imported components	Other	Research grants
Denmark	—	—	Credit guarantees 15 yr loans for up to 80% of price	Yes	Yes	Turnover tax exemption	Yes	Duty re-imbursed	—	—
U.S.A.	—	Up to 60% of construction costs. Operating subsidy	Credit guarantees 25 yr loans for up to 25% of price at 3½%. Ships trading abroad only	—	Yes	Tax concessions for rebuilding and conversion	Yes	—	Ban on importing ships for domestic trades	Yes
Spain	Subsidy for home orders	—	Yes	Yes	—	Partial exemption from value-added tax	Yes	For export ships only	Tariff	—

example, the U.S.A. government, in order to cover the additional expenditure by American shipping firms in the construction and operation of their vessels as compared with the expenditure incurred for the same purposes by owners of vessels under the flags of other maritime nations. It is said that differential subsidies are advanced by the U.S.A. government to shipping firms owning modern, large, and speedy vessels.

The basic argument of the U.S.A. government is the defence requirements for sea transport facilities. According to this argument, U.S.A. transoceanic transport facilities, including modern dry-cargo ships, have to be retained for defence purposes in operational condition during peace-time in spite of the fact that equilibrium freight rates are insufficient to cover their costs and, at the same time, enable entrepreneurs to make a normal profit. Thus, the additional revenue required by American shipping firms for building and maintaining tonnage in the required operational state is made good by the American taxpayer through governmental subsidies. It is not within the framework of this study to examine the validity of this argument.

It should not be difficult to see why differential subsidies are a limiting factor so far as the free competitive functioning of the world tramp freight market is concerned. Tramp ships which, on account of their high building and operating costs, could not have survived competition are maintained in operation. Differential subsidies to firms owning cargo liners also have an effect on the tramp shipping industry because uneconomic liner tonnage in operation restricts the substitutability of the liner by the tramp.

The various tonnage stabilization schemes proposed by some shipowners are, in effect, a form of internal subsidy to be advanced to tramp shipping firms owning old and uneconomic tonnage for the purpose of keeping it out of the market. However, this point will be discussed later in a separate chapter.

The other facilities offered by national governments to their shipbuilders and shipowners that are shown in Table 18 are self-explanatory. Nevertheless, before we consider the validity of the argument of Greek shipping circles to the effect that flags of convenience are the only device for protecting the competitiveness of the 'Greek Ship', it will be advisable to comment on the significance of such flags in relation to costs.

2. Flags of convenience in relation to labour costs

One of the main determinants of the different levels of operating costs of vessels under different national flags is, of course, the differences that exist in labour costs. In order to be able to throw some light on this significant topic, we propose to examine briefly the variations that exist—so far as vessels under different national flags are concerned—on the following points:

    (a) The number of crew employed.
    (b) Level of wages, etc.
    (c) Other terms of employment.

    (a) During 1964 an attempt was made by *Fairplay* to construct a comparative table with regard to the number of crew employed under various national flags. The editors of the magazine thought, in our view correctly, that in order to indicate the real position the table should not be based upon the legal requirements of the maritime nations in this respect but on information furnished by the shipping firms themselves.

As is well known, legal requirements of traditional maritime nations in respect of the qualifications and minimum number of crew do not differ drastically. Nevertheless, such countries as Panama, Honduras, Liberia, Lebanon, etc. (otherwise called in the shipping world as PANHOLIB countries) do not have the necessary apparatus of mercantile services or even consulates abroad which would enable them to enforce their legislation on maritime matters. Thus, shipping firms operating tonnage under flags of convenience are practically free to maintain their own standards so far as the numbers, qualifications, and terms of employment of officers and crew members are concerned. In the circumstances *Fairplay*'s view that the relative facts can only be established by direct contact with the shipping firms themselves can only be regarded as correct.

The results of this inquiry cannot be considered as very satisfactory because the magazine did not receive a sufficient number of replies to its questionnaire from the shipping firms. Nevertheless, from the replies received it became possible to construct the table which appears in the next page. As can be seen, the table does not refer to tramps but to tankers of dead-weight tonnage in the neighbourhood of 35 000 and 70 000. This is so because tankers are vessels of more or less the same specification and differences in the number of crew cannot be attributed to differences in their hull, engine, or auxiliary machinery.

In the original table there are no figures as far as Greek vessels are concerned, the reason for this being that not one of the offices representing Greek shipping interests thought it correct to reply to the questionnaire. Thus, the figures which appear in

Table 19. Number of crew serving on vessels of different national flags

State of registration (flag)	DECK Officers	Crew	ENGINE Officers	Crew	CATERING DEPARTMENT Officers	Crew	TOTAL
Tankers about 35 000 t.d.w.							
U.K.	6	16	9	10	1	10	52
Japan	4	15	6	13	2	8	48
Denmark	5	19	13	8	1	12	58
Sweden	6	13	6	15	1	7	48
Belgium	6	12	11	3	0	4	36
Netherlands	6	12	9	7	1	7	42
Panama	4	8	4	6	0	3	25
Liberia	6	12	5	11	0	6	40
U.S.A.	5	13	5	9	1	6	39
Greece	6	13	6	13	—	7	45
Tankers about 70 000 t.d.w.							
U.K.	6	22	10	21	0	11	70
Japan	4	18	6	16	2	7	53
Denmark	5	19	13	8	1	12	58
Sweden	6	13	6	15	1	7	48
Belgium	6	12	11	3	0	4	36
Netherlands	6	13	9	8	1	7	44
Panama	4	8	4	10	0	3	29
Liberia	6	17	7	12	1	5	48
U.S.A.	6	12	6	11	1	8	44
Greece	6	16	6	15	—	9	52

Sources: *Fairplay, Naftica Chronica*, 1 May 1964, and private sources.

Table 19 with respect to Greek vessels are the product of our own private research in shipping offices and amongst Greek officers who have served on vessels of approximately the same specification.

In view of what has been pointed out it may be risky to generalize on the figures given in Table 19. Nevertheless, the data contained in the table, as well as the information that is freely circulating in the shipping world, may be considered as a safe basis which enables us to arrive at the following conclusions on the subject:

(1) The number of crew serving on cargo vessels does not depend only on its size, type, and specification, but it also depends on its flag.

(2) The number of crew on vessels under flags of convenience is, as a rule, smaller than the number of crew on vessels of the same size and type that are under the flags of traditional maritime nations.

(3) The gap that exists—so far as the number of crew is concerned—between flags of convenience and the flags of traditional maritime nations is tending to narrow.

Although the figures given for the Liberian flag in Table 19 may be considered for those who are well versed in the subject, as a proof of our third point, it is necessary to elaborate a little.

In the first place, it should be mentioned that the figures given in the table for tankers under the Panamanian flag can hardly be considered as evidence in support of the third point. These figures are based upon information given to *Fairplay* with respect to some tankers of American ownership under the Panamanian flag. Their degree of automation is not given.

As *Fairplay* remarks, the number of crew engaged for vessels of the same size and type and under the same flag differs from company to company. Broadly speaking, so far as vessels under flags of convenience are concerned, we may differentiate between those shipping firms which follow the policy of manning and maintaining their tonnage well and those which do not. Most probably the majority of shipping firms owning or managing modern tonnage under flags of convenience belong to the first of these two categories. Thus, cases, such as the one indicated in the table with reference to the Panamanian flag, cannot be regarded as representative.

This point may be seen more clearly from the number of crew employed on Liberty ships which are vessels of more or less the same size and specification. As is well known, the number of crew serving on this type of tramp, in the case of the British and other Western flags, is on the average above 35. The number of crew on Liberties under the Greek flag varies from 30 to 32. The number of crew on this type of tramp under flags of convenience is usually from 29 to 32.

However, during the low freight rate periods after Suez and even as late as 1960–2, there were Liberty ships trading under flags of convenience with as few as 26 seamen on board.[1]

This practice which, according to the experts could have serious consequences so far as safety is concerned, was widely condemned at the time in various governmental, industrial, and union circles. Moral as well as real pressure applied by some of these institutions, and the press, has contributed to the decrease in the number of such cases at present.

However, apart from these institutional factors, there also exist serious economic ones which cause the continuous narrowing of the gap in the number of crew engaged between flags of other maritime nations and flags of convenience. It is widely accepted—at least so far as modern tonnage is concerned—that the long run costs of a vessel which is inadequately manned and, therefore, not well maintained, will tend to be higher than those of a vessel with a full complement.

Moreover, the quantity and quality of output of labour employed on vessels is another factor which affects the level of operating costs. As we shall shortly see, productivity of labour is closely related to scales of wages and other terms of employment. Nevertheless, it must be stated at this point, that in present-day conditions it is exceedingly difficult, if not im-

---

[1] Furthermore, it should be added that during 1966–9 Liberty ships were purchased in the West, fixed for one voyage to the Far East and then sold to Far Eastern yards, mainly Formosa for scrapping. Although this kind of commercial transaction proved rather profitable, it has been reported that the number of crew employed was in some cases, less than 20. Such vessels before commencement of their last voyage were registered under various flags of convenience including the Sudanese flag.

possible, for tramp shipping firms managing vessels under flags of convenience to engage qualified officers and experienced seamen if they follow the policy of manning their vessels insufficiently.

Thus, it may be stated that owing to maintenance costs and automation the gap existing between flags of other maritime nations and flags of convenience with regard to the number of crew employed will continue to narrow.

(b) The tables at the end of this chapter give a clear picture of the position regarding wages, etc., during the mid-sixties for tramp ships under the British, Greek, and Liberian flags. If we make the rather realistic assumption that total pay to seamen serving on vessels under the British flag is not substantially different from that of the other Western European maritime nations, then it may be stated that the existing differences in the rates of pay for seamen between continental flags and flags of convenience are essentially marginal.

This is actually a new development. During the first years of the post-war period, when the economies of some of the Western European nations were characterized by the existence of a certain degree of unemployment, it was possible for tramp shipping firms operating tonnage under flags of convenience to engage Greek, German, Italian, Spanish etc. officers and seamen at rates of pay which were lower than those agreed between shipowners and the unions of European maritime nations.

As a result of the economic recovery of European maritime nations on the one hand and the unprecedented expansion of all maritime industries—particularly after the Suez affair—on the other, the position changed and, at present, there exists a serious world-wide shortage of qualified officers and skilled seamen.[1]

---

[1] Another factor which has contributed to the present world-wide shortage of seamen is that relatively large numbers of workers from maritime countries (such as, for instance, Greece, Italy, and Spain), with relatively under-developed national economies have emigrated to countries with advanced industrial economies. For instance, in the case of Greece, during 1961–3, more than 300 000 workers emigrated mainly to Western Germany and Australia. It should be added that this figure does not include the considerable number of Greek seamen who are working more or less permanently on vessels of other maritime nations. Neither does it include the relatively very large number of deserters from Greek and Greek-owned flag of con-

Thus, it is now difficult for a tramp shipping firm that operates tonnage under flags of convenience to engage qualified officers and skilled seamen if it is not prepared to pay wages, etc. at rates which approximate those of other maritime nations.

As a rule the quantity and quality of output of labour that is employed by firms which offer low rates of pay and manage vessels that are inadequately manned is extremely low. It is now widely accepted that in the long run the operating costs of vessels on which uncertificated officers and a large proportion of inexperienced and unlicensed (that is to say unskilled) men are serving tend to be higher than those of vessels of the same age and specification that are adequately manned by certificated officers and skilled seamen receiving wages and benefits which are in accordance with the rates prevailing in the labour markets of the traditional maritime nations. It seems that relatively high productivity depends upon high wages and vice versa.

Indeed, it is not difficult at all to distinguish between a vessel which is adequately manned and has a satisfied crew from another which is insufficiently manned. It is highly likely that big parts of the sides of the latter will be dirty and rusty because the usual maintenance work which consists of chipping, scraping, and painting has not been carried out satisfactorily. Most probably the position will be the same so far as the deck plates are concerned. As is well known, negligence of this kind of maintenance work leads to the relatively speedy thinning out and deterioration of the plates.

Furthermore, maintenance work on the winches and generally all the working gear on deck would be imperfectly carried out. There are numerous examples of delays in the loading and discharging of cargo vessels as a result of neglecting maintenance work on deck.

If the number of crew in the engine room is insufficient, it is highly likely that the boilers will not be clean and that maintenance work on the auxiliaries will be badly carried out—resulting in the deterioration in thermal efficiency, and so on.

venience ships. Such desertions take place mostly in Australian, U.S.A., and Canadian ports. The deserters are usually unskilled seamen of the lower ranks.

Furthermore, on account of various reasons the number of Indian and Hong Kong Chinese seamen who work on cargo vessels under the British flag at rather low rates of pay is now dwindling.

We may, therefore, safely conclude that in view of the reasons stated above the existing differences in the rates of pay between Continental flags and flags of convenience will tend to narrow.

(c) Seamen are also entitled to other benefits as a result of their services. Legislation of maritime nations with respect to such benefits as leave pay, sick pay, compensation for injury, unemployment benefit, pensions, etc., varies in detail. Furthermore, most tramp shipping companies have their own rules in this respect, which also differ in detail. In other words, there are firms that may pay to their officers, wages which are smaller than those indicated in Table 20 (in terms of constant prices), but which may be more generous so far as leave pay and retirement bonuses are concerned. On the other hand, there are firms that pay their officers on the scale indicated in Table 20 (in terms of constant prices), permit them to take their wives on board over prolonged periods of time but do not pay bonuses on retirement, and so on. Some firms grant such benefits to some of the lower ratings who have served over long periods of time, such as chief stewards, cooks, bosuns, greasers, etc. On the other hand, there are many tramp shipping firms which endeavour to follow the policy of granting benefits strictly according to the relative legal provisions of their countries.

It is not within the scope of this study to examine the significance of the existing differences in the legislation of various maritime nations and in the rules of the various shipping firms regarding seamen's benefits. What is important from our point of view is the fact that unless tramp shipping firms are prepared, one way or the other, to incur the cost of such benefits they cannot employ efficient seamen in the long run.

The present position with respect to benefits so far as shipping firms operating tonnage under flags of convenience are concerned is not different from the one indicated regarding rates of pay. The following example may illustrate this significant point.

The Greek Seamen's Pension Fund (N.A.T.) was founded a century ago. Shipowners and seamen of cargo vessels under the Greek flag contribute at present to this fund 7.5 per cent and 8.5 per cent of the seamen's basic monthly wages respectively. Before 1955 there were practically no tramp shipping firms

Table 20. Scales of monthly wages for officers and crew (for tramp ships 10 000–12 000 t.d.w.)

Rank	English			Greek			Liberian		
	£	s	d	£	s	d	£	s	d
Master	210	0	0	225	0	0	225	0	0
Chief officer	110	0	0	110	0	0	105	0	0
Second officer	80	0	0	80	0	0	80	0	0
Third officer	65	0	0	70	0	0	70	0	0
Wireless operator	100	0	0	110	0	0	110	0	0
Apprentice officer	15	0	0	21	10	0	21	0	0
Bosun	52	0	0	44	10	0	44	10	0
Carpenter	52	10	0	44	10	0	44	10	0
Able seaman	41	10	0	40	0	0	40	0	0
Ordinary seaman	31	5	0	23	0	0	23	0	0
Chief engineer	205	0	0	220	0	0	220	0	0
Second engineer	105	0	0	115	0	0	115	0	0
Third engineer	80	0	0	85	0	0	85	0	0
Fourth engineer	65	0	0	75	0	0	75	0	0
Electrician	83	0	0	85	0	0	85	0	0
Apprentice engineer	47	0	0	35	0	0	35	0	0
Donkey greaser	45	12	6	46	10	0	46	10	0
Greaser	42	15	0	44	10	0	44	10	0
Fireman	42	15	0	42	0	0	42	0	0
Wiper	41	10	0	30	0	0	30	0	0
Chief steward	58	12	0	44	10	0	44	10	0
Cook	52	10	0	49	0	0	49	0	0
Assistant steward	25	2	6	23	10	0	23	10	0
Assistant cook	25	2	6	23	10	0	23	10	0

Sources: *National Maritime Board Yearbook 1964*; *Greek Collective Agreement 1964*; Greek Employment Agreements for vessels under flags of convenience, and private sources.

As it appears from the table, in the case of officers, particularly Masters and chief engineers, wage rates tend to be much higher than those specified by agreements between national shipowners associations and unions. Also in the case of Greek and Liberian flags, the wage rates for deck-boys are £13 10s 0d and £11 10s 0d respectively. However, the possibilities of engaging young seamen at such rates are few.

Since the above agreements were signed there has been a constant trend for higher wages both in real and money terms.

representing Greek interests, and operating vessels under flags of convenience, contributing to this fund. Consequently, many Greek seamen serving on such vessels and wanting to get their pension in full were 'buying their service' by paying to the N.A.T. in full both the shipowners' and their own contributions. However, as a result of international pressure by the seamen's unions, the press, and other institutions, and also because of the gradually growing shortage of qualified seamen after 1959, there are now only about one hundred Greek-owned vessels under flags of convenience whose owners are still unwilling to pay contributions to the N.A.T. pension fund.

It may therefore be safely stated that, in present conditions and due to the factors indicated above, tramp shipping firms operating tonnage under flags of convenience—if they wish to follow the policy of maintaining their tonnage well—have to incur the additional cost of paying benefits to the seamen employed by them at a level which is not much different from the one of continental maritime nations.

3. Other operating costs

It has been seen that the existing differences in the scale of wages and other terms of employment of the labour factor for vessels under flags of convenience and for those of other maritime nations are not very significant at present. The number of crew employed on vessels under flags of convenience tends to be smaller than the one of vessels under flags of the other traditional maritime nations. On the other hand, it should be pointed out that for various reasons, such operating costs as insurance, provisions, etc., tend to be higher in the case of vessels under flags of convenience.

For example, insurance premiums and club calls are higher in the case of Panholib flag and Greek flag vessels than those under Continental flags. According to some underwriters and to the management of some Protection and Indemnity Clubs, this is so because the rate of casualties in the case of Panholib and Greek fleets is higher and, therefore, claims are heavier. Although both Underwriters and Clubs do not, unfortunately, publish their rich and useful statistical data, it may be assumed that in the case of marine insurance this point of view appears to be correct—particularly with regard to relatively old fleets during the last two decades. During the early and mid-sixties the cost of provisions was, as a rule, higher in the case of Greek and Panholib vessels than in the case of the British. The average cost of victualling per person per day on Greek vessels on which the crew were well-fed tended to be 10s or above, whilst on British vessels it was 9s at the maximum. The average cost of victualling per person, per day on vessels under flags of convenience on which the crew were well-fed was definitely above 10s and was higher when crew members were of more than one nationality (for example: British officers, Hong Kong Chinese crew; British flag, Hong Kong registry).

Thus, it may be safely concluded that the level of operating costs of vessels under flags of convenience that are maintained well is not considerably lower than the one for other maritime nations.

The following significant development may be taken as a proof of this.

During 1957, the Greek government decided to take such steps as were necessary in order to attract Greek-owned flag of convenience tonnage to the Greek register.

...instead of trying to solve the problem by discriminatory practices, the Greek Government felt that, in a free world, the best solution would be the adoption of a shipping policy minimizing the advantages offered by flags of convenience and founded on a basis in line with sound maritime tradition. A shipping policy providing such compensatory treatment for the Greek vessels would be sure to bear fruit for the Greek registry and also, what is even more important, encourage foreign capital to invest under the Greek Flag.[1]

Thus, the Greek government decided to grant a 'tax holiday' period of seven years for newly constructed vessels destined for registration under the Greek flag on completion of their building. A 50 per cent tax reduction for a five-year period was granted for vessels of more than seven years of age that should be

[1] This is part of an extract from the first edition of the *Shipping Bulletin* published by the Greek Ministry of Mercantile Marine and quoted in p. 31 of the *Annual Report 1957* of the Chamber of Shipping of the U.K.

transferred from flags of convenience to the Greek flag. For vessels with an age less than seven years transferred to the Greek flag, either the five year 50 per cent tax reduction period was to be applied or the 'tax holiday' period until they had reached the seven year age limit. This was left to the shipowners preference. Vessels transferred or registered under the Greek flag and owned by foreign companies, such as for instance, Panamanian ones, were considered as 'foreign capital'.[1]

This policy proved partially successful. In the two-year period which ended in December 1959, the Greek merchant fleet grew from 0.6 million G.R.T. to 3.3 million G.R.T., the latter figure including a very considerable amount of tonnage transferred from flags of convenience. Needless to say that if this flag transfer presupposed any significant increase in operating costs, shipowners would have followed the alternative of keeping their tonnage under flags of convenience. However, as may be gathered from Table 17, when the tax holiday period was over the Greek flag began to lose its popularity amongst entrepreneurs and during 1964 and 1965 there was a decline in the total of Greek-owned tonnage under the Greek flag. Some vessels were re-transferred to other flags.

The position of American-owned tonnage under flags of convenience is somewhat different in this respect. It has already been pointed out that, for obvious reasons, operating costs in general and labour costs in particular of vessels under the U.S.A. flag are considerably higher than those under Continental flags. Thus, a considerable number of American shipping firms have followed the alternative of using flags of convenience.

During the late fifties U.S.A. shipowners using flags of convenience formed an organization called the American Committee for Flags of Necessity. It was stated by the committee that the purpose of the use of flags of convenience on the part of American owners was to equate operating costs with those of other maritime countries.

As in the case of Greek tramp shipping firms, there have been numerous reports in connection with unfair practices on the part of American firms using flags of convenience. It is well known,

[1] See various 'Government Approval Acts' in the *Greek Government Gazette* during the period 1958–64.

for instance, that seamen's unions in the United States have filed with the National Labour Relations Board, charges of unfair practices against owners who refused to enter into collective agreements on wages and working conditions. Furthermore, although the figures indicated in Table 19 with respect to American-owned Panamanian-flag ships must be considered as examples of extreme cases, it would seem that the numbers of crew employed on such ships may be less than those of the generally accepted standards. It has been seen that such short-run pecuniary economies lead to higher maintenance and repair costs in the long run.

However, what is more important from our own point of view is the implicit assumption in the statement by the Committee for Flags of Necessity that, by using such flags, the cost of American-owned vessels can be equated with those of other maritime nations and that, therefore, the country of registration of a vessel is the only factor which determines the level of its operating costs. Such factors as managerial know-how, experience in navigation and labour efficiency in maintenance work due to long maritime tradition, and so on, do not seem to be taken into account. Although there are no statistics available in respect of the costs of American-owned ships under flags of convenience, it is our opinion that, in view of such factors as those mentioned above, in the long run they will tend to be higher than those of vessels under the flags of other maritime nations—even though they may continue to be smaller than those of American vessels under the U.S.A. flag.

4. Additional remarks

The facts given in this chapter indicate quite clearly that the use of a flag of convenience is a device that, due to special conditions prevailing during the first twenty years after the second world war, was widely used by shipowners of Greek, American, and other nationalities, for it enabled them to keep labour costs at a relatively low level.

Supply and demand conditions in the labour markets have now changed and, therefore, it may be said that so far as operating costs are concerned, flags of convenience whenever used are not likely to reduce long-run operating costs to any marked extent. As already indicated the only exception to this is American-owned tonnage.

What is the present difference in operating costs between a well-maintained modern tramp ship (or bulk carrier or tanker) under the Greek flag or under a flag of convenience and a vessel under the British flag of the same specification and age? In terms of money costs this difference at the present time varies between 10 per cent to 20 per cent at the maximum. Needless to say, this difference is primarily due to price differences in the labour markets of the two countries.

However, the figures that are usually given for operating costs refer to money costs. If costs were assessed in terms of use and the way of use of scarce resources, the figures under consideration may well be quite different. For example, it is likely that in a given period the work load of the British seaman is quite different from the work load of the Greek seaman, both in quantitative and qualitative terms. It is highly likely that the work load of the British seaman will consist of navigating the ship from one point to the other and of doing some basic maintenance work, whilst the work of the Greek seaman will consist of navigating, maintaining and, to a large extent, repairing the ship—for example, in continuous surveys, cleaning of boilers, and so on.

This comparative advantage in relation to the labour factor has contributed significantly in the profitability and rapid growth of Greek shipping under all flags as well as in maintaining the 'competitiveness' of the Greek ship, particularly the tramp ship under the Greek flag. In the circumstances it would have been natural to expect that an employment policy would have been applied by the Greek State in the field of maritime industries which would have aimed at protecting this important comparative advantage. Unfortunately, this does not seem to be the case.

It has been pointed out that the device of flags of convenience is of importance also with regard to revenue maximization and taxation. Furthermore, political considerations constitute a factor in the choice of flag. For example, it has been stated that during the early fifties when there was political instability in Greece, American creditors were recommending to Greek entrepreneurs the use of the Liberian flag instead of the Greek one. It has been reported that during the early sixties a vessel which was actually of Bulgarian ownership was registered at the port of Tahiti. This vessel was partly manned and managed by Greek personnel and the aim of the experiment seems to have been the acquisition of know-how by the Bulgarian personnel. In the late fifties the U.S.S.R. became a charterer of considerable dimensions for Greek-owned tanker tonnage. The terminal costs at Black Sea ports were higher for vessels under Panholib flags than those under the Greek flag. At the same time Soviet maritime authorities seemed to prefer Greek registered tonnage. Thus, several tankers were transferred from the Liberian to the Greek flag (some of these transfers were carried out at Suez and Alexandria whilst the tankers were proceeding to Black Sea ports). Insufficient information is available to decide the real ownership of vessels registered at the port of Hong Kong.

Consequently, the time when the national flags of such territories as Liberia, Panama, Honduras, Lebanon, Costa Rica, Bahamas, Hong Kong, Gibraltar, and so on will cease to be of interest to shipowners of other nationalities does not depend only on the criteria of cost minimization and revenue maximization, but it also depends on the level of taxation as well as on political considerations.

There exists, at the present, a movement to transform other flags into flags of convenience. For example, during 1968 the transformation of the Greek flag into another 'Panholib' flag was fully completed. Articles 1 and 2 of 'Obligatory Law' 378/1968 'On the Supplementation of Law 89/1967' concerning the establishment in Greece of foreign commercial and industrial companies specifies that such companies will be exempted fully from any tax or fiscal obligation or contribution whatsoever so far as revenue obtained from vessels is concerned. Thus, Greek shipping entrepreneurs are now in a position to establish the 'main offices' of their 'foreign', i.e. Panamanian, companies in Greece, and operate their tonnage from Piraeus or Athens or any other port of the Greek mainland or the islands. Moreover, Law 465 of 1968 reduces taxation of vessels to the level of other

Panholib flags. For example, Article 2 of this law reduces taxation of vessels 10–20 years old to 20 cents per N.R.T. per annum. Vessels 0–10 years old are exempted from tax. Vessels that are less than 30 years old, if they are transferred under the Greek flag are exempted from tax for a five-year period starting from the day of their registration.

Another interesting example in this connection was the effort of the authorities of Gibraltar during the sixties to transform the British flag (Gibraltar registry) into another Panholib flag. The Gibraltarian tonnage tax was at a comparatively higher level than the fiscal obligations of the Panamanian Companies to the Panamanian and the other national authorities. However, the use of the British flag for tramps that could be chartered by the liner companies (and especially the British liner companies) was a definite advantage. Competition in freight rates is officially

Table 21. Monthly wages of an able seaman

	BRITISH FLAG				GREEK FLAG			
Year	Basic A			Total B	Basic A			Total B
	£ s d			£ s d	£ s d			£ s d
1951	22 0 0			26 0 0	30 0 0			31 0 0
1956	29 10 0			34 0 0	35 0 0			37 4 0
1959	33 5 0			38 0 0	35 0 0			37 4 0
1961	35 15 0			43 0 0	38 0 0			39 5 0
1964	41 10 0			47 0 0	40 0 0			41 6 7

Sources: (a) Chamber of Shipping of the United Kingdom *Annual Report 1962–3*, p. 200.

(b) *The National Maritime Board Yearbook 1964*.

(c) Greek Collective Agreements between Union of Greek Shipowners Athens and the Panhellenic Federation of Maritime Unions 1951, 1956, 1961, 1964.

Column A of the table shows basic wages paid both in the case of the British and the Greek flag. In the case of the British flag column B indicates the maximum that a sailor may receive in the form of basic wages, 'efficient service pay' and payments for holding certificate and for 'compounded compensation' for work on Saturday afternoon. In the case of the Greek flag column B includes 'leave pay' after a year's service on the same vessel or on vessels owned by the same firm. For sailors, leave pay amounts to 12 days per annum at basic wage rate.

Table 22. Overtime rates (per hour)

Rank	British flag			Greek flag		
	£	s	d	£	s	d
Officers	0	6	5	0	5	0
Bosun	0	5	1	0	3	4
Carpenter	0	5	1	0	3	4
Donkeyman	0	5	1	0	3	4
Cook	0	4	10	0	3	4
Chief steward	0	4	10	0	3	4
Other ratings	0	4	10	0	3	0
Boys	0	2	6	0	1	6

Sources: (a) *The National Maritime Board Yearbook 1964.*
(b) Greek Collective Agreement 1964. In the case of the Greek flag, if a seafarer is ordered to work in excess of 12 hours per day (i.e. 8 hours normal duty plus 4 hours overtime) he must be paid overtime at double the fixed rate.

eliminated in the liner's industry. Nevertheless, each liner company aims at reducing the cross-elasticity of demand between its own service and that of its competitors by advertising and trying to promote special qualities for its own fleet which at times includes time-chartered tonnage. Consequently and *ceteris paribus* from the point of view of reliability, it is to the advantage of the liner company to charter and advertise cargo vessels under the British flag. The significance of this fact was realized by some non-British entrepreneurs who, in order to secure the alternative of prolonged employment for their vessels in the remunerative liner market, established shipping companies at Gibraltar.

The authorities at Gibraltar agreed to the employment of foreign crews (including the Master, chief engineer, wireless operator, chief officer and second engineer) on vessels registered at the port of Gibraltar and also to foreign terms of employment for these crews. However, this policy was not in accordance with British maritime legislation and practice. Difficulties were experienced by such vessels when in British territorial waters (as well as when calling in the ports of some of the Commonwealth countries). They were considered as some sort of 'pirate ships'. In spite of this, as reported in maritime circles, the Chief Minister of Gibraltar continued with the submission of memoranda to H.M. Board of Trade stressing the importance to the local economy of the development of a Gibraltarian flag of convenience fleet.

It is not advisable in a book of this nature to discuss the problems created in the economies of maritime nations as a result of the use of flags of convenience. So far as the question of taxation of vessels is concerned, all that may be said is that flags of convenience constitute a basic factor for the state of disequilibrium that exists in this respect—taking international merchant shipping as a whole. It is quite clear that the question of flags of convenience calls for serious attention by maritime economists and governments of maritime nations.

Chapter 7

Fluctuations in the Tramp Freight Market

In chapters 1–6 of this book we have discussed the structure of the industry, the basic characteristics of the demand for and supply of tramp shipping services, and the costs of operation of the tramp shipping firm. The competitive or substitution relationships that exist between the tramp, the tanker, the cargo liner, and the bulk carrier have been described in some detail. Also, we have already discussed topics such as ships' measurement, flags of convenience, and flag discrimination.

Each subject would in itself stand major investigation using all the tools of economic analysis. Here we have only given an introduction so that we may concentrate on a discussion of what seems to be the most important economic phenomenon of the tramp shipping industry, namely the tendency of freight rates to fluctuate sharply.

1. Introduction

The year 1869, which witnessed the opening of the Suez Canal, provides a convenient starting-point for the study of fluctuations in freight rates in modern times.

As has already been pointed out, during the hundred years of freights covered in Tables 8, 9, and 10 of the Appendix there have been very significant changes both in the supply of and the demand for tramp shipping services. During this period there have been big changes in the size and type of tramp ships and their substitutes, the method of their propulsion, the means of loading and discharging, the trading routes, the nature of cargo carried, and so on. Consequently, even on the assumption of constant prices, it is not realistic to attempt direct comparison between the freight paid in 1869 to a sailing vessel carrying grain over the traditional trading route Black Sea–U.K. with the freight payable in the 1960s to a modern diesel-engined tramp ship carrying grain from, let us say, Durban to Yokohama. However, Tables 8, 9, and 10 of the Appendix give a clear indication of the sharp fluctuations that have occurred in the tramp freight market during the last hundred years.

Table 8 of the Appendix gives the values of the freight index numbers and the 'Statist' index number for wholesale prices for the years 1869 to 1936 to base 1869= 100, the general trend for each as shown by a seven-year moving average, the absolute deviations from the general trends and the deviations for each year expressed as percentages of the general trend. The figures of Tables 9 and 10 for the period after the second world war are those of the British Chamber of Shipping.

Dr Isserlis, who is responsible for Table 8, has made a comparison of his figures with those of the U.K. Chamber of Shipping Index for tramp freights (voyage charter) for some of the pre-war years. The comparison has revealed some discrepancies. As Isserlis points out, these may be owing to the fact that his assumption that half the sum of the highest and lowest freight rates on any particular route during the year could be used to represent the mean freight rate on that route for the year, may not be absolutely correct.[1] Our discussion in the subsequent sections regarding tramp freight rate trends will be mainly based on the figures contained in these three tables. In looking at the figures contained in Tables 8, 9, and 10 of the Appendix two observations may be made:

(a) Periods of high freight rates coincide with world or local war periods.

(b) Fluctuations in freight rates tend to synchronize with those of international trade.

2. The effects of war

It is necessary to comment on these two observations before proceeding to a discussion on the nature of fluctuations in freights generally.

[1] See L.Isserlis, 'Tramp Shipping Cargoes and Freights', *Journal of the Royal Statistical Society*, May 1938.

It is widely maintained in the shipping world that one of the (main consequences of war) so far as the tramp shipping industry is concerned, is that freight rates rise to very high levels. On the basis of the available data this view appears to be correct.

For instance, during the South African war the British government met its increased tonnage requirements by chartering in the open market. As a result, extremely high rates were rapidly established. Again, during the first and second world wars, freights rose to high levels as the following time charter rates indicate:[1]

Table 23. Monthly time charter rates during the first months of the First and Second World Wars

July	1914	4s	July	1939	5s	6d
December	1914	10s	December	1939	18s	0d
July	1915	14s	July	1940	22s	0d
December	1915	25s	December	1940	24s	0d

At the beginning of the second world war, i.e. September 1939, all ocean-going British ships were requisitioned under the Defence of the Realm Act. Later on, during the course of the war, most ocean-going vessels belonging to the allied European maritime nations were requisitioned at rather remunerative rates by the British and U.S.A. governments, whilst the Liberty ships built in the States also remained under government control. Thus, the self-regulating tramp freight market mechanism was temporarily suspended. The relationship between high freight rates and wars is not indicated merely by the experience of the two world wars, but by limited conflicts in various parts of the world. As already pointed out by L. Isserlis and H. Griparios, 1898–1900, 1912, 1926, 1937, and 1951 were so-called 'peace-time' years enjoying high freight rates. However, it should be mentioned that the Spanish-American war was in progress in 1898, the South African war in 1900, a Balkan war in 1912, the Spanish civil war in 1937 and the Korean war in 1951. One could of course add the Suez crisis as one of the factors for the high freight rates that prevailed during 1956–7 and again the closure of the

[1] See H. Griparios, *Tramp Shipping*, p. 62.

same canal in 1967 which caused a short-run rise in the level of tramp, tanker, bulk carrier, and liner rates (i.e. time charter rates).

War situations constitute an external factor which exercises direct and drastic influence both on the supply of and the demand for tramp shipping tonnage. As a war situation develops, active and available supply are reduced for one or more of the following reasons:

(a) The destruction of tonnage at sea or in port by the belligerents. One may mention in this connection the initial stages of the second world war, i.e. 1940–1, when a rather considerable quantity of tonnage was destroyed by submarines and aircraft.

(b) The lengthy deviations that take place from the traditional maritime routes in order to avoid enemy submarines and aircraft, thus adding to the length of the voyage.

(c) When a war assumes world-wide dimensions, ocean-going vessels do not as a rule move by themselves but in convoys. The organization of a convoy and the fact that during the course of the voyage all vessels must travel with the average service speed of the slowest unit participating, results in a considerable loss of time.

(d) Long delays in ports which may be due to: (i) congestion, (ii) enemy raids, (iii) destruction of the means of loading and discharging (cranes etc.), and of warehouses, (iv) shortage of labour in ports. Also, some ports which are exposed to enemy raids are not used and vessels have to deviate from their normal course in order to load or discharge at other ports which are safer.

(e) Insufficient manning of vessels, due to shortage of competent officers and skilled seamen, which results in damages and stoppages. Such shortage is created—in spite of the loss of tonnage—because of several reasons: many seamen lose their lives, others participate in other branches of the war effort and others are unable to continue their profession because their countries are occupied by the enemy.

The other consequence of war preparations and war situations as such is that the demand for tramp shipping services increases.

In addition to the greater demand for transport of bulk commodities at the stage of war preparations, tramp shipping tonnage is utilized also in order to carry materials necessary for the
war effort.

The level of tramp freight rates does not fall sharply as soon
as a war is terminated. This is due to the fact that on the one hand
there is a higher demand for tramp shipping facilities as the
reconstruction effort in many countries gets under way, and on
the other there is a relative shortage of tonnage.

Thus, it may be said that the high freight rates prevailing
during war and early post-war periods are due to the fact that
war constitutes an external or exogenous factor which causes the
demand for tramp shipping services to rise and the supply of
tonnage to decrease. It follows that any other abnormal situation
that would exercise an influence of basically the same nature on
both blades of the scissors would also cause the same symptoms
so far as the level of tramp freight rates is concerned. But *it does
not follow* that the popular credo in the shipping world to the
effect that freight rates can rise decisively *only* as a result of war
or warlike situations is correct. On the other hand, it may be
argued that in the absence of wars or any other factors of similar
nature, the sharp upward trends in freight rates that are caused
by such factors will tend to disappear.

3. Fluctuations and the trade cycle

In his article 'Tramp Shipping Cargoes and Freights' Isserlis
points out:

Apart from minor fluctuations during the latter part of this period
the peaks have occurred in 1873, 1881, 1888, 1900, 1907, and 1912. These
may be compared with the peaks for trade fluctuations in general given
by Pigou, 1872, 1882, 1890, 1900 and 1907. The agreement is close, and
there is also, with some interesting exceptions, good agreement in the
deviations from the general trends shown by the two series.[1]

This characteristic tendency of the fluctuations in the tramp
freight market to synchronize with those in international trade
is also apparent in the period between the two world wars as

[1] See *Journal of the Royal Statistical Society*, May 1938, and Table 8 in the Appendix.

well as in the period after the second world war. For instance, the high freight rates that prevailed during the years 1916–17–18, 1926–7, and 1929 coincided with the periods of prosperity in the countries with industrially advanced economies and the relatively high volume of international trade that characterized these periods (which have been called the 'war prosperity period').[1] On the other hand, the very low freight rates of the 1930s coincided with the depression period.

In chapter 2 we have commented on the relationship between the volume of international trade and the demand for tramp shipping facilities. No detailed analysis is therefore needed in order to explain the fact that fluctuations in freight rates tend to synchronize with trade cycle fluctuations in industrially advanced countries.

Fluctuations in economic activity in the industrially advanced countries cannot be regarded as something that is entirely isolated from the rest of the world. On the contrary, there exists a close interdependence between trade cycle movements in various countries through foreign trade. An expansion or a contraction in business activity of a big industrial country can affect other countries; firstly, through a direct increase or decrease in the demand of the country undergoing the fluctuations; secondly, through an increase or decrease in the demand of the primary producing countries.

Industries depending on foreign trade more than others, such as the tramp shipping industry, are more sensitive to such international fluctuations. An expansion or a contraction in international trade leads to an increase or decrease in the volume of international seaborne trade and, consequently, to an increase or decrease in the demand for tramp shipping services.

Since fluctuations in freight rates tend, as a rule *and up to a certain degree*, to coincide with those of international trade, it could be assumed that they have a common original cause. In fact, an *ad hoc* explanation can usually be found for each period of prosperity and depression provided that sufficient knowledge

---

[1] See Diagram 'Business Cycles since 1831' in L. P. Ayres, *Turning Points in Business Cycles*, and in J. A. Estey, *Business Cycles*, chapter v.

FLUCTUATIONS AND THE TRADE CYCLE

is available about the conditions prevailing at the time. Thus, as has already been indicated in another context—the high freights of 1873 and 1874 can be accounted for by the high demand for tramp shipping facilities on the part of France and Germany for the restoration of their disturbed trade after the Franco-German war; the 1900 and 1936 high level of freight rates is connected with the high demand for tonnage during the South African and Spanish civil wars, and so on.

Nevertheless, the fact remains that it is comparatively easy to find explanations for the various stages of a trade cycle and for the various stages that the freight market has passed through, but it is practically impossible to determine precisely the duration or the amplitude of a trade cycle which is in progress or of the future movements of tramp freight rates.

Consequently, the only realistic conclusion that we can safely arrive at on the basis of the foregoing argument is that trade cycles in countries with advanced national economies and cycles in international trade (which are their result) affect the magnitude of the demand for tramp shipping services, and for this reason tramp freight rate movements tend, up to a certain degree, to coincide with those of international trade.

Nevertheless, this should not be taken to mean that cyclical fluctuations in advanced industrial countries constitute the only exogenous factor that may effect the demand for tramp shipping facilities and, therefore, the level of freight rates at any given period of time. As we are aware tramp shipping develops within the framework of a dynamic world and there are many factors of a physical, technological, political, economic, or social nature that can exercise a direct and significant influence on the level of tramp freight rates. For instance, the expectations for and the actual conclusion of the agreement between the U.S.A. and the U.S.S.R. for the export of grains from the former to the latter (1963–4) which has had a significant effect on the level of tramp freight rates cannot be considered as an exogenous factor that had anything basically in common with trade cycles in advanced industrial countries.

It has been mentioned that freight rate movements are also affected by endogenous factors, that is to say, factors originating from within the industry. However, it will have been noticed that up to this point we have commented only on the importance and the nature of the external factors.

Actually, external factors produce a chain reaction which does not end with a rise or a reduction of the level of tramp freight rates. Thus, we think that in order to be able to understand fully the causes, the nature, and the main consequences of fluctuations, a further look at some of the basic properties of the tramp freight market mechanism becomes necessary.

Chapter 8

Tramp Shipping Services: Supply and Demand

1. The concept of equilibrium

In order to understand price fluctuations and the mechanics of price formation in the market it is essential to apply the concept of equilibrium.

The world tramp shipping industry could be said to be in stable long-run equilibrium if freight rates the world over were offering no inducement to entrepreneurs either to add new units to their fleets or to withdraw the existing ones from the market without replacement. In this state freight rates would be such that there would be no advantage for entrepreneurs outside it to enter the market by creating new firms nor for shipping firms to leave the industry. The availability and requirements for tramp shipping services would be equal. Average freight rates for the various tramp shipping services required would be equal to the average costs incurred for producing these services. Each one of the existing tramp shipping firms would fix its vessel or vessels at such rates that the revenue obtained from each additional voyage would be just enough to cover the cost for producing this additional service—including normal profit. In other words, marginal cost, i.e. the cost per additional voyage, would be equal to marginal revenue.

Fig. 6 shows the equilibrium position of the industry. If the industry were in equilibrium, output in million ton-miles would have settled at the point where the demand curve DD intersects the minimum point of the industry's long-run supply curve SS. Total output in million ton-miles would therefore be OM and the average level of freight rates OF.

Needless to say, such a long-run permanent state of equilibrium has never been attained nor is it likely to be. There have been only brief periods of time when the availability and

Fig. 6. The equilibrium position of the tramp shipping industry

requirements for tramp shipping tonnage have tended to match. As we have already pointed out, new developments of an economic, social, political, physical, or technological nature intervene all along the way, changing the position of the ultimate equilibrium.

Fig. 7 shows how a tramp shipping firm maximizes its profits when the industry as a whole is not in equilibrium. If the tramp shipping firm produces OM_1 ton-miles, it will itself be in equilibrium because marginal cost equals marginal revenue at that

Fig. 7. Profit maximization by the tramp shipping firm when the industry is in disequilibrium

192

point and its profits are maximized. However, at that output the average revenue of the firm $M_1 Q_1$ will be in excess of its average cost $M_1 N_1$ and it will therefore be earning more than normal profits; new firms will be attracted in the market by excess profits so that the industry will not be in equilibrium. As new firms come in, total supply will expand in the long run and the level of freight rates will fall so that the individual firm's demand curve will fall until it touches the average cost curve at its lowest point and profits are back to normal. However, if the tramp shipping firm produced OM_2, average cost and average revenue would be equal, profits would be normal and the industry would be in equilibrium. Nevertheless the firm would not be maximizing its profits. At output in ton-miles OM_2 the marginal cost of production $M_2 Q_2$ would be in excess of the marginal revenue $M_2 N_2$ and the firm would be reducing its total profit with every additional unit it produced after OM_1. Whatever other situation is postulated, then, either the industry or the firm will be in a state of disequilibrium, and average freight rates will continue to change. Only when average freight rates are equal both to marginal and minimum average cost will both the individual firm and the tramp shipping industry as a whole be in a state of complete balance.

The absence of stable equilibrium should not be taken to indicate that the functioning of the tramp freight market mechanism is not characterized by the inevitable tendency towards long-run equilibrium, a tendency of the industry to adjust itself to demand requirements. When profitability prospects are high the industry expands. When expectations for profitable trading are poor the rate of expansion gradually diminishes and when prospects for future trading do not seem to be either good or bad the magnitude of the fleet is maintained more or less on the same level. Thus, irrespective of the influence of exogenous factors it may be said that there exists a long-run tendency towards equilibrium position.

Let us consider what has been the position in respect of the supply of tramp shipping tonnage since the end of the second world war. Broadly speaking, up to and including the sixties, the actual position so far as the supply side of the tramp freight market was concerned appears to have been one of numerous representative ships on the one hand, which were more or less of the same age and specification, and on the other of the fewer and older units that were becoming more and more costly to run plus the modern ships which were to take the place of the representative ships later on. For instance, taking the first decade after the second world war as a given period of time, we may classify the pre-war built tramps as the old ones, the Liberty ships as the representative productive units of the industry and the rather few larger and faster tramps built at the end of this decade as the modern units. More specifically, it may be stated that the representative tramp ship was the dominant type of vessel which in effect (and together with demand) determined the general price level in the market. Had long-run average freight rates been below the average operating costs of such vessels, then it would not have been possible to move the world's goods.

Let us now assume momentarily that at a given point of time the supply of tramp shipping tonnage consisted only of representative units with the same fixed and variable costs. Furthermore, we will assume that at the same point of time the freight market was at a relatively low level. Most of the existing tramp shipping tonnage was trading, but shipowners were finding it difficult to cover their variable costs. However, owing to the influence of some external factor, the demand curve for tramp shipping services in trading route A, let us say Canada–U.K.–Continent, shifted upwards suddenly. We know from Chapter 2 that the first symptom of such a development will be that freight rates for cargoes carried over route A will rise rather sharply. Consequently, tonnage will be withdrawn in the first place from the neighbouring routes, let us say trading routes B and C, and will be fixed to load cargoes at the loading ports of route A. In this particular example we may suppose that trading routes B and C are Hampton Roads–U.K.–Continent and South America–U.K.–Continent. The withdrawal of tonnage from routes B and C, as well as expectations for the future development in the market, will naturally cause rates to rise in these routes. Eventually, new tonnage will be chartered for voyages in routes B and C and the effects of the increase in the magnitude of demand in route A will be transmitted through the price mechanism to all trading routes as well as the lay-up berths.

As the data contained in Table 11 of the Appendix shows, the tramp freight market offers ample evidence that tramp freight rates over various trading routes tend to move in the same direction. Therefore, broadly speaking we may state that 'this path of movements' of tramp freight rates may be taken as an expression of the inherent tendency of the tramp freight market mechanism to readjust itself under a given set of conditions.

If we return for a moment to our example and if we assume that for a given long-run period there was no other exogenous or endogenous influence on the tramp freight market mechanism (i.e. after the one which caused freight rates to rise starting from trading route A), then we could safely state that new tonnage would have been entering trading routes A, B, C, etc. until tramp freight rates the world over would have reached such a level that shipping firms would not be induced either to transfer their tonnage from one route to the other or withdraw their vessels from trading. Nevertheless, as we have seen, other events are taking place and disrupt the process of adjustment. Thus, equilibrium position in the various routes is either attained as a passing phase or not attained at all.

2. Supply, demand, and freight rates in the short run

In chapter 3 it was pointed out that the supply of tonnage does not substantially expand or contract in the short run, but that it tends to be inflexible. It has been seen that at least between 12 and 18 months must normally elapse between the ordering of new tonnage and its eventual delivery to the owners. When the shipyards are fully occupied the intervening period may be as long as 3 or 4 years. As Tables 11 and 13 of the Appendix indicate, over short-run periods, owing to external causes the demand for tramp shipping facilities is capable of varying quite substantially one way or another.

The data contained in Tables 11, 12, and 13 of the Appendix may be taken as evidence that, over various short-run periods, variations in the magnitude of demand or shifts in the demand curve constitute the causal factor for the changes that occur in the price level.

The variations in freight rates indicated in these two tables must be attributed not only to variations in the demand for transport of the bulk commodities mentioned therein, but also to variations in the magnitude of the overall demand for transport of cargoes in bulk. For instance, Table 11 in the Appendix shows that between 1954 and 1955 there was an increase in freight rates for coal in the U.S.A.–Continent route. During the same period the volume of U.S.A. coal exports increased from 12 926 000 tons to 51 256 000 tons. However, this sharp increase in the volume of the U.S.A. coal exports explains only partly the upward trend in freight rates. It should also be taken into account that, as shown in Table 2 (chapter 2), between 1954 and 1955 world seaborne trade of dry cargoes increased from 390 to 450 million metric tons and world seaborne trade as a whole, i.e. including liquid cargoes, increased from 710 to 800 million metric tons.

Thus, it may be stated that an increase in the magnitude of demand for tramp shipping services can cause a rather sharp rise in freight rates, whereas a decrease in the magnitude of demand can result in rates falling to low levels.

However, it could still be argued that the data given above as well as in the tables still do not prove the point because they do not indicate whether or not there has been any reduction in the supply of tramp shipping services during the period under consideration. In fact, the supply of tramp shipping tonnage had just begun to increase during 1954–5. Up to 1954 the supply of tramp shipping tonnage consisting mostly of Liberty and Empire type of ships as well as of pre-war built vessels remained more or less static, its magnitude being during 1954 about 14 995 000 t.d.w.

Year	Supply of tramp ships in t.d.w.	New buildings annual increase in t.d.w.	Total annual increase in t.d.w.
1955	16 797 000	435 000	—
1956	18 620 000	726 000	1 823 000
1957	21 179 000	2 100 000	2 559 000
1958	23 570 000	2 351 000	2 391 000
1959	24 798 000	1 023 000	1 228 000

It was only after 1954 that, as a result of the continuous increase in the demand for transport of bulk cargoes, the supply of tramp shipping tonnage began to rise.[1]

Consequently, it can be safely stated that short-run changes in freight rates are a direct result of variations in the magnitude of demand for tramp shipping facilities.

3. Supply, demand, and freight rates in the long run

The nature of the factors that cause the supply of tonnage to expand or contract in the long run has been discussed in chapter 3. However, we must now make some additional comments on two points.

(a) It has been stated in chapter 3 that there is a time-lag between the shipowners' decision to expand their fleets and the date of delivery of the new vessels. At least between 12 and 18 months must normally elapse between the ordering of new tonnage and its eventual delivery to the owners. When the shipyards are fully occupied the intervening period may be as long as 3 to 4 years.

(b) As already indicated, owners' expectations tend, as a rule, to be high when the freight market is at a high level, whilst when the freight rates are at low levels prospects for future developments are not optimistic. A policy of 'wait and see' is usually followed by shipowners in the rather prolonged periods of low freight rates and the belief that firms which do not appear 'very sound' financially will not be able to go on much longer seems to be widespread in the industry. Thus, it is expected by entrepreneurs that when freight rates are again high there will be fewer competitors in the market and, consequently, they will again be able not only to restore, but to improve the position of their firms.

Most orders are given to the shipyards during the relatively short periods of high freight rates, whilst during the usually prolonged periods when the market remains at low levels, new orders are much fewer.

[1] Sources: Westinform *Shipping Report*, no. 133, and O.E.E.C., *Maritime transport* 1959.

There is ample evidence to suggest that the level of freight rates has been the basic criterion in shipowners' minds when deciding on their expansion schemes. However, it would be an over-simplification to say the expectations of the present 'captains of industry'—and particularly the more experienced ones—are exclusively based on the existing level of the market at a given period of time.

The period after the second world war (unlike the period after the end of the first world war) proves that the tramp shipping firms already established in the market took other considerations into account so far as their investment plans were concerned. For example, during the first years after the second world war and during the course of the Korean war, when freight rates were at high levels, tramp shipping firms did not proceed with ambitious schemes of expansion. There were several factors which led entrepreneurs to the conclusion that a cautious policy must be followed in respect of new investments. The most important of these were the following:

(*a*) The existence of the government-owned U.S. 'Reserve fleet'. The numerous Liberty ships belonging to the American government, that have been laid up practically since the end of the war, could at any time, as a result of a political decision, be sold or leased to independent owners or transferred in some other way from the available to the active supply.

(*b*) The re-entry into the tramp freight market of the Liberty ships that were used as substitutes for cargo liners over prolonged periods because of tonnage shortage in the liner market.

(*c*) The relatively slow recovery after the war in the sphere of international seaborne trade which was due to various factors, economic as well as political.

(*d*) The existence of credit restrictions.

(*e*) (1) The level of employment of the European shipyards which was high because of orders for cargo liners, passenger liners, and tankers. (2) The policy followed by the shipyards of some countries of not agreeing in advance with owners on the price and (in some cases) date of delivery of new buildings. (3) The initial doubts of many shipowners of well-known maritime nations with respect to the reliability of Japanese shipyards.

Nevertheless, in spite of the fact that long-run considerations are now taken more into account by entrepreneurs and their managements in decision-making, as the period after the first closure of the Suez canal demonstrates, the development of the industry is still characterized by an endemic tendency to over-invest during periods of high freight rates.

On the basis of the foregoing it should not be difficult to see how an external factor can cause prices in the market to fluctuate sharply.

If, as a result of the influence of external factors, the demand for tramp shipping services rises, freight rates will also rise rather sharply. The magnitude and duration of such an increase of demand and of prices—other things being equal—will depend primarily on the influence of the factor. Such a change in demand and price conditions is bound to have serious repercussions on the supply side of the market. Entrepreneurial expectations tend to be high during periods of high freight rates and, therefore, ship-owners may decide to expand their fleets. Moreover, during the same period new firms will enter the market. As the history of the industry proves, during periods of 'prosperity' entrepreneurs tend to over-invest. In the end, as a result of this endemic tendency for over-investment, surplus tonnage is created in relation to immediate demand requirements. Thus, the average level of freight rates is brought down to relatively low levels over prolonged periods of time. In other words, the fact that freight rates fluctuate sharply stems from the difficulty in recon-ciling the supply of and the demand for tramp shipping services. Whilst the supply at any point of time tends to be inelastic, the demand is capable of varying most significantly one way or the other.

Chapter 9

Main Characteristics and Consequences of Fluctuations

1. Stages in fluctuations

As shown in Fig. 8 each fluctuation in the industry may be separated into different stages. The level of average freight rates, that is to say, the level of prices for tramp shipping services, is commonly considered as the basic criterion in determining the different stages of each fluctuation.

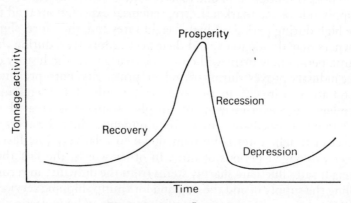

Fig. 8. Stages in fluctuations

Thus, it is generally maintained that when average freight rates are at a high level the industry is passing through a period of prosperity, and when average freight rates are at a low level the industry is passing through a period of depression. The usually brief period of time during which freight rates are rising may be called revival or recovery periods and the usually brief period of time during the course of which freight rates are falling may be termed the recession period.

On the basis of past experience it can be safely stated that the prosperity stage is, as a rule, longer than the stages of recession or recovery and lasts for several months. The duration of the depression stage is usually measured in terms of years.

There is no ground for assuming that the stages of future fluctuations will or will not conform to the time periods broadly indicated above.

Changes in the level of prices for tramp shipping services are the basic but not the only criterion with regard to the different stages of each fluctuation. We must therefore examine the other significant characteristics of the different stages of each fluctuation. In doing so it will become possible to obtain a clearer understanding of how various factors that cause the fluctuations also affect the scarce resources used by the industry.

2. Utilization of capital

The prosperity stage is characterized by a relatively high degree of utilization of capital resources whilst, on the other hand, one of the main features of the depression stage is the existence of idle capital.

Supply tends to be inelastic during the downward trend of the freight market, that is to say during the beginning of the recession stage. This is due to the fact that shipowners endeavour to keep their vessels trading as long as the losses incurred are no greater than the cost of idleness. Moreover, at the beginning of a recession period some of the industry's entrepreneurs may take the short-run decision to keep part of their tonnage trading even though losses are expected to be higher than the cost of idleness. Such short-run decisions are taken if it is expected that competitors will soon proceed with the laying-up of their tonnage and, therefore, 'the market will improve'.

Since demand, which remains at a relatively low level during the depression stage, is satisfied mostly by relatively modern tonnage, a large number of the other tramps must be expected to proceed to lay-up berths, either because of complete lack of employment or because the level of freight rates clearly indicates that if new fixtures are to be concluded marginal cost will be greater than marginal revenue and the difference will be greater than the cost of idleness for the same period of time.

Older tramps, which happen to be on the average of smaller size and lower speed are more costly to operate. Thus, as may be seen from Tables 24 and 25, the greatest proportion of vessels which are laid up on account of lack of employment at a given point of time are the older ones.

Table 24. World shipping laid up for lack of employment at the beginning of May 1963. Age distribution

Year of build	DRY CARGO		TANKER		TOTAL	
	No.	Gr. tons	No.	Gr. tons	No.	Gr. tons
1937 and earlier	82	260 185	8	53 744	90	313 929
1938	6	16 005	1	7 949	7	23 954
1939	13	67 109	1	9 986	14	77 095
1940	4	16 334	2	10 638	6	26 972
1941	8	49 397	1	12 874	9	62 271
1942	25	158 766	4	37 657	29	196 423
1943	117	823 945	18	187 616	135	1 011 561
1944	104	714 333	15	141 676	119	856 009
1945	32	191 344	12	115 039	44	306 383
1946	8	44 097	1	8 187	9	52 284
1947	5	21 739	—	—	5	21 739
1948	9	39 985	2	12 176	11	52 961
1949	3	13 443	5	43 205	8	56 648
1950	3	21 900	5	51 865	8	73 765
1951	3	17 318	3	31 544	6	48 862
1952	2	4 401	1	16 127	3	20 528
1953	5	37 579	1	11 365	6	48 944
1954	2	8 937	—	—	2	8 937
1955	4	23 894	—	—	4	23 894
1956	4	32 815	—	—	4	32 015
1957	5	38 016	—	—	5	38 016
1958	1	6 903	—	—	1	6 903
1959	1	18 123	—	—	1	18 123
1962	2	10 994	—	—	2	10 994
Totals	488	2 637 562	80	752 448	528	3 390 010

Source: The Chamber of Shipping of the U.K. The table is compiled from information received at Lloyd's, but excluding *inter alia* coasters and certain vessels normally engaged on short voyages.

Table 25. World shipping laid up for lack of employment at the beginning of May 1963. Size distribution

Gr. tonnage range	DRY CARGO		TANKER		TOTAL	
	No.	Gr. tons	No.	Gr. tons	No.	Gr. tons
Under 1000	12	9 081	2	1 181	14	10 262
1000–1999	48	73 271	1	1 413	49	74 684
2000–3999	52	150 832	2	5 519	54	156 351
4000–5999	43	219 007	3	15 973	46	234 980
6000–7999	269	1 928 430	8	56 302	277	1 984 732
8000–9999	16	138 373	11	100 216	27	238 589
10 000–14 999	4	43 337	51	539 657	55	582 994
15 000–19 999	2	34 118	2	32 187	4	66 305
20 000–24 999	2	41 113	—	—	2	41 113
Totals	448	2 637 562	80	752 448	528	3 390 010

Source: The Chamber of Shipping of the U.K. The table is compiled from information received at Lloyd's but excluding *inter alia* coasters and certain vessels normally engaged on short voyages.

In considering the data of Tables 24 and 25 we must note that the figures given refer to world shipping and dry-cargo vessels as a whole and not to tramp ships in particular. The tables show that the greatest number of units laid up were those that were constructed during 1943 and 1944 and had a tonnage of 6000–7999 G.R.T. Thus, both the year of construction and the size suggest that they were tramp ships of the Liberty type. In reading the tables it must be borne in mind that in 1963 the Liberties still constituted about 40 per cent of the world tramp shipping fleet whilst the pre-war built vessels were below 12 per cent of the world merchant fleet.

Thus, the figures under consideration must be taken only as a rough indication to the effect that the greatest proportion of tramp ships and vessels in general which are laid up, on account of lack of employment at a given point of time, are the older ones whose direct costs of operation are higher than those of new ones.

It should also be pointed out that Tables 24 and 25 do not refer to a depression stage but to a short-run period, during the course of which tramp freight rates were temporarily on a relatively low level. The difference between a short-run period, during which tramp freight rates may fluctuate temporarily on a relatively low level, and an actual depression period, lies in the fact that during the latter the lay-up figures are massive and include many of the average or representative units of the fleet—and even some modern ones—for their owners find it extremely difficult to secure profitable employment.

Thus, during the depression stage some of the most modern units of the world tramp fleet may remain laid up whilst a certain number of the older tramp ships may continue trading. For example, the following modern tramp ships under the Liberian flag, owned by Greek interests, remained laid up during the depression stage of 1957–60: *Avgi*, built 1956, G.R.T. 10 312, laid up at Baltimore, 29 January 1958; *Nymphe*, built 1954, G.R.T. 8062, laid up at Toronto, 26 February 1958; *Pan*, built 1956, G.R.T. 10 486, laid up at Rotterdam, 10 August 1958.[1]

These are exceptions to the rule that tramp ships and cargo vessels in general which are laid up on account of lack of employment at a period of low freight rates are the older ones which are nearly always more costly to operate.

An examination of the reasons for these exceptions may be of some interest. Older vessels which are trading during a depression may be on a long time charter concluded during the prosperity stage. Time charter rates tend to follow, up to a point, free market rate trends. During prosperity, time charter rates tend to be lower than single voyage rates. Owing to their commitments or other commercial considerations, it is the policy of many shipping firms to time charter a certain percentage of their tonnage during prosperity in order to avoid the risk of laying up possibly the whole of their fleet during depression. Also, from considerations of the same nature, shipowners endeavour especially during the brief recession period, to charter their tonnage on a long-run basis. Fixtures of this sort enable owners to cover the operating costs of their units comfortably or with difficulty. Thus, some of the older tramps that are, for example, suitable for entering the liner market may be trading, whilst other more modern units have already been laid up.

The location of a vessel under construction or while trading is

---

[1] See *Naftica Chronica*, 15 October 1958, and also Lloyd's Shipping Indexes for the same period, i.e. February 1958 to October 1958.

another factor that may cause idleness in the case of modern and economic tonnage during periods of low freight rates. For example, if we assume that the construction of a tramp ship was completed in Japan at a period when the tramp freight market was 'inactive' so far as the Far Eastern routes were concerned, but that there was some tonnage activity in the Atlantic route, then it is perfectly reasonable to conclude that whilst the newly-built ship might have had to lay-up temporarily, the cargoes available for transport on the Atlantic might well have been carried by older tramps with higher operating costs per ton-mile.

The best example of which we are aware with regard to the significance of the locational factor in entrepreneurial decisions as to whether modern tramp ships should continue trading or not during a depression is that of the M. V. *Nymphe*. This vessel remained at the port of Venice discharging her cargo from 14 to 24 February 1958, i.e. a period of low freight rates, during which the demand for tramp shipping services on the Atlantic and on the other areas near the Mediterranean sea was at a very low point. Owing to the seasonal factor also entrepreneurial expectations were rather poor for the short run. Thus, it was decided to send the M. V. *Nymphe* to lay up at Toronto and repatriate her Greek crew to their home port at a relatively low cost. An example of a tramp ship, the construction of which was completed during a low freight period and thus was sent to lay-up temporarily, is the M. S. *Egton*, built 1962, British Flag, G. R. T. 9958.

The financial position of the shipping firm is an important factor in this respect. If entrepreneurs are under heavy commitments they may decide to trade their ships during low freight periods irrespective of the risks involved. However, if they are not under heavy commitments the cost of idleness of a modern tramp ship does not constitute a serious problem. Hence, their ships may be sent to the lay-up berth until such time that market prospects are better.

In examining the interesting phenomenon of the laying up of modern ships during low freight periods it should be emphasized that such ships may remain laid up for reasons that are not the direct result of market developments such as, for instance, lengthy repairs and detentions. Moreover, some of the modern ships may be relatively small in size and less economical to operate than others of larger size which may have been built a few years earlier. For example, the relatively modern but small tankers *Atlantic Duke*, built 1952, G.R.T. 10 930, and *Olympic Rainbow*, built 1956, G.R.T. 13 934, both under the Liberian flag, remained laid up during 1958. Furthermore, there may be modern specialized vessels which remain laid up due to lack of employment in their own special field of maritime transport.

It has been pointed out already that although the world tramp freight market mechanism closely resembles the theoretical model of perfect competition, it is also characterized by the existence of some imperfections. One of these imperfections which has not been mentioned earlier originates from the political realities of our time and becomes apparent during recession and depression periods. For example, some of the governments of Eastern countries, because of politico-economic considerations, offer time charter or consecutive voyage rates which, during low freight periods, are slightly higher than those offered by other sources and which enable shipowners, if they employ their vessels with them, to obtain a revenue which is higher than the minimum operating costs of their vessels. In such circumstances some shipowners decide to disregard the political aspect and charter their vessels, thus minimizing the risk of leaving the tramp freight market temporarily or even permanently. One may mention as examples in this connection the role of the Chinese government as a charterer during 1958 or of the U.S.S.R. and Cuban governments during the low freight periods of the early 1960s.

Tables 26 and 27 give a clear indication of the extent to which capital resources remain unused during the stages of depression. Table 26 shows the quantity of tonnage laid up—as a percentage of national fleets—during the depression of the 1930s at its highest level (i.e. during 1933) and Table 27 shows the quantity of laid-up tonnage at the end of the major post-war depression in the tramp freight market, i.e. 1958-9.

Tonnage laid up at its highest level during the depression of the 1930s (G.R.T. in 1933) totalled over 14 million tons, or about $19\frac{1}{2}$ per cent of the world fleet. During the depression that occurred after the first closure of the Suez Canal, and specifically

Table 26. Quantity of tonnage laid up 1933 (in 1000 G. R. T.)

Flag	U.K.	U.S.A.	Ger.	France	Neth.	Nor.	Italy	Greece	Others
Tonnage laid up	3356	3425	1270	922	209	801	863	570	2067
Percentage of Fleet	18.1	25.5	30.5	25.9	27.3	19.2	25.7	34.7	—

Table 27. Percentage laid up 1958–9

Country	Percentage of fleet
United Kingdom	6
Norway	10
Sweden	4
Netherlands	3
Germany	4
Italy	18
Denmark	5
France	3
Greece	36
Panama	23
Liberia	20

during August 1968, less than 96 million G. R. T. were employed out of a total of 119 million G. R. T. of world shipping—the laid-up total being 23 million G. R. T., that is to say, approximately 19 per cent of the world fleet.[1]

It will be noted in the first place, that the above figures refer to merchant shipping as a whole (with the exception of some coasters and some small ships engaged on short voyages), and secondly that they are based on the gross registered tonnage of vessels and not on their deadweight tonnage which, as we know, is a better indicator of cargo-carrying capacity. However, in the

[1] The sources for the data contained in the tables and in the last paragraph of the text are Westinform *Shipping Report*, no. 118; Chamber of Shipping of the U.K., *Annual Reports 1957–62*; *Naftica Chronica*, 1958, and the annual report of the Executive Council of the Union of Greek Shipowners, Athens 1960, p. 10.

absence of accurate data for the tramp shipping industry as such, the figures under consideration may be accepted as giving a broad and, perhaps, modest estimate of the actual degree of unemployment of capital resources in the tramp shipping industry during the stage of depression.

The prosperity stage is characterized by a high but not full utilization of capital resources. Average freight rates may exceed equilibrium point, but this upward trend in prices does not automatically induce individual shipping firms as well as governments to recommission all their tonnage, particularly when it is old or uneconomic to operate. Entrepreneurs' decision making in this respect does not depend only on the prevailing level of the freight market but also on owners' expectations for the industry's future in the long run.

For example, during the prosperity stage of 1929 when freight rates were at a high level 3 000 000 G.R.T. remained laid up, nearly two-thirds of this being in reserve in the U.S.A. Also, as is well known, the greatest part of the government-owned American reserve fleet remained laid up during the whole post-war period, that is to say, even during the course of relatively short-run periods when it could be trading profitably. The total of the U.S.A. reserve fleet amounted, during the 1950s and early 1960s, to approximately 12 700 000 G.R.T. (i.e. 12 000 000 dry-cargo ships mostly Liberties, and 700 000 G.R.T. tankers).[1]

We may state that during the prosperity stage utilization of capital resources reaches its maximum, whilst the stage of depression is characterized by massive figures of laid-up ships. During the usually brief stage of recession the degree of utilization of capital resources is reduced, and vice versa, during the usually brief period of recovery or revival it increases. The history of the tramp shipping industry seems to indicate that the phenomenon of fluctuations should be regarded as a normal hazard and firms should expect to have to meet the problems involved. The degree to which capital resources may remain unused differs from firm to firm and it mainly depends upon

[1] The sources for the above figures are Westinform *Shipping Report*, no. 118, and Chamber of Shipping of the U.K. *Annual Reports 1959–62*.

such factors as the timing of when the firm decides to order or purchase its tonnage, or to dispose of some of its ships, the substitutability of the productive units owned, and the chartering policy followed by the firm.

3. The labour factor

Variations in the quantity of capital utilized are accompanied by variations in the quantity of labour employed in the industry. During the depression stage unemployment of seamen of maritime nations reaches wide dimensions, whilst during the prosperity stage labour shortages, particularly of qualified officers and skilled seamen, become acute.

The supply of labour available for the maritime industries differs from one maritime nation to another, both in a quantitative and qualitative sense. The supply of labour for the tramp shipping fleet of a nation depends on many factors, some of which are of a non-economic nature, For example, it depends on the number of population, the geographic position and maritime tradition of the country, the existence or non-existence of a trade union movement, the educational system, the habits of the people, the level of development of the national economy, the degree of employment of labour by inland industries, the terms of employment that a tramp shipping firm is prepared to offer in comparison with the terms of employment offered to labour by entrepreneurs of inland industries, the wages and other benefits that tramp shipping firms are willing to pay for officers, skilled and unskilled seamen as compared with the wages and other benefits that entrepreneurs of other maritime industries of the country are willing to pay, and so on.

As already indicated in chapter 6, in addition to national markets for labour there already exists, although in an imperfect form, an international market. Seamen from countries with developing economies and a relatively high degree of unemployment sign on various ships—some of them being under flags of convenience. Their terms of employment are considerably lower than those offered to seamen of advanced industrialized nations. This imperfect market is at the present time expanding.

For example, it has now become fashionable amongst owners of vessels under flags of convenience to engage Philipino and Indonesian seamen. The 'migration' of seamen from countries with developing economies on foreign flag ships has, no doubt, its advantages and disadvantages so far as the seamen themselves and their national economies are concerned. Probably the most serious disadvantage is that at the depression stage—or even at a short-run period of low freight rates—such seamen have practically no other alternative than repatriation to their own countries. Thus, if the number of seamen of a nation with a developing economy that have joined foreign ships is relatively large, their massive repatriation during a depression may create an economic and social problem for the state in question. This is particularly so if the crew employment agreements of the seamen with the foreign companies does not provide for unemployment and social security benefits—which is usually the case. For reasons that have a sound economic basis many developing countries are following the alternative of creating their own merchant fleets. In this connection it should be pointed out that merchant shipping and particularly tramp shipping has its 'ups' as well as its 'downs'. Thus, a depression in the international freight markets will inevitably create considerable unemployment of capital and labour resources.

The following data concerning unemployment of Greek seamen during periods of low freight rates is available.

The number of Greek seamen of all ranks who worked on Greek vessels during 1932 was, according to the statistical data of the relative Department of the Ministry of Mercantile Marine, 15,500. In addition, about 3,000 seamen on the average remained unemployed. From those that were able to secure employment about 10,500 worked on steamships and 5,000 on sailing ships. Thus the unemployed seamen during 1932 were 19 per cent out of all those engaged in the nautical profession. This percentage was lower in 1931 when unemployment reached 13.5 per cent that is to say, there was an increase in the unemployment of seamen by 5.5 per cent.

The figures for laid-up Greek vessels during the course of the same years were as follows.

During 1931 there were 81 steamships laid up, their tonnage (G.R.T.) being 201 000, i.e. 15 per cent of the existing Greek tonnage, but during

1932 there were 118 steamships laid up of 346 000 G.R.T., i.e. 26 per cent of the existing Greek tonnage.[1]

Table 28 shows the number of unemployed Greek seamen during the years 1947 and 1958 when the tramp freight market was at low levels.

Table 28. Number of unemployed Greek seamen, 1947 and 1958

Month	1947	1958	Month	1947	1958
January	3564	4978	June	2227	7740
February	3586	5473	July	2202	7833
March	3549	6369	August	2243	8762
April	3461	6946	September	2640	8201
May	3565	7288	October	3240	8766

Source: the Greek 'Employment Bureau for Maritime Workers'.

The total number of Greek seamen was about 45 000 in 1947 and 65 000 in 1958. Consequently, during October 1947 the percentage of unemployment was about 7.2 per cent and during October 1958 about 13.5 per cent.

There are several reasons why these figures should be taken only as a rough indication of the actual position. Registered seamen with no previous experience, who were seeking employment at the time (i.e. in 1947 and 1958), are not included in these figures. In the after-war period some of the large shipping firms followed the policy of keeping on their payrolls (i.e. at basic pay) not only their efficient Captains but also some of their most capable and highly qualified engine room officers. Such officers although essentially unemployed were not included in the records of the employment bureau of the Ministry of Merchant Shipping. Seamen are a relatively mobile factor of production. Thus, in this particular case, a considerable number of seamen secured alternative employment soon after their discharge from tramp ships or tankers either in the expanding liner industry of their country (particularly on passenger vessels and cargo liners

[1] The source of the data is the *Survey of Greek Merchant Shipping* for 1933, pp. 228 and 260–1.

in 1958) or they 'migrated' by joining vessels of other nationalities. If these alternatives had not existed the percentage of unemployed Greek seamen due to the depressed state of the tramp and tanker freight markets during these periods would have been higher.

The degree of employment of labour in the tramp shipping industry is determined by the level of the freight market. The depression stage is characterized by large unemployment of seamen of various nationalities, whilst during the stage of prosperity the problems of engaging competent officers and reliable crew members becomes rather difficult.

4. Minimum and maximum costs

During periods of low freight rates shipping firms endeavour to reduce their operating costs to the minimum, whilst during the period of prosperity—usually a period of rising prices—these costs rise inevitably to their highest level.

The remuneration of crew members (wages, overtime, payments for extra work, long-service bonus, leave pay, etc.) of three vessels under the Greek flag belonging to two highly reputable Greek shipping firms have been examined both in periods of prosperity and depression and the results of our examination are given below:

The monthly remuneration of the crew of vessel A, a well-maintained Liberty ship of about 10 000 t.d.w.

1957 (prosperity stage)	£2032
1959 (beginning of recovery)	£1750

The monthly remuneration of the crew of vessel B, a tramp ship built in 1954 of about 10 000 t.d.w.:

1957	£1993
1958	£1700

The monthly remuneration of the crew of motor vessel C, a tramp ship built in 1954, of 11 300 t.d.w.

1957 (prosperity stage)	£2292
1958–(depression and	
1959 revival)	£1800–1820

The effort of shipping firms to run their vessels as cheaply as possible during periods of low freight rates does not manifest itself only in the amounts paid to crew members, but in all operating costs such as insurance, maintenance, provisions, stores, etc.

The operating costs of several tramp ships during prosperity and depression have been examined. In our opinion—provided that such vessels remain maintained properly, adequately insured, with a full complement, and their crews properly paid and fed—the difference between minimum and maximum operating costs can only be in the neighbourhood of 7 to 9 per cent.

Needless to say, instances of vessels trading not in accordance with existing safety regulations are more numerous in depression than in prosperity. It is said, not without justification, that such instances are mostly due to relatively small shipping firms operating tonnage under flags of convenience. As in other transport industries there seems to be a close connection between safety and commercial viability.

Rate fluctuations in the tramp freight market have a pronounced effect on the original cost, that is to say the price of new or used tramp ships.

Fig. 9. shows fluctuations in the price of cargo ships.[1] These are assessed on the basis of the average price of an 11 000–13 000 t.d.w. cargo ship—as estimated by *Fairplay*—the ship having the following main specifications: Diesel engine developing 6500 i.h.p. to give a sea speed of 15 knots as an open shelter decker and slightly less in the closed condition. Dimensions: 460 ft (between perpendiculars) by 64 ft by 40 ft to shelter and 31 ft to upper deck. Deadweight: 11 000 tons on a draught of 27 ft as an open shelter decker and 13 000 tons on a draught of 30 ft as a closed shelter decker.

Fig. 9. also shows trends in the building cost of a 24 000 t.d.w. bulk carrier with the following specifications. Dimensions: 550 ft (b.p.) by 75 ft by 47 ft. Deadweight: 24 000 tons on a draught of 33 ft. The propelling machinery consists of a super-charged diesel engine developing 8500 i.h.p. in service to give a speed of 14¾ knots.

As pointed out in *Fairplay*, the data on which Fig. 9 is based

[1] See 'Fluctuations in Shipping Values', *Fairplay*, 1 January 1965, pp. 94–5.

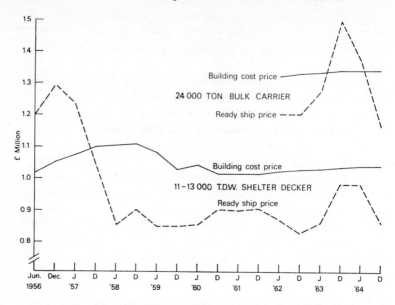

Fig. 9. Fluctuations in the price of cargo ships 1956–64

may not reflect accurately real market prices during the actual time periods under consideration. Average prices as assessed by *Fairplay* include 'full overheads and a fair profit margin, and therefore, are much higher than would be quoted at the present time (i.e. 1964–5) in open competition'. However, in the absence of other relative data the figures under consideration may be accepted as a rough guide to the degree of variation in the price of new ships which is demonstrated in Fig. 9.

Fig. 10 shows the variations that occurred in the average price of Liberty ships from 1951 up to and including 1963 and it is based on data contained in Table 12 of the Appendix. It will be noted that this table also contains data for the year 1950. However, Fig. 10 is based on the average price of Liberty ships during the month of March of each year under consideration and data for March 1950 are not available. Also for 1951 we take the highest average price for the year which was £590 000 in December.

Some useful conclusions may be drawn from the above two figures as well as from the data contained in Table 14 of the Appendix.

Fig. 10. Fluctuations in the price of Liberty ships 1952–63

As a rule, fluctuations in the price of tramp ships closely follow those of the tramp freight market. During prosperity the demand for tonnage (new and old) increases, and thus, the price of tramp ships reaches its highest point. During the brief recession period the price of tramp ships follows the downward trend of the freight market. During the depression stage when the demand for tonnage, new and old, is at a minimum the price of ships reaches its lowest point, but eventually it begins to rise during recovery.

It should be pointed out, however, that over various periods of time there may be other economic factors in operation which may prevent the tendency of ships' prices to follow freight market trends from becoming apparent. One such factor is, of course, building costs. For example, if the price of scrap-iron or labour costs are rising, the ability of shipyards to reduce their prices during a recession in the tramp freight market will be reduced. Another factor is the international liquidity problem. For example, during late 1968 and early 1969 the price of second-hand tramp ships and liners remained at relatively high levels although tramp freight rates were maintained at relatively low levels. One of the reasons for this development was the fact that shipowners were prepared to sell their tonnage only at a high price because their expectations about the future value of the dollar and the pound were low. Nevertheless, on the whole, the price of tramp ships tends to follow freight market trends.

As may be noted from Fig. 9, the price of ready ships is higher during prosperity than the building cost price, but, on the other hand, it is lower when freight rates tend to be low. This interesting phenomenon is simply due to the fact that shipowners want to obtain early delivery of new tonnage during prosperity with a view to concluding as many fixtures as possible 'whilst the going is good'. On the other hand, when the freight market is at a low level—and shipowners' expectations tend also to be low, as a rule—shipping firms neither proceed with new orders nor do they want to obtain delivery of their new tonnage in the short run.

Fig. 10 shows the fluctuations in the average price of the Liberty-type tramp ships which is a typical example of price trends in the second-hand market during the fifties and the early sixties. The price of these vessels reached its maxima points during the periods of the Korean war and the Suez crisis. During the depression of the late fifties and during the short-run low freight rate periods in the sixties the price of Liberties reached its minima points which, in view of their advanced age, was approaching their scrap-iron value.

During the prosperity stage when expectations of entrepreneurs are high the demand and, therefore, the price of old vessels rises, and during periods of low freight rates, when prospects for the employment of scarce resources are also low, the demand, and therefore, the price of old tonnage necessarily falls.

The low price of old tonnage during the depression stage does not, as a rule, induce owners to send their vessels to the scrap yard. Shipowners keep their vessels for as long as possible in the hope that the tramp freight market will rise again enabling them to recommission or to sell their vessels at a better price.

It would have been natural to conclude this section by stating that—as has already been made abundantly clear—fluctuations in the price of tramp ships closely follow those of the freight market and that during a depression stage all operating costs tend to reach their minimum level whilst during prosperity they remain at higher levels. However, we have to stress that entrepreneurs' expectations constitute an important factor that influences fluctuations in the price of ships. We think that the following example demonstrates this point quite clearly:

The influence of the U.S.S.R.—American grain-deal talks on ship sale and purchase can be clearly seen in Harley Mullion and Company's report on that market for October–December 1963. Early in the quarter the Liberty vessel *Suncampomella* (survey of 1961) was sold to Greek buyers for £65,000, but prospects of greater trade advanced owners' ideas for this class of tonnage to £125,000. The urgency of the situation lessened, however, when ratification of the grain contract was delayed and at the end of the year the Liberty ship *Panagiotis Coumantaros* (Survey 6/1961) fetched only £107,500 from her Greek buyers.[1]

5. Mobility of capital

In chapter 1 it was pointed out that putting 'all eggs in one basket' is not considered to be a wise policy by shipowners. Shipowners including owners of tramp shipping tonnage invest, as a rule, in other industries which are thought to be less speculative. The object of such investments in the short run does not appear to be profit maximization. It is widely maintained amongst the industry's entrepreneurs that investments in other economic sectors can have a balancing effect on single- or multi-service producing shipping firms, particularly during periods of recession and depression when losses may be incurred. On the other hand, during periods of prosperity the expected rate of return in shipping is higher than in other economic sectors, and thus, new capital moves into the industry. Consequently, maritime industries in general, and tramp shipping in particular, are characterized by a relative mobility of capital resources.

Taking the existence of fluctuations in the tramp freight market as a fact, it is realistic to assume that capital movements to and from the industry are mainly determined by the following factors:

(*a*) The expected rate of return on capital as compared with other industries.

---

[1] *Fairplay*, 9 January 1964, pp. 53–4.

(b) The speculative character of the tramp shipping business as compared with other businesses.

(c) The availability and cost of managerial and technical know-how.

It will be seen shortly, that in the long run the average rate of return of capital invested in tramp shipping has been a relatively high one. This very fact has invited capital to move into the industry from many and varying sources, mainly during the prosperity stage. Thus, at periods of high freight rates, when expectations tend to be high, credits are obtained from ship-yards, banks, insurance companies, and other financial institutions by entrepreneurs who are already established in the market, enabling them to proceed with their replacement and ex-pansion schemes. Moreover, the same facilities are provided to entrepreneurs who possess some knowledge and experience on maritime questions and are seeking to enter the market. In addition, entrepreneurs who are engaged in business connected with the industry in various ways, such as industrialists who may be in need of tonnage for the sea transport of raw materials for their own factories, shipping firms owning tonnage that belongs to other maritime industries (for example, coastal shipping, small liners, etc.), shipping managers, captains, chief engineers (and sometimes officers of lower ranks), suppliers of bunkers, stores and provisions, etc., invest in the industry either as independent owners by (usually) buying from the second-hand market or as shareholders in medium or large enterprises owning modern tramps. Also, in view of the expected higher rate of return on capital and, as a rule, through the medium of shipping firms already established in the market, entrepreneurs who have no previous direct connection with tramp shipping enter the market during periods of prosperity.

One of the main causal factors for capital withdrawals from the industry has been stated at the beginning of this chapter. The existence of fluctuations in the freight market makes tramp shipping a profession that is more speculative than others. Thus, owners of tramp shipping tonnage follow, as a rule, the policy of investing in other economic sectors where investments are thought to be safer even though the rate of return on capital is expected to be definitely less than from the tramp shipping industry during prosperity.

The other main causal factor for capital withdrawals from the industry is, obviously, profit maximization. For example, investments made by multi-service producing shipping firms, owning tramp shipping tonnage in the ship repair and ship construction industry, have as their long-run objective profit maximization (or cost minimization).

Capital resources move out of the industry along the following two directions:

(a) By investments in such neighbouring industries as tankers, bulk carriers, liners, passenger vessels including ferry-boats and roll-on-roll-off ships, tugs, whaling fleets, shipyards, marine insurance, banking, provisions and stores suppliers, shipbroking enterprises, inland transport, etc.; and

(b) By investments in various economic sectors which are not connected in any way with merchant shipping.

6. Profits

The period of prosperity in tramp shipping is commonly called amongst Greek nautical circles the 'epoch of the fat cows'. Obviously this popular Greek expression signifies that during prosperity 'fat', i.e. large, profits are made. Indeed, there exists sufficient data to support the widespread view that tramp shipping provides opportunities for profitable investment, and that during the comparatively brief period of prosperity the rate of profit tends to be abnormally high.

The following passage supports this view:

The closing year of the century has been a memorable one for the shipping industry... in respect of the vast trade done and the large profits safely housed. The almost universal division of abnormal dividends and large reserves set apart has restored this most important trade of the country to a very sound and wealthy position after the severe strain it had passed through from 1888.[1]

[1] See Angiers' *Fifty Years Freights*, entry 31 December 1900. For freights see Table 8 of the Appendix.

Table 29. Fifty years of

Period five-year averages	(1) Paid-up capital	(2) Debentures, loans, etc.	(3) Reserves	(4) Book value of fleet	(5) Profit on voyages
	£	£	£	£	£
1904–1908	8 608 632	3 892 040	—	12 661 860	921 486
1909–1913	10 078 439	5 668 818	—	15 480 886	2 267 483
1914–1918	13 229 492	8 775 012	—	19 608 484	5 581 064
1919–1923	22 562 176	12 471 974	—	36 863 451	3 815 048
1924–1928	26 802 107	10 959 605	14 289 079	42 100 509	2 914 700
1929	18 134 035	8 564 998	8 399 164	29 226 184	1 466 690
1930	16 748 121	8 400 577	8 170 103	24 478 792	1 363 064
1931	15 722 698	7 712 101	6 668 071	22 418 769	607 023
1932	14 585 461	5 887 248	6 399 196	19 611 259	626 325
1933	14 001 163	5 331 014	5 915 158	18 330 350	155 023
1934	14 636 389	5 811 210	4 826 803	19 223 343	88 653
1935	12 189 426	4 165 692	4 667 256	16 489 400	499 235
1936	12 451 926	3 914 198	3 681 434	16 177 984	1 082 889
1937	11 462 193	3 707 252	4 738 176	14 322 118	2 237 009
1938	12 178 135	2 860 526	6 156 943	14 717 444	4 546 688
1939	12 342 350	2 356 095	6 360 305	13 987 380	1 805 425
1940	12 451 034	3 365 569	7 543 344	13 107 426	1 736 263
1941	11 023 218	4 392 839	8 537 563	10 488 437	1 924 369
1942	11 784 770	5 196 986	13 195 335	10 602 441	1 575 303
1943	11 867 440	5 875 004	16 306 476	10 557 309	1 553 067
1944	11 756 420	6 265 460	17 887 130	11 367 087	1 355 398
1945	10 533 180	5 964 322	15 581 997	11 436 118	1 457 883
1946	10 129 270	4 207 348	18 303 998	9 057 898	1 269 300
1947	9 263 200	6 416 022	20 213 049	11 045 006	6 088 667
1948	9 893 420	7 692 427	21 596 569	11 096 106	6 863 104
1949	8 005 436	7 086 244	18 514 226	11 796 283	4 984 642
1950	11 731 075	6 614 470	24 381 426	16 910 209	4 100 991
1951	11 354 661	4 257 274	23 540 081	18 342 532	4 146 991
1952	13 043 488	10 716 139	34 221 478	21 693 126	13 324 182
1953	13 899 032	11 881 040	37 326 334	23 567 555	9 862 462

Source: *Fairplay*, 14 January 1954, and Tables 8 and 9 of Appendix (1869= 100, and for

British cargo-boat earnings

(6) Freight Index	(7) Amount £	DIVIDEND Percentage on capital	DIVIDEND Percentage on capital plus reserves	no.	(8) FLEET Tonnage G.R.T.	(9) Depreciation written off £	(10) Depreciation at 5% £
50	321 764	3.74	—	463	1 410 023	322 079	760 896
58	573 160	5.69	—	545	1 852 934	1 158 752	945 972
414	1 929 667	14.59	—	502	1 912 136	2 143 198	967 377
256	1 779 972	7.89	—	361	1 300 883	1 298 995	1 593 838
117	1 386 980	4.80	3.13	477	2 108 137	1 485 809	2 004 646
115	928 391	5.12	3.49	489	2 070 359	605 487	1 525 013
93	652 398	3.89	2.62	454	2 075 038	537 215	1 542 367
90	241 438	1.53	1.08	431	2 026 890	531 834	1 472 126
88	229 905	1.58	1.09	387	1 850 556	551 887	1 226 534
85	135 380	0.97	0.68	361	1 733 980	349 398	1 193 389
85	208 246	1.42	1.07	347	1 701 940	134 304	1 190 607
88	178 545	1.46	1 06	316	1 495 455	342 239	1 026 291
103	260 435	2.09	1.52	309	1 404 487	673 578	1 005 275
—	481 733	4.20	2.97	294	1 404 959	1 071 893	954 583
—	1 123 207	9.22	6.13	329	1 664 945	2 510 317	1 005 488
—	683 399	5.54	3.65	297	1 405 711	1 164 765	911 369
—	787 343	6.32	3.94	289	1 373 310	718 744	846 020
—	778 369	7.06	3.98	214	1 034 249	1 045 339	717 508
—	837 506	7.11	3.35	206	986 705	833 844	686 481
—	843 657	7.11	2.99	210	1 019 550	947 107	673 078
—	826 913	7.03	2.79	235	1 127 744	937 246	706 072
—	711 981	6.76	2.72	171	858 302	989 463	700 339
—	805 304	17.95	2.83	131	739 479	1 633 046	542 677
—	1 269 023	13.70	4.31	153	848 487	4 476 460	735 027
111	1 548 055	15.68	4.92	155	883 706	4 559 589	826 858
87	1 216 861	15.20	4.59	150	856 186	2 842 928	877 436
72	1 304 418	11.12	3.61	165	986 082	3 426 330	1 194 783
151	1 365 069	12.02	3.91	131	793 060	2 428 800	1 248 647
163	1 726 796	13.24	3.65	140	881 424	969 728	1 478 919
128	1 926 637	3.86	3.76	146	892 766	623 342	1 668 640

the after-war period 1948= 100).

It appears that the profits made during the prosperity stage of 1898–1900 more than compensated for the preceding eight years of relatively low freights. The passage quoted below suggests that the profits made during the last years before the second world war, and particularly during 1936, more than compensated for the losses that were incurred during the depression of the thirties.

It is estimated that for the period 1936–1938 the improvement in freights, particularly in 1937, produced sufficient earnings for Tramp Shipping Companies to provide for depreciation for those years and leave a balance almost sufficient to make up arrears of depreciation for the years 1930–1935.[1]

During the middle and the late fifties the greatest percentage of tramp shipping tonnage was under Panholib flags and under the Greek flag. Unfortunately, there is no published data available to show the profits made by tramp shipping firms owning tonnage under these flags. During the fifties the operating costs of ships under these flags (i.e. basically labour costs) were lower than those under flags of Western European maritime nations. Thus, profits made by the owning companies were higher. For example, the profits made by well-maintained relatively modern tramp ships under Panholib flags during 1956–7 on voyage account (i.e. freights collected less operating costs) were in the neighbourhood of £1500–2000 per day. As is well-known, the earnings of Liberty ships, particularly during the periods of the Korean war and the period 1956–7, were not only sufficient to cover operating and capital costs, but they formed the financial basis for the expansion schemes of many Greek-owned tramp shipping firms and for their impressive entry into the tanker, bulk carrier, and liner industries.

Table 29 shows the earnings of British cargo boats over a period of half a century, that is to say from 1904 to 1953. The source of this table (with the exception of the figures entered in column 6 which originate from Table 8 of the Appendix) is *Fairplay*, 14 January 1954.

The table includes cargo boats of all types. It is not clear whether all earnings made by British enterprises owning tramp

[1] See Chamber of Shipping of the U.K. Report, *Shipping Policy—Fact Finding Enquiry, Deep Sea Tramp Fact Finding Committee*, 7 December 1936, p. 5.

and liner tonnage are included, but taking into consideration the tonnage figures given in column 6 we must assume that this is not so. Moreover, it is not clear whether any losses of enterprises that have left the market during the period under consideration are taken into account. We presume that they are not. Thus, the data contained in the table must be taken as a rough guide of the actual position for the total earnings of British firms owning cargo boats. Column 1 of the table shows the amounts of capital paid up, that is to say sums paid into the business by shareholders. Column 2 shows sums borrowed by the business, and column 3 shows the reserves of the enterprises in question, i.e. sums accumulated from revenues collected. The book value of the fleet, i.e. original cost less provision for depreciation, is given in column 4. Column 5 shows profits made on voyage account, i.e. freight collected less operating costs. Column 6 indicates the level of freight rates. Column 7 shows dividends paid to shareholders in their total amount, as a percentage of capital and as a percentage of capital plus reserves. Column 8 shows the magnitude of the fleet in units and in terms of G.R.T. Column 9 shows the actual depreciation charged in the accounts and column 10 shows depreciation on a 5 per cent basis. Columns 5, 6, and 7 should be considered as the most significant, for they indicate rather clearly that during periods of high freight rates big profits are made and large dividends are paid.

Some useful conclusions may be drawn on the basis of the facts given in this chapter. In the first place it would appear that, as expected, the fortunes of the entrepreneurs in the industry depend upon the level of the freight market and fluctuate accordingly. Secondly, the facts indicate that, during the relatively brief stages of prosperity, large profits are made on the average which enable shipping firms as a whole to cover the original cost of their investments and, at the same time, to compensate them for their long run costs in the lean years in which profits may not be made at all.

Thus, on the basis of the experience of a century or so, it could be concluded that tramp shipping has been a remunerative transport service, because the resulting revenues have been sufficient to cover all those costs which, but for its provision, would not have been incurred either directly or indirectly, in the short or in the long run.

7. The endemic tendency to over-invest

The 'green light' for investment in the industry is given by the level of freight rates. When the average level of freight rates is high, and consequently, the revenues collected higher than costs, entrepreneurs expectations lead to over-investment, that is to say, to the creation of tonnage which is more than adequate to satisfy demand requirements for a given period of time. This endemic tendency to over-invest has characterized the economic life of merchant shipping, and of tramp shipping in particular, over various periods of time. Let us, therefore, examine the significance of this economic phenomenon in some detail. In the *Annual Report 1958–1959 of the Chamber* of Shipping of the U.K., under the title 'The Growing Crisis for British Shipping' one may read the following paragraphs:

In the world today there are 114 million gross tons of merchant shipping including the U.S. reserve fleet. A year ago the figure was just under 107 million, so that in twelve months there have been added to an already 'over-stocked' market nearly 7½ million tons, of which 4 million consisted of tankers. Most of this new tonnage was probably ordered when freights were recovering from the 1952/1954 depression and had started the upward climb which reached its peak at the end of 1956. By the time this new tonnage was reaching the market, freights were beginning to fall and the fact that the rate of addition far exceeded the extent to which world trade expanded in 1958 meant that freights were forced down further. In these circumstances it is, perhaps, surprising that the amount of world shipping laid up in 1958 was not more than the peak figure of about 8 million tons.[1]

Table 30 shows the magnitude of new orders given to the shipyards of the major shipbuilding countries of the world for the period 1954–36. In chapter 2 it has been demonstrated that during the same period the demand for transoceanic transport services kept increasing more or less steadily. However, orders for the construction of new tonnage began to rise sharply only

[1] See *Annual Report 1958–1959 of the Chamber of Shipping of the U.K.*, pp. v, 17.

Table 30. Sea-going merchant ships under construction and on order 1954-63 (in 1000 G.R.T.)

Country of build Year	GREAT BRITAIN G.R.T.	Index	F.R. OF GERMANY G.R.T.	Index	JAPAN G.R.T.	Index	SWEDEN G.R.T.	Index	WORLD TOTAL G.R.T.	Index
1 January 1954	5331	100	1421	100	482	100	1572	100	13 053	100
,, 1955	3947	74	1417	100	787	163	1489	95	11 249	86
,, 1956	4417	83	2651	187	3097	643	1690	108	17 821	137
,, 1957	5188	97	4872	343	5067	1051	3016	192	29 248	224
,, 1958	5734	108	5425	382	5080	1054	3853	245	34 494	264
,, 1959	5373	101	4193	295	3784	785	3271	208	27 295	209
,, 1960	4116	77	3268	230	3136	651	2833	180	22 314	171
,, 1961	3296	62	2467	174	2254	468	2256	144	17 975	138
,, 1962	2551	48	2275	160	3537	734	2330	148	18 656	143
,, 1963	2068	39	1802	127	3487	723	1747	111	16 294	125
1 October 1963	2143	40	1692	119	5423	1125	2226	142	18 721	143

Source: *Fairplay*, 9 January 1964. The data for the period 1 January 1954 to 1 January 1963 has been obtained from the American Bureau of Shipping, and for 1 October 1963 from *Statistik der Schiffahrt*, no. 11/1963.

after freight markets reached excessively high levels, i.e. during 1957–8.

If we assume that 1954 was a year of normal growth for the merchant shipping industries, that is to say, that the rate of expansion of supply was more or less adequate to replace old vessels being withdrawn from the markets and also to satisfy the additional demand requirements of the future, then the endemic tendency for over-provision of capital, as it manifested itself during 1957–8, when the rate of new tonnage created reached 29 248 000 and 34 494 000, i.e. 124 and 164 points above normal, can be noted without fail.

On the other hand, shipowners were rather reluctant to send old and uneconomic tonnage to the scrap-yards. As shown in Table 31, the breaking up of old tonnage only began to assume considerable proportions from 1959 onwards.

Table 31. Tonnage of merchant ships broken up and lost 1956–61 in G.R.T.

Year	Broken up	Lost through casualty	Total
1956	528 000	249 000	777 000
1957	730 000	271 000	1 001 000
1958	1 452 000	348 000	1 800 000
1959	3 125 000	282 000	3 407 000
1960	3 285 000	358 000	3 643 000
1961	3 727 000	471 000	4 198 000

Source: Chamber of Shipping of the U.K. *Annual Report 1962–3*.

It may be justly argued that, although the above figures and their variations are representative of merchant shipping as a whole, they may not be so with respect to the tramp shipping industry alone. However, the data contained in the last part of chapter 8, section 3 is sufficient to show that the tendency to over-invest manifests itself in the industry in the same way as in other maritime industries. The annual increase in the supply of tramp ships began to be of sizeable proportions from 1957 onwards. It should be added, however, that in later years (1960–6) the tendency to over-invest has become much more pronounced in the bulk carrier's industry.

Thus, on the basis of the foregoing, it may be stated that in the absence of any subsequent variation of demand during a period of high freight rates, the duration of the prosperity stage or the 'boom' is largely determined by the endemic tendency to over-invest and by the rapidity with which new tonnage can be created in relation to the magnitude of the original increase of demand which has stimulated the general rise in freights.

In assessing the significance of the endemic tendency to over-invest, we should not be led to the conclusion that this endogenous factor constitutes the only basic cause for the existence of fluctuations in the tramp freight market. A full and thorough analysis of fluctuations must take into account all factors that affect the interplay of supply and demand for tramp shipping services in a given period of time. For example, from Table 2 we note that during 1957 the quantity of dry cargoes transported by sea was 500 million tons. However, the relative figure for 1958 was 30 million tons less, i.e. 470 million metric tons. The downward trend actually began during the last four months of 1958. It is necessary to take into consideration also that, according to various estimates, during the same period of time there has been no decrease in the volume of general cargoes. In chapter 2 we have discussed the rather sensitive nature of the demand for tramp shipping services and the consequences that may be brought about—so far as the tramp freight market is concerned—by a relatively small fall in the volume of international seaborne trade of bulk commodities. Hence it should only be mentioned at this point that the downward trend, i.e. the recession, in the freight market during the late fifties originally began as a result of a temporary fall in the demand for tramp shipping services which was due firstly to the decline of the transatlantic coal trade and secondly to the re-opening of the Suez Canal. However, the prolongation of the period of relatively low freight rates after 1959, when the magnitude of demand began to increase again, was due to the creation of new tonnage capacity which was more than adequate to satisfy the gradually increasing demand requirements.

The demand, supply, and price relationships that were described above with particular reference to the period 1956-9 do not constitute unusual economic phenomena. A careful look at the industry's picture during the early thirties suggests that such relationships occur at the end of every period of prosperity.

It is clear that a decrease in the demand for tramp shipping facilities brought about a temporary decline in the volume of international trade—or even a decline in the rate of its growth—combined with an increase in the creation of new tonnage that is brought about by the endemic tendency to over-invest are sufficient to cause the supply of tonnage to outstrip demand. Thus, tramp freight rates remain at a low level over prolonged periods of time.

As is pointed out in Westinform's Report, no. 118, which is entitled *Lessons of the 1930s*:

Rates did not rise above this break-even point until most of the vessels had been scrapped; in fact rates did not begin to rise until after the world fleet's decline had reached bottom, although the recovery in trade had begun a year earlier.

As already indicated, the stage of prosperity is characterized by the relatively large investments made for the construction of new ships. Furthermore, prosperity is marked by expansion in the activities of all enterprises connected with tramp shipping, such as shipbuilding firms, ship-broking firms, ship's agents, and stores and provisions suppliers, underwriting, average adjusters firms, and so on.

In short, during prosperity, orders are given by firms which cause the expansion of the industry's capacity to an extent which is greater than demand requirements.

Chapter 10

Tonnage Stabilization Schemes

1. Introduction

As shown in Tables 8, 9, and 10 of the Appendix, over the last hundred years or so tramp freight rates have shown a tendency to fluctuate sharply. After relatively brief periods, lasting from some months to two years or so, of exceptionally high freight rates, the market remained, for several years following at relatively low levels and during depression periods unemployed factors of production assumed considerable proportions.

In other words, it may be said that the tramp shipping industry has displayed, in a rather acute form, fluctuations of the same nature as those experienced in the past by other industries and by entire national economies of industrially advanced states. The symptoms of the stage of depression in tramp shipping can also be compared with those of other industries. Depression shows itself as a situation in which there is over-provision of tonnage, in which costs tend to equal and/or exceed the price level, in which the firms engaged in the industry find that their earlier expectations are not justified by the state of the market, in which earlier errors of anticipation are revealed.

The shifts between average prices which afford very profitable trading and average prices at which even owners of representative tramps cannot earn interest and depreciation suggest that the functioning of the freight market is not characterized by the existence of a stable equilibrium and that demand requirements do not, as a rule, equal the supply of tramp shipping tonnage available.

The difficulty in adjusting supply to demand requirements is due, in the first place, to the nature of demand. As pointed out in detail, the magnitude of demand depends upon the variations of the volume of international seaborne trade of bulk commodities. Such variations, which determine in the main the degree of employment of scarce resources in the industry at any point of time, are due to various exogenous factors which stem from the economic, political, social, and physical environment of nations.

No less important, however, is the inelasticity of supply, which must also be taken into consideration. The inelastic nature of the supply of tramp shipping services is due to the period of time required for the construction of ships, to the magnitude of shipbuilding capacity available, to the duration of the useful life of tonnage once it has been built, to the insistence of the industry's entrepreneurs on keeping their vessels trading during recession periods for as long as the losses incurred appear to be smaller or equal to the cost of idleness, and to their normal propensity to resist sending old and uneconomic tonnage to the scrap-iron yard. This inflexibility makes any immediate adjustment of the supply of tonnage to demand requirements a practical impossibility.

Explanations have been given as to why fluctuations in the industry tend to synchronize with international trade cycles, but it has also been indicated that in general it appears that tramp shipping depressions last longer than trade slumps and also that the actual variations are much more pronounced in the case of the tramp shipping industry.

Reasons have been given in chapters 2 and 3 as to why, as a consequence of the derived and marginal character of the demand for tramp shipping services and the inelasticity of supply, any discrepency between supply and demand would not have to be very great in order to cause tramp freight rates to fluctuate considerably on a world-wide basis. Even a decline in the rate of growth of international seaborne trade of bulk commodities when combined with an increase in the creation of new tonnage may be sufficient to cause the supply of tonnage to exceed demand requirements and thus cause rates to move downwards sharply.

The amplitude and duration of a fluctuation cannot be predicted with any degree of precision while it is actually happening. This is due to the varying nature and strength of the exogenous factor which affect the volume of international seaborne trade of bulk commodities and, therefore, the magnitude of demand for tramp shipping facilities. On the basis of data given in the Appendix it would appear that the fluctuating tendencies of the tramp freight market were more regular before the first world war and less so after the end of the second world war.

The effects of wars on the demand and the supply of tonnage as well as on freight rates have been examined. It may be realistic to assume that in the absence of major wars the increase of the demand for transport of bulk commodities over various routes may be of a more regular and gradual nature, and the relative shortage of supply of tonnage, whenever it occurs, less acute than the one experienced in the early periods after the end of major wars. However, this should not be taken as a forecast (or prophecy) either for the absence of future variations in demand or for the elimination of fluctuations from the tramp freight market. It should always be borne in mind that even a temporary decrease in the rate of growth of international trade is sufficient to cause tramp freight rates to fluctuate downwards sharply. Therefore, fluctuations must be looked upon as a normal hazard of the industry.

It has been seen that the supply of tramp shipping services has displayed a tendency to oscillate irregularly and that one of the major factors for this phenomenon is decision-taking with regard to provision of tonnage by entrepreneurs during the stage of prosperity. The fact that the shippers, i.e. the users, have no alternative but to pay high freights during the period of boom allows entrepreneurs in the industry to make high profits. In the circumstances, like any other market functioning under competitive conditions and for as long as there is an advantage anticipated by entrepreneurs, new investments are made. Firms that are already in the market expand further and new ones make their appearance.

It is in this respect that the decisions of the entrepreneurs do not seem to be consistent with users' wants. Within given periods of time there are shifts which lead to the employment of

231

resources in greater quantities than the ones required by users. Hence, users are able to secure low prices, but on the other hand the unemployment of factors of production engaged in the industry assumes considerable dimensions. Nevertheless, as in the case of other competitive industries, in the long run supply tends to adjust itself to demand requirements and the over-sufficiency of tonnage is eventually eliminated.

Shipowners as well as management and chartering depart-ments of tramp shipping firms, particularly those with a long tradition in the industry, are aware of the continuous tendency of the freight market to fluctuate. This knowledge is mainly the product of the wealth of their experience and of freely circulating information, not necessarily organized in a scientific manner. In other words, it is widely known and accepted in the tramp shipping world that in the absence of wars the stage of prosperity is bound to be a relatively short one and that a long period must elapse before the next period of high freight rates. This knowledge has had the following consequences. It has in-duced entrepreneurs:

(a) to obtain or order as much tonnage as possible during the stage of prosperity, and
(b) to keep old and inefficient tonnage.

At least up to the present, in the case of many tramp shipping firms, the basic criterion for investment does not seem to have been whether the industry's prospects for the next ten or twenty years are reasonably good. Expectations have tended to be high during the prosperity stage and the criterion for investment seems to have been that large profits must be secured whilst the going is good, if they are to be secured at all. Hence, new tonnage is ordered or acquired during prosperity.

Consequently, during the course of each prosperity period or after its termination, relatively large numbers of bigger and faster tramp ships enter the market. Such modern tramp ships can produce the same service at a lower cost per ton-mile than the old tramps, most of which are to be found at the lay-up berths after the end of the prosperity stage.

In spite of these developments entrepreneurs tend to keep old and unremunerative tonnage in the hope that it will be once more operated profitably when freight rates rise again. In other words, up to the present the criterion for scrapping old tonnage has been based on entrepreneurs' expectations with regard to the next prosperity stage.

2. Tonnage stabilization schemes

The knowledge that tramp freight rates fluctuate continually has led a considerable number of the industry's entrepreneurs to the thought that the economic effects of the depression stage could be eliminated by the application of a 'Tonnage Stabilization Scheme'.

Schemes for the rationalization of tonnage, as they were then called, were first developed and attracted the interest of a considerable number of tramp owners during the 1930s. It should be noted that, ever since, such interest is mainly shown during periods of low freights.

Broadly speaking, the aim of the various tonnage stabilization schemes has been to restrict the magnitude of active supply by withdrawing tonnage from the market and to fix minimum freight rates which are higher than those prevailing in the market—during the recession or the depression stage.

Consequently, the proposals were that members of the scheme were to be obliged not to conclude fixtures for their vessels below the specified rates in the scheme. Tonnage laid up and belonging to members of the scheme would be compensated by the creation of a fund. In order to induce shipowners to scrap old tonnage, some of the schemes have provided for special compensation in this respect. Tonnage that was trading and belonging to members of the scheme was to contribute a proportion of earnings to the fund.

Fig. 11 shows the object of the various schemes. It is assumed that there is a period of low freight rates. A given quantity of tramp shipping tonnage has been laid up and, in view of a temporary decrease in demand requirements, average freight rates are at a low level, i.e.f. This level of freights enables only modern low-cost tonnage to cover costs and make a profit on

Fig. 11. The object of tonnage stabilization schemes

voyage account. The total quantity of tonnage capacity employed is OT and the total revenue of the industry is OfPT.

The aim of all schemes proposed so far has been to bring freight rates to the f_1 level, thereby raising the industry's total revenue to Of_1XT_1, either by fixing minimum rates or by organizing withdrawals of tonnage capacity from the market. The expectation has been that the additional revenue that would result ($Of_1XT_1 - OfPT$)—if the overwhelming majority of tramp shipping firms joined the scheme—would be sufficient to cover the compensation of laid-up tonnage and at the same time, enable owners of tonnage still trading to make a bigger profit on voyage account.

3. Detailed proposals of schemes

In 1935, a Pricing Fixing Committee was established. The Committee had the support of a considerable number of tramp shipping firms belonging to British shipowners and shipowners of other nationalities. Minimum freight rates were fixed on a limited number of trading routes, leaving others to fall. It has been maintained that the scheme operated successfully from 1935 to 1939 and that since this was so during the thirties there should be no reason why a new scheme could not now be applied with the same degree of success. We think that in order to discuss this point the following factors should be taken into account:

(a) The Committee began to operate at the end of the depression stage. As we have seen, because of external factors freight rates rose to profitable levels from 1936 onwards, thus making the observance of the minimum rate of nominal importance. The picture might have been different if the depression stage had lasted for a longer period of time. It should also be pointed out that a few members of the scheme thought it fit to violate the agreement and conclude fixtures below the rates specified.

(b) The Committee had the support of the British and other governments. As the 'Committee on Deep Sea Tramp Co-operation' of the International Chamber of Shipping has put it:

We recognise that minimum freight schemes were operated internationally in the years 1935 to 1939 and were attended by a considerable measure of success. Present-day conditions are, however, very different to those prevailing in the pre-war years. Another point of importance is that the 1935/1939 scheme was buttressed, so far at any rate as a substantial portion of the world tramp fleet was concerned, by government support.[1]

(c) The difference in the size and speed of existing tramp ships is greater today than in the thirties, making any agreement on minimum freight rates extremely difficult.

Thus, even if we assume momentarily that the scheme was operated successfully in the late 1930s—so far as the industry was concerned—it does not follow that this would happen now.

The idea of co-operation amongst the industry's entrepreneurs with a view to 'stabilizing' freight rates by restricting the magnitude of active supply 'to immediate tonnage requirements' again came to the fore during the first major depression after the end of the second world war. By then, there were several schemes proposed by National Shipowners' Associations:

---

[1] See *Report of Committee on Deep Sea Tramp Co-operation*, p. 5, International Chamber of Shipping, November 1958.

(a) The U.K. and Italian schemes were similar in principle suggesting the creation of a fund by contributions from particular members out of which compensation would be paid to owners of laid-up ships. Neither of these two schemes called for the observance of minimum freight rates.

(b) The Greek scheme which envisaged the automatic laying-up of tonnage under a 'Gentleman's Agreement' whereby participants undertake 'not to trade their dry-cargo vessels at a loss.' The Greek scheme was linked with the compulsory observance of a minimum freight rate plan before laid-up vessels recommenced trading, and embodied a penalty payment for participants who failed to keep the agreement. This scheme neither required contributions from owners of trading ships nor did it provide for the payment of compensation to the owners of laid-up tonnage.

(c) Japanese shipping circles had also been discussing measures for the laying-up of a block of Japanese flag deep-sea tramp tonnage.

With these schemes in the background, and some of the representatives of national shipowners' organizations actively campaigning for the creation and application of a scheme as soon as possible, the International Chamber of Shipping at its annual meeting, during April 1958, decided to invite tramp owners to a special meeting for an exchange of views 'on the desirability or practicability' of co-operative action on an international basis.

This special meeting was held in London during May 1958 with the participation of tramp owners' representatives from twelve maritime nations. It was concluded in the meeting that:

... The broad aim of any co-operative scheme should be one which would encourage and assist owners to match the volume of tonnage in commission to trade requirements; to keep any surplus tonnage laid up until market conditions improve; and to break up tonnage which is likely to remain uneconomic.[1]

In order to achieve this objective, the meeting recommended the application of a scheme which was mainly based upon the U.K. and Italian schemes.[2] The purpose of the scheme was:

[1] See Report of Committee on Deep Sea Tramp Co-operation, p. 3.
[2] The U.K. scheme had been worked out in detail in 1950 under the title Tonnage Stabilisation Association Limited.

236

to relate available tonnage to the volume of traffic moving while, at the same time, leaving individual owners freedom of action to operate at whatever they regarded as economic rates of freight. Owners would pay into a common pool a percentage of freights received by them on charters made after the scheme became operative.[1]

These payments, less administrative expenses, were to be distributed in the following manner: firstly, in compensation for laid-up tonnage and secondly, in compensation payments for tonnage sold for breaking up, thus encouraging shipowners to restrict the volume of active supply 'until conditions improve'.

During the course of the meeting a proposal was made to the effect that owners should undertake not to order new vessels unless they sold for scrap two old units of similar deadweight. This proposal was rejected, for it was thought that it would introduce 'an element of compulsion' unacceptable to prospective members.

It was also decided in the meeting that at the time no international agreement could be obtained for the operation of a minimum freight rates scheme. Finally, it was decided to form the organizational apparatus which would administer the scheme, that is to say, 'International Tonnage Stabilisation Association Ltd.'.

The scheme did not gain widespread support amongst tramp owners. From the start, Scandinavian shipowners did not show any real interest in the scheme whilst British tramp owners were not advocating its speedy application. The immediate application of the scheme was suggested mainly by a group of Greek shipowners who were thought to have over-expanded their enterprises during the Suez period.

No important steps were taken by the organization during 1959 when the demand for transport of bulk commodities increased considerably, and as a result the level of tramp freight rates also increased.

As has already been indicated, during 1960 freight rates fell to rather low levels. This reduction in the level of freights was due to the increase in the magnitude of the available supply of tonnage. A large number of new dry-cargo vessels, bulk carriers, and tramps were completed during the course of the year.

[1] See *Report of Committee on Deep Sea Tramp Co-operation*, p. 6.

Furthermore, owing to prevailing conditions in the tanker market, a considerable number of tankers and super-tankers were participating in the grain trade.

In the circumstances, a meeting of the Association was held during summer 1960. It was decided that tramp shipowners should be invited to enter tonnage to the Association 'with the intention of setting the scheme into operation'.[1]

The salient points of the scheme were given as follows:

(i) Initially the scheme was to be open to deep-sea dry-cargo tramp ships of not less than 5000 tons deadweight and members were obliged to offer for entry all eligible tonnage, whether trading or laid-up, under their ownership or management. The governing body of the Association (the Council) would, however, have discretion to accept the entry of other ships or types or classes of ships.

(ii) The scheme was not linked with any form of minimum freight or compulsory laying-up scheme. Every owner was to retain his complete independence and be at liberty to trade or to lay up his vessels as he preferred without consulting the Association.

(iii) Contributions to the Association were to be payable on freight engagements entered into after the commencement of the scheme.

(iv) In addition to a freight percentage, members were required to pay an entrance fee as well as an annual subscription not exceeding £100 per ship. Entrance fees and subscriptions were to be used for the administrative expenses of the Association.

(v) The levels of both contributions and allowances were left to be assessed by the Council 'in the light of prevailing circumstances'. On the assumption that freights would be at the level indicated by the U.K. Chamber of Shipping Index for May 1960, the approximate level of contributions of gross freights on voyage charter were estimated as follows:

About $1\frac{1}{4}$ per cent if 10 per cent of entered tonnage were

[1] See Circular of the International Tonnage Stabilisation Association Ltd., dated 12 July 1960.

laid up and the remaining 90 per cent were contributing.

About 2 per cent if 15 per cent of entered tonnage were laid up and the remaining 85 per cent were contributing.

About $3\frac{1}{4}$ per cent if 25 per cent of entered tonnage were laid up and the remaining 75 per cent were contributing.

Since the gross receipts of a vessel on voyage charter are normally at a higher level than those of a similar vessel on time charter, it was estimated that the rate of contribution on time charter hire would be levied at a correspondingly higher level than on receipts for voyage charters.

(vi) A ship would require to be laid up for 90 consecutive days before qualifying for a laid-up allowance. The object of the 90 days qualifying period was to dissuade the frequent movement of a ship out of and back into lay up at every fluctuation of the freight market.

It was estimated by the Provisional Council of the Association that at least 75 per cent of eligible world tramp tonnage would be required for the successful operation of the scheme.

Although the scheme proposed did not provide for the fixing of minimum freight rates but for a system of collection and distribution of allowances to owners of laid-up tonnage with a view to restricting the magnitude of active supply, the response on the part of shipowners was a poor one.

During 1960 the Council of the Association forwarded application forms to tramp shipping firms through their national organizations. These were aiming at establishing the number of shipowners 'favourably disposed in principle towards co-operative action along the lines of the Tonnage Stabilisation Scheme'. The number of favourable replies received represented a percentage of tramp tonnage which was considerably less than that estimated as necessary for the successful functioning of the scheme. Furthermore, it was stated at the time that a considerable number of those tramp shipping firms completing the application and giving favourable replies to the questions asked did so on the understanding that these were not to be taken 'as binding'.

Interest in the scheme was revived during 1962 and 1963. It

was stated at the time that in view of the increase in the available supply of tonnage, British tramp owners had become more interested in the practical application of the scheme. Nevertheless, the annual general meeting of the Association for 1962 was rather inconclusive. The following comment of the representative of the Greek Shipping Co-operation Committee, London, is, we think, enlightening in this connection:

United Kingdom representatives waited to hear the views of the other countries before they spoke. Having regard to what was said at the Meeting, although even in the case of the U.K. there was more desire at present to support the scheme; nevertheless, in view of the absence of 'a burning enthusiasm' in favour of the scheme, they were not encouraged to advocate further steps for the time being.

Following further discussion, it was pointed out that unless Tankers joined the scheme there was little chance of the scheme succeeding. Another serious point militating against the scheme was the enormous building programme of large bulk carriers by the Scandinavian Countries, which is encouraged by taxation concessions, far in excess of world tonnage requirements. No hope can be held that the Scandinavian bulk-carrier owners will agree to join the scheme.

It was agreed that an approach be made to the Tanker owners in order to find out whether they would be willing to join the scheme if it was decided to put it into operation.

The Chairman, in conclusion, stated that although there is more desire at present to put the scheme into operation, there was, however, no 'burning enthusiasm' for it. He repeated the previous view, that unless 75 per cent of the World Tramp Tonnage agreed to join, the scheme could not be expected to succeed.[1]

During March 1963 application forms were sent out by the Association explaining the main provisions of the scheme, which basically remained the same, again asking tramp owners to participate.[2] Table 32 shows the replies to this application on the part of tramp shipping firms of various nationalities.

As Table 32 indicates, the response on the part of owners was rather poor. The big difference between columns III and VI is explained by the fact that since the replies to the application

[1] Circular no. 986, dated 29 April 1962, of the Greek Shipping Co-operation Committee, London.
[2] See Circular letter of the International Tonnage Stabilisation Association Ltd., dated 27 March 1963.

were not to be considered 'as binding', many owners, who later declined to apply for membership, originally thought it correct to give their approval to the scheme. However, as shown in the Table, shipowners' participation in the scheme did not actually amount to more than 15 per cent of the total ocean tramp shipping tonnage which was estimated by the Association to be 30 214 000 t.d.w. at the time.

Table 32. Tonnage participation in stabilization scheme (1964)

Country	Total Eligible Tonnage 8.5.63	DEADWEIGHT (000) REPLIES TO QUESTIONNAIRE OF 27/3/63			Applications for membership to 28/4/64
		Yes	Conditional	No	
I	II	III	IV	V	VI
Belgium	113	—	—	—	—
Canada	—	(Included with U.K. figures)			20.7
Denmark	555	36	—	427	—
Finland	156	—	—	156	—
France	626	—	527	99	257.4
Germany	2011	1172	478	361	466.5
Greece	8500	3026	424	43	305
Italy	1860	972	220	—	795.7
Japan	2900	298	873	970	—
Holland	590	533	—	57	358.5
Norway	5677	718	961	1968	36
Spain	402	224	—	—	—
Sweden	1635	1078	79	—	6.1
Swiss	186	—	143	—	—
U.K.	5003	3819	98	355	2239.7
Others	—	214	—	—	110.7
Totals	30 214	12 090	3803	4436	4596.3

Source: Circular no. 1121 of the Greek Shipping Co-operation Committee dated 13 May 1964.

It will be noted that the total eligible tonnage is not equal to the total of columns 'yes', 'conditional', and 'no'. This is explained by the fact that there were shipping firms owning eligible tonnage which did not reply to the questionnaires of the Association.

During 1963, when there was an improvement in the level of tramp freight rates, several differences amongst shipowners became apparent so far as the scheme was concerned. Japanese owners pointed out that they were not in a position to join because of 'government reorganization of the shipping industry and government control'. Greek owners of Liberty ships stated that they were not interested in the scheme because laid-up allowances were low and they would prefer to keep their tonnage trading. Norwegian owners, on the other hand, thought that the scheme would be a 'home of rest for Liberties'. By 1964 not one of the national shipowners' organizations showed any real enthusiasm for the scheme.

In the circumstances, a meeting of the Provisional Council of the International Tonnage Stabilisation Association was held in London on 29 April 1964. A statement was issued to the Press afterwards in which it was mentioned that the Provisional Council was still convinced that the scheme 'was sound and sensible' for all tramp ships. However, it was decided at the meeting that: 'Until such time as there was evidence of greater support for its co-operative scheme, no further steps should be taken to bring it into operation.'[1]

It is not difficult to understand why the scheme failed to attract the support of the majority of tramp owners. Some of the reasons may have already become apparent in previous chapters. The main reasons were, however, as follows:

(a) The knowledge on the part of shipowners and their managers of the competitive and speculative nature of their profession (which made them think that the scheme would not work anyway!). It has been seen that entrepreneurs concentrate their efforts in maximizing profits whilst the going is good in order to be able to face future 'crises', that is to say, prolonged periods of low freight rates. A stabilization scheme the operation of which pre-supposes additional financial obligations on the one hand, whilst on the other it may assist in the prolongation of the life of old tonnage owned by competitors is basically foreign to the policies followed by the majority of individual tramp shipping firms.

At times the argument has been advanced amongst circles near the industry that if the 'spirit of co-operation' existed amongst owners of tramp ships, as it does amongst liner firms,

[1] Source: Circular of the International Tonnage Stabilisation Association Ltd., no. 191/13/ZA dated 4 May 1964.

then a tonnage stabilization scheme would not have been more difficult to put into operation than a conference. Needless to say that this view disregards completely the different market structures of the two industries. The liner market is character-ized by its oligopolistic structure. Thus, it is possible for a few sellers to exercise some control over local markets and agree on rates for various commodities over different trading routes.

(b) The existing differences in the size and speed of tramp ships which are far greater now than they used to be during the inter-war period. Tramp shipping firms owning modern and efficient tonnage are, as a rule, in a position to trade their vessels without loss even during depression stages. Thus, entrepreneurs who own modern and efficient tonnage and expect to make large profits as soon as the next prosperity stage sets in—when con-siderable quantities of old and unremunerative tonnage would inevitably have left the market—do not see any benefit in joining the scheme.

It may be argued, quite correctly, that tramp shipping firms which own exclusively modern tonnage may not be very num-erous and, consequently, what has been pointed out above may not reflect the thoughts of the majority of the industry's entre-preneurs. However, it is common knowledge in the shipping world that during periods of low freight rates, if necessary, part of the revenue obtained from modern tonnage is used by firms to 'finance' payments towards the costs of idleness of their old tonnage (or towards the losses accrued if old tonnage is kept trading). In other words, it may be said that each firm, as a result of the existence of fluctuations, is in a sense organizing its own 'tonnage stabilization scheme' which aims to put it in Mr Onassis's terms, to 'weather away the storm' and remain in the market. The fact that, as a rule, most firms are in a position to make their own financial arrangements with a view to remain-ing in the market can hardly be considered as an inducement to join the scheme proposed by the Tonnage Stabilisation Associa-tion.

In fact it could be argued that the only firms that would obviously benefit from a tonnage stabilization scheme are those that own mostly old tonnage and those that have over-expanded during prosperity.

Thus, the existence of differences amongst tramp shipping firms in respect of the size, speed, and age of tonnage that they own as well as the possibility of making arrangements to 'weather away the storm' independently, are factors which hamper co-operation amongst shipowners with a view to restricting the volume of active supply.

(c) The scheme proposed by the International Tonnage Stabilisation Association and which aims at the creation of a high degree of monopoly in the tramp freight market does not seem to take into account the price effects of substitution.

The following comments of the provisional Council of the Association are enlightening:

(i) *Tankers*: Tankers tonnage in grain trades. It is also encouraging to record that active steps are now being taken to promote a co-operative scheme in the tanker trades. If such a scheme is successfully adopted this should reduce the volume of tanker tonnage employed in the grain trade.

(ii) *Cargo liners*: It has always been envisaged that support for a co-operative scheme of this nature would be likely to be forthcoming from the cargo liners since they would benefit from an improvement in world tramp freights.

(iii) *Bulk carriers*: It should not be inferred from the foregoing that... tonnage on long-term charter is wanted in the scheme simply because it would contribute to the pool. Indeed, it is hoped that Owners of such tonnage will not, for this reason, refrain from joining the scheme. They would by joining, give the scheme their moral support besides making a small contribution to it by way of entry fees and annual subscriptions. Moreover, they would stand to benefit from the scheme as and when their long-term commitments come to an end.[1]

Although the Association did not reach the stage of having to face seriously the question of substitution of the tramp by productive units belonging to the neighbouring industries, the comments given above may be considered as representative of the thinking of the provisional council in this respect. A glance at the facts is enough to show that the provisional council did not take into account seriously the price effects of competition from without—if the scheme were put into operation.

[1] See Circular letter of the International Tonnage Stabilisation Scheme dated 27 March 1964.

(1) A scheme fixing minimum tanker freight rates which had the support of a considerable number of independent owners was put into effect during summer 1963.[1] The operation of this scheme had no appreciable effect so far as participation of tankers in the grain trade is concerned. Substitution of the tramp by the tanker continued to be determined, as before, by the level of the two freight markets. For example, during summer 1964, when the tanker freight market was at a relatively low level, this form of substitution assumed considerable proportions.

(2) Whilst it is correct to say that cargo liner firms would stand to benefit if the scheme was applied successfully (for, if necessary, liners could function profitably as tramps or take Case cargoes at higher rates), this represents only one side of the question. However, so far as the other side is concerned, it must be taken into account that, if as a result of the successful application of the scheme, tramp freights remained at relatively high levels, liner companies would also have to pay high time charter rates in order to attract tramp tonnage whenever necessary. This may explain the relative indifference of the majority of liner firms so far as the scheme was concerned.

(3) There is nothing to suggest that the provisional council was expecting firms operating bulk-carrier tonnage actually to participate in the scheme. Neither can it be said that the statement previously quoted to the effect that the owners of these vessels would stand to benefit 'as and when their long-run commitments came to an end' represented a serious attempt on the part of the Council to persuade them to apply for membership. Needless to say, that no positive results could be expected from such an attempt. Depending on the magnitude of demand in their own market, bulk carriers usually of the smaller sizes (i.e. 18 000–34 000 t.d.w.) may function as tramps over short- or long-run periods. Since bulk carriers are vessels of larger size, greater speed and therefore, lower operating costs per ton-mile, they are in a position to compete successfully with traditional tramps on all those routes where there is a demand for transport of relatively large quantities of bulk cargoes and which have the necessary terminal facilities. Thus, the scheme

---

[1] See Circulars of the 'Intertanko', i.e. International Tanker Recovery Plan. Membership about 3 000 000 t.d.w.

did not offer any tangible benefit in the short, or in the long run, to induce owners of bulk carriers and generally of modern and large dry-cargo tonnage to join. Hence, in their view, the scheme was asking the efficient and far-seeing shipowners to support the less efficient. It was nothing else but a 'home of rest for the Liberties'.

The scheme obtained the support of only a minority of tramp owners. Thus, the Tonnage Stabilisation Association did not reach the advanced organizational stage when it would have to study seriously the question of substitution and its price effects in the tramp market. Had this stage been reached, it would have become obvious to the governing body of the Association that it may not be possible to restrict the entry of productive units belonging to neighbouring industries into a free competitive market.

The substitution of the tramp by vessels of the neighbouring industries is of a marginal nature, but its effects on freight rates are not insignificant. It is, therefore, realistic to assume that the price effects of substitution in the tramp market would probably have neutralized to a large extent those of a stabilization scheme if it were put into operation.

(d) Many of the shipowners who originally developed an interest in co-operative action (i.e. during 1958) maintained that it would not be advisable to put a scheme of minimum freight rates into operation. Apart from the fact that many tramp owners were saying that it would be undesirable to 'maintain an artificial state of affairs' in the world tramp freight market, it was thought that it might be impossible to overcome the technical difficulties that would arise by attempting to put a minimum freight rates scheme into operation. The main technical difficulties under consideration were the following:

(1) The difficulty of determining scales of minimum rates which would be generally acceptable and which would apply equitably to the wide range of tramp shipping tonnage operating under many different flags in the transoceanic trades.

(2) The practical difficulties of taking account of and maintaining a minimum freight scheme in view of the many forms of

tramp charterparty and in view of the different specific conditions applying to individual trades.

(3) The reluctance of the great majority of owners to consent to submit themselves to any form of international control in the operation of their ships.

Some of these technical difficulties would not have to be faced if the scheme providing only for laid-up allowances and compensation for the breaking up of old and unremunerative tonnage were put into operation. However, if the scheme proposed by the Association had been put into effect, there can hardly be any doubt that difficulties of the nature described above would have had to be faced.

The fixed and variable costs of tramp ships which may be of the same specification but are registered under different national flags are not the same. Furthermore there are differences in the size, speed, and age of tramp ships. Also the cost of idleness is not the same in all lay-up berths the world over.

Taking into consideration these differences it would have been difficult to compute a generally acceptable scale of contributions and laid-up allowances to be applied equitably to all tramp ships. Also, it should be pointed out that no agreement was reached during discussions on the amount to be paid as compensation with a view to inducing owners to send their old and uneconomic tonnages to the scrap-yard. Thus, this part of the scheme remained in abeyance.

It is obvious that if difficulties on the above technical points were to be overcome, more information concerning costs would have to be furnished. However, it is highly doubtful whether owners would have agreed to supply such information to the permanent governing body of the Association.

It seems certain that co-operation amongst tramp shipping firms aiming at the restriction of the volume of active supply during periods of low freight rates and based upon a minimum scheme providing only for allowances to cover lay-up costs may not represent a practical proposition at the present time. This is mainly due to the following factors:

(i) The entrepreneurs' awareness of the competitive and speculative nature of their business.

(ii) The existing differences in the size, speed, and age of tramp ships leading to different degrees of interest on the part of different firms in the scheme.

(iii) The impossibility of controlling or minimizing competition from without and its effects on freight levels.

(iv) Technical difficulties that would develop in applying the provisions of the scheme equitably to the wide range of tramp tonnage registered under many different national flags.

Thus, it may be concluded that stabilization schemes were an attempt by sections of the industry to smooth out fluctuations. However, the attitude of the industry as a whole has shown the difficulties involved in putting such schemes into effect.

The short- and long-run effects of schemes, which restrict the active supply of tonnage and aim at maintaining tramp freight rates at a level higher than they would have been if they had been determined by the free interplay of supply and demand, are not in the interest either of the user of tramp shipping facilities, i.e. the shipper, or of the millions of ultimate consumers of the bulk commodities transported.

Classical tradition teaches us that this inconsistency between the industry and the consumer is not an isolated phenomenon:

The interests of dealers in any particular branch of trade or manufacturers is always in some respects different from and even opposite to that of the public. To widen the market and to narrow the competition is always the interest of the dealers. To widen the market may frequently be agreeable enough to the interest of the public, but to narrow the competition must always be against it, and can serve only to enable the dealers by raising their profits above what they naturally would be, to levy, for their own benefit, an absurd tax upon the rest of their fellow citizens.[1]

4. Conclusions

Although the tramp ship has been replaced by the bulk carrier on a number of major routes, there is no evidence to suggest that tramp shipping is a declining industry. On the

[1] See A. Smith, *The Wealth of Nations*, p. 250, edited by E. Crossman (published by the Modern Library, New York).

contrary, with the gradual increase of world seaborne trade and particularly the growth in the volume of foreign trade of the developing countries, the demand for tramp shipping services will continue to rise in the long run.

The development of tramp shipping during the course of a century proves that fluctuations are a normal hazard of the industry. The facts disclosed in this chapter have shown quite clearly the difficulties in putting into effect the tonnage stabilization schemes that have been proposed by some sections of the industry with a view to smoothing out fluctuations. Consequently, we think that the inevitability of the ups and downs of the freight markets and their adverse effects on the factors of production engaged in the industry must be taken into account by the governments of maritime nations in the formulation of their maritime policies.

There is evidence that buoyant freight markets have, on many occasions, led to undue optimism in the ordering of ships. Having regard, however, to the inevitability of ups and downs and the dependence of net earnings on the results of decades of trading, is a short-run boom really any more propitious a time for investment and optimism than other periods? In times of boom purchase prices of all commodities, including ships, are likely to be higher than in time of relative depression. The wisdom or otherwise of an investment in a vessel depends essentially on long-run profitability rather than temporary booms. There is no short cut to uninterrupted prosperity.

Appendix

Table 1. Monthly expenses of a T2 tanker laid up (during 1958). G.R.T. 10 400, N.R.T. 6300, 16 500 t.d.w., Greek flag

	£	s	d	£	s	d
Crew wages, 5 men	248	0	0			
Greek Seamen's Pension Fund	19	17	0			
Victualling at 8s 6d per man per day	63	15	0			
Insurance						
Port risks and club calls	149	3	0			
Stores	45	0	0			
Nightwatchman, agency, and sundries	65	0	0			
Radio maintenance and radar rental maintenance	35	12	0	626	7	0

That is £20 17s 6d per day or £7516 per annum.

Table 2. Daily running expenses of a tramp ship (during 1952). G.R.T. 5173, N.R.T. 3192, 8200 d.w.t. Built 1919. Greek flag

	£	s	d	£	s	d
Crew expenses						
Wages, overtime, and bonus for extra work	74	9	4			
Greek Seamen's Pension Fund	6	0	0			
Repatriation expenses	1	0	0			
Master's expenses in ports		16	0			
Victualling 36 men per 10s per person	18	0	0	100	4	4
Stores and spares						
Deck, engine, and cabin	19	0	0	19	0	0
Maintenance and repairs	17	0	0	17	0	0
Insurance						
Marine insurance on hull and machinery, etc.	25	15	0	25	15	0

Table 2 (*cont.*)

P and I Club; calls, franchise, unrecoverable						
items, deserters, detainees, etc	11	0	0	11	0	0
Management						
Management	3	10	0			
Superintendent engineer	2	0	0	5	10	0
Incidentals	1	10	0	1	10	0
				180	0	4

Table 3. Daily running expenses of a tramp ship (during 1957, Liberty type). G.R.T. 7174, N.R.T. 4322, 10 200 t.d.w. Built 1943. Greek flag

Crew expenses	£	s	d	£	s	d
Wages, including overtime and bonus for extra						
work	75	0	0			
Greek Seamen's Pension Fund	5	10	0			
Victualling	17	12	0	98	2	0
Stores and spare parts, etc.						
Deck, engine, and cabin	25	0	0			
Electronic equipment	3	15	0	28	15	0
Insurance						
On hull, machinery, etc.	43	10	0			
Club: calls, plus unrecoverable items	18	0	0	61	10	0
Maintenance and repairs	25	0	0	25	0	0
Management						
Office	3	10	0			
Superintendent	3	10	0			
Incidentals and sundries	1	0	0	8	0	0
				221	7	0

Table 4. Size of vessels and number of crew employed

The manning scale of well-maintained tramp ships and bulk carriers belonging to Greek owners of 4501 t.d.w. and upwards is fixed as follows:

(A) *Navigating officers and radio officers*

Vessels t.d.w.	Master	Chief Officer	Second Officer	Cadet	Radio Officer
4 501–6 500	1	1	2	—	1
6 501–9 000	1	1	2	—	1
9 001–13 000	1	1	2	1	1
13 001–17 000	1	1	2	1	1
17 001–30 000	1	1	2	1	1
30 001–40 000	1	1	2	1	1
40 001–	1	1	2	1	1

(B) *Deck ratings*

Vessels t.d.w.	Boatswain	Carpenter	Sailors	Deck Boys
4 501–6 500	1	—	7	—
6 501–8 000	1	1	7	1
8 001–11 000	1	1	8	—
11 001–13 000	1	1	8	1
13 001–17 000	1	1	9	1
17 001–30 000	1	1	10	1
30 001–40 000	1	1	11	3
40 000–	1	1	12	4

(C) *Engineers*

Vessels t.d.w.	Chief Engineer	Second Engineer	Third Engineer	Electrician	Apprentice Engineer
4 501–6 500	1	1	2	—	—
6 501–8 000	1	1	2	—	—
8 001–11 000	1	1	2	1	1
11 001–13 000	1	1	3	1	2
13 001–17 000	1	1	3	1	2
17 001–30 000	1	1	3	1	3
30 001–40 000	1	1	3	2	4
40 000–	1	1	3	2	4

Table 5. Daily running expenses of a tramp ship (during 1955). G.R.T. 3553, N.R.T. 2159, 6400 t.d.w. Built 1922. Greek flag

	£	s	d	£	s	d
Crew expenses						
Wages	45	10	0			
Overtime	5	0	0			
Greek Seamen's Pension Fund	4	10	0			
Victualling	10	17	6			
Repatriation, etc.		10	0	66	7	6
Stores and spares						
Deck, engine, and cabin	15	0	0	15	0	0
Insurance						
Hull, machinery, etc.	22	0	0			
Club: calls, plus unrecoverable items	7	4	5	29	4	5
Repairs and maintenance	16	0	0	16	0	0
Management						
Office, Superintendent engineer, and incidentals	7	0	0	7	0	0
				133	11	11

Table 6. Daily running expenses of a 31 500 t.d.w. modern bulk carrier (Diesel Sulzer engines) under the Greek flag, 1966

	£	s	d	£	s	d
Crew expenses						
Wages and overtime	117	0	0			
Pension Fund, etc.	14	0	0			
Repatriations and substitutions	3	0	0			
Victualling	23	0	0	157	0	0
Insurance						
Hull, machinery, and freight	49	0	0			
War risk, P and I Club, and non-recoverable items	28	0	0	77	0	0
Maintenance and repairs						
Repairs	40	0	0			
Spares	24	0	0			
Stores	50	0	0	114	0	0
Management						
Office expenses and superintendence				11	0	0
				359	0	0

APPENDIX

Table 7. Port charges and the size of vessels; re: Port of Genoa

Pilotage

For the first 500 gross tons (minimum) compulsory charge 21 000 Lire

Gross tons	Lire per gross ton
501–1000	2.60
1001–3000	1.85
3001–5000	1.70
5001–7000	1.25
7001–9000	1.05
9001–10 000	0.55
Over 10 000	0.15

Mooring and unmooring service

Vessel's G.R.T.	Mooring or unmooring (Lire)	Ship shifting—2 operations unmooring and mooring (Lire)
0–250	760	1 370
251–500	3 020	4 620
501–1 000	4 620	6 830
1 001–2 000	6 120	8 400
2 001–3 000	7 260	9 110
3 001–5 000	8 390	11 310
5 001–7 500	10 090	13 190
7 501–10 000	11 520	14 640
10 001–15 000	12 880	18 140
15 001–20 000	15 930	21 910
20 001–30 000	21 900	25 670
Over 30 000	25 560	29 960

Table 7 (*cont.*)

Towage	Vessel's G.R.T.	Lire
	0–500	7 000
	501–800	9 000
	801–1 200	11 000
	1 201–2 000	16 000
	2 001–3 000	23 000
	3 001–4 500	29 000
	4 501–6 000	36 000
	6 001–8 000	44 000
	8 001–10 000	57 000
	10 001–13 000	68 000
	13 001–16 000	80 000
	Over 16 000	88 000

Source: *Italy: Port Expenses and Information*, published by the Mediterranean and Overseas Shipping Agency S.P.A., Genoa. For more details in connection with port charges see *Ports of the World*, 13th ed., edited by Sir Archibald Hunt. *Shipping World*, no. 1.

Table 8. Index numbers of tramp shipping freights and wholesale prices 1869–1936 (base year 1869)

	FREIGHTS				WHOLESALE PRICES			
Year	Freight index	Seven year moving average	Devi-ation	Devi-ation per cent	Price index	Seven year moving average	Devi-ation	Devi-ation per cent
1869	100	—	—	—	100	—	—	—
1870	103	—	—	—	98	—	—	—
1871	102	—	—	—	102	—	—	—
1872	103	105	− 2	− 1.90	112	104	− 7	6.73
1873	117	104	13	12.50	113	103	10	9.71
1874	108	104	4	3.85	104	103	1	9.97
1875	99	102	− 3	− 2.94	98	101	− 3	− 2.97
1876	98	100	− 2	− 2.00	97	97	0	0
1877	99	95	4	4.21	96	94	2	2.13
1878	91	92	− 1	− 1.09	89	92	− 3	− 3.26
1879	85	90	− 5	− 5.56	85	90	− 5	− 5.56
1880	87	86	1	1.16	90	88	2	2.27
1881	87	81	6	7.41	87	86	1	1.16
1882	81	77	4	5.19	86	83	3	3.61
1883	75	74	1	1.35	84	81	3	3.70
1884	64	71	− 7	− 9.86	78	78	0	9

Table 8 (*cont.*)

Year	FREIGHTS				WHOLESALE PRICES			
	Freight index	Seven year moving average	Devi- ation	Devi- ation per cent	Price index	Seven year moving average	Devi- ation	Devi- ation per cent
1885	63	69	− 6	− 8.70	73	76	− 3	− 3.95
1886	59	68	− 9	− 13.24	70	74	− 4	− 5.41
1887	65	67	− 2	− 2.99	69	72	− 3	− 4.17
1888	76	66	10	15.15	71	72	− 1	− 1.39
1889	75	65	10	15.38	73	71	2	2.82
1890	64	65	− 1	− 1.54	73	71	2	2.82
1891	63	64	− 1	− 1.56	73	70	3	4.29
1892	55	62	− 7	− 11.29	69	69	0	0
1893	60	59	1	1.69	69	68	1	1.47
1894	58	58	0	0	64	66	− 2	− 3.03
1895	56	58	− 2	− 3.45	63	65	− 2	− 3.08
1896	56	60	− 4	− 6.67	62	65	− 3	− 3.08
1897	56	62	− 6	− 9.68	63	66	− 3	− 4.45
1898	68	62	6	9.68	65	67	2	2.99
1899	65	61	4	6.56	69	68	1	1.47
1900	76	60	16	26.67	77	69	8	11.59
1901	57	59	− 2	− 3.39	71	70	1	1.43
1902	49	57	− 8	− 14.03	70	72	− 2	− 2.78
1903	49	55	− 6	− 10.91	70	73	− 3	− 4.11
1904	49	52	− 3	− 5.77	71	74	− 3	− 4.05
1905	51	50	1	2.00	73	74	− 1	− 1.35
1906	52	49	3	6.12	79	75	4	5.35
1907	54	50	4	8.00	82	76	6	7.89
1908	45	51	− 6	− 11.76	74	78	− 4	− 5.13
1909	46	55	− 3	− 16.36	76	80	− 4	− 5.00
1910	50	57	− 7	− 12.28	80	81	1	− 1.23
1911	58	59	− 1	− 1.69	82	82	0	0
1912	78	81	− 3	− 3.70	87	96	− 9	− 9.38
1914	67	219	− 152	− 69.41	87	110	− 23	− 20.91
1915	199	318	− 119	− 37.42	110	126	− 16	− 12.70
1916	365	376	− 11	− 2.93	139	144	− 5	− 3.47
1917	695	420	275	65.48	179	168	11	6.55
1918	751	434	317	73.04	196	178	18	10.11
1919	490	424	66	15.57	210	182	30	16.48
1920	374	390	− 16	− 4.10	256	181	75	41.44
1921	166	308	− 142	− 46.10	158	175	− 17	− 9.71
1922	130	216	− 86	− 39.81	134	167	− 33	− 19.76

Table 8 (cont).

| Year | FREIGHTS | | | | WHOLESALE PRICES | | | |
	Freight index	Seven year moving average	Devi-ation	Devi-ation per cent	Price index	Seven year moving average	Devi-ation	Devi-ation per cent
1923	123	165	− 42	− 25.45	132	156	− 24	− 15.38
1924	121	129	− 8	− 6.20	142	137	5	3.65
1925	110	122	− 12	− 9.84	139	132	7	5.30
1926	133	119	14	11.76	129	129	0	0
1927	122	115	7	6.09	124	125	− 1	− 0.80
1928	112	111	1	0.90	122	116	6	5.17
1929	115	108	7	6.48	117	108	9	8.33
1930	93	101	− 8	− 7.92	99	101	− 2	− 1.98
1931	90	95	− 5	− 5.26	85	96	− 11	− 11.46
1932	88	92	− 4	− 4.35	82	91	− 9	− 9.89
1933	85	90	− 5	− 5.36	81	87	− 6	− 6.90
1934	85	—	—	—	84	—	—	—
1935	88	—	—	—	86	—	—	—
1936	103	—	—	—	90	—	—	—

Source: L. Isserlis, 'Tramp Shipping Cargoes and Freights', *Journal of the Royal Statistical Society*, May 1938.

Table 9. Index of tramp shipping freights of the U.K. chamber of shipping

Year	Jan.	Feb.	Mar.	April	May	June	July	Aug.	Sept.	Oct.	Nov.	Dec.	Annual average
						1948 = 100							
1948	111.3	104.5	105.5	107.7	104.6	99.8	99.4	100.7	97.2	98.8	88.8	86.8	100.0
1949	87.1	100.5	95.0	94.6	99.7	86.7	73.3	70.6	71.6	69.8	66.5	72.8	82.3
1950	72.8	75.5	75.8	74.4	71.4	74.3	78.8	86.6	89.0	95.8	97.6	115.7	84.0
1951	151.9	164.7	180.6	176.8	203.8	179.0	179.6	149.3	166.5	190.4	172.4	168.5	173.6
1952	163.9	157.3	137.7	109.4	110.9	99.1	90.2	79.2	87.0	94.2	99.0	98.8	110.6
						1952 = 100							
1952	146.4	140.6	122.4	108.4	195.8	91.2	73.5	71.2	76.3	84.9	88.0	83.7	100.0
1953	79.3	80.0	83.2	85.6	82.2	73.8	75.8	73.9	73.9	77.5	73.8	71.5	77.5
1954	71.9	77.6	77.4	75.8	77.4	77.6	79.7	80.1	90.6	99.5	110.4	115.5	86.1
1955	115.1	119.8	113.7	110.2	122.6	128.0	130.0	129.9	138.1	148.9	135.5	140.1	127.7
1956	144.3	140.3	147.2	151.6	162.2	155.5	155.2	157.9	156.1	153.6	171.4	189.4	157.0
1957	173.7	167.6	145.5	134.3	116.6	109.9	101.9	86.9	81.6	80.7	82.3	71.6	112.7
1958	64.9	64.0	63.3	62.7	64.6	66.5	66.6	65.0	65.7	70.4	76.4	74.6	67.1

Source: *Annual Reports* of the Chamber of Shipping of the U.K.

Table 10. Index number of tramp shipping freights. Voyage charter.
(1960 = 100)

	1962	1963	1964	1965	1966	1967	1968
January	96.9	93.1	128.6	116.1	124.1	100.5	134.5
February	95.2	94.1	110.7	117.1	126.1	103.1	122.0
March	96.9	97.5	107.0	124.1	122.4	106.2	131.7
April	99.4	100.7	109.5	122.3	123.4	103.7	123.2
May	97.9	109.9	110.3	130.5	113.3	109.8	112.7
June	84.4	105.9	107.4	125.7	110.9	113.5	126.0
July	78.4	101.1	108.4	130.6	107.8	138.0	119.0
August	79.4	104.8	105.3	128.1	108.0	113.2	123.5
September	81.0	110.4	105.6	134.1	104.2	125.8	119.1
October	84.3	134.8	118.8	128.9	105.8	139.8	119.4
November	87.5	128.0	120.0	127.3	104.1	146.3	128.0
December	87.8	127.8	113.7	133.5	111.5	145.8	126.9
Year	89.1	109.0	112.1	126.5	113.5	120.5	123.8

Source: *British Shipping Statistics 1968–9.*

Table 11. Coal exports and freight rates

Year	U.S.A. tons	U.K. tons (excluding coke, fuel, and bunkers	Poland metric tons (including bunkers)	Hampton roads– Holland		Cardiff– River- Plate (per ton)		Poland– Buenos Aires (per ton)	
				s	d	s	d	s	d
1949	32 785 000	13 915 916	26 776 000	50	0	37	6	—	
1950	29 360 000	13 550 632	26 473 000	51	6	43	1	57	6
1951	33 193 000	7 806 569	26 004 000	81	6	97	6	160	0
1952	24 477 000	11 750 860	24 333 000	39	6	85	0	108	9
1953	14 098 000	15 656 580	24 299 000	32	6	35	0	45	7
1954	12 926 000	15 507 609	24 289 000	35	6	32	6	48	0
1955	51 256 000	14 343 193	24 026 000	58	0	—		70	9
1956	51 054 000	11 216 995	19 299 000	82	6	—		—	
1957	76 342 000	9 996 694	13 353 000	55	0	—		40	6
1958	50 279 000	5 762 755	16 205 000	23	0	32	3	36	6

Source: Data obtained from *Tramp Shipping Freight Rates 1949–58.* The sources of information in respect of the quantity of exports of the countries under consideration are given in the above publication as follows: United States Embassy, London; Accounts relating to trade and navigation, U.K.; Commercial Counsellor of Polish Embassy in London.

Table 12. Monthly highs and lows of freight rates during 1956 (in shillings per ton)

| | Ore Marmogoa to Antwerp/Rotterdam range | | Grain West Australia to U.K. | | Coal Hampton Rds. to Holland etc. | | Coal Rotterdam to West Italy | | Grain South Africa to Antwerp/Hamburg range | | Grain St. Lawrence to U.K. | | Grain River Plate to Antwerp/Hamburg range | |
	H	L	H	L	H	L	H	L	H	L	H	L	H	L
	s d	s d	s d	s d	s d	s d	s d	s d	s d	s d	s d	s d	s d	s d
Jan.	100 0	100 0	170 0	170 0	71 0	69 6	27 6	26 9	116 6	116 6	80 0	80 0	125 0	125 0
Feb.	104 6	104 6	160 0	157 6	72 0	67 6	27 0	26 6	112 6	103 9	82 6	82 6	132 6	125 0
March	110 0	110 0	175 0	170 0	75 0	71 3	29 0	28 0	112 6	112 6	95 0	83 9	155 0	127 6
April	—	—	180 0	175 0	77 6	73 6	—	—	125 0	118 9	100 0	95 0	160 0	147 6
May	115 0	115 0	177 6	160 0	79 0	74 6	34 6	34 6	122 6	112 6	96 0	92 6	167 7	162 6
June	107 6	107 6	170 0	150 0	79 0	66 0	39 0	39 0	117 6	110 0	85 0	77 6	141 3	141 3
July	—	—	155 0	150 0	71 6	67 0	35 6	35 0	122 6	105 0	95 0	79 9	150 0	137 6
Aug.	—	—	—	—	71 0	68 6	—	—	127 6	122 6	87 6	87 6	150 0	143 6
Sept.	—	—	180 0	180 0	75 0	69 0	34 0	34 0	132 6	132 6	90 0	85 0	150 0	145 0
Oct.	122 6	122 6	180 0	175 0	76 6	93 0	36 0	34 0	132 6	131 3	95 0	80 0	160 0	150 0
Nov.	—	—	185 0	185 0	105 6	79 6	37 0	34 0	136 3	133 9	115 0	102 6	162 0	153 9
Dec.	—	—	220 0	200 0	116 0	98 0	36 0	36 0	170 0	170 0	—	—	188 9	177 6

Source: The data for the above table is obtained from the *Daily Freight Register* publication *Tramp Shipping Freight Rates 1949–58*. Although the above figures are crude ones, we think that they offer a clear indication of the permanent tendency of freight rates to move in parallel.

Table 13. Grain exports and freight rates

Year	Australia (tons)	Canada (in thousands of bushels)	Year	Argentina (metric tons)	W. Australia–U.K. average freight rate for each year (per ton) s d	Churchill–U.K. average freight rate for each year (per Q.R.) s d	River Plate–Hamburg range (per ton) s d
1948/49	2 777 633	308 949	1949	3 501 300	79 0	10 1½	39 10½
1949/50	2 542 061	243 980	1950	4 213 900	51 6	9 5½	43 6
1950/51	2 876 492	273 753	1951	3 223 465	147 6	26 3	100 7½
1951/52	2 205 892	472 766	1952	980 441	77 0	13 6	63 9
1952/53	2 368 230	542 076	1953	4 739 460	93 0	51 3	67 6
1953/54	1 694 483	441 530	1954	7 325 238	86 6	52 4½	89 6
1954/55	2 260 582	370 689	1955	4 934 069	126 0	77 6	106 0
1955/56	2 600 156	406 524	1956	4 628 964	174 0	95 0	156 10
1956/57	3 233 497	409 352	1957	4 745 925	134 0	63 0	118 9
1957/58	1 536 438	560 830	1958	4 816 126	69 0	48 9	55 7½

Source: Data obtained from various tables of the *Daily Freight Register* publication *Tramp Shipping Freight Rates 1949–58*. The original source of information in respect of freight rates is the *Daily Freight Register*. The original sources of information in respect of the grain exports are the following: Australia: Australian Overseas Trade Bulletin; Canada: The Canadian Wheat Board, London; Argentina: Office of the Economic Counsellor, Embassy of the Argentine Republic, London

Table 14. Fluctuations in the price of Liberty ships 1950–63

Years	Three-monthly periods	Price in £	Years	Three-monthly periods	Price in £
1950	October	200 000	1957	June	250 000
1951	January	210 000	1957	September	225 000
1951	March	—*	1957	December	230 000
1951	June	400 000	1958	March	135 000
1951	October	485 000	1958	June	145 000
1951	December	590 000	1958	September	160 000
1952	March	355 000	1958	December	120 000
1952	June	315 000	1959	March	69 000
1952	September	260 000	1959	June	70 000
1952	December	220 000	1959	September	72 000
1953	March	280 000	1959	December	110 000
1953	June	237 000	1960	March	117 500
1953	September	180 000	1960	June	85 000
1953	December	172 000	1960	September	100 000
1954	March	175 000	1960	December	105 000
1954	June	195 000	1961	March	106 500
1954	September	200 000	1961	June	120 000
1954	December	250 000	1961	September	143 000
1955	March	285 000	1961	December	130 000
1955	June	310 000	1962	March	85 000
1955	September	325 000	1962	June	60 000
1955	December	400 000	1962	September	55 000
1956	March	450 000	1962	December	55 000
1956	June	500 000	1963	March	55 000
1956	September	550 000	1963	June	66 000
1956	December	670 000	1963	September	90 000
1957	March	500 000	1963	December	115 000

Source: Data obtained from *Naftika Chronika*, 1 January 1964, p. 85.
* Not available.

Bibliography

1. Books

Bain, J.S., *Pricing Distribution and Employment*, Henry Holt, and Company, New York.

Bes, J., *Chartering and Shipping Terms*, Uitgeverij v/h C.De Boer Jr., Amsterdam.

Bratt, E.C., *Business Cycles and Forecasting* (3rd edn.) 1948, Richard D. Irwin Inc., Chicago, Illinois.

British Petroleum Co. Ltd., *Our Industry* (3rd edn.), Britannic House, London.

Clarke, W.V.J., *Cole's Shipmasters' Handbook to the Merchant Shipping Acts* (6th edn.), Brown, Son and Ferguson Ltd., Glasgow.

Daily Freight Register, Tramp Freight Rates 1949–58, London.

Estey, J.A., *Business Cycles*, Prentice-Hall Inc., New York.

Goss, R.O., *Studies in Maritime Economics*, Cambridge University Press, 1968.

Griparios, H., *Tramp Shipping*, Thomas Nelson and Sons Ltd., London.

Haberler, G., *The Theory of International Trade with its Application to Commercial Policy*, Macmillan Company, New York.

Hanidis, B., *Cargo Liners and Conferences*, Athens, April 1958 (in Greek).

Hempel, S.C., *Your Ship and its Maintenance*, J.C. Hempel's Foundation, Copenhagen, 1963.

Hitachi Zosen's, *Economical Mammoth Tanker*, Hitachi Shipbuilding and Engineering Co. Ltd.

Hurd, A., *Ports of the World*, The Shipping World, London.

Labberton and Marks, *Marine Engineers Handbook* (1st edn.), New York.

Lambert Bros (Shipping) Ltd., *Container Ships*.

Lammeron, W.A.P. van, *Ships and Marine Engines*, vol. iv (2nd edn.).

Lipsey, R.G., *An Introduction to Positive Economics*, Weidenfeld and Nicolson, London.

Marshall, A., *Principles of Economics*, (8th edn.) Macmillan & Co. Ltd., London.

Meij, J.L., *Depreciation and Replacement Policy* (Studies in Industrial Economics), North-Holland Publishing Company.

Meyer, J.R., Peck, J.P., Stenason, J., Zwick, C., *The Economics of Competition in the Transportation Industries*, Harvard University Press, Cambridge, Mass., 1959.

Milne, A.M., *The Economics of Inland Transport*, Sir Isaac Pitman & Sons Ltd., London.

Organisation for Economic Co-operation and Development, Maritime Transport, 1959, 1961.

Reed, T., *Table of Distances*, Thomas Reed & Co. Ltd., Sunderland.

Reed's *Practical Mathematics for Marine Engineers* (8th edn.), Thomas Reed & Co. Ltd., Sunderland.

Robbins, L., *The Great Depression*, Macmillan & Co. Ltd., London, 1934.

Robinson, J., *The Economics of Imperfect Competition*, Macmillan & Co. Ltd., London, 1948.

Shipbuilder's Assn. of Japan, *Shipbuilding and Marine Engineering in Japan 1957–1958*.

Smith, A., *The Wealth of Nations* (ed. E. Cannau), Modern Library, New York.

Stigler, G.J., *The Theory of Price*, Macmillan Company, New York, 1947.

Sturmey, S.G., *British Shipping and World Competition*, Athlone Press, London.

Thornton, R.H., *British Shipping* (2nd edn.), Cambridge University Press.

Wigham-Richardson & Co. Ltd., *Lloyd's Calendar*, Armadores House, London.

2. Articles

Cufley, C.F.H., 'Trends in the Bulk Trades', *The Syren and Shipping*, 3 July 1963.

—, 'Economic Research as an Aid to Planned Shipowning', *The Syren and Shipping*, 4 July 1962.

Isserlis, L., 'Tramp Shipping Cargoes and Freights', *Journal of the Royal Statistical Society*, May 1938.

Lewis, W.A., 'Interrelations of Shipping Freights', *Economica*, February 1941.

Ponsonby, G.J., 'Depreciation with Special Reference to Transport', *Economic Journal*, March 1956.

—, 'Pinpointing the Benefits of More and Better Roads', *Road International*, Winter 1956–7.

—, 'What is an Unremunerative Transport Service?', *Institute of Transport Journal*.

Razdobudko, J., 'Soviet Sea Shipping', *Fairplay*, 11 January 1962.

Seland, J., 'On Forecasts and Forecasters, Pitfalls in Predicting Tonnage Demand', *The Shipping World*, 13 January 1960.

Sturmey, S.G., 'Economics and Liner Services', *Journal of Transport Economics and Policy*, May 1967.

Svendsen, A.S., 'The Revival of the Freight Market', *International Design and Equipment*, January, 1960.

Trace, K., 'Underdeveloped Countries: Shipping Problems and Policies', *The World Today*, May 1969.

Vernouil, A., 'Seaboard Steel Industry and Shipping', *Journal de la Marine Merchande et la Navigation Aerienne*, 1963 volume.

3. Magazines and Newspapers

Fairplay, 1953–65.

Financial Times, 13 May 1959, 2 June 1960, 19 March 1962.

Mercantile Marine Review (Epitheorisis Emporicou Nafticou, Athens), 1933, June–July 1937.

Naftilia (Shipping), 1960–66.

Naftica Chronica (Nautical Chronicles), 1955–66.

Nea Economia (New Economics, Athens), January 1959.

Shipbuilding and Shipping Record, 4 January 1962.

Shipping World, 1962–4.

The Marine Engineer and Naval Architect, December 1961, April 1962.

The Motor Ship, 1962–3.

The Syren and Shipping, January editions 1961–4. (also 4 July 1962 and 3 July 1963, see 'Articles').

Hellenic Shipping International, January–April 1970.

4. Reports, Documents, and Unpublished Material

Chamber of Shipping of the United Kingdom, *Annual Reports 1957–65*, 7 December 1968, and Circulars 1958–64.

Fearnley and Egers Chartering Co. Ltd., 'World Bulk Carriers', Surveys 1966–9.

Goss, R.O., 'Some Financial Aspects of Shipping Conferences', paper given at Transport Economist's Seminar, Ealing Technical College, London, May 1970.

—, 'The Size of Ships', paper given at the College of Europe, April 1970.

Greek Government, Government Gazettes, Re-approval Acts for Flag Transfers 1958–60.

Greek Ministry of Mercantile Marine, Acts, Decrees, and Collective Agreements regarding Greek Seamen, Athens 1951, Piraeus 1956, 1959, 1961, 1962, 1964.

Greek Shipping Co-operation Committee, London, Circulars 1940–64.

H.M. Stationary Office, *Committee of Inquiry into Shipping Report*, May 1970.

International Chamber of Shipping, *Report on Deep Sea Tramp Co-operation*, 1958.

International Tonnage Stabilisation Association Ltd., Circulars 1960–4.

Jacobs, J.I.Ltd., 'Market Summary' Circulars issued by the Chartering Department of John I. Jacobs & Co. Ltd., London, 1959–65.

—, 'World Tanker Fleet Review', 31 December 1965.

Lloyd's Register of Shipping, *Annual Report for the Year 1959*, 'Two Centuries of Service'.

National Maritime Board, *Yearbooks 1961–64*.

Netherlands Shipowners' Association, 'Maritime Freights and Commodity Prices', March 1960.

Norwegian Government, Economic Survey 1962.

Sulzer Bros., Booklet no. e/22, 02, 7.1. December 5.

Sturmey, S.G., *On the pricing of tramp ship freight rates*, Occasional Papers
    Series, University of Lancaster.
Union of Greek Shipowners, Circulars 1950–64, and *Annual Reports 1962–3*.
United Nations Conference on Trade and Development, *Level and Structure
    of Freight Rates, Conference Practices and Adequacy of Shipping Services*, 1968.
—, *Establishment or Expansion of Merchant Marines in Developing Countries*.
Westinform, *Shipping Reports*, nos. 133, 188, 223, 280.

Index

KT-164-325

800 655 088

THE TRIAL
of
ADOLF HITLER

A crowd outside the Bürgerbräukeller, shown here in 1923.
"In Bavaria, there is no politics without beer," wrote the Catalan
newspaper *La Veu de Catalunya*.

ALSO BY DAVID KING

Death in the City of Light: The Serial Killer of Nazi-Occupied Paris

*Vienna, 1814: How the Conquerors of Napoleon Made Love,
War, and Peace at the Congress of Vienna*

*Finding Atlantis: A True Story of Genius, Madness, and
an Extraordinary Quest for a Lost World*

THE TRIAL
of
ADOLF HITLER

The Beer Hall Putsch

and

the Rise of Nazi Germany

◆━━━━━◆━━━━━◆

DAVID KING

MACMILLAN

First published 2017 by W. W. Norton & Company

First published in the UK in paperback 2017 by Macmillan

This edition first published 2017 by Macmillan
an imprint of Pan Macmillan
20 New Wharf Road, London N1 9RR
Associated companies throughout the world
www.panmacmillan.com

ISBN 978-1-4472-5111-8

Copyright © David King 2017

The right of David King to be identified as the
author of this work has been asserted by him in accordance
with the Copyright, Designs and Patents Act 1988.

All rights reserved. No part of this publication may be reproduced,
stored in a retrieval system, or transmitted, in any form, or by any means
(electronic, mechanical, photocopying, recording or otherwise)
without the prior written permission of the publisher.

Pan Macmillan does not have any control over, or any responsibility for,
any author or third-party websites referred to in or on this book.

1 3 5 7 9 8 6 4 2

A CIP catalogue record for this book is available from the British Library.

Printed and bound by CPI Group (UK) Ltd, Croydon, CR0 4YY

This book is sold subject to the condition that it shall not, by way of
trade or otherwise, be lent, hired out, or otherwise circulated without
the publisher's prior consent in any form of binding or cover other than
that in which it is published and without a similar condition including
this condition being imposed on the subsequent purchaser.

Visit **www.panmacmillan.com** to read more about all our books
and to buy them. You will also find features, author interviews and
news of any author events, and you can sign up for e-newsletters
so that you're always first to hear about our new releases.

To Van King, in loving memory

This was the most important political trial of the twentieth century. It opened the way for Hitler's criminal regime.

—OTTO GRITSCHNEDER

Contents

Part II: The Courtroom

MUNICH, 1923–1924: CAST OF CHARACTERS

Amann, Max Staff sergeant in Hitler's regiment during the First World War. He now manages the business operations for the Nazi Party office.

Bechstein, Helene Wife of a Berlin piano manufacturer and an influential society hostess.

Berchtold, Josef Cigar dealer who commands the newly formed Stosstrupp Hitler, or "Hitler Assault Squad."

Brückner, Wilhelm Leader of the Munich regiment of Storm Troopers.

Danner, Jakob Ritter von Major general, commander of the Munich city garrison.

Ebert, Friedrich A Social Democrat Party functionary who became the first president of the German Republic.

Ehard, Hans Deputy prosecutor in the trial of Adolf Hitler and later prime minister of Bavaria.

Esser, Hermann A young journalist and rabble-rousing orator in the Nazi Party.

Feder, Gottfried Owner of a construction firm and early economic adviser to Hitler.

Frank, Hans Law student who marched with a Storm Trooper unit.

Frick, Wilhelm Head of the political intelligence office at the Munich police.

Gademann, Otto Defense lawyer for Hermann Kriebel.

Göring, Carin Swedish aristocrat who fell in love with Hermann Göring and helped him escape Munich after the putsch.

Göring, Hermann Flamboyant wartime pilot and socially prominent recruit to the Nazi Party who commands the Storm Troopers.

Götz, Georg Defense lawyer for Wilhelm Frick.

Graf, Ulrich Bodyguard to Adolf Hitler.

Gürtner, Franz Bavaria's nationalistic minister of justice.

Hanfstaengl ("Putzi"), Ernst Harvard-educated scion of a prominent publishing family.

Hanfstaengl, Helen Niemeyer American-born wife of Ernst Hanfstaengl who hides Hitler from the police.

Hemmeter, Walther Defense lawyer for Ernst Pöhner and Robert Wagner.

Hemmrich, Franz Prison guard at Landsberg.

Hess, Rudolf Student at Munich University who already shows a fanatical loyalty to Hitler.

Himmler, Heinrich A young member of Captain Röhm's paramilitary squad, the Reichskriegsflagge, or "Imperial Battle Flag."

Hitler, Adolf Thirty-four-year-old Austrian-born demagogue and fanatical anti-Semite who chairs the Nazi Party.

Hoffmann, Heinrich Photographer who enjoys the exclusive right to photograph Adolf Hitler.

Holl, Alfred Defense lawyer for Friedrich Weber.

Imhoff, Sigmund Freiherr Major in the Bavarian state police.

Kahr, Gustav Ritter von Bavarian politician appointed to the newly created position of general state commissioner with expansive executive powers.

Knilling, Eugen Ritter von Bavaria's conservative prime minister who had played an important role in appointing Gustav von Kahr as general state commissioner.

Kohl, Karl Defense lawyer for Wilhelm Brückner.

Kriebel, Hermann Lieutenant colonel (retired) who serves as military commander of the Kampfbund, or "Combat League."

Leybold, Otto Warden at Landsberg Prison.

Lossow, Hermann von Head of Bavarian military. He works closely with the general state commissioner, Gustav von Kahr, and the head of the state police, Colonel Hans von Seisser.

Ludendorff, Erich Quartermaster general for the German Army during the First World War and idol to the far right.

Luetgebrune, Walter One of two defense counsels for General Erich Ludendorff. The other one was Willibald von Zezschwitz.

Maurice, Emil Matchmaker, chauffeur, and brawler in the Stosstrupp Hitler, or "Hitler Assault Squad."

Mayer, Hellmuth Defense counsel for Friedrich Weber. He is joined by Alfred Holl.

Murphy, Robert Twenty-nine-year-old American vice consul who went from one beer city, Milwaukee, to another, Munich.

Neithardt, Georg Superior court director and presiding judge in the trial of Adolf Hitler.

Pacelli, Eugenio Papal nuncio in Munich and later Pope Pius XII.

Pernet, Heinz Stepson to General Erich Ludendorff.

Pöhner, Ernst Former president of Munich police who serves as a judge on the Bavarian Supreme Court.

Roder, Lorenz Defense attorney for Adolf Hitler. He also helps defend Ernst Pöhner and Wilhelm Frick.

Röhm, Ernst Captain in the Reichswehr who heads the paramilitary society Reichskriegsflagge, or "Imperial Battle Flag."

Rosenberg, Alfred The viciously anti-Semitic German Balt editor of the Nazi newspaper, *Völkischer Beobacher.*

Scheubner-Richter, Max Erwin von German Balt intriguer active in Munich's far right and Russian émigré circles.

Schramm, Christoph Chief counsel for Captain Ernst Röhm.

Schweyer, Franz Bavaria's minister of the interior who had long been critical of Hitler and the Nazi Party.

Seeckt, Hans von Commander-in-chief of the German Reichswehr.

von Seisser, Hans Ritter Head of Bavarian state police, close ally to Gustav von Kahr and Hermann von Lossow.

Stenglein, Ludwig Chief prosecutor in the Hitler trial. His deputy was Hans Ehard.

Streicher, Julius Headmaster of a Nuremberg elementary school and publisher of the virulently anti-Semitic *Der Stürmer.*

Stresemann, Gustav Chancellor and then foreign minister of Germany.

Wagner, Robert Student at Munich's infantry officer training academy.

Weber, Friedrich Veterinarian and political leader of the paramilitary society Bund Oberland.

Zezschwitz, Willibald von One of the two defense counsels for General Erich Ludendorff.

Prologue

A large crowd gathered on the usually quiet Blutenburgstrasse west of Munich's city center. Mounted guards, plainclothes detectives, and two battalions of state police troops patrolled outside the redbrick building. Nobody was allowed to enter without the proper stamped pass and accompanying photo identification. Once inside, in a small room down the long corridor, security personnel checked for hand grenades in purses or daggers in stockings.

It was February 26, 1924, the first day of the anticipated high-treason trial that would mesmerize the country. According to tips picked up by the Munich police, thugs and hooligans planned to swarm into town, disrupt the proceedings, free the accused, and perhaps even stage another insurrection.

Just before eight thirty that morning, the defendant, Adolf Hitler, entered the packed courtroom. He wore a black suit with an Iron Cross First Class and an Iron Cross Second Class pinned to his jacket. His hair was slicked to the left and his mustache was clipped short and square, in a style derided as "a snot brake."

He stood five-nine and tipped the scales at 170 pounds, the heaviest he had been in his life. Still, he looked small and insignificant, concluded a reporter for Berlin's *Vossische Zeitung*—and much less imposing in person than was suggested by the photographs circulated by the banned National Socialist Party. On the way to his seat in the front, Hitler stopped to kiss the hands of a few women in the audience. It must have been his Austrian manners, a correspondent for Paris's *Le Matin* said.

Nine of the ten defendants had come that morning, like Hitler, from their temporary holding cells in the building. The tenth and final defendant, however, arrived by limousine. This was Gen. Erich Ludendorff, victor of the eastern front in the First World War and architect of the bold strategy that almost won the war in the west. Instead, his series of risky offensives in the spring of 1918 had exhausted Germany's dwindling resources and, some critics added, doomed the country to defeat.

Stern and stout with close-cropped white hair, Ludendorff seemed like the archetypal brash and arrogant Prussian. He strode into the room, "proud and sneering," the United Press correspondent put it, as if serenely aloof from the world around him. His thin mustache swirled up over a hefty double chin emerging from his high collar. Ludendorff took his seat in the front next to Hitler, looking, as German nationalist Kurt Lüdecke later said, like "a tower that defies the world."

To try the country's most prominent commander for high treason was certainly going to be a sensation. But few people in the courtroom that morning expected that the real star to emerge in the legal drama would be the private first class at his side.

On the eve of the trial, Adolf Hitler was a minor, if ambitious, local party leader idolized by a relatively small number of supporters. His name was still sometimes misspelled in the international press, and his background bungled—if he was mentioned at all, that is, besides in jest at leading his followers in what the *New York Times* dubbed a "Bavarian Opera Bouffe." Once the trial began, those days would be numbered.

As the judges prepared to make their entrance, the two sets of doors on the side of the room were shut as a safety precaution. The foreign correspondent of the Associated Press watched Hitler and Ludendorff shake hands and chat amicably beforehand. Ludendorff looked cool. Hitler, on the other hand, appeared agitated and showed signs of emotional strain. There was good reason for his concern.

If the verdict were guilty, Article 81 of the Criminal Code stipulated a maximum punishment of life imprisonment. But for Hitler, who was born in Austria and still did not have German citizenship, there was a second relevant law. Section 9, Paragraph 2 of the Law for the Protection of the Republic called for foreigners convicted of high treason to be deported after serving their sentence.

Would Hitler now be convicted, imprisoned, deported, and then forgotten?

This was the fate he feared the most on the morning the trial began.

PART I

THE BEER HALL

1.

BÜRGERBRÄUKELLER

At the edge of large cities, where streetlamps are scarce and policemen walk by twos, are houses where you mount till you can mount no further, up and up into attics under the roof, where pale young geniuses, criminals of the dream, sit with folded arms and brood . . .

— THOMAS MANN, "AT THE PROPHET'S"

November 8, 1923

At about ten o'clock on a chilly, gray morning, the normally late-rising Adolf Hitler woke with a splitting headache and a sharp pain in his mouth. For days, he had refused to seek medical help for his tooth-ache. There was no time, he said, for a trip to the dentist.

The thirty-four-year-old Hitler rented a small back bedroom in an apartment at Thierschstrasse 41. About eight feet by fifteen feet, the room was sparsely decorated, with little more than a chair, a table, a bookcase, and a large bed with a headboard that partially blocked the single window. Drawings were tacked up on the walls, and worn rugs covered the linoleum floor. He rarely entertained visitors there, though for his most recent birthday, he had packed the space with flowers and cakes decorated with swastikas in whipped cream.

After belting his trench coat and looping his riding whip around his wrist, Hitler rushed over to the offices of the *Völkischer Beobachter*, the

National Socialist Party newspaper, at Schellingstrasse 39. This was just north of Munich's medieval center and a few blocks away from one of the city's grand boulevards. In the bare, whitewashed room on the second floor sat the introspective thirty-year-old editor, Alfred Rosenberg, a Baltic German who already thought of himself as the philosopher of the party. He wore a violet shirt with a brown vest, a blue jacket, and a bright-red tie. A pistol lay on his desk, serving as a makeshift paperweight to a stack of papers.

Rosenberg was deep in conversation with another member of the party, the thirty-five-year-old half-American, Ernst Hanfstaengl, a tall and flamboyant Harvard-educated dilettante who came from a family that owned a prominent art-reproduction firm. The two men discussed the morning's paper, which, in the runaway inflation that gripped the country, cost 5 billion marks. This was still 3 billion marks cheaper than its Socialist rival, the *Münchener Post*.

Rosenberg and Hanfstaengl stopped their conversation when they heard Hitler stomping up and down the corridor, shouting, "Where is Captain Göring?"

No one knew. Hermann Göring was often late, or out of the office enjoying lunches with friends, usually at Munich's most expensive restaurants. That morning, however, Göring was at home in the suburb of Obermenzing with his Swedish wife, Carin, who was suffering from pneumonia.

Rosenberg and Hanfstaengl rose when Hitler entered the room. Hitler swore the men to secrecy and went straight to the point: Rosenberg was to draw up a series of posters and spearhead a special edition of the newspaper. Hanfstaengl would be in charge of alerting the foreign press in his most subtle, discreet manner about the importance of being at the Bürgerbräu beer cellar that evening without revealing why. After that, both men were to report there at seven sharp and bring their pistols.

"The moment for action has come," Hitler said. "You know what that means."

• • •

AROUND EIGHT O'CLOCK on that black, virtually starless night, a flashy red Benz pulled up to the entrance of the Bürgerbräukeller, located about a mile south of the city center. Beer halls, like this one, were popular venues for political meetings, with promises of ample food, drink, space, and, it was hoped, a lively atmosphere conducive to rallying the party faithful. They were also, increasingly, providing opportunities for disrupting the gatherings of rivals.

But the crowd that night was far larger than anyone had expected. There had been only one small notice in a single newspaper, *München-Augsburger Abendzeitung*, and about fifty invitations, mostly sent at the last minute. An estimated three thousand people, however, had thronged its premises for that night's political rally.

Munich city police officers had been turning people away for the last forty-five minutes. A crowd now spilled outside onto the stone steps below police lines and onto the street, stretching as far away as the tram tracks.

The door to the Benz opened and out came Hitler, only to be, as he put it, "mobbed by a huge crowd," yelling and pushing its way forward, hoping that he would help them gain entrance. He was only a guest himself, Hitler said, and had no authority to issue invitations. He walked straight ahead to the arched gateway into the beer hall.

With Rosenberg in tow, Hitler entered the Bürgerbräu's banquet hall, a dark, gloomy room permeated with a haze of cigarette and cigar smoke. At the far end, a brass band thumped out oompah music. Waitresses, loaded with armfuls of beer steins, circulated around the wooden tables. Wafts of oxen steak and sauerbraten filled the air.

There were politicians, diplomats, journalists, bankers, brewers, and businessmen, many of the men in dark suits or military uniforms and the women in furs, jewels, and long evening dresses. The cloakroom was lined with swords, top hats, and military dress coats. All the political and patriotic elite of Germany's preeminent beer city seemed to be present, said a reporter from *Münchener Zeitung*.

That is, except for the evening's speaker, Bavaria's general state commissioner, Gustav Ritter von Kahr, who was scheduled to address his supporters in what was expected to be an important talk. He was already more than thirty minutes late and the crowd was getting restless.

Kahr, a short, dark-haired sixty-one-year-old man in a black frock coat, finally entered the crowded hall. He was accompanied by Bavaria's highest-ranking military commander, the monocled and saber-scarred Gen. Otto Hermann von Lossow, who appeared in uniform with dress sword at his side. Both leaders managed to reach the front of the room only with the help of a police escort.

After a brief introduction by the event's organizer, a tobacco merchant named Eugen Zentz, Kahr stepped up to the podium to give, or rather read, his speech. It was long, dry, and poorly delivered. He spoke of the rise and rule of Marxism, and how Munich would have to resist this "contagion" and "quintessential evil." A police informer in the audience compared this speech to a history lecture as dry as straw.

"Does anyone understand what Kahr is talking about?" Hitler asked, also unimpressed.

As planned, Hitler, Rosenberg, and a small circle of supporters had gathered in the vestibule. They looked too conspicuous, Hanfstaengl thought, after he finally gained entrance, bringing a few newspaper reporters with him. He maneuvered his way to the bar and returned, carrying a round of beers that cost billions of marks.

"In Munich," Hanfstaengl later said, "no one will suspect anyone with his nose in a stein of beer of having ulterior motives."

Leaning against a column, Hitler sipped and waited.

AT AN EMPTY factory yard on a nearby street, a twenty-six-year-old cigar dealer, Josef Berchtold, was passing out rifles, machine guns, stick grenades, and ammunition. The small, elite unit he commanded was the Stosstrupp Hitler, or the Hitler Assault Squad, which had been founded six months earlier and consisted of men selected primarily for their courage and loyalty.

Trained for street fights or confrontations in closed spaces such as a beer hall, this squad of about 125 men was often used for "specially dangerous work," such as serving in the vanguard of an action, or coming in at the end to mop up. They wore a field gray military uniform, high black boots, and a ski cap adorned with a silver death's head on a red background. The Stosstrupp Hitler would form the original core of the SS, or Schutzstaffel, the murderous "protection squad" of the Nazi Party.

Next to Berchtold was a broad-shouldered man wearing a steel helmet adorned with a large white swastika and sporting an officer's sword at his side. This was the thirty-year-old captain Hermann Göring, a war ace who had succeeded Baron Manfred von Richthofen as commander of the renowned Flying Circus squadron when the "Red Baron" crashed in April 1918. Göring had joined Hitler's party almost one year before, becoming instantly its most socially prominent member.

Göring was not yet the overweight morphine addict with a ring on every finger who looked like a "madam of a brothel," as Rebecca West later described him. He was a dashing, swaggering thrill-seeker celebrated in Munich salons as a "knight of the air." He had received Germany's highest military decoration, the Pour le Mérite, and boasted of personally shooting down no fewer than twenty-seven planes in his career. After the war, he had moved to Denmark and then Sweden, where he worked as a stunt flyer, a charter pilot, and a sales representative for the Fokker airplane manufacturer.

Eight months before, Göring had been named leader of the large and often disorderly Sturmabteilung—the Storm Division or "Storm Troopers." This organization, founded in early 1920 as a "hall protection" force for the National Socialist Party, had developed into a "Sports and Gymnastics" section that focused on training its men in boxing, jiu jitsu, and calisthenics. It had since taken on a more militaristic organization with companies, battalions, and regiments, and received its name in honor of an elite German commando unit of the First World War.

The Storm Troopers wore gray, mainly war surplus uniforms, with ski caps, wind jackets, and a ten-centimeter-wide red band with an encircled swastika on the left arm. Their infamous brown shirts—inspired by the attire of German colonial troops in East Africa—would appear in the coming months and be officially adopted in 1926. An American who observed these gangs goose-stepping down the streets of Munich and shouting, "Death to the Jews!" called them the "toughest roughnecks" he had ever seen.

Under Göring's command, the Storm Troopers excelled at the improvised weapons of a beer hall brawl: broken chair legs, heavy steins, and concealed knives, blackjacks, billy clubs, brass knuckles, and firearms. "Cruelty impresses," Hitler said, instructing the troops in this private army never to leave a fight "unless carried out dead."

While Göring and Berchtold discussed last-minute arrangements, one of their men returned from reconnoitering the area to report that the police had finally dispersed the crowd in front of the Bürgerbräu. The entrance was now clear. What's more, only about a dozen municipal police officers had been spotted outside.

Berchtold glanced at his watch. He and Göring ordered everyone onto the waiting trucks.

MOMENTS LATER, THE glow of headlights was illuminating a dimly lit side street off Rosenheimerstrasse. A convoy of four flatbed trucks pulled up to the Bürgerbräu's front entrance, stopping in the middle of the street.

"Out of the way—you there!" Josef Berchtold shouted at the handful of Munich police officers. The Stosstrupp Hitler bounded out of the first vehicle, wielding tommy guns and bayonets. Several of the policemen thought that the men were the German Army. The police were, as the commander Berchtold put it, "amazed and unprepared"—and soon also overpowered.

Göring drew his sword and jumped off his truck's running board. He shouted something about the Berlin government being overthrown and his men only recognizing the regime of Ludendorff and Hitler. Two dozen men followed him into the building, yelling, "Heil Hitler!"

By 8:25 p.m., about one hundred men had dispersed throughout the premises to block exits, seize telephones, cover the windows, and line the walls in the main room. A small group carried swastika banners, and a handful of other men carted a heavy machine gun over the gravel path into the beer hall.

Hitler had by now removed his trench coat to reveal an oversized black morning coat. Pinned to his chest were an Iron Cross First Class and an Iron Cross Second Class. He took a last sip from his beer stein, and, it was said, smashed it to the floor. Drawing his Browning pistol and pointing it toward the ceiling, Hitler walked in the direction of the banquet room.

Immediately behind him was his bodyguard, Ulrich Graf, or "Red," a forty-five-year-old butcher and former amateur boxer who sported a bushy handlebar mustache. Several other men followed. "Watch out so that we don't get shot in the back," Hitler said to Graf.

At the podium, the speaker, Gustav von Kahr, looking up from his stack of papers, saw "a kind of narrow path" cutting its way through the crowd. He first thought it was Communist hecklers, as did General von Lossow, who was seated with several military officers near the steps to the stage.

The shouting sounded like an argument that was quickly escalating. "Halt!" "Get back!" "What do you want?" Patrons stood on the round wooden tables and chairs hoping to discover the cause of the commotion. Karl Alexander von Müller, professor of history at Munich University, saw a sea of steel helmets in the smoke-filled room. He could also make out the blood-red swastika bands on their arms.

Kahr stood frozen. The men, carrying an array of firearms, pushed their way forward, knocking over chairs and tables, sending plates of food and steins of beer to the floor. For the shocked audience, it looked like they were about to witness an assassination.

At this point, the occasional scream gave way to confusion and panic. The Storm Troopers had assembled the heavy machine gun in the vestibule, its barrel aimed at the crowd.

When he reached the front, about five or six steps from the platform, Hitler stood on a chair and shouted something, probably demanding silence, though his voice was lost in the tumult. A pistol was fired into the ceiling. Several eyewitnesses near the stage said the shot came from one of Hitler's associates, perhaps his bodyguard. The crowd was still not silenced, so Hitler raised the Browning into the air and pulled the trigger, sending a second shot into the ceiling.

Hopping down from the chair, he scrambled across a table toward the stage. A policeman, Maj. Franz Hunglinger, blocked his way. Hitler lowered the pistol to the officer's forehead and ordered him to step aside. Col. Hans Ritter von Seisser, the head of the state police, motioned for the officer to obey.

"The national revolution has broken out!" Hitler screamed from the front of the banquet room. Six hundred armed men have surrounded the beer hall, and no one is to leave. The governments in Bavaria and Berlin have been overthrown, he shouted in a shrill, rasping voice, and the army barracks and police headquarters have been occupied. All of this was, of course, a bluff, but he hoped that it would be true soon enough. He was sweating considerably. He looked crazy, drunk, or both.

He turned to three of Bavaria's most powerful men, all in the front: Gustav von Kahr, General von Lossow, and Colonel von Seisser. Hitler wanted them to join him in a small side room that Rudolf Hess had booked earlier that day. It would take only ten minutes, he said.

The leaders hesitated but then complied, slowly exiting the banquet hall.

2.

STARVING TRILLIONAIRES

It was quite a thrill to raise a trillion.
—ROBERT MURPHY, US VICE CONSUL TO MUNICH,
PLAYING POKER IN THE AUTUMN OF 1923

Nestled at the foot of the Alps, Munich was an opulent, baroque, and neoclassical gem teeming with cafés, cabarets, beer gardens, art galleries, and opera houses. Its population had soared over the last century, rising from a provincial marketplace of 34,000 people to a royal metropolis of about 600,000. The king of Bavaria, Ludwig I, and his successors of the Wittelsbach dynasty, had enriched the city with lavish cultural patronage that earned Munich the sobriquet "Athens on the Isar."

In 1871, when Prussian chancellor Otto von Bismarck united Germany into a single state for the first time in its history, Munich had been brought virtually kicking and screaming into the federation. Prussia dominated the new country—its territory alone surpassed the other twenty-four states *put together.* Munich suddenly found itself on the periphery. No longer the capital of a sovereign state, it had become a distant third to the larger, richer, and more influential northern cities of Berlin and Hamburg.

As if to compensate for this loss of status, Munich reveled in its uniqueness as a city of art and beer, warmth and hospitality. By the turn of the century, Munich had drifted further away from the capital. Broad social and cultural differences separated the more traditional, agricultural, and easygoing Catholic south from the militaristic, industrial, and brash Protestant north. One of the worst insults in Munich was to call someone a "Prussian pig."

The First World War had strained this already tense relationship to a breaking point. Like many places in Germany, Munich had at first welcomed the war with enthusiasm, expecting the struggle to be both victorious and short. Instead, the war had dragged on and brought a host of hardships: scarcities, rationing, the black-market economy, and the proliferation of ersatz commodities that made its coffee taste like turnips and beer like dishwater. The British blockade had exacerbated all the difficulties. Some three-fourths of a million people around the country died from malnutrition.

The capital, in addition to creating unrealistic expectations, had overextended the federal bureaucracy in the management of the war effort. In the process, it had become an easy target for the hungry and discontented. In fact, for many people in Munich, Berlin had begun to appear as more of an enemy than the Allied Powers. It was the Prussian government that both launched and lost the war. News of German victories on the battlefield, moreover, had been so amplified—and defeats so heavily censored—that the surrender came as a genuine shock.

The country paid a terrible price in the 1,560 days of war, suffering around 2 million deaths, and almost 5 million casualties. By the fall of 1918, the war was costing the country 136 million marks a day. The government, which had financed the war by borrowing, was deep in debt. Interest payments alone exceeded the entire prewar federal budget. The economy was in shambles, infrastructure in tatters, and trust in authorities shattered.

Then, after all the bloodshed and sacrifice, the Berlin government dared to sign the Treaty of Versailles. At the stroke of a pen, Germany would be stripped of 10 percent of its population, 13 percent of its territory, all of its overseas colonies, and virtually its entire military except for a token 100,000 men. The country was to have no airplanes, submarines, tanks, heavy artillery, or ships larger than 10,000 tons either.

Article 231 declared Germany alone responsible for the war and saddled it with a reparations bill that would eventually surpass $33 billion. For many Germans, it was a "peace of shame" and an unparalleled national humiliation.

The monarchy and Great Power status were gone. Germany was no longer the continent's richest and most powerful state. The victorious Entente prattled on about the principle of national self-determination, but then, when it redrew the map of Europe, handed over German-speaking populations to France, Belgium, Italy, Denmark, the re-created kingdom of Poland, and the new state of Czechoslovakia. A wide gulf indeed seemed to separate the victors' lofty ideals and their actions, which were loudly criticized as hypocritical and unjust.

To the horror of monarchists and militarists alike, Germany was now a republic for the first time in its history. Worse for them, it was ruled by the country's first Socialist leadership, as the Social Democratic Party had recently come to prominence in Berlin and several industrial cities in the north and west. The Socialist leaders of the young republic had been ushered into power in time to sign the armistice, allowing the German military to avoid the stigma of defeat and, at the same time, providing Munich another reason to despise the politicians of Berlin.

BY THE AUTUMN of 1923, postwar disillusionment was extreme. After five years of turmoil, the country teetered on the verge of anarchy. Rival political factions clashed in a veritable civil war. Law and order seemed to have disintegrated, or withered away. Communists were rising in Saxony, Thuringia, and in the port of Hamburg. There were separatist movements afoot in Bavaria and the Rhineland.

Munich's far right hoped to restore the monarchy and military greatness. The radical left wing, inspired by Lenin and the Bolsheviks in Russia, wanted to launch a revolution. Mainstream parties, caught in the ever-shrinking middle, worked to buttress the shaky republic. The bulk of the population, alienated and embittered, drifted further to the extremes. Germany was becoming, as Social Democrat Paul Löbe warned, a "democracy without democrats."

In Bavaria, the problem was compounded by the loss of many privileges the state had enjoyed under the kaiser. The Weimar Republic had, at a stroke, removed Bavaria's control of its railway system, postal service, and tax collection. The once-proud kingdom, many of its citizens felt, had lost its way.

All this uncertainty about the future was reflected in the instability of the currency. War expenditure and its financing by loans had caused the German mark, which stood at 4.2 to 1 US dollar on the eve of the war, to fall to more than 8 marks to a dollar in December 1918. This was only the beginning. In January 1923, when Germany fell behind its reparations payments, the mark had plummeted to almost 18,000 to a dollar. France at once accused Germany of being in default and invaded the Ruhr, home of eight-tenths of Germany's remaining coal, iron, and steel. German workers fought back with a state-sponsored program of "passive resistance" that centered on a general strike. To support them, Berlin started printing even more money.

Almost two thousand printing presses were soon churning out currency day and night. The German mark now spiraled out of control. In July, it traded at an exchange rate of 350,000 and then 1 million on the first day of August. A week later, the mark had dropped to more than 4.5 million, soon passing into millions, billions, and hundreds of billions, ultimately hitting rock bottom in December 1923 at 6.7 trillion marks to a single dollar. Germany had succumbed to one of the most devastating cases of hyperinflation ever experienced in a modern industrial economy.

Two weeks before Hitler stormed the beer hall, a loaf of bread cost a staggering 1.8 billion marks; now it was 32 billion and rising. The price of a single egg would soon be the equivalent of approximately 1,000,000,000,000 eggs before the war. In the nightmare of hyperinflation, the life savings of the middle class had been wiped out. Years of thrift had been in vain.

In this monetary apocalypse, big business exploited its workers, paying them a pittance that deteriorated in value by the minute. Wheelbarrows of marks would not suffice for basic subsistence. Foreigners with hard currency, meanwhile, snapped up real estate, or family heirlooms, for obscene bargains. Germany had become a nation of starving trillionaires. The German republic, by debasing its currency into worthless scraps of paper, had robbed its people of its wealth, and had become, Hitler said, the "biggest swindler and crook [of all]!"

For many nationalists, Italy's Fascist leader Benito Mussolini served as a model for solving the German crisis. In October 1922, he had marched on Rome and seized power, or at least that was how the legend came to enshroud the operation. In reality, Mussolini's small force of poorly armed and -equipped supporters, perhaps 20,000 strong, had ground to a halt outside the city, where the Italian Army could easily have crushed them. The king, Victor Emmanuel III, had simply appointed Mussolini as prime minister. Still, a myth had emerged that would long inspire right-wing extremists to look to an energetic and dynamic brand of leadership to solve national problems.

"If a German Mussolini is given to Germany," Hitler said to a journalist for London's *Daily Mail* on the eve of the putsch, "people would fall down on their knees and worship him more than Mussolini has ever been worshipped." This journalist was unimpressed. In private, he dismissed Hitler as another "hot-air merchant." But Hitler had in fact decided to follow in the fascist footsteps and march on Berlin.

Such a move, several advisers urged, was necessary. Hitler had spoken of revolution for so long—and criticized rival leaders for empty posturing so loudly—that failure to deliver could be disastrous for him and the party. As the leader of the Munich Storm Troopers, Wilhelm Brückner, said, the day was coming when he would no longer be able to restrain his men. Hitler, characteristically, reduced his options to an either-or scenario: Act or lose face to someone who would.

The original plan had been to strike on Saturday night, November 10. This was, after all, the weekend, which Hitler believed was the best time for a revolution. Authorities would be away from their desks, police would be reduced to a minimal staff, and the lighter traffic would not impede the movement of his trucks and troops. More symbolically, the following morning, when they expected to achieve success, would mark the fifth anniversary of the hated armistice that ended the First World War.

By November 7, however, Hitler had changed his mind. He had received word of Gustav von Kahr's rally the following night at the

Bürgerbräu, and he feared that this event might prefigure a major announcement, possibly the unveiling of Kahr's own plans to march on Berlin or even declare Bavarian independence. But even if the speech produced no major result, which was more likely, Hitler predicted, all the prominent leaders of the Bavarian regime would be together at the beer hall at the same time—and easy pickings for his bold plan to persuade them to join him in the march north.

In any event, Hitler decided that, given the unprecedented chaos, he could not wait and risk being upstaged, or outmaneuvered. Such an opportunity might not appear again. He ordered the attack to commence within twenty-four hours.

3.

FOUR BULLETS

The National Socialist Storm Troopers were, for example, not a gentleman's club.

—LT. COL. HERMANN KRIEBEL

As the armed men escorted the three Bavarian leaders out of the banquet hall, stepping over the machine gun in the vestibule, Göring's Storm Troopers were busy rounding up the Munich police, nicknamed the "blue police" for the color of their uniform. There were some 1,500 members on the squad, but only a small force of about 40 men had been on duty that night. Göring's men had no trouble capturing the vast majority of the policemen on the premises.

At a front table near the guests of honor, a lean young man in an old Bavarian military uniform stood on a chair. This was Rudolf Hess, a twenty-nine-year-old student at Munich University. He pulled out a sheet of paper that Hitler had earlier handed him and began to read.

It was a list of names that included Bavaria's prime minister, Eugen Ritter von Knilling; three members of his cabinet; and the president of the police, Karl Mantel. Hess asked all of these people to step forward. Each one was to be arrested. Why the hostages would be held was not communicated.

Hess took charge of the prisoners. Quiet, shy, and introspective, Hess often struck people as aloof, if not morose, rarely smiling or even looking anyone in the eyes. Like many other prominent early members of the party, Hess had been born outside Germany, in his case, Alexandria, Egypt, where his father owned a wholesale export business. He had lived abroad until age twelve, when he was packed off for boarding school at Bad Godesberg on the Rhine.

During the war, Hess served in a Bavarian unit (though not Hitler's regiment, as widely claimed), and then had become a pilot. The two men met only in 1920; Hess had been elated by one of Hitler's speeches. Since joining the party on July 1 of that same year as member 1,600, Hess was active on its emerging "intelligence division" and eventually received command of a Storm Trooper battalion. Otherwise, Hess continued to study geopolitics, write poetry, enjoy classical music, pursue his interests in astrology, and above all, draw closer to Hitler.

Hess had been staying at his family estate in Fichtelgebirge when Hitler summoned him. He hurried back to Munich, having been instructed earlier that morning to capture the Bavarian prime minister and several cabinet members. "An honorable and important assignment," Hess said.

He escorted the seven new captives up a narrow staircase to a room on the second floor of the beer hall near the residence of its manager, Korbinian Reindl. Three Storm Troopers, armed with rifles and hand grenades, joined them, while two other men stood sentry in the corridor. Hess waited for further orders.

Downstairs, meanwhile, the bodyguard Ulrich Graf handed Hitler another stein of beer and then double-checked his loaded Mauser pistol.

"No one leaves this room alive without my permission," Hitler shouted to the Bavarian leaders in the side room. Sweating and waving his pistol in between sips of his beer, which helped clear his dry throat, a legacy of a poison-gas attack he had suffered at the end of the First World War, Hitler addressed these men as if he were rallying a mass audience.

There would be a new German government, Hitler said, adding that he would lead it himself. General Ludendorff would take charge of the army and Hitler offered a place in the regime to each of the three Bavarian leaders.

"I know that this is difficult for you gentlemen," Hitler said, "but the step must be taken." He tried to rationalize his move that night as making it easier for the leaders to assume their roles. "I have four bullets in my pistol," Hitler then said, "three for my collaborators, if they desert me, and the fourth one for me." Tomorrow morning, Hitler repeated, placing the pistol at his temple, would see either success or death.

Colonel von Seisser reminded Hitler of a promise he had made earlier in the year not to make a putsch.

"Yes, I did," Hitler said, "but forgive me for the sake of the Fatherland." He gave no other explanation for breaking his word.

When Lossow turned to whisper something to his colleagues, Hitler forbade them from speaking with one another.

Was Ludendorff really involved in the plot? Lossow asked, no doubt wondering why he was absent.

He had already been contacted, Hitler said, and would soon arrive.

Kahr reminded everyone of his difficulties in joining the new government, given that he and his Bavarian colleagues had been, as he put it, "taken out of the auditorium under heavy guard" and the people would lack confidence in them. He hadn't even been allowed to finish his speech.

Hitler looked indecisive and insecure. Then, all of a sudden, he darted out of the room as if an idea had just struck him.

No one said a word. Kahr stood by the window, deep in thought. Lossow, now leaning against the side of a table, smoked a cigar. Seisser was near the door. Kahr broke the silence: "How incredible that they would spirit me away like this. . . . You can't just hold up someone like a bandit!"

AT HIS TABLE near the front of the banquet hall, Munich University history professor Müller was talking with friends. Someone asked if Hitler really thought he could succeed by riding roughshod over everyone. Another person noted that Kahr now had the heaven-sent opportunity he had long desired; that is, he could join a conspiracy to create a new nationalist government without having to take responsibility for planning or leading it.

"There must be some disagreement," Müller said. "Didn't Hitler say it would all be settled in ten minutes, and then they'd be back?"

The crowd was getting restless.

"That's German loyalty?" someone shouted. "That's German unity?"

"South America!" one cried.

"Theatre!" yelled another.

Others whistled and booed, or even mocked Hitler's appearance. With his ill-cut black frock coat, he drew comparisons to a headwaiter, a concierge at a small hotel, a tax collector in his finest clothes, and a nervous provincial bridegroom on his wedding day.

Hermann Göring mounted the stage, pistol in hand, to calm the volatile audience. Hitler had "the friendliest intentions," he shouted over the din. Göring too would have to fire a shot into the air to gain the crowd's attention. He tried to assure the audience that Hitler's move was "in no way against Kahr," or the army or the police. It was aimed instead at "the Berlin government of Jews." This elicited a round of applause.

The people simply had to be patient. A new Germany was being born. Besides, Göring said, his booming voice carrying throughout the hall, "You've got your beer. What are you worrying about?"

Despite Göring's clumsy attempt to calm the crowd, many people in the banquet room did worry about the safety of the Bavarian leaders, and their own. The Storm Troopers had seized control of the building, lining the walls and covering the exits, all of them, heavily armed and their faces, as General von Lossow later put it, "distorted with ecstasy." Professor Müller, for one, feared that the Storm Troopers would also keep everyone locked up all night. Worse still was the risk that someone in the overcrowded beer hall would make a stupid or reckless act, causing a panic and, ultimately, a bloodbath.

4.

GERMAN ULYSSES

This is more than just a lost war. A world has come to an end.
—WALTER GROPIUS

As Hitler left the side room, he turned to a small, bald man wearing a pince-nez and told him that it was time to fetch Ludendorff. This man, First Lt. Dr. Max Erwin von Scheubner-Richter, was one of the many shadowy figures who flocked to the fledgling National Socialist Party.

An engineer by trade, with a specialty in chemistry, Scheubner-Richter was a thirty-nine-year-old German Balt from Riga with many social connections. He had come to Munich in 1910, bringing his newlywed aristocratic wife, Mathilde von Scheubner, nearly thirty years older. They had met during the uprising of 1905 when his cavalry unit was posted to guard her father's estate. He legally took his wife's name, becoming Scheubner-Richter (his family name was Richter).

During the war, Scheubner-Richter had volunteered for a Bavarian light cavalry regiment, and then, in December 1914, joined the German consulate in Erzurum, Turkey. He was soon promoted to vice consul, and in this capacity he would witness the genocide of the Armenian people. His diplomatic cables back to Berlin described in horrifying detail how the Ottoman regime scapegoated its Armenian minority in the aftermath of its military defeats at the hands of the Russians.

Entire villages were emptied and plundered; the women and children marched away in caravans for "resettlement" only to face hunger, disease, and massacre, their bodies strewn along the roadside, burnt and butchered with bayonets. His dispatches, along with his official protests at this slaughter, remain one of the valuable early eyewitness accounts of this humanitarian tragedy that killed anywhere from 300,000 to 1.5 million Armenians.

Paradoxically, Scheubner-Richter's outrage at this persecution and genocide of a minority coexisted with a rabid anti-Semitism that only became more prominent over time. Transferred to the Baltic, where he served as press officer for the German 8th Army, Scheubner-Richter deplored the effects of the Russian Revolution. Bolshevism, he argued, was nothing more than terror, plunder, slavery, and starvation that aimed to exterminate the middle and upper classes and annihilate Western civilization. It was also, he claimed, a Jewish-led conspiracy.

In October 1920, Scheubner-Richter created an elite secret society, the *Aufbau*, or Reconstruction, to build an alliance between German and Russian nationalists. The goal was to fight "international Jewry," overthrow the supposed Jewish regimes in Russia and the Weimar Republic, and, ultimately, restore the monarchy in *both* Moscow and Berlin.

It was in this right-wing conspiratorial atmosphere that Scheubner-Richter first came in contact with Munich's National Socialist Party, which was not yet widely known by the shortened nickname of Nazis. The organization, only four years old, was originally one of about forty similar right-wing extremist groups emerging in the chaos of postwar Munich. Like many of its nationalistic rivals, the young party was known at the time more for what it opposed than what it advocated: It was anti-republic, anti-parliament, anti-Communist, and anti-Semitic.

Yet at the same time the party had some considerable strengths on a tactical and organizational level. It boasted a political office with a strong focus on propaganda. Its paramilitary wing, the Storm Troopers, was being militarized, making them one of Munich's first political parties to have a veritable private army. They aggressively recruited youth, which brought dynamism and zeal. By one modern estimate, two-thirds of its membership in November 1923 were under the age of thirty-one. And of course there was the party's main attraction: a speaker who could fill the beer halls and whip the throngs into a frenzy.

Scheubner-Richter had gone to hear Hitler speak for the first time on November 22, 1920, on a tip from a fellow Balt, Alfred Rosenberg, whom he had known back in Riga, where they had belonged to the same fraternity. Scheubner-Richter had joined the Nazi Party shortly thereafter and, like Rosenberg, became a fixture on the scene. They gave the impression of a powerful clique, or "Baltic Mafia" within the echelons of the party.

For the next three years, Scheubner-Richter rendered many services to Hitler. He cultivated Munich's sizable right-wing Russian and Ukrainian émigré community, many of whom were old tsarist noblemen who had fled the revolution and civil war. He stirred up anti-Bolshevism, and solicited donations from his contacts among conservative industrialists and landlords who feared the rise of left-wing parties. He also took advantage of his royal connections, including no less than Bavaria's crown prince, Rupprecht, and Russia's Grand Prince Kirill. Hitler acknowledged Scheubner-Richter's contributions: "All the others are replaceable," he later said, "but not him."

Indeed, Scheubner-Richter had been one of the many people encouraging Hitler to launch the beer hall putsch. Drawing upon the lessons of the Bolshevik Revolution, he noted how Lenin and a small, determined minority could, by a daring act, change the course of history. Mussolini had done the same in Italy and Mustafa Kemal (later given the surname Atatürk) had in Turkey as well. The right-wing conspirators in Munich could not fail either, he argued. The corrupt regime of Berlin was tottering. It was time to sweep it away.

At Hitler's command, Scheubner-Richter pressed through the Bürgerbräu lobby now swarming with Storm Troopers. Three men joined him at his side: his butler, Johann Aigner; Ludendorff's valet, Kurt Neubauer; and Ludendorff's own stepson, a young veteran and pilot in the war named Heinz Pernet.

Outside, they passed a line of trucks, barricading the front entrance of the beer hall, to prevent possible police reinforcements. A trolley car in the distance rang its bell incessantly for the vehicles to move out of the way.

Waved through by a Storm Trooper, the men headed off on the fourteen-mile drive to pick up the general whose support was critical to the success of the plan.

THAT NIGHT, GEN. Erich Friedrich Wilhelm Ludendorff was at home in his upstairs study. He had been pacing up and down the room, rather than sitting at his writing desk, as was his habit in the evening. Shortly after eight thirty, the telephone rang and a voice on the line announced that his presence was "urgently desired" at the Bürgerbräu.

When he asked what was happening, Ludendorff later said, he was only told that he would soon be informed. He claimed that he had not recognized the caller, nor, for that matter, known of Hitler's intentions in advance. (The caller had been Scheubner-Richter.)

Fifty-eight years old, General Ludendorff was struggling to adjust to his life as a civilian. He had been a soldier or a cadet since the age of twelve, when he entered a military academy in Holstein. Born in Kruszewnia in the West Prussian province of Posen in today's Poland, Ludendorff was the son of an impoverished merchant—not a nobleman—despite the many incorrect references to him, then and later, as "von Ludendorff." As a commoner, Ludendorff was unable to enter the prestigious cavalry and joined instead the German Great General Staff, earning his red stripes in 1894.

Ludendorff had made his name in the first month of the First World War, pulling off an unexpected victory at the citadel of Liège. He won bigger still at Tannenberg on the eastern front, encircling a larger Russian army and seizing more than 90,000 prisoners. Ludendorff and his superior, Gen. Paul von Hindenburg, would later knock Russia out of the war altogether, thereby consolidating Ludendorff's reputation as a grand strategist.

H. L. Mencken, then a foreign correspondent in Germany, described Ludendorff as a man of intelligence worth "ten Kaisers." He elaborated on his impressions of the general during the summer of 1917 in a piece for the *Atlantic Monthly*:

> Once his mind is made up, he gets to business at once . . . He has imagination. He grasps inner significances. He can see around corners. Moreover, he enjoys planning, plotting, figuring things out. Yet more, he is free of romance. Have you ever heard of him sobbing about the Fatherland? Or letting off pious platitudes, like Hindenburg? Of course you haven't. He plays the game for its own sake—and he plays it damnably well.

Ludendorff was hailed, Mencken said, as "the esoteric Ulysses of the war."

To many people who encountered him at headquarters, however, Ludendorff appeared arrogant, cold, and aloof, and incapable of compromising or admitting a mistake. He could not bear being contradicted either. He would scowl at subordinates, a category in which he seemed to include almost everyone, especially civilians, and he wore his monocle so frequently that he was rumored to sleep with it. His trademark lack of humor had become its own source of amusement.

Ludendorff had not always been so ambitious and harsh, his wife, Margarethe, said. She remembered a time when he had been "cheerful and free from anxiety," his facial expression not yet frozen into "that look of unbending obstinacy." It was the experience of war, she thought—and probably also the immense fame that it brought—that had hardened him into an overbearing and feared man, whose feelings "had been turned to ice."

But as the German Army collapsed on the western front and critics of his bold offensives gained influence, Ludendorff had suffered his own near mental breakdown. Unable to sleep, he flew into rages at the least provocation and succumbed to crying fits without consolation. Ludendorff's reliance on alcohol deepened and he indulged in fantasies, imagining the Spanish flu then hitting the trenches would decimate the enemy, paving the way for a miraculous German triumph.

In October 1918, Ludendorff found himself dismissed from the army.

"The Kaiser has sacked me," he told his wife, dumbfounded at the turn of events. His dismissal, coupled with the German defeat the following month, had been, he said, "the bitterest moments of my life." The former commander now fled in disguise, with false beard, dark glasses, and a fabricated passport, to Denmark and then to Sweden, where he stayed in a country estate at Hässleholm.

"No human fate has been as hard as mine," Ludendorff later wrote, comparing himself to the ancient Carthaginian general Hannibal, who after the wars with Rome went into exile and took poison. He had nothing to look forward to, Ludendorff said, feeling at war with himself and the world. He spent his days taking long walks in the woods and brooding over his wartime experiences for a series of memoirs that he later wrote.

In February 1919, Ludendorff returned to Germany, regretful that he had not acted more decisively at the end of the war, and, as he put it, "snatched the dictatorship for [himself]." One year later, after he joined a poorly planned attempt to install a right-wing military regime in Berlin, the so-called Kapp Putsch, Ludendorff was forced again to admit defeat. He boarded a train for Munich in the summer of 1920, richer, he said, for the lessons he learned from the experience. Ludendorff was welcomed with open arms in Kahr's Bavaria.

Ludendorff had become obsessed with the idea that Germany had not lost the war—certainly not because his own reckless gambles on the western front had exhausted its manpower and resources, and certainly not, either, because his insistence on unrestricted submarine warfare helped bring the United States into the struggle. Instead, his country had been "stabbed in the back." Left-wing politicians had cowardly sold out the country, surrendering first on the battlefield and then a second time when they signed the Versailles Treaty. Germany, as a result, lay weakened and exposed, while foreigners waited, like vultures, to pick at its carcass.

The general saw the same sinister forces of treason and cowardice at work again in the postwar world, undermining his country's moral fiber. He blamed the decline and fall of Germany, above all, on the Jews, the Bolsheviks, and the Catholics, all of whom he equated with unwelcome foreign influences. He joined Scheubner-Richter's secret society *Aufbau*, and, in March 1921, met Adolf Hitler for the first time. It was Scheubner-Richter who introduced them.

Hitler was soon praising Ludendorff in public as "Germany's greatest commander." He spoke of how Ludendorff's recent book, *War Leadership and Politics*, helped him understand many important facts about the modern world, not least how the Jewish international conspiracy had been exerting powerful influence in France and England, if not also controlling the Allied governments. Ludendorff, in turn, admired Hitler for his "driving determination" and called him the only political leader left with any common sense.

By the summer of 1923, Ludendorff had turned his villa outside Munich into a veritable Nazi party headquarters—his wife compared the activities to "the continual coming and going in a pigeon loft." The general had covered up his conspiratorial endeavors well, she added. He went out to his garden, and, like an old pensioner, pruned roses, watered flowers, and cared for the lawn, seemingly aloof from the swirl of intrigue plotted around him.

When the delegation from the beer hall reached the exclusive neighborhood of Sollen-Ludwigshöhe, their car turned onto Heilmannstrasse and pulled up to the estate at Number 5. The driver blew the horn. Scheubner-Richter hopped out of the backseat and went inside with Heinz Pernet. Ludendorff greeted them in a brown tweed hunting jacket. To save time, he said, he decided not to change into uniform.

They were indeed in a hurry, but there was almost certainly another motive for the general's unaccustomed lack of formality. If the conspiracy failed, Ludendorff the civilian would plead ignorance of any plots against the state.

After a brief talk in the book-lined study adorned with a wartime painting of the general peering over maps with Hindenburg, Ludendorff slipped on his overcoat, grabbed his green fedora, and climbed into the car. They raced off in the foggy night, as Ludendorff put it, at a "whirling speed." Snow had begun to fall.

5.

"LOUD, RAW, AND SCREECHING"

*I have often had to make quick decisions in difficult situations,
and I did so here too.*

—GEN. ERICH LUDENDORFF

hen Hitler returned to the banquet room—late, alone, and without the triumvirate as he had promised—he found an increasingly restless audience that threatened to turn on him. There were a few jeers and catcalls. Hitler demanded silence, reminding the crowd of the machine gun in the vestibule.

Hitler then reassured the audience, as Göring had tried to do, that the national revolution was not aimed at Kahr's Bavarian regime, the police, or the army; it was only against the Berlin government of "the November criminals." After announcing his new cabinet, dropping the name of the still-absent General Ludendorff as the commander-in-chief of his proposed army, Hitler promised that they were ready to "begin the advance against Berlin, that Babylon of wickedness."

Where did the crowd stand?

The loud cheers left no doubt, noted an off-duty police officer sitting at a table in the middle of the hall. He also heard cries of "Heil Hitler!"

Hitler then asked the men and women in the beer hall to send a message to the Bavarian leaders Kahr, Lossow, and Seisser, who, at that moment were, he claimed, "struggling hard to reach a decision." He was careful not to reveal just how much the leaders had resisted. "May I say to them that you will stand behind them?"

The speech was unoriginal—and the orator "loud, raw, and screeching," noted a reporter from the Swiss newspaper *Neue Zürcher Zeitung*, but the crowd roared its assent. Professor Müller deemed this speech a masterpiece. He had never seen such a drastic change sweep an audience. In fact, it seemed to him almost magical, spellbinding. Hitler had completely changed their mood, "[turning] them inside out like a glove," or, as Hanfstaengl put it, played them like a master on a Stradivarius.

THE THUNDERING APPROVAL reverberated back into the side room. His mission accomplished, Hitler returned to the captive leaders. "Did you hear that ovation out in the hall?" he asked.

Outside in the beer garden, a young Hitler supporter named Max, or "Marc" Sesselmann was talking to one of his friends who stood guard. When he stepped into the light of the inside room to admire the man's gun, Sesselmann happened to look through the window. To his surprise, he had a view of the back room where these negotiations were taking place. Kahr was then sitting at a round table with his head in his hands and staring out in the distance. Sesselmann thought he looked terrified.

The impasse dragged on, with the men in the back room unable to reach an agreement and the people in the banquet hall growing restless. Suddenly, there was another round of cheers and shouts, along with salutes and the clicking of boots. Someone shouted the military order, "Attention!"

General Ludendorff had arrived at the Bürgerbräu. A colleague in the audience, Maj. Gen. Karl August Ritter von Kleinhenz, thought he looked graver than at any time he had ever seen him before. Hitler greeted Ludendorff at the door of the side room.

"Gentlemen, I am just as surprised as you are," the general said, addressing the Bavarian leaders without even bothering to look over at Hitler. It was a show of disdain that did not go unnoticed.

Why did Ludendorff appear grumpier than usual?

He may have disapproved of Hitler's move and considered it premature. He might also have been upset that Kahr, Lossow, and Seisser had been forced out of the banquet hall at gunpoint. Or he may have been disappointed that he, a decorated general, would be taking orders from a private first class. On the other hand, it could all have been a pretense to cover up his own involvement in the operation.

Ludendorff never admitted any involvement in the planning stages of the putsch, but many years later, his son-in-law Heinz Pernet, who rode with him to the Bürgerbräu, confirmed that he had not been left in the dark. At any rate, however much he knew in advance, Ludendorff now unquestionably joined Hitler. He spoke of a "great national *völkisch* movement" beginning that night and he asked the triumvirate, as he put it, "to cooperate with *us*." He reached out his hand to the leaders.

Lossow was the first to side with the general; he grasped his saber and gave his assent in a low voice, almost a whisper. Seisser, looking like he had been waiting for someone else to make the first move, also offered his hand. Kahr, however, remained aloof. He felt "personally wounded" by Hitler's gruff manner. Ludendorff tried to persuade him to relent, adding that Kahr could not "forsake the German people in this hour."

This putsch either would not work, Kahr objected, or it would not last. If only Hitler had had the patience to wait another week or two, the prospects would have looked much brighter.

At this point, the men in the side room were joined by Ernst Pöhner, a justice of the Bavarian court and a former police chief who had been sitting at a reserved table in the banquet hall with his former colleagues from the department. Pöhner had been an important supporter of the Nazi Party during its early growth. It was in his capacity as president of the police that he had been asked if he realized that murderous right-wing thugs stalked Bavaria and he gave his notorious reply: "Yes, yes, but far too few of them!"

Pöhner had been summoned to the side room because he knew Kahr better than anyone else close to Hitler. Pöhner and Kahr had worked together since March 1920, when Kahr had come to power.

"I can't take part [in this putsch]," Kahr insisted, identifying himself as a monarchist who needed the king's permission before taking such a dramatic step. By this, Kahr meant the approval of Crown Prince Rupprecht, heir to the throne of the kingdom of Bavaria, which had been abolished at the end of the First World War.

"Your Excellency, that is precisely my point of view," said the lanky six-foot-two Pöhner, looming over Kahr. They had a duty, as faithful servants of the king, to act in the monarchy's best interests. Kahr looked "very distraught," Pöhner thought, and the men in the room succumbed to a "painful silence."

Hitler chimed in to say that he was acting to correct the wrongs inflicted on the crown by the criminals who overthrew the royal dynasty. Besides, Hitler added, could they really return to the banquet hall and announce that this was all "just a mistake [and] there will be no revolution tonight after all?"

After approximately forty to fifty minutes, Kahr relented. He accepted a position under Hitler on the condition that he would serve the new government as "a viceroy of the monarchy."

As voices of the old army and police, Ludendorff and Pöhner had been instrumental in forging whatever agreement had been struck in the back room. They also helped convince the cautious leaders of the state to return to the banquet hall and share the platform with members of the Nazi Party. "Put on an act," Lossow later claimed to have whispered to his colleagues.

While the men prepared to reenter the banquet room, filled to capacity with supporters and Storm Troopers alike, Kahr suddenly seemed to waver, overcome by second thoughts. Hitler turned to his reluctant ally and promised him applause from the hall unlike at anytime in his life. Kahr shrugged it aside. At any rate, Hitler told him, "There is no turning back now!"

6.

SPARKLING METROPOLIS

Previously, the beautiful, comfortable city attracted the best minds of the Reich. How could it be that they were now gone, and in their place, everything that was rotten and evil and could not make it elsewhere, fled as if magically drawn to Munich?

—LION FEUCHTWANGER, *Erfolg*

Ten years before, it would have been difficult to imagine Adolf Hitler meeting such a prominent figure as General Ludendorff, let alone the two men forging an alliance. Hitler had arrived in Munich for the first time on May 25, 1913, as a down-and-out twenty-four-year-old Austrian painter. He had carried all his belongings in a single black suitcase.

Answering a handwritten note attached to a window that offered "furnished rooms to rent to respectable men," Hitler walked up a dark staircase to the small, third-floor attic above the tailor shop at Schleissheimerstrasse 34. He was accompanied by a man he had met three months before when he lived in a men's home in Vienna: an unemployed twenty-year-old shop assistant named Rudolf Häusler.

The room, barely eight feet by sixteen feet, lay on the western edge of Munich's bohemian district of Schwabing. Artists, it seemed, were everywhere, lugging easels, paint boxes, rolled-up canvases, and portfolios. Already by the late nineteenth century, this district had boasted more painters and sculptors than Berlin and Vienna together.

Hitler wanted to be one of these artists. He went to work painting postcards and watercolors, mostly of Munich's monumental structures: the medieval Frauenkirche, with its three-hundred-foot spires; the massive beer hall, Hofbräuhaus on the Platzl; the Italianate Feldherrnhalle, or Hall of Field Marshals, on the Odeonsplatz. He would then peddle his wares in cafés and beer halls, and on and street corners around town. The word "kitsch" is believed to have been coined in Munich at this time to describe cheap keepsakes sold to tourists.

Unlike many artists in the quarter, Hitler did not usually work outdoors in the natural light. He preferred to paint at his easel in his room, by his window overlooking a school playground. He used postcards or pictures that the landlord's twelve-year-old son, Josef Popp Jr., or "Peppi" fetched for him as models, tipping him with coins or sweets. Hitler would call his first fifteen months in Munich "the happiest and by far the most contented" of his life.

He had liked Munich immediately. It was, as he later put it, "a German city," and stood in sharp contrast to Vienna, where he had lived for the last five years and despised as "a Babylon of races." Hitler's landlady, Anna Popp, however, remembered her new tenant not so much exploring the city as shutting himself up in his room like a recluse. When he did venture out, he would often bring back sausage or a pastry. Otherwise, he spent most of his time there painting and reading.

No one in the household ever recalled him receiving a visitor or any personal mail, other than an occasional letter from his younger sister, Paula, in Vienna. He did not seem to make any close friends either. A couple of people in the Schwabing neighborhood remembered Hitler, including a baker at a shop around the corner, who recalled mainly his sweet tooth, his polite manners, and his clean frock coat, which his tailor landlord regularly pressed for him.

There is no evidence that Hitler devoured the philosophical works of Plato, Karl Marx, or Arthur Schopenhauer at this time, as he later claimed. Peppi, however, recalled checking out library titles at the nearby

Bayerische Staatsbibliothek on his behalf, such as Clausewitz's *On War* and the *Illustrated German Naval Almanack*. Once the landlady asked her lodger how this reading would help his painting.

"Dear Frau Popp," she said he had answered, "does anyone know what is and what isn't likely to be of use to him in life?"

AT THE TIME of Hitler's arrival, Munich had indeed been enjoying a lively "golden age" of art and culture. It was here that Hitler's favorite composer, Richard Wagner, had written the operas *Tristan und Isolde*, *Die Meistersinger*, and *Das Rheingold*. It was here too that Gustav Mahler, driven out of Vienna because of anti-Semitism, had debuted his Eighth Symphony with a choir of 858 singers and an orchestra of 171 members.

Many other artists had come to Munich to soak up its atmosphere and enjoy its then relatively cheap rent. The Norwegian playwright Henrik Ibsen lived for a time at Schellingstrasse 30, down the street from future headquarters of the Nazi newspaper. It was in Munich that Ibsen shifted exclusively to prose writing, with contemporary themes and Norwegian settings, and crafted many of his pioneering plays of social realism, including *A Doll's House*, *Ghosts*, *The Wild Duck*, and *Hedda Gabler*. The American writer Mark Twain, likewise, lived briefly at Nymphenburgerstrasse 45, where he wrote *A Tramp Abroad* and completed his masterpiece, *The Adventures of Huckleberry Finn*.

Of course since Ibsen's departure in 1891, Munich artists had pioneered several other modernist aesthetic movements with an avant-garde flair. In music, Richard Strauss had ventured into atonal and dissonant pieces that dispensed with melody and harmony. In painting, Paul Klee and Wassily Kandinsky had experimented in the realm of the abstract, the latter in particular revolutionizing modern art with his quest for "pure painting" that transcended the painstaking, naturalistic representations that Hitler admired.

In many other ways, Munich was on the cutting edge of the modernist and avant-garde. Munich's "Blue Rider" Group, named after the celebrated Kandinsky painting, had launched the bold color schemes that illuminated German Expressionism, and a young group of breakaway architects and interior designers were turning the city into a center of Art Nouveau exuberance. Munich's secession movement had emerged well before its more high-profile counterparts in Vienna and Berlin.

Hitler's adopted city had been the first to host a solo exhibition of Pablo Picasso's paintings, and the first, no surprise, to stage the early plays of its own Bertolt Brecht. Munich, at this time, boasted more cabarets than Berlin or anywhere else in Europe east of Paris. In the back room of a Schwabing tavern on Türkenstrasse was the innovative and influential, if short-lived, cabaret known as the Eleven Executioners. Its performers—wearing crimson robes and hangman masks—assaulted conventional society, putting its morals and platitudes on the chopping block and indulging in judgment as sharp as the executioner's blade.

For more than half a century, Munich had been a cosmopolitan and tolerant bastion that had proved welcoming to foreigners, outsiders, and freethinkers alike. The anarchist playwright and poet Erich Mühsam described the people who flocked to the cafés and cabarets of Munich's bohemian quarter:

> Painters, sculptors, writers, models, loafers, philosophers, religious founders, revolutionaries, reformers, sexual moralists, psychoanalysts, musicians, architects, craftswomen, runaway girls of good family, eternal students, the industrious and the idle, those with a lust for life and those who were world-weary . . .

Just two blocks away, on the same street as Hitler, lived a carpenter who had rented a room to a Russian émigré. He called himself Herr Meyer, but his real name was Vladimir Ilyich Ulianov, and he had moved to Munich in 1901 where he assumed the name Lenin. For a year and a half, in between intellectual debate and games of chess often at the Schwabinger Café, Lenin had published revolutionary pamphlets *What Is to Be Done?* and the paper *The Spark*. Lenin's Munich work, which was smuggled back into tsarist Russia, would help him win many new recruits, including Joseph Stalin. It would entice Leon Trotsky to move there, which he did for six months in 1904.

Munich had been a progressive and, at the same time, a decadent city that set itself apart from the kaiser's stiff-laced, rule-bound Berlin. Just prior to Hitler's arrival, Munich resident Thomas Mann had published *Death in Venice*, a novella about middle-class decay that captured the fin-de-siècle ambience. At that time too an impoverished former Hamburg high school history teacher who had recently moved to Munich named Oswald Spengler had begun transferring the theme of dissolution-writ-large onto Western civilization, in his landmark treatise, *The Decline of the West*. In this work, Spengler tried to turn history into philosophy and even prophecy, predicting the imminent demise of the West and the rise of a new Caesar, whom the mobs would follow blindly.

BUT DECLINE TOO had eventually settled upon the sparkling metropolis. By the early 1920s, Munich was attracting fewer painters, writers, musicians, and artists than at any time over the previous half century. It was spawning instead a different crowd with a far more violent agenda. The city was to be the scene of a fierce clash between the modernist avant-garde and its militaristic, xenophobic rear-guard reaction—a battle for Munich that would leave a lasting impact on Germany and the world.

For years before the First World War, some artists had already moved away from a scene that seemed to rest on its laurels and, as several artists complained, force its creative spirits to conform to its own brand of non-conformity. The war had only accelerated this trend. Blue Rider painters Franz Marc and August Macke volunteered to fight, and both died on the western front. Kandinsky left for good in 1914. The pacifist piano player Hugo Ball moved with his wife, Emmy Hennings, to Zurich, where, in 1916, they founded the café Cabaret Voltaire and created the art protest movement known as Dada.

Writers and actors who remained in Munich struggled, as many publishing houses and theaters closed, or cut back on their productions. The lack of coal made it difficult to operate in the winter months, and the severity of war made residents reluctant to splurge on theatre or the latest novel. Worse still, the city's renowned cosmopolitan flair began to buckle under the rising xenophobia. Shakespeare, Molière, Racine, George

Bernard Shaw, and other artists from enemy countries would no longer be welcome on its stages.

On November 7, 1918, as the German war effort collapsed, Munich became the first German city to remove its rulers, ousting the Wittelsbach dynasty after more than 750 years. King Ludwig III had fled the palace by night, with one of the princesses wrapping the crown jewels in a hand-kerchief and the king lugging a box of cigars. The royal family had to hire a rental car, because their chauffeur had joined the revolution. Ludwig would eventually reach safety in Hungary, never to return to Munich.

Swept into power was an unlikely revolutionary, Kurt Eisner, a fifty-six-year-old theatre critic for the Socialist paper, *Münchener Post*. He had been delivering a speech to a crowd at the Theresienwiese, a large park where the city hosted the Oktoberfest celebrations, and not far from the statue of Bavaria, which had been the world's largest standing cast bronze sculpture until the Statue of Liberty. Eisner fired up the crowds to storm the military barracks, seize its weapons, and then occupy key locations around town, such as railway stations, newspapers, and the Mathäser beer hall. No one had resisted.

"Isn't it wonderful that we have made a revolution without shedding a drop of blood!" Eisner said.

Pale and scruffy with a long, salt-and-pepper beard, and wearing a tiny pince-nez and a dirty frock coat, Eisner looked, as one journalist put it, "like every philistine's idea of every bohemian." What's more, this idealistic man was not even from Munich or Bavaria. He was a Jew from Berlin.

Eisner's inaugural celebration that November set the tone for his planned "realm of light, beauty and reason." He had the Munich Phil-harmonic, conducted by Bruno Walter, play Beethoven's "Leonore Over-ture." A troupe of actors performed a scene from Goethe's *Epimendes Erwachen*; a chorus sang a section of Handel's *Messiah*; and the entire spectacle concluded with the audience joining Eisner in singing a poem he had composed himself called "Hymn to the Peoples." The former drama critic was indeed staging his own surreal theater production, but as Berlin's Socialist paper, *Vorwärts*, predicted, "The curtain will come down and it will be all over."

Despite the grand spectacle, the basic underlying economic and social problems remained unaddressed. Eisner's popularity plummeted. In the parliamentary elections in early 1919, his party won less than 3 percent of the vote. Then, on the morning of February 21, when Eisner was walking from his office in the Montgelas Palace to the parliament building, probably to resign, he passed a doorway where a twenty-two-year-old right-wing cavalry officer waited with a gun. This man, Count Anton Graf von Arco auf Valley, stepped out of the shadows and fired two shots, one hitting Eisner in the head and the other in the back. He died immediately.

Overnight, many of the people who had criticized Eisner mourned him as a martyr, and his supporters maneuvered to exploit the sudden popularity swing. The twenty-five-year-old anarchist poet Ernst Toller took charge, along with his friend the playwright Erich Mühsam and other regulars of Schwabing coffeehouses. Idealism ran rampant.

Once again, while many people lacked jobs, housing, and even food, the leaders of the regime called for the creation of new forms of art. Education was to be reformed by the Shakespearean scholar Gustav Landauer, who planned to abolish university tuition, exams, degrees, and titles, along with the study of history, which was denounced a threat to civilization. Primary education, by contrast, would be centered on the writings of Walt Whitman. "The world," the reformer proclaimed, "must become a meadow of flowers in which everyone can pick his share."

But this Bavarian Arcadia was not to be. After one week of power, these "coffeehouse anarchists," as they were dubbed, would be pushed aside by a more extreme group of revolutionaries: Bolsheviks, who scoffed at this bourgeois reform and instead demanded a real revolution. The new Red Army raided Munich banks, businesses, printing presses, and private homes, requisitioning money, food, clothing, jewelry, and other goods at will. It disarmed the police and population, handing the seized weapons to workers who swore an oath of loyalty to the regime.

The most controversial act of the revolution took place on April 30, 1919, when the Munich Red Army seized a number of Bavarian aristocrats and murdered them at the Luitpold Gymnasium, Albert

Einstein's former school. This act of violence, which was soon joined with sensational exaggerations that claimed the soldiers butchered the bodies and hacked off genitals, would long play a role in the propaganda of the far right.

By early May, four weeks into the Bolshevik rule, an army of right-wing freelance fighters hired by the German republic marched into Munich to restore order. This semiofficial volunteer force, known as the Freikorps, would be far more brutal than the revolutionaries had ever been, killing at least six hundred "Bolsheviks," real or imagined. Still, despite the bloodshed, the Freikorps were celebrated as liberators.

Munich's so-called Bolshevik regime, on the other hand, would be remembered by many people mainly for its "red terror" and its rumored Jewish leaders. Right-wing politicians would long exploit memories of this upheaval as an excuse to propagate virulent anti-Semitism and impose authoritarian rule. One of those leaders was Gustav von Kahr.

After seizing power in a coup of March 1920, Kahr had begun to turn Munich into a "cell of law and order." He welcomed right-wing extremists to settle in the region and many of them, in turn, joined the paramilitary societies emerging in the aftermath of the war and revolution. Kahr also organized many of these bands into a loose coalition called the *Einwohnerwehren*, or citizens' militia, that would soon surpass three hundred thousand men. Kahr would use this volunteer home guard in everything from law enforcement to border patrol. They were necessary, he said, like "a fire brigade."

Kahr had won clout in extremist circles for his support of the *Einwohnerwehren*. But France started to protest this "secret army"—and Berlin, under pressure from the Allies, demanded that Bavaria dismantle it. Kahr had pledged to stand or fall with this citizens' militia, but while the latter were disbanded, the politician had remained in power. This lasted until September 1921. Overwhelmed by unpopularity among his right-wing base, Kahr resigned.

Many former members of the *Einwohnerwehren* had then gone off to join new, more extreme and xenophobic paramilitary societies emerging in its ashes, such as the Nazi Storm Troopers.

As Germany sank deeper in crisis in the fall of 1923, the Bavarian government declared a state of emergency and appointed Kahr to the newly created position of general state commissioner, with broad executive powers that verged on the dictatorial. Kahr was going to be, as one contemporary put it, an umbrella to be used during the storm and then quietly put away.

But there was no clear consensus on how exactly Kahr was to steer Bavaria out of the catastrophe. Some supporters wanted him to use his new authoritarian powers to restore the Bavarian monarchy and declare independence. Others lobbied for the creation of a new, larger "Danubian monarchy" that joined with Austria and the southern German states of Baden and Württemberg. Still others preferred that Bavaria march on the capital of Berlin, remove its left-wing leaders, and impose a dictatorship to restore the country's greatness.

Within this cacophony of voices were some disgruntled Bavarians on the extremist fringe who had come to believe that Kahr was too reluctant to make any significant move at all, that is, without being forced to act.

7.

HARVARD'S GIFT

It's a far cry from Harvard to Hitler, but in my case the connection is direct.

—ERNST HANFSTAENGL

Watching the Storm Troopers shove the prime minister and the other dignitaries upstairs, Ernst Hanfstaengl feared that the hooligans might hurt the hostages, or, at the least, damage the image of the party in the eyes of the foreign correspondents. He decided to check in on them.

After stopping at the bar and plunking down his last billions of marks in his pocket on a round of beers, he climbed the steps to the small room. Each man accepted the brew, except for the minister of the interior, Franz Schweyer, who refused to share a drink with his captors. At least, Hanfstaengl thought, the men were not being harmed.

Ernst F. Sedgwick Hanfstaengl was one of the more singular men who had joined Hitler. A thirty-six-year-old cosmopolitan with a mop of thick black hair, Hanfstaengl was a six foot-four-inch tower nicknamed since his youth "Putzi," or "Little Fellow." On his father's side, he descended from three generations of privy councilors to the duke of Saxe-Coburg-Gotha. On his American mother's side were two Civil

War generals: John Sedgwick, whose statue stands at West Point, and William Heine, a pallbearer at Abraham Lincoln's funeral.

Putzi had lived for sixteen years in the United States, most recently as the manager of the New York branch of his family's art-printing and reproduction business. Thanks to his work at this shop, which he had moved to the corner of Fifth Avenue and Forty-Fifth Street, Putzi had gotten to meet many people, including Henry Ford, Charlie Chaplin, and J. Pierpont Morgan. Before that, as a student at Harvard, he had befriended T. S. Eliot and Theodore Roosevelt Jr., the eldest son of the president. Putzi, a talented piano player, liked to tell about the evening he got carried away carousing at a stag party in the basement of the White House and broke "seven bass strings [inside the] magnificent Steinway Grand."

In the summer of 1921, Putzi; his wife, the American-born Helen Niemeyer; and their infant son, Egon sailed to Europe on board the SS *Amerika*. Germany, they discovered, was "a madhouse," seething with political and economic intrigue. By the end of the following year, as he pursued his studies in history at Munich University, he had met Hitler at one of his beer hall speeches. Putzi had been awestruck, marveling at how Hitler showed complete mastery over the audience. That night, Putzi had been so excited that he could not sleep.

He had pledged a loan on the spot, promising a monthly allowance that the Nazi Party used to buy two rotary presses for its *Völkischer Beobachter*. At a time when many German newspapers were contracting or facing closure, Hitler's paper expanded to a daily publication for the first time in its existence. It also took on a larger format and boasted a new masthead, thanks to Putzi, who hired a cartoonist from the left-wing satirical magazine *Simplicissimus* to improve its design. He claimed credit for the paper's new motto reflecting its ambitions to appeal to the masses struggling in the economic turmoil: "Work and Bread."

For the last couple years, Hitler had been a regular guest at the Hanfstaengls' three-room apartment on Gentzstrasse in Munich's bohemian quarter of Schwabing, just north of the university. Hitler had come there so often that Putzi dubbed it Café Gentz. Hitler liked to indulge his notorious sweet tooth, dipping a piece of chocolate in his coffee or devouring pastries piled high with whipped cream. Putzi had helped introduce him to Munich's fashionable society, becoming, as one Nazi put it, "the upper crust" in Hitler's pot pie.

Although Putzi rejected the idea that he had taught Hitler manners, he was not without influence on his emerging new style. He weaned Hitler away from his black, broad-brimmed "gangster hat" and the clunky old army boots in which he stomped around in their drawing room. No matter how hard he tried, however, Putzi had no success convincing Hitler to ditch the toothbrush mustache—that "ridiculous little smudge," as he called it.

Now again, Putzi found himself trying to refine Hitler's rough edges, this time for the international press. He had his work cut out for him. The American foreign correspondent Hubert Renfro Knickerbocker, a twenty-five-year-old Texan, spoke for many of his colleagues when he summed up his first impression of Hitler: the distant stare, the little wisp of a mustache, the lock of hair dangling on his forehead, the way he stuck out his jaw in a pose calculated to show determination. "I broke out laughing!" Knickerbocker said.

Several of the foreign correspondents at the beer hall that night, including Knickerbocker, had come, thanks to Putzi. He had spent part of the late morning tracking down reporters in Munich's most elegant hotels and restaurants. At the Hungaria, Putzi had dined with the *Chicago Daily Tribune*'s Larry Rue, a rising star in the world of foreign correspondents—he used his aviation skills and his own plane to fly to the continent's hot spots. Over a fine meal of caviar, pheasant, and raspberries and cream, washed down with brandy and coffee, Putzi assured the reporter of a "journalistic delicacy" that night at the Bürgerbräu that would not disappoint.

CHIEF INSPECTOR PHILIPP KIEFER, the fifty-four-year-old head of Munich police's Criminal Division, watched the events unfold at the beer hall with increasing concern. He had been in the cloakroom at about eight thirty when he heard the tumult and then a gunshot. Turning toward the vestibule, he saw a long line of uniformed men with carbines or machine guns rushing into the building.

Many members of Kiefer's thirty-officer team, he soon learned, had quickly been apprehended by the Nazis. Other officers had put on swastika armbands to show support for Hitler's cause. One of them, Josef Gerum, had even been spotted helping the Storm Troopers erect the machine gun in the vestibule.

Hoping to muster reinforcements, Kiefer was brusquely ordered by one of Hitler's men not to leave or enter the building; no one would be allowed to do so. He then slinked away to look for the telephone in the kitchen, but alas, it was already in use. Unwilling to risk further delay, Kiefer decided that, given the chaos, he might be able to sneak out into the beer garden and then, once there, slip past the Storm Troopers unloading weapons from their trucks. This time, his plan worked. He found an unguarded exit in the kitchen and he was soon on the street.

At the 15th Precinct station, a few blocks south, Kiefer put in a call to headquarters. The line was busy. When he finally got through by calling the main duty room, Kiefer reported that armed men had occupied the Bürgerbräu and blocked off the surrounding area, trapping all the patrons and his patrolmen inside. As chief inspector, he was "completely powerless."

The officer on duty, Capt. Fritz Stumpf, said he would call back.

Kiefer waited.

After ten long minutes, the phone rang.

It was Dr. Wilhelm Frick, the head of Department VI, the office for political intelligence and security at the Munich police. After hearing the report from the beer hall, Frick was unambiguous in his instructions: "There is nothing really you can do." Frick reminded the inspector that many important decision-makers were at the beer hall, including the president of the police and several members of the government. They will know what to do.

Kiefer was stunned. Did this official not understand that those men had been taken captive?

Earlier that evening, Frick had been hanging about at the station long past the end of his shift. He had been asking police officers whether they planned to attend the rally. Now he seemed to be stalling and avoiding making any decision that might relieve the outgunned and outnumbered officers at the Bürgerbräukeller. The priority, he said, was "to avoid bloodshed." His refrain was "Wait for instructions."

Forty-six years old, with graying, close-cropped hair, Frick had worked his way up to chief of Munich's political police. He had started at the district headquarters on August 1, 1915. Since then he had risen through the ranks, chasing war profiteers and black-market racketeers. Frick had completed a doctorate in jurisprudence and briefly practiced law. He was married with three children under the age of twelve. All this was well known among his colleagues at headquarters. But what few of them knew was that Dr. Wilhelm Frick had recently joined the Nazi Party.

8.

THE NEW REGIME

*The rabble has to be scared shitless. I can't use an officer;
the people no longer have any respect for them. Best of all
would be a worker who's got his mouth in the right place . . .
He doesn't need much intelligence; politics is the stupidest
business in the world.*

—DIETRICH ECKART

At the sound of "Heil!" from the back of the banquet hall, the procession of Bavarian leaders and their National Socialist escorts returned from the side room and made its way to the platform.

Gustav von Kahr was the first to speak in a series of oaths, proclamations, and pledges of loyalty that struck several people in the audience like a call to freedom out of Friedrich Schiller's play *Wilhelm Tell*. With "heavy heart," Kahr said, he accepted the call to serve his country in "the hour of its gravest distress" and assume responsibility for "guiding Bavaria's destiny as viceroy of the monarchy." The applause was enthusiastic, a police informer in the crowd noted. Professor Müller thought this was by far the loudest and most enthusiastic cheering of the night.

After shaking Kahr's hand so forcefully, almost yanking or pumping it, Hitler triumphantly announced the new government, to thundering cheers. He then said that he would fulfill the vow he made five years earlier, when he lay in a military hospital at Pasewalk, recovering from a mustard-gas attack: he would "know neither rest nor peace until the November criminals have been overthrown." He was ready to build on "the ruins of the wretched Germany of today . . . a Germany of power and greatness, of freedom and magnificence."

Shouts of "Heil Hitler!" roared through the gallery.

Each of the men of the new regime, when signaled, pledged their cooperation, as Hitler put it, to purge Berlin of the criminals whose treason had dishonored the country and slaughtered its people. Ludendorff, speaking briefly in his best "mailed fist" style, repeated his claim to have been surprised at the revolution, but embraced the hour at hand as "the turning point of our history." Putzi, his large frame standing on a chair, translated the speeches for the foreign correspondents.

Professor Müller watched Hitler, standing on the stage, almost giddy with delight. Ludendorff also looked moved, his face betraying a conviction that this was a profound historical moment and, at the same time, a determination to meet the challenges of the future. The audience burst into a lively rendition of "Deutschland über Alles," which had been adopted as the national anthem the previous year. Ernst Pöhner, standing on the platform with Hitler's new government, said that this was the most rapturous applause that he had witnessed since the declaration of war in August 1914.

Not everyone, however, was swept up in the hysteria. A police informer overheard someone in the audience quip that the only thing missing was a psychiatrist.

WITH THE NEW national government proclaimed, Hitler was ready to release the crowd. Everyone wanting to leave the beer hall would first be questioned. Good German patriots would be allowed to go. Those who were not—foreign correspondents, Communists, or anyone suspected of being an enemy of the new regime—would be detained. He asked Göring to oversee the process.

Hitler went to check on Hess and the captive Bavarian prime minister and his cabinet, whom, he suspected, would never support the revolution.

He apologized for the "inconvenience" they had experienced and promised them no harm, making a point of not looking at the Bavarian Minister of the Interior, Franz Xaver Schweyer. This man had long opposed the Nazis, denouncing them in public for their "unilateral, unscrupulous, and terroristic nature." Schweyer was also someone to whom Hitler had given his word the previous year never to make a putsch.

Schweyer approached Hitler "like an angry schoolmaster." He pecked his finger on Hitler's chest and admonished him for his broken promise.

Hitler turned and headed to the door without responding.

Then he ordered Hess to take the men away.

9.

"SAFELY DELIVERED"

*If active people could only grasp the significance of what they
do—and the inactive of what they don't do—then humanity
would cease to be its own worst enemy.*

—ERNST TOLLER

Munich's nightlife was coming into full swing. Crowds emptied
out of the grand opera house after the evening's performance of
Beethoven's *Fidelio* and from the Theater am Gärtnerplatz for *Madame
Pompadour.* Trolleys dropped off revelers ready to blow billions at downtown restaurants, bars, cabarets, and cinemas.

Among them was a young American from Wisconsin named Robert Murphy. A muscular six-foot-two with a shock of red hair, Murphy
was the twenty-nine-year-old US vice consul. He was in fact serving as
America's highest-ranking authority in Bavaria, since his boss, the consul
general, had been promoted and relocated. Murphy and his wife, Mil-
dred, lived on the Prinzregentenstrasse, across the square from where
Hitler would later reside.

The Murphys had arrived in Munich two years before, and the diplomat had helped reestablish America's first consular relations with Germany since the war. He and a small staff had retrieved office furniture

from storage and reopened the consulate on Ledererstrasse. Its previous quarters had been rented from a student fraternity.

Murphy had first met Hitler in March that year. The locale of the interview—"a cold, bare office with a light bulb hanging from the ceiling"— reflected the fledgling status of the Nazi Party. Murphy was not impressed. He did not think Hitler had a chance of winning over sophisticated Bavarians. With $50,000, he later told a US House Select Committee on Intelligence, they could have wiped out the entire Nazi organization.

Murphy's diplomatic career had begun on April 23, 1917, only seventeen days after the United States had entered the First World War. His first post had been to neutral Bern, Switzerland, where he served as a code clerk and worked alongside the future head of the CIA, Allen Dulles. After the war, Murphy returned to the States and completed his law degree at George Washington University.

Murphy had never expected to embark on such a path. His father, a railroad steam fitter of Irish descent, had a fourth-grade education, and Murphy had grown up in a tough Milwaukee neighborhood. It was a scholarship to Marquette that changed his trajectory, and he soon scored high enough on his civil-service exams to secure a position with the Postmaster General's Office in Washington, DC. His desire to serve his country and see the world had led him into international relations.

At the Munich consulate, Murphy's work typically consisted of writing economic reports, processing passport extensions, and chasing down signatures to complete the paperwork for an average of four hundred visa applications a day. Now, however, Murphy had a major event to report. He based his telegram, marked "urgent" and "confidential," to the Secretary of State on an eyewitness account from the beer hall:

ACCORDING [TO] HITLER TASK OF THIS GOVERNMENT IS TO MARCH ON BERLIN, WAGE TWELFTH HOUR FIGHT; ASSERTED THAT THE DAWN WOULD SEE EITHER NEW NATIONAL GOVERNMENT OR THE DEATH OF SPEAKER.

Washington, he reasoned, must know of these developments.

. . .

ACROSS TOWN THAT night, some fifteen to eighteen hundred men had come out to the large and historic Löwenbräukeller for a "comradely festive evening." The insignia and armbands on display identified many of the men present as members of various paramilitary societies that had joined together into an alliance.

This was the Kampfbund, or Combat League. Founded less than two months before, the organization consisted of three radical right-wing groups that pledged to fight Jews, Marxists, pacifists, democrats, and supporters of the Treaty of Versailles. The charter members were the Nazi Storm Troopers, the closely related Bund Oberland, and the newly formed Reichskriegsflagge, or "Imperial Battle Flag," who were hosting the event that night.

The banquet hall was decked out in the white-red-black colors of imperial Germany, as well as the white-and-blue of Bavaria. Eagle and swastika standards stood in the front. Two bands had been playing military marches and opera overtures.

Hitler, the political leader of the Kampfbund, was supposed to speak to the crowd, *Völkischer Beobachter*, the Nazi newspaper, had announced. Stepping up to the podium instead was Hermann Esser, a twenty-four-year-old journalist, who had been dragged out of his bed, where he lay sick from jaundice and asked to stand in for Hitler. A former editor of the *Völkischer Beobachter*, Esser was deemed one of the most vivacious speakers in the party. He was a notorious rabble-rouser, or as a colleague put it, "a demon speechmaker, though from a lower circle of hell."

At some point before nine p.m., as Esser ranted on about the perils of "Jewish big business," a pay phone had rung and a voice on the line relayed two words: "Safely Delivered." The call came from the kitchen phone at the Bürgerbräu. The message—a coded reference to the birth of the German revolution—was rushed into the banquet room and delivered to a man in uniform sitting at the head table.

This was Capt. Ernst Röhm, the leader of the Reichskriegsflagge and a former staff officer under General von Lossow. With sandy brown hair and green eyes, Röhm stood five-feet-five inches tall, with a barrel chest and prominent scars across his chin, cheek, and nose. He had received about a dozen other wounds in his military career. He was, as colleague Kurt Lüdecke put it, "the living image of war itself."

Röhm had drifted into the Nazi orbit as one of its early members. He had been one of only 111 people present at Hitler's first major talk on October 16, 1919. After joining the party three months later, Röhm had become one of the closest men to the aloof and distant Hitler. He was one of the few people who addressed him with the intimate form of *du*.

With his immense prestige in nationalist circles, Röhm had helped make Hitler credible to soldiers in the German Army as well as to war veterans who had been decommissioned by the Versailles Treaty and now flocked to Munich's fighting societies. Röhm, a die-hard Bavarian monarchist, had also served as a key figure in the paramilitary underground. He not only hid weapons and war materiel deemed illegal by the Treaty of Versailles, he dispersed them to the societies as desired. For his services, he had earned the nickname "The Machine Gun King."

Overjoyed by the success at the Bürgerbräu, Röhm hopped onto the stage in the middle of Esser's speech and whispered something in his ear. Esser then announced the news of the revolution to the audience, many of whom had been putting back beer after beer.

After a brief silence, the crowd erupted in a deafening celebration. They shouted, cheered, and embraced, and many members of the military in attendance ripped off the republican insignia from their caps. People also jumped up onto chairs and tables. Musicians in a brass band danced around the stage and then blasted "Deutschland über Alles." Röhm struggled, in the joyous roar, to sound the call to join Hitler and Ludendorff.

With both bands blaring, one in front of the marchers and the other in the back, the Löwenbräu carousers poured out into the street for a raucous procession to the Bürgerbräu. The sensation attracted many people who rushed out of cafés to see the source of the commotion. The spectators cheered and shouted encouragement. At the front of the procession, just behind the tuba players, was a twenty-three-year-old assistant at a chemical fertilizer plant carrying the fighting society's battle flag. He sported a gray ski cap, thick rimless glasses, and a toothbrush mustache. His name was Heinrich Himmler.

ON THEIR MARCH to the beer hall, Captain Röhm dispatched a small detachment of Munich Storm Troopers to the Franciscan Abbey Church of St. Anna in central Munich. The unit's commander was Wilhelm Brückner, a tall and broad-shouldered thirty-nine-year-old political science student who had once been one of the country's top tennis players. Brückner led a few men into the twin-spired, neo-Romanesque church and descended through a stone corridor to a cellar lit by candles. A vault inside was filled with rifles.

A few days before, the monks at the abbey had been told that these weapons were to be safeguarded in case of a Communist uprising. There did not appear to be any such threat that night, thought the abbot Father Polycarp. He began to doubt their intentions, and went to telephone his friend Gustav von Kahr, for advice.

The Storm Troopers, however, did not wait for a reply; they just pushed their way into the vault and started seizing the stock. They forced the monks to pass the 3,300 infantry rifles down a human chain that stretched from the cellar to the trucks in the public square. Other monks supplied coffee and rum. All these weapons, it was clear, had been forbidden by the Versailles Treaty, and hidden there to avoid seizure by the Allied authorities.

That was also the case for the weapons stored at the Corpshaus Palatia, the home of a student dueling society. The porter, Andreas Mutz, was woken up to see young Heinrich Himmler and a group of soldiers from the Reichskriegsflagge standing outside the building. When the porter opened the door, the men pushed him aside and dashed down to the basement. They helped themselves to the cache of rifles, ammunition, helmets, and other supplies that fellow members had locked away in the society's bowling alley.

Afterward, Himmler and his gang marched off to rejoin Röhm and proceed to the Bürgerbräu. Along the way, a motorcycle messenger pulled up with orders for another, bolder, operation: Röhm's men were to seize control of the War Ministry, the command post of General von Lossow, and secure it as the headquarters for planning the attack on Berlin.

The military commander on site was in no position to stop Röhm and more than a hundred armed men had he wanted to, and it was by no means clear that he did. He said afterward that he had not wanted any bloodshed and had accepted the claims that Lossow and Kahr supported the putsch based on Röhm's rank and reputation. Not a single shot was fired. The Bavarian War Ministry was occupied in the name of Adolf Hitler.

WHILE RÖHM'S MEN swept through the church and the house of the student dueling society, some of their Kampfbund allies were also on the move. Hitler had sent a detachment from the Bund Oberland to retrieve weapons from the Army Engineer Barracks.

Formed from the Freikorps Oberland in October 1921, the Bund Oberland had grown into one of the largest and most powerful of the paramilitary bands. Its members took an oath to fight for the "greatness of the German Reich" and resist the Treaty of Versailles, the "death sentence on the German race." The society recruited heavily in the Bavarian highlands. Its symbol was the edelweiss.

The Bund Oberland had already scheduled maneuvers for the evening, as they did every Tuesday and Thursday (as well as Saturday afternoon), and so they had not expected to encounter any resistance. After gaining the arms, the Oberlanders were to seize control of the central railway station to prevent, as one member put it, "the rabble of racial alien Jews from the East from riding away at the last moment in a mad rush, loaded with foreign exchange."

But according to a report that arrived at the Bürgerbräu, the men had still not arrived at the train station several hours after the order had been given. The cause of the delay was not immediately clear. Spellbound by the string of successes so far that night, an overconfident Hitler made a snap decision to go there to evaluate and solve the problem himself. Leaving the beer hall at that time, however, would be a major blunder.

At the Army Engineer Barracks, Hitler found the situation worse than the reports indicated. The officer in charge of training, Capt. Oskar

Cantzler of the first company of the 7th Engineer Battalion, had managed, with only a handful of men, to lock all four hundred members of the Oberland contingent inside the training hall.

The wily captain had achieved this success in a disarmingly simple way. When the Oberlanders requested the weapons for training, Cantzler had become suspicious. If they really wished to practice maneuvers with arms, he had said, then they would have to remain indoors. The Oberland commander, Max Ritter von Müller, angrily—and rashly—marched the entire troop inside the drill hall. Cantzler then locked the door. Hitler's men were trapped. There were of course no weapons there, and should the men try to muscle their way out, Cantzler set up two machine guns aimed at the entrance.

Then, when Hitler arrived, Cantzler refused to open the barrack gates. Furious, Hitler briefly considered resolving this embarrassing imbroglio by rolling down artillery and blowing the gatehouse to smithereens. He probably abandoned the idea when he realized that he could just return to the beer hall and have General von Lossow order the release of the Oberlanders.

Not only did Hitler waste precious time with his fruitless expedition to the Army Engineer Barracks, he then discovered upon his return to the Bürgerbräu that Kahr, Lossow, and Seisser had disappeared.

General Ludendorff had decided that the three Bavarian leaders looked exhausted. He then released them, accepting their word of honor that they would meet him at the War Ministry later that night to coordinate the march on Berlin.

Hitler could not have imagined that Ludendorff would allow these men to leave the beer hall, though he was probably not at first as concerned as often portrayed. He too had taken the Bavarian leaders at their word that they would support the revolution. He had, after all, three thousand witnesses to their pledge of loyalty.

Hitler's adviser, Scheubner-Richter, on the other hand, was more troubled. He asked Ludendorff if he had really expected the Bavarian leaders to return, given that they had been released "without a guard."

Ludendorff, unused to having his decisions questioned, forbade him, or anyone else in the room, to doubt the word of a German officer.

10.

COUNTER-PUTSCH

The leaders of the National Socialists did not possess the requisite skill for their leadership roles.
—HANS FEIL, MUNICH POLICE REPORT, DECEMBER 18, 1923

Scheubner-Richter was not the only one to express concern over Ludendorff's decision. This was "sheer madness," said Hermann Esser, upon arriving outside the beer hall after his speech at the Löwenbräu. "Who let the fellows go? . . . Who is responsible for this nonsense?"

Putzi was also incredulous. He had learned enough from his studies in history to realize that aspiring revolutionaries simply do not allow the leaders of the established government to remain free. He and Esser retreated inside the beer hall, where on Esser's account, they consoled themselves with another round of drinks.

The banquet room was, by this time, mostly empty, except for the Storm Troopers and Nazi Party members still loitering about drinking beer and munching on remaining sausages. Tables and chairs lay helter-skelter where they had been overturned. Broken glass littered the place. It looked like Munich after the carnival.

A hole in the ceiling was pointed out as the shot that started the German revolution. One party member, Marc Sesselmann, had gathered the shards of the beer mug that Hitler supposedly shattered before storming the stage. The beginnings of a new mythology surrounding the beer hall putsch were already forming.

About eleven p.m., three cars filled with Hitler, Ludendorff, and other conspirators plotting the German revolution left the beer hall to coordinate strategy at the newly seized War Ministry. They still expected the three Bavarian leaders to meet them there and plan the attack on Berlin.

Gustav von Kahr, however, was not headed to the War Ministry. He chose instead to return to his apartment attached to his office in the rambling neo-Gothic structure on Maximilianstrasse, the center of political authority in Munich. He faced a major dilemma.

For six weeks, since his appointment as general state commissioner, a virtual dictator tasked with countering the unprecedented economic turmoil, Kahr had resisted Berlin at times with open defiance. He was not opposed to the overthrow of the republic—he was a notorious monarchist—and at times, he seemed on the verge of joining, if not planning, a coup d'état himself. But this putsch, he feared, would fail. Unfortunately for him, he had supported it in front of a packed beer hall.

Walking up the stairs, he greeted his daughter and handed her his coat. He asked for some tea and, after a quick change of clothes, went to his office in Room 125 on the third floor. Several of his advisers were already rallying forces to resist Hitler.

Kahr appeared shaken. He had had no choice or alternative, he said, explaining his apparent agreement with Hitler at the Bürgerbräu. He then blamed the police for failing to take proper precautions, which was ironic, given that it had been Kahr who instructed them to diminish their presence that night. He had not wanted it to look like he needed to be protected from his own people.

The situation was far from hopeless, said one of his advisers, Eberhardt Kautter, a veteran soldier who led a local unit of the paramilitary Bund Wiking [Viking League], which was a successor to one of the infamous Freikorps groups, the Marinebrigade Ehrhardt. Hitler had acted unwisely, Kautter said, with too narrow a base of support for Bavaria, let alone all of Germany. If Kahr moved quickly, they could still emerge victorious. He had a suggestion.

Kahr should suspend the Weimar constitution and proclaim a

dictatorship with himself as a viceroy, or deputy, of the ousted king. He could make the case to the public that this was necessary to combat the Communist threat. Several paramilitary societies would certainly join this cause—he had already mobilized his own Bund Wiking. The people would likewise rally to their side. Hitler and Ludendorff, outmaneuvered, would either have to subordinate themselves to Kahr's leadership or they would be overtaken by the momentum of the revolution.

As Kahr considered the proposition, he no doubt realized that the top priority was to find out where his colleagues, Lossow and Seisser, stood on the Hitler putsch. The three Bavarian leaders had not had the chance to speak freely without the presence of the Nazis.

During the discussion, the phone rang. It was neither Lossow nor Seisser, but instead Kahr's vice premier and sometime rival, Franz Matt, the minister of education and culture. Matt had skipped Kahr's speech at the beer hall that night, allegedly for a dinner party with the archbishop and the papal nuncio in Munich, Monsignor Eugenio Pacelli, who would later become Pope Pius XII.

"What does Hitler actually want?" Matt asked.

"The famous march on Berlin," Kahr said.

Good luck with that, Matt replied sarcastically. By the end of the conversation, Matt reached the conclusion that Kahr was either committed to Hitler's plot or unfit to fight it. Either way, he was not to be trusted.

That night, Matt would propose to fellow cabinet members that they should retreat sixty miles north to Regensburg on the Danube. There they could rule as the legitimate government and ensure the integrity of the state. In the chaos of the moment, however, this meant only that there would be yet another faction vying for power.

MEANWHILE, FORCES OPPOSING the putsch were emerging at police headquarters.

At about 9:15 p.m., the state police major Sigmund Freiherr von Imhoff had just wrapped up teaching a class on riot control. He was about to leave the building when a detective ran in "breathless" with news of Hitler's attack at the beer hall. Rumors often circulated in Munich's hothouse atmosphere, but Imhoff realized that this was no exaggeration.

Frick was still preventing any significant police action with his rhetoric of caution. Imhoff, realizing where his colleague's true allegiance lay, pretended to agree, but as soon as Frick left the room, he started working the telephones.

Imhoff placed the entire *Landespolizei*, or state police (also known as the "Green Police," given the color of their uniform), on high alert, and he took responsibility for dispatching other units to guard Munich's telegraph office, the telephone exchange, the central post office, and key government buildings and bridges in case of attack.

The quick action of this state police major would safeguard vital communications centers. What's more, this feat was accomplished despite the vigilance of Dr. Frick, who kept popping into the office to check on him, while trying in his stiff, awkward way to appear nonchalant.

Imhoff scored another success that night when he managed to reach the commander of the Munich city garrison, Maj. Gen. Jakob Ritter von Danner at his home and inform him of the emergency. Danner came at once to the police station, where he too feared sabotage under Dr. Frick and soon left for his office in the neo-Baroque building that housed the Army Museum. Like Imhoff, he planned to oppose Hitler with all his authority.

As a decorated commander whose career had begun with the German expeditionary force in China during the Boxer Rebellion, Danner abhorred the putsch as an indefensible act against legitimate state authority. He was also angry at his immediate supervisor, General von Lossow, for not only succumbing to the temptations of politics but also failing to put the despicable Nazi rogues in their place. Lossow, he said, was "a sad figure of a man," and, above all, "a coward."

When Danner arrived at his office, he realized that the city garrison was not safe either. The War Ministry was already occupied by Röhm's Reichskriegsflagge, and Storm Troopers had been spotted marching nearby around St. Anna's Church. Danner decided to set up a new command center for the fight against Hitler outside Munich's center, in the northwestern part of the city: a wooden communications hut deep inside the 19th Infantry Regiment barracks.

After ordering military reinforcements from Augsburg, Landsberg, Regensburg, Nürnberg, and elsewhere, Danner then gave explicit instructions to each commanding officer: Under no circumstances were they to obey General von Lossow. Without explicitly doubting his commander's loyalty, Danner said that the general should be regarded as "a prisoner" and all his communications ignored. In other words, commanders should follow orders from Danner personally, or in his name alone.

11.

INITIATIVE

We must seize the initiative, or the others will.
—ADOLF HITLER TO ERNST PÖHNER

With guns in hand, Rudolf Hess and the Storm Trooper detachment loaded seven men onto a truck parked outside the Bürgerbräu beer hall: the Bavarian prime minister, three members of his cabinet, an adviser to Crown Prince Rupprecht, and two policemen, including the president of the police Karl Mantel. The distinguished captives were then driven away in the direction of the forest of Grosshesselohe.

The caravan stopped at a gravel driveway of a large house adorned in the gingerbread style at Holzkirchnerstrasse 2. This was the home of Julius F. Lehmann, the founder of the prominent publishing firm J. F. Lehmanns Verlag, which specialized in medical texts as well as nationalist, anti-Semitic works. Lehmann had agreed to open up his property on the recommendation of his son-in-law, Dr. Friedrich Weber, a young veterinarian who served as the political leader of the Bund Oberland.

"Please regard yourselves as my guests," Lehmann said.

Privately, he was not too happy about the last-minute decision to house the hostages at his villa. "This cuckoo's egg was laid in my nest by my dear son-in-law," he said.

Each of the "guests," as he called them, was assigned a different room in the cold, unheated house. Two Storm Troopers stood guard outside each makeshift cell, while other men patrolled the garden and the surrounding woods in case the police discovered the location and tried to free the men. A machine gun was placed outside, aimed at the road, and another one in the hallway at the front door. Conversation was strictly prohibited, and Hess warned the leaders that the Storm Troopers had instructions to shoot, should anyone attempt to leave the premises.

IN CONTRAST TO the seized War Ministry, which was now swarming with Röhm's men, the Nazi Party office on Corneliusstrasse was strangely quiet. It gave no signs of being its usual bustling chaos of "conspiracy and intrigue" as Putzi dubbed it. Only three people were there: the twenty-four-year-old assistant business manager Philipp Bouhler, and two typists also in their early twenties: Else Gisler and Anna Schürz.

Bouhler had advised the two women to eat an early supper because there was going to be a heavy workload that night. Five hours later, however, the typists were still waiting at their desks. They had long since finished the correspondence and other clerical duties. No further instructions had arrived, nor, for that matter, had there been any other signs of activity, until sometime after eleven p.m., when Bouhler rushed into the office and told them to gather their belongings. They were moving to a new location.

Their boss, Max Amann, the business manager of the party, had found more luxurious headquarters for the nascent regime. Amann had been Hitler's staff sergeant in the war, and still acted like one. He was short and blond, with his neck disappearing into his shoulders. He was, as Putzi's wife, Helen, put it, "ruthless, hardheaded . . . [and] entirely without scruple." One party member, the story went, had found himself bear-hugged and tossed out of the office for daring to ask to look into the accounting books.

Years later, the American wartime espionage organization the OSS, a precursor to the CIA, would sum up Amann as "a commonplace man [who] knows himself to be commonplace" and yet did not shy away from making decisions well beyond his expertise. Hitler, it added, had patterned his leadership skills on this bullying and sometimes brutal staff sergeant.

Earlier that night, Amann had barged into a bank and claimed the property on behalf of Hitler's government. He knew the selected financial institution, the Siedelungs- und Landbank at Kanalstrasse 29, well. He lived on the fourth floor of the same building and had previously worked at the bank.

Their swank offices would complement the military operations planned at the War Ministry. One room was to be set up for the new finance department, which was to be led by Dr. Gottfried Feder, an engineer and building contractor who had been one of the oldest members of the party. It was Feder who had spoken at the Sterneckerbräu on the evening of September 12, 1919, when Hitler attended his first party meeting. The topic was "How and by What Means Can One Abolish Capitalism?"

As the provisional head of the new finance committee, Feder planned to freeze all bank accounts in the country; earlier that afternoon, he had taken the precaution of withdrawing his own savings deposits. That evening, when Hitler stormed the stage at the beer hall, Feder had felt as if he had just awoken from a dream.

Another office in the bank was reserved for the propaganda center, which would be led by Julius Streicher, a short, bald, and bull-necked publisher of the vicious anti-Semitic tabloid *Der Stürmer.* Streicher had arrived in Munich that evening, after leaving the elementary school in Nuremberg, where he worked as a senior master.

A third room was set aside for Hermann Esser, the speaker at the Löwenbräu rally. Esser had been summoned there to craft a proclamation of Hitler's government for the newspaper and party posters. That was why the typists had been kept waiting at their desks.

In the early morning hours, the first of the Nazi proclamations would hit the streets triumphantly announcing the new government and the end of "the most shameful period in German history." Some were signed using the earliest known reference to the future title: Adolf Hitler, German Reich Chancellor.

Later ones would issue inflammatory calls to action, declaring "open season . . . on the scoundrels responsible for the treason of November 9, 1918." Fellow patriots, the blood-red posters announced, should do their duty and capture the president of Germany, Friedrich Ebert, and his government ministers—"dead or alive."

As AMANN SET UP shop at the bank, Hitler sent Ernst Pöhner to make arrangements with his former colleagues and staff at police headquarters.

Upon arrival, Pöhner sought out his old friend and protégé, Dr. Wilhelm Frick, and took him into the office of the police president Karl Mantel, who was still held hostage by the Storm Troopers. Yes, Pöhner said magnanimously, this was now Frick's office.

The proposal of Frick as the new police president had actually been made in the back room of the Bürgerbräu by Gustav von Kahr, who knew how closely Pöhner and Frick had worked together. In May 1919, just two weeks after taking charge of the police, Pöhner had named Frick as head of its powerful political division. Pöhner divided his staff into two categories: men of promise, who were the officers, and the rest, who were assumed to aspire to little more than a paycheck and job security. He called them the "whores."

In Pöhner's mind, Frick was clearly an officer. He showed independence, carried out responsibilities with diligence, and proved his strength of will. He was no "weather vane," as Pöhner put it. The close collaboration of Pöhner and Frick made them as inseparable and complementary as Castor and Pollux of classical mythology.

Captain Röhm explained the analogy. Pöhner was an intelligent hothead, "energetic, bold, and quick to make a decision," though would readily change course if he met stiff resistance. Frick, on the other hand, showed a subtler, icy intelligence that proved most tenacious in the face of a challenge. The two men had carved out a formidable power base within the Munich police. Hitler expected that they would do so again on his behalf.

In the office of the police president, Pöhner and Frick plotted how to introduce the new Hitler regime to the people it claimed to represent.

They decided to summon Munich's leading editors and publishers to a midnight press conference in the library of police headquarters.

When everyone had arrived, Pöhner appealed to the patriotism of the newspapermen, warning of possible repercussions if they did not see "reason" and portray the events that night in an appropriately positive fashion. The leaders of Hitler's new regime should be praised for steering the country out of the nightmare of 1918. If the editors showed responsibility in their work, or "discipline," as Pöhner put it, there would be no censorship or other unpleasant consequences.

When Pöhner opened the forum to questions, Paul Egenter of the royalist *Bayerischer Kurier*, wanted to know if Kahr had secured the support of Crown Prince Rupprecht when he referred to himself as the king's deputy. This was a good question—the answer was no—but Pöhner tried to evade it. Pöhner also dodged the follow-up question asking for comment on the fundamental contradiction between Kahr's monarchism and Hitler's "republican-dictatorial" ambitions.

Fritz Gerlich, the editor of *Münchner Neueste Nachrichten*, wanted to know about early reports of Jewish men and women being harassed by the Storm Troopers. The Jewish factory owner Ludwig Wassermann had been detained as he tried to leave the Bürgerbräu, and was being held hostage.

Pöhner was completely indifferent.

12.

BARBARIAN HORDES

We do not have the right or authority to execute—yet.
—HERMANN GÖRING, NOVEMBER 9, 1923

Earlier that night, the Bürgerbräu had succumbed to a hostile and threatening atmosphere. The first sign of a darkening mood had come early. When the event organizer introduced Gustav von Kahr, his call for a bright future was met by a heckler who shouted out, "Without the Jews!" and the crowd cheered. Later, the Storm Troopers searched the banquet hall for people to detain, like sword-wielding, pistol-bearing "Ukrainian pogromists," noted the special correspondent of the Jewish Telegraphic Agency, Dr. Matatyahu Hindes.

After Göring ranted about Berlin's "Jewish" government, the Storm Troopers assembled foreign correspondents near the front and held them at gunpoint. "The pressmen were all Jews," they taunted. When one of the reporters demanded their immediate release, Hitler was overheard dismissing them: "We waited five years, surely the pressmen may also wait." The worst moment came when the members of the crowd near Hindes started singing nationalist songs and shouting: "What a pity there are no Jews here to kill!"

The Jewish Telegraphic Agency correspondent eventually took

advantage of the disorganization in the beer hall to escape through one of its unguarded side doors, probably the one in the kitchen that other reporters had discovered. He must have left the premises wondering if the troops at the beer hall were about to carry out a threat recorded in another dispatch by the Jewish Telegraphic Agency three days earlier: "Ludendorff and Hitler declare war on Jews."

ACROSS TOWN, THE crack of shattered glass emanated from a building at Altheimer Eck 19.

Members of the Nazi Party's elite shock troops, the Stosstrupp Hitler, were pouring out of trucks, blocking off the cobblestone lane outside the offices of the rival Social Democratic paper, *Münchener Post*. The Nazis hated this "Jewish paper" for its history of critical reports and exposés of their own activities. They called it *Münchener Pest*, or the "Munich Plague," and the "Poison Kitchen," tapping into centuries-old imagery that had been used to scapegoat Jewish minorities and incite pogroms against them.

With a gun pointed at the head of the newspaper's business manager, the commander of the troops, Josef Berchtold, demanded that he open up the iron gate. Once inside the building, the assault squad started destroying desks, knocking over filing cabinets and bookcases, tossing ink onto the walls, and cutting telephone lines.

Other members, wielding rifle butts, attacked the four large display windows. An estimated 320 glass planes—or 380 by a later prosecution count—were broken in this frenzy of destruction. Postcards were later made depicting the demolished offices.

"We forced [open] the doors of this place, ransacked the building, and flung all the printed stuff we could lay hands upon out into the street," Berchtold later said. This included personnel records, mailing addresses of subscribers, account information of advertisers, half-finished manuscripts, and any picture or bust of a Social Democratic leader or a flag of the republic. Then they torched the property in a gigantic bonfire.

During the operation, a policeman arrived to stop the senseless attack.

More likely, he had come to make sure that the men did not damage the printing presses, because Hitler had decided to hand them over to the Kampfbund's paper, *Heimatland*.

The Stosstrupp Hitler hauled away a full load of equipment, including five or six typewriters, several stacks of documents, and an estimated 6 trillion German marks looted from a cash box. They did not overlook the garage, where they tried to steal the paper's only automobile. Unable to get it started, they settled for running off with its spare tires.

One of the members of the assault squad found the home address of the newspaper editor and the leader of Munich's Social Democratic Party, Erhard Auer, and they decided to attack him next—this had probably been one of the objectives from the start. As Berchtold and his men returned to the trucks, a red-black-white swastika banner flew from the second-floor balcony of the Socialist paper, its offices reduced to what one Nazi eyewitness described as "smoking ruins."

At about twelve thirty a.m., fifteen to twenty members of the Stosstrupp Hitler bounded up the steps to the editor's fourth-floor flat at Nussbaumstrasse 10. Pushing their way inside was Hitler's chauffeur, Emil Maurice, or "Maurizl," a twenty-six-year-old watchmaker by trade and the first leader of the Storm Troopers.

"Where is your husband?" Maurice asked, holding a pistol to the face of the editor's wife, fifty-five-year-old Sophie Auer.

She said she did not know.

Relying on threats of violence, Maurice demanded that she answer the question and then gave the woman a push, knocking her backwards, nearly to the ground. A couple of his men locked her up in a room while they searched the apartment.

Actually Erhard Auer was not at home. Acting on a tip about the threat to his life, he had gone to the apartment of a friend and fellow social democrat, the lawyer Wilhelm Hoegner, who lived on Schellingstrasse. Auer was in fact staying one block away from a main Storm Trooper gathering spot.

Auer's elder daughter, Sophie, asked the intruders to be as quiet as possible because her own two-year-old daughter was sleeping. Maurice, ignoring the request, asked who the father was as he rummaged through their closets, laundry, and bedding. He then smashed up a cupboard and turned over bookshelves, apparently looking for weapons or valuables as much as any clue for the whereabouts of the editor. "We are the masters and we govern now," Maurice boasted.

Before Berchtold ordered his men to stop, Maurice and his cronies had opened the safe and seized its contents, which consisted of little more than a few letters to President Ebert, some papers on the Nazis, and their daughters' old report cards.

Some of the papers would be brought back to the beer hall as if it were a grand triumph, but the leaders of the assault squad were clearly disappointed. They had not found Auer, or any clue of his whereabouts. Instead, they consoled themselves by carrying off his revolver and an older pistol. They also took the husband of Auer's other daughter Emilie, Dr. Karl Luber, as a substitute hostage until they could find the editor who had dared to criticize the Nazis as a party of terror and racism.

OTHER ATTACKS WERE being reported around Munich that night, and not all of them were ordered or coordinated by the leaders of the putsch. One group was led by Ernst Hübner, a young bank clerk who had been drinking at the Donisl beer hall, opposite the town hall, oblivious to the events at the Bürgerbräu. Many drinks later, he ran into some friends from the Bund Oberland who had gone off on their own looking to attack "Jews and other enemies of the people." Hübner decided to join them.

As an officer in this organization, Hübner took charge of the gang and led them to the crowded café at the Fürstenhof Hotel. "All Jews out!" he shouted. No one stirred. Apparently, the manager said, trying to diffuse the situation, no Jews were present. The Oberland hooligans then marched on looking for Jews to harass at the Spatenbräu restaurant and the Excelsior Hotel.

Police reports, unfortunately, provide only a small and incomplete picture of the attacks that night, and some errors have occasionally entered into later accounts of the putsch. One of the most glaring is the claim that the wanton destruction had disturbed Hitler so much that he sought to curb the violence and even expelled some of the offenders from the party for smashing up a Jewish shop or delicatessen.

The source for this claim can be traced back to the testimony of Police Staff Sgt. Matthäus Hofmann. Hofmann, however, was a member of the Nazi Party (and a close enough associate to be chosen by Ulrich Graf to keep Hitler's dog when the latter went to prison). Still, what the policeman said does not indicate that Hitler had intervened in favor of Jewish victims.

For one thing, the attack on the Jewish delicatessen did not take place on the night of the putsch, Hofmann claimed, but at some undetermined date beforehand. Even more, Hitler's anger had not been aroused by the scale of the violence, the degree of suffering, or even the poor impression that this incident would make on the public. The reason for Hitler's rebuke of the offending Storm Troopers was that the latter had removed their party badges before they ransacked the place.

For Munich's Jewish community, the putsch would be a night of terror. Gangs, like those under Hübner, were prowling downtown and near the train station, seeking out Jews to rob or attack. Some resorted to searching for Jewish-sounding names on letterboxes or thumbing through the Munich phone book. They smashed windows of shops, such as a Jewish-owned clothes store on Franziskanerstrasse, and dragged away Jews they found.

It is not known how many Jews suffered this harrowing experience. Historian Erich Eyck suggested that twenty-four had been taken hostage. The figure may well have been higher. One man who was at the beer hall, in the vicinity of Hitler, thanks to his position as valet to Scheubner-Richter, said in his unpublished memoir that the arrests of the city, coupled with the detentions at the banquet hall, led to the "provisional custody" of sixty-four Jews. The hostages would spend the night at the Bürgerbräu, many of them fearing for their lives.

13.

MIDNIGHT IN MUNICH

The peacocks need to be plucked, before they fall over their own feathers.

—HERMANN GÖRING

In Berlin, Chancellor Gustav Stresemann and the finance minister Dr. Hjalmar H. G. Schacht were finishing a late-night supper in a private dining room at the Hotel Continental. At eleven thirty p.m., as they moved on to dessert, a messenger shuffled over to their table and whispered to the chancellor that the press was reporting of "a putsch in Munich." Stresemann, apologizing, rushed out to an emergency meeting at the Reich Chancellery.

Bold, bald, and brilliant, Stresemann was one of the most talented statesmen in the Weimar Republic. He was hard at work that autumn, his first months in power, trying to steer the country out of the madness of inflation and isolation. At the same time, he had an unpredictable streak. The British ambassador, Viscount D'Abernon, said he had "more than a dash of recklessness" and "a pronounced predilection for the unorthodox." Stresemann, he added, "might have been Winston Churchill's brother."

Stresemann was joined by Friedrich Ebert, the first president of the German Republic. The fifty-three-year-old Social Democrat had an eighth-grade education. He had worked as a saddle maker and in other crafts before buying a tavern in the city of Bremen and becoming active in trade unions. In February 1919, Ebert had unexpectedly won the young republic's first national election. He had, since then, presided over four and a half years of extreme instability, and was vilified by political opponents on both the left and right.

President Ebert, Chancellor Stresemann, and their advisers hashed out a hurried response to this latest crisis in Munich. They imposed censorship on news from Bavaria, froze financial transactions, and secured roadways, railway stations, and other communications links with the unstable southern state.

A key factor in the outcome of the Hitler putsch was clearly going to be the German military. Would the soldiers obey the commands of the republic, which they had sworn to defend, or would they rally to the conspirators led by nationalist idol General Ludendorff?

President Ebert put the question directly to the chief of Army Command, the fifty-seven-year-old Col. Gen. Hans von Seeckt, a former chief of staff under August von Mackensen and organizer of the German victory in Russia, Turkey, and the east. Seeckt had already deployed military forces to quash Communist revolts in Hamburg, Saxony, and Thuringia. But would the notorious right-wing leader do so against this revolt?

"Mr. President," the general reportedly said, staring out behind the monocle at his left eye, "the Reichswehr will obey me."

But would it? Many people, including Chancellor Stresemann, were not so certain. Reports were already trickling in of German units defecting to Ludendorff and Hitler. And even if most of the troops did obey, what exactly would General von Seeckt command? He was believed by many people to be plotting for power himself. He was certainly no friend of the republic. It was not without reason that the inscrutable general with the monocle was nicknamed "The Sphinx."

That night, faced with the specter of revolution and civil war, President Ebert invoked the infamous Article 48 of the Weimar constitution—a safeguard that enabled a leader to wield emergency executive powers in situations in which "the public safety and order in the German Reich . . . were seriously disturbed or endangered." Ebert would invoke this authority no fewer than 136 times, a reliance that did not help the legitimacy or stability of the fragile republic.

Ebert then handed over this emergency power to General von Seeckt. The process took only minutes. Never before in modern German history has so much authority been legally granted to a military leader in such a short period of time.

THE FUNDAMENTAL QUESTION for Berlin was, of course: What would Hitler do, if he somehow succeeded in reaching the capital?

Would he and his conspirators proclaim the independence of Bavaria? Some of his supporters clearly wanted this, but it was unlikely. The putschists of course wanted to remove President Ebert and his cabinet, but would they dismantle the republic, and if so, would they replace it with a dictatorship or a restoration of the monarchy? If the latter, which dynasty: the Wittelsbachs of Bavaria or the Hohenzollerns who had ruled Germany until the end of the First World War? Kahr was a notorious supporter of the former, Ludendorff of the latter. There were many open questions, and the men in Munich remained vague on the specifics.

What's more, there were fears that a German revolution would, as Hitler promised, repudiate the Versailles Treaty and immediately end all reparations payments. Yet even if the putsch collapsed, there was now the risk that the French would use this incident—and Ludendorff's participation in the affair—as a "welcome pretext" for imposing harsh disciplinary actions. This was the view of Cardinal Pietro Gasparri, Secretary of State of Pope Pius XI. The putsch might also inspire Bavarian separatists, the cardinal warned, prompting "unforeseeable consequences" for both Bavaria and Germany.

France, no surprise, was proving vigilant. After hearing the news of the putsch, the French ambassador to Germany, Pierre de Margèrie, dispatched a communiqué to Berlin, stressing that his country had not spent four years of blood and treasure in the First World War to defeat "Prussian militarism" only to allow its rebirth in the guise of a "National dictatorship of men who have sworn to tear up the Treaty of Versailles." Britain, the ambassador added, would likely share this position.

Back in Munich, Captain Röhm was barking orders around the War Ministry in preparation for the supposed meeting with the Bavarian leaders. After securing the premises, Röhm had set up the anteroom outside Lossow's office as the war room, or headquarters for planning the attack on Berlin.

When Ludendorff and Hitler arrived, everything was ready for this important meeting. But where were Kahr, Lossow, and Seisser?

They were supposed to have appeared at the ministry by now. Calls to Kahr's office went unanswered, or worse still for their nerves, the line remained busy. Indeed, when the phone was answered, someone would say Kahr was on the way there or over to the Army Engineer Barracks, or he was on the other line, which, after a long wait, would be inexplicably cut. The same went for Lossow and Seisser.

Ludendorff was not worried about the missing Bavarian leaders, because they had given their word. Hitler was still not overly concerned either. At the same time, signs of anxiety began to show. Putzi recalled how Hitler, still wearing his belted trench coat from the venture into the city, started to "[pace] up and down like a desperado."

General von Lossow was certainly keeping many people guessing about his whereabouts, and indeed his motives.

One group that did not expect to see him that night was his staff at the city garrison. After issuing a series of orders, Lossow's subordinate, Gen. Jakob von Danner entered an office on the second floor. To his astonishment, he found General von Lossow, who had just arrived by automobile from the Bürgerbräu.

"Your Excellency, surely all that was a bluff, was it not?" Danner asked.

Of course it was, Lossow said, answering with such anger and indignation about Hitler's "vile raid" in the banquet room that at least a few officers present thought he blamed himself. He walked back and forth across the room, "extraordinarily excited and outraged," as state police captain Hans Bergen said, and apparently uncertain how to proceed.

As much as Danner mistrusted Lossow, however, he knew that he needed him, if for nothing else than to gain access to the resources under the command of his colleagues Kahr and Seisser. The latter, for instance, as head of the state police, had the largest force currently available in the city, including some 1,800 men at the barracks. And until the military reinforcements arrived, these state police troops would be essential for maintaining control in Munich and waging the struggle against Hitler.

The overarching priority then, Danner said, was to move to a more secure location in the army barracks of the 19th Infantry Regiment. Messages were sent to Kahr at his office and Seisser at the police barracks urging them to come at once. From the refuge of the new command center, which would be set up in the one-story wooden communications hut, Lossow, Danner, and their staffs would prepare for the struggle to suppress Hitler's uprising.

14.

ORDINANCE NO. 264

I did not want to show my cards too early.
—GUSTAV VON KAHR

By the early-morning hours of November 9, 1923, probably around or not too long after one a.m., Kahr, Lossow, and Seisser had reached the new counter-putsch command center. Two important pieces of information had arrived as well. First, they learned that the Bavarian crown prince, Rupprecht, strongly disapproved of the putsch. Second, they received notification that General von Seeckt, the head of the military in Berlin, also opposed "this crazy mutiny," as he called it. He ordered the Bavarian authorities to suppress the rebellion at once, or he would do it for them.

At 2:50 a.m., more than four hours after leaving the beer hall, the three Bavarian leaders sent a joint statement to radio stations around the Reich:

GENERAL STATE COMMISSIONER VON KAHR, GENERAL VON LOSSOW, AND COLONEL VON SEISSER REJECT THE HITLER PUTSCH. STATEMENTS EXTORTED IN BÜRGERBRÄUKELLER GATHERING BY FORCE OF ARMS ARE INVALID. CAUTION ADVISED AGAINST MISUSE OF THE ABOVE NAMES.

The Bavarian leaders also composed a longer text for posters that attacked Hitler's "deceit and breach of promise," and pledged to act decisively to quash this act of betrayal.

At this point, the Nazi Party and their Kampfbund allies were declared illegal and dissolved. Kahr's decree, Ordinance No. 264, also ordered the confiscation of all currency, weapons, armaments, vehicles, and other property belonging to these banned parties, and stipulated that any member of them could face up to fifteen years in prison. General Ludendorff, Hitler, and their supporters were, in the words of a subsequent order, to be arrested "on sight."

Various proclamations repudiating Hitler were quickly printed and posted around town. They would, however, have to compete with the posters the Nazis were pasting up, announcing the success of the Hitler-Ludendorff-Kahr-Lossow-Seisser regime. Hitler's men had a large lead in the battle of the kiosks.

Worse still, the triumvirate would have to counter newspaper accounts too, which would soon hit the street. Kahr's adviser and speechwriter, Adolf Schiedt, the editor of *Münchener Zeitung*, had warned that the newspapers would be able to report only what its writers had observed at the beer hall; namely the Bavarian leaders' speeches in support of the revolution. Munich would, in other words, read page after page in the morning papers describing the alliance of Kahr, Lossow, and Seisser with Hitler, but not one word of their disavowal. Schiedt urged them to stop the presses to avoid "the immense danger" of confusing the entire country.

Although the Bavarian authorities had agreed that this was a good idea, no one, in the chaos of the night, had gotten around to doing anything about it. At some point between three and four that morning, Schiedt finally gained access to a telephone and called his publisher, Hans Buchner, who also served as chairman of Munich's association of editors and publishers. "Publication of the morning newspapers throughout Munich is forbidden," Schiedt said, asking him to relay the order to his colleagues, along with news that violators would be punished by death.

The publisher's response to this astonishing order was not recorded, but he dutifully started making calls to his colleagues around town. He woke Fritz Gerlich, editor of the *Münchner Neueste Nachrichten*, who had gone to bed after the midnight press conference at the police library.

Gerlich told him that he had already printed at least thirty thousand copies of his paper, and they were about to be delivered. It was impossible to stop it, he said. He could not comply, even if he had wanted to.

The editor then called Ernst Pöhner to complain about this last-minute attempt to suppress free speech.

But Pöhner was surprised at the news as well.

He had not given any such order, Pöhner said, emerging from his post–press conference nap. He was certain that Kahr had not done so either. It must be a mistake. Unable to return to sleep, Pöhner tried to call his right-hand man, Wilhelm Frick, at police headquarters.

Several other people had been inquiring about Frick too, the duty officer at the switchboard said, but he was not in his office or his apartment, and no one knew where he was.

Minutes later, the editor called Pöhner back to confirm that, after some investigation, he knew for a fact that the order to stop the presses had indeed been given by Kahr's office. Pöhner was taken aback by this revelation. Kahr was his old friend. Surely he would not issue such a proclamation without informing him. Still, he started to worry. Where was Frick? It was not like him to leave his post without informing his staff.

As Pöhner ruminated over these developments, the doorbell rang. It was Max von Scheubner-Richter who had been sent to bring Pöhner to the War Ministry. Something was amiss, the visitor said. Hitler needed him immediately.

15.

"I AM NOT A COWARD"

I fear that your dream will soon be over.
—EBERHARDT KAUTTER TO A SUPPORTER
OF THE HITLER-LUDENDORFF PLOT

One of the first orders of the Bavarian authorities after they reunited at the infantry barracks had been to arrest Wilhelm Frick. The commander of Munich's state police, Col. Josef Banzer, and his chief of staff, Maj. Sigmund von Imhoff, were only happy to oblige because they had long been suspicious of his motives. Their task was made easier when, at about three thirty a.m., Frick walked into their office, asking if they had any news about the triumvirate.

Banzer tried to carry on a casual conversation as Imhoff discreetly left to find backup. When he returned, Frick started to leave the room. Imhoff blocked the door.

"Herr Frick, I'm awfully sorry, but I must do my duty," Imhoff said.

Banzer clarified what this meant: Frick was under arrest.

"On whose orders?" Frick asked.

"The government's."

"But which government, Colonel?"

Frick was thunderstruck. Could it really be on orders from Gustav von Kahr, the same man he had promised support for Hitler's regime only hours before?

Two police officers, called in by Imhoff, escorted Frick to another room in the building. The next task was to arrest Pöhner.

As Scheubner-Richter and Pöhner arrived at the War Ministry, the rooms and corridors were crowded with soldiers, some of them smoking, chatting, or just trying to sleep. On the third floor, Hitler was talking with Röhm, accusing the absent General von Lossow of betraying them. Virtually everyone in the room agreed, except for Ludendorff, who still refused to believe that a German officer would break his word.

To extricate themselves from the crisis, Hitler put his hope in the art of persuasion. There would be official posters of the new regime, 100,000 of them, soon to be plastered around town. There would be speeches by fiery demagogues like Julius Streicher and a call for fourteen rallies all around Munich. There would be articles and proclamations by Hermann Esser. The *Völkischer Beobachter* and other Munich papers would bring the news to breakfast tables around Munich. "Propaganda, nothing but propaganda," Hitler said.

At the new offices in the occupied bank, Esser was hard at work on just that. His text of the forthcoming announcement for the newspaper, coupled with its rapid composition despite his illness, would earn him praise from Hitler's men:

> The revolution of the November criminals has ended today . . . Five years have passed since the day the heroic German people were stabbed in the back by yelling, miserable deserters and criminals who had escaped from our prison. The national traitors lied to the trusting people, promising them peace, freedom, beauty, and dignity . . . And what came of that?

Esser went on to depict the hunger and misery of the people who lay exposed to the ravenous exploitation of "speculators, profiteers, and political frauds," as well as the criminal politicians in Berlin who surrendered the country's assets. Thanks to the dictated peace of Versailles, 17 million Germans had been "torn from us, and ignominiously dishonored." In the meantime, the fact that "a former brothel-keeper," he said, referring to President Ebert, "has usurped the title of Reich President besmirches the honor of the German People and the German Republic."

"One would have to be an idiot to expect help from such places."

Despite the ringing triumphalism in his proclamations, Esser was worried. After dropping off the copy to the offices of the newspaper, where Alfred Rosenberg was anxiously awaiting it, Esser had shared his concerns with his friend, the photographer Heinrich Hoffmann, at his studio across the street.

"It's all over," Hoffmann remembered him saying as he sat there in an armchair. Ludendorff and Hitler, he added, had made the fundamental mistake of letting the Bavarian leaders leave the beer hall. Lossow would rally the army—and Seisser the state police—for a massive counterstrike. The Nazis, by contrast, were losing momentum.

Hours in, the putsch certainly seemed to be unraveling. It was marred by poor planning, hasty decisions, and a reliance on slapdash improvisation that showed a remarkable lack of attention for detail. Haphazard communications and a preference for lengthy talk and grandiose proclamations also dogged their efforts. The change of plans at the last minute, rushing up their action to November 8, had prevented them from utilizing effective preparation and organization, let alone from securing enough allies. As a result, the National Socialists had failed to obtain a powerful base of support to counter the influential military, industrial, and economic resources arrayed against them.

Hitler and the leaders of the putsch were stuck in a surreal fantasy world, where desire was perceived as reality and they were unable to admit that the Bavarian leaders would not be cooperating with them. By six o'clock that morning, they would have no choice but confront the facts of the situation.

This realization came by way of a mutual acquaintance, a fifty-five-year-old instructor at Munich's Infantry School, Col. Ludwig Leupold. After being awoken at the academy with news that General Ludendorff wished to speak with him, Leupold had come over at once to the War

Ministry. A long wait later, Leupold was taken into a small room alone with Ludendorff and Hitler. General Ludendorff expressed his frustration with Lossow for keeping them waiting almost seven hours. Telephone calls went unanswered; messengers failed to return. Ludendorff asked point-blank about Lossow's whereabouts.

He was not coming, Leupold said. He went on to confirm that Lossow had given orders for the army to resist Hitler and his supporters.

Ludendorff looked astonished, Leupold later said. The general must have been the last person to realize that Lossow was not going to join them.

Ludendorff then asked the instructor to make a personal appeal to Lossow to keep his word of honor.

Before the meeting wrapped up, Hitler launched into a tirade, shouting that he had worked for four years for Germany and he was "prepared to fight for [his] cause." He ranted, "I am not a coward!" As for Lossow, if he tried to destroy his work for Germany, the Bavarian general would forfeit his "right to exist."

All this braggadocio aside, Hitler must have realized that it would be difficult for his men to defend the War Ministry against the mobilized Reichswehr. They decided to move back to the Bürgerbräu. The putsch was returning to the beer hall where it had begun. And there, on Hitler's natural turf, they would prepare for a final confrontation with the authorities, whatever that would be. The Nazis apparently had no plan, let alone an alternative or contingency should their efforts fail. Once again, they would have to improvise.

On the way to the beer hall, Hitler would first stop by his apartment and change his clothes. Ludendorff and other plotters would meet him at the Bürgerbräukeller. Röhm was asked to remain at the War Ministry and to hold it at all costs.

16.

HOUR OF DECISION

If people gave him advice or warned him he used to say, "I shall go my own way." Where that way would lead him he neither saw nor dreamed.

—MARGARETHE LUDENDORFF

After a long night, about one thousand Storm Troopers and Kampf-bund men lay about the beer hall, passed out on the floor, hunched over tables, or stretched out on chairs pulled together. For the fortunate ones, there was breakfast of dark rye, cheese, wurst, and black coffee, much of it plundered from a restaurant across the street. Hitler, by contrast, had enjoyed two fried eggs, a slice of liver loaf, a couple pieces of bread, and a cup of tea.

Foreign correspondent Larry Rue, who had spent the night at the *Völkischer Beobachter* offices, was allowed inside the occupied beer hall that morning. The premises, he thought, resembled a war camp with rations, munitions, and supplies. Young men had started practicing maneuvers in the garden, and almost everyone, albeit hungry and exhausted, believed that the attack on the republic had succeeded.

Hitler, Ludendorff, and a handful of advisers had retreated to a small private dining room on the second floor. In contrast to the high spirits among the men outside, the mood there was dour. "It's looking very seri-ous for us," Hitler said earlier that morning to his bodyguard, Ulrich Graf.

Ludendorff, still in the same tweed jacket, nursed a glass of red wine amid a haze of stale cigar and cigarette smoke. Hitler had changed to a dark double-breasted suit underneath his belted trench coat. A corre-spondent for the *New York Times* saw Hitler that morning, poring over a map of Munich and looking "obviously overwrought and dead tired."

Hitler presented himself as the leader of the new dictatorship, but he "scarcely seemed to fill the part," the *New York Times* correspondent added. He seemed only a "little man in an old waterproof coat with a revolver at his hip, unshaven and with disordered hair, and so hoarse that he could scarcely speak." Ludendorff, on the other hand, appeared "extremely friendly," though "anxious and preoccupied as he talked with Hitler and some other political advisors." The general expressed his desire to secure the recognition of England, and above all, spoke about the "future glory of new Germany."

Clearly, Hitler and Ludendorff differed on the nature of their dilemma and the proper course of action. Hitler's awe for the general was dimin-ishing. He no longer acted with the sycophantic demeanor that one col-league compared to an orderly tending to a general, or a waiter looking after his most prominent patron. Did Hitler already blame Ludendorff for allowing the Bavarian leaders to leave the beer hall?

Hitler said only that he wished he could have spoken to Kahr, Los-sow, and Seisser one more time. Ludendorff would return the rebuke, pointing out that Hitler should never have forced the men into the back room with a pistol. He had believed that they were all in agreement.

So there they were, with their prospects dimming, their enthusiasms fading, and their leadership paralyzed, uncertain how to proceed. Hitler stuck to his idea of a propaganda campaign and sent the fiery anti-Sem-ite Julius Streicher into Munich to "speak at every street corner." He put Hermann Göring and Max Amann in charge of sending out Storm Troopers to pick up posters from printers and paste them all over town.

As for money, which they desperately needed to pay their supporters, Hitler ordered a gang of Storm Troopers to raid two shops, the Jewish-owned Firma Parcus on Promenadeplatz and the E. Mühlthaler and

Company on Dachauer Strasse. These businesses were selected because they represented a convenient way to obtain a lot of money quickly: they printed banknotes.

The Storm Troopers would return that morning with 14,605 trillion marks in twenty crates, which were stacked up almost five feet high on the stage where the band had performed the previous evening. Actually the band was still there, but it played only sporadically and without inspiration. The musicians were tired and hungry, grumbling that none of the financial windfall was coming their way.

Hitler issued one last order that further alienated Ludendorff. He sent a personal emissary to Crown Prince Rupprecht in Berchtesgaden to appeal to him on the grounds that he alone could convince Kahr to support the revolution. Ludendorff was no supporter of the Catholic Wittelsbach royal dynasty, but Hitler believed that Rupprecht's help could be a decisive factor in their success.

OUTSIDE, SNOW CONTINUED to fall on the cloudy and chilly morning. The streets were empty, except for people hurrying on to work, as if it were any normal Friday. Munich certainly did not seem to be in the throes of a revolution.

For most people in town, news about the Bürgerbräu had come only with the newspaper. "The Victory of the Swastika" headlined the Nazi *Völkischer Beobachter*, rhapsodizing on Hitler's triumph over "five years of the most atrocious shame and disgrace" perpetrated by Jews and the Jewish regime. A new age had been launched, the paper said. The German eagle was about to soar.

Alfred Rosenberg had planned the edition carefully. He praised each of the leaders of the revolution: Hitler and Ludendorff, of course, but also the Bavarian authorities who had joined them on the stage. Kahr was the model civil servant, faithful to his country and people; Lossow emerged as "the brave military leader"; and Seisser stood out as someone whose hard work and steadfast support had helped reawaken the spirit of "the new National Socialist Germany." They were men about to make history.

Copies of the early papers were snapped up quickly. Munich's most influential daily, *Münchner Neueste Nachrichten*, also carried a lively account of this apparent triumph. The press would certainly help the nascent, fledgling putsch, as Kahr's adviser Adolf Schiedt had warned, spreading information of the event that was some twelve hours old, and also providing encouragement to the leadership that their cause was not yet lost.

Elsewhere, news of the putsch arrived too late for many European newspapers to report anything other than the barest account. In Paris, *Le Matin* noted that General Ludendorff had been proclaimed dictator and Munich fascists had imprisoned the leaders of the Bavarian government. There was a widespread fear, *Le Petit Parisien* added, that the revolutionaries would repudiate the Treaty of Versailles. The London *Times* and several British newspapers warned of Germany disintegrating into civil war.

Across the Atlantic, newspapers took advantage of the time difference to print more details of the events. "Adolph [*sic*] Hitler's troops have begun an offensive movement toward Berlin," reported the *New York Times*, in one of its six articles that morning on the putsch. Most of the newspapers, German or international, emphasized the role of General Ludendorff, who was of course the most famous man in the plot. Hitler's own *Völkischer Beobachter* was one of the few papers that cited Hitler's name first.

Some papers resigned Hitler to the role of minor support, as "Ludendorff's aide," as the *New York World* put it. Other papers, like the *Daily News*, misspelled his name as "Hittler" or, like *New York Tribune*, misidentified him as a lieutenant. *Time* magazine, then in its first year of publication, labeled him a Bavarian royalist. *La Croix* referred to him as "General Hitler."

But Hitler was not a general, a royalist, or a Ludendorff aide, and he was certainly not on his way to Berlin. He was still on the second floor of the Bürgerbräu beer hall, pacing back and forth, trying to find a way to salvage a revolution spinning out of control.

. . .

ERNST RÖHM AND several other high-ranking associates were, meanwhile, transforming the Bavarian War Ministry into a Nazi fortress, ringing it with barbed wire, sharp steel obstacles, and machine-gun defenses at its windows. Other members of his force stood guard at its entrances and patrolled the courtyard. Deep inside the building, in the war room on the third floor, they were waiting.

No order or information had come from Hitler and Ludendorff for hours. Nothing had arrived from Ernst Pöhner at police headquarters either, where Hitler had sent him to check on Frick, or from General von Lossow, who should have been there by now. Röhm felt, as he later put it, "alone, abandoned, and perplexed by developments."

Dogged by this lack of communication, Röhm would soon face a large Reichswehr force mobilized by Gen. Jakob von Danner and reportedly on the way toward the War Ministry. Some of these troops were already rumbling up Ludwigstrasse: Two infantry battalions, three artillery batteries, and a trench mortar company, along with eight armored cars and a large contingent of state police detachments. Army snipers scrambled into strategic posts on nearby roofs, or at upper-story windows. There they remained, also waiting for orders.

DESPITE INITIATIVES TO suppress the putsch, Hitler still possessed more men and weapons than Munich's authorities commanded at this time. Hitler's Storm Troopers and Kampfbund forces totaled some 4,000 men; the government, by contrast, had only 2,600 troops at hand, 1,800 of whom were in the state police.

But military reinforcements were arriving en masse from around Bavaria. State police units were taking up positions already secured on bridges and main pathways into the city center. Hitler's early advantage in troops was fading.

In the private dining room on the second floor, Hitler, Ludendorff, and the team debated strategy. Lt. Col. Hermann Kriebel, the military commander for the Kampfbund, called their prospects "hopeless," and pressed for an "orderly retreat." Göring agreed, provided that they used the opportunity to regroup in order to attack at a more favorable opportunity.

In the meantime, he suggested that they move their base of operations to Rosenheim, some forty miles south of Munich near the Austrian border. The city was, relatively speaking, a bastion of Nazi support. It had hosted the first branch of the party outside Munich, and Göring knew its streets well too, because he had been born and raised there.

At first Hitler supported this plan, but then he waffled, counting on the Bavarian crown prince to come to his rescue, or trusting in the power of propaganda to swing things in his favor. Ludendorff, however, opposed both Hitler's preference for waiting and Göring's plan to retreat to Rosenheim. He scornfully dismissed the latter as driving the national revolution into the ditch of some forsaken "dirt road."

Sometime after eleven a.m., news arrived that the state police was tightening its hold around the city, including a barricade on the bridges over the Isar that command the entrance into the city center. The leadership would soon have to make a decision. They could not simply stay at the beer hall, or they would end up under siege, like Röhm.

Ludendorff proposed that they organize a demonstration, or a public show of strength. They should march their supporters through the city, rallying the people to join them or, at the least, cheer them on. This would also counter the lethargy and boredom of idling about the premises without direction. Nothing was worse for morale than just waiting while the enemy grew in strength and gained in position.

Perhaps a show of popular support would convince Kahr, Lossow, and Seisser to abandon their intention to oppose them. Surely, too, it was reasoned, the army would not shoot at a procession led by such a popular national figure as General Ludendorff. "The heavens will fall before the troops fire on me," Ludendorff had told a colleague the previous day. The soldiers would, it was hoped, flock to the banner of the swastika. With a little luck, nationalist momentum might push Hitler to Berlin, just as it had propelled Mussolini to Rome.

The time for hesitation and indecision was over, Ludendorff said. "We march."

17.

IN THE COURTYARD

*Since I am a wicked and immature man, war and unrest,
like it or not, appeal to me more than the orderly life of your
respectable burgher.*

—CAPT. ERNST RÖHM

Göring went to issue instructions to Josef Berchtold, the commander of the Stosstrupp Hitler, for one final raid. The troops were ordered to capture the mayor of Munich, Eduard Schmid, and the members of the city council who belonged to the Social Democratic Party, or as his colleague Lieutenant Colonel Kriebel dubbed it, the "Red, Redder, and Reddest party."

But the expedition of about fifty men struggled to reach the city center thanks, ironically, to Hitler's handpicked orator, Julius Streicher. His rabble-rousing in the Marienplatz, Munich's largest square, had caused a major traffic jam.

The new government will "hang Jewish profiteers from the lampposts," shouted Streicher, standing on the backseat of an open car. Hitler would shut down the "Jewish" stock exchanges and nationalize all banks. He promised bread for the hungry and justice for the scoundrels who had robbed, rather than ruled, them. The "time of shame is over," Streicher screamed.

After navigating around the masses, many of them chanting "Heil Hitler! Heil Ludendorff!" the Stosstrupp Hitler detachment finally reached the town hall.

Berchtold selected a dozen of his men with machine guns and rifles, barged into the building, dashed up the steps, and, tearing into the room, shouted that the council was under arrest. All Socialists, Marxists, and Jews were ordered to rise. No one moved.

Instead, one of the city council members, Deputy Mayor Hans Küffner, had the audacity to ask: What is your definition of a Socialist?

The sixty-two-year-old deputy mayor was seized by the collar and thrown against the wall. Councilman Albert Nussbaum, clasped by the wrist and the back of his jacket, was struck by the barrel of a gun to his left temple. Each council member was dragged outside, passing an angry mob that had been worked up by demagogic rants. The people spat, shoved, and shouted insults, urging the captors to show no mercy.

Heinrich Hoffmann, a former wartime aviation photographer who had been named a couple months before as Hitler's personal photographer, had bicycled to the square with his camera and glass plates of film. He snapped a chilling portrait of the mayor and the seven city council members being loaded onto a truck for a journey to the Bürgerbräu.

During the commotion, the Rathaus-Glockenspiel rang in the eleven o'clock hour with the dance of mechanical jesters and knights.

LESS THAN A mile north, the German Reichswehr moved toward the occupied War Ministry. The state police covered their flanks and rear. Nearby houses had been occupied with machine guns placed in windows, their barrels aimed at the front door of the stone building.

Röhm's men held their positions around the War Ministry and its courtyard. One of them, Heinrich Himmler, raised the Reichskriegsflagge banner at the barbed-wire barricade on Ludwigstrasse. Machine guns peered out of the windows toward the advancing army. His men, Röhm said proudly, were going to be "blood brothers unto death."

As the two sides settled down to a standoff, the Reichswehr commander of the operation, General von Danner, sent in a number of negotiators, carrying white flags of truce, to try to reason with the putschists and give them one last chance to leave the building peacefully.

One member of the delegation was Captain Röhm's previous commander and mentor, Maj. Gen. Franz Xaver Ritter von Epp. Epp had led one of the most powerful Freikorps units, the "Freikorps Epp," that had helped quash Munich's Communist uprising in 1919. He had also raised some 60,000 Reichsmarks for the Nazi Party to purchase its newspaper. Epp was, in other words, a power broker with prestige in extreme right-wing circles.

With a crowd of spectators watching, some of them shaking fists at the negotiators, Epp and his colleagues passed Röhm's men standing guard and made their way inside the War Ministry.

Resistance was futile, the negotiators were overheard telling Röhm. Kahr, Lossow, and Seisser had decided to fight the putsch with the full might of the state. Röhm was "totally outnumbered and outgunned," Epp said, and had no choice but to surrender. Röhm refused. He had his orders and he would only stand down on Ludendorff's command.

But the putschists had already won, claimed one of the negotiators. Berlin had invoked Article 48 and handed supreme power over to General von Seeckt. They promised Röhm "an honorable surrender."

Röhm asked to speak with their commander, General von Danner, and a two-hour cease-fire was arranged to allow for their negotiations at the state police barracks on Türkenstrasse. Minutes after he left, however, shots were heard outside the War Ministry.

It was disputed, of course, who fired first. The Reichswehr claimed that the gunfire came from Röhm's men in a wing of the occupied building; Röhm's men said that they did not fire a single shot, and that it was the Reichswehr who had occupied the third floor of a garage facing the rear of the ministry. Years later, however, Röhm admitted that a hothead who had served alongside his men might have been responsible.

The first shots turned into a volley, seventeen shots from the state-police side alone. Two Reichswehr soldiers, crouched by a wall on the nearby Kaulbachstrasse, were wounded. In the eastern courtyard of the War Ministry, one of Röhm's men, a young bank employee, Martin

Faust, was also struck, the bullet penetrating behind his right ear. He fell face forward to the ground.

Faust's superior, Lt. Theodor Casella, raised his right hand high in the air and yelled for everyone to hold their fire. He rushed to Faust's side unarmed only to take a bullet in his thigh. Both of the men were retrieved by Himmler and his comrades. Faust was already dead, and Casella died that afternoon after being transported to the nearby Klinik Josephinum. The Beer Hall Putsch had claimed its first lives.

18.

HITLER'S FOREIGN LEGION

Don't go along, Herr Rosenberg. This is pure suicide.
—ADOLF MÜLLER, PRINTER

Ernst Pöhner, the former president of the Munich police, was sup-posed to be working on a plan for Hitler's government to end the runaway inflation. One of the priorities was to stop the "flight of capital from Jews and political enemies." A meeting to hash out the details had been set for eight a.m. Pöhner, however, did not show.

When his colleague Marc Sesselmann called his apartment to check on him, Pöhner's wife, Margarethe, came on the phone, in great excite-ment. "You do not know then?" she asked. Kahr's support had collapsed, Hitler's men had been betrayed, and Pöhner had been taken into custody. Authorities had already searched their apartment, "like pigs," rummag-ing through desks and emptying out file cabinets. "Flee to safety," she advised. "It's all lost!"

Pöhner had indeed been arrested that morning. After learning of the triumvirate's resistance, Hitler had sent him to police headquarters, where he could use his contacts and secure the building for the revolu-tion. State police officers Banzer and Imhoff, however, had immediately arrested him, just as they had Frick. It felt, Pöhner said, "like a blow from a club."

The Nazis were down to two main centers of resistance: the beer hall and the War Ministry. But in which building were Hitler and Ludendorff? asked the morning edition of *Berliner Tageblatt*. It was still not known when the newspaper went to press.

As the clock ticked closer to noon, some 2,000 men were gathering in an irregular and slapdash formation outside the Bürgerbräu. At the front stood the two standard-bearers, one of them holding a black-white-red banner emblazoned with a swastika, the other the Bund Oberland's white edelweiss on a blue diamond.

Just behind them stood Adolf Hitler in his trench coat, with rumpled fedora in hand and a Browning pistol holstered at his side. To his immediate left was Scheubner-Richter; to his right, General Ludendorff. Behind them followed Lieutenant Colonel Kriebel, Ulrich Graf, and Hermann Göring. The marchers were about to embark on what Hitler would later call "the most desperately daring decision of [his] life."

"Things look ugly," Scheubner-Richter said to Rosenberg, his old friend who had just arrived from his office at the *Völkischer Beobachter* to take up his position near the front. Scheubner-Richter also expressed his concern to Hitler that this might be their last walk together.

The early-morning snow had now stopped and a faint sunshine tried to peer through the gloomy and gray sky—the rising sun of German freedom, as one marcher put it. For hours now, the state police had marshaled its forces and deployed them at strategic points to consolidate their control over the railway station, telegraph, and telephone exchange. The legitimate government also held the police station, which Hitler had tried unsuccessfully to take.

But Göring had a plan to counter the growing strength of the Reichswehr and state police. He wanted to march the recently seized mayor and city council members in the procession. If the police dared to fire on them, Göring would threaten "to execute all the hostages." And if the police cooperated, the politicians could still be used as valuable leverage and exchanged for their own captured men, Pöhner and Frick.

When he heard of this scheme, the leader of the Stosstrupp Hitler,

Josef Berchtold, or someone near him, protested that the hostages weren't "worth a bullet" and suggested that his men bludgeon them instead. Hitler, however, ended the discussion by sending the prisoners back to captivity at the Bürgerbräu. He did not want any martyrs.

About this time, the midday newspaper *Münchener Zeitung* hit the stands. Right before going to press, the editor and Kahr speechwriter Adolf Schiedt had managed to insert news of the Bavarian leaders' rejection of the putsch. The paper also printed a brief commentary criticizing Hitler's deceit and broken promises. "Hitlerputsch—the Rape of Kahr" ran the headlines. The Bavarian state was ready to assert its power.

The Nazi marchers, many of them hungry and hungover from the long night in the beer hall, headed northwest toward the city center, waving the swastika banner and singing their anthem, "Sturm-Lied": *"Germany, awake! Break your chains in two!"* The song's composer was Dietrich Eckart, the translator of Henrik Ibsen's *Peer Gynt* and the author of its popular adaptation to the German stage. Eckart had missed the storming of the beer hall, and so watched the procession from the sidewalk near the Isartor train station.

All the while, traffic continued to flow, outside of a few bottlenecks, and trolleys were still picking up and dropping people off for their Friday-morning activities. The marchers passed through the surreal city. Nazi sympathizers followed them, Lieutenant Colonel Kriebel said, "like a swarm of bees." Street vendors catered to the crowds that already seemed to be celebrating victory, while musicians blared their trumpets and beat their drums.

One of the men in the procession, Hans Hinkel, recalled years later "the deep joyful enthusiasm" that marked the occasion. "We [were] workers, students, officers, burghers, craftsmen, old and young," he said, all united in an elevated and exalted earnestness.

Posters were still up proclaiming the German Revolution, as were those announcing the Bavarian authorities' repudiation of it. Some people stopped to watch, cheer, or shout "Heil!" Others laughed. The young law student Hans Frank, setting up a machine gun that day at the Museum Bridge, was asked by an onlooker if his mommy gave him permission to play with such dangerous toys.

FIFTEEN MINUTES INTO the march, Hitler's procession reached the Ludwig Bridge over the Isar River. The "Green Police," or state police, had arrived about one hour earlier with a small contingent of thirty men armed with heavy machine guns and orders not to let the putschists pass.

Many of the men marching down the hill toward the bridge also believed that the police would either join them or they would stand aside. The commander of the state police on-site, Lt. Georg Höfler, how-ever, ordered his force into formation and shouted for the putschists to halt. Göring ignored him. The police then loaded live ammunition, as commanded.

"Don't shoot at your comrades," Göring yelled to the line of police-men at the bridge.

Before the police had time to respond, a trumpet blared and Berch-told's Stosstrupp Hitler troops charged, pushing the police aside, seizing their weapons, and, in some cases, attacking them with rifle butts. Other people in the procession spit on the officers and insulted them. At least twenty-eight policemen were taken captive and marched back to the beer hall, their hands on their heads. This was described by later Nazi propaganda as "police fraternization."

Crossing the bridge over the Isar, Hitler's procession continued west-ward down Zweibrückenstrasse, where the crowds were appearing, many of the people waving swastika banners or joining in the march. "The mood of the city," as eyewitness Johann Aigner put it, "was with-out exception favorable to our venture." The marchers passed through the Isartor Gate and then onto the broad Tal, toward the narrow streets of the city center.

Historian Karl Alexander von Müller watched the rowdy proces-sion from a street corner at the Marienplatz. Ludendorff strode forth, he thought, as "one of the greatest generals of the old German army." The men behind him, by contrast, seemed like "a motley rabble . . . all helter-skelter." They looked like "desperate revolutionaries," or as some said derisively, like Hitler's foreign legion. Even Hans Frank, marching with the men, thought they looked like "a defeated army that had not fought anybody."

Carl Zuckmayer, the young playwright, eating lunch on the Marien-platz, saw the procession as a riotous victory celebration, like a second Oktoberfest.

19.

BLOOD LAND

If you cross the Rubicon, you also have to march on Rome.
—ADOLF HITLER, FEBRUARY 26, 1924

Shortly after eleven that morning, Putzi left the beer hall for the office of the party newspaper, *Völkischer Beobachter*. The prospects of success looked so dismal that he decided to return home and, as he put it, "prepare for a get-away." While packing, his sister Erna called with news of the march into town, and Putzi, not wanting to miss out, changed his mind and set out to rejoin the procession. It was near the Pinakothek art museums that he encountered a mob fleeing toward him, away from the Odeonsplatz.

"It's terrible, Herr Hanfstaengl," one Storm Trooper told him. "It's the end of Germany!" The army had opened fire on the patriots, he said, and it was a massacre. Ludendorff had marched the followers into the Marienplatz. But he did not stop there, as many people in the procession assumed. Neither did he wheel the men around and double back to the beer hall via one of the side streets, as other people in the procession had expected, including his military planner, Hermann Kriebel.

Instead, he turned right onto Wienstrasse and then took another right onto Perusastrasse. Ludendorff never fully explained his reasoning.

"At certain moments of life," the general later said, "you act instinctively and do not know why." Were they headed to relieve Röhm, under siege at the War Ministry, and perhaps link up the two armies?

This seems likely, but along the way, as several eyewitnesses in the procession overheard, Ludendorff had been warned by a policeman that the state police troops and a tank lay just ahead on the Odeonsplatz. Ludendorff may well have acted on this tip, though without following the rest of the advice—namely, to avoid this concentration of force by continuing down the broad Maximilianstrasse. So, instead, the marchers were led onto Residenzstrasse, a narrow street that passed the royal palace and, presumably, had the advantage of approaching the police from the rear.

The commander of the second company of state police on the Odeonsplatz was 1st Lt. Michael Freiherr von Godin, a twenty-seven-year-old Bavarian nobleman. His brother Emmerich had been Hitler's regimental commander at the end of the war and, in fact, made the official request for Hitler to receive his Iron Cross First Class.

The Nazis, Godin knew, could not be allowed to pass from the narrow streets into the broad space, where they could exploit their sizable numerical superiority—about 2,000 to 100.

As the marchers came down the Residenzstrasse, rifles, pistols, and bayonets were on full display. The rank and file shouted, cheered, and sang a nationalistic anthem, "O Deutschland hoch in Ehren" [Oh, Germany, high in honor], their voices amplified as they bounced off the walls of the palace in the lane.

At the end of the street, which opened onto the Odeonsplatz, a machine gun was mounted on the Feldherrnhalle and the state police were crouching among the statues. First Lieutenant von Godin scrambled some of his men over to face the procession. He ordered the marchers to halt.

The procession continued in defiance of his commands.

"Don't shoot, Ludendorff and Hitler are coming," shouted bodyguard Ulrich Graf. The National Socialists kept marching straight into the muzzle of the guns. Hitler locked arms with Scheubner-Richter. They braced themselves as they walked forward.

. . .

No ONE, THEN or later, has satisfactorily answered the question of who fired the first shot. The putschists would blame the police, and the police the putschists. Godin said that his company used only "rifle-butt and baton" until the first bullet whizzed by his head and struck Sgt. Nikolaus Hollweg of the state police in the head. Before Godin could give the order to fire, he claimed, the police responded as if in a single volley. Hitler's men did likewise, in a thunderous roar echoing off the narrow street.

It is difficult to find many credible nonpartisan eyewitnesses who confirm the story. One retired schoolteacher was trying to pass a police cordon near the Feldherrnhalle when she heard loud shouting and crying of "Heil!" of the oncoming marchers. Then, all of a sudden, an array of policemen in steel helmets was crouching down around her and one of these men, she was certain, had shot first.

The student Arno Schmidt, also in the area that morning, described an officer rushing forward, dropping to a knee, and firing first—and not into the air, but with his gun held "perfectly horizontal." It was also the police, several witnesses added, who held guns in firing position when they first heard the shots, while Hitler's men did not.

Putsch veterans would add that they had been packed so closely together in the lane that it would have been difficult to shoot without hitting their own men. Many of the guns, moreover, had no firing pins, removed, perhaps, by the monks in an act of sabotage. Other men in the procession had no ammunition. Before marching, Hitler had given the order to unload, but it remains unclear how many people obeyed him. Many of the putschists had either not heard the command or disregarded it altogether.

Berchtold, who had returned from bringing the police captives back to the beer hall, arrived in time to witness what happened next. The singing and shouting had been interrupted by a shot and then a "hideous racket of a machine gun!"

After that, "all was horror, agony, and confusion."

The police fired furiously at the marchers from in front and on the flank: At the Odeonsplatz, the balcony of the Feldherrnhalle, the tower of the Residenz, and the alley behind the Palais Preysing. Everything happened "lightning-fast," Ludendorff said, describing the short but fierce battle that raged in the street.

Hitler was one of the first to fall. He was either pulled down, presumably by Scheubner-Richter or by his bodyguard, or he instinctively sought cover as he would have done as a dispatch runner under fire in the First World War. He grabbed his left shoulder in wrenching pain, fearing he had been shot. The blood on him was in fact from Scheubner-Richter, who had been hit in the lungs and died immediately. The bullet missed Hitler by about one foot.

The leader of the Nazis hit the ground with so much force that he dislocated his shoulder. His bodyguard, Ulrich Graf, was severely wounded as he covered Hitler, possibly saving his life. Graf took bullets in the lungs, the chest, both thighs, and his right arm, which had been shot through from the elbow to the shoulder. Several other men were lying on the pavement beside him. One large man in a dark coat, covered in blood, he believed, was Ludendorff.

Göring was shot in the thigh and groin. He crawled behind a stone lion at the royal palace, twisting in agony. Several colleagues rushed to his aid. Rosenberg also went down, looking for cover, but soon found himself being used by a fellow Nazi as a sandbag as he fired at the police. Rosenberg eventually scooted away to safety, near the same stone lions. He looked over at a putschist lying on the sidewalk, with his head blown off, brains flowing out, "steaming." His body was still jerking.

Lieutenant Colonel Kriebel, seeking shelter, ran toward the Feldherrnhalle. He noticed a man in a dark-brown overcoat, covered with blood and thought it was Ludendorff. The two battle flags lay in the street, covering two other dead men. Kriebel also recognized Scheubner-Richter, dead. A policeman, Kriebel recalled, stood over a fallen comrade and fired three times, "each shot jolted the body from the street into the air."

Several shots then came at Kriebel from a palace window, all of them missing and probably lodging into a wall of the Feldherrnhalle. He decided to lie low, as if he were hit, hoping that the firing would stop. In the commotion, Kriebel remembered thinking he'd soon be struck, and cursing the police.

The firing seemed to be coming from all sides. Many of the marchers fled into doorways, or turned around, retreating into their own ranks and thereby increasing the chaos and panic. Hans Rickmers of the Bund Oberland saw a woman in a fur coat beside him fall to a knee and another woman in a raincoat hit the ground. At that point, he felt the blow to the back of his head, and staggered off eventually finding his way to a physician and a bottle of schnapps in a room above an automobile club. He heard the rumor there that Ludendorff had been killed and felt, as he later said, hate, anger and despair. He died three weeks later.

The head of Munich's Storm Troopers, Wilhelm Brückner, took refuge in a chemist's shop. Of all the street battles he had fought, he later said, "the most disgusting was this blood land at the Odeonsplatz." He was, as he put it, "completely crushed."

The putschists were fleeing wherever they could. Otto Engelbrecht of the Bund Oberland ran to the restaurant Bauerngirgl; Johann Prem, who had joined in the march after finishing his night shift at the post office, fled to the Ministry of the Interior, where he banged on the windows of the porter's lodge until someone opened the door. He had been hit by shots grazing his knee, chin, and right shoulder. Karl Kessler of the second company of Storm Troopers made it unscathed to a nearby café. A colleague he found there was less fortunate. He had been shot in the head.

"This is madness!" Storm Trooper Richard Kolb shouted.

Despite the rumors, Ludendorff had neither been killed nor wounded. In fact, he was soon praised for maintaining his composure, marching forward undeterred by whizzing bullets. Oxford historian John W. Wheeler-Bennett called his supposed bolt-upright stance "the last gesture of the Old Imperial Army." Not every eyewitness, however, agreed that the reality lived up to the emerging legend.

American vice consul Robert Murphy, who happened to be watching nearby, swore that Ludendorff behaved as everyone else: He "fell flat to escape the hail of bullets." He was only human, and acted with the instinct of the battlefield. Several other eyewitnesses agreed with this description. In fact, a counter-rumor soon circulated that Ludendorff had remained on the ground, pretending to be dead and raised himself only when directly ordered by the police. At any rate, Ludendorff probably returned quickly to his feet and marched straight across the square to the police. Not a single bullet touched him.

Ludendorff's valet, Kurt Neubauer, on the other hand, was shot in the stomach, as he apparently jumped in front of the general, and tumbled over, foaming at the mouth. Scheubner-Richter's valet, Johann Aigner, who crept over to help, felt warmth on his neck and found blood on the back of his head. He thought that he, too, had been hit, but the blood was from a man beside him who had been shot in the throat.

Many of the police officers did, as commanded, aim for the ground, but the bullets had ricocheted against the pavement and walls, chipping off granite, and implanting razor-sharp pieces of stone in flesh and bone.

"Everywhere people were going down," Josef Berchtold remembered, "writhing on the ground in agony, dead and dying, while the guns still rattled death and murder into their stampeding midst . . . [the] dead were trampled under people's feet throwing [tripping] the living down; blood flowed everywhere over the grey pavement. The whole thing was a ghastly debacle. Shrieks and cries rent the air, and ever that insane firing went on."

Dr. Friedrich Weber, flattening his body against the wall of a house in the narrow alley, began to cry. It was a slaughter.

By the time the smoke had cleared, less than one minute after the shooting began, all that was left of the beer hall putsch was a trail of destruction. The march to Berlin had ended, one mile away, at the Odeonsplatz. Bloody, mangled bodies of the dead and the dying filled the street.

Twenty people were killed, including four state policemen: Nikolaus Hollweg, Friedrich Fink, Max Schoberth, and Rudolf Schaut, the latter having been married only five months before. The owner of a toy shop, Oskar Körner, who had donated a sizable part of his profits to the Nazi Party and marched in the third row, had been killed. Many were wounded, probably more than one hundred. Dr. Ferdinand Sauerbruch, a professor of surgery, and his staff at Munich University Hospital would struggle to save the lives of nineteen people rushed to the emergency room.

One young man who had been shot in the head remained unidentified for several days. After his death, he was discovered to be neither a marcher nor a member of the state police; he was a waiter named Karl Kuhn who had been walking across the square on his way to work. An Englishwoman, Suzanne St. Barbe Baker, hoping to extend her stay in Munich at the British consulate, was more fortunate. She escaped the "battlefield" of the Odeonsplatz by crawling to the safety of a café that had every windowpane shattered.

Police apprehended as many marchers as possible, first those lying there cursing authorities and groaning in pain. Ludendorff surrendered, shocked and appalled that the state would fire upon him and the men he regarded as Germany's true patriots. He refused to acknowledge attempts to address him as "Excellency," or General, and swore, in his disdain, never to wear the German military uniform again.

One other person hit—the large man in the front in the dark coat mistaken for Ludendorff—was one of Ernst Pöhner's friends, Theodor von der Pfordten, chief magistrate of the Bavarian Supreme Court. In his pocket was a bloodstained draft of a constitution for the new Germany. It set out a draconian authoritarian regime that called for, among other things, the abolition of parliament, the removal of Jews from the country, the confiscation of Jewish wealth, and the confinement of the regime's enemies in what he called "collection camps." It was a chilling premonition of what was at stake that morning on a narrow street outside the royal palace.

20.

FLIGHT

Ludendorff Arrested. Hitler Makes His Escape.
—*Daily Mail* (BRISBANE), NOVEMBER 11, 1923

At some point in the melee, Hitler staggered to his feet and scrambled for safety. Dr. Walter Schultze, chief of the Storm Trooper medical corps, whisked the dazed leader away to a car, waiting near the Finance Ministry on Max-Josef-Platz. An eyewitness saw the vehicle speed away carrying a very pale passenger.

Stunned and disoriented, with severe pain in his shoulder, Hitler had few real options. He had been so confident in the success of his plan that he had not bothered to sketch even a rudimentary contingency or alternative. Now that the march had ended in an utter fiasco, he had to improvise his retreat.

Several of his men had been killed and wounded, and Hitler had run away, as one former Freikorps man and later prominent anti-Nazi, Friedrich Wilhelm Heinz, put it. "Adolf the Swell-Head took off . . . and left his men in the lurch . . . Did you expect that he'd do anything else?"

A story was later circulated to cover for Hitler's lack of valor. He was said to have spotted a young boy bleeding on a street corner and left the scene to save him. In later Nazi accounts, he was even said to have carried the ten-year-old away (with his dislocated shoulder!).

Other lies and half-truths circulated to explain Hitler's behavior. It was said, for example, that he had been forced to race away, with the police in pursuit, firing machine guns at his car, and that was what prevented him from returning to the beer hall to check on his men. Hitler certainly seemed to be a poor contrast to Ludendorff, who had not abandoned his comrades, and, it was widely if improbably claimed, walked straight into the gunfire without a trace of fear.

Göring, wounded in the upper thigh and groin, writhed in pain near the stone lions outside the royal palace. Supporters carried him down the street to a courtyard of the Residenzstrasse. Two men in the building, Robert and Martin Ballin, Jewish owners of the Royal Bavarian Furniture Factory, agreed to take him in, even though the injured man was the commander of Hitler's Storm Troopers. Robert's wife, Bella, who had experience caring for the wounded in the First World War, administered emergency aid in the upstairs salon.

One of their neighbors, a physician named Dr. Emil Neustadt, had watched the procession from a window on Theatinerstrasse. After the shooting, he went into the street, which was soon nearly empty, except for men in uniform running back and forth. Against one wall leaned a handful of Storm Troopers, "partly covered in blood, their clothes torn open, and groaning in pain." The physician went to work with injections on two of the most severe cases, who were already nearly unconscious. He never learned their names or their fates.

Putzi dashed down Arcisstrasse when a car, racing by, slammed on its brakes. Inside sat his friends Hermann Esser, Dietrich Eckart, and Heinrich Hoffmann. He hopped in and they headed to the photographer's studio, where they split up to leave town separately. Putzi obtained a false passport with the help of another friend, Adm. Paul von Hintze, and soon passed across the border.

One group of putschists fled to a girls' school near the Odeonsplatz, where they hid in closets and under beds. Other Storm Troopers headed to a pastry shop, Konditorei Rottenhöfer, and concealed weapons and ammunition under ovens, in flour sacks, cake boxes, and behind coffee machines. Hans Frank and his cronies entered the Eiles Coffee Roasting Company, hiding their SA gear in the back and pretending that they had spent the morning chatting over coffee.

Thirty-one suspected putschists were arrested by the police and placed in "protective custody," pending charges. Another two hundred and three people were quickly picked up for lesser offenses, such as insulting authorities or disseminating revolutionary pamphlets. Arrests would continue for some time. By two o'clock, Röhm had surrendered. His men, ordered into the courtyard of the War Ministry, were divested of their arms and ammunition, along with their insignia, allegedly ripped off the uniforms. Röhm was bitter as he joined other leading Nazis taken into captivity.

The police sealed off the Odeonsplatz and Residenz area; the pavement was strewn with dead bodies and discarded swastika flags and armbands. Pigeons were chased away from the corpses, which were brought into the palace courtyard. The wounded were taken there as well for emergency dressing. The more serious cases had been rushed by automobile to the hospital.

"I was close to madness," the valet Johann Aigner said, after being allowed into the restricted area thanks to a sympathetic policeman. He saw the bodies now lying side by side near the entrance gate to the Residenz palace. Among them were Scheubner-Richter and his good friend Kurt Neubauer, Ludendorff's valet. "I was sick in my soul and totally shattered."

Immediate reports of the street fighting were vague and often contradictory. Many newspapers, including Berlin's *Vossische Zeitung*, Paris's *Le Figaro*, and the London *Times* described Hitler and Ludendorff holed up to the bitter end in the War Ministry. *Le Petit Parisien* identified the site of the siege as the Prince Arnulf Barracks near the Pinakothek museums, reporting how the army captured both Ludendorff and Hitler. In another piece in the same issue, it noted correctly that Hitler had been wounded, but had escaped.

Some of the early rumors suggested that Hitler had fled to Rosenheim, Troenum, or somewhere in the Isar valley. Monarchists gathering in eastern Munich were said to be sheltering him in preparation for making a last stand. *Le Petit Parisien*, by contrast, announced that he had already crossed the border into the Tyrol. "All's well that ends well," wrote its foreign correspondent, because Hitler was returning to the Austrian hole from which he had emerged.

• • •

AT THE HANFSTAENGL family villa in the middle of the village of Uffing, some thirty-five miles south of Munich, Putzi's wife, Helen, was finishing supper with her son Egon in the second-floor living room. Shortly
after seven p.m., one of her maids came in to say that someone was quietly knocking at the door.

She had already locked up the house and closed the shutters in the
wake of rumors warning of "dangerous elements roaming the countryside." She walked downstairs to speak to the strangers from behind the
bolted door. "To my utter amazement," Helen later said, "I recognized
the weak, but unmistakable voice of Hitler."

She described the sight in her doorway: "There he stood, ghastly pale,
hatless, his face and clothing covered with mud, the left arm hanging
down from a strangely slanting shoulder." Dr. Schultze and the first-aid
men were trying to hold him up, though she said they hardly looked
much better. "Pathetically rampaged" was how she put it.

The men had indeed toyed with the idea of fleeing to Austria. Hitler
is often believed to have outright vetoed that option, presumably for his
dislike of his home country, but according to the doctor in the car, that
was not what happened. They were headed to Austria, like many other
putschists, but somewhere on the road to Garmisch, probably near Mur-
nau, their automobile had broken down.

Given the police search, Hitler and the two other men decided not
to risk a walk to a mechanic in town, and instead took advantage of
the nearby woods for cover until nightfall. At some point during the
wait, Hitler had remembered the Hanfstaengl property in Uffing. They
had asked the chauffeur to deal with the car and renew contact with
Göring—they had no idea of the extent of his wounds. Hitler, Schultze,
and the orderly then set off on foot, avoiding the main road.

After what must have been a grueling trek given Hitler's shoulder
injury, they finally arrived at the villa. Helen took the men upstairs to
her living room.

"*Also doch?*" she asked, meaning "So it's true, after all?"

Hitler just lowered his head.

Helen asked about her husband, whom she had not seen or heard from since the morning.

Putzi had been at the newspaper office at the time of the march, Hitler thought, and suggested that he would probably soon arrive.

Hitler was in a poor state, his nerves raw. He was exhausted after two sleepless nights. He spoke of the deaths of Ludendorff and his bodyguard Ulrich Graf, which he believed was true and said he welcomed his own death as a delivery from his misery. At the same time, he blamed the failure of the putsch on General Ludendorff for allowing the triumvirate to leave the beer hall and sabotage the plan. Then, abruptly changing his mood, he swore to "go on fighting . . . as long as breath was in him."

Helen suggested that Hitler, who was apparently running a temperature, try to rest. The doctor and his first-aid man helped him upstairs to an attic bedroom, where they worked to set his swollen left shoulder. It had been dislocated and fractured at the upper arm socket. The excruciating cries of pain from behind the closed doors, Helen said in her unpublished, handwritten notes, could be heard all the way downstairs.

A short while later, Hitler was huddled in the attic lined with books, wrapped in English traveling rugs that Putzi had taken to Harvard and usually kept atop a wooden chest. The first-aid man went to sleep in another guest room upstairs in a part of the house that they had renovated the previous summer. Dr. Schultze and Helen, in the meantime, discussed the strange turn of events that morning after the march to the Odeonsplatz and weighed their options.

They of course had no idea how successful the chauffeur would be repairing, or hiding, the broken-down car, let alone reaching Göring. What they did know was that the police would be patrolling the main roads, streets, and railways in search of Hitler, and news of strangers traveled quickly in the close-knit village of Uffing. Hitler could not stay there indefinitely.

21.

HOSTAGE ORDEAL

Dear Rosenberg, from now on you will lead the movement.
—ADOLF HITLER, NOVEMBER 11, 1923

Göring was planning his escape. Thanks to Bella Ballin, who had rendered emergency care in her apartment in central Munich, he had been able to call his wife, Carin, who got out of her sickbed with a raging fever and raced over in a taxi to meet him at the office of Nazi sympathizer Dr. Alwin Ritter von Ach.

From there, the Storm Troopers helped carry Göring—wrapped with "furs and blankets" and "delirious" from the pain, as Carin recalled—to a car for his flight, sixty miles south to Garmisch. They spent two days lying low there among friends until they had to leave as curious onlookers began to mill about hoping to catch a glimpse of the wartime pilot who commanded the Storm Troopers.

Lieutenant Colonel Kriebel tried to help Göring by placing his name on the list of the dead, which was published in *Münchner Neueste Nachrichten*. Other popular dailies picked up the story, with *München-Augsburger Abendzeitung* asking if the famous flier had been "the twentieth casualty." Police, however, kept up the search.

At the Bürgerbräu, Göring's assistant, Julius Schaub, meanwhile, stood guard over the kidnapped mayor and city council members.

Around one p.m., one man of the Stosstrupp Hitler returned from the march in a highly agitated state with blood on his face. He was furious at the authorities. He accused them of a bloodbath, slaughtering Hitler, Ludendorff, and many other marchers. The hostages, fearing acts of retribution, were loaded onto an open truck and hauled off out of town toward the southeast.

When councilman Albert Nussbaum tried to speak with one of the guards, a Storm Trooper officer came up with his pistol: "Another word and I'll shoot both of you."

The truck stopped in the middle of a forest. The mayor and councilmen, of course, expected the worst. But to their relief, the captors only wanted their civilian clothes, not their lives. After complying with the demands, handing over hats, jackets, and coats, the hostages were driven away to a tavern in the nearby village of Höhenkirchen.

The mayor and the politicians were soon freed for good. According to a police report, this resulted from the actions of a clever town hall employee who had been following the Storm Troopers' truck in an automobile. When he caught up with them at the tavern where they had stopped, he told the kidnappers that the councilmen had to return to their offices as soon as possible to sign the papers authorizing payment of unemployment relief. The Storm Troopers, clearly not wanting to be blamed for any delays in disbursing payments, bought the story. In exchange for a promise not to reveal any details of their captivity, the councilmen were released. The mayor was driven back to his office and the other members of the council were packed off on the next train to Munich.

AT THE PUBLISHER Julius Lehmann's villa, meanwhile, Rudolf Hess and the kidnapped cabinet ministers also began to hear rumors of the failed putsch. Ludendorff was presumed dead, and Hitler "shot in the head," and several other colleagues were said to have been killed or even decapitated in the massacre. The early reports seemed confirmed when one group of Oberlanders passed by in their flight from authorities, bringing along a bundle of 20 trillion Reichsmarks from their raid on the printing presses.

This was the most terrifying moment, the hostage, prime minister Eugen von Knilling later said of the ordeal. The villa's owner was also alarmed. Even if the Storm Troopers did not seek revenge, he feared that the police would arrive for a siege and the Storm Troopers would make a desperate last stand.

Despite the guns in the garden, it would be difficult to remain there. Police would no doubt discover the location, and the food and supplies in the villa would not last for any length of time. Hess, then, had an alternative plan. He decided to take two prominent hostages—the minister of the interior, Franz Schweyer, and the minister of agriculture, Johann Wutzlhofer—to a more secure location, high in the Alps, probably in a ski lodge or hut. From there, these men could be used for bargaining.

At 4:10 p.m., Hess left with his two captives, a handful of Storm Troopers, and the package of 20 trillion marks. He was headed for Bad Tölz, where he knew a veterinarian from the Bund Oberland who could guide them into the mountains.

Uphill and downhill, they went through dark forest groves with not a soul in sight. Four times that night, the hostage Schweyer counted, Hess would stop the car, shine the headlights into the woods, and go off with one of the Storm Troopers. The government minister feared that they were looking for a place to execute them.

The drive became more difficult on the narrow, winding paths, covered with snow and not intended for automobiles. The fog and darkness made the dangers more acute, and in the end they had to turn back. Conditions were too poor to reach the hut. They did not have the necessary climbing equipment, and the two aged hostages were not up for the challenge.

They settled instead for a nearby house. Hess and his guide set out to locate and inspect it, leaving the hostages alone with the Storm Troopers and 20 trillion marks. Time passed slowly in the cold automobile. Hess was gone for more than an hour.

During that wait, the Storm Troopers, clearly tense and impatient, got out of the car and deliberated. Moments later, they returned, and to the surprise of the hostages, drove away in the direction of Munich. Along the way, the car stopped at Holzkirchen, and the Storm Troopers abruptly released the hostages. And just like that, the frightening ordeal for the two cabinet members had ended. The trillions of marks, on the other hand, were never found.

The remaining five prisoners that Hess had left behind at the publisher's villa were also freed Friday night. For the first three hours after Hess's departure, there had been moments of high tension. Power had been cut off, and there were fears of a siege, if not also a shootout with authorities. The Storm Troopers, however, had simply drifted away, leaving the villa individually or in small groups. Lehmann eventually called the police to let them know about the high-ranking hostages in his house.

When Hess returned to where he had left the car, he was shocked to find that it had disappeared. He looked all over for the hostages and their keepers. He blamed himself for their disappearance. Like Hitler, Hess was soon talking of suicide. Instead, he contacted his fiancée, Ilse Pröhl, and hid out with friends until the spring of 1924.

22.

NEW NOVEMBER CRIMINALS

*Without the applause of the Munich beer drinkers, he was
unable to act.*

—OTTO STRASSER ON HITLER

By the early afternoon of November 9, the police had cleared out the remaining Hitler supporters from the Bürgerbräu beer hall. They also freed the last prisoners, who had been held in a private room on the second floor, and seized the stockpile of weapons and ammunition, which filled almost four trucks.

Estimating the wreckage to the beer hall, the Bürgerbräu manager would later send a bill to the already-banned Nazi Party totaling 11,344,000,000,000. In addition to the enormous quantities of food, beer, and coffee consumed, there was a long list of charges for missing and broken items: 143 beer steins, 80 glasses, 98 stools, 2 music stands, 1 mirror, and 148 sets of cutlery. Oddly, there was no mention of any holes shot out of the ceiling.

At around three p.m., Lossow sent word to Gustav von Kahr: "Excellency, the Ludendorff-Hitler Putsch has been broken." But this was not exactly how it looked in the center of Munich.

Demonstrators had poured into the Odeonsplatz, chanting "Heil Hitler!" and "Down with Kahr!" Several people raised fists at the police and shouted insults, calling them "traitors," "bloodhounds" and "Jew protectors." One of the officers, Capt. Johann Salbey, remembered how the crowd "yelled, whistled, jeered, and threatened." He answered by ordering his men to show their batons and arrest the worst offenders.

Another officer, staff sergeant Alfons Gruber, hoped to calm the crowds by instructing his men to pour eighteen tankards of water to wash away the blood outside the Feldherrnhalle. All the while, the dead bodies remained in the courtyard of the Residenz Palace. Police requested that no one attempt to move them until nightfall because of the growing unrest in the city.

Some Storm Troopers were indeed reassembling. They were spotted around the city center singing and shouting. Crowds were gathering outside the hospital and National Theater, while others appeared to be headed to the Residenz Palace, where they believed that Ludendorff was being held, and, authorities feared, they would attempt to free him. The threats of violence would become more menacing, and state police deemed it unwise to dismount the machine guns on street corners.

Rumors circulated that Hitler, hiding out in the mountains, would return in triumph, like a modern King Frederick Barbarossa. He was said to have been spotted in a hunting lodge in Otterfing in southern Bavaria or in Kufstein in the Tyrol. Others suspected that he had decamped to one of the small Austrian villages between Innsbruck and Salzburg. At any rate, wherever he was, many people believed he was rallying supporters for a grandiose plan to surround Munich and enact vengeance.

By 6:00 p.m., police reported approximately 1,000 "Hitler people" marching toward the railway station. By 8:45, there was a mob of 1,500 to 2,000 milling about outside the offices of *Münchner Neueste Nachrichten*. The police feared attacks against the newspaper comparable to the devastation at the *Münchener Post*.

Citizens seemed out of control, leading to widespread fears of riots and plundering. In the eastern part of Munich, mounted police lowered lances and charged the crowd, the *Chicago Sunday Tribune* reported. Five people were carried away on stretchers and several others were less seriously wounded, including reporter Percy Brown of London's

Daily Graphic, who was beaten trying to capture a photograph of the turmoil.

Many residents of Munich were bitter at the Bavarian authorities for suppressing the national revolution and unleashing its "Danube Cossacks" on the people. They would agree with Stosstrupp Hitler commander Josef Berchtold, when he later complained of the "sheer reactionary cowardice" and "the betrayal of the whole thing." Demonstrations against Kahr and the treasonous triumvirate continued all night and into Saturday.

Police patrolled the streets, cordoned off the main squares, and manned gun nests on the roofs of public buildings. No public gatherings of more than three people would be permitted, and neither would pamphlets, handbills or posters that did not originate with the officials. Curfew was imposed at 8 p.m. Cafes, restaurants, and beer halls had to close by 7:30 p.m., and all other forms of public entertainment, such as theatre, concerts, cinema, and dances, were forbidden. The main train station was locked down, out of fear it would be used for Hitler's impending attack on Munich.

WHILE THE POLICE attempted to secure the city center, the national and international press were conducting a postmortem on the failed putsch. "General von Ludendorff," the *New York World* began on November 10, making the common mistake of ennobling the general with a false *von*, was "the most dangerous man in Germany for the last four years." Now, however, he had come "to the end of his rope":

> Driven mad by ambition to reunite Teutonic peoples into a solid fighting force which yet would conquer the world, Ludendorff allied himself with Hitler. When Hitler went off half-cocked last night, declaring the Fascist revolution in Munich, Ludendorff was dragged down with him.

The putsch had then "collapsed like a punctured balloon . . ."

The state police action marked "the end of the buffoonery," Ernst

Feder wrote for *Berliner Tageblatt*—a "second Ludendorff putsch" that failed even more abjectly than the first attempt in 1920 to seize power in Berlin. The putschists' efforts reminded him of a childish prank that was flawed strategically as well as tactically. Crying out for revenge against the "November criminals," Hitler and Ludendorff had become, in fact, November criminals themselves.

There was still not much reliable information about Adolf Hitler's whereabouts or even his background. On November 10, the *New York Times* ran one of the most detailed accounts yet, identifying Hitler as a sign painter and "alien agitator" from Austria and not even "a German of Germany." Hitler's age, however, was identified as thirty-nine (it was thirty-four), his place of birth located outside Vienna (it was Braunau on the River Inn), his military service depicted as in the Austrian Army (it was the Bavarian List Regiment), and his first arrival in Munich in January 1922 (it was May 1913).

More accurately, the *New York Times* identified Hitler as a master beer hall orator with an abundance of energy. He excelled at exploiting grievances. All of the country's resentments and frustrations were woven by Hitler into a portrait of Germany succumbing to Communists and traitors, who were, in turn, subservient to Jews and industrialists. Hitler was a demagogue extraordinaire. He had built up his small political party from a core of Bavarian veterans of war, the report noted, parading them around at his speeches for dramatic effect.

The state of affairs worried France's *République Française*. The paper cautioned its readers from concluding that the beer hall putsch was a simple battle between republic and monarchy, much less a clash between pacific democracy and military reaction. It was instead a war between two different visions of dictatorship, and the most dangerous one, it believed, was not the one suppressed at the Odeonsplatz. Several papers on the left agreed with this assessment. Hitler, in his defeat, looked ludicrous and less menacing than the state authorities who had stopped him. This illusion would only grow in the upcoming months.

23.

TESTAMENT

Breach of promise here, breach of promise there.
—München-Augsburger Abendzeitung

As Gustav von Kahr tightened his grip over the city, the Munich police raided the Nazi Party headquarters at Corneliusstrasse 12. The team conducted a thorough search of the premises, confiscating all the property of the illegal organization. They hauled off an array of office equipment and furniture—desks, filing cabinets, bookshelves, cupboards, typewriters, and a Schapirograph, or duplicating machine used to run copies.

Police also seized the artwork that had adorned its walls. There were several landscapes and still-lifes, reflecting to some extent Hitler's own choice of subject matter as a painter. There were also portraits of Frederick the Great, Otto von Bismarck, Field Marshal Hindenburg, and of course, Adolf Hitler. More surprisingly, the police found two pictures of "Gypsies," one of a young boy, the other a girl, which they believed were the private property of one of its members.

Among other removed items were library books, cigar boxes, a pair of shoes, seven bags of potatoes, a Mifa bicycle, a hunting rifle with ammunition, and a vast amount of Nazi Party stationery, which the police later used as scratch paper. The most valuable objects seized were the seven automobiles and trucks, including Göring's Mercedes and the red Benz that had brought Hitler to the Bürgerbräu. The six iron safes on the premises, however, proved to be empty. One man in the party, Ludwig Ess, had already carried off the identification cards of the party's 55,787 members.

By this time, authorities had discovered indisputable evidence of Nazi ties abroad. This had come to their attention after a dramatic arrest at the Austrian-Hungarian border on the night of the putsch. The man apprehended was Ferenc Ulain, a rabid anti-Semitic leader of an extreme right-wing group that called itself Awakening Hungary.

Searching Ulain's baggage, the police had found a "preliminary agreement" between Hitler's forces and the Hungarian organization, which wanted to launch its own putsch in Budapest. Both the German and Hungarian right-wing organizations shared much in common, not least anti-Semitism and their hatred of the Versailles peace settlement. Hungary too had been carved up, losing no less than two-thirds of its territory and some 3.5 million people to neighboring states.

This contract in Ulain's possession had been brought to Budapest by one of Hitler's men on November 2, 1923. According to the agreement, Hitler would provide soldiers and weapons from the secret stashes hidden from the Allies. Hungary, in return, would send over agricultural products from its vast landed estates. Hitler could then use this source of food to win over the German masses—a foreshadowing, in effect, of his popular job-creation measures in the 1930s by skewing the economy toward military production.

There was another element to the plot. The Hungarian society had planned to round up all the Jews in the country and then send word to international organizations that, if the Allies or anyone intervened, the hostages would be slaughtered.

This international alliance, however, had failed in both Munich and Budapest. Yet with the lingering economic and social malaise, the embers of unrest still smoldered under the ashes.

. . .

MUNICH HAD BEEN shaken to its core. All hopes of a national rebirth, *Münchener Zeitung* noted, continuing its pro-Kahr stance, had been dashed, thanks to Hitler's rash, ill-advised move. Hitler was dismissed in many circles as a demagogue spewing a grotesque and pathological ideology. The publisher of *Deutsche Zeitung* described him as "a hysteric . . . [who had fallen victim] to the devil of a prima donna vanity."

On the streets, however, it was a different matter. Kahr appeared to be the most hated man in Bavaria.

The prime minister, Eugen von Knilling, fresh from his release from captivity, called a cabinet meeting on the afternoon of November 10 to discuss whether the government should retain Kahr in his post. He also proposed that Lossow and Seisser be removed from the military and state police.

Franz Gürtner, the minister of justice, spoke up in favor of Kahr and then asked: What exactly would be the grounds for his dismissal?

He had supported the putsch, Knilling said bluntly, and swore his dramatic oath on the podium.

There was some question whether Kahr was actually serious, Gürtner countered. And if this were in fact a strategy, he added, could anyone criticize him? Deception aside, Kahr, Lossow, and Seisser had made it possible for the military and state police to suppress the putsch.

No, they had not, someone interjected. This point was often forgotten, then and later, but it was true. By the time Kahr, Lossow, and Seisser returned to their offices from the beer hall, their subordinates Danner and Imhoff had done the lion's share of the work summoning reinforcements and securing Munich's vital buildings and communication centers.

The parameters for the upcoming debate on the role of Bavarian leaders in the putsch were being outlined in broad terms in this confidential cabinet meeting. Then, as the minutes recorded, the conference was interrupted by loud shouting on the streets outside: "Down with Kahr! Up with Hitler!"

• • •

BACK AT UFFING, Hitler decided to escape to Austria. To avoid being caught by police patrols, his first-aid man had been sent to Munich wearing an old jacket and hat of Putzi's and lugging a bag of butter and eggs. He looked as if he had been visiting relatives in the countryside and so, it was hoped, would slip by under the watch of the police.

His task was to find Helene Bechstein, the wife of the rich piano manufacturer who lived in Berlin though often came to Munich where she owned property as well as a suite in the Four Seasons Hotel. Hitler had met this prominent society hostess in June 1921 and Bechstein had become one of Hitler's most valuable supporters. It was through her that he had come to meet many influential people in Bavaria, including Richard Wagner's widow, Cosima, and the Wagner circle in Bayreuth. Bechstein was someone with the power, money, and social connections to spirit him out of the country.

So after the orderly made his way to catch the Munich train at a nearby village, Dr. Schultze had waited an appropriate interval and then left in the opposite direction for a train at a different station. The physician's goal was to bring back a surgeon to treat Hitler's shoulder.

Hitler and Helen Hanfstaengl, in the meantime, spent most of Saturday, November 10, waiting for the arrival of the physician and the getaway car. They were on edge, and too excited to eat—that is, except for the toddler Egon, who behaved in his usual rambunctious ways.

The priority, Helen knew, was to make sure that neither the two maids nor her son Egon leaked a word about their houseguests.

As evening approached, the physician had returned with a friend in a borrowed car, but they were no more successful with Hitler's swollen shoulder. They left once more for Munich. Hitler and Helen were again in the empty house, waiting and wondering.

Little news trickled in.

The wait seemed interminable.

Around eleven p.m., after she had gone to bed, Helen was woken by her cook, who said someone was outside. The visitor claimed to be Captain Göring's gardener and wanted to deliver a message allegedly from General Ludendorff to "someone who was staying at our house." Helen, suspicious, pretended not to know what the stranger was talking about, and shooed him away to a nearby inn, promising to contact him if anyone came.

Was it possible that the chauffeur had already reached Göring?

Helen rushed upstairs to tell Hitler. The description sounded like the gardener, he thought, but he was not certain. They decided that Helen would call the man in the morning and invite him inside the villa. Hitler was confident that, watching undetected upstairs, he would be able to tell.

The next morning, when the man came, Hitler determined that he was in fact the gardener, and joined him in the downstairs sitting room. Helen never learned the purpose of the visit, which was brief and concluded with Hitler retiring upstairs for a nap. Putzi always suspected that this man was really an informer, hoping to tip off police on Hitler's whereabouts.

On Sunday, November 11, instead of celebrating victory over the republic, Hitler was still hiding out in the Hanfstaengl attic. He wore a borrowed pair of white pajamas and a dark-blue terry-cloth bathrobe, an oversized garment that fit Hanfstaengl but dwarfed Hitler. It must have suited his hurt shoulder. Hitler joked to Helen that his baggy attire made him feel like an ancient Roman senator.

Around noon, Hitler, Helen, and Egon had their first and only good meal of his stay. Hitler seemed to be in better spirits, joking with Egon that the boy needed a "blond, blue-eyed sister." Helen took the toddler up to his crib for a nap and then returned to her guest. Hitler had started pacing the sitting room, rambling about the beer hall putsch and wondering about the fate of his comrades. He spoke of the certain mistakes he made in the putsch and swore that next time he would not repeat them.

Where was the Bechstein car to take him to Austria?

Helen offered to contact her plumber, whom she knew was an ardent Nazi supporter and in possession of a motorcycle. Hitler could hide in the sidecar underneath an array of pillows, blankets, and tarpaulin. No one would suspect a thing. Hitler declined.

. . .

By the late afternoon, with the shutters closed and curtains drawn, Hitler was again pacing up and down the room, "silently, moodily," Helen remembered. At about five o'clock, her mother-in-law called with news that the police were searching her house outside Uffing. That large and isolated residence was certainly a likely hiding spot.

They searched for it for two hours until one of the eleven officers on the property overheard the telephone conversation between Helen and her mother-in-law. He grabbed the receiver and demanded to know who was on the line. When Helen identified herself, the policeman asked if she knew the whereabouts of her husband and when was the last time she saw Adolf Hitler.

"Today," Helen answered. Surprisingly, she made no attempt to cover for her houseguest.

"Caught!" was all she wrote in her unpublished account.

Helen went to the second-floor living room to tell Hitler that the police would no doubt be on their way to the villa. Hitler then, as she put it, "completely lost his nerve."

"Now all is lost," she remembered him shouting. "No use going on!"

He then lunged for his pistol, which was on a cabinet. The story went around (and made its way into history books) that Hitler, panicking, nearly committed suicide. According to Putzi, the source of the tale, Hitler did make an attempt to end his life. Helen, however, had saved him by seizing the gun with a "ju-jitsu trick" that Putzi had taught her after he had learned it from a Boston policeman during his Harvard years. She then supposedly sent the weapon flying into a barrel of flour.

Helen, by contrast, in her handwritten notes, told a different and more plausible story. She simply grabbed his arm and removed the gun, calmly, if firmly, reprimanding Hitler for such unproductive, defeatist thought at only the first setback. She made no reference to disarming Hitler by any jiu jitsu technique. When Hitler sat down and put his head in his hands in despair, she took the opportunity to get a hold of the gun and then hid it in the first place she could think of: deep inside a barrel of flour, which was on a completely different floor of the house. Years later,

Helen had come to wonder if she had really prevented Hitler's suicide, or whether it was just another "one of his many melodramatic gestures."

When she returned to the room, Hitler was still sitting there, head in his hands, in a state of dejection. As they waited for the police to arrive, Helen offered to take down any instructions to his followers, "while there was still time." Hitler then hurriedly dictated his "political testament," outlining his choice of successors.

The new chairman of the party was a surprise. It was not Göring, Hess, Amann, or other prominent figures of the putsch. It was not Anton Drexler, the cofounder of the party; nor, for that matter, Julius Streicher, who had a note from Hitler, scribbled in haste at some point on the night of the putsch, granting him authority for "the entire organization." Hitler probably meant only for propaganda, but Streicher would soon argue that this meant for the entire Nazi Party.

Hitler's choice was instead Alfred Rosenberg.

Helen must have been shocked. Like her husband, she had long disliked him and saw him as a cold, cynical figure who did not have the leadership abilities to manage a newspaper, let alone a party. Rosenberg was, as Röhm's deputy, Karl Osswald, put it, a coward who "showed more shit than patriotic feeling."

Even Rosenberg would be surprised at his election. "Hitler had never taken me into his confidence as far as organizational matters were concerned, and now I was to assume control at this critical moment!" he wrote in his memoirs. It was as if Hitler had intentionally picked an unpopular mediocrity without charisma to avoid creating a threatening rival. At the same time, it is probably more likely that Hitler just made a snap decision under pressure and chose one of the few people remaining around Munich whose loyalty would be unquestioned.

Hitler's testament, like the pistol, was hidden in the barrel of flour in anticipation of the police, whose arrival was imminent. The sound of truck engines and the barking of dogs announced their approach. Officers quickly surrounded the house. The twenty-nine-year-old 1st Lt. Rudolf Belleville from the district of Weilheim walked up to the door. He had no special desire to be there.

For one thing, it was a Sunday and much of his staff was on holiday.

He'd had to borrow a truck from a local brewery for his mission. For another, the policeman had served with Rudolf Hess as a gunner in his air unit of the First World War, and, in 1920, had joined the Nazi Party. The last thing he wanted was to arrest Adolf Hitler.

Belleville knocked and asked if he could search the property. Helen escorted him up to the attic and, after a brief hesitation, opened the door. A senior government official, Johann Baptist Loritz, described what happened next:

> In the room stood Hitler in white pajamas, his arm in a bandage . . . Hitler stared at him absent-mindedly. On hearing the announcement that he had come to arrest him, Hitler reached out his hand and declared that he was at his disposal.

At this point, as the temperature outside had dropped, Helen offered to loan him some of Putzi's warmer clothes. Hitler refused and was helped on instead with the large, loose-fitting bathrobe. This was his attire, with his trench coat hung over his shoulders, as the police escorted him towards the door.

Little Egon, escaping from the maids in the kitchen, shouted at the "bad, bad men" taking "Uncle Dolf" away. Hitler patted the boy on the cheek and shook hands with Helen and her two maids. Without another word, Hitler turned and left with the guards.

Roughly an hour after the police drove off with their captive in the commandeered brewery truck, another vehicle pulled up at the villa. It was Max Amann bringing the Bechstein car that was supposed to take Hitler to Austria.

24.

CURTAINS

We have to be careful about who are his jailers, or he will make
them a speech and have them cheering for the revolution.
—GEN. OTTO VON LOSSOW

The prison guard Franz Hemmrich lay sleepless in his quarters, listening to the ticking clock and the rhythmic steps of a colleague patrolling the corridor. It had rained so hard that night that it shook the windowpanes. There was a simultaneous ring of the bell and a knock on the door. An assistant announced that the warden wanted to see him immediately.

Upon arrival, Warden Otto Leybold handed him a telegram announcing that Hitler had been taken prisoner and would arrive that night. Arrangements had to be made. A detachment of thirty-two soldiers from the Bavarian 7th Division was being sent over to reinforce security, in case Hitler's supporters tried to break him out of prison. There would be patrols, machine-gun nests in the courtyard, and new telephone lines installed connecting directly to the army barracks in case of an emergency.

Hidden away in the Alpine landscape some forty miles west of Munich, Landsberg am Lech looked more like a country estate or relic of the medieval past than a modern state prison. Yet this institution, with its two onion-domed towers and the large front gate, was only fourteen years old. It housed up to five hundred inmates in its four main wings, which were laid out in the shape of a cross with a central watch station at its hub. The "panopticon" model of prison architecture allowed guards to view every prisoner, but not the reverse.

But it was not to this part of Landsberg Prison that Adolf Hitler was headed.

Landsberg had, since 1919, taken on the second task of housing political prisoners and convicted duelists. They were placed in what was called "fortress confinement" (*Festungshaft*), a form of *custodia honesta*, or "honorable custody." Established in Bavaria in 1813, this type of punishment had been reserved for lesser crimes of more privileged social classes. Unlike the prison (*Gefängnis*) or its more severe form (*Zuchthaus*) with its emphasis on silence, solitary confinement, and hard labor, fortress confinement did not carry the same stigma or impose the same demands as the other institutions.

Landsberg's prisoners in honorary confinement had their own wing in a separate, modern two-story annex, called the *Festung*, or "fortress." In this wing, which was connected to the main prison by a corridor, the inmates did not have to wear uniforms, receive a mandatory haircut, clean their cells, or endure many other usual restrictions. They did not even have to remain in their rooms.

During daylight hours, they could visit fellow cellmates, entertain visitors for six hours a week, and enjoy a minimum of five hours a day of movement. They could decorate their cells with pictures or flowers, as well as purchase cigars, cigarettes, wine, and a daily ration of one liter of beer at the canteen. Fortress confinement stood at the apex of the German penitentiary sentence, and, as such, meant essentially "the loss of liberty with the supervision of the prisoner's activity and way of life."

Just before ten thirty that evening, the heavy, nail-studded entrance gate cranked open for the awaited prisoner. The Landsberg guard, wearing a cap, a dark-blue uniform with epaulettes, and a belt with dangling keys, went down to the entrance. He described his first impressions of

Adolf Hitler as he entered: "A dark hair strand fell across his pale face ... A pair of hard eyes stared out into the void."

A file was prepared for Hitler, who became Prisoner No. 45: "Catholic, 34 Years old, Father was a customs official in Linz. A. H., born April 20, 1889 in Braunau on the Inn, Upper Austria (Austrian), single. Occupation: supposedly writer, previously artist ... Parents: both dead. He has no epistolary contact with his sister in Vienna. He lives in Munich, Thierschstrasse 41." The file also listed his service in the 16th Reserve Infantry Regiment and his military awards.

Flanked by several police officers and a dog on a leash, Hitler was escorted to Cell 5 on the second floor—one of the largest and brightest in the wing. Nine feet by twelve feet, the room had an iron bed with woolen blankets, a nightstand, a table, a desk, a cupboard, and a couple of chairs. During the day, the sun streamed through the barred windows and bathed the whitewashed walls with light. This was Landsberg's so-called celebrity cell. The previous occupant, Anton Graf von Arco auf Valley, the assassin of Munich's Socialist leader, Kurt Eisner, had been moved to quarters in the infirmary to make way for the new prisoner.

After refusing the offer of bread and soup, Hitler went to lie down. He was exhausted and clearly still in pain. The prison physician, the sixty-six-year-old Dr. Josef Brinsteiner, diagnosed him as suffering from "a dislocation of the left shoulder with a fracture in the humeral head, and, as a result, a very painful traumatic neurosis." The doctor expected that this injury would "result in a [permanent] partial rigidity and pain in the left shoulder."

But there was a discovery in store for the physician when he continued his physical examination. Hitler suffered from cryptorchidism, a medical condition in which a testicle fails to descend into the scrotum. This claim was first made in the scholarly world in 1968 by the Russian writer Lev Bezymenski, supposedly based on the Soviet autopsy of May 1945, but historians have long been skeptical. Many scholars in the West saw it as a petty attempt to emasculate Hitler. But the Landsberg doctor had no ideological ax to grind, and in fact he was quite partial to Hitler. And so, thanks to this newly recovered report, the Russian assertion appears surprisingly to have merit.

• • •

FROM THE FIRST moment he heard of the putsch, the correspondent for an Argentine newspaper, *Argentinische Tag- und Wochenblatt*, Carl Christian Bry, had been flabbergasted. Hitler and his cohorts had wanted to overthrow the government, but were they in a government ministry, the military barracks, or even at the police department? It was at a beer hall. "That is typical for Hitler and for Munich," he mocked.

On November 9, Bry had hurried down to pick up a copy of the Nazi newspaper, *Völkischer Beobachter*, and marveled at its "treasure trove" of unintentional humor. Ridiculous, pompous phrases jostled next to hateful insults about Jews, all of this driving a narrative that read like some inferior crime novel. Now that the putsch had failed and Hitler had been arrested, Bry was pleased to report that he had not "overestimated Hitler." Still he had never expected Hitler to meet such a "quick end."

Did Hitler really think, Victor Serge wrote in the Communist press agency Correspondance Internationale, that he could fire "a few revolver shots into the ceiling" of a Munich beer hall and expect to become "something like a new Emperor of Germany?" This so-called revolution, Reuters predicted, would be remembered as one of the briefest on record.

Hitler was indeed being consigned to the history books. The Nazi Party had been banned, and its members, fleeing into exile, were to succumb to division and quarrel. Hitler's career seemed to be finished, almost as fast as it had begun. He certainly believed it was. The beer hall putsch was well on its way to becoming a joke.

"This Bürgerbräu coup d'état was the craziest farce pulled off in memory," concluded the *New York Times*. "Beer and oratory" had inspired a slapdash, amateurish troupe better suited for the "comic opera stage than for a serious effort to overthrow the Berlin Government." *Le Petit Parisien* dubbed the performance sheer vaudeville; *Le Matin* compared it to a "carnivalesque adventure."

The end had come for "charlatan Hitler," as *Vossische Zeitung* called him. *Frankfurter Zeitung* had printed the party's obituary, and Cyril Brown at the *New York Times* concluded that "the amateurish and abortive putsch in Munich . . . definitely eliminates Hitler and his National Socialist followers."

THE REHABILITATION OF Gustav von Kahr, meanwhile, was afoot. Kahr would remain in power, thanks largely to the support of minister of justice Franz Gürtner. Other members of the council had gone along with Gürtner, for the moment accepting his reasoning that this was not the time to remove Kahr because that would look like Hitler had won.

That evening, Prime Minister Knilling and Gürtner went over to speak with Kahr, Lossow, and Seisser. It was another stormy meeting. The three Bavarian leaders defended their actions on the night of the putsch without qualification, and argued that they should not resign but instead take advantage of the state of confusion to secure more power for Kahr. Seisser used the words "supreme power."

Despite Gürtner's success in saving Kahr, the Bavarian cabinet remained uncertain about how to proceed. The prime minister clearly wanted to remove Kahr, Lossow, and Seisser, but he realized that they would resist and he was not confident that authorities had enough power to force them out. Besides, as other cabinet members emphasized, the government needed to maintain a united front against the onslaught of propaganda that the far right would unleash.

Over the next few weeks, Kahr, Lossow, and Seisser would launch their own multipronged assault to sway opinion in Bavaria. They banned right-wing papers sympathetic to the Nazis, such as *Heimatland* and Julius Streicher's *Der Stürmer*, and, in the process, took advantage of the moment to abolish the Communist Party that had long been critical of the regime. Prohibitions and then stricter censorship of the Socialist press followed, though the ambitious plan to stop debate would later come back to haunt them.

Outside Bavaria, particularly in papers that were Socialist or leaning to the left, Kahr was believed to be far closer to the Nazis and the extreme right than he wanted to appear. He had played with fire and then acted surprised that he got burnt. Others wondered if Kahr had not so much backed out of a commitment as he had "sold out" Hitler, succumbing to the temptations of German industrial barons, or, alternatively, the monarchical-Jesuit clique that supported the crown prince and favored Bavarian separatism. Some even claimed that Kahr had betrayed Hitler because a rich Jewish rug merchant had bribed him with seven Persian rugs.

"Helmets and rifles glittered everywhere," Franz Hemmrich said of the new military presence at Landsberg. Fellow guard Otto Lurker likewise recalled the clang of weapons and heavy steps in the corridors. With so many soldiers milling about the premises, Hitler claimed that he had feared that he was going to be executed by a firing squad.

He probably changed that opinion, if in fact he ever believed it, when he heard that the state prosecutor would be coming to question him as part of his fact-gathering mission in the pretrial investigation. But Hitler refused to cooperate. He threatened to commit suicide and then went on a hunger strike that lasted at least a week and perhaps a total of ten days.

Guards tried to convince him to eat, resorting to typical methods of leaving food in his cell and not retrieving it until they brought the next meal. They also used a variety of arguments to reach the stubborn prisoner, who, as Hemmrich later recalled, just "sat there, like a small, shrunken pile of misery, badly shaved . . . listening to my simple words with an apathetic, tired smile." During this time, Dr. Brinsteiner recorded that Hitler's weight had dropped from 160.9 pounds (73 kg) upon arrival to 149.9 (68 kg).

The prison psychologist, Alois Maria Ott, remembered how despondent Hitler had become when he examined him on November 19, 1923. Hitler complained about the treachery of his supporters and the German people, adding that all his suffering on their behalf meant nothing. He was ready to leave all of them to wallow in the mess they had made and show them how poorly they would fare without him. "I've had enough," Hitler said with a white clump of saliva on his mouth from the long rant. "If I had a pistol, I would take it."

Hitler was apparently expressing these melodramatic sentiments with many people who visited him at Landsberg. Anton Drexler came later that month and found the thin, pale prisoner sitting by the window— "thinner, and weaker and whiter" as his hunger strike had worn him down. Hitler, moreover, seemed to go out of his way to give the impression that he could not accept the fact that sixteen of his own men had died under his leadership.

"He was utterly in despair," Drexler later said. He complained that all the efforts building up the party—"all our work and planning and striving, and stinting and scraping and saving"—had come to naught. Hitler's gloom was contagious, Drexler added, though he did take credit for supposedly helping Hitler not give up, no matter how difficult their prospects seemed.

Hans Knirsch, a German who had established the Sudetenland Nazi Party in Czechoslovakia, also found the prisoner "awfully depressed" on his visit of November 23. Knirsch tried to reassure him that the party and its program would collapse without him. Hitler just shook his head and, Knirsch recalled, "timidly asked who would continue to follow a man with such a fiasco behind him." He had "no right to go on living," Hitler added, after causing so much loss of life, and saw no other option for himself other than "death by starvation."

As he related it, Knirsch scolded Hitler for imagining that he could just abandon his supporters and argued instead that the putsch was actually a victory. In the short run, it raised national spirits. In the long run, it would help lead to their ultimate triumph because failure served as a necessary component of struggle and a prelude to success.

Many other guests would leave feeling, as Drexler and Knirsch had, that they had encouraged Hitler, or even prevented him from committing suicide. According to Putzi, his wife, Helen, fell into this category. She sent a message to Hitler, he said, reminding him that she had not talked him out of suicide at their villa only to let him "now starve himself in Landsberg." Besides, if he persisted with this plan, he would just be doing what his enemies most wanted. She may have sent a note to Hitler, but there is no trace of a visit from her in the prison archives or of any such encouragement in her unpublished memoir.

There is, however, record of a different, somewhat more unusual visitor to Landsberg who did in fact cheer up the depressed prisoner. On December 3, 1923, a guest signed in a large German shepherd named Wolf—a birthday present that Hitler received the previous year.

25.

TRIALS BEFORE THE TRIAL

I must confess that he did not, at that time, strike me as a significant, much less a brilliant, man.

—HANS EHARD, DEPUTY PROSECUTOR,
AFTER HIS FIRST INTERROGATION OF HITLER

General Ludendorff was indeed allowed to return to his villa at Sollen-Ludwigshöhe for house arrest. Barricading himself in his study, Ludendorff worked hard on his defense. His wife, Margarethe, said he worked harder now than he had on the eve of the putsch. He also entertained freely, receiving supporters and strangers alike, clearing off space from the coffee table piled high with books, magazines, and newspapers. "He attached importance to every story they [the guests] told or any comment they made," she said, adding that he viewed it all as "parts of a mosaic."

Surprise, disgust, amusement, and amazement vied for primacy in public discussions of Ludendorff's poor judgment in joining this half-baked putsch. The general might commit suicide out of shame, his critics speculated, rather than face the further indignity of a trial for treason. Ludendorff's epitaph was already being written: "A good soldier wrecked on the reefs of fantastic politics."

Göring, meanwhile, had crossed into Austria and now lay recuperating in a private clinic in Innsbruck. Weak from loss of blood and lack of sleep, he endured the excruciating pain from the gunshot wound, which had become infected, perhaps from the grime picked up when the bullets ricocheted off the muddy stones near the royal palace. He drifted in and out of consciousness, imagining he was again fighting a street battle and biting his pillow in between unnerving cries and groans.

It was at this time that Göring received his first morphine shots. They would soon become a daily habit, launching an addiction that would persist for years. It would soon send him to the Långbro insane asylum in Sweden, and, in his many attempts at treatment for his expensive craving, he would turn to binge eating and gargantuan meals for which he later became notorious.

On December 24, Göring left the clinic on crutches strung out on morphine, shaking, and "white as snow," as Carin put it. The Görings still could not return to Munich, where their villa was being watched, their mail being read, and their bank accounts frozen. They moved into the hotel Tiroler Hof, where Storm Troopers gave them a Christmas tree, every candle adorned with white, black, and red ribbons. The Tiroler Hof afforded them their accustomed luxury, thanks to the generosity of the proprietor and other supporters.

Most of the other Nazi exiles, by contrast, roamed about "like tramps," as Putzi put it. Putzi was then using a false passport, along with a disguise of dark glasses and a new set of "Franz-Josef mutton-chop whiskers." He had been helped across the border into Austria by a group of railway workers, many of whom had moved to the right politically during the economic chaos. One of these men put him up in a small flower-shop in Kufstein, where he slept on the floor underneath rows of chrysanthemums.

Among other things, Putzi used his time in Austria to visit Hitler's forty-year-old half-sister, Angela Raubal, who lived in poverty on an upper-floor apartment on Schönburgstrasse in Vienna. At the age of twenty, she had married Leo Raubal, a tax official in Linz, though the marriage was cut short by his premature death seven years later. Angela was now raising her three young children.

Putzi was surprised by their living conditions. Inside, behind the door she barely opened, which he attributed to embarrassment, was a place of squalor. Putzi invited her and her eldest daughter to a café, where he found Angela shy and her daughter, by contrast, graceful and uninhibited. This was the sixteen-year-old Geli, the future mistress of Adolf Hitler.

That December, Angela crossed into Germany and visited Hitler in prison. She found her half-brother in a better state than she had expected. His arm was healing, given his regular program of massage, although he still could not raise it higher than shoulder-level or move it without pain. He had been eating again; his first meal after his hunger strike had been a bowl of rice.

Gifts had been piling up in his cell. There was a five-volume edition of the writings of German philosopher Arthur Schopenhauer (1920), a German dictionary, an unidentified book in a "foreign language," as well as paper, two quill pens, and a penholder. All of these had been sent on December 4 by Hitler's lawyer, Lorenz Roder, a forty-one-year-old Munich public defender whom Hitler had met in 1922. Roder had then represented Hitler's colleagues who had attacked a rival speaker at a beer hall.

Just before Angela's arrival at Landsberg, someone had brought a Christmas package from Winifred Wagner, the English wife of composer Richard Wagner's son, Siegfried. It included a wool blanket, a jacket, long underwear, socks, sausages, zwieback crisp bread, and a copy of her husband's libretto for *Schmied von Marienburg*. Hitler's high spirits, several visitors noted, were returning.

The *New York Times* ran a piece on his detention at Landsberg. "[It] is by no means an unpleasant place of confinement," the story began, noting the privileges the incarcerated enjoyed, such as books, exercise, and a progressive approach that placed few onerous restrictions on its prisoners. Hitler was taking full advantage of this leniency, except for exercise, which he refused to do at that time on account of his shoulder. The trial, it reported, would not take place anytime soon because Bavarian authorities were waiting for Hitler's popularity to subside.

But Hitler's popularity showed no signs of significant decline, at least in many right-wing and nationalist circles. Some of these supporters were urging the government to grant a pardon, or offer some kind of amnesty. Dr. Richard Graf du Moulin Eckart, a professor in the German philology and history department at Munich's Technische Universität, put the question directly to Gustav von Kahr in a private meeting. The Bavarian leader rejected the proposal.

An internal government memorandum had a more insightful plan for addressing the problems raised by Hitler and the putsch. The note recommended a three-pronged strategy that emphasized an aggressive prosecution of the plot's ringleaders, a complete disarming of the private paramilitary bands, and a concentrated effort to discover and then block the flow of funds that sustained their newspaper, pamphlets, office of twenty employees, and their wide range of propagandistic activities. To what extent this advice would be heeded remained to be seen.

That Christmas, Blute Café in Munich's bohemian quarter of Schwabing staged a tableau vivant entitled *Adolf Hitler in Prison*. As the curtain rose, the audience glimpsed a man sitting alone at a desk, his head in his hands, and his back turned to the audience. Snow fell outside his window. An angel flew into the lonely cell bringing an illuminated Christmas tree. Offstage, a men's choir sang "Silent Night."

At the climax of the performance, the man slowly turned around to face the audience. Many in the café thought for a second that this might be Hitler himself. The photographer Heinrich Hoffmann was proud of his success in choosing a suitable actor for this role. The lights were switched on and several people, with teary eyes and muffled sobs, Hoffmann said, quickly put away their handkerchiefs.

THE TRIAL, IT was announced in December, would be not by jury, but by a tribunal of judges. "It is generally felt," the *New York Tribune* reported, "that [Hitler] will be executed." Other observers, like the American vice consul in Munich, Robert Murphy, predicted a long imprisonment and then deportation.

Hitler was still not cooperating with authorities. After threatening suicide and launching a short-lived hunger strike, he now refused to talk. The prosecutor, Ludwig Stenglein, a conservative Bavarian in

his fifty-fourth year, was getting nowhere with the recalcitrant prisoner until he handed over the questioning to his deputy. This was Hans
Ehard, a young lawyer from a Bamberg Catholic family who looked
much younger than his thirty-six years of age. Ehard had just been promoted to the position the previous month. In fact, he had only served in
this capacity for seven days when Hitler stormed the beer hall.

Ehard, however, would prove to be an inspired choice. As a boy, a son
of a local government official, Ehard had wanted to be a judge. At law
school in Munich and Würzberg, he had shown his potential, graduat-
ing magna cum laude. He had served during the war as a clerk for the
military court, moving with his regiment to Russia, Serbia, and France,
and earning an Iron Cross Second Class among other medals.

Since then, he had moved to Munich with his wife, Anna Eleonore,
or Annelore, the daughter of a brewery owner, and their three-and-half-
year-old son, Carlhans. Ehard loved to read and play the cello in a string
quartet, though he would have less time for these pursuits. He had just
been handed the most high-profile case of his career.

The young prosecutor was a thinker. People often criticized him, he
later said, for not being energetic enough, or hesitating too long before
a major decision, and he understood those criticisms. That was his tem-
perament. It was deliberate, reflective, and methodical. "Know yourself
and always control yourself" was one of his mottos. Another was to "recognize what is important, hope for the best, and do what is possible."
Ehard would, of course, need every advantage that hard-earned perspective could provide given the ordeal that lay ahead.

On December 13, 1923, the young prosecutor took the train to Landsberg to see if he could, as Stenglein put it, "get something out of Hitler."
It would be a long day. Ehard sat across a small table from Hitler, who
took his seat in a wicker chair, his arm still in a sling.

Ehard asked if Hitler was still in pain.

There was no answer.

Was he prepared for the talk? Ehard next asked.

Hitler just stared at him, his pale-blue eyes "hard and repellent,"
shooting daggers of hate. Ehard felt that Hitler, as he later put it, "was
going to eat me."

Ehard advised him of his right to hire a lawyer.

There was still no response.

He was only here to do his job, Ehard continued, still speaking calmly as possible and treading carefully as if he were handling "a raw egg."

"I have nothing to say," Hitler eventually declared, turning toward the wall. He would not be deceived by any lawyer tricks, he added, and everything that he had to say was going in a memoir that he planned to write.

When Ehard pressed further, asking about his actions, accomplices, and background, Hitler did not budge, claiming that he would not "jeopardize [his] political career by giving you a statement."

Cooperation was in his own interests, Ehard countered, as well as those of his fellow accused. Hitler shrugged. He had his own role in history to consider and the verdict of this court meant nothing to him.

Ehard then had an idea. He asked the stenographer to pack up the typewriter and leave the room. He put away pen and paper. Claiming to be intrigued by his politics, Ehard said he wanted to talk. "There'll be no record, no protocol," he said. "We'll just talk."

As Ehard later put it, this simple ruse worked "like a charm."

Hitler launched into a long political harangue as if he were addressing a beer hall full of fanatical supporters rather than a single prosecutor in the prison's visiting room. He could not answer a simple question with a clear, concise response, spewing invective and sometimes also spraying saliva around the room. Ehard later joked that he could have used an umbrella.

The torrent ran on for five hours. At the end, the prosecutor thanked Hitler for "the illuminating interview" and went to type up every point he could remember. It would be a document fifteen pages in length. This was an important start, providing insight into Hitler's upcoming strategy, but Ehard feared that Hitler would, as he threatened, save his best arguments for the trial.

By January 1924, the prosecution had narrowed the number of main defendants to ten. In addition to Adolf Hitler, there would be Gen. Erich Ludendorff, still under house arrest; Lt. Col. Hermann Kriebel, the commander of the Kampfbund and alleged military planner of the putsch; Ernst Pöhner, the judge and former police chief; Dr. Wilhelm Frick, his close ally in the police department.

The leaders of three prominent paramilitary societies that comprised the Kampfbund were also included: Capt. Ernst Röhm of the Reichs-kriegsflagge; Friedrich Weber of the Bund Oberland; and Wilhelm Brückner, leader of the Munich Storm Troopers. The last two defendants were young, minor figures in the plot: Ludendorff's stepson Heinz Pernet and Robert Wagner, a student accused of helping rally cadets at Munich's infantry officer training academy to the putsch.

Each of the defendants was going to be charged with the crime of high treason. This was defined by Article 80 of the law code as the attempt to change the constitution of Germany or of its federal states with the use of violence. (Treason, by contrast, was the divulging of state secrets to a foreign power.) The penalty for a conviction of high treason would be life in prison or fortress confinement.

But what about the death of four policemen, the kidnapping of government ministers, the assault on Jewish citizens, the theft of trillions of marks, and attacks on the *Munich Post*? Significantly, there were no charges for any of these crimes. This strategy of focusing the case solely on the question of high treason would generate considerable criticism.

What's more, why was the trial taking place in Munich?

Technically, the trial of Adolf Hitler should never have been held there. A special state court, the Staatsgerichtshof, had been established in Leipzig on July 21, 1922, with the passage of the Law for the Protection of the Republic, to try cases of high treason. The Social Democratic–controlled parliament had pushed for this legislation to counter the wave of political upheaval and murder that culminated with the assassination of Germany's Jewish foreign minister, Walther Rathenau.

Bavaria, however, had refused to recognize this law. It was a matter of principle, its advocates argued, emphasizing the necessity of clinging to state's rights, or what remained of them, against the encroachments of the central government. Besides, it already had its own institution for punishing crimes against the state: the so-called People's Court, which had been set up in Bavaria in November 1918 as an emergency measure to prosecute defendants caught in the act of committing a nonpolitical crime, such as murder, manslaughter, rape, burglary, arson, or looting. This institution had since then expanded its jurisdiction to other offences, including cases of high treason.

The People's Court, reestablished in July 1919, had another unusual feature. It circumvented the traditional legal system with its emphasis on quick verdicts without the right of appeal. The name of the institution derived from the fact that this court operated as a tribunal of five judges: two professionals and three laymen selected from the male population. In practice, however, the presiding judge had a large say in the appointment of the men on the bench. This influence, coupled with the total absence of any judicial review, made the presiding judges of the People's Court, as one Munich lawyer put it, virtual "judicial kings."

It was this institution that the Bavarian Ministry of Justice now insisted had jurisdiction in this case. But the problem with the People's Court was that, since the Weimar Constitution had gone into effect in August 1919, local judicial organs like this had become unconstitutional and illegal. Many people suspected that Bavaria's stubborn refusal to comply with the constitution was because its authorities hoped to protect the defendants or, more likely, hide some secrets of their own.

Kahr, Lossow, and Seisser had certainly seemed tainted by their complicity in the plot, no matter how much they emphasized that they had suppressed the revolt. With a nudge from authorities, eager to distance themselves from the fiasco, they cast the events of November 8–9, 1923, in official statements as the "Hitler putsch." Hitler, for his part, was only glad to oblige, claiming responsibility, no matter how much this inflated his own role in the affair.

But why did Berlin, clearly in the right legally, not press the matter? For one thing, insisting on federal jurisdiction would probably have required the use of force, which authorities, in the aftermath of the putsch, wanted to avoid. Stresemann's government had also lost a vote of confidence on November 23, 1923, and the chancellor had resigned. New elections were imminent. Politicians in Berlin were in the meantime reluctant to enter the Munich hornet's nest and force a measure that would be enormously unpopular with many voters in Bavaria.

For Berlin, then, allowing the trial to proceed in Munich seemed to offer the path of least resistance. For Munich, however, the problems were only beginning.

To start with, there was no courtroom large or secure enough for such a monumental trial. Authorities ignored Munich wits who suggested that they hold it in the Bürgerbräu. They also dismissed other proposals as impractical, such as holding the trial in a small town outside the city such as Straubing, or even at Landsberg Prison. The rejection of the latter, however, had come after the warden, in a burst of enthusiasm, had started renovating the second floor of the fortress in preparation of the proceedings. He had already selected a double cell for Ludendorff's use and handpicked a guard to serve as his valet.

By February 1924, the Bavarian Ministry of Justice had settled on the Reichswehr Infantry School as the location for the trial. Once the site of the Bavarian Army's war academy and later a prestigious officer-training academy, this institution had been shut down after the beer hall putsch because the vast majority of its cadets had joined Hitler and marched under the swastika banner to overthrow the government.

Rumors circulated that the trial would last only a few days before the compromised Bavarian authorities would put an end to what would surely be an embarrassing spectacle. Others predicted that the trial would never make it that far, most likely postponed or canceled at the last minute. Gustav von Kahr was said to be the Machiavellian power behind the scenes, the Dr. Frankenstein of Munich, or the tinkerer who had created a monster that would crush him.

Clearly Bavaria preferred a quick, quiet trial out of the spotlight. The less attention, the better. Hitler, on the other hand, wanted quite the opposite. Putzi remembered one conversation with Hitler on a visit to his cell before the trial. "What can they do to me?" Hitler asked, with little Egon sitting in his lap and munching on sweets. He only needed to reveal the collaboration of the Bavarian authorities and the entire basis for the prosecution would shatter.

The People's Court had scheduled the trial to open on the morning of February 18, 1924. But a few days before, the proceedings were abruptly postponed, just as several skeptics had predicted. Then, on the day the trial was supposed to begin, there was some other dramatic news: Both Gustav von Kahr and General von Lossow had resigned from office.

Berlin had long been exerting pressure on Bavaria to remove its highest-ranking military commander for his "mutinous" actions. By this point, the Bavarian cabinet no longer supported him, nor did it wish to retain Kahr, who, in turn, had grown weary of the office. It had, in his opinion, brought responsibility for difficult problems without granting him enough power to solve them.

But if these moves were somehow supposed to silence rumors of a high-placed scandal and cover-up, they did not succeed. Munich was now a cauldron of speculation and rumor-mongering. All of this was, of course, made worse by the lack of forthright communication from the government.

Various patriotic societies rallied support to stop the trial, which they predicted would cause national disgrace. One prominent group of war veterans appealed to no less than Field Marshal Paul von Hindenburg. The famous leader, however, declined to intervene on the grounds that he knew his wartime colleague, General Ludendorff, would not want any special treatment.

As the new opening day of February 26 approached, many people questioned if the trial would in fact begin. If so, would it be held entirely behind closed doors? Other people wondered if the witnesses would dare to show up. Kahr, for one, was receiving death threats. He changed offices, hired bodyguards, and refused to appear at the opera or theatre unless he remained backstage surrounded by detectives. One story said the subpoena for the trial had reached him in his latest hiding place: an insane asylum.

Several defendants were, likewise, reported to be in poor health and unable to testify. Hitler needed surgery for his shoulder injury, and his supporters were trying to seek another postponement. Others said he needed mental help to treat his depression. Frick was complaining of insomnia, heart palpitations, shortness of breath, and thoughts of suicide. Pöhner had been rushed to the hospital for an undisclosed gastrointestinal disorder, prompting wild speculation that he had been poisoned.

According to *Völkischer Kurier*, three or four of the defendants had launched another hunger strike.

Of the many rumors in the cafés and beer halls of Munich on the eve of the trial, one of the most fantastic—and feared—was the threat that diehard Nazi thugs and hooligans would swarm into town, infiltrate the courtroom, overpower security, and whisk away the defendants in preparation for a planned second putsch. This time, the Hitlerites warned, they would not fail.

Bavaria called in reinforcements in military and state police, and promised to be ready.

PART II

THE COURTROOM

26.

"WE WILL NOT HURT GERMANY!"

Let justice be done, even though the world might perish.
—GEORG NEITHARDT, PRESIDING JUDGE

February 26, 1924

A long line of men and women in thick winter coats snaked its way down the sidewalk to the main entrance of the sprawling red-brick building. Two guards stood at the door, while mounted state police patrolled the streets outside the high walls of the castle-like structure. Barbed wire, steel cordons, and approximately fifty other state police troops had blocked off traffic, except for pedestrians and official vehicles.

Spectators fortunate enough to possess one of the rare authorized passes that cold, snowy morning crossed the security lines, ascended a staircase, and walked down a long corridor lined with still more state police troops armed with carbines. There were two additional body searches before entering the makeshift courtroom on the second floor. "Never in my long career," said the foreign correspondent for *Le Gaulois*, "have I encountered such police measures."

Inside the drafty room, the former cadet dining hall, four large windows let in the winter sun, casting an almost reddish glow on the wallpaper and the heavy oak beams adorning the ceiling. The gallery was packed. There had not been an empty seat since about eight o'clock that morning. The correspondent for the right-wing *Das Bayerische Vaterland* had one complaint: There were too many women in the audience. The reporter for *Markt Grafinger Wochenblatt* had another one: too many foreigners.

The room, roughly fifty-three feet long and thirty-eight feet wide, seemed too small to serve as a venue for such an important judicial proceeding. Acoustics, moreover, were poor, *Berliner Tageblatt* added. Only sixty of an estimated three hundred reporters requesting press passes received admittance, leaving the majority of the arriving correspondents, columnists, cartoonists, and other feature writers out of luck. The journalists with passes were then crammed together in the middle of the gallery, behind the elegantly dressed and well-connected citizens who had secured the most advantageous seats.

Ten small tables stood at the front of the room, five for the defendants and five for their counsel. Behind them lay a row of seats for the witnesses, who would be pooled mainly from the military, state police, civil service, and former teaching staff at the academy. Lecterns from a former classroom in the building had been brought in for use during the trial. A reporter for the *Münchener Post* discovered that the one originally intended for the prosecutor's table had sported swastikas scrawled in ink until authorities discreetly exchanged it for a cleaner one the day before the opening session.

Just before eight thirty that morning, a phalanx of police officers escorted the ten defendants down the corridor into the courtroom. At the front of the procession was General Ludendorff in a dark-blue suit, not his military uniform that he had sworn in disgust never to don again. He kept his hands in the pockets of his jacket, which looked new to a reporter for *L'Ouest-Éclair*, and sat down at a small table at the front.

Some journalists thought he appeared reserved and haughty, surveying the audience from a lofty summit, scorning everything in the world below him. Others detected a supreme annoyance, as if he were irritated by the audacity of the court to bother him with its trivial activities. Still others speculated that the general's rigid posture masked a deep-seated anxiety that the proceedings would not enhance his reputation. Writers of right-wing and nationalist sympathies, on the other hand, saw only a good soldier stoically awaiting his fate.

Adolf Hitler followed a few steps behind the famous German, carrying a thick leather briefcase under his arm. His blue eyes scanned the room for supporters, who were very much in attendance. He sat down at the same small table as Ludendorff, making a show of deference to the general. A reporter for *Völkischer Kurier* thought Hitler looked well rested from his stay in prison.

"Was this provincial dandy, with his slick dark hair, his cutaway coat, his awkward gestures and glib tongue, the terrible rebel?" asked *Chicago Daily News* correspondent Edgar Ansel Mowrer, upon seeing Hitler for the first time in the courtroom. "He seemed for the world like a traveling salesman for a clothing firm."

Suddenly everyone in the room rose, the rubbing of the chairs on the wooden floor sounding like a "swarm of bees" escaping a hive. Five judges in dark, flowing robes made their entrance, along with two alternates. Each member of the tribunal took his seat in a leather chair behind the twenty-foot-long baize-covered table underneath the chandeliers in the front of the room.

The presiding judge, wearing the traditional high beret, was Georg Neithardt, a fifty-three-year-old Superior Court director, the highest rank of a trial judge in the German legal system. Scion of a noted Munich businessman, Neithardt had earned a reputation as a judge who opposed liberal and democratic tendencies, even at that time, when judges, as a profession, were notorious for harboring authoritarian sentiments. Severe and dignified with a white goatee trimmed to a point, Neithardt seemed to have stepped out of the court of Kaiser Wilhelm II.

Born on January 31, 1871, only thirteen days after Otto von Bismarck declared the birth of the German Reich at the end of the Franco-Prussian War, Neithardt had come of age during the spectacular growth of German military and industrial might. He never seemed to have reconciled himself to his country's defeat in the First World War or the democratization under the Weimar Republic. In fact, if anything, he had moved further to the right, and his verdicts reflected an increasingly ideological bias.

Would justice be served in the Hitler trial? Absolutely not, the foreign correspondent for the French Communist paper *L'Humanité* predicted.

Not in the courtroom of this right-wing Bavarian reactionary, who would be joined on the bench by judges suspected of being more extreme: a fifty-seven-year-old Superior Court counselor, August Leyendecker; three lay judges, Philipp Herrmann and Christian Zimmermann, both in the insurance business; and Leonhard Beck, a bookbinder and owner of a stationery shop.

The work of Weimar statistician Emil Julius Gumbel suggested that the French paper had a point. His analysis of political murder trials between 1918 and the summer of 1922 showed an unmistakable bias. Right-wing defendants received a not-guilty verdict in no fewer than 326 of 354 cases. There were no death penalties and only one life sentence. Left-wing defendants, by contrast, were judged innocent in only 4 of the 22 cases, receiving 10 death penalties and 3 life sentences. The length of the sentence also confirmed the double standard: fifteen years on average for the left, four months for the right. Weimar may have created a republic, but it had not removed the judges of the kaiser's regime who interpreted its laws.

At 8:52 a.m., without so much as a greeting or an introductory statement, Judge Neithardt began the roll call of defendants. Adolf Hitler, age thirty-four, identified as a Munich writer from Braunau, Austria; Erich Ludendorff, who spoke up to correct the spelling of his hometown of Kruszewnia; Ernst Pöhner, who nodded when asked if he had recovered enough from his recent illness to follow the proceedings. A British foreign correspondent, G. Ward Price of the *Daily Mail*, thought he saw the presiding judge give a quick smile to the defendants.

Already that morning, rumors circulated that Neithardt had shown extraordinary deference to the defendants, praising Ludendorff in private as "the only positive that Germany had left" and telling Hitler how sorry he had been not to have met him earlier. The rumors would gain such currency that the judge would soon feel compelled to address them in court. He would deny categorically that he had greeted Hitler that way. The correspondent for *Le Petit Parisien* watched some members of the audience smile in disbelief.

The judge was, in this case, almost certainly telling the truth, because he and Hitler were no strangers. In January 1922, after Hitler had attacked a rival Bavarian politician giving a speech at the Löwenbräu beer hall, he had appeared before Neithardt, facing three to six months in prison. Neithardt, however, had mitigated the sentence, ordering only a single month's incarceration, a token fine, and probation until March 1, 1926. The fact that Hitler had a prior conviction—and that he was still on probation at the time of the beer hall putsch—were only a few of the many relevant pieces of information never revealed during the trial.

AFTER THE ROLL CALL of defendants, Neithardt instructed the prosecution to read the indictment. "On November 8, 1923, in the Bürgerbräukeller in Munich," began Hans Ehard, taking up the duty for his boss. It was only appropriate that Ehard would open. Not only was he a more forceful speaker, but the hardworking deputy had almost certainly drafted most of the document himself. Ehard would soon earn praise, as the *Bayerischer Kurier* put it, for having the finest mind in the courtroom.

Hitler had conquered the beer hall with military precision, Ehard recounted, laying out the basis of the indictment. After declaring the current Bavarian government deposed, Hitler had attempted to establish a new regime that would serve as "the springboard for the Reich government." Once the conspirators reached the capital, they planned to begin "the final reckoning" with the Berlin politicians whom he called "the criminals who are destroying Germany."

Ehard grouped all ten defendants together, each one charged with high treason, except for one, Heinz Pernet, the stepson of General Ludendorff who was accused only of being "an accessory to the crime of high treason." Then the prosecutor took on each defendant individually.

Hitler was, Ehard said, "the soul of the whole undertaking."

Ludendorff was singled out for spreading word among discontented patriots that he would lend his name and his talents as a decorated general to support the putsch. This was, moreover, not a spontaneous decision in the heat of the moment but rather a premeditated act. "It is our supposition," Ehard said, "that Ludendorff had been accurately informed of this planned undertaking well before November 8."

Ehard continued hammering the defendants for more than one hour. The text, which ran to forty-two closely typed pages, carried a punch as it outlined the arguments and the evidence of guilt. Not everyone agreed. Hitler sympathizers would find the prosecutor "offensive," as defendant Captain Röhm later put it, and at least one foreign correspondent in the audience found his mind wandering off. He recalled mainly being struck by the fact that he had never heard so many references to beer in a legal document before.

AT ABOUT TEN TWENTY that morning, the chief prosecutor, Ludwig Stenglein, made a strategic request. Calling the case "a threat to national security and public order," he asked the judge to exclude the audience from the rest of the trial.

For prosecution and defense alike, the stakes were high. If the trial was moved behind closed doors, Hitler would lose one of his most valuable assets. He could, of course, still launch into speeches and interrogate witnesses at will, as permitted in German law, and, "erupt like a volcano" in the witness box, as one observer put it, but all his dramatic performances would be for the benefit of only a handful of people.

Hitler's defense attorney, Lorenz Roder, objected to the prosecution's motion. The German people had a right to reach a decision about the guilt or innocence of the defendants for themselves, and would clearly be alienated by a last-minute maneuver to hold the trial behind closed doors. The country would not be damaged by a public examination of the facts; on the contrary, it would be served. Three defense lawyers supported him in this argument.

Neithardt ordered the courtroom emptied so that the prosecution's motion for secrecy could be discussed in private. Once this was done, Stenglein stressed that, in the course of proving his case, he would have to introduce facts that risked exposing links between the German military and members of Munich's paramilitary societies—links that might be scandalous and almost certainly in violation of the Versailles Treaty, which had limited the size and scope of German armed forces.

Could the Hitler trial, he implied, lead to an international incident and perhaps even war with France, Britain, or any other member of the victorious alliance responsible for enforcing the treaty? This was a delicate matter. The court was, as Stenglein noted, "trying the case before an immense public, which includes virtually the whole world."

No, objected Weber's defense lawyer, Dr. Alfred Holl, a short and wiry former pilot who stood with the help of a cane after having lost a leg at the Battle of Verdun. The opinions of the vast international audience were irrelevant to the trial. "There is no harm," Holl said, "if the French and the English know that there are people in Bavaria ready to clean out a Berlin pigsty."

Everyone wanted to hear the defendants' explanations for their actions that night in November, seconded Willibald von Zezschwitz, a defense lawyer for General Ludendorff. This was necessary because the charges against his client could only be described as "monstrous," and he should have the right to defend himself in public.

General Ludendorff, not one to hold his tongue, joined the debate, soon moving off-subject and launching an attack on the indictment itself. He had been "deeply shaken" when he read the charges, he said, in a hoarse and surprisingly high-pitched voice, and then proceeded to call the document itself an act of high treason. "If I were a prosecutor," Ludendorff added, "I would take action against this prosecutor!"

"That's going a little too far," Judge Neithardt said.

As the debate over the proper procedure raged on, Adolf Hitler spoke up for the first time and promised that he and his fellow defendants would show discretion. As soldiers who fought for their country, Hitler said, "We do not want to conduct our defense in such a way that Germany might be harmed."

At the same time, Hitler wanted to draw a distinction between causing "damage to Germany" and "damage to a few men, who, by their own behavior, have most severely harmed Germany." All he asked for was the opportunity to defend himself in public. "We will not hurt Germany!"

Quick to realize the risks of allowing a beer hall demagogue take the stand, the prosecutor called Hitler's appeal to "public interest" a thinly disguised ploy to gain an audience for his antics and cause a sensation in the courtroom. Two defense advocates objected.

During the commotion, Hans Ehard shouted over everyone, reminding the court that the prosecution was simply performing its duty. He then turned to General Ludendorff and said that he, if anyone, should appreciate the importance of carrying out one's obligations. What's more, Ehard did not take kindly to accusations of high treason. If Ludendorff ever repeated this outrageous charge, he added, "the prosecution will of course dutifully react in the sharpest way possible."

Many people again started speaking all at once.

"The prosecution does not intend to be accused of treason!" Ehard shouted out in the din.

Judge Neithardt promptly suspended the debate and read out a court order requiring everyone in the room to keep quiet about the discussion. He then retreated to his chambers with the rest of the tribunal to deliberate on the motion to hold the treason trial behind closed doors.

Just before lunch, he emerged to announce the decision.

"The trial is to be public."

But he added a qualification. "The court will decide, from case to case, whether the exclusion of the public is necessary."

This compromise, while offering a sop to the prosecution, would lead to many motions to move the proceedings into secret session—and the frequency and timing of these requests would all but ensure a great deal of skepticism and cynicism about the fairness of the trial and the motives of the judges. Hitler would exploit this situation with consummate skill.

There was another, far more significant, consequence. Hitler would now not only be able to address the courtroom, but also, thanks to the sensational headlines and extensive media coverage, reach a much larger and more prominent audience than ever before. Hitler may have lost the battle of the beer hall, but Judge Neithardt had just handed him a second chance to win his war for power. The prosecution of a little-known writer from Braunau, Austria, was on its way to becoming one of the most momentous and significant trials of modern history.

27.

DEFENDANT HITLER

I made the decision to defend myself and fight back to my last breath.

—ADOLF HITLER, FEBRUARY 26, 1924

Reopening the trial before a courtroom brimming with anticipation, the presiding judge called Hitler to the stand. All eyes turned to the leader of the banned party, his hair neatly parted, his light-blue eyes staring straight ahead, and his long, tapering fingers seeming out of proportion to his average-sized hands. He would use them theatrically, like an actor. His face, according to a reporter for Munich's *Allgemeine Rundschau*, resembled "a rather dashing Austrian sergeant."

As was customary in German criminal law procedure of the time, the presiding judge led the interrogation. The questions, however, stemmed largely from the prosecution. The judge was therefore, during this stage of the proceedings, supposed to be speaking for Stenglein and Ehard.

One of the first concerns in the biographical introduction was confirming that the Austrian-born Hitler was not a German citizen, and consequently, if convicted of high treason, subject to be deported.

"When I came to Munich in 1912," Hitler said, describing his arrival in Germany, "it was not for my training [as an architectural painter]. I was already finished with that. But I had to earn my bread myself." He expressed his goal, at that time, of becoming an architect and master builder.

No one caught it, but Hitler had just succeeded in misleading the court about one aspect of his past that he would hide his entire life. He had not come to Munich in 1912, but a full year later. This lie probably helped him conceal the fact that he had left Austria without registering for military service and authorities had been pursuing him on grounds of desertion. The German police had finally arrested Hitler in January 1914 on a tip from their Austrian colleagues and sent him back to report to authorities in his home country. On February 5, 1914, however, Hitler had failed the mandatory entrance examination. The Austrian recruitment panel had pronounced him "unfit for combatant and auxiliary duties, too weak." Hitler's deception on the witness stand had spared him from revealing this embarrassing episode.

So without this knowledge or without investigating his past thoroughly, the court went on instead to emphasize how Hitler had served the *German* Army with distinction. Neithardt read out his record. Hitler had volunteered in August 1914, served the entire four years of the First World War in a Bavarian infantry regiment, and earned a number of decorations, including the coveted Iron Cross First Class that he wore that morning. Hitler's military file summed up his standing as "Very Good."

The impression given in the courtroom was that Hitler had spent the war fighting in the trenches. There was not one word of his actual primary duties, which, after November 1914, consisted of serving as a battalion dispatch runner (*Meldegänger*) for the 16th Infantry Regiment. He of course came under fire in his line of duty, but he spent most of the war behind the front lines, carrying messages from staff headquarters to battalion command leaders.

Unlike his comrades in the trenches, Hitler enjoyed, for the most part, dry feet, a dry uniform, and dry woolen blankets. His food was more edible, his drink more abundant, even if he preferred only tea sweetened with ersatz honey. There was no mold growing on his leather message pouch. Lice, mice, and rats were further removed from his experience, not to mention the frostbite, typhus, and imminent threats of enemy bombardments. "Rear Area Pig" was how the veteran "front hogs" labeled the relatively more privileged men like Hitler.

The judge asked about Hitler's wounds "fighting for the Germans."

"For war injuries, I suffered a shrapnel in my left thigh and later gas poisoning," Hitler said, both of which were true. The first wound occurred on October 5, 1916, when a grenade exploded at the entrance to the dugout where the dispatch runners stayed. The second happened two years later, on the night of October 13–14, 1918, outside Ypres, when a British mustard-gas attack burned his skin, damaged his retina, and caused him to cough up blood. He was at first "completely blinded," he told the court, and feared that he would never see again.

At 11:53, only minutes into the public proceedings, Neithardt called a break for lunch. Under the judge's careful questioning, Hitler had made an unmistakable first impression as a good German patriot who had volunteered for military service, earned high distinctions for his bravery, and nearly died for his sacrifices on behalf of his adopted country. This was a peculiar opening for a trial of a non-German citizen charged with high treason.

DURING RECESSES IN the proceedings, police escorted the defendants back to their cells on the other end of the second-floor corridor. Eight rooms had been allocated there for their accommodation, and two others had been set aside for use during meals and breaks by defendants who were not required to remain there: General Ludendorff, who returned every evening to his villa, and Ernst Pöhner, who, given his illness, was granted this privilege as well.

Hitler was accommodated in Room 160 near the far end of the corridor. The space was simple and Spartan. The one luxury in this former cadet dorm room was a white tablecloth with a vase of posies. For the duration of the trial, Hitler and the defendants were allowed two hours of daily exercise in the rear courtyard or, occasionally, in the academy's gymnasium. They could also smoke, if desired, and drink beer in moderate amounts.

There were rooms set aside for the judges and court staff, prosecutors and press, witnesses and the various units of the criminal police and security service. Roder and the defense counsel also had their own room for breaks. This was accessible by a door in the back of the courtroom. The lawyers had also rented a suite on the third floor of a building down the street. The huge workloads, it was predicted, would not allow them much leisure time, let alone the opportunity to return home.

When the court reconvened at 2:30 p.m. for the afternoon session, Judge Neithardt asked Hitler to make his opening statement.

"Your Honor," Hitler began, standing in the front of the courtroom with his Iron Cross First and Second Class pinned to his black coat. As the correspondent for Berlin's Socialist *Vossische Zeitung* noted, Hitler would put on a strong performance that showed unquestionable skill— the reporter called him "a genius" at appealing to the proletariat.

Hitler started off in a courteous and restrained manner, almost nervous. As he progressed with his statement, *Frankfurter Zeitung* observed, he assumed the sharp and harsh tones of a commando barking orders with excitement. The rawness of his voice softened and amplified at will, rising to a shout or falling again, nearly breaking, at an emotional crescendo, into a hoarse shrill. All of this, the correspondent added, he exploited to dramatic effect.

It was a dazzling performance, *Markt Grafinger Wochenblatt* said. The foreign correspondent for *La Croix* thought Hitler addressed himself less to the judges than to the audience, and posed as a modern tribune of the people. A reporter for *L'Écho de Paris* compared him to a charlatan hawking his wares on a street corner.

With confidence and verbosity in no short supply, Hitler often grew animated in the witness box. He underscored his statements by raising one hand in the air, index finger skyward, or lifting up both hands, palms facing each other, as he glanced toward the ceiling. At other times, he pointed directly and aggressively at the state prosecutor. His fervor was reflected in the intensity of his gaze. It was not difficult, a reporter for *Le Petit Parisien* concluded, to imagine this man's success with young Bavarians in a beer hall.

Hitler would talk for at least three hours that afternoon. The audience in the courtroom would receive its first impression of Hitler's autobiography, and this carefully crafted statement stands as a chilling display of fact management.

Defendant Hitler began by returning to a part of his past that was clearly a source of pride and a valuable component of his defense: his military service. Reminding the courtroom of his "Very Good" rating, based on six years of service, Hitler boasted of how he had learned as a soldier "to respect his superiors, contradict no one, and obey blindly."

Hitler's emphasis on his own military background was so pronounced that New Zealand's *Auckland Star* referred to him throughout its piece without irony as "Lieutenant Colonel Hitler." A journalist for the British United Press identified him as "Herr Von Hitler."

After trying to show he had the character of a soldier, not a traitor, Hitler spoke of his youth as his second formative experience that shaped his outlook. At age seventeen, he had moved to Vienna, where he had been, as he put it, "forced to earn my own bread." Hitler would repeat this phrase several times that afternoon. His vocabulary would, as several journalists pointed out, alternate between low German phrases and the expressions of a self-taught man.

In Vienna, Hitler said he had discovered two major crises of the modern world. The first was "the great misery and great poverty of a broad strata of people"; the second was the "racial problem" that rendered the masses vulnerable to what he called "the greatest enemy and adversary of all Aryan humanity." Hitler made no mistake that he had left the city of renowned diversity as "an absolute anti-Semite."

Hitler would later expand on this theme, emphasizing the rise of his own anti-Semitism in Vienna and claiming that his hard lessons there provided the "granite foundation" for his world view. This idea, which he made a cornerstone of his autobiography, would persist in biographies for years, though historians have begun to question the accuracy of this statement.

For one thing, not a single verifiable anti-Semitic comment from Hitler can be traced back to his Vienna days (September 1907 to May 1913). His closest friend at that time was Jewish (a copper polisher named Josef Neumann); his art dealer was Jewish (Samuel Morgenstern); and his customers were overwhelmingly Jewish, as Nazi researchers in the

1930s learned to their discomfort. The people nearest to Hitler in Vienna remembered no anti-Jewish statement whatsoever, and in fact several were adamant that he had not yet developed this hatred.

Instead, Hitler's earliest known anti-Semitic comments derive from the time after his move to Munich. By the fall of 1919, he was regularly spewing hateful comments about the Jews in his political speeches, raising the possibility that Hitler's rabid anti-Semitism more likely emerged in the aftermath of Germany's defeat in the First World War, the outbreak of the left-wing revolutions in Munich, and the indoctrination courses he took with the German Army in 1919.

If that is the case, then why did Hitler try so hard on the witness stand (and later in *Mein Kampf*) to trace the origin of his own hatred to Vienna? One likely reason would soon be clear enough.

Hitler had not returned to Munich with his battalion in March 1919, as he would claim. It was instead in January that year, or at the latest mid-February. The missing four to six weeks coincided with the rise of Munich's revolutionary left-wing regime—and, as German historian Anton Joachimsthaler proved, Hitler had served it.

He was a *Vertrauensmann*, or representative, of the Demobilization Battalion of the Second Infantry Regiment to the Revolutionary Council that seized power in the chaos following Germany's defeat. One of his duties was to deliver "educational," or propaganda, material to win over soldiers to the left-wing regime. Hitler had also won an election later that spring, becoming deputy battalion representative to the revolutionary worker-soldier regime, or Munich's "Red Republic."

Many of Hitler's colleagues, from Hermann Esser to Emil Maurice, had also belonged to Socialist parties during Munich's brief revolution. Unlike them, however, Hitler never admitted any support. He avoided the subject, sticking to vague claims of how he had opposed the upheaval. When forced to confront the topic, since he was now on the witness stand, he manipulated the chronology, preventing the truth about his past from being discovered.

Then, without pausing, Hitler embarked on a vicious tirade on the dangers of these left-wing ideologies. Marxism in particular, the defendant said, growing animated, threatened civilization wherever it emerged. It taught good German citizens to raise their fists at authority and seek to carve out "a state within a state"—ironically, the same charges that the prosecution was now making against him.

The presiding judge did not interrupt Hitler's long-winded rant. Many of the members of the audience no doubt shared these sentiments. No objection was made when Hitler called the Communists "not even human," or when he raced ahead to his unqualified conclusion: "Germany will only be saved when the last Marxist has been converted or crushed!"

Do not be fooled, warned Berlin's Communist paper *Die Rote Fahne*, highlighting the defendant's attempts to dupe the unsuspecting public with his manufactured tales of personal suffering and his "socialism for dummies." The paper would later dub Hitler and his ilk "the racist rat catchers," spewing an ideology of "despair and confusion" calculated to attract the vulnerable masses.

Hitler had indeed wasted no time in turning his treason trial into a stage for Nazi propaganda. He was also painting a self-portrait that would appeal to his followers. Tracing his anti-Semitism and right-wing roots back to his years in prewar Vienna served him well, helping conceal his earlier involvement with a rival party that he was now so fiercely denouncing.

THAT AFTERNOON, THE crowd in the Munich courtroom supported Hitler, the London *Times* reported. The Nazi "movement," as Hitler liked to call the party, was not founded "to gain seats in parliament." Its purpose was instead to change the fate of Germany.

He simply could not sit by as the country was, as he put it, "cut up and slashed into pieces." France had seized the Ruhr, Germany's industrial heartland, and strove to dismantle the once Great Power into a series of smaller, weaker states. The German republic mismanaged the crisis from day one. Then, with runaway inflation, Germany descended into economic madness. Millions of people had lost everything—"practically robbed," as he put it, "of their last marks from their pockets."

The German people were starving, and lands that could have been used to feed them had been given away by the cowardly government. Still, the hardships continued to grow "from hour to hour." Was this why, Hitler asked, 2 million young German patriots had died in the war?

Hitler had struck many similar points over the last four years in talks around Munich's beer halls, but this time, his audience would be magnified beyond anything he had ever experienced. Reporters from the leading newspapers of Germany, France, Britain, the United States, and many other countries were taking down his words and transmitting them for millions of readers around the world. This was publicity that he could never have hoped to purchase.

As Neithardt made no effort to rein in the defendant, Hitler roamed across subjects at will, speaking more like a propagandist or agitator, *Münchener Post* noted, than a defendant. Enjoying the limelight, Hitler eventually found his way to the putsch by lecturing the court on how to wage war.

Victory, he said, required a state to marshal its resources both at the front and back at home, and that had been the fundamental aim of his men at the beer hall. Ludendorff would ensure triumph in the field, while Hitler would rally the people to the cause. He was the drummer of the movement. He looked congenial, the Swiss newspaper *L'Impartial* said, noting his swagger, even if he came across as bombastic and theatrical.

Feeding off the audience, Hitler went on boasting about how he had shown what he could achieve with the Nazi Party. He claimed that he had transformed it from a group of six men in a back room of a beer hall into a movement of millions. This was another lie that Hitler would repeat in *Mein Kampf* and on many later occasions. The minutes of the first meeting that Hitler attended on September 12, 1919 show that there had been forty-one people there, or slightly higher, counting Hitler and the men who came with him. And the Nazi party files that had been salvaged from its office before the police search reveal that the membership was 55,787, not millions. Yet Hitler's misleading statement would draw admiration in the right-wing press.

"I must categorically state," Hitler said, continuing his vigorous self-promotion, "that I refuse to be modest about something that I know that I can do. If someone believes that he is called to do something, then he has the obligation to do it!"

Hitler then turned on the Bavarian leaders who had shared the stage with him at the Bürgerbräu. Kahr had agreed to join them, he said. Seisser had spoken of the national revolution as an imminent explosion for which they had only to prepare the powder and light the fuse. Lossow, likewise, seemed in agreement, or, as Hitler scoffed, at least never refused. They had all shared the same ambition to march on Berlin. The only difference, Hitler said, was that these so-called leaders lacked "the will to make the leap"—like a "horse that lost its courage before the hurdle."

So if he and his fellow defendants committed high treason, Hitler concluded, then the Bavarian triumvirate must also be guilty of this crime. "For all these months, nothing else was discussed other than that for which we now sit in the dock."

But unlike Kahr, Lossow, and Seisser, who now hid from the consequences of their words and deeds, Hitler seemed prepared to stand up for his actions and beliefs. "I did not come to this courtroom to deny anything," he bragged. "I alone bear the responsibility and also every consequence." At the same time, he balked at pleading guilty to the prosecutor's specific charges because, as he put it, "There is no high treason against the traitors of 1918!"

Before closing his statement, Hitler made one last appeal. He reminded the court of his service defending Germany both in the war as "an obedient soldier and also in the homeland." What's more, he added, "since my youth, I have never felt like an Austrian." He saw himself instead as the best kind of German who "wanted the best for his people." He asked the court to allow him to remain in the country.

Many newspapers would cover the trial like a prizefight. Hitler had clearly won the first round. In a legal sense, however, the prosecution also had good reason to be pleased. Hitler had, in his long rant, provided what Stenglein called "exhaustive evidence of his guilt." The prosecutor then had the last word of the day before Neithardt sounded the bell: "Examination of the witnesses will reveal more."

28.

CONFESSIONS AND DISTORTIONS

*I had already by then come to the conclusion that, in Bavaria,
it was absolutely impossible to know who was master and who
was servant.*

—ERNST PÖHNER

Wednesday, February 27, 1924, opened the second day of the trial.
Photographers and camera crews were allowed to shoot only
outside the building, provided that they had obtained a special permit.
Political rallies had been banned at the Löwenbräu and other nearby beer
halls. The police once again blocked off surrounding streets, prompting
protests from local residents and shops. A motorcycle dealer was particularly incensed about disruptions to his business.

Security staff scrutinized the rainbow of passes that granted admission to the proceedings: green for the prosecution, defense counsel, and
court officials; yellow for state authorities; brown for prominent guests
and relatives of the defendants; blue for members of the press, or alternatively, white if the reporters had access only to the press room. The cards
for the public were handed out on a temporary basis, usually valid for a
single day or a half day. Neithardt himself issued the cards.

The presiding judge was already being criticized for showing a bias
in the distribution of these prized passes. One known Communist who

had arrived from Berlin was curtly rebuffed, while spectators with right-wing sympathies seemed to have much less difficulty securing a seat. Neithardt would soon be accused of packing the audience with what Munich's *Allgemeine Zeitung* called "the scum of the Hitler crowd."

The police presence at the Munich trial appeared to have increased even further than on the first day. The grounds of the building complex, the adjacent streets, and the corridors outside the courtroom virtually swarmed with men in spiked and steel helmets with grenades festooned in their belts and rifles slung over their shoulders. This "state of siege," the *New York Herald* mocked, was far more threatening than the beer hall putsch had ever been.

Laughs about the "beer patriots" and their miniature "beer hall revolution" certainly remained in vogue. "Putsch Trial Called Joke," headlined the *Vancouver Sun*. Hitler and his men had sworn to remove Socialist, Communist, and Jewish enemies, the United Press correspondent wrote, but only succeeded in staging a comic opera with his "ludicrous beer cellar putsch." *Le Petit Journal* enjoyed the irony of patriotic Bavarians rushing off to follow an archrival Prussian like Ludendorff and a "Czechoslovakian" like Hitler.

Despite the dismissals in Berlin, Paris, and elsewhere, Hitler and his co-defendants remained popular in Munich and glowing reviews for his speech the day before were pouring in from the right-wing press. "It was either do or die at the Blutenburgstrasse," observed a reporter for *Das Bayerische Vaterland*. Hitler had appeared in top form and, he added, emerged as the most brilliant agitator he had ever seen.

The anti-Semitic writer of *Das Bayerische Vaterland* was also pleased to hear the defendant's renewed attacks on the Jews, which reminded him of "the old Hitler." By this moniker, he meant the rabid rabble-rouser of the years 1919 to 1921, before Hitler had taken control of the Nazi Party and, in the opinion of the reporter, moderated his rants to appeal to a wider audience.

It was this popularity that had in part prompted authorities to house the defendants in the former academy for the duration of the trial. In addition to security, this arrangement, it was hoped, would prevent embarrassing scenes of crowds cheering the defendants every day upon their arrival and departure.

Ludendorff, however, received preferential treatment. The former commander was free to return each night to his villa, and the *Daily Express* in London was already labeling the trial "a farce" that should be subtitled "the Whitewashing of Ludendorff." The general would probably be found not guilty, its correspondent predicted, and sent off, like a mischievous little schoolboy, asked politely "not to do it again."

Papers on the left, in particular, took pleasure in how Hitler had attacked his fellow right-wing, conservative Bavarian leaders. Berlin's Socialist *Vossische Zeitung* asked, like Hitler, "Why was Kahr not arrested?" The French Communist *L'Humanité* also scrutinized the Hitler-Kahr relationship, even as it ran a photo supposedly of Hitler that was in fact the wrong man. It was Gustav von Kahr.

By the second day of the trial, the court was already behind schedule. The first four defendants were expected to have testified by now, but instead, Hitler's speech had taken the entire afternoon. The digressions, diversions, and other distractions were only beginning.

At 8:35 a.m., Judge Neithardt called the second defendant to the stand, Dr. Friedrich Weber, the president of the Bund Oberland, one of the most financially solvent of the radical right-wing paramilitary organizations that had emerged after the war. This group had developed from the brutal Freikorps Oberland, which had helped suppress Munich's Communist Revolution in 1919 and left-wing agitation in the Ruhr in 1920. In Neithardt's introduction, the defendant sounded like a freedom fighter.

After the putsch, Weber had published a pamphlet called *The Truth* that set out provocative allegations of complicity on the part of the Bavarian triumvirate. Several newspapers had picked up the story, forcing a spate of official denials. Still, Weber's allegations had not gone away, and, as the sympathetic *Der Oberbayer* put it, they would be hard to counter, given Weber's reputation as a man of honor.

A tall and thin clean-shaven man who looked young even for his thirty-two years, Dr. Friedrich Weber worked as a research assistant on the veterinary faculty at Munich's Technische Universität. He seemed like a student himself, thought Munich's *Allgemeine Rundschau*. He wore small, round eyeglasses and spoke in a calm and succinct manner. This was a contrast, it was said, to Hitler's "big speech," as Berlin's *Vossische Zeitung* labeled it, referring to its length, not its distinction.

Weber's testimony that morning would, among other things, shed light on the motives of some of the first people to support Hitler. In his experience, Weber said, the fighting societies attracted two extremes of recruits. On one side were the German patriots who wanted to restore the monarchy and the imperial traditions, which had been taken away from them at the end of the war. On the other were the Germans who pressed for more populist and revolutionary aims, such as abolishing aristocratic titles and eliminating class barriers. These were people with vastly different agendas, but there were three things that united them. The audience, *Le Petit Parisien* correspondent noted, hung on closely to his statements.

First and foremost stood their hatred of the Versailles Treaty as a dictated peace that had unjustly stripped them of population, territory, resources, and dignity. Second, before they could "break the fetters of this disgraceful" document, they had to defeat the so-called greatest enemy to German freedom, which he identified in a single sweep as "Marxism, Jews, and this democratic parliamentary system with its worship of the masses and majorities." Without dealing with this threat at home, German patriots risked marching off to war only to suffer another "stab in the back." This led to their third unifying point: the need to "launch a crusade for spiritual and moral renewal first of ourselves and then, through us, to as many of our people as possible."

This was the path to a new, free Germany—and the best hope for this future was Adolf Hitler, Weber said. It was a ringing endorsement.

Under questioning by Neithardt, Weber confirmed many of the points Hitler had made on the stand the previous day. The plotters of the beer hall putsch had expected to have the support of the Army of North Germany based on the prestige of General Ludendorff. An alliance between the military and their fighting societies, they were confident, would cause the Berlin government to crumble, with "nothing left to do but submit to this pressure and disappear from the scene."

Indeed, Hitler would never have acted, Weber suggested, if he had not believed that he enjoyed the full support of the Bavarian military and the state police. He told of several meetings that he had personally attended with both General von Lossow and Colonel von Seisser in preparation for this operation.

"When did you first receive reliable notification [of the change in allegiance of the Bavarian leaders]?" Neithardt asked.

"We never received a reliable notification," Weber said. "We found that out only when they shot at us."

Neithardt asked Weber if he had expected any other outcome.

If Kahr, Lossow, and Seisser had not "broken their word in such a shameful and disgraceful manner," he answered, "it is obvious that our final objectives in Germany would have been obtained."

AFTER THE PRESIDING judge wrapped up his questioning of Weber by inquiring about the age of the defendant's two young children, Arnold and Friedrich, the second prosecutor, Hans Ehard, took over and managed at once to ruffle Weber's composure.

Did the defendant know, Ehard asked, about the extensive plans of Hitler and the conspirators to pressure Berlin for what he called "your own objectives?"

"I protest against the phrase 'to pursue our own objectives,' Weber said. "We never pursued our own goals, but always German ones alone."

"My, you seem very sensitive," the second prosecutor taunted. Then he went further by questioning Ludendorff's reputation: "Haven't you ever heard that General Ludendorff has very little influence in the army, particularly in North Germany?"

Many people in the audience stirred at this statement. "Outrageous!" shouted one member in the gallery. Another one said no such disrespectful question should be asked in a German courtroom. A reporter for Le Matin watched Ludendorff stand up in the tumult and complain about this personal insult.

Neithardt chastened the young prosecutor, reminding him that he had to keep order in the courtroom.

Ehard, undeterred by judge and audience alike, said he was pursuing a crucial point.

It was Weber, however, who won the applause of the gallery when he delivered a long monologue on the respect, indeed reverence, he felt for Ludendorff, whom he identified as the greatest commander not only in the First World War, but in all German history.

"Good, that's what I wanted to know," Ehard said.

"Actually you wanted to know something else," countered defense attorney Karl Kohl, jumping to his feet and speaking in a tone that came off as disrespectful. The short, powerfully built advocate with a barrel chest and a booming voice congratulated Weber on his dignified response to the prosecutor's insults. The audience cheered again. Neithardt pounded the gavel. They were not at the theater, the presiding judge said.

When the commotion died down, Weber stated that, contrary to various allegations, he had never heard that Kahr, Lossow, and Seisser had been forbidden to talk to one another in the back room. The defendant spoke with such poise and assurance that it came as a surprise, when only minutes later, Ehard tripped him up by asking a simple question: Had he heard what Lossow said to one of his assistants when they entered the side room?

They were not allowed to speak, Weber said, before he realized the contradiction and tried to correct himself. Hitler's attorney, Lorenz Roder, rushed to his aid. The Bavarian leaders were free to move about the room, weren't they?

Weber affirmed that.

But wasn't a guard posted at the door, Neithardt asked.

"Outside the door."

"So that the gentlemen couldn't leave the room?"

Weber was caught again.

IN THE AFTERNOON session, the Bavarian judge and former Munich president of police, Ernst Pöhner, took the stand. At age fifty-four, he was one of the oldest men in the dock: balding, clean-shaven, and sporting a pince-nez on his once broken nose. The reporter for Berlin's *Vossische Zeitung* thought he looked more Bohemian than German.

Like Hitler, Pöhner made no attempt to deny his role in the affair. He related how Hitler had come to him on the eve of the putsch, outlining the plans for the march to Berlin and asking for his help to facilitate the operation. Pöhner admitted his own role in the back room of the beer hall, persuading Kahr to join Hitler. He never saw any evidence whatsoever of any games, pretensions, or even reservations from Bavaria's leaders.

Pöhner spoke on the stand slowly and carefully, with minimal gestures, and kept his left hand behind his back, clenched into a fist. He was measured and matter-of-fact, speaking simply and, apparently, without a shred of remorse. How, he asked, could General von Lossow, as an officer, swear obedience to a commander like Ludendorff and then deliberately deceive him? It was more likely, Pöhner argued, that Lossow had joined the putsch but later regretted it and made up the story of "putting on an act."

The defense lawyers wanted to keep questioning Pöhner about his relationship with Kahr, particularly given their work together in March 1920 in the attempted overthrow of the republic. The judge was visibly troubled by this line of questioning, suggesting that they save it for the secret session.

But Hitler's defense attorney, Lorenz Roder, persisted, arguing that it was "simply unfathomable" to imagine this subject to be a matter of pressing national security. The court would disgrace itself by moving important testimony to private session and "give the impression that protective hands shielded Kahr." Ludendorff's lawyer agreed.

Stenglein objected to the line of questioning altogether. "I do not think that these questions have any essential significance for assessing the question of [the defendant's] guilt." The prosecutors would have cause to repeat this statement many times over the course of the trial as the defense pursued a strategy of exhausting and overwhelming the prosecution by drowning the case with myriad distractions and irrelevancies.

By the end of the day, when the judge asked Pöhner if he would have liked to have marched against the state, he said that he most certainly would have. Berlin politicians were criminals and "murderers" who had seized positions of power that did not belong to them and had gorged themselves on the spoils. Pöhner then again caused more commotion in the courtroom when he said to the judge with a smirk: "We have been carrying on that business you call 'high treason' for the last five years!"

29.

BEHIND CLOSED DOORS

I have tried calmly and soberly to ask Hitler a question.
—HANS EHARD

On the morning of Thursday, February 28, 1924, the audience encountered an unexpected delay. Snow blanketed Munich, just as it had much of the continent from the Pyrenees to the Apennines, and General Ludendorff's car had apparently gotten stuck on his way to court.

The defendants passed the time by chatting with one another and reading reports. Around nine twenty a.m., as the excitement and flashing photography outside the building signaled, the German commander had arrived thanks to a ride from a supporter. Still, the proceedings did not open. A reporter for the French news agency Agence Havas believed that someone had misplaced the keys to Room 130, where the tribunal kept the minutes of the trial.

Lt. Col. Hermann Kriebel finally took the stand as the accused military planner of the beer hall putsch. Age forty-eight, Kriebel was a burly man with bushy eyebrows and broad shoulders who looked spruced up, as a reporter for *Le Petit Parisien* put it, like a groom on his wedding day. The journalist knew the defendant from his work covering nationalism in Germany, and concluded that he had never met a German who harbored a deeper hatred of France than this "Bavarian colossus."

Kriebel retraced his career as a soldier, focusing on the misfortune at the end of the war, not least in being ordered to accompany the German armistice mission to Spa in Belgium. It had been a humiliating and searing experience. He had never forgotten the sense of rage and frustration of fighting on the western front against "a ruthless, merciless enemy capable of every kind of villainy" while at the same time suffering attacks from "bands of traitors" at home.

Then he had watched with disgust as the same traitors who broke their oaths to the German kaiser were rewarded with positions of power in the new republic. He spoke of his time after the war in French-occupied Palatinate, cursing the signatories of the armistice, the "November criminals," for preventing him from thrashing the opposing French general, and, as he put it, "[giving] such a fellow what he deserved." At this phrase, Neithardt halfheartedly admonished the defendant to show more restraint.

A reporter for the French nationalist newspaper *L'Action Française* noted that Kriebel was proving to be as much of a fanatic as Hitler, whose name he misspelled as "Hittler." Several international journalists were still incorrectly spelling the chief defendant's last name. *Le Gaulois* and Germany's Telegraphen-Union wire service would persist in giving Hitler an extra *t* long into the trial, though this was becoming increasingly less common.

Under the guise of his biographical introduction, Kriebel treated the courtroom to a series of anecdotes about the decline and fall of modern Germany. At the armistice in Spa, he recounted how, as his train left the station, he shouted out the window with a clenched fist: "See you in a few years!" The Belgians reacted "with a storm of indignation, yelling, stone throwing, and pistol shots." At that point, Kriebel said, he vowed "not to rest" until he achieved what he had proclaimed at the train station.

Kriebel spoke as "a convinced Bavarian" who wanted to annex Austria, or "German Austria," as he put it, and restore his country's power and reputation. In this stance, he shared a lot in common with Hitler. But it was not Hitler's ideas or even his position on this question that primarily attracted him. It was something else entirely, Kriebel said, though he hesitated to speak of it in public.

Judge Neithardt took the hint. So the audience, after sitting through the morning delay, had not heard fifteen minutes of testimony before they had to vacate their coveted seats for another one of the trial's many secret sessions.

THE TRIAL WAS being eagerly followed in Great Britain, France, Italy, Spain, Switzerland, Scandinavia, the United States, and as far away as Argentina and Australia. Several foreign correspondents, particularly from Paris, took a skeptical view of the presiding judge's move of the proceedings behind closed doors.

Le Petit Parisien guessed that Kriebel's testimony, to which the public was not privy, would delve into the secret army that Germany was believed to be building up in defiance of the Versailles Treaty. Several other papers speculated that Kriebel would reveal how much the German Army had supported Hitler in his planned attack on the republic. At any rate, many people concluded, the discussion would probably be very much worth hiding.

Kriebel's closed-door testimony would indeed have provided fodder for a feast of headlines. He began by giving his perspective on the value of the German patriotic societies in what he called the inevitable "great war of liberation which we will one day have to wage, whether we want to or not." There were, however, several fundamental misconceptions about these societies.

The general public, of course, imagined that the nationalist paramilitary organizations were being assisted by the military and police. In truth, it was the reverse. Kriebel praised the everyday Germans who, at great personal risk, hid weapons from the Allied investigators trying to enforce the Treaty of Versailles. It was a thankless task, he said, that at any moment might bring the prosecutor to their door, an indirect slap in the face to Stenglein and Ehard. German patriots were acting bravely, despite the laws passed by their own "criminal government" to constrain them.

"Lieutenant Colonel!" Neithardt said. "You spoke about a criminal government. I cannot allow that."

The defendant then explained why he had supported Hitler. The German military needed to attract the masses, especially the members of the working class. The problem was that, since the end of the war, the workers had flocked overwhelmingly to the Socialist and Communist parties. None of the German patriotic, or nationalistic, parties or leaders could win them, he soon noticed, except for one person: Adolf Hitler.

Hitler's charisma and speaking skills, coupled with his "tremendous power of the will," put him in a unique position to help Germany prepare for the inevitable next war. He won both the young workers who would fight and the older ones who would forge weapons and produce materials for the military. As Kriebel put it, "We can wage no war of liberation without such workers."

This forthright admission in closed session yields some insight into one reason why certain military officers were first attracted to the beer hall demagogue whose opponents all too often underestimated or even dismissed him as a Chaplinesque buffoon. Kriebel then delved into more detailed testimony that would have been explosive if it had reached the public.

The Bavarian leaders, he testified, had positively been informed of the preparations for the march to Berlin. Colonel von Seisser had even helped train his men. Kriebel described a meeting with Seisser in October 1923, when they pored over the map of Germany and planned marching routes and deployment areas on the way north to the capital.

The plan was to seize power, Kriebel said, with the help of the "border police," which were none other than members of various patriotic fighting societies. Seisser had approved of the project. Everything had been so clear, he said. As late as October, there was "no doubt that we would march to Berlin."

He pulled out the exact order, dated October 16, 1923, that his men had received for the march and then offered to pass it out.

"Now?" Neithardt asked. He warned that such a document would by law have to be surrendered to the court.

Kriebel handed the document to the judge anyway. A map was added to illustrate the routes to the capital.

Stenglein looked over the paper. Was this really about mobilization?

"And its preparation as well," answered Kriebel.

Ehard asked who drafted this plan.

"It comes from Berlin."

Ehard examined the order. It was striking, he said, that, given the implications, Colonel von Seisser did not make any reference to this order in any of his pretrial statements.

"That is not striking," Kriebel countered. They had the full cooperation of the Bavarian authorities.

Fellow defendants Dr. Weber and Ernst Pöhner confirmed that the emergency police had served as a cover for the paramilitary societies who were mobilizing for the march north.

One of the judges on the bench warned the defendants not to repeat this information in public.

Hitler had some additional information to inject into the closed session. The Storm Troopers had also been trained by the German military. This was done in the army barracks, and when his group later overwhelmed capacity, the state police had provided facilities. They had been cooperating with authorities in this way since January 1923, when the French had invaded the Ruhr and the military establishment began to fear they might soon have to go to war. The training had intensified in the fall.

In fact, Hitler said, the military and the state police were pressuring *them* to act. By November 1923, the Storm Troopers were restless. It was impossible, he added, to restrain his men after all this talk of war and the training at the barracks.

"They were trained in the barracks?" Neithardt asked.

Yes, Hitler said, adding that the instruction took place with the knowledge and support of Bavarian authorities, who also provided some uniforms.

"By officers of the Reichswehr?"

"Yes, by officers of the Reichswehr."

This was a clear violation of the Versailles Treaty. If such information reached the press, Kriebel said at one point during the secret session, "everyone would then march against us, even the Eskimos." The risk of an international scandal was no exaggeration. The French had marched into the Ruhr with less provocation.

AT 2:37 THAT afternoon, when the court reconvened behind closed doors, Kriebel's lawyers submitted a series of confidential documents outlining mobilization and marching plans. It was patently absurd, Kriebel said, that his men would consider fighting the German military and state police. They were their allies, not their enemies.

Hitler spoke up in support of his colleague, coming out with another revelation about his actions that he did not want to say in front of the public. He admitted to ordering the thefts at the printing presses, claiming that he had been promised funds by the military at the "moment of mobilization." On the morning of November 9, however, he had not been able to reach General von Lossow. The money was needed to help his men buy breakfast and prevent acts of violence.

"I considered it an absolute matter of course that, in such a case, you do what is necessary," Hitler said.

When Ehard asked about the feasibility of the march to Berlin, given its major international consequences, Hitler responded with a long monologue that swept across centuries of international relations and Great Power politics. He outlined how France had long sought "the Balkanization of Germany," by dividing it up into smaller, controllable parcels. Britain too had used Germany as a pawn in its classic balance-of-power calculations, trying to prevent any one country from dominating the continent. "Once it was Spain, later the Netherlands, then France, and lastly, us." Germany's only hope against such determined enemies was to exploit any rift between them, as their own self-interests would continue to diverge and conflict.

Hitler went on to criticize Berlin for failing its people with its lack of nationalism and fighting spirit, which caused the defeat in war and the current misery. World history, he added, confirmed that capitals cannot lead a national revival. It was not Constantinople that produced Atatürk, but Ankara; it was not Rome that gave rise to Mussolini, but northern Italy. That would also, Hitler said, be the case for Munich and the rebirth of Germany.

What's more, given the scale of the crimes committed against Germany, Hitler did not expect a peaceful solution. On the contrary, it would require "a tremendous, unprecedented exertion of force [and] perhaps even a great deal of bitter suffering." He, for one, was prepared to die for his cause. He regretted nothing. He vowed to attempt a putsch all over again if necessary; he was convinced they would have succeeded if only the Bavarian leaders had not failed them.

The prosecutor asked if Hitler imagined that he had the support of a majority of the population.

No, of course not, Hitler sneered. History was not made by majorities but by an individual, or "hero," he said, who often acted in opposition to the larger public and imposed his will on society. He was no traitor and neither were his colleagues. "High treason is the only crime which is punished by its failure."

On that note, Hitler went on, still uninterrupted by the presiding judge, to warn the prosecution. "Do not believe that this trial will destroy us! You can calmly lock us up—you can do that. But the German people will not destroy us. Our prisons will open and a time will come when today's accused become the accusers!"

30.

THE DEFENSE ATTACKS

Ludendorff towers over this quagmire of lies, deception, and broken promises. He will always stand proud. No pearls fell from his crown because he fell in with robbers.

—LT. COL. HERMANN KRIEBEL

The trial was splashed across the headlines around Germany and the world. For many left-wing newspapers, particularly in Berlin and northern Germany, it seemed Hitler and company were starring in a grotesque circus or sensational theatrical production. Right-wing southern German papers, like the *Rosenheimer Anzeiger*, countered that Berlin had expected the trial to be "a party," when in fact the proceedings were better styled "Tragedy at Munich."

The audience had filled the dark, somber courtroom more slowly than usual the next morning, February 29. Many people were expecting another lengthy delay, or perhaps also a quick resort to a secret session. Others wondered about the focus on extraneous details in this strange trial. "If the public sessions are to be merely devoted to anti-French and anti-Belgian speeches," a reporter for the London *Times* wrote, referring to Kriebel's testimony, "there must be little reason why the proceeding should be continued at all."

The spots reserved for the public and press were actually half-empty when Hitler entered on the morning of Leap Day, 1924, walking briskly and looking in all directions. Ludendorff followed him, accompanied by his counsel and a team of defense lawyers shuffling behind, the rustle of their gowns swishing across the floor.

München-Augsburger Abendzeitung had praised the defendants for their restraint in avoiding sensitive issues that might harm German interests, but added that the same could not be said for their lawyers. Christoph Schramm, chief counsel for Captain Röhm, had taken offense. All the lawyers faced the challenge of defending their clients without compromising national security. As a good German, he said, he wanted it to be clear that he and his colleagues prioritized the interests of the Fatherland.

He also wanted to draw attention to an article in the *Völkischer Kurier* that told the story of a man on a Munich streetcar who happened to sit between two cartoonists who had attended the trial. One of them, described as "apparently a Bulgarian or Hungarian, or at least a typical Slav," had drawn an unflattering portrait of one of the judges on the bench as a deceitful trickster; the other one, identified as a Jew, had sketched a lampoon of Ludendorff as a shrew with a gaunt face and hollow cheeks, staring emptily into space. Schramm wanted the judge to banish "such men" from the courtroom. Neithardt agreed.

While they were on the subject of the press, prosecutor Ludwig Stenglein took exception at an article that portrayed him as listening to Hitler's speech with an unremitting smirk on his face. For the record, he said, it was untrue. Berlin wits, however, must have sympathized, wondering how anyone could keep a straight face in this bombastic travesty of a trial.

Lieutenant Colonel Kriebel resumed his testimony. For the benefit of the public, excluded from almost the entirety of the previous day's proceedings, Kriebel explained in a discreet, censored fashion his role as military commander of the forces that conquered the beer hall. His restrained discussion carefully avoided any reference to the inevitability of another war, the training his men had received from the military, or anything else that might provoke the wrath of the international community.

After accepting full responsibility for his actions, Kriebel described the motives of Hitler and the fellow conspirators in a way that showed the complicity of the Bavarian authorities. He told the court of a conversation with Lossow two days before the night of action, when the latter pledged to support a march, provided it had a 51 percent chance of success. Kriebel then showed his disdain at this reasoning as unbecoming of a soldier, let alone the highest-ranking military commander in Bavaria. Had the German Army espoused the same sentiment in the last war, they would have surrendered in August 1914.

This was why Hitler's men stormed the beer hall. They came, he said, to open the door for the three procrastinating triumvirs—and then deliver a well-timed kick to push them through it. He saw this action also, changing metaphors, as a "springboard" and "a little nudge" to help the leaders overcome their fear of jumping into the water.

The defendant acknowledged that he had come up with the code phrase "Safely Delivered" to signal the successful and bloodless birth of the revolution at the Bürgerbräu. He also admitted writing the phrase on the paper the police found, but not making or ordering any phone calls to Captain Röhm or Dr. Frick.

Neithardt reminded him that the words "First report to Frick," were also on the paper, as was the word "Löwenbräukeller." Was this phrase telephoned to the beer hall?

"In a word, no."

The judge told him that the prosecution had identified the lieutenant who made the call.

"I mean, if that is known to the public," Kriebel backtracked, "then I will admit it."

This minor point of dispute illustrates a strategy that the defendants would exploit to devastating effect. They would sometimes deny a fact in the courtroom and then, if corrected, claim that they were merely covering up to protect "national security." It was a win-win scenario for the defense and yet another challenge that Stenglein and Ehard faced in the prosecution of Adolf Hitler.

LIKE THE DEFENDANTS before him, Kriebel seemed determined to exonerate Ludendorff from any responsibility for the putsch. The German commander was furious at the Bavarian leaders, he testified, because their betrayal not only doomed the revolution to failure but they had never given any warning before the state police fired upon them. This testimony provoked a fierce response among members of the gallery.

Kriebel went on to praise Ludendorff for his honor, which he contrasted with Kahr's, Lossow's, and Seisser's shocking lack of it. The defendant was also appalled by the police. When one officer heard the rumor that Ludendorff had been killed, one policeman had said, "That was the best solution."

The audience in the courtroom jeered at this revelation.

"Outrageous!" someone yelled.

"Shame on him!" shouted another person.

"That is no officer!"

The judge pounded his gavel.

The prosecutor also objected. "I would like to ask you not to forget that this is only a one-sided account that consists of the most serious personal attacks." He urged that "such extremely harsh comments" at least be reprimanded and the court reserve judgment until it could hear the other side.

Now Judge Neithardt took issue with the prosecutor. "I do not believe it is the concern of the public prosecutor to reprimand the presiding judge in a session." His tone, *Berliner Tageblatt*'s correspondent said, came across as "very harsh," and the judge's words were met with shouts of "Bravo!"

The defense attorney Karl Kohl, emboldened by the judge's rebuke, decided to take aim at the prosecutor. Kriebel's negative opinion of the Bavarian leaders was shared by "all decent men in Germany," the lawyer said, wondering aloud if Stenglein also thought of himself as a decent person.

"That is going too far!" Neithardt said. "That is a personal attack that I cannot tolerate."

After tempers cooled, Kriebel emphasized the alleged peaceful intent of the march to the city center. The men, he repeated, had been ordered to unload weapons and refrain from shooting. They had no desire whatsoever to fight the Reichswehr or state police, which should be obvious, he added, given their formation. No experienced military commander would march troops packed so closely together through narrow streets in range of enemy fire.

The prosecution did not ask him how much, if at all, the leaders had tried to enforce these nominal orders among their hungry, somewhat disgruntled men who, by their own admission, were desperate and hard to control. Nor did it ask why the men bothered to carry heavy, cumbersome, and menacing weapons if they were supposed to be engaged in a peaceful demonstration.

Instead, Hitler's defense counsel, Lorenz Roder, pressed ahead with a series of questions that confirmed Kriebel's attendance at several meetings with Kahr, Lossow, and Seisser in the first ten months of 1923. Then Roder asked point-blank if the defendant would have acted on November 8–9 had he not been confident that his good friend Colonel von Seisser was involved.

"I would not have taken any action against my old friend," Kriebel said, referring to his thirty-five-year friendship with the colonel that dated back to their youth. "I was absolutely rock-solid convinced that he was participating."

On that note, defense counsel Karl Kohl wanted to stress that the state police had not given a single warning before firing on the marchers. Kriebel said they had not.

What's more, the defendant said, there was little the marchers could do. They could not shout orders to their men in the deafening noise. Even if they could have, the mass of people behind them prevented them stopping or turning around in the narrow streets. On the other hand, had the marchers been allowed to proceed another fifty meters into the open square, Kriebel claimed, the peaceful demonstration would have ended naturally and the death of twenty men could have been avoided.

The defense attorney Kohl was now fired up. "According to the sentiments of our people, the events at the Feldherrnhalle must be called 'murder!'"

The presiding judge did not say a word, much less object. Other defense lawyers jumped to their feet to agree. Kohl's words had gone off, a reporter for *Völkischer Kurier* said, like a bomb in the courtroom.

31.

A MASTERPIECE OF IGNORANCE

Is Ludendorff a super-patriot?
—Calgary Daily Herald

L udendorff's admirers clung to the hope that their patriotic idol would not have to endure a public session of the trial. His critics did not think he would take the stand either. Given the concern for national security, they said, Neithardt would probably have to call a closed session for Ludendorff too, because the irritable and unpredictable general would be a loose cannon, likely to say anything that popped into his head. So at three o'clock that afternoon, the courtroom buzzed with anticipation when it was clear that Ludendorff was indeed going to testify in public.

The general, still refusing to put on his military uniform, wore a blue suit with a single Iron Cross First Class pinned on his chest. During his long speech, lasting perhaps as much as three hours, Ludendorff would raise his horn-rimmed eyeglasses onto his forehead as he flipped through his typewritten statement, copies of which he had scrupulously sent beforehand to journalists. He would then lower his spectacles to the tip of his nose and peer through them at the judges. Ludendorff was no orator, it was often said, and as Berlin's *Vossische Zeitung* added, he apparently had no desire to become one.

He would hesitate, stop in midsentence, fumble about in his stack of papers scattered about him looking for a particular sheet. He was sweating, his hands trembling, and he looked very uncomfortable. The discomfort was not nervousness, some nationalist supporters explained; it was fury as a result of the betrayal of the state leadership.

"I cannot express myself as Hitler did yesterday in his marvelous speech in closed session," Ludendorff said in his rasping, high-pitched voice, which did not carry well in the courtroom. He did, however, share Hitler's assessment of Germany's plight as being caused not by foreign powers, but "by our own guilt."

He attacked three domestic enemies in particular for causing the country's decadence and ruin. First, he singled out the Marxists, or Communists, who had opposed the German military during the war and regretted its victories on the battlefield as "detrimental to the interests of their party." Second, he attacked Jews for spoiling the German race, physically and morally, and claiming that they deserved no more influence in national affairs than other foreign peoples, like the English or French. Third, he blamed the Catholic Church, calling it another negative influence that undermined the country's liberation and future rebirth.

This statement was received in complete silence.

Reporters for right-wing papers like *Rosenheimer Anzeiger* called the general's talk "a new high point of the trial." Many other correspondents would scoff at the pompous and disjointed statement that Thomas R. Ybarra of the *New York Times* dubbed "a masterpiece of political ignorance."

As for his relationship with the triumvirate, Ludendorff retraced familiar territory, dwelling on his "great confidence" in General von Lossow and his absolute certainty that the defendants had worked together with the Bavarian leaders. They had seemed full of conviction. Ludendorff's impression was of high-ranking, ambitious politicians who were accustomed to wielding power and reluctant to relinquish it.

Ludendorff went on to depict the march as a peaceful attempt to persuade the people—"a procession of enlightenment." It all changed, he said, when they were shot at by the police. Hitler's party had become a victim of "betrayal, treason, and attempted murder," but Ludendorff predicted it would ultimately draw renewed strength from "the blood of martyrs."

This racial rejuvenation was essential for the rebirth of the country, he urged. They did not want a Germany under the thumb of France, or, he ranted, the Marxists, Jews, or Catholics. "We want . . . a Germany that only belongs to the Germans—a strong, powerful Germany that is also a haven of peace as it was in the age of Bismarck."

How exactly he would achieve this strong nation-state, however, remained an open question. In the opinion of many left-wing papers, Ludendorff had only one solution: He wanted the power for himself. The defendant was a dangerous man, Berlin's *Vorwärts* wrote. He was the incarnation "of the spirit that brought Germany to ruin."

Neithardt was about to wind down the day's session when Ehard managed to ask the general if he did not realize that his actions during the putsch not only harmed the authority of the state of Bavaria but also Germany.

"That was only against the government officials," he said.

Ludendorff drew some polite applause in the courtroom. The commander who had never lost on the battlefield, an admiring right-wing reporter claimed, left the witness box still unvanquished. That afternoon, when the general's car drove away, the staff at the Löwenbräu beer hall stopped it and brought him a stein of beer.

CAPT. ERNST RÖHM had few complaints as he sat in the former dorm room of the military academy down the long corridor from the courtroom. Food and drink were certainly superior to the fare he had endured in the building as a cadet in 1907. A sampling of the menu during the trial included beer, wienerwurst, sauerkraut, pretzels, cheese, rye bread, and other Bavarian specialties. This was, it was said, part of a conscious strategy by the court administration to dissuade the defendants from launching another hunger strike.

To Röhm's pleasure, the defense attorneys had been aggressive. The legal team might have coordinated their strategy and tactics more effectively, he thought, and perhaps made decisive use of their superiority in numbers, but he did not want to quibble. They had kept the prosecutors off-balance, and the trial seemed to be shaping up well.

Röhm was also enjoying seeing his fellow defendants again. The Munich courtroom was the first time they had all been reunited since the putsch. Hitler, in particular, was in high spirits, undoubtedly relieved, Röhm thought, that his colleagues did not blame him for the beer hall fiasco and they had come to the trial ready to fight.

Just after 8:40 in the morning on March 1, 1924, Röhm took the stand. He arrived in uniform, his short light-brown hair carefully parted in the middle, and wore a pince-nez for the questioning. His strategy, he later said, was just to remain true to himself and his men, and above all avoid walking down what he called "the road of humiliation and penance."

The defendant opened with a sweeping statement that set the tone for his testimony that day:

> Your Honor, I should justify myself today. I must say that I still cannot comprehend that I should have to defend myself for a deed that is so natural to me, that I wouldn't know how I could have acted otherwise on November 8, 1923.

Did he not count as crimes, reporters asked, high treason, the seizure of government buildings, the taking of members of the government as hostages, the theft of trillions of marks, and the death of four policemen?

Röhm spoke with a haughty, crisp intonation, his concise responses delivered in a somewhat choppy flow. He seemed stiff and pompous, his lower lip locked in insolence.

He looked like a stereotypical Prussian soldier, the correspondent for *La Justice* thought, adding that he sounded like one too. *Berliner Tageblatt* found him "rather uninteresting," except perhaps as a specimen of the type of mercenary, or freebooter, emerging in postwar Germany.

"I am an officer and a soldier," Röhm said, explaining that he wanted his thoughts and actions judged in this light—this was also how he would later open his memoir. His words came out with a "peculiar snort-like sound," probably a result of the wounds to his nose during the war, or the rudimentary plastic surgery he had received.

Röhm seemed to take pleasure in emphasizing his reverence for the royal dynasty that he credited with building up Germany into a Great Power. During this time, he boasted that he had never forsaken his oath to serve the king. Attempts to release him from that sacred commitment had been "very disheartening." He had refused them, unable to understand how other soldiers could abandon their word of honor.

Loyal to the ousted king, Röhm came across as even more blindly obedient to Hitler, marveled a reporter for *Allgemeine Rundschau*. Röhm went on describing the heady early days when the Nazi party consisted of only a dozen men meeting in a tavern on Dachauer Strasse. Röhm's disdain for the republic was boundless. He called the president of Germany "Comrade Ebert." Neithardt made no attempt to chastise him.

The audience did not seem as interested in this testimony as it had been with Hitler or Ludendorff. It was positively dull, several journalists noted, fighting off sleep as Röhm descended into the minutiae of the mutiny. "Dismal weather outside, dismal boredom [inside]," *L'Écho de Paris* said. For once, he added, many people in the courtroom apparently yearned for a closed session to relieve them from the tediousness of the testimony.

Neithardt asked if Röhm had ever considered the legality of his actions.

He and his men had cheered rather than contemplated, Röhm answered.

"It is understandable that you were very pleased. But did you not give any thought to whether the affair was legal?"

"No," Röhm repeated. "Our enthusiasm was extraordinary."

His attorney, senior counsel Dr. Christoph Schramm, the father of one of Röhm's men in the Reichskriegsflagge, brought up the question of stolen food and other supplies belonging to the War Ministry.

Röhm said there had been no plundering whatsoever.

Judge Neithardt cut him off, dismissing this line of questioning as irrelevant. Several reporters in the audience had the impression that the judge was not so much keeping the proceedings focused on the question of high treason as trying to cover up a scandal. This was not farfetched.

During one of the trial's closed sessions, Röhm admitted that as much as three-fourths of the money stolen from the printing presses during the putsch had disappeared. The banknotes had been in an office at the War Ministry when his men surrendered, he said, blaming the pilfering on the state police and Reichswehr troops who took over the building. The matter was not resolved.

Nor was the investigation into the thefts at the army storehouse during the occupation by Hitler's men. A list of missing property totaled more than 5,700 items, including 299 shirts, 528 pairs of socks, 125 field caps, 87 uniform caps, 87 pairs of infantry boots, 78 pairs of riding boots, 65 steel helmets, 65 armbands, 49 pairs of leather gloves, and a variety of other goods from songbooks to carbine halter straps.

Röhm was not pressed either, when he insisted on claiming that his activities at the Löwenbräu were independent of the events of the Bürgerbräu, and he had no knowledge whatsoever of the code "safely delivered" that had been telephoned to his men. The questioning of the defendant was anticlimactic and unrevealing.

THE NEXT DEFENDANT to make an introductory statement was Wilhelm Brückner, a tall, powerfully built leader of three battalions of Munich Storm Troopers who had helped secure the Bürgerbräu. Despite his imposing stature and somewhat stylish air, the forty-year-old student of political science did not make a good impression with many reporters in the room. The correspondent for Berlin's *Vossische Zeitung* saw him as "a rather confused political chatterbox" who raced through his muddled ideas with an ill-mannered cynicism and shocking callousness.

Like many of the Storm Troopers under his command, Brückner was drawn to Hitler by his "ruthless combat against Marxism." He clearly despised this ideology and other left-wing doctrines, stopping himself at one point in the middle of a sentence from calling the slain Socialist leader, Kurt Eisner, a pig. The National Socialists had taken up the battle against these internal enemies, and Hitler seemed the only one, in the deplorable state of affairs, who could, as he put it, "rescue Germany."

One secret of Hitler's success, Brückner said, was his ability as "probably the first person to give our despondent youth an ideal again." This, in turn, inspired older, disillusioned Germans to regain hope for the country. What a contrast Hitler had seemed to the current lot of rulers who proved to be incompetent in the face of chaos and shuddered in fear of the Allies.

"We wanted and needed people who had an exuberant love of the Fatherland along with a fanatical hatred and a fanatical zeal," Brückner stated. Hitler was attracting men and women with these qualities like no other leader in Germany, and what's more, he was drawing them from a broad swath across society: the middle class, civil servants, merchants, students, and workers. Brückner had the "greatest faith" in Hitler before the putsch, he said, but this confidence had been strengthened immeasurably the last three months in prison.

In the end, Brückner remained defiant. Thinking everything over in prison, he concluded:

> I must really say I am proud, as a German—awfully proud—that I took part on November 8 and 9. Today, if I were in this situation again, I have no doubt that I would follow my leaders, Ludendorff and Hitler, in exactly the same way.

As with Röhm, several reporters rightly dismissed the cross-examination as short and uneventful. The day ended with the defendant expounding on his statement that, in his opinion, the constitution of the Weimar Republic did not exist.

32.

CUP OF BITTERNESS

He got us rolling, suddenly stopped, and then we rolled over him.

—ROBERT WAGNER, ON GENERAL VON LOSSOW

The trial of Adolf Hitler, wrote the young Austrian novelist Joseph Roth, was unfolding with a morbid sense of unreality. The main defendant was an illiterate upholsterer who called himself a writer and everyone believed him. He ranted for hours about his insignificant life, and the fawning press printed every detail with diligence. His associate was a disgraced general plucked from history's "register of the dead," who had then taken the stand and proved only one thing: He read nothing other than military books. Captain Röhm, however, had surpassed them all in stupidity. Could this man really believe, Roth asked, that the German Army could not have lost the war?

The real problem in the case, *Fränkischer Kurier* countered, was the "incomprehensible ineptitude" of the court in allowing foreigners to sit in on this German affair. *Deutsche Tageszeitung* agreed. Enemies everywhere were showing a little too much glee in the display of Germany's troubles. Democratic papers like Cologne's *Kölnische Zeitung*, by contrast, objected to the peculiar focus of this trial: Why was the republic being questioned more than the defendants?

At 8:52 a.m. Monday, March 3, Judge Neithardt opened the next session of the controversial, polarizing proceedings. Day six was going to be another surreal spectacle that blurred the lines between judge, prosecution, and defense.

One of the defense counsels, Heinrich Bauer, the fifty-seven-year-old representative of Heinz Pernet, immediately stood up and complained about the coverage of the trial in two left-wing Munich newspapers. The defense was not, he said, indulging in the "most superfluous" speeches full of "pomposity and personal ambition so as not to be outstripped by the other defense lawyers." They sought only to find the truth, he claimed, hoping that Neithardt would confiscate the passes of the offending reporters.

Karl Kohl raised a more substantial point. Taking up the previous day's allegation that the Bavarian leaders had committed nothing less than murder, Kohl had tracked down the official police handbook and read out the proper procedure for confronting marchers in a peaceful demonstration.

Three attempts must be made, either by a bugler, a drummer, or a signalman, each time, followed by a clear warning from the ranking officer. The police must then allow time for the crowd to disperse. None of these regulations were followed. Instead, the police had immediately fired on the demonstrators, even when the march included a German field marshal and many war veterans. Such actions were unfathomable.

"There can be no doubt whatsoever that the bloodshed at the Odeonsplatz, which the public calls murder, must be charged to the accounts of Herr Kahr, Seisser, and Lossow!" He called for the immediate arrest of the three leaders.

Speeches like this were quickly earning Karl Kohl a reputation as the most aggressive of the defense advocates. "Fiery" was the word the London *Times* used. Kohl did not consider his words before he uttered them, a reporter for the extreme right *Völkischer Kurier* even acknowledged. He was a headline-making machine eager for the spotlight, and he was succeeding. Audience excitement peaked whenever he spoke.

Stenglein, for the moment, deflected this dramatic maneuver. "A preliminary inquiry on the incidents at the Odeonsplatz is pending," he stated, confident in the innocence of the authorities. Neithardt moved the proceedings on before the defense could pursue its agenda of derailing the Hitler affair into a murder trial against the leaders of state.

The defendants who would appear this day were minor figures in the plot. First came Lt. Robert Wagner, the twenty-nine-year-old cadet accused of rallying his fellow infantry academy students to Hitler. He had been the first of the defendants to wear his military uniform to the courtroom, and he did so again as he took the stand. He looked trim and dashing, said a sympathetic reporter for *Völkischer Kurier.*

Like several other defendants in the trial, Wagner traced back the moment he began to despise Socialists and Communists to the revolutionary upheaval of 1918 and 1919. He then offered a surprising first-person account of an encounter with the nephew of the president: "Staff Sergeant Ebert," who had supposedly started a mutiny among the men of his regiment. The experience made Wagner, as he put it, drink from his overflowing cup of bitterness.

Wagner's comments drew considerable attention in the press, but this so-called "Staff Sergeant Ebert" was not the president's nephew, or even a relative at all. In reality, the president had lost two sons in the war, and a third one had been wounded. The fact that the man in the defendant's story was an imposter was not public knowledge at the time, leaving the court to ponder about the supposed nephew of the beleaguered president betraying his country.

Discussing the events at the officer academy, Wagner explained how he and his fellow students had no doubt that the Bavarian authorities had supported the putsch. General von Lossow, who had led the school until 1922, had ordered the cadets to attend Hitler's meetings. Lecturers at the academy had likewise informed them that Kahr was ready to march on Berlin and wished Hitler would stop standing on the sidelines.

Wagner was providing some tantalizing glimpses behind the scenes of Bavarian nationalism. As his testimony progressed, Wagner acknowledged that he did not accept the charges of high treason because, as he put it, the constitution no longer existed. What's more, Germany would never be free as long as the Social Democratic government remained in power and tried to solve national problems by "conferences and negotiations."

At various times during the testimony, the reporter for Berlin's *Voss-ische Zeitung* noticed that several officers in the front of the courtroom in military uniform looked uncomfortable.

When the defendant started to relate his experiences at the Infantry Academy on November 8, the prosecutor moved for the court to enter closed session.

The defense advocate, the thirty-seven-year-old Walther Hemmeter, objected. Although the story might be dreadful in its implications, there was no reason to exclude the public, he argued. Nothing in Wagner's testimony could possibly threaten national security.

The judges, however, decided in favor of the prosecution and cleared the courtroom.

IN THE CLOSED session, Wagner argued that his cadets at the academy had not failed in discipline, obedience, or loyalty to their country when they had joined the putsch. On the contrary, they had just been following orders. Their actions on November 8 seemed the culmination of months of clandestine training and preparation on behalf of the German strug-gle for freedom. Were they to betray *that*?

Ehard asked the defendant, if he, as an army officer, had given his oath to the constitution.

Wagner admitted that he had.

How well was he, Ehard asked, fulfilling this obligation?

Wagner tried to claim he had not broken his oath. What he and his fellow cadets did was correct because the head of the Bavarian military supported the movement. From that moment, they had entertained no doubts whatsoever about the legality of the act.

The presiding judge then reminded the defendant that he had pre-viously testified that, in his opinion, the constitution "no longer existed."

Ehard, turning to the judge, said he was glad that they were in secret session because of the sight of a young officer of the Reichswehr, like the defendant, disrespecting the constitution would make a poor impression. What would Germany, let alone the world, think of such blatant disregard for the law?

"Was that a question or a reprimand?" asked Judge Neithardt.

The defendant, unable to remain quiet, jumped in to attack Ehard. The second prosecutor wanted to dwell upon his youth, Wagner said, even though "the difference in age [between them] is not so considerable." (Ehard looked young for his age. At thirty-six, he was seven years older than the defendant.)

Besides, if the prosecution was so concerned about the poor impression of the trial, Wagner's lawyer said, it should deal with the real odor of scandal rising from the case: The state wanted to single out his client as a criminal while approximately 250 other people at the academy "from the commander to the youngest officer" who strove for the same goal were allowed to remain free. The same also went for the Bavarian leaders Kahr, Lossow, and Seisser.

As the dispute turned into another round of attacks on the authorities, defense lawyer Lorenz Roder said that his client Hitler had noticed one of the representatives of the Reichswehr had been sending signals to the prosecution. He wanted this interference stopped immediately.

Stenglein said he was unaware of any such signs.

The trial cannot continue this way, the presiding judge said. It was embarrassing for everyone. He made no attempt to find out if the military representatives were in fact attempting to communicate with the prosecution. Instead, he resorted to his usual refrain of urging caution and discretion.

When the public session reopened at about eleven thirty a.m., Wagner retraced his testimony without mentioning anything that might be construed as compromising national security or embarrassing to the military. His bowdlerized account, deemed bland and unimportant, drew relatively little comment in German and international press.

After an unexpected delay, during which time the defense counsel huddled together to discuss strategy, the next defendant to take the stand was Ludendorff's stepson, Heinz Pernet. His testimony clarified little

and ranked as among the dullest thus far, judged the foreign correspondent of Agence Havas. Pernet had remained in the background, both in
the putsch and the trial—and that minor role best suited him, concluded
Bayerischer Kurier. The Hitler trial, with its sensational outbursts, inces-
sant quarreling, and increasingly frequent use of closed sessions, was
taking a turn for the worse.

33.

DR. FRICK

I dismissed all the officials because I assumed that the dance would begin the next morning.
—DR. WILHELM FRICK

"Comedy, comedy, deplorable comedy," André Payer wrote in *La Presse*, criticizing the trial as a ridiculous farce in which the audience already knew the script and the actors' talent no longer sufficed for their roles on the stage. Ludendorff in particular had seemed miscast. He looked aged and exhausted. He lacked common sense. He poured out a barrage of "words, words, words," as the *New York Times* correspondent Thomas R. Ybarra put it, but succeeded only in giving "a black eye to extreme German nationalism."

Ludendorff had staged a "phantasmagoria" highlighting the Catholic, Marxist, and Jewish menace, wrote the Swiss *Neue Zürcher Zeitung*. Yet most of the ire against the general clearly focused on his portrait of Catholics as enemies of the German state—not a popular stance in a country with a sizable Catholic population.

The papal nuncio in Munich, Monsignor Eugenio Pacelli, had been monitoring this trend for some time. He wrote in a dispatch to the secretary of state, Cardinal Pietro Gasparri, condemning the attempts by the Nazis to turn the people against the Church and pope, and to paint the

Jesuits as a sinister international freemasonry. The propaganda, like the Nazi movement, was "vulgar and violent," though he was not surprised given the bile spewed for months by its newspaper.

The archbishop of Cologne was one of the first to protest at Ludendorff's statement, noting the role that countrymen of his faith had played in the building of the German state. *Bayerischer Kurier* printed a lengthy retort to Ludendorff's "battle against Rome." Many newspapers, from the *Corriere d'Italia* in Rome to the *Daily Mail* in London, carried excerpts of this rebuttal, recounting many valuable services Catholics had rendered the country.

Was it not Pope Benedict XV and his secretary of state, Cardinal Pietro Gasparri, who intervened to stop the Allies from putting Kaiser Wilhelm II, Hindenburg, and many prominent German generals on trial as war criminals? One of the men spared had been Ludendorff himself.

What about all the Catholic soldiers who had served their country under Ludendorff's command and died on battlefields across the continent? What, for that matter, about all the Jewish soldiers who had also served and died for Germany only to be vilified by their commander? Ludendorff's speech was, *Time* magazine wrote, "ineloquently written and ineloquently read." Even worse were its ideas. London's *Observer* called them simply grotesque.

Ludendorff had launched his offensive in the courtroom hoping to show the malice of others, but succeeded only in "revealing his own true nature," Germany's Catholic Center Party paper, *Germania*, wrote. Could anyone listening to Ludendorff's speech in the Munich courtroom possibly have the impression that he was a distinguished general possessing a great mind? He seemed at best a young staff officer. *Vossische Zeitung* thought more of a deranged infantry cadet. *Vorwärts* just called him an ass.

The correspondent for *L'Écho de Paris* outlined a theory for Ludendorff's bizarre behavior. Based on a series of interviews with the defendant over the years, he summed up the general as "an impulsive and ambitious man" embittered by his condemnation to a peripheral role in the republican regime. In this frustration, Ludendorff had become desperate—and gullible—enough to be taken in by a mediocrity like Hitler.

Others went further, reminding that it was Ludendorff's poor judgment that had caused Germany to lose the war. He did not understand his countrymen, or apparently much of the world, as if he were stuck in the age of Bismarck. Even some of Ludendorff's supporters suggested that the general had gone astray. "Regrettable," wrote *Deutsche Allgemeine Zeitung.*

The Hitler trial was also inspiring some reflections on the nature of the far-right movement in Germany. It was difficult to understand "the Hitler-Ludendorff mess," *Vorwärts* wrote, without distinguishing two emerging camps the trial had thrown into the spotlight. One was overwhelmingly Catholic and monarchist, finding its main enemies in Berlin, or closer to home, with Social Democrats and Communists. The other traced its spiritual roots to Nietzsche and racist theorists like Arthur comte de Gobineau and Houston Stewart Chamberlain. Adopting the swastika as its symbol, this latter racial group espoused a rabid anti-Semitism that also, to a lesser extent, incorporated anti-Christian views. It was this second group that cheered Ludendorff's tirade.

What this analysis might have added was that while Ludendorff was dividing his far-right base, Hitler was not. He straddled both of these groups, just as he was already showing a talent for holding together an unlikely coalition of ruffians who flocked to the Storm Trooper battalions on one hand, and more law-abiding, middle-class supporters who had been devastated by the hyperinflation on the other. Ludendorff was losing his eminence, while Hitler began to bask in the fallout. There was already a rumor in Munich that Hitler would take advantage of his rising popularity to run for Parliament.

First, however, he would have to come through the trial without a lengthy prison sentence and deportation.

THE TENTH AND final defendant to make an opening statement was Dr. Wilhelm Frick. As head of Department VI, the political intelligence office for the Munich police, Frick was accused of "dereliction of duty" for failing to alert the state police and security forces to the crisis at the Bürgerbräu.

The forty-six-year-old defendant was suave, elegant, and, as a correspondent for *Berliner Tageblatt* put it, "tall and thin as a poplar." Frick had been amused by the attention that the trial had received. He had become, as he wrote to his sister, an accidental European celebrity. But there would be no sign of humor or wit when he took the stand.

Frick began by stating his political views, concentrating on his conception of the state as the embodiment of power: "Without [it], a state has no authority, dignity, prestige, or governmental policy." This principle of power—both at home and abroad—had guided him in his career. "I have never in my life, even for a moment, let myself be misled by Marxist, pacifist, or democratic ways of thinking," he boasted.

Frick had nothing but contempt for the current German government, which he regarded as impotence personified. The regime functioned at the mercy of a "hopeless party system." In international relations, it could only stagger—like "a game ball"—"from one hostile kick to another, and exhaust itself in pathetic whining for enemy or foreign aid, and in powerless, hence ridiculous, protests."

One of the most striking parts of Frick's testimony occurred that afternoon, in a casual, almost offhand, remark about his work as head of the political division of the Munich police. Frick admitted that he had used his position, since 1919, to support the young Nazi Party—this at a time when the organization was, as he put it, "still small and would have been easy to suppress." Frick had chosen Hitler's party because it had gained a foothold among the "Marxist-infected workers" and therefore showed promise as "the germ of Germany's renewal."

On November 8, Frick had been at police headquarters at the time of the putsch because he had meetings there until six thirty that evening. He remembered debating whether to attend the rally at the beer hall. "I had already heard enough fine speeches," he said, and did not expect anything different. Then, after dinner, he changed his mind and decided to go. On the way out, however, he saw that the evening newspaper had already arrived and figured that it must have been later than he thought. He opted to stay at the office and work.

Frick offered an explanation for each instance that the prosecution accused him of failing to carry out his duty. "He admits nothing, he concedes nothing" was how Berlin's *Vossische Zeitung* summed up Frick's strategy of excuses and evasions. He spoke like he expected to be treated as a hero, the reporter added, albeit one who had refused to face any dangers that night.

Above all, in Frick's view, the burden of the blame for the fiasco of the beer hall putsch fell squarely on the Bavarian authorities and the general state commissioner, Gustav von Kahr, in particular. If only Kahr had informed them of his change of heart, then Frick told the court that he could have shared the news with the editors at their midnight press conference and prevented the needless bloodletting outside the Residenz Palace.

34.

FIRST WITNESSES

I think it was Herr Hitler who stated that the testimony [of the witnesses at the beer hall] might, to a certain extent, not be credible because they were perhaps under the influence of alcohol.

—GEN. FELIX LUDWIG COUNT BOTHMER

After six days of the trial, the defendants had finally completed their opening statements. Criticism of the proceedings, meanwhile, was increasing. Every day, *Münchener Zeitung* noted, Hitler and his cronies entered the courtroom cheerful and confident, spewing the same political extremism. They spoke without fear of interruption for apparently as long as they wished or, alternatively, clammed up in silence, if they preferred. Then, at times of pronounced tension, Neithardt intervened and conveniently moved the court into closed session.

The police had been complaining about the insults the department had endured at the hands of the defendants without Neithardt so much as "lifting a finger" to stop them. The military made a similar criticism, as did several members of the Bavarian cabinet, who were angry at the spectacle.

"The defendants were not questioned; they held speeches," the minister of the interior, Franz Schweyer, snapped at the cabinet meeting on

March 4. They just said whatever they wanted. The judge's indulgence had gone so far, the minister reported, that Neithardt had apparently allowed one of the defendants, Dr. Weber, to leave captivity for a stroll through town over the weekend.

The press was having a field day with the trial. If he were the presiding judge, a reporter for *Das Bayerische Vaterland* said, he would put an end to the mockery. On the other hand, he recognized some untapped potential for the proceedings. The trial should be recorded and broadcast—the first German radio station had hit the airwaves in Berlin four months earlier. That way, the world could hear, and not just read about, the outrageous antics, and the court could sell advertising. Hitler's stentorian voice, he joked, could be used to plug toothpaste or treatment for hemorrhoids.

Stenglein, likewise, came under fire. *Das Bayerische Vaterland* attacked the prosecutor as a pathetic creature who allowed the defendants to praise their own deeds, or rather crimes, *ad nauseam*, and insult Bavarian authorities without fear of retribution. The Socialist *Münchener Post* did not disagree. Exaggerating the relative obscurity of the prosecutor, the paper predicted that this trial—his "debut," it was dubbed—would likely be his finale.

Stenglein's sympathizers, by contrast, cautioned against the rush to judgment, at least until the tribunal had heard the quality of the witnesses that the prosecution had assembled. On Tuesday, March 4, 1924, the trial entered its second phase with the summoning of the first witnesses and the weighing of the evidence.

There was, however, a slight delay that morning caused by the security staff having to scrutinize the variety of spectator passes and entrance cards. Then came the now-customary series of gripes and complaints. This time, Hitler's lawyer, Lorenz Roder, raised some serious objections.

Roder first wanted to protest against certain deliberate attempts to suppress the facts and influence witnesses. This had begun on November 9, 1923, with the control of Bavarian newspapers, which, he alleged, not completely unfounded, were instructed not to print any account of the affair that conflicted with the official view sanctioned by Gustav von Kahr.

Then, after silencing opposition, Roder said, two documents were circulated that outlined the Bavarian government's approved version of events. One was the so-called white-blue pamphlet, an anonymous forty-six-page piece that drew its nickname from Bavaria's traditional colors. The other was a secret report, signed by General von Lossow. Both the pamphlet and the memorandum had been disseminated among high-ranking officers in the military, the state police, and various officer clubs. Each of these leaders was instructed about the "facts" of the case and encouraged to share them with their staffs.

Roder pulled out a copy of the report, marked "Secret!" and "Confidential!" Leafing through it, Hitler's advocate read out a highlighted passage instructing that no reproductions or excerpts were to be made. He had examined this document and compared it to the witness's pretrial interrogations, Roder continued, with the audience enthralled. "I found that Colonel von Seisser's [pretrial] statements match this document, page-by-page, nearly word-for-word."

He read out a passage that proved his point.

The presiding judge, clearly troubled, tried to stop Roder, advising him to wait and confront the witnesses with his discovery.

Roder reminded the tribunal that he was speaking about a concentrated effort to influence the trial's witnesses—and the court should know this fact *before* it examined their testimony. He also claimed that, based on his investigation, the report must have been distributed by the triumvirate, probably General von Lossow and composed by Colonel von Seisser, or at least one of his subordinates in the state police.

What's more, Roder wanted to point out some other peculiarities. German law stipulated that each witness had to make his statements independently, but that had clearly not occurred. Kahr, Lossow, and Seisser had each been questioned at the end of the pretrial investigation, and then been allowed to read and even make use of the previous testimonies for their own statements. He promised that he could prove these strong allegations.

Neithardt stopped him again, calling it unwarranted at this time.

Roder, however, persisted, seconded now by Ludendorff's chief counsel, Willibald von Zezschwitz, who took the discussion one step further. The "striking agreement" between this confidential report and the indictment could be explained, he said, by the simple fact that both documents probably came from the same source: the prosecution. Four other defense attorneys quickly concurred.

At this point, Stenglein jumped to his feet and forcefully denied that his office had any connection with this document. Neither he nor anyone on his staff had anything to do with the drafting or dissemination of this classified report.

Regardless of its origins, Ludendorff's second defense counsel, Walter Luetgebrune, pointed out that this document had in fact been sent to many witnesses scheduled to testify. At the least, it should be read out for the benefit of the court.

The judges went into deliberation to consider the motion.

In the meantime, the foreign correspondent for the Associated Press noted with surprise that the defendants were allowed to roam at will. Adolf Hitler, playing the gallant, kissed the hands of women in the audience in his "foppish manner," as *Allgemeine Zeitung* put it. He was also spotted talking to a man who had drawn attention to himself for his clothes: he wore a field-gray officer coat adorned with the imperial black-white-red cockade that was a direct insult to the Weimar Republic. Had the judges lost complete control of the courtroom?

Neithardt emerged to announce that the pamphlet would not, at this time, be read. He promised to allow it later, subject to his discretion. That moment would never come.

Before the judge could summon the first witnesses of the trial, the prosecutor motioned for a closed session. Testimony of these witnesses, all members of the Reichswehr, might threaten national security.

The defense objected. The court did not need to convene behind closed doors, Ludendorff's attorney Zezschwitz said; what it needed to do was prevent the members of the military in the audience from unduly influencing or perhaps even intimidating the witnesses. He therefore urged the presiding judge to remove *them* from the courtroom.

At this, two members of the military in the audience stood and requested permission to remain present for the duration of the testimony.

The judge deliberated a second time that morning, and, after five minutes, returned to agree once again with the prosecution. The public would be turned away. Neithardt also agreed to allow the military representatives to remain in the room.

ENSCONCED IN CLOSED session, the first of almost a dozen scheduled witnesses that morning took the stand. This was fifty-eight-year-old Gen. Hans Tieschowitz von Tieschowa, commanding officer of the Infantry School whose cadets had supported the putsch.

The witness explained that the infantry cadets' seemingly treasonous actions on the night of November 8 stemmed from the fact that they believed in the imminence of the great national uprising. The students had been so swept away by their patriotism that they had not realized that they were in the process of committing a crime against the state.

As the questions veered further away from the defendants on trial for high treason and more onto the possible complicity of the Bavarian leaders in the affair, Neithardt dismissed the witness. The second person to testify in the trial, still in closed session, was Col. Ludwig Leupold, the instructor at the Infantry School who had come to Ludendorff early on November 9 and conveyed the news that Lossow was now opposing the putsch.

The questioning did not go anywhere, until Ludendorff interrupted to ask the witness if he remembered him promising not to shoot at the Reichswehr or state police, and then requesting that this message be relayed to General von Lossow.

Leupold confirmed it.

Had Lossow, in turn, wanted to send any message to Ludendorff, perhaps a warning that the Reichswehr planned to open fire?

No, he had not, the witness testified.

The presiding judge decided to end Leupold's testimony and dismiss the other nine witnesses from the Reichswehr infantry academy as unnecessary. For once there was no objection from *either* the prosecution or the defense. Stenglein and Ehard had little to gain from testimony that would likely damage the reputations of the Bavarian leaders, their chief witnesses, if not further implicate them in the putsch. Roder and the defense team, likewise, saw the closed-door proceedings offering minimal opportunity for the strategic maneuvering and dramatic antics that they had in store.

At 2:52 that afternoon, when the court reconvened for the public session, a parade of witnesses from the Munich police would pass before the tribunal, prompting the press to dub it "The Day of the Police." Eleven witnesses appeared in rapid succession, though many of them added little more than confusion to the proceedings.

One of the witnesses, the forty-two-year-old chief of the political police division, Friedrich Bernreuther, had to admit that, thanks to Frick's intervention, he had not been informed of the events at the beer hall. He testified further that duty required an officer, when hearing reports of a crisis of that magnitude, to alert the state police, the city commandant, the security team, and the criminal police.

"What specifically happened, I do not know," Bernreuther said.

Stenglein and Ehard knew exactly what had happened. Frick had done nothing of the sort.

Another witness, Dr. Heinrich Balss of the Munich police political division, had seen Frick being offered the position as the president of the police. At that moment, he had looked Frick in the eye and remembered being struck by the defendant's genuine surprise and lack of pleasure at the promotion. He also confirmed that Frick had neither referred to himself with the new title nor allowed anyone else to do so.

Had Hitler, Ehard asked, claimed to take over leadership of Germany or did he only claim to be the drummer of the movement?

The witness said he did not exactly remember. He had read so much in the newspaper. As Ehard pressed him, Hitler interrupted to say that he had most definitely announced his intention to "assume the political leadership of the provisional national government." He pulled out a copy of the *Münchner Neueste Nachrichten* and, with the spotlight on him, the courtroom was treated to the spectacle of Hitler reading aloud from his own reported speech at the beer hall.

Hitler then turned to the prosecutor and, suddenly overcome with excitement, bellowed out, as if he had been transported back to the Bürgerbräu: "My quarrel and reckoning with the November criminals remains essential to me, Herr Prosecutor, if not now, then in the time to come!"

There was a loud commotion in the courtroom.

35.

THE PROSECUTOR'S MISFORTUNES

*"I cannot elaborate any further on what was discussed behind
closed doors"—a statement like that in a public talk is enough
to cause some conclusions, that, under the circumstances,
could be extremely harmful.*

—LUDWIG STENGLEIN

By early March, the carnival season was in full stride in Munich, but
the biggest carnival in town, it was said, was the Hitler trial. Berlin's
Vossische Zeitung called it the most fantastic political event in Germany
in years. *L'Écho de Paris* labeled it "a parody of justice."

The presiding judge, Neithardt, appeared to be overwhelmed by the
burdens of the trial. He sat there almost motionless in his chair, as if
exhausted from the ordeal, fighting off fatigue or even sleep in the rising
temperatures in the room. One or two journalists thought that he dozed
off during testimony.

A more frequent criticism was made against Neithardt's perceived
biases in favor of the defense. He was polite and deferential, indeed too
much so. *Le Canada* was struck by how Neithardt addressed Ludendorff
in court as "Your Excellency." Actually he used the titles of all the defendants, that is, except for one: Adolf Hitler. The chief defendant lacked

one, and so remained "Herr Hitler." This glaring difference probably only enhanced Hitler's image as a man of the people.

Le Petit Parisien also mocked the presiding judge's fawning approach as "Monsieur Hitler, would you like to be questioned?" After that, *La Presse* added, he did not dare to ask even the most innocuous question without wrapping it in a coat of qualifications. The journalist H. R. Knickerbocker thought Neithardt literally shook in fear, his white goatee quivering, when he finally summoned up the resolve to reprimand a defendant.

Neithardt, moreover, made no attempt to stop Hitler, or his outbursts, or those of his fellow defendants, even when they addressed the ousted ruler as "His Majesty the king," and disparaged the republic. Vienna's *Wiener Zeitung* found the sight of a young officer in uniform like Wagner criticizing the president to be particularly repugnant.

Critics assailed the trial on a number of other fronts as well. Many left-wing and center papers despised the unwarranted and unproductive reliance on secret sessions in the name of "national security." It made a poor impression both in Germany and abroad. *Der Tag*, on the other hand, lauded the court for this same reason, giving the trial one of its rare praises that did not involve Hitler. The presiding judge was, the paper concluded, rightly safeguarding state secrets from foreign observers eager to discover how many cannons, machine guns, and other war materiel the Reichswehr commanded.

On March 6, Neithardt readmitted the audience at 9:15 a.m. for the trial's short but stormy eighth-day session. He began by reading out a number of letters protesting various parts of the testimony, particularly some of the accusations that the Bavarian Army and state police had collaborated in the beer hall putsch. The presiding judge agreed that the representatives of the maligned authorities must be given an opportunity to speak for themselves.

Defense counsel Walter Luetgebrune complained about drawings of his client General Ludendorff as a grumpy old man in the French newspaper *Le Matin*. These deplorable and witless "scrawlings," as he called them, "without doubt do not deserve the name 'caricature.'" He praised Neithardt for expelling people like that from the courtroom.

The lawyer also protested against other international articles that lampooned Germany and its patriotic citizens. The *New York Herald* came particularly under fire. In a piece entitled "The Leader of the Beer Revolution," the American paper had mocked the revolt for lasting less than thirty minutes and ending "when Hitler fled in fear of his life and the dignified General Ludendorff cried, 'I surrender.'"

Another defense counsel, Karl Kohl, stood to make a protest. It was not actually on behalf of his client, the Munich Storm Trooper commander Wilhelm Brückner, but rather of his friend, Capt. Wilhelm Weiss. Kohl was referring to the former publisher of the banned *Heimatland* and then editor of its successor *Völkischer Kurier*, who had been arrested on suspicion of having participated in the putsch. Kohl attacked the prosecution for pursuing an "arrest craze" that concentrated on innocent people, like Weiss, while allowing the real guilty parties to remain free.

The judge interrupted, "We are not dealing with the Weiss affair, but with the affair of Hitler and his comrades."

The issues were related, Kohl insisted in his booming voice spiced up with a soft Bavarian accent. This was a question of an unparalleled abuse of power on the part of Gustav von Kahr. If arrests are to take place, Kohl asked, why shouldn't the person responsible for the shedding of blood on November 9 also be arrested?

Some members of the audience cheered and Neithardt rebuked the defense counsel again for his irrelevant and insulting comments. Kohl snapped back that he would save the discussion for his closing statement because the court needed to know the truth.

At this point, Stenglein stood up, visibly upset and losing his composure. After uttering something unintelligible, the prosecutor's voice became clear and distinct. "During these proceedings, I have repeatedly been the object of scathing attacks," Stenglein said, now in a halting, sharp staccato tone. His voice grew louder and more forceful as he spoke of trying hard to maintain dignity and answer the constant injurious, often personal, insults with restraint. "But today enough is enough!"

The audience, used by now to melodramatic outbursts in the trial, watched in shock at what happened next.

Stenglein, fuming with rage, said that he could no longer participate in this trial. He turned to Hans Ehard and asked him to take his place for the remainder of the proceedings. With that, he grabbed his briefcase and stormed out of the courtroom, slamming the door behind him.

The courtroom was silent. Audience, defendants, and judges looked around in confusion. The startled deputy prosecutor moved for a recess.

The presiding judge, trying in vain to prevent another headline-grabbing scandal, rebuked the defense counsel for his "expressions of an insulting nature."

Kohl accepted the reprimand, but when he started to defend his position, Ehard interrupted to repeat his call for a recess, and then he too walked out of the courtroom.

"There will always be enough prosecutors!" Kohl taunted.

The gallery burst into laughter. Several people applauded and shouted "Bravo!"

"Prosecutor Humiliated" ran headlines as far away as Auckland, New Zealand. Thomas R. Ybarra of the *New York Times* described the scene as causing "an uproar," adding that German republicans were now calling the Hitler trial "the most scandalous ever conducted in Germany."

The extreme right-wing press launched yet another personal attack on Stenglein and Ehard. What an "extraordinary display of prosecutorial sensitivity," the *Völkischer Kurier* scoffed. It was unprecedented disregard of duty for a state prosecutor to throw in the towel and run away from the courtroom. Hitler, Ludendorff, and the defendants faced insults every day at the trial—the trial itself was an insult!—and yet they did not flee.

Many people, however, sympathized with the beleaguered prosecutor, who day after day faced the hostile atmosphere of the tribunal. A reporter for *Bayerischer Kurier* praised Stenglein for having the "patience of an angel." In the end, he could no longer tolerate the lack of impartiality that had dogged the "monstrous trial" from the beginning.

The prosecutor's frustrations, *Vossische Zeitung* added, illuminated the state of the proceedings like lightning. Hitler and his codefendants posed as "German heroes," while the judges, either out of sympathy or impotence, sat in silence at the extraordinary spectacle of a prosecutor powerless to prove their guilt. Stenglein was right to walk out, *Berliner Tageblatt* concluded. This was the only dignified response in his power against this "scandal of justice of the most serious kind."

Others suspected that Stenglein might be relieved to escape a difficult trial that would sooner or later force him to assume the thankless task of prosecuting many elite figures of the Bavarian government. The prospects for justice, in any case, looked dim. Many people were openly saying that the best hope for this trial, with its "unprecedented vaudeville-esque character," as *Le Petit Parisien* put it, was to move it out of Munich, far away from Judge Neithardt's courtroom.

36.

PRIORITIES

*A far more serious scheme to alter the existing constitution of
Germany was being planned, and presumably still meets with
the approval of the extreme nationalists.*
—LONDON *Times*, MARCH 13, 1924

The Hitler trial, *Vossische Zeitung* noted, was reading like a serialized
novel. The proceedings, which were supposed to have lasted only
two weeks, were now estimated to carry on another three weeks. The
prosecution was expected to call around 80 witnesses and the defense
another 150. Some newspapers reported an even higher number. France's
Agence Havas topped everyone with its prediction that, thanks to a typo,
put it at "more than 2,000."

On March 7, 1924, Neithardt called the courtroom to order. Karl
Kohl's apology on behalf of his fellow defense lawyers—and probably
more than a little help from the minister of justice, Franz Gürtner—had
persuaded Stenglein to return to the courtroom. The judge reiterated
his desire to conduct the proceedings in a worthy manner and banish
all incidents "incompatible with the dignity of the court." Otherwise, he
threatened to try each of the defendants separately. All was soon calm,
as *L'Écho de Paris* noted with amusement, as if the glimmer of blue skies
had peeked through the thunderclouds after a storm.

But despite the attempts of judge and lawyers to act as if nothing had happened, several newspapers, such as *L'Humanité*, detected the whiff of a scandal. The sudden and unexpected harmony suggested that the judges, prosecutors, and defense lawyers were closing ranks to prevent the disgraceful trial from being transferred to the state supreme court in Leipzig, which many critics had called a likely and welcome solution to the burlesque of justice at Munich.

The *Münchener Post* was particularly skeptical that this superficial reconciliation would last. The defense counsel may be forced to make his own humble walk of repentance to Canossa, the reporter said, referring to the Holy Roman Emperor Henry IV, who sought Pope Gregory VII in 1077, only to be kept waiting for three days in a snowstorm, but that did not change the fact that the cards seemed stacked in its favor.

As the presiding judge prepared to call the morning's first witness, Hitler's lawyer, Lorenz Roder, offered a suggestion. While recognizing the tribunal's prerogative to summon witnesses in any order it desired, Roder proposed that the court forgo a series of witnesses who could only testify about what they saw or heard at the beer hall. Instead, Neithardt should call to the stand the three men who could exert significant influence on the trial: Kahr, Lossow, and Seisser. Their testimony would allow the court to discover whether their actions were "sheer hypocrisy" or "serious collaboration," and, in the process, fulfill the mandate of the People's Court to reach a verdict as swiftly as possible.

Neithardt ignored the suggestion and called the next witness, as planned.

This was Adolf Schiedt, editor in chief at the *Münchener Zeitung*, Kahr's director of the press, and coauthor of the general state commissioner's speech the night of the beer hall putsch. Roder objected that this man was not impartial. As Schiedt was one of Kahr's employees, he should be regarded not so much as a witness as an accomplice to the crime of high treason. The judge ignored him a second time.

Schiedt was visibly uncomfortable, speaking haltingly and in a low voice. He justified the meeting at the beer hall on the night of November

8, 1923, as "useful, indeed necessary" to provide Kahr with the opportunity to show his determination to wage a "battle against Marxism." This event was intended to rally his supporters, many of whom had been frustrated at the lack of progress in establishing a nationalist regime in Berlin.

That evening, however, Schiedt had found the crowd outside the beer hall much larger than he had expected, given the nature of the talk. He had made his way with difficulty to his reserved seat near the front of the banquet room. After Hitler's arrival and the series of oaths to the new national government, Schiedt feared that he was in fact witnessing a revolution.

Did he think that Kahr had been pretending?

No, he did not, the witness said, though he had begun to wonder, and eventually concluded that he could not explain Kahr's behavior. When the Storm Troopers finally released the crowd, Schiedt left the beer hall feeling a sense of depression and uncertainty.

Defense counsel Kohl, then using the witness to attack Kahr, asked how the Bavarian leader's acceptance speech as "viceroy of the monarchy," could be reconciled with his sworn oath to uphold the constitution of the republic.

Neithardt refused to allow the question, but he was interrupted by three defense lawyers all shouting at once.

"That will not do!" Neithardt said.

Schiedt went on to field a series of questions, or as the foreign correspondent for *Le Petit Journal* put it, be "harassed by rather unfriendly inquiries of twelve lawyers." At one point, when the presiding judge asked Schiedt if he had spoken to anyone before planning the rally at the beer hall, the witness hesitated and then flat-out refused to answer. To further surprise, Judge Neithardt accepted the rebuff without hesitation, as *L'Humanité* noted, suspecting that he was covering up a scandal that went back to Kahr.

The French paper was not the only one to draw this conclusion. In Berlin, Rudolf Breitscheid of the Social Democratic Party stood up in the Reichstag and said that Kahr, Lossow, and Seisser belonged in the dock with Hitler. At the very least, had the Bavarian regime shown a modicum of vigilance and foresight, the beer hall putsch would never have happened. It was essential to investigate the allegations of high-level collaboration to overthrow the German republic.

IN THE MORNING and afternoon session, a total of seventeen witnesses appeared in rapid succession before the court. Most of these were eye-witnesses at the beer hall, and also, clearly, strong supporters of Kahr, Lossow, and Seisser.

The next witness, Gen. Felix Graf von Bothmer, illustrated this pattern. "My impression of the affair," Bothmer said, speaking of Hitler's attack, "was that it was a well-prepared, brutal ambush that could not have been thwarted by any preventive measures." He saw no evidence of any genuine participation on the part of Kahr and the triumvirate, he continued, with a commanding presence that, for once, *Le Gaulois* noted, the defense did not interrupt.

Professor of history Alexander von Müller, who had been sitting near the stage, disagreed. Not for a minute had he believed that the triumvirate's participation in the putsch was an act. Nor had anyone else sitting near him. Hitler, Ludendorff, and the Bavarian leaders were far too serious for that. History seemed to be unfolding.

Another witness, Karl Sommer, a senior councilor in the Foreign Ministry and author of several memorandums on the putsch, testified to the terror he felt when Hitler invaded the banquet room. He had first feared that this was an assault from the far left, prompted by Kahr's anti-Marxist rally.

"The senior councilor appears to be reading out a speech!" Hitler's lawyer objected.

"I am not reading, but I consider myself justified to make my statements and assist my memory with the help of notes."

This was not the only document that the witness had read. He also clearly knew the white-blue pamphlet and the confidential memo that had circulated among supporters of Kahr, Lossow, and Seisser. Almost every witness from the military and state police thus far had likewise read them.

Many of them also gave the impression that they were more interested in defending the actions of the Bavarian leaders than answering questions about the case. The result was ambiguity and confusion, as Roder had predicted. The session dragged on until almost eight o'clock, as the correspondent for *Le Temps* put it, without much interest.

But in fact, the judge's steering of the questioning sheds light on an important dynamic emerging in the Munich trial. Neithardt has been traditionally portrayed as a nationalist who favored Adolf Hitler. This is not inaccurate, but the presiding judge had another, more important, priority that has been overlooked. He was, it would soon be clear, concerned foremost with protecting Kahr, Lossow, and Seisser—and by extension, the reputations of the Bavarian administration, military, and state police that they had commanded. And it was this shielding of high-ranking authorities that would afford Hitler his extraordinary opportunity at the Munich trial.

München, den 7.November 1923.

Euer Hochwohlgeboren

bitte ich hiermit um Ihre Beteiligung an einer Vertrauens-
kundgebung für den Herrn Generalkommissar in der am

Donnerstag, den 8.November

abends 1/2 8 Uhr

im Bürgerbräukeller, Rosenheimerstrasse, stattfinden-
den Versammlung bayerischer Erwerbstände und vaterländischer
Vereinigungen. Exzellenz von Kahr hat zugesagt, bei dieser Ge-
legenheit eine grosse programmatische Rede zu halten.

Mit deutschem Gruss!

r. Henz

Vorsitzender des Heimatdienstes Bayern.

Top: Rare surviving copy of an invitation to the Bürgerbräu beer hall on the night of November 8, 1923.

Center: The Stosstrupp Hitler, the shock troops who overpowered the police and seized control of the beer hall.

Bottom: Members of the Stosstrupp Hitler take Munich's city councilmen hostage.

Captain Ernst Röhm's troops barricade the captured War Ministry. The soldier holding the banner is young Heinrich Himmler.

Mounted police clear the streets on the morning of November 9, 1923. Rumors circulated that Hitler had been killed or had withdrawn to rally supporters for another attack on Munich.

The official transcript of the Hitler trial spans nearly 3,000 pages.

Adolf Hitler addresses the court. At the small table, stenographers record the proceedings.

Hitler and his lawyer, Lorenz Roder (right), who was not paid in full for his legal services until after Hitler came to power. This drawing, and the following two, are rare illustrations of the Hitler trial by the artist Otto D. Franz.

Above: Deputy prosecutor Hans Ehard (right) faced formidable challenges in his efforts to prosecute Adolf Hitler. On the left sits chief prosecutor Ludwig Stenglein.
Right: Presiding judge Georg Neithardt. Thanks to his right-wing sympathies as well as the extensive media coverage, Hitler would reach an audience at the trial far larger than anything he had ever before experienced.

A never-before-published sketch by Carl August Jäger captures a fretful Hitler during the trial as he faced deportation from Germany.

Who was on trial, critics asked, Hitler or the Weimar Republic? This illustration of the tumultuous proceedings has not been published since it appeared in *Münchner Neueste Nachrichten* in 1924.

Photography was prohibited inside the courtroom, though a handful of people smuggled in cameras. This is one of the better shots of the trial in session.

Top: Hitler, Ludendorff, and codefendants in discussion during a break.

Center: Security was again heightened as the trial approached its conclusion.

Bottom: Adolf Hitler and fellow defendants assemble in the courtyard before the announcement of the verdict: (left to right) Heinz Pernet, Friedrich Weber, Wilhelm Frick, Hermann Kriebel, Erich Ludendorff, Adolf Hitler, Wilhelm Brückner, Ernst Röhm, and Robert Wagner. One defendant, Ernst Pöhner, was absent.

Top: Photograph of Hitler's cell, which was later decorated with the props of a typewriter and Nazi flag. After Hitler was released, fellow defendant Ernst Pöhner briefly served time in this cell.

Center: Hitler in his cell at Landsberg.

Bottom: At Landsberg, Hitler read, entertained visitors, and worked on his book, *Mein Kampf.* Hitler called his time in prison his university education at state expense.

Adolf Hitler and fellow inmates while away the hours at Landsberg. Emil Maurice, standing, played in the prisoner band. Hermann Kriebel, cup in hand, wrote for the prisoner newspaper. On one occasion, the inmates performed a parody of the trial, which ended by sentencing Hitler to deportation—from Landsberg.

Left: Hitler walks in the garden with Emil Maurice, his chauffeur and first leader of the Storm Troopers. Landsberg prisoners had plenty of time to reassess (and reinvent) the past and plot the future.

Below: On December 20, 1924, Hitler leaves Landsberg as a free man.

37.

"PECULIAR GENTLEMEN"

Hitler is not even a Mussolini in a waistcoat.
—Arbeiterwille (GRAZ, AUSTRIA),
FEBRUARY 28, 1924

Saturday, March 8, 1924, the tenth day of the trial, opened in secret session with Neithardt's warning never to divulge the contents of the proceedings. The plan was then to readmit the public and interrogate the next seven witnesses, six from the Reichswehr and one from the state police.

Col. Hans Etzel, a fifty-four-year-old commander of the 20th Infantry Regiment in Regensburg, took the stand in the closed-door session. On the day before the beer hall putsch, Etzel said, he had attended a meeting at the War Ministry. General von Lossow had discussed the possibility of a Hitler attack and made it clear that he would order the Bavarian military to resist if that hotheaded maverick struck prematurely.

The presiding judge asked the witness if he recalled General von Lossow rejecting Hitler's plot with the words "We are not taking part in this insanity."

Etzel confirmed that the word "insanity" had been used. He also testified that Lossow preferred an authoritarian regime set up by unnamed allies in Berlin, rather than one by Hitler and Ludendorff. The problem was that no one in the north seemed prepared to act.

Neithardt asked the witness if he recalled a couple of other statements Lossow had allegedly made about Hitler. One of them read: "With Hitler, [success] is doubtful because he believes that he can do everything alone." Etzel confirmed that it had been said.

"Evidence that Hitler is the German Mussolini, as he believes, has not yet been produced."

Etzel had heard that too.

At 10:30, Neithardt invited the public to return to the courtroom. Before the next witness took the stand, General Ludendorff wanted to make a statement.

It was necessary, the commander stated, to correct the misleading impression that the prosecution had tried to convey to the court, namely that he and his fellow defendants had attacked the Reichswehr. Nothing could be further from the truth. Nine of the ten men accused of treason in this trial had served in the military (the exception being Dr. Frick). "We see the Reichswehr as a continuation of the old army," the general said.

The fundamental problem for Germany, Ludendorff continued, lay not with the defendants but with *their* enemies who sought to harm the reputation of the country and its military. "In our love of the Fatherland, in our love of the Reichswehr, in our concern for honor and glory of the Reichswehr, we will take on every one of them!"

Shouts of "Bravo!" came from the audience.

Who were these enemies Ludendorff boasted of wanting to fight? Were they the prosecution, or perhaps the Communists, Jews, and Catholics whom he targeted earlier in the trial? This time, as if mindful of his many critics, he chose not to identify them.

Maj. Gen. Karl von Hildebrandt took the stand, ready to rebuild the reputation of Ludendorff. As he retraced familiar territory, Hildebrandt added one interesting comment about General Ludendorff's approach to Hitler—articulating a delusion that would later be repeated by many ambitious politicians during Hitler's rise to power: Ludendorff believed that he was the only one who could influence Hitler.

Ludendorff, the witness added, was neither an enemy of the Wittelsbach dynasty nor of Bavaria. On the contrary, he respected the southern land with its robust, patriotic population and its "mountains, lakes, and marvelous countryside." He was not, in other words, the stereotypical Prussian officer as his enemies tried to paint him.

The witness closed his testimony by interpreting Ludendorff's controversial words on Catholic enemies in the country as an attack on the Catholic Center Party, not on the Pope, the Vatican, or people of faith. At this point, Hitler could not remain out of the spotlight any longer; he told the court that he too was a Catholic.

As ON THE previous day, the first high-ranking witnesses each spoke with restraint and vigilance, as if striving not to admit any unsanctioned testimony. Some, like the chief of staff at the War Ministry, Lt. Col. Otto von Berchem, lashed out to defend the honor of the military for its role in suppressing the putsch.

"I believe that you can perhaps understand that we had finally had enough of people insulting us and spitting at us for a matter in which we only did our damned duty," Berchem said, before correcting himself, "our difficult duty." This comment drew commotion in the gallery.

Moments later, Ludendorff interrupted the witness to point out that the order to seize the War Ministry in the name of Hitler had been signed by none other than General von Lossow.

Berchem hesitated. There had been an order, he said, but that was four months ago. He could not remember every command that had passed his desk. "And neither could Your Excellency."

There were loud jeers from the audience.

He was only stating a fact, the witness said. Ludendorff could not recall every single order he had given four months ago.

Alfred Holl, defense counsel for Friedrich Weber, expressed his indignation. He had other questions for Berchem, but given this witness's willful disparaging of a German hero, he would refrain from asking them. He received more cheers from the spectators.

These defense lawyers were "peculiar gentlemen," noted *Berliner Tageblatt*. They took offense when witnesses like Berchem answered their questions with facts, or diverted them from their efforts to turn a trial of confessed traitors against the republic into a forum for insulting

222 THE TRIAL OF ADOLF HITLER

the government, the military and the state police. Most peculiar of all, however, was Judge Neithardt.

Why did he not take action against the hecklers who applauded Ludendorff and jeered at this witness? The building was, after all, swarming with police. Why not remove the offenders and, at minimum, confiscate their passes to the trial? Clearly, Neithardt's sympathies with the defendants—and even more, his reluctance to provoke them into exposing Bavarian state authorities' violations of the Versailles Treaty and their own plots against Berlin—prevented him from taking charge of the proceedings. If Neithardt could not preserve the dignity of the court, *Berliner Tageblatt* argued, the German government should stop this "judicial comedy," and move the case to the state court in Leipzig, where it belonged.

THE LATE-MORNING SESSION had almost as many "incidents" as revelations. The last witness to take the stand that day was Sigmund Freiherr von Imhoff, the police major who had played a valuable role in suppressing the putsch by placing units on alert and securing strategic locations around town. He had also arrested defendants Frick and Pöhner.

Before the judge could finish swearing in the witness, Hitler's lawyer, Roder, demanded that he halt the ceremony. As this was a trial of high treason, this witness should stand trial himself. It had been proven in secret session, Roder claimed, that the actions of the ten defendants on the night of the putsch paled into insignificance compared to the treason of men in authority like Major Imhoff. The audience, not privy to the "evidence" presented in closed session, could only imagine what this man had done.

Stenglein objected.

Despite the impression the defense tried to give, Imhoff said, the police had been eager neither to fire on Hitler's men nor to join them. Their duty was to oppose any violent attempt to overthrow the government, regardless of the political persuasions of the revolutionaries.

Roder asked the witness if he knew of any "secret orders" that Colonel von Seisser had given the state police.

Imhoff said he could not answer this question in public.

As the questioning continued without the witness budging, defense lawyer Walther Hemmeter also insinuated that Imhoff knew more about official collaboration in the beer hall putsch than he had testified. "I want to be careful here," Hemmeter said, hinting in vague and ominous terms about certain unidentified meetings with authorities.

"I actually do not know what you are alluding to," Imhoff replied.

The defense counsel was again exploiting the judge's concern for national security, his reliance on secret sessions, and people's ignorance of proceedings behind closed doors.

By the end of the day, defense attorney Holl requested that the court bypass the myriad redundant questions and tangential witnesses and settle the disputes by calling the Bavarian leaders Kahr, Lossow, and Seisser to the stand. This time, to the surprise and pleasure of many spectators in the audience, the presiding judge said that their cross-examination would start on Monday morning.

38.

A DANGEROUS GAME

I attached no significance to the matter. It was almost as if Hitler had distributed positions and said: You be kaiser, you be pope, and you be king.

—GEN. OTTO VON LOSSOW

On March 10, 1924, the court would begin hearing the testimony of the Bavarian authorities who had become central to the defense. Tensions ran high. Police cordons and security checks returned with vigor, prompting Munich wits to dub the courtroom "the occupied territory."

The morning session opened with the usual slew of protests, clarifications, and corrections. Defense lawyer Georg Götz wanted to refute the charge in the *Deutsche Allgemeine Zeitung* that the defense counsel's loud, brash pleading and repeated interruptions were proving nothing— that is, except for the necessity of restricting the freedom of lawyers. The advocates' success lay not, he said, in confusing witnesses and distracting the court from its task of evaluating evidence but rather in trying to establish the facts. He could not help it if some members of the press might get lost in the complexity of the case.

After repeated demands to call Kahr, Lossow, and Seisser to the stand, it was ironic that one of the defense counsels, Otto Gademann, now protested this move. As "manipulators of the entire undertaking," Gademann said, these men should only appear in court to stand trial for their own crimes of high treason.

Hitler's lawyer, Lorenz Roder, disagreed with his colleague. Still he thought Gademann had a point: the Bavarian leaders were under no circumstances "unbiased and impartial." Roder wished that they would be honest and acknowledge their own role in the affair, admitting that they share the same responsibility as the defendants, if not more, because they had pulled the strings that set the plot in motion.

It was now the prosecution's turn to object. All these allegations lacked evidence, Stenglein said, and the dispute raged on until Neithardt called Gen. Otto von Lossow to the stand. At this point, the room became quiet—a "dead silence," *Berliner Tageblatt* said, with all eyes glued to the courtroom door. General von Lossow entered, slowly walking to the stand, carrying a stack of papers. His tall, slender frame was draped in a black frock coat, as he was prohibited from wearing the military uniform after his dismissal. At age fifty-six, he looked fit, energetic, and ready for a fight.

Judge Neithardt reminded the witness that he could exercise his right not to incriminate himself and refuse to answer any question that he deemed potentially damaging. The presiding judge also instructed him to be mindful of comments that might affect Germany's foreign relations.

Lossow would speak all morning, often briskly with his booming, melodious voice filling the room—it could have filled the Albert Hall in London, said the correspondent for the *Daily Telegraph*. He did not sit at the table, as did many witnesses, but walked around the front of the room, returning from time to time to the lectern he had arranged to have placed there for his notes.

Lossow spoke like a Bavarian officer accustomed to salons and drawing rooms. At the same time, he was often visibly moved, punctuating his words with sharp, angular gestures and baring his teeth almost like a snarling attack dog. He also tended to avoid making eye contact with most of the defendants, though he would sometimes lock eyes with Hitler or Ludendorff, shooting a piercing gaze through his pince-nez, which the correspondent for *L'Écho de Paris* said suggested he would have preferred to "cross swords" with them.

From the outset General von Lossow admitted that he had made attempts to forge an alliance with unnamed powerful figures in the north, who also, as he put it, wished for the rescue of Germany from "increasingly impossible conditions." Their plan had been indeed to establish a national directorate, or a right-wing regime with "dictatorial authority." But their goal, he stressed, was not a putsch.

It was instead a legal and constitutional maneuver based upon invoking the infamous Article 48 of the Weimar Constitution. This act, which allowed for the establishment of a temporary dictatorship in a time of crisis, would be used 136 times before the end of Friedrich Ebert's presidency in February 1925, contributing in no small way to the destabilization of the republic.

The problem with their plan had been Berlin. Politicians and allies in the capital dragged their feet, and, in the process, allowed an outsider like Hitler to act. Lossow did not mince his words:

> These were people who, in political and patriotic meetings, could not talk big enough to prove their national activism; people who in their overheated patriotism had forgotten how to think soberly; people whose driving force was political ambition.

These people took it up in speeches that seemed "a bit childish." They had lost all reason. Foremost among these men was Adolf Hitler.

The witness had known Hitler for only about nine months before the putsch, but offered an astute assessment of a young man in a hurry. "In the beginning, Hitler's well-known enchanting and suggestive eloquence made a great impression," Lossow said. "It is readily apparent that Hitler was right in many ways, but the more I listened to Hitler, the weaker this first impression became."

He then elaborated upon the deterioration of his respect for the National Socialist leader, which would soon manifest itself into outright contempt:

> I noticed that his long talks almost always contained the same points: One part of his remarks is obvious to every nationally-thinking German, and another part of them bore witness that Hitler had departed from a sense of reality and proportion for what is possible and achievable.

As such, the witness said, Hitler's talk lost its influence on anyone with a sober frame of mind and an ability to withstand the assault on reason.

Talking with Hitler was, likewise, an impossible affair. It was Hitler who did the speaking, and, for anyone else in the conversation, General von Lossow added, it was difficult to make a comment, let alone an objection. Hitler was a poor listener who struggled to heed advice when it conflicted with his preconceived notions or agenda.

At first, Hitler had shown a lack of personal ambition, speaking of himself only as a drummer wanting to prepare the way for "the one who is to come." By October 1923, however, Lossow could not avoid sensing a change. Hitler was now strutting about the Munich stage as the "German Mussolini" and *the One* who would bring about the regeneration of his adopted country.

Lossow admitted seeing Hitler on several occasions and even learning of his plans. He explained this involvement as an attempt to influence a powerful propagandist who seemed to be the only person who succeeded in reaching the workers. Lossow's goal was to bring Hitler, as he put it, "down to earth." He went on to admit his role in a frank way: They did not want to "suppress the Hitler movement violently," but rather build on what he called its "healthy core" and guide it in a more productive way toward plausible, realistic goals.

In the end, Lossow had discovered that Hitler was simply not suited to leadership, and certainly not a dictatorship. He was adept at drumming up a cause, but showed little talent for much else. Essentially, the witness concluded, Hitler was only "a swashbuckling little ward politician."

Unfortunately, Lossow's insights into the flaws of Hitler's style of leadership and the forces driving this man forward were lost in resonant headlines and the barrage of speculation about Lossow's own bloodied hands in the putsch. Still, Lossow's testimony offers insights into how prominent figures, even those free from anti-Semitism, could become enamored by a reckless and hate-filled figure like Hitler—and then prove willing to shield and coddle him. What they hoped to receive in return was his influence on the street. It was a dangerous game, as Lossow was one of the first to learn.

THERE WERE MANY errors and distortions in the testimony of Hitler and the defense, Lossow said. To refute all of them, he added with a flash of anger, "I would have to talk for days."

He went on for several more hours that day. The stories of his own alleged agreements with the putschists, or plans for their move against Berlin, were, Lossow said, "pure invention." He described going to the beer hall on November 8 expecting nothing more than another political rally for Gustav von Kahr. He did not worry about any special precautions, nor, for that matter, had he even bothered to bring a handgun.

When Hitler pushed his way to the podium, Lossow testified that he had been overcome by "a plethora of thoughts and feelings." He felt "outrage and the deepest contempt" at this devious attack that meant not only betrayal but, worse, threatened to upset their own plans for the patriotic movement. Lossow watched the unraveling of their plot with "deep sorrow." The crisis that could have assured their success was being squandered.

"What was to be done?" Lossow asked.

First, the triumvirate could not challenge Hitler in the beer hall because he had too many armed supporters. Any accident or rash move could cause one of the hooligans to panic and open fire, unleashing "a general and senseless shoot-out." With the same reasoning, Lossow said, he had concluded that the triumvirate could not resist Hitler in the back room either.

Shouts from hecklers in the gallery interrupted his testimony. Neithardt threatened to adjourn the court if order were not restored.

"The Fatherland had to be saved from grave danger," Lossow explained, justifying his actions that night. His strategy, he admitted, was "to deceive Hitler and his comrades, just as [Hitler] had deceived Kahr, Seisser, and me."

He conceived of this plan, he said, standing on the platform. He knew his colleagues Kahr and Seisser would go along with it, given their "quick glances and brief, whispered remarks." On their way out of the beer hall with the Storm Troopers, Lossow said he uttered the words "Put on an act!" The three of them then waited until they could gain their freedom and resist Hitler with their full powers. This was their duty, no matter how unpleasant or embarrassing it was.

Lossow went on to ask why Hitler and his men portrayed them in the witness box with "contempt . . . [as] pitiful creatures, and complete idiots," and yet they wanted "to assign to us the most important offices of state." How could this paradox be resolved?

The puzzle, however, was not as difficult as he hoped to convey. The men on trial had wanted Kahr, Lossow, and Seisser as allies in the autumn of 1923. Then, when Hitler's ill-conceived plans to storm the beer hall failed to win over Munich authorities, let alone topple the government in Berlin, they were quick to exploit the Bavarian leaders' self-acknowledged duplicity, and blame the disaster on them.

When Neithardt opened the floor for cross-examination, defense attorney Alfred Holl said that he had a list of "hugely important questions," but he would wait until after the court had heard the testimony of Seisser and Kahr. That was Hitler's plan too, though he jumped to his feet and yelled to commotion in the gallery: "Herr Lossow's statement is false and inaccurate!"

The session ended at 6:33 p.m.

39.

AVOIDING THE RUBBLE

In short, everywhere we looked, we saw only a smoking heap
of rubble, destruction, and, in the end, complete collapse.
—GUSTAV VON KAHR

After weeks of snow, day twelve, March 11, 1924, opened with promises of spring and high expectations for the trial. Gustav von Kahr,
the former general state commissioner, was supposed to take the stand,
dispel allegations about his complicity in the putsch, and, in the process,
clear up many ambiguities and contradictions still dogging the Hitler
trial. It would not turn out that way.

Exiting an automobile at the side entrance, Kahr ducked a camera
crew hoping to film his arrival. Shortly after nine a.m., as the presiding
judge and tribunal entered the courtroom, Kahr walked in inconspic-
uously, bowed quickly to the bench, and took his place at the podium.

Sixty-one years old, he was a short and stocky dark-haired man with
a bushy mustache that he sometimes turned upward. His hair was oiled
and parted in the middle. His large head plunged into rounded shoulders and he scanned the room with calculation and a scowl that cartoonists adored. Kahr appeared, as *L'Ouest-Éclair* put it, "a true peasant of
the Danube."

Some people thought he seemed tense and reserved, as he relied

heavily on his notes. Others, like *Bayerischer Kurier* said he was inscrutable with a classic poker face. Kahr's voice was hesitant and weak, though
it eventually gained strength even as it remained monotone. He sketched
a brief history of the economic turmoil and political chaos that plagued
Germany in the fall of 1923, prompting the creation of his powerful
executive office in Bavaria.

Judge Neithardt told the witness to stop reading his statement.

Accepting the reprimand, Kahr went on to speak about how he had
sought solutions to the crisis through "political pressure," not military
force. He described how his office had begun to hear rumblings of a
Hitler-Ludendorff putsch in September 1923, but opposed this crude
approach as "abysmal and catastrophic" for Bavaria and Germany. He
foresaw it leading to civil war and perhaps also war with France and her
allies.

Moreover, Kahr asked, did Hitler and his cronies not realize that
the army lacked "clothing, footgear, equipment, ammunition, weapons,
and money?" This argument seemed to be geared, more than anything,
toward reassuring the international community that Germany was not
rebuilding its military in violation of the Versailles Peace Treaty.

"My first reaction was rage and loathing," Kahr said of Hitler's
storming of the rally. He was furious that his patriotic regime would
suffer an attack by supposedly "nationally minded men," and he felt "a
deep grief and anxiety" when he realized that this reckless act could
lead to "the most staggering catastrophe for our domestic and international politics."

He had thought of trying to win over the beer hall crowd that had
been cheering his speech. Of course, he was no match against an orator
like Hitler, but what really deterred him was the presence of many tense,
armed Storm Troopers, who, in their state of excitement, would not be
reluctant to use their weapons. He had feared "unspeakable misfortune
and a bloodbath."

Kahr described how he had whispered to Lossow and Seisser at the
podium, urging them to find a means of escape. He remained calm, he
said, thinking of the greater good of the people. They decided to win
their freedom by playing this game of high-stakes charades.

Judge Neithardt again asked the witness to stop reading his statement.

The foreign correspondent for Paris's *Le Matin* would rebuke Kahr for a different reason. He was describing the same events in virtually the same way as Lossow, sometimes even word for word.

Kahr went on explaining his actions on the night of the putsch. At every stage of the affair, the witness recounted the evening in a way that portrayed him as a selfless leader with no ambition other than serving the greater good of the public.

About 11:25 a.m., Judge Neithardt asked if anyone had any questions.

Stenglein proposed that they move to a secret session.

With no objection, Neithardt removed the public from the courtroom.

IN A LONG session, Kahr admitted increasing the size of the Bavarian Reichswehr, not as a prelude to the putsch, as the defense alleged, but as a necessary safety precaution to the threat of a Communist uprising. He also admitted reinforcing the Reichswehr with some volunteers from the patriotic societies. This had been done to help the police prevent attacks from Communist insurgents in Saxony and Thuringia, he insisted, not to prepare for a march on Berlin.

When the presiding judge opened the floor to questions, Ludendorff asked how many battalions the regime had planned to supplement the Reichswehr.

Kahr said he did not know.

Before he answered the question himself, Ludendorff pointed out the fact that the order for the reinforcements that Kahr mentioned was issued on October 9 and yet its execution had not occurred until more than two weeks later. If this mobilization was really about an urgent Communist threat, why had he waited so long to act?

Kahr could not explain the cause of the delay.

"Aren't you privy to this at all?" Neithardt asked.

"No."

Ludendorff raised more doubts when he asked Kahr if he knew that the Reichswehr order (Ia Nr. 800/23) repeatedly used the word "operation," not "action," as would have been the case if it had intended only a police maneuver. "Operation," Ludendorff noted, is a military term.

Kahr said he did not remember the order. "It may have passed through my hands, but I do not recall it."

Ludendorff then called attention to the fact that the Reichswehr was not being increased, as Kahr implied, by only a small number of volunteers. It was being *tripled* in size. How else could Kahr explain this expansion of the military?

"I don't know," Kahr said.

Under further questioning, Kahr pleaded ignorance or argued that the matter did not fall under his purview. All he knew was what Seisser sometimes told him.

What did Seisser say? Neithardt asked.

"I don't remember."

Kahr would continue to deny, evade, and act ignorant in a long, difficult session. Sometimes the defense exacerbated his discomfort by calling out that they could not hear, or did not understand, his response.

Kahr refused to answer one question about the police stockpiling ammunition in late October on account of the need for secrecy—an irony not lost on the defense, who reminded him that they were in closed session.

"This is indeed remarkable," Judge Neithardt finally said, exasperated by the succession of unanswered questions.

At one point, the frustrated Kahr told the judge, "I was dealing with official responsibilities from morning until late in the evening and did not concern myself with such small matters."

AFTER ALMOST A three-hour recess, the trial resumed in public session at 4:10 p.m. for the long awaited cross-examination of Gustav von Kahr. This was, however, going to be another heady cocktail of denials, evasions, and distortions if not outright falsehoods. Any hopes for clarity in the Hitler trial would, for the moment, again be dashed.

Neithardt opened by asking the defense counsel to be selective and systematic in its questioning. Roder asked if the typewritten document Kahr had been reading that afternoon had been copied and distributed.

Those were simply his notes, Kahr said, adding that a few other copies might exist.

Upon further questioning, Kahr admitted that he had given copies to Lossow and Seisser. It was important, he said, "to check if everything that I said here corresponds with reality."

Roder asked if the three Bavarian leaders had met to discuss their testimony.

Kahr denied it.

Before Roder could continue his questioning, the judge cut him off. Hitler then blurted out a series of questions about Kahr's appointment as general state commissioner. Neithardt stopped him too.

This time, Roder and Hitler were not simply playing upon the prejudices of the gallery. They were in fact introducing a shift in legal strategy. That is, if they could not implicate Kahr and the triumvirate as active co-conspirators in the putsch, they now planned an alternative line of attack. It went like this: The indictment charged the defendants with attempting to change the constitution by force. But this was impossible because the constitution had ceased to exist at the moment Bavaria appointed Kahr general state commissioner.

Stenglein immediately objected. "The authority of the general state commissioner clearly derives from the [emergency] decree."

Actually, Roder countered, he could not find evidence for that interpretation in any law or ordinance gazette, or any other official document. Perhaps Kahr or someone on the prosecution team could enlighten the court with the reasons for drawing that conclusion.

Neithardt called a quick recess, prompted by this unexpected argument. The tribunal returned for their ruling that this line of questioning could not continue on the grounds of "national security." Roder tried to rephrase the question, but the judge stopped him a second time. Growing frustrated, the judge interrupted yet again to ask if the defense had any other questions.

Roder rattled off a list of questions he wanted to ask Kahr about the legal basis of his authority and the constitutionality of his actions. Kahr, once again, seemed to be on trial, not Hitler, and the former government official was struggling to counter the impression that he had a history of overstepping his authority, which, as another defense lawyer, Hellmuth Mayer, argued, represented "the crucial point of the trial."

Neithardt called his tribunal a second time that afternoon into chambers and, after deliberation, returned to prohibit the defense from asking these questions.

When Roder started on the same subject, Neithardt yet again ruled him out of order.

Determined to make his point, Roder then wanted to know if Kahr really opposed the putsch, as he claimed, why did he wait almost five hours [it was closer to four] before informing his fellow cabinet members of his intention to resist the putsch?

"That was not so simple," Kahr said, though he failed to enlighten the court on how and why the matter was more complicated than the defense implied.

As this tough day for the prosecution drew to a close, the defense continued to cast doubt on Kahr's credibility as a witness and his status as an innocent victim of the beer hall putsch. Neithardt appeared to be as worried about the reputation of this prominent figure as he was about the impressions of the trial, and with good reason.

40.

DAY THIRTEEN

I assume that the court is prepared to allow the defense counsel to speak here, too.

—LORENZ RODER

The *Völkischer Kurier*, vying for the readership of the banned Nazi and Kampfbund papers, had long been putting the charges Hitler, Ludendorff, and their fellow defendants faced in quotation marks. Were their actions, it asked, really "high treason"? The paper's answer was brash: "We do not give a damn!"

Other, more important, factors were at play, it argued, such as Germany's gratitude to its national heroes and the state's abuse of power when it stabbed patriots in the back and then fired upon them in the street. Rhetoric swirled and readers snapped up papers as soon as they hit newsstands. The question of guilt in this case, *Völkischer Kurier* concluded, was simply too important to leave to judges and state bureaucrats. It should be decided by the people.

Day thirteen of the Hitler trial would center on the testimony of Col. Hans Ritter von Seisser. Shortly after nine o'clock, the tall and slim forty-nine-year-old took the stand, carrying a thick portfolio of documents. He wore the uniform of the state police that he commanded and came ready to defend the military, state police, and

Bavarian authorities, all of whom had their reputations attacked at the trial.

Neithardt opened the session by announcing that a preliminary inquiry had been instigated against Seisser, Kahr, and Lossow. (It would be quietly dropped weeks later.) The presiding judge then instructed the witness to be brief and make his statement without reading. "Nervous tension" loomed over the proceedings, wrote Thomas R. Ybarra in the *New York Times*. The correspondent for *Le Figaro* was reminded of the charged atmosphere of a thunderstorm.

Immediately, Seisser went on the offensive. Adolf Hitler was, he said, a young man who had succumbed to the applause of the masses. At first, he had seemed content with being "the drummer" for a cause; now, his ambitions had grown to the extent that he placed himself at the forefront of the nationalist movement as "the man, who, alone, could steer the fate of the country." Bavaria was, for Hitler, "only a means to an end." He sought quite simply a dictatorship in Berlin, with himself at the pinnacle of power.

Seisser, no surprise, impressed many reporters in the courtroom as a more honest and forthright witness than Kahr. He emphasized how the triumvirate could never work with Hitler, who, he reminded the court, had essentially agreed on their incompatibility. Kahr's train was headed to Paris, Hitler had once told Seisser, while his own went to Berlin. They could work together only if Kahr changed course.

The witness testified to a series of meetings that had widened the chasm between the Bavarian leaders and Hitler. One of the more important ones had taken place on November 1, 1923, when Hitler, after making long, repetitive speeches, reaffirmed his pledge never to make a putsch. Seisser explained:

> [Hitler] repeatedly promised me . . . when I warned him against violent acts: "I will not take any action against the Reichswehr and the Landespolizci; do not think that I am so stupid. I will make no putsch, I promise you that."

Seven days later, Hitler broke his word. The three Bavarian leaders had trusted him and fallen right into his trap.

After a motion to move into closed session was overruled, Seisser attacked the defense counsel for citing evidence given behind closed doors and then vastly inflating its importance before an audience not privy to the details of the discussion. "That is an easy method to influence public opinion," Seisser noted.

Neithardt politely stopped him in a voice low and hardly audible.

Several defense lawyers stirred, with Roder speaking over everyone: "It is my opinion that the colonel was summoned as a witness, not as a public prosecutor!"

When Seisser was asked to continue with his testimony, he described for the court Hitler's "ill-starred, senseless raid" at the beer hall. His scorn was scarcely concealed, and his voice, at first clear and distinct, now often rose with indignation.

Hitler tried to justify his actions as necessary for Germany, the witness said, but this so-called rescue of the Reich would have led to its destruction. In the west, the French and the Belgians would have mobilized; in the east, the Czechs and the Poles. Germany would then face a two- or possibly a three-front war, without a national army or sufficient resources. This emphasis on lack of military preparation was of course for public consumption. The Allies were not supposed to know any of the clandestine actions that might violate the Versailles Treaty.

As a result, Seisser concluded, playing to both national and international audiences, Germany would fight with "nothing but enthusiastic men willing to make sacrifices." This would have led to another defeat of Germany and the loss of "our last possession and our last hope." Such were the stakes for the Bavarian leaders, the witness said, when they sought to rescue the country "in its darkest hour."

When Hitler had barged into the Bürgerbräu, Seisser continued, the audience hanging on to his every word, the putschists had, in this single move, wiped away years of hard work and planning on behalf of the nationalist cause.

Like Kahr and Lossow before him, Seisser claimed that he had decided to oppose Hitler while standing on the platform at the banquet hall. According to the witness, Lossow had indeed whispered the words "play act." Seisser also acknowledged that they understood one another using quick glances and furtive nods of the head.

Seisser then raised one fundamental point often overlooked in the fireworks of the trial: If Hitler and the triumvirate really had forged an agreement, why was it necessary to storm into the beer hall and risk the lives of three thousand Germans? This was something that Hitler could never satisfactorily explain, for a good reason. His move that night—despite the months of negotiations with the triumvirate and a considerable amount of common ground—had been made without their support.

Hitler sat through the testimony squirming with impatience.

"What insolence!" Hitler said moments later, loud enough for the gallery to hear.

Colonel von Seisser then "reddened with anger," as the foreign correspondent for *Le Gaulois* noted, and demanded that the judge rebuke Hitler for his outburst. A shouting match then echoed throughout the courtroom. The foreign correspondent for Agence Havas estimated that the chaos lasted a full ten minutes.

When the presiding judge finally regained order, he rebuked Hitler for his inappropriate remarks. Roder tried to argue that Hitler was merely giving instructions to his lawyer. A reporter for *Berliner Tageblatt*, however, had watched the two men whispering during Seisser's testimony and distinctly remembered Hitler turning his head and making the critique. At any rate, there were no repercussions for yet another incident in Neithardt's courtroom.

Seisser went on to explain one question that many people had asked about the Bavarian leaders: Why did they not alert Ludendorff of their change of plans and avoid bloodshed? This was simple, Seisser said. They had come to distrust the general, fearing that he had become loyal only to Hitler and, at the same time, realized that they had no choice other than to fight. "It would have been entirely inappropriate in a military sense and downright foolish to announce the battle before you were pre-pared for one." The stakes were too high not to win.

Besides, Hitler and Ludendorff knew of the official opposition to their plans between five and six o'clock that morning. They had plenty of time to call off their march. After Seisser hammered home these points, Stenglein made a motion to exclude the public.

Alfred Holl of the defense objected. The prosecution was calling wit-nesses and then, immediately after the testimony, motioning for a secret session and thereby leaving the presentation to remain "unchallenged throughout the country." This one-sided portrait was misleading the public.

The judge objected not at the prosecutor tactic, which was transparent enough, but at the charge that the public was being deceived. Closed ses-sions took place on national-security grounds alone, Neithardt claimed. If he allowed sensitive details to be aired in the public, *that* would be treason.

Holl then requested, and received, a twenty-minute recess to prepare for the closed session that the judge had just called.

When the court resumed, the defense spoke up on cue, hurrying to make a few points while the public and press were still in attendance.

Hitler went first, denying every one of the colonel's allegations about him and promising to refute them at the first opportunity. Pöhner fol-lowed, complaining about Seisser's "misrepresentation of the historical events," and Ludendorff agreed that the witness had embellished his tes-timony with "a construction after the fact."

Roder then took over, describing Seisser's testimony as riddled with errors and lies. When the judge objected to this "improper" criticism, Roder swore that he would prove it at the end of the testimony. In the meantime, he wished to protest that the triumvirate, or the trio of trai-tors, was being sheltered under the guise of national security.

"The high treason of the gentlemen is being sheltered?" Neithardt asked. Was that criticism against the court?

Having aired his allegation, Roder shifted the object of his criticism onto the state prosecutor, saying that the guilt of the high-profile wit-nesses only seemed to be treated behind closed doors.

Stenglein was furious, jumping to his feet to deny any such protection of the Bavarian leaders.

"Scandalous!" Ehard was overheard muttering in frustration.

As tensions rose, Neithardt and the tribunal recessed to weigh the merits of calling for another secret session. On their return, Neithardt ruled again in favor of the prosecution. The public was once more ushered out of the courtroom.

41.

A PUTSCH, NOT A PUTSCH

Defendants, witnesses, judges, and lawyers . . . At Munich, there are only accomplices.
— DE VILLEMUS, *L'Écho de Paris,* MARCH 13, 1924

Despite all the jokes about its comic-opera qualities, the "Hitler adventure" had come close to provoking an international crisis. Speculation was rampant, particularly outside Germany, that Kahr, Lossow, and Seisser had abandoned the putsch not so much because of its improbable odds of success, but rather due to the realization that, even if the conspiracy proved victorious, it would probably not bring any lasting advantage.

The overthrow of the Berlin government would have constituted a clear violation of the Versailles Treaty. Bavaria, it was predicted, would be one of the first places to suffer a foreign invasion. The German Army, limited to 100,000 men and the hastily trained patriotic societies, would be no match for France, Europe's greatest military power, which would, in turn, likely be backed up by an international coalition.

What's more, how had Reichswehr weapons, equipment, and ammunition ended up in Hitler's hands? No answers were emerging, and it was difficult to avoid noting how often Neithardt called a closed-door session whenever a military witness took the stand. "Germany is arming," the

Chicago Daily News concluded without qualification, in a report that outlined the country's secret preparations for war.

The German chancellor, Gustav Stresemann, tried to calm international concerns. To the outrage of nationalists, however, he blamed the Great War on Germany's blustering and blundering. That was the old Reich, he claimed. The new republic was returning to its roots as the most peaceful country in Europe.

The trial, meanwhile, spent the rest of the morning in secret session, contradicting the chancellor's pledge. Colonel von Seisser launched into an exposition of state-police preparations as an auxiliary force on the northern border that had been indeed, as the defense alleged, reinforced by members of some patriotic societies, including the Bund Oberland. At another point, Seisser conceded that the triumvirate had drafted a plan to purge the civil-service administration in Berlin.

That afternoon, a group of spectators from the trial were riding home on a Munich streetcar. Nothing was being revealed to the public, they complained. Everything of importance took place behind closed doors, where they suspected that the defense counsel had proven that Bavarian authorities planned an attack on Berlin. Disillusionment about the proceedings and the responsibility of the leaders was clearly not fading.

On day fourteen of the trial, Gustav von Kahr returned to the stand for his postponed public cross-examination. Otto Gademann, a defense lawyer well versed in the clandestine military preparations, began with an inquiry into the witness's authority and responsibility.

Kahr brushed off most of the questions as irrelevant, redundant, or already answered in secret session. He went on to claim that any talk of a putsch by the Bavarian leaders must be understood as a desire to suppress it, not join it. Then, when asked about the words "on to Berlin," Kahr said that expression did not mean a march on the capital, but rather an attempt to prevent Bavaria from seceding from Germany.

At this point, Hitler interjected that the witness was abusing the German language by taking simple words and giving them a new meaning. March to Berlin did not mean a march to Berlin, and a putsch was not a putsch. "If the gentlemen today are allowed to give these utterly clear words and terms a completely different meaning," Hitler said, the court should not convict him or his fellow defendants. All their testimonies were based on definitions that apparently ceased to be valid.

Judge Neithardt, on multiple occasions, stopped Hitler and the defense lawyers from asking questions, on the grounds of preserving "national security." So Kahr went on, as before, evading issues, denying detailed knowledge of events, and referring the matter to colleagues. Repeatedly, Kahr deflected responsibility or minimalized the significance of his own actions.

How ironic, noted defense lawyer Kohl, that this witness, the "Bavarian Bismarck," did not seem all that knowledgeable about his post, or above hiding behind a smokescreen of blatant ruses. Frustrated, the lawyer blurted out that he could not take it anymore.

"Whether you can put up with it or not is entirely irrelevant," Judge Neithardt said. "The witness has the obligation to tell the truth."

The defense returned to the topic of the now notorious handshake between the witness and Hitler in the banquet hall. This might have been a minor point in the grand scheme of the case, but the defense magnified its importance out of proportion. Victory on this detail might help compensate for their earlier failure to pin down Kahr on the larger question of complicity.

As Kahr denied that he had used both hands in the gesture, Hitler jumped up from his chair and proceeded to describe the scene in detail. He started to lose control. Kahr sat impassively. The calmer Kahr remained, the more furious Hitler became. He was soon almost shouting at the witness: "Am I now a liar or not?"

Kahr, still looking straight ahead, without making eye contact with the defendant, coolly said that he had no recollection of the gesture as Hitler described it. But everyone in the beer hall had seen it, defense counsel Georg Götz said. "I will remember it in one hundred years' time!" The courtroom erupted into applause.

Hitler, smelling blood, rattled off a series of questions to Kahr about his actions on the night of the putsch. The judge asked Hitler to slow down and lower his voice, because his excitement was threatening to disrupt the "dignity of the court." Minutes later, however, Hitler was again shouting and calling the witness a liar.

Roder, apologizing on behalf of his client, explained that Hitler's fervor stemmed from the fact that his honor was at stake. He then tried to turn this point to his advantage, asking the judge to require Kahr to face Hitler, "eye to eye," and confront the hard truth about the events of November 8–9. This was a reference to the witness's body language that day, sitting in his chair, staring down at the floor, out into the distance, or anywhere, away from the gaze of the defendants.

The judge declined to force a showdown. Instead he would soon be chastening Hitler again for his language. The beer hall orator had won the day, *The Outlook* concluded, "by sheer lung power."

If Kahr had appeared melancholic and listless at the opening of his testimony, as *München-Augsburger Abendzeitung* concluded, he now looked like the image of misery itself. This was the verdict of the right-wing nationalist newspaper *Deutsche Presse*, which was, as usual, quick to slam the fallen leader.

Kahr's supporters, on the other hand, later said that he had skillfully maneuvered through a series of devious traps, each one trickier than the last. Hitler and Ludendorff's legion of lawyers had shamelessly transformed the Munich courtroom into an Inquisition or a medieval torture chamber.

Another view is that Kahr had survived the interrogation thanks to his strategy of denial, evasion, and continual stonewalling, as well as the assistance of the presiding judge. It was Neithardt, after all, who had granted Kahr the privilege of deciding what, if anything, fell into the category of "executive privilege" or posed a threat to "national security." The witness was, in other words, given wide latitude in answering or avoiding a question as he saw fit.

Neithardt had repeatedly come out in favor of the Bavarian leader, overruling questions that might implicate the authorities further in the putsch. This courtroom management, however, did not help the reputations of the authorities. To many Germans, Kahr, Lossow, and Seisser seemed to have betrayed either Germany or the putschists, or both, only to escape responsibility by abandoning the patriotic foot soldiers who fought their battles. Now, to the further outrage of citizens across the political spectrum, the Bavarian puppet masters seemed to enjoy the shield of the presiding judge.

246 THE TRIAL OF ADOLF HITLER

Neithardt, in trying to safeguard the authorities and the institutions under their command, had handed the rabble-rousing defendant a remarkable opportunity. Hitler could now stand up in defiance to the powerful, unpopular figures of both Berlin and Bavaria—and, in the process, turn his trial for high treason into grand theatre with himself in the starring role as the true patriot and martyr to his national cause. This performance was received with growing applause in the courtroom and accolades in the press.

42.

BLOW-UP

German Versus German, Plot and Counterplot
—Auckland Star

O n day fifteen of the trial, it was General von Lossow's turn to face his cross-examination. His earlier testimony had been met with mixed results. On one hand, he had exposed the brutality and disloyalty of the putschists. On the other, he had failed to refute the accusation that he had been conspiring against the republic. The image in the Munich courtroom was "not pretty," *Berliner Tageblatt* concluded.

With biting sarcasm and a knack for quick repartee, Lossow lashed out at defendant and advocate alike. The witness first wanted to draw a distinction between his goal—a legal, authoritarian regime based on the emergency powers granted by Article 48 of the Weimar Constitution—and the simplistic misrepresentation that reduced it to a "putsch." He had no desire for a military dictatorship, he said, certainly not one that involved Adolf Hitler.

Lossow tried to exploit the powerful antiestablishment sentiment swelling up in the gallery. For one thing, he championed the right of a general to refuse orders of a corrupt government, meaning, of course, Berlin. He referred to the economic and social crisis during the nightmare of hyperinflation:

Our soldiers are not there for the purpose of perpetually shooting starving people to death merely because you [politicians] are not capable of establishing a decent government.

Like Kahr, Lossow said that his use of the word "putsch," or coup d'état, was supposed to be viewed as a means of exerting pressure on the capital.

So, defense counsel Holl asked, "The defendants did not conceive of the putsch any differently than Your Excellency?"

This provoked amusement in the audience, many of whom were now sporting an array of new fashion accessories; "Brooches, necklaces, chatelaines of hand-carved gold and silver in the form of a *Hakenkreuz* [swastika]," the *New York Herald* reported, had become "all the rage."

Several times that morning, the courtroom erupted in laughter, prompting Judge Neithardt to pound the gavel and threaten to expel the boisterous crowd from the gallery. The defense attorneys, all the while, kept the pressure on the witness, giving the impression that he, not Hitler, was on trial.

Röhm's counsel, Christoph Schramm, wanted to know why all the threads of the grand conspiracy against the republic converged in Munich.

"How do you know that the threads converged in Munich?" Lossow replied. He corrected himself, saying that he did not think that they did, and then concluded that he knew for a fact that they did not. The web of intrigue was also being spun in Berlin and in other parts of the Reich.

Didn't the witness expect to receive a position in the new regime?

"No, never!" Lossow said. Referring to himself in the third person, he continued: "I have already expressed my view that General von Lossow has come into politics quite against his will and desire, and he yearns for the day when he can clear out."

Another lawyer asked him if he had called the leaders in Berlin "only eunuchs and castrati too cowardly to make a decision."

Lossow admitted that he had probably said something along those lines, but regretted that the phrase had now, thanks to the lawyers for the defense, spread outside the closed room in which he had intended it to stay. His anger was rising. Minutes later, Lossow was banging on the table, refusing to answer another question that he deemed tangential. The judge asked him to show more composure.

"I would be grateful if unnecessary questions were not posed!" the witness snapped back.

Lossow was, as the correspondent for Agence Havas put it, "a tough opponent." During his interrogation, he walked up and down in the open space in front of the judges' bench, his hands behind his back. He gave the impression of power and confidence. Like Kahr, however, he sometimes evaded or answered questions in ways that raised concerns about his credibility.

When Hitler asked the witness to identify the people who first conceived of the proposed authoritarian regime, Lossow at first balked, flatly refusing to answer the question. He then said he did not know, only to reverse himself and claim that he had learned it afterward in "confidential talks."

"We are obliged to tell the court confidential matters clearly and openly," Hitler said. Then, at the top of his lungs, Hitler demanded that the presiding judge not allow the witness to avoid his question.

Neithardt calmly ordered Hitler to control himself and struck his question as irrelevant to the trial.

At this point, defense counsel Walther Hemmeter motioned for a brief recess to reevaluate strategy because, as he put it, the witness on the stand seemed to be controlling the trial.

The presiding judge took the criticism in stride, but Hemmeter was not finished. He protested General von Lossow's unseemly behavior, pacing up and down the front of the room, shouting as if he were in the army barracks. The lawyers for the defense were not his recruits.

Besides, what was the legal basis for the witness's refusal to answer?

"The witness has already said that he considered himself bound on account of the confidential character of the conversation," Neithardt said.

"That is not in the code of procedure."

"I know that as well," Neithardt said, shrugging off the objection. He then said that he refused the question because it was not relevant.

On the contrary, Holl said, it went to the heart of the defense. If the

Bavarian leaders had devised the plot against Berlin, as they were prepared to show, then Hitler, Ludendorff, and their codefendants were simply carrying out orders.

Once more, the presiding judge ruled the question irrelevant.

Unfazed, Hitler tried again. Perhaps Lossow actually did not know the answer to the question. Would it be possible, then, to ask him the name of the person, or people, whom he believed had conceived of the idea to establish an authoritarian regime in Berlin? Neithardt ordered a brief recess to consider this question.

At 11:15 a.m., Neithardt returned to the courtroom and refused Hitler's question.

Hitler lost his temper. "Far be it from me to criticize the decision of the court," Hitler began, his voice quickly rising to a shout. The events of November 8 were simply the "product of the treasonable activity of Lossow, Kahr, and Seisser!"

There was stirring again in the gallery.

"You have no right to criticize in this way," Neithardt said. "Rightly or wrongly, the court has already made its decision." He urged the defense to confine its statements to facts, and Hitler in particular to keep his voice down. Moments later, however, Hitler and Lossow were again at daggers drawn.

The American journalist H. R. Knickerbocker would later recall this remarkable scene: Hitler jumping to his feet, shouting at the witness, and then, overpowered, falling back to his seat "as if he had collapsed under a physical blow." It was the only time in his long career of covering foreign affairs, the Pulitzer Prize–winning journalist later said, that he had known of Hitler being shouted down. This was a slight exaggeration, but there was an element of truth, and the scene ended with another incident.

The "lively confrontation," as *Le Figaro* called it, began when Hitler challenged Lossow to admit that he had felt threatened in the backroom of the beer hall. Hitler told the court that the witness was treated not as a hostage, but rather as the future military leader of the new nationalist regime.

Hitler pressed on, emphasizing months of solidarity between his supporters and the Bavarian leaders against Berlin, that is, until the moment when the putsch hung in the balance and the politicians betrayed them. The judge again asked Hitler to speak "a little more calmly." Everyone in the room could hear him just fine.

How many times would Neithardt have to reproach Hitler for shouting, interrupting, insulting witnesses, or repeatedly asking questions the judge had already ruled inadmissible? Outside the courtroom, Neithardt was overheard complaining that it was impossible to silence Hitler.

At one point, Hitler admitted that he had in fact given his word not to make a putsch without informing Colonel von Seisser in advance. But then he went on the offensive and forced Lossow to admit that there had been certain reservations and conditions attached to his promise. One of those was that, in case of an unforeseen event, he would no longer be bound by his pledge.

General von Lossow, haughty from the start, now dismissed the defendant with the confidence of an aristocratic officer rebuking a private first class commoner. It was still a broken promise and a surprise attack. Hitler's denials in court meant nothing. Lossow accused Hitler of having a bad conscience. The crowd became disruptive.

"Lieutenant General!" Hitler said, visibly angry, he needed no "bad conscience" because the only broken promise in this affair was made by Lossow. Hitler had just contradicted himself, but the audience did not care. There was a loud and long stirring in the gallery, including a round of applause. The witness, by now furious, grabbed his belongings and marched out of the courtroom.

Some people said that Lossow had asked to be dismissed, but if so, few, if any, heard him. The judge then reprimanded Hitler for his "gross impropriety," and immediately stopped the proceedings.

For many spectators in the Munich courtroom, General von Lossow gave the impression of an impetuous German officer throwing a tantrum. Hitler seemed yet again to be standing up to the lies, cowardice, and treason in the echelons of power. Left-wing readers from Berlin to Paris, on the other hand, wondered who was behaving more reprehensibly: the reactionaries like Lossow, the radical extremists like Hitler, or the court system that oversaw the deplorable circus.

43.

HINTS

The witnesses for the prosecution have become witnesses for the defense.

—KARL KOHL

After losing his temper and stomping out of the courtroom, General von Lossow was scheduled to retake the stand on Saturday morning, March 15, 1924. The first question in the mind of virtually everyone in the audience, *Bayerischer Kurier* thought, was: Would he return? The answer came at 8:30 a.m., when the presiding judge opened the session. General von Lossow was nowhere to be seen.

Instead, Neithardt read out a note from the absent witness explaining that he refused to come back to the courtroom for reasons that were, as he put it, "clear to anyone who was present at the conclusion of [yesterday's] session."

Roder requested that the court order Lossow to face his cross-examination, but the presiding judge ignored him and called the first in a series of inconsequential witnesses. The morning progressed slowly—an irony, given that the proceedings were rumored to be wrapping up by the end of the following week. *Welt am Montag* was reporting that Neithardt had confirmed this timetable to several lawyers in private.

The trial would indeed have to hurry to reach a verdict, because the emergency judicial institution that tried the case, the People's Court, was set to expire on April 1, 1924. This was a compromise that Bavaria had made with Berlin to keep the trial in Munich and then, in return, let the People's Court quietly disappear from the scene.

So with the pressure of time looming, it was striking that a plethora of minor witnesses took the stand to offer secondary testimony that ventured in almost every direction except the one that might clarify the facts of the case. The trial was not so much building to resolution as branching out into a number of irrelevant and distracting digressions.

What's more, a glance at the witnesses thus far gave the impression that the court focused too much on the testimony of the privileged and the powerful. Where were all the workers, craftsmen, day laborers, and other people who had been in the city that night and the following morning in November? The Bavarian state association of hairdressers, for one, had formally protested this elitist bias. What facts were *not* being aired in Neithardt's courtroom? Others, however, wondered what facts actually had been.

L'Écho de Paris predicted that the Hitler trial—as many newspapers had long ago begun calling the proceedings, rather than the Ludendorff trial—would cause the Munich judges to live on in legal fables and cautionary tales. The name "Bavarian trial" would become synonymous with a travesty of justice. *L'Humanité* speculated that the charade would end with the sentencing of the judges themselves to ten years in the fortress prison.

Still, the parade of unimportant and often irrelevant eyewitnesses continued. The most revealing information that day was shared by the fifty-four-year-old retired cavalry captain Friedrich von Schirach, whose testimony raised many eyebrows.

In the middle of his statement that the march to Berlin was not meant to be a literal attack, the witness made a passing reference to the fact that Judge Neithardt had hinted that he should avoid this topic. This startling claim was quickly followed by both the judge and the prosecution motioning to move the examination into secret session.

Behind closed doors, Schirach admitted knowing of the order sent from the War Ministry [Ia 800, dated October 26, 1923] that reinforced the infantry regiment with three battalions of volunteers from the fighting societies. This was the same document about which Ludendorff had previously grilled Kahr. The men of Schirach's paramilitary group, the V.V.V. Munich, had been overjoyed, convinced that this summoning of the troops was the beginning of the long-anticipated attack on Berlin.

Stenglein asked if the order had been executed.

"The volunteers reported. They were referred to the War Ministry." They were then to proceed to the barracks of the 19th Infantry for inspection at ten a.m. on November 11, 1923.

"Why did it not happen?" Neithardt asked.

"Because the events of the eighth and ninth came to pass."

Under questioning, Schirach affirmed with confidence that several combat societies were prepared to march alongside the Bavarian Army, unite with nationalist allies in the north, and then use their combined strength to persuade the president and his cabinet to resign. If the politicians had refused, they would have been forced out.

Hitler wanted to confirm the witness's testimony. As a political leader, he had received "precise reports day after day about the state of affairs." Everyone under him was "obviously convinced that this was *the* advance—and, to be sure, I emphasize that quite purposely," he said, because this was no metaphoric or imagined advance. They were headed for Berlin.

What really convinced him was the marshaling of artillery batteries. The Bavarian leaders would not have needed such a concentration of cannons and howitzers if it had contemplated applying only political pressure on the capital.

The problem in this plan, Hitler continued, had been Gustav von Kahr. He was a weak, indecisive politician who lacked the ability to shoulder the burdens of leadership. Instead of waiting for him to fail, Hitler had decided to march into the Bürgerbräu and demand the "political leadership" for the upcoming battle.

Shouts came from the prosecution bench.

Hitler talked over them. "[Kahr's] weakness would have become Germany's doom!"

For years, Hitler had said that he wanted nothing more than to be a drummer of the nationalist movement. But in this outburst, he had yet again admitted that he aspired to something more.

Neithardt, meanwhile, tried to stop Hitler from talking and hurried up the debate past these uncomfortable allegations about Bavarian government complicity in the putsch. He was also trying to forego the calling of additional witnesses.

As the proceedings wound down for the day, Neithardt further alienated the defense by refusing to force Lossow to face his cross-examination. Defense lawyers Gademann, Holl, Roder, and Hemmeter again demanded his return to the stand. The questions they needed answered were essential to the defense, they claimed.

Neithardt, unmoved, fined Lossow fifty marks for his "unauthorized absence," or, failing that, five days' imprisonment.

At 1:20 p.m., the presiding judge closed the session for the week, leaving many people to wonder how the trial could possibly conclude in the next five days. Outside, meanwhile, a number of young Germans were protesting against Gustav von Kahr and in favor of Adolf Hitler. This was a sign of things to come.

44.

HITLER'S BODYGUARD TAKES THE STAND

This is not the type of trial that takes place every week in the People's Court.
—ALFRED HOLL, TO WHICH THE JUDGE REPLIED,
"THANK GOD!"

In Berlin, the British ambassador, Edgar Vincent Viscount D'Abernon, sat down for a chat with Gustav Stresemann, the former chancellor who had recently been named Germany's foreign minister. Talk turned quickly to the trial of Hitler.

Stresemann had been struck by the many "revelations" emerging from Munich. Clearly, the danger to Germany and Europe had been "infinitely greater than the general public realized." The British ambassador recorded in his diary:

> [Stresemann] himself had always known that Germany had been within an ace of a serious and successful 'putsch' from the Right, but official circles in Berlin had hitherto underrated the danger the country had gone through.

Kahr's plots against the republic, Stresemann realized, had been "not less subversive." Hitler's hasty move had derailed their efforts.

Many diplomats in Munich were also following the sensational trial. The minister of Württemberg, Carl Moser von Filseck, when he attended a session in early March, had been repulsed when the defendants entered the courtroom, laughing, chatting, and greeting one another and the public. There was no attempt to chasten them. The atmosphere was riotous, and their arguments reckless. His colleague Robert Murphy at the US embassy would later sum up their stance as "insolent bravado."

On Monday, March 17, Hitler's trial appeared on the cover of Munich's satire magazine, *Simplicissimus*. The "Red Dog," as it was nicknamed, depicted a dainty Hitler, nose in the air, straining with torch in hand to set a government building ablaze. He sits on the shoulders of General von Lossow, who, in turn, balances on the back of Gustav von Kahr. The latter, at the same time, calls for the police. In the distance, a shooting star rises in the sky. It is in the shape of a swastika.

That morning, the proceedings entered its fourth week. Hitler's advocate, Lorenz Roder, opened by lodging a complaint against someone rumored to be writing a book on the trial. This author was said to be collaborating with a military official, who was bartering information he gained from the secret sessions in return for a daily payment and a portion of the book's profits. The plan was to expose the inside story of the Hitler trial.

Roder found this story credible, given the high public interest and the amount of sensitive material that had already been leaked to the press. Neithardt agreed to investigate. As the suspected informant, Col. Joseph Schraudenbach, was present that morning, the courtroom was treated to the spectacle of the presiding judge questioning a man pulled from the audience.

Schraudenbach admitted at once that he had placed an advertisement in the newspaper offering his services as a writer and photographer for any book project about the trial. He made no attempt to deny the claims that Roder made, except for one: He swore that he would never divulge any classified information.

As for the notes he had taken during closed sessions, Schraudenbach explained that this was to ensure the accuracy of his account. Not a word, he promised, would be published. To avoid an inadvertent mistake, he had enclosed all this sensitive material in parentheses. Roder accepted the explanation, as did Neithardt. The colonel was allowed to continue his collaboration, though he would soon pull out from the venture as a result of a contractual dispute.

Public opinion in Munich strongly favored Hitler and the defendants. The Bavarian leaders were regarded as the real traitors in this trial of patriotism, and, as the correspondent for *Le Temps* noted, they no longer dared to appear in public. Rumors circulated that General von Lossow had received more challenges to duels than he could ever fight. *Time* magazine noted that one of the challengers was believed to be the defendant Lieutenant Colonel Kriebel.

During this day's long session, Roder made a dramatic move. To support his position that Kahr's plan was no metaphoric or hypothetical enterprise, he motioned to call four new witnesses: the president of Germany, Friedrich Ebert; Foreign Minister Gustav Stresemann; the head of the military, General von Seeckt; and the minister of defense, Dr. Otto Gessler. There was no way the presiding judge was going to comply with this request, but several journalists ran with it. Roder's flamboyant antics made headlines around Germany and the world.

So did the blatant disregard for the German constitution that afternoon. One witness, Eberhardt Kautter, a high-profile adviser to Kahr, opened his testimony by asking permission to make a statement. He then outlined the historical background of the putsch in a way that served largely to justify the acts of both Kahr and Hitler. There was no objection, either, when he described the Weimar constitution as "the gag on the will of the people."

In the afternoon session, Hitler's bodyguard, Ulrich Graf, took the stand. This was the first time he had seen Hitler since the beer hall putsch, when he had possibly saved his life. For weeks afterward, Graf had remained in the hospital, and, as he put it in his unpublished memoir, hovered between life and death. He was also depressed: Hitler was in prison, the Nazi Party appeared to be "smashed," and his life savings had been wiped out by the hyperinflation. "Difficult days," he said.

The bodyguard covered familiar ground on the storming of the beer hall, but then he added some little-known details about the talks in the back room. The questioning was, as *Berliner Volks-Zeitung* put it, "quite interesting." Although he had not been able to hear the entire conversation, Graf testified that he had witnessed enough to believe that Lossow and Seisser had come to an understanding with Hitler even before Ludendorff had entered the room.

This impression of solidarity was strengthened, he added, when he watched the defendant Dr. Weber give a cigarette to Colonel Seisser, prompting General von Lossow to ask for one as well.

"Was the meeting that cheerful?" Neithardt asked.

Yes, Graf said, adding that the mood was quite different from the one described in the newspapers. What's more, Hitler's success with the triumvirate had been easier than he had expected. They didn't really have to drink that much, he remembered thinking.

As for the march into the city center, defense attorney Christoph Schramm wanted to know if the witness had informed the state police troops at the Odeonsplatz that Ludendorff was with them.

Yes, Graf said, describing how he had shouted out, "This is Ludendorff! Do you want to fire on your general?" At this point, the shots had come. From behind he had still heard the marchers singing "Deutschland über Alles."

Perhaps the police had not been able to hear him amid the noise and confusion?

Impossible, Graf said. "I did not just shout it—I roared it."

The questioning continued without a major revelation until Hitler spoke up in favor of his bodyguard and called him "a most upright, loyal, and sincere man." Graf would, Hitler added, "allow himself, at any time, to be shot dead for me." He nearly had been. Graf's young daughter Gretl was still nursing him back to health, and the witness left the courtroom, overjoyed by this praise.

The day would wind down with a discussion over whether to call the remaining witnesses. The presiding judge was trying to conclude the testimony as soon as possible. The prosecution, on the other hand, wanted to summon at least one more witness, and the defense had its own list. All this only threatened to cause the trial to descend into a labyrinth of testimony and counter-testimony. The judge recessed the court at 5:12 that evening, promising to announce his decision soon.

45.

VOLTE-FACE

I already foresee that this trial, like all the great public trials, is going to be roughed up . . . according to all the rules of the art.

—WALTER LUETGEBRUNE

At the beginning of the trial, Ludendorff had been heralded as a strongman in the tradition of Frederick the Great or Otto von Bismarck. But by day eighteen, the general was losing his luster. While Hitler roared with his "guttural thunder" and basked in the media spotlight, Ludendorff was receding into the shadows.

The general's first appearance on the stand had alienated a large number of people, including many of his own supporters. He had exposed himself, the United Press correspondent said, as both a "thickhead politician" and "a moral coward"—"Ludendorff the Clueless" said *Augsburger Postzeitung*. The statement the general was about to make, when Neithardt allowed him to retake the stand, certainly did not enhance his reputation.

Ludendorff began by identifying himself as a monarchist who had consoled himself with the realization that Germany's royal crown would never be restored until the people wanted it. What he expected in the meantime was a temporary and transitional dictatorship, like the ones, he said, that had been installed during wartime in France, England, and the United States. This comment about these Western authoritarian regimes left some observers wondering about his mental health.

Neithardt asked Ludendorff if he had known of Hitler's plans before he arrived at the beer hall.

No, Ludendorff said, he had not. He also denied that he had ever considered participating in "a military march on Berlin." His objective was only to apply "moral coercion."

Neithardt repeated the question, asking for confirmation because this new statement blatantly contradicted Ludendorff's previous testimony on three main points: that he had joined the planned national revolution; that he found out about the plot on the way to the beer hall; and that he had aspired to conquer the capital.

"I have heard so many things and have had so many impressions that I really do not know the details any longer," Ludendorff said.

The correspondent for *Le Petit Journal* put it differently: "Ludendorff denies what he confessed."

Ludendorff's current position—particularly his argument that the march to Berlin was only a metaphor—sounded suddenly in conformity with the official line espoused by Kahr, Lossow, and Seisser. Some papers, like Berlin's *8-Uhr-Abendblatt*, had long predicted that Ludendorff would change sides, deserting fellow defendants to save his own skin.

Sometimes Ludendorff tried to iron out the glaring contradictions in his newly revised confession; other times he made no attempt, or simply appealed to ignorance. No, he had not known that the ministers were detained in the beer hall. No, he had not realized that Hitler wanted to depose the president, and that was certainly not his own aim. All the sudden excuses and denials struck several reporters as pathetic and ill becoming of a man of his stature. "The brave general," *L'Humanité* said, "trembled in fear of a condemnation."

At one point, Adolf Hitler came to the general's assistance. Ludendorff had been tapped as the new military commander, he said, because there was no one better qualified. As for the political leadership, Hitler accepted the blame for the actions at the beer hall, just as he claimed its credit: "I am now the political leader of young Germany," Hitler said, boasting that he had started the nationalist movement four years ago and had ever since drummed up support on its behalf.

His goal for November 8–9, 1923, Hitler said, was to launch "an immense wave of propaganda" that would overwhelm the renegade Socialist and Marxist regime in Berlin. Modesty and discretion were ill placed in such an enterprise because, Hitler added, "the man who can do something has the damned duty and obligation to carry it out." Kahr was in way over his head. "In the final analysis, statecraft is not applied political science. You must be born with it."

When Ehard reminded the court of the major domestic and international consequences for this action, Hitler said that that was exactly his intention. He wanted to destroy the government that, he claimed, had illegally desecrated Germany for five years and held the country captive to its "international, Marxist, defeatist, pacifist, democratic" agenda. The goal of the putsch, he repeated, was patriotic. If the court thought otherwise, it should impose the death penalty.

Hitler's speech made an impression on the courtroom. "Munich's great treason trial," Thomas R. Ybarra wrote in the *New York Times*, "has come the full circle." General Ludendorff, a lifelong Prussian militarist and renowned commander retreated from his involvement in the putsch, whereas Hitler, a private first class, "brazenly avowed his intention to march on Berlin . . . and sweep away the German Republican Government by force of arms."

The general had behaved on the stand like he did when he wrote his books: he tried to absolve himself of all responsibility. Hitler, on the other hand, seemed invigorated as he shouldered "the lion's share of the blame." Ludendorff, the aged hero of the past, came off as not knowing, seeing, or choosing anything, pointing his finger everywhere—that is, except at himself. His less-distinguished comrade, by contrast, was ready to take responsibility for his mistakes as well as those of his colleagues.

Above all, this surreal and "amazingly paradoxical spectacle" raised a question. Was this man with the Charlie Chaplin toothbrush mustache dominating the Munich courtroom, a reporter for the *Vossische Zeitung* wondered, the face of "young Germany"?

• • •

LUDENDORFF HAD THE distinction of being the last person to testify in the high-treason trial. At 10:35 a.m., after conveniently allowing the general to make his volte-face, Neithardt announced his decision that no other witness would be called to the stand. The long list of remaining witnesses, drawn up by the lawyers and predicted by the press, would never be heard. The presiding judge was finally, *Vossische Zeitung* noted with irony, acting with decisiveness.

No wonder cynicism about the trial was pervasive. Neithardt was protecting the reputation of Ludendorff, it was widely said. He was also trying to prevent full knowledge of the putsch from reaching the public, several papers added. The trial seemed indeed to be a sordid tale of scandal, intrigue, and injustice, with responsibility for the cover-ups probably reaching high in the Bavarian state, probably the minister of justice, Franz Gürtner, himself.

Neithardt's next move did not reassure his critics either. After dismissing the last witnesses, he cleared the public from the courtroom to discuss the prosecution's proposal to hold the rest of its proceedings behind closed doors.

Deliberation would last one and a half hours. Much of the debate consisted of arguments not too dissimilar from the ones made on the first day of the trial. This time, however, Neithardt leaned toward excluding the public from the closing statements. The people could lay no special claim to their right to attend the trial, he said, when "a higher interest" such as national security, is at risk.

No fewer than six defense attorneys pressed for a final round of openness. The German public, engrossed in the progress of the case and invested in the execution of justice, would not benefit from the final arguments being given behind closed doors. Nor, it was argued, would the international audience. As Schramm put it, "the whole world has followed the trial with the most rapt attention."

Another proponent of an open session, of course, was Adolf Hitler.

Suppression of information, he argued, would not stop the demand for knowledge. If the court insisted on enshrouding the proceedings with secrecy, less reputable sources would flood the market with inferior work. What's more, it would only be understandable if many people, hoping to support the defendants, divulged classified information, not realizing the damage they might do to Germany.

If none of the arguments thus far had convinced Neithardt, Ludendorff's defense advocate Walter Luetgebrune had one that might: The procedures of German criminal law protected the defendant's right to "vindicate themselves before the world"—and, as he emphasized, a verdict could be overturned if this mandate for a public trial was not met.

This brought Hitler back into the debate and his comment soon turned into a tirade. Hitler wanted to stress that if he and his colleagues had "committed crimes, we acted in good faith and in burning love for our fatherland." So, of course, he assured Neithardt, that if the public were allowed to hear the closing arguments, he and his fellow defendants would not reveal any sensitive information. But, he added, he would never shy away from the struggle against leaders who defiled the country. On the contrary, Hitler said, "we want to shout it out to the world!"

He also wanted to make it clear that the primary goal of Germany must be to break free of the Versailles Treaty. This was, he argued, the only way they could save the country and rebuild a strong defense against their ring of enemies. Hitler then attacked the Munich trial itself as a misfortune because it pitted good Germans against one another, everyone "fighting like the Niebelungs." Stenglein would understand this position well, Hitler then suggested, because the trial "forces him to act as the prosecutor."

Interestingly, Stenglein made no attempt to deny or refute this allegation.

This speech, one of Hitler's most political thus far in the trial, was delivered for the benefit of prosecutors, defendants, tribunal, and a small number of mostly military observers in the closed-door session. It was a foretaste, indeed almost an audition, for his grand performance—that is, if the tribunal decided to open the doors to the public.

46.

"GOOD TIMES FOR TRAITORS"

My good gentlemen, acquit Herr Hitler!
—LORENZ RODER

After a public holiday and a day without a session, the court readjourned at 9:15 on the morning of Friday, March 21. Neithardt first wanted to address recent rumors that the court's closed sessions had been convened to protect the reputation of a powerful person. The *Frankfurter Zeitung* believed this was Crown Prince Rupprecht of the Wittelsbach dynasty.

The allegations were absurd, Neithardt said. He did not know of any influential person exerting influence on the trial, and assured the public that the crown prince had not even been discussed. This speculation was the product of the thriving rumor mill that surrounded the secret sessions and a sign of what was to come should the trial wrap up behind closed doors.

That was why, the judge announced, he would reject the prosecutor's motion to exclude the public from the rest of the proceedings. The court would move to closed session if necessary, but in the meantime he urged everyone yet again to show caution and discretion in all their public statements.

It was time for the closing arguments. The prosecution went first.

Stenglein began by promising to concentrate on facts, not on personal opinion, political issues, and what he called all the irrelevant "accessories which have taken up so much room in the proceedings." He then launched into a lengthy exposition on the German patriotic movement as riven with strife and discord. Each faction harbored a deep suspicion of its rivals, even as they all shared an "ardent, burning impatience" to restore the country to its former magnificence.

This patriotic movement—like many other manifestations of youthful enthusiasm—could benefit from more patience and prudence. Stenglein urged its followers to seek a certain kind of fortitude: "a hard, tough, and iron patience, which works in silence, rejoicing in the deed and confident of the future, as it waits with clenched teeth until the seed has ripened and the hour has come."

The root of the problem for contemporary Germany lay in the "decay of state authority" and the decline of respect for the law, all of which boded ill for the country. Still, he emphasized that "a high, perhaps morally legitimate goal does not justify the use of criminal means." Committing an act for the love of country does not make it legal. The Weimar Constitution remained "the foundation of the Reich," and its many opponents, however much they might feel justified, "should never be allowed to alter or remove the constitution by violence."

The defense, Stenglein continued, wanted to focus on the actions of the Bavarian authorities, but they were irrelevant to the case. This statement surprised many people in the room—the correspondent for *Le Petit Parisien* called it "stupefying." Then, after arguing irrelevancy, Stenglein spent several minutes defending the reputation of the men in power.

The prosecutor eventually turned to the question of the individual defendants. These men alone bore "responsibility for the events and their consequences." Foremost among them was Adolf Hitler. At this point, the closing statement became more peculiar and controversial:

> Arisen from humble origins, Hitler proved his German cast of mind as a brave soldier in the Great War. He was filled with a genuine, blazing enthusiasm for a great German Fatherland. After the war, with painstaking work,

he created from the smallest beginnings a great party: the National Socialist Workers' Party.

"I have no judgment to render on his party's politics," Stenglein said, even as he just called it "great."

Each word seemed carefully chosen. The Austrian defendant, at risk of deportation, was commended by the prosecutor for his "*German* cast of mind" and his "honest efforts to inspire belief in the *German* cause." Hitler had provided hope to an "oppressed and disarmed people," Stenglein said, despite the plethora of evidence of rearming that had been submitted in secret session.

The prosecutor's statement at times sounded like an apology, or even a eulogy. It certainly did not sound like a condemnation. Indeed, the defense lawyers later thanked the prosecutor for his portrait. There was almost nothing on the loss of life, or other consequences of the acts of high treason. Few prosecutors, it has been said, have made such a weak and imbalanced closing argument.

Stenglein then came to his point, which was also uttered as if grudgingly extracted:

> As human beings, we cannot withhold our respect from Hitler. Yet as grave as his crime is, so great, too, is his guilt.

Stenglein adopted a similarly laudatory approach to Ludendorff. He praised him as "a real man, a brave soldier," whose "renown as a general [remains] untouched." Bravery and heroism aside, however, the general had violated the law, and therefore, needed to be punished. Ludendorff, "a model of the stern, unswerving performance of duty, will understand that best."

The only question was whether the general should be charged with high treason, or merely aiding and abetting the crime. Stenglein proposed the milder option, laying out his case that the general did not know of the plot in advance and only joined once it was set in motion. Significantly, all these conclusions were based on Ludendorff's second, revised confession that the court had allowed him to make.

After summing up the case against Hitler and Ludendorff, Stenglein handed the closing statement over to his assistant Ehard, who wrapped up the case against the other eight defendants. Stenglein then proposed the punishments:

Hitler: 8 years
Pöhner, Kriebel, and Weber: 6 years
Ludendorff, Röhm, and Frick: 2 years
Wagner and Brückner: 1 ½ Years
Pernet: 15 months

All of this was to be "fortress confinement," the traditional punishment for major political crimes. Time already spent in custody awaiting trial should be deducted from the sentence.

When the proposed punishments were read out, the reporter for *Deutsche Zeitung* detected a current of emotion running through the audience. The crowd seemed particularly upset about the idea of confining Ludendorff in a fortress. This was not likely to happen, many newspapers predicted. "Class justice" reigned in Munich, reminded *L'Humanité*.

To the *Vorwärts* reporter in the courtroom, Stenglein seemed to be balking at prosecuting the defendants. Stenglein's voice struck the foreign correspondent of *L'Humanité* as gloomy and "as little convincing as possible"—that is, when he was not paying tribute to the men on trial. The *Daily Telegraph* concluded that his speech contained "as many compliments as condemnations." The prosecutor seemed to show more conviction and enthusiasm when he spoke of "extenuating circumstances" than about the crime of high treason itself.

Many people were indeed appalled by the closing statement and the proposed punishment. They did justice neither to the crime nor to the memory of the victims. The suggested penalty seemed, as *Le Matin* put it, token and a mere formality—and yet another sign that Germans were living in what *Berliner Volks-Zeitung* called "good times for traitors."

. . .

AFTER NEITHARDT RECESSED the court, Roder received almost four hours to put the finishing touches on his defense of Adolf Hitler. Roder's closing argument, estimated at three and a half hours in length, would pack a rhetorical punch.

"Six years ago today, the great spring offensive began," Roder opened, referring to the German attack at the end of the First World War. Most of the defendants had risked their lives in this struggle for "Germany's greatness, freedom, and honor." Today these veterans were waging a different battle, Roder said, this one "for their own personal honor." The same noble sentiments of patriotism and duty that drove these men into the trenches of the western front led them into the dock in Munich, charged with treason.

The weapon in the current battle would be what Roder called the most powerful and worthy one at their command: the Truth. But this was not a fair fight. The defendants faced the superior force of the Bavarian authorities, who cast them into jail to await trial and then proceeded to tarnish their reputations. Kahr's regime had censored official newspapers, suppressed the nationalist papers, and, either directly or indirectly, disseminated the authorized version of the events in propagandistic pamphlets and memoranda.

The lawyer shifted gears, speaking again as much to the gallery as the bench:

> Gentlemen of the court, you have heard Hitler speak repeatedly the last few weeks. You have looked into his soul. You have learned from his speeches that he is not a cowardly and untrustworthy man, but someone who speaks the truth with the most brutal lack of consideration for his own interests. He has concealed nothing.

His client had readily "admitted his guilt and taken responsibility," Roder said, as he stressed the importance of context. Hitler was standing up to the economic turmoil, the French invasion of the Ruhr, and the repeated humiliations of their country at the hands of the international community. Germany was threatened to be torn apart. Enemies at home, meanwhile, stirred. Berlin seemed powerless. Respectable citizens across the country began to feel an "immeasurable bitterness" at this regime.

"What happened here," Roder said of the beer hall putsch, "can only be understood from these conditions."

In fact, if there was a crime of high treason, Roder went on, it did not happen on November 8, 1923. It took place weeks earlier, in a series of meetings, intrigues, and plots spun in the highest circles of Bavarian government by none other than Kahr, Lossow, and Seisser.

Now his client Hitler—portrayed as a pawn in "the struggle of the men in Munich against the government ministers in Berlin"—was taking the fall. This was absurd, Roder argued, and, to add insult to injury, the Bavarian leaders had been called as witnesses to his guilt. They should not appear in court in any other capacity than as accomplices, or more exactly, as the "principal offenders" who had launched the struggle that led to Hitler and his codefendants being prosecuted for high treason.

At this point, Neithardt objected.

Roder went on attacking the credibility of the Bavarian triumvirate. He retraced the events at the Bürgerbräu, from the banquet hall to the back room, emphasizing the harmony between the authorities and the defendants. Then, after pledging their word and sealing it with a handshake, the Bavarian leaders set about their cold betrayal, prompting Roder to read out a passage from Machiavelli's *The Prince* on the cunning ruler who exploits the appearance of honesty to his advantage.

As for the march to the city center, it was no act of aggression. It was a desperate, last-minute attempt to prevent the German patriotic movement from collapsing from acts of betrayal. The leaders made no attempt to warn the defendants of their change of heart, Roder said; in fact, they had actively prevented it when they detained Hitler's messengers. So young men, filled with patriotic sentiment, marched in a peaceful procession to the Odeonsplatz, singing "Deutschland über Alles" as authorities shot them down. No surprise, then, that frustrated and embittered German citizens blamed the leaders for this tragedy and accused them of murder.

Neithardt stopped him again, ordering him to refrain from such "provocative and rabble-rousing remarks."

As it was already past seven o'clock that night, Roder moved toward his conclusion. "Here was a man," he said, referring to his client, Hitler, "who put his strength, his mind and his hand to use for a cause that he believed was right." He and his colleagues had, in short, collaborated with Kahr, Lossow, and Seisser. There was nothing in the criminal code that suggested that obeying Bavaria's highest civil and military authorities was a crime.

The stakes in this trial were enormous, Roder said.

> You are allowing a man, who has stood up with every fiber of his being for the German people, the German state, and German Greatness, to keep on doing so. This motion means that you will return this man to his work . . . He is the one who will liberate future forces; he will lead the way to further growth and prosperity of our great German fatherland.

"My good gentlemen," Roder urged, "acquit Herr Hitler."

47.

FROM MUNICH TO VALHALLA

When German Republicans have nightmares nowadays, they
dream they are in Bavaria.
        —THOMAS R. YBARRA, *New York Times*

On March 22, the twentieth day of the trial, defense attorney Alfred Holl presented the summation for Dr. Weber. In another strongly nationalist speech that drew applause from a rowdy audience, Holl traced the roots of the beer hall putsch back to the "so-called Treaty of Versailles." This infamous document, as he put it, enshrined the "biggest lie" of world history when it blamed Germany alone for the war and saddled it with penalties unparalleled in "sadistic malice."

The patriots in the dock, by standing up to the ambitious Berlin politicians who signed this treaty and sold out Germany, had hoped to reverse the depressing postwar saga of "cowardice and corruption." This was a goal shared by millions of Germans. "If that is high treason," Holl said, "then the prisoners' box must be lengthened by several kilometers!"

The judge stopped him, refusing to allow the words "cowardice and corruption."

"I am at a loss for any other expression," Holl said. "In any case, it captures the feeling of all Germans."

Minutes later, Holl resumed his attack on the Weimar Republic as born in "treason and perjury" and lacking any shred of legitimacy. No one objected, either, when he assailed its constitution as unconstitutional. As for the bloodbath at the Odeonsplatz, Holl said many people in the street were understandably wondering, "What kind of a Fatherland . . . orders its nationally minded youth to be shot at?"

Several international reporters listened with astonishment. "Bavaria is the bête noire of Germany," Thomas R. Ybarra wrote in his next piece for the *New York Times*. The city of Munich, as evidenced by the reactions in the gallery, was rampant with anti-Republican sympathies tantamount to high treason.

After Holl finished his speech, Judge Neithardt called for a thirty-minute recess. Four defense attorneys asked for more time to craft their final arguments. When the judge refused, Roder claimed it was necessary because three of the defendants were ill (Pöhner, Frick, and Röhm). The judge accepted this reason, adjourning the court for two days.

Munich police, in the meantime, picked up warnings of a riot should Ludendorff and Hitler be pronounced guilty. Planned vacations for the Bavarian military and state police were canceled, and security around the Blutenburgstrasse was increased. The verdict was expected within the week.

OVER THE NEXT few days, the court would hear closing arguments from twelve defense lawyers. Many of these speeches were long, tedious, and repetitive, and focused on defendants other than Hitler and Ludendorff. For the first time in weeks, there were several empty seats in the gallery.

Even some of the defendants were absent. Wilhelm Brückner and Lieutenant Colonel Kriebel were excused from the proceedings because of a supposed sickness. On Tuesday, March 25, Hitler would join them because he was said to be exhausted. The Meistersinger of the trial probably had to go lubricate his throat, mocked the *Münchener Post*.

The defendants found it strenuous to participate in court proceedings for ten hours a day, Roder complained, as if that had been the norm.

Perhaps the judge could relieve some of the strain by giving a longer midday recess.

"Or the pleadings of the defense could be shortened!" Neithardt said, to the amusement of the tribunal.

One of the recurring themes in the closing statements was once again the alleged failure of the Weimar Republic. Another was the treason of the Bavarian leaders. If the court wished to reach a just verdict, Schramm argued, it would have to punish Kahr, Lossow, and Seisser, as well as all the defendants, or none of them. If it opted to prosecute, it would then, in the interests of fairness, have to indict several thousand other people at the beer hall. It was ridiculous to single out his client, Ernst Röhm, for a guilty verdict. He was compared to a putsch supporter whose assistance that night consisted of pouring hot coffee.

Schramm then added another challenge to the prosecution's stance. Citing a precedent back to the supreme court in 1916, the lawyer argued:

> If legislation no longer corresponds with the feelings of the people, it has become obsolete, and the legislator has neglected his responsibility . . . In such a case, it is the noblest task of the judge to interpret the law in a way that mitigates against the sense of injustice.

This trial was the epitome of such a case, Schramm said. He urged the judges to listen to German public opinion, with its unanimous and indignant rejection of these charges.

Karl Kohl was scheduled to give the final defense counsel summation of the trial. Wading through a number of Latin maxims, emotional appeals, and legal wrangling, the outspoken and unrestrained advocate presented the putsch as an alliance of men of action, like Hitler, Ludendorff, and the codefendants, and men who failed to keep their word, like Kahr, Lossow, and Seisser. The defense counsel summed up one extreme perspective in provocative terms: "For the majority of the German people, the Weimar Constitution means nothing other than dynamite for the blasting of the German Reich!"

There was, strikingly, no objection from the bench or the prosecution.

Kohl ended the talk by making a reference to old Teutonic legends in Richard Wagner's operas. Hitler was a "second Siegfried of the new Germany, the man who slays the Marxist dragon and frees the German worker from Marxist syphilis." Now he had to fight for his honor and freedom. Given the overwhelming evidence in favor of the defendants, Kohl said, he would neither beg nor plead for a verdict of innocence. He would demand it.

ON THE MORNING of March 27, 1924, journalists and ticket holders alike arrived early in the former dining hall of the officer academy, hoping to beat the crowds pouring in for the twenty-fourth and final regular session of the dramatic trial. The prosecution and defense counsel had made their closing statements. The defendants would be given the opportunity to take the stand, as per German law, to say anything they wished to add before the tribunal went into deliberation.

Lieutenant Colonel Kriebel stood to make the first statement.

Given his military background, he explained, he had opted for a tactful defense, carefully avoiding any leak of sensitive material that might endanger national security. He stood by his own record, even if much of it could only be cited in closed session, and took full responsibility for his actions on November 8–9, 1923.

Pöhner followed, framing the entire debate around the issue that he first raised on the stand—namely, the legitimacy of the government and its laws, or lack thereof, since 1918. Ironically, he criticized the prosecutors for trying to sensationalize his case and refused to admit that he had committed high treason. He would never act in any way against the genuine authority of the king, the ardent monarchist added, blatantly insulting the republic.

The real treason, Pöhner argued, had occurred with the overthrow of the kaiser and the establishment of the republic by what he called a pack of "Jews, deserters, and paid traitors to the German people." These men had no legitimate authority, he spewed, because they were an "alien race" who had deceived the people and usurped power. Pöhner drew

laughter from the audience on a couple of occasions by derisively referring to the president of Germany as "Fritz."

Pöhner's close ally, Dr. Frick, spoke next, still claiming to have ful-
filled all his obligations at police headquarters the night of the putsch
and averted a catastrophe. Like Kriebel, he boasted that he would not
change a thing and awaited with confidence the judgment of the court.
Weber also emphasized that he and his colleagues had coordinated their
actions with the legal authorities of Bavaria. He realized that he was
making strong accusations against the leaders, but that was unfortunately the only conclusion he could reach. These were, he said, shameful
criminals who had stabbed Germany from the back during "its struggle
for existence."

One of the most prominent proponents for this "stab-in-the-back"
theory, General Ludendorff, spoke next, claiming that he would add
nothing to the statements of his distinguished colleagues and counsel.
He proceeded instead to give a brief history lesson. He reminded the
court that he was respected for "grand battles and brilliant campaigns"
as well as for predictions of national catastrophes. He now wished to
sound the alarm again, calling for every patriotic German to support
the movement of the nationalistic far right because, in his view, it alone
could save Germany from its distress.

General Ludendorff painted a dismal portrait of the ramifications for
the country should this movement not succeed: "We will be lost—lost
forever!" Germany would suffer a fate worse than the humiliating and
shameful Treaty of Versailles. He urged the court to heed his warning
and "hear the cry of the German soul for freedom." The defendants
must be acquitted.

Ultimately, though, it did not matter what verdict Neithardt's court
rendered, Ludendorff said. "World history will not send men who serve
their Fatherland to prison; it will send these men instead to Valhalla,"
the hall of slain heroes in Norse mythology.

This unusual claim made headlines around the world. "Ludendorff
Exalts Himself with Gods," headlined the *New York Times*. At the
same time, its correspondent, Thomas R. Ybarra, praised the general's
talk for having "a ring of dignity and eloquence." Unlike his previous

appearances on the stand, the general had dispensed with the "laborious attempts to whitewash himself and blacken everybody else." The short, somewhat hesitant and stumbling talk, he added, elicited "a tremendous ovation" from the Munich courtroom.

Ludendorff sat down and his colleagues, Röhm, Brückner, Wagner, and Pernet would all decline the right to make a final address to the court. This gave the last word to defendant Adolf Hitler.

48.

FINAL WORDS

It goes without saying that I am less interested in being acquitted by you [the court] than in being exonerated in the eyes of all my comrades!

—ADOLF HITLER

When Hitler had appeared in the room earlier that morning, the audience had reacted with extraordinary enthusiasm, the men standing to attention and several women waving handkerchiefs. For most of the talk, the *New York Times* correspondent Thomas R. Ybarra observed, Hitler "poured out a torrent of eloquence," much of it "uttered at the top of his lungs."

This was the speech, more than one hour in length, that remains one of the most underrated of Hitler's career, capping a four-week media bonanza in which he had taken an increasingly prominent role in the proceedings and its coverage. Hitler began by touching on some issues already mentioned, though laying them out in even more starkly black-and-white images.

Weimar was founded on "a crime of high treason," Hitler asserted, continuing the assault on the republic. He then heaped praise on his adopted country under the kaiser. Before the war, Germany had boasted an army and civil service that stood as the envy of the world. Twenty-six states had struggled for four and a half years to defeat it, and this large international coalition did not succeed until the very end, when the country collapsed, or as he explained it, the army had been betrayed by "a stab in the back."

It was at this point that the revolution erupted with its Socialist leaders promising "a life of pleasure, beauty, and dignity in abundance and less work than before." What a sad disappointment, Hitler jeered. The German people, now starving and homeless, had been "driven into the streets in despair." When the government lost patience, the so-called people's representatives ordered the Reichswehr to whip and even fire upon the people. The masses had nowhere to go. The middle classes had been wiped out. A lifetime of savings had disappeared into wheelbarrows of worthless paper.

As the country suffered one catastrophe after another, the leaders of the republic remained subservient to the Allied powers and preached the virtues of the Versailles Treaty.

They promised world peace, but what did Germany get: "A world peace over fields of our dead bodies!"

They promised disarmament, but it was the disarmament of Germany alone so that it could be plundered easier. The other countries remained armed to the teeth.

What about the right of self-determination? "Yes, a right of self-determination for every black tribe!" Hitler fumed. But 17 million Germans had been transferred to other countries against their will and were now ruled by foreign governments.

And the promised League of Nations? It was a league that guarantees only the corrupt peace treaty, not a body that would produce "a better world for the future."

Hitler then attacked Germany's so-called people's regime, which did not dare ask what the people really thought—and selected a president who was himself opposed by the majority of its population. In short, in the last five years of the Weimar Republic, a great deal had been "snatched away from the German nation." They had become "outcasts of this world" and the government in Berlin merely an "executive body for our outside tyrants."

Now, after such a bitter legacy, this so-called government was daring to haul "German heroes of old into court, in chains . . . heroes, who have done nothing other than fight for their fatherland." He cited an author he had been reading in prison, Clausewitz, who noted how a heroic people would prefer to perish in an honorable struggle rather than voluntarily accept disgrace.

Hitler turned to the prosecutor's closing statement bemoaning the decline of state authority and respect for the law. But who was responsible for creating and maintaining that authority? The state that had been built by German monarchs, Hitler said, answering the question himself, with another hat tip to the royalists he courted. This work was continued over time, particularly under leaders such as Frederick the Great and Otto von Bismarck, until the efforts collapsed in the treason at the end of the war.

This lack of leadership among the revolutionaries who ended up in power both reflected and in part caused the decline of the country and the eradication of respect for the law. The German people saw how the legal system did not treat everyone equally. Many citizens went hungry, no matter how hard and long they worked, while a small group of people profited obscenely at their expense. It was difficult to avoid the conclusion that the laws were not uniformly applied. There was something fundamentally wrong, Hitler said, when such a system catches "the small-time thief, while the great assassins of our people go undetected!"

No wonder such a state of degradation prevailed, he exclaimed, when the supreme law of the land had become the Versailles Peace Treaty. This document proscribing "immorality in 440 articles" had caused citizens, who had obeyed the law all their life suddenly to become unruly or even criminal. The real criminals, meanwhile, controlled the government, even though they had destroyed the German currency and ruined the economy.

Respect for the law would only return when Germany overcame this catastrophe—when a prosecutor, Hitler said, thumping the table, would stand up in court and accuse the president of Germany, Friedrich Ebert, and his companions of "high treason and . . . of destroying a nation of 70 million people!"

At this statement, Judge Neithardt finally interrupted the defendant.

Hitler went on spelling out the necessary conditions under which respect for the law would return. One of the most provocative prerequisites was his assertion that a prosecutor of the future would have to restore "the inner harmony between his duty and his human sentiments." This meant prevailing over the current situation, where every prosecutor stood "at odds with himself," having to choose between being "a lawyer or a human being." It is striking that neither Neithardt nor anyone else in the room objected to these assertions.

Hitler shifted gears onto the postwar world, where Germany was only a pawn in the chessboard of diplomacy. Foreign powers may have seized their weapons, but they would never destroy their spirit of resistance. Hitler was determined, no matter what, he said, to drum up patriotism, and he did not care if this meant igniting hatred against enemies who had surrounded and infested the country. He spoke in particular of the Marxists and what he called "the racial tuberculosis of the people in the international Jews."

It was such enemies, Hitler added, who had heckled and attacked him in beer halls, calling him all sorts of names like "reactionary, warmonger, murderer and mass murderer." One thing he was not, however, was a demagogue. If he had been, he told the court that he could have taken an easier road to success. "Believe me, I would also have been received in the other camp with open arms!" Was this curious, little-noticed statement a reference to his work in early 1919 as a supporter of the Socialist regime?

Now almost shouting, Hitler ranted on about how he had not acted out of ambition or opportunism, unlike many politicians he knew. For him, he said, it was about a sense of duty. He criticized General von Lossow again, when the Bavarian war minister said that Hitler "only wanted to be a propagandist and alarmist of the people."

> How petty small people think! Gentlemen of the court, rest assured that I do not view the achievement of a ministerial position as worth striving for.

He had a goal "a thousand times greater than becoming a minister": He would be the drummer of the people and "the shatterer of Marxism."

He mocked the pretensions of the ambitious seekers of honors, preferring to follow in the footsteps of his favorite composer, Richard Wagner, who had refused to put any title on his tombstone.

Unlike Kahr, who had been thrust out of his league, Hitler said he was doing what he personally had to do. It was all about one's calling, and he had found his, even if it now sounded far more ambitious than he had just claimed:

> I take the view that, just as a bird must sing because it is a bird, so must the man born for politics enter politics, whether he is in prison, in a dungeon, or in freedom; whether he sits in a silk chair or he must settle for a hard bench. He is born to it . . . and the destiny of his people will stir him from early morning until late at night.

Likewise, he argued: "Anyone who is a born dictator will not have to be 'urged,' but wants it himself; he won't be pressed forward, but presses himself forward." That, moreover, is his duty.

The defendant reaffirmed the goals for the national revolution, which did not oppose the republic, he claimed. It only went against its "ignominious content." That is, he wanted to reform this regime, create order in the national budget, toss out the slackers, and launch the real struggle against "the enslavement by the international stock market" and "the cartelization of our entire economy." He had also hoped to remove the "iron shackles of outside enemies" and restore the right and duty of Germans to serve their country in arms.

Were these objectives, Hitler asked, high treason?

Hitler made two final requests to the court. First, he wanted to assume all responsibility for the actions of his men, who had only followed his orders with the unquestioned obedience that the party demanded. Second, if the court wished to pronounce him guilty, he asked it to overlook Article 9 of the Law for the Protection of the Republic that required foreigners convicted of treason to be deported.

This appeal was not for his sake, he claimed, but for the shame and humiliation that history would later attach to such a wretched decision.

After reminding the court yet again of his services to Germany during the war and his eagerness to repeat these contributions, Hitler disputed Stenglein's remark that the beer hall putsch had been a failure:

> It would have been unsuccessful if only one mother had come to me and said, 'Herr Hitler, my child has fallen and you have him on your conscience. But I can assure you that no mother has come. On the contrary, ten—ten thousand others—have joined our ranks.

"The hour will come when the masses who are now on the streets with our swastika . . . will unite with those who, on November 8, made a stand against them." How happy he had been to learn that it was the state police who fired on his men, not the army, as their disgrace would have been too much to bear.

The judge finally objected at this charge of "defilement" against the state police.

Hitler ignored him. "The army which we have trained up grows faster from day to day and hour to hour, and we nurture the proud hope that these fierce hordes will become battalions, the battalions again to regiments and then to divisions. The old cockade will be retrieved from the dirt and the old flags will flutter again." Several people in the audience were moved to tears.

Hitler's rhetoric aimed to seduce his targeted audience: the rural and royalists, the students and veterans; the disgruntled and the alienated; people who hated the Versailles Treaty; the middle classes who had been devastated in the hyperinflation; workers, craftsmen, and artisans continuing to struggle in the class system still reeling from the economic plight; people looking for something or someone to blame for their anger and resentment.

Hitler was also, in the process, painting an alternative vision of the future—one that centered on a restoration of German power and reputation, served by him, once again in the pose of the drummer or, more exactly, for those who listened closely to his words, leader of the people. He had carefully avoided Ludendorff's mistakes in the courtroom, particularly the general's critiques of Catholics. Instead, Hitler honed his message for his intended audience, which by now had expanded well beyond the beer halls and the courtroom in Munich.

Looking straight at the presiding judge, Hitler closed what was arguably one of the most important talks of his career:

> Even if you pronounce us guilty a thousand times, the eternal goddess of the eternal court [of history] will smilingly tear up the proposition of the prosecutor and the verdict of the court; *she* will acquit us!

With this, Hitler sat down. The courtroom was now silent.

"The trial is concluded," announced presiding judge Georg Neithardt.

As the tumultuous last day of the four-week trial closed, the audience cheered the defendants with a thunderous ovation. Some people surged forward, eager to shake hands with them after what *Le Matin* called the unabashed triumph of Adolf Hitler.

The verdict would not be read until 10:00 a.m. on April 1, 1924, which was five days away. Until then, the public had little to do but wait—that is, wait, speculate, and as *Das Bayerische Vaterland* suggested in classic Munich style, perhaps drink a good beer.

49.

ENDINGS AND BEGINNINGS

If Germany cages in a man, like Hitler, whom the prosecutor had called honest, brave, and selfless, then you have to believe scoundrels [are in control] . . . I believe England would be happy to have Hitler and Ludendorff.
—A BRITISH WOMAN, IN AN OPEN LETTER TO STENGLEIN, *Grossdeutsche Zeitung*

All weekend, discussions raged in cafés, shops, and beer halls about what the *Miesbacher Anzeiger* had already dubbed the most significant political trial in the history of Munich. The popular cabaret performer Weiss Ferdl celebrated the defendants before a massive crowd at the Hofbräuhaus: Hitler and his colleagues "courageously . . . confess their deed; they've nothing to conceal. Tell me, what have they done wrong? Can it really be a crime to try to save one's fatherland from disgrace and despair?"

By the end of the trial, Hitler had radiated an enormous confidence, firmly convinced of his own historical importance. *Vorwärts* saw this "measureless hubris" as evidence that Hitler was nothing less than a psychopath. *Frankfurter Zeitung* focused more on the effects of his speech on the crowd, marveling at how this simple, half-educated "virtuoso of rhetoric" whipped the crowds to a frenzy and "moved thousands to tears." Along the way, he hit every note on the scale: outrage, pain, indignation, enthusiasm. There was nothing subtle about this man or his speeches.

For Charles Bonnefon in *L'Écho de Paris*, the Hitler trial had seemed straight out of the fourteenth century. Rival chieftains, each commanding a private army, stalked the land in "the struggle of everyone against everyone": There were Hitler and Ludendorff; Kahr and the Bavarian authorities; President Ebert and his cabinet; General von Seeckt and the German Army. Were they witnessing the "apotheosis of the feudal age?"

The foreign correspondent for Philadelphia's *Public Ledger* preferred a different image, calling this Munich's own "Alice in Wonderland" trial. The entire cast, from Hitler "the would-be Mussolini" to Kahr the "ex-dictator," seemed like the queen and the pack of cards in the Lewis Carroll novel: "collapsible when not taken seriously."

But it was essential to take these men and their actions seriously, the *Vancouver Sun* had advised. If the tribunal wanted the Munich court to regain respect, it had to deal firmly with the Prussian general, the "Austrian scene painter," and their ragtag band of misguided, hate-filled cronies. A young republic like Germany should "avoid prosecution for high treason as long as possible," but once it initiated the process, its justice system "must carry [it] through energetically." This was especially true of this republic whose legitimacy was questioned by a large number of brash, outspoken opponents.

If there was ever a case so clear-cut, then surely it must be this one, *Vorwärts* concluded. The defendants had confessed—even boasted—of their own guilt. Yet given the course of the proceedings under Judge Neithardt, who could say with certainty that these men would receive a guilty verdict?

Only Hitler would be punished, it was widely predicted, and this was because of his theatrical defiance of Berlin, Bavaria, and the Entente. Robert Murphy at the US consulate, for one, thought Hitler would receive a prison sentence and then, as required by law, be deported to

Austria. His friend Eugenio Pacelli, the nuncio for the Vatican and future Pope Pius XII, agreed. At the least, it seemed, Hitler would not be making problems for quite some time.

GIVEN THE POLARIZING nature of the proceedings, authorities feared the outbreak of demonstrations, brawls, or even riots at the announcement of the verdict. That week, certain newspapers on both the left and far right, like the Socialist *Münchener Post* and the extremist *Grossdeutsche Zeitung*, had been banned from publishing. Munich authorities had also outlawed the distribution of any political pamphlet, poster, handbill, or even a printed notice of the verdict.

On one hand, the police were pleased that the announcement of the tribunal's decision would not take place over the weekend when, thanks to increased leisure time, the size of the crowds would be larger and the risks for trouble magnified. On the other hand, the reading of the verdict had been moved to another date that might prove problematic: It was to take place the same day as the birthday of nationalist icon Otto von Bismarck.

That weekend, informers tipped off police about a riot being plotted at the Augustinerbräu, and a telegram arrived from Augsburg warning the presiding judge that the Nazis would most emphatically refuse to accept any guilty verdict. Hate mail had poured in from as far away as the United States, calling Stenglein "a pathetic bastard." There were even death threats to his deputy, Hans Ehard. In this overheated atmosphere, authorities decided not to take any chances.

On Monday March 31, several leaders of the police met at the library of the headquarters at Ettstrasse to plan the strategy for controlling the final session of the trial. Emphasis was placed on minimalizing the opportunities for disturbances or, if they broke out, stifling them immediately. The police were to show no toleration whatsoever of protests or applause. Large gatherings were to be prevented around Blutenburgstrasse, and a close watch placed on railroad stations for arrivals in Munich.

The Reichswehr was put on high alert and reinforcements were called in from neighboring towns in Bavaria. Guards were also posted at key sites around Munich, in fear of a possible attack, including the French consulate, the residences of government officials, and above all, the homes of Judge Neithardt, the tribunal, and the prosecutors.

THE VERDICT IN the trial would, of course, be final. There was no appeal in the People's Court. *Time* magazine, then in its first year of publication, recapped the proceedings for the benefit of its readers, summing up the arguments Hitler and his codefendants made for why "they should not be decapitated, hung, or otherwise extinguished for high treason":

> They say in effect, "We were not the only ones [who committed the crime]. The highest Bavarian officials were in the plot, but got out when they thought it would fail. One of them was Kahr, another Lossow, etc. So there!"

Despite the jocular tone, the reporter admitted that he found this argument credible.

In fact, the number of people compromised in the beer hall conspiracy was believed to be so high that, *L'Intransigeant* reported, the Bavarian Ministry of Justice did not know what to do. Rumors swirled of deals behind the scenes to ensure the acquittal of Ludendorff, Hitler, and the other defendants.

As for the triumvirate, they had fled Munich before the end of the trial. Some said they went to Italy and others to Corfu, Greece, or Switzerland. At any rate, few were surprised. The Bavarian leaders had shown themselves to be small men, *Allgemeine Rundschau* said. Rather than take responsibility for their actions, they had preferred to hide behind official secrecy and seek shelter in loopholes of the law. Did not their flight from Munich confirm their guilt, or cowardice, or both?

It was hardly a surprise, either, that the court had allowed the Bavarian leaders to leave the country when investigations of their own alleged treasonous activities were pending. Neithardt had been quicker to protect Kahr, Lossow, or Seisser than he had the constitution.

No trial in recent memory had been quite like this one, *Bayerischer Kurier* concluded. Its main defendant had acted like "a man possessed," *Vorwärts* added. The Berlin reporter related a conversation overheard at the trial when a man in the audience had praised Hitler as a master speaker who strode forth like a colossus of classical antiquity. This defendant could, if he wished, the man added, "cause a world to collapse."

So as Hitler was emerging from the debacle of the putsch more powerful than ever, the question for the court remained: Would he be at the end, or the beginning, of his career?

50.

NOMEN EST OMEN

If I had to conduct this trial again, I would not lead it one iota differently than how it happened.

—GEORG NEITHARDT

On Tuesday morning, April 1, 1924, the courtroom on the second floor of the former military academy was so crowded that even members of the audience with legitimate admission cards were turned away. Journalists, likewise, struggled to find a seat in their own reserved section. In the gallery sat government officials, military officers, and, it was often noted, a great number of women. Everyone was waiting for the verdict, the correspondent for *Berliner Tageblatt* said, with "breathless excitement."

The atmosphere in the courtroom resembled an opera gala or a fashionable theatrical premiere. Hitler was likened to the star of the performance, or perhaps even a saint. The foreign correspondent for the *Daily Telegraph* heard a couple of women in the audience expressing their desire to bathe in Hitler's bathtub.

As large flower bouquets for the defendants piled up in the guardroom, they had assembled for a photograph in the rear courtyard of the building. Hitler appeared in his dark suit underneath his pressed trench coat, and clasped his hat in his right hand. The other man in a suit was Dr. Frick.

The rest of the defendants donned military uniforms adorned with an array of crosses, medals, cordons, and other insignia of the country's highest honors. General Ludendorff wore the German uniform that he had sworn never to put on again. One defendant missing from the shot was Ernst Pöhner, who was allowed to skip the announcement of the verdict, given his gastrointestinal illness.

Would these decorated defendants now be punished for committing high treason against the state? Controversial too was the appearance of Dr. Friedrich Weber. He sported a dress sword and the blue cap of the banned Bund Oberland. Wearing this attire was yet another show of contempt at the law of the German republic, though Judge Neithardt would make no objection when he saw Weber.

The first of the trial participants to take his seat in the front was the brash defense lawyer Karl Kohl. At ten a.m., or shortly thereafter, the defendants entered the room, Ludendorff in front, followed by Hitler, and the entourage of lawyers. The prosecutors came immediately afterward.

At five minutes after ten, Judge Neithardt and the tribunal took their seats in the large leather chairs at the long wooden table. Neithardt looked grave and nervous. After five weeks of high anticipation, the verdict was read with little fanfare.

Hitler, the judge began loudly and slowly, was pronounced guilty of high treason. Stirring and murmurs of disapproval emanated from the gallery, as did cries of "Unacceptable!" and "Scandalous!" Outside the building, beyond the barbed-wire blockades, a large crowd had gathered, despite official orders to the contrary. These people would soon shout and curse when the news arrived from reporters rushing out to file their stories.

Three of Hitler's codefendants received the same verdict: Weber, Kriebel, and Pöhner. The punishment would be five years in prison and a small fine, though the sentence was reduced for time already served since the arrest, which, in Hitler's case, meant a reduction of four months and two weeks.

For defendants convicted of high treason, Article 81 of the German penal code required lifelong imprisonment in a penitentiary or a fortress prison. The Munich court, however, had invoked extenuating circumstances that permitted the sentencing of five to fifteen years, and opted for the absolute minimum penalty. It then interpreted the law in such a way that Hitler and his fellow conspirators would be eligible for parole after only six months.

Five of the other defendants—Brückner, Röhm, Pernet, Wagner, and Frick—were ruled guilty of the lesser charge of aiding and abetting high treason. Although each man would technically receive one year and three months' imprisonment, the judge deducted the time already spent in prison since their arrest and struck the remainder of their sentences in favor of probation. So, in other words, if they stayed out of trouble until April 1, 1928, these five defendants would never have to spend another day in prison.

As for General Ludendorff, he was acquitted of all charges.

"Bravo!" was shouted from the audience.

"Heil Ludendorff!"

There was applause.

Neithardt spent the rest of the short morning session, per German legal procedure, providing the justification for the verdict. The triumvirate at the center of the trial may or may not have been involved in the putsch, the presiding judge read. It did not matter. They were not on trial at this time. "The only question to be decided is the guilt or innocence of the defendants."

Hitler, Kriebel, and Weber had conceived the plan of the beer hall putsch, the court had determined. Pöhner was added to this list of plotters because he went along with the scheme and accepted a position in the new regime. The fact that Ludendorff also accepted a position, however, was not addressed.

Neithardt explained that the court believed the general had come to the beer hall convinced that he was acting in support of Gustav von Kahr's government, though this same justification had not exonerated the other defendants. This reasoning also contradicted Ludendorff's first statements on the subject. Neithardt then, incredulously, concluded that Ludendorff had not realized that he was committing high treason:

A whole range of eyewitnesses have testified that Ludendorff was so moved on the platform that he hardly paid
attention to the events around him.

The tribunal interpreted the events in the backroom in a similarly
unlikely fashion, concluding that Ludendorff might have thought he
was going along with Kahr's regime, though this left the question unanswered why, if that were the case, the general had spent so much time
persuading Kahr to accept a position in a government that he was supposed to be leading.

As for the other defendants, found guilty of high treason, or attempting to change the constitution by the use of physical force, as set out in
Articles 81 and 82 of the Criminal Code, Neithardt explained why the
tribunal decided to consider extenuating circumstances: The defendants
had acted in a "purely patriotic spirit . . . [with] the noblest, unselfish
motives." What's more, they believed that they had the consent of the
Bavarian authorities.

So despite the risks of the enterprise, including a possible civil war
and foreign invasion, Neithardt concluded that the minimum sentence
sufficed for this crime. After all, the law against treason seemed to him
to be quite unsparing. This viewpoint had not previously stopped him
or other judges of the Weimar Republic from issuing harsher sentences
against left-wing conspirators.

In a recent treason trial before the People's Court, for example, the
left-wing Jewish journalist Felix Fechenbach was sentenced to eleven
years in prison with hard labor. He also lost his rights as a citizen for
ten years. Two of his codefendants, Sigismund Gargas and Karl Heinz
Lembke, received twelve and ten years in prison respectively. Verdicts
with such bias in favor of radical right-wing defendants prompted the
German historian Karl Dietrich Bracher to call the Weimar justice system "the wellspring of the Third Reich."

German nationalists were thrilled with the outcome, at least with
regard to General Ludendorff, Captain Röhm, and the several other
defendants who would walk out of the courtroom as free men. Bavaria's *München-Augsburger Abendzeitung* and Berlin's *Deutsche Zeitung*

praised the court for reaching a decision that all right-thinking, patriotic Germans wanted. Berlin's *Lokal-Anzeiger* called the judgment
Solomon-esque.

Deutsche Tageszeitung likewise celebrated the verdict from both a
legal and sentimental point of view, emphasizing the "noble motives"
of the defendants. Hitler and his supporters had reacted against foreign
oppression and the swelling up of national patriotism. The court had
spared Germany from the miserable spectacle of sending "its greatest soldier" to prison, *Deutsche Allgemeine Zeitung* wrote. The principal critique was the ruling on Hitler and his closest colleagues, which
Kreuz-Zeitung called simply harsh.

Many people were, of course, horrified at this verdict. From beginning to end, Berlin's *Die Zeit* summed up the whole affair—the beer hall
setting, its almost slapstick bumbling, and its ridiculous punishment—as
a purely Bavarian phenomenon that itself could not be construed as anything but high treason. Had Hitler and comrades never appeared before
court, *Köln Volkszeitung* said, the damage to the state would have been
less than it was after Neithardt's verdict. April 1, 1924 would forever
mark a "black day" for Bavarian and German legal history.

Nomen est omen! Did not the day's moniker—April Fool's—foretell
all? Berlin's *Vorwärts* called the outcome a disgraceful joke. "The verdict
in the Munich high treason trial is a farce and a mockery," *Frankfurter
Zeitung* concluded, and Zurich's *Neue Zürcher Zeitung* made a point of
reminding its readers that this embarrassing verdict was no hoax, but
actually "Munich justice." It was, *Le Petit Parisien* wrote, a "comedy of
justice" without precedence.

Blood had been spilled, human lives had been lost, and the legal, constitutional regime of the republic had been attacked, *Berliner Tageblatt*
reminded. Yet the defendants stood up in court and praised their actions,
swearing to repeat them if necessary. And these included five members
of the military, a high-ranking police official, and a judge. Reactionaries
may celebrate, *Das Bild* said, but republicans could only cover themselves
in "shame and sorrow." Was not high treason against the government
and its constitution, the London *Times* asked, a crime worthy of more
than six months in prison?

Outside of the far-right nationalist and racist press, criticism of this judgment was scathing indeed. Munich's *Allgemeine Zeitung* noted that the verdict on Ludendorff only made sense if the court judged the general innocent by virtue of his senility or feebleness of mind. Did not his incoherent babblings on the stand lend credence to this explanation?

It was simply ludicrous, *Augsburger Postzeitung* observed, to imagine that the commander of the German armed forces in the First World War could have been so overtaken by the confusion of events in a Munich beer hall not to realize that he had bungled into an act of high treason. The anarchy of the trial at Munich reflected what *Vossische Zeitung* called the "political mess of Bavaria." What was to become of Germany?

Germania hazarded a guess. The people who tried to overthrow the republic were going to be walking out of the building and likely go back to the beer halls to plan a more effective assault. The verdict seemed like a veritable invitation for other extreme right-wing sympathizers to commit high treason. This was no minor "miscarriage of justice," *Vorwärts* wrote, but a judicial catastrophe that threatened the legitimacy and the security of the state.

Alfred Oulman, writing in *Le Petit Bleu*, feared additional consequences. He implored the international community and France in particular to be more vigilant than ever before. They should, he urged, pounce at the first sign of German aggression or movement across the borders of its neighbors.

GIVEN THE SENTENCING and the early eligibility for parole, one police detective later calculated on the back of a piece of scrap paper that Hitler and his fellow convicted traitors might well escape nine-tenths of their already lenient punishment.

Why had Hitler received such a light sentence? What role had Neithardt's sympathies for the defendants played? Had Hitler been offered a deal in return for his cooperation not to expose *in public session* the full extent of the Bavarian government's actions against both the Weimar Republic and the Versailles Treaty? It is certainly not out of the question (and Hitler's codefendant Ernst Röhm did claim that he had been approached with a vague offer if he agreed to show what he called a "reasonable reserve" in the courtroom). The distinguished Weimar lawyer Max Hirschberg concluded that the verdict in the trial, particularly in the case of Ludendorff, showed that it was a pre-arranged affair: "Never before had Justice, even in Bavaria, revealed itself so shamelessly as the whore of fascism."

But the perversion of justice wasn't over. Article 9, paragraph 2 of the Law for the Protection of the Republic mandated that foreigners convicted of high treason, after serving their time, be deported from Germany. Neithardt, however, chose to ignore this law. He explained his reasoning:

> Hitler is a German-Austrian [!] He considers himself to be a German . . . [He] thinks and feels like a German. He voluntarily served for four and a half years in the German Army, and by his outstanding bravery before the enemy, earned high-ranking war decorations. He was wounded and damaged his health.

As a result, the judge ruled that mandatory expulsion would serve no purpose in this case. Hitler would be allowed to remain in Germany. This interpretation was, as jurists then and later noted, a clear violation of the law.

Loud bravos emanated from the gallery.

Hitler must have been relieved. He would soon renounce his Austrian citizenship so that, should he face legal difficulties again, he could not be deported. Hitler would in fact be stateless until he became a German citizen in the summer of 1932—only six months before he came to power.*

The defendants who were free on parole were requested to stay in the

---

* Despite Hitler's denials, there was apparently a short-lived plan among his advisers to arrange a marriage to a German woman to gain citizenship and prevent another threat of deportation.

courtroom until all the reporters and spectators had left. At 11:10 a.m., Neithardt was ready to close the trial.

At this point, the morning went from absurd to bizarre. General Ludendorff stood and started protesting his own acquittal. He wanted to join his colleagues in their punishment, calling the verdict "a disgrace, which this uniform and these decorations did not deserve!"

"Heil Ludendorff!" shouted several people in the gallery. "Heil Hitler!"

Neithardt gaveled, trying to call Ludendorff to order over what the reporter for Agence Havas described as a "storm of applause." Several correspondents noted that the presiding judge looked genuinely confused at this outburst. It took some time for him to gain control of the courtroom. Neithardt ordered the police to identify the hecklers, so he could sentence them to three days in jail. The policemen, apparently not exerting much effort, could not find them.

As Neithardt tried to clear the courtroom, an official approached General Ludendorff requesting that he leave by a side exit to an automobile waiting in the courtyard. The hope was clearly to avoid a scene in the front of the building, where the crowds were growing. They had already started shouting "Heil Hitler!" and singing nationalist anthems.

Ludendorff—his face "blood red" with anger, noted a *Berliner Volks-Zeitung* reporter—refused to leave through the side door and haughtily challenged the official to arrest him. The presiding judge ordered the general to comply, but again this had no effect.

"I am a free man now," Ludendorff said, ignoring authorities.

The general pushed through the corridors, now filled with spectators cheering the defendants, and he exited by the front door to what the *New York Times* correspondent Thomas R. Ybarra called "a wild ovation." The crowds outside, despite the warnings of the police, pressed forward to the barricades. Ludendorff's wife waited in the vehicle, which was now covered with flowers tossed by "the throngs of his delighted admirers." On the hood of the automobile was a small black, white, and red German imperial flag.

Along the road from the Infantry School, people cheered the

nationalists, while shouting, "Down with the republic!" Others waved handkerchiefs from windows and yelled abuse at Kahr, Lossow, and Seisser. The mob was becoming increasingly unruly. In the northwestern part of the city, a few injuries were reported when the mounted police charged at protesters with their rubber-coated truncheons.

Hitler had, in the meantime, been escorted to a room on the second floor, where he was to await transport to prison. He walked up to the window, smiled, and waved to the crowd, which then erupted into a frenzy of applause.

PART III

PRISON

51.

CAESAR IN CELL 7

In the welter of German politics, there is no saying what strange, perhaps unexpected figure, or figures will emerge into prominence.
—*The Saturday Review*, MARCH 22, 1924

That afternoon, Munich police transported Hitler back to the fortress wing of Landsberg Prison. A laurel wreath with black-white-red ribbons soon hung on the whitewashed wall of the second-floor common room as a potent reminder of his victory in Neithardt's courtroom.

The name and image of Adolf Hitler would mean something different in the spring of 1924 than it had just six months earlier. A book published about Hitler that year summed up the change in his reputation among a growing segment of the population. Georg Schott's *Das Volksbuch vom Hitler* celebrated the defendant as nothing less than a prophet, a genius, a man of humility, a man of will, an awakener, and leader of German youth. The language was sometimes nearly mystical in its frightening veneration of the new nationalist hero.

Hitler had also won support in much higher circles than he was accustomed to. On May 8, 1924, two Nobel Prize winners in physics, Philipp Lenard and Johannes Stark, wrote an article in *Grossdeutsche Zeitung* expressing their admiration. Just as the scientists honored Galileo,

Kepler, Newton, and the great illuminators of the past, the physicists wrote, "We marvel and honor in the same way also Hitler, Ludendorff, Pöhner and their comrades." These men had stood before the court as "God's gifts from the distant past when races were purer, people were greater, and minds less deceived." Both Nobel laureates planned, from now on, to follow Germany's "man of the people."

Fresh from the trial, the banned Nazis, regrouped under the banner of the "Völkisch Block," won big in the spring elections. Three of the defendants—Ludendorff, Röhm, and Frick—ran for the Reichstag and they were all elected. In all, thirty-two of the thirty-four candidates of the former National Socialists and their fellow extremists won seats. In the Bavarian Landtag vote just five days after the trial, the right-wing block fared even better, receiving no less than 17 percent of the vote in the region and the support of an estimated one-third of the population in Munich. This was by far the strongest performance the extreme right would show until the Nazi "breakthrough election" of 1930.

Hitler's speeches at the trial, thanks to the indulgence of Neithardt and the detailed reporting in the media, had won him far more recognition than he had ever received before. His popularity, a Munich police report concluded, had "only increased by [the defendants'] conviction and their quasi-martyrdom."

The forced seclusion of prison would, likewise, serve Hitler far better than it would Germany or the world. Not only would Hitler have time to reflect on his successes and mistakes in the putsch and his career— something he rarely showed any great talent for or inclination to do—he would also enjoy the fawning admiration of his supporters. These fellow prisoners would flatter his vanity, feed his ambitions, and contribute in many other ways to the National Socialist echo chamber dangerously emerging at Landsberg. All of this would take place behind the high walls of the fortress, safe from the risk of opposition or contradiction from the outside world.

Hitler had been punished with fortress detention, the mildest form of incarceration in the penal system. His prison number was changed— now that he had been convicted—to 21, and he moved into the large

Cell 7. It was spacious and bright, with a view of the garden and, beyond the surrounding twenty-foot-high stone wall, the expanse of the countryside and a distant road where cars zoomed by. Hitler, an automobile enthusiast, would soon be daydreaming about vehicles and highways.

Lieutenant Colonel Kriebel occupied neighboring Cell 8 to the right, and Dr. Weber the smaller one nearby at 9. Other prisoners at Landsberg would call this collection of units "the commander's wing."

Two other prisoners also moved into this section. The first was Emil Maurice, convicted in a separate trial for his role in the putsch. The second was Rudolf Hess, who, after hearing about the lenient verdicts doled out, had turned himself in to Munich police on May 12. The People's Court, on the last day before it finally expired, ruled Hess guilty of high treason and sent him to share the same fate as Hitler.

Landsberg would undoubtedly afford Hitler the most comfortable lifestyle that he had thus far experienced. He settled down into a routine marked by considerable privilege. At six in the morning, when the prison guards changed shifts, Hitler's cell door was unlocked and he was allowed to roam the wing.

Fellow prisoners served him breakfast at seven in the common room, where there was a table for six, usually with a white tablecloth. A few feet away were an iron stove, a double sink, and a simple mirror on the wall. A couple of wicker chairs were placed in a corner. After breakfast, which was often coffee, bread, and oatmeal with butter and marmalade available for purchase, other prisoners carried away the dishes. These were the *Kalfaktoren*, or prisoners from the main penitentiary, who counted themselves fortunate for this job. They would tidy the rooms, make the beds, shine shoes, and clean up after meals, finishing off whatever food or drink remained.

At 8:00 a.m., Hitler and his circle of fortress inmates were allowed use of the prison's parallel bars, vaulting horse, and other gymnastics equipment. The slim and athletic Dr. Weber sometimes served as coach and instructor. The prisoners could also race, wrestle, practice jiu jitsu, and perform calisthenics—and they competed in everything from foot races to stone- and club-tossing. Rudolf Hess lost no time, upon his arrival at

Landsberg, winning a reputation as one of the better athletes in these prison games. In one such contest, the prize was a leather-bound edition of Norse sagas with an inscription from Adolf Hitler.

There were also opportunities to box. An amateur boxer in Cell 2, Edmund Schneider of the Stosstrupp Hitler, had convinced the Landsberg Prison staff to provide him with a sack of sand as a makeshift punching bag. He then taught the art of boxing to the prisoners. In one match, Hitler's chauffeur, the experienced brawler Emil Maurice of Cell 6, and another member of the Stosstrupp Hitler, Hermann Fobke of Cell 11, nearly beat each other senseless. Prisoner Hans Kallenbach said he had rarely, if ever, seen Hitler laugh so much. After that bout, Hitler was said to limit the combat sports to wrestling, though this still sent the inmates limping back to the infirmary.

Hitler usually refrained from participating in the training and competitions himself, remaining a spectator, or at times, according to the prison warden, a referee of the matches. Shoulder injury aside, it is doubtful that Hitler would have joined his fellow prisoners for long. He was not interested in strenuous physical activity and apparently believed that a leader could only lose the respect of his supporters in such competitions.

After the morning exercise, Hitler and the Landsberg prisoners had access to the fortress library and garden. Some of the inmates would play cards, board games, or gamble away their snacks, cigars, or cigarettes. Lieutenant Colonel Kriebel, when he was not playing chess, liked to work in the garden, striding across the grounds in overalls and a wide straw hat like "a Brazilian coffee planter." Hess sometimes chopped wood, trying to balance his time, he wrote home, between being a "worker of the brain" and a "worker of the fist."

Hitler preferred to walk the nearly two-hundred-meter-long gravel lane between the buildings and the wall. This path, one of two in the area, led past bushes, spring flowers, fruit trees, and the garden, which he could see from his window above. Hitler walked often in the company of Emil Maurice or Rudolf Hess. This was soon dubbed "the Hitler Path."

At eleven a.m., mail was distributed, and, for Hitler, the letters and packages arrived en masse. Each item received at the prison was brought to the duty room and spread over the large table. For seemingly innocent goods like clothes, the stitching was supposed to be examined, and for bread, cakes, or wurst, a guard would cut a slice to make sure it did not conceal any messages, weapons, or tools that might aid an escape. In practice, this control was no doubt lax.

The guard Hemmrich described how the prisoners opened the packages. Lieutenant Colonel Kriebel "attacked" the wrapping like a commander concentrating his forces on the strongest point of the enemy, that is, the most resilient string. Weber, by contrast, approached the package like a puzzle, untangling "every blessed knot with the utmost care and patience." Hitler remained in between the extremes, supposedly varying his method, depending on the parcel and its sender.

The highlight of the day, of course, centered on the main meal, which was served at midday in the common room. Fellow prisoners remained standing behind their chairs until someone signaled Hitler's arrival by shouting "Attention!" Hitler then made his way to the head of the table, shaking hands and greeting every person. Adorning the wall behind them was a blood-red swastika banner that had been smuggled into the prison. The prisoners hid it under a tub, if they heard a guard coming. The staff looked the other way because the show of party insignia violated Landsberg ordinances.

After the meal, the prisoners of the main penitentiary again removed the dishes. Hitler and his circle were free to smoke, using the old cigarette cartons as ashtrays. A nonsmoker, Hitler preferred fruit and cakes. The chats ended abruptly when Hitler rose from his chair and returned to his cell to read or answer correspondence. He also drew. He sketched imaginary museums honoring the First World War; he drafted architectural plans for a theater, national library, and university; he designed stage sets for several Wagner operas, Puccini's *Turandot*, and Shakespeare's *Julius Caesar*.

During the early afternoon, some prisoners read, napped, or played cards or other games. Around four thirty p.m., after an afternoon tea or coffee, the prisoners would again have access to the garden. Supper was served at six in individual cells, often wurst or pickled herring, with boiled potatoes or potato salad, along with a half liter of wine or beer available for purchase. This small ration, prisoner Hans Kallenbach said, inflicted the hard drinkers with Tantalus-like tortures, even as the administration found a way to increase the daily limit in return for work in the prison garden or on the grounds.

Finally the fortress inmates enjoyed another hour of exercise with races, slingshot contests, and ball games, and then the chance to chat again in the evening over tea or ersatz cocoa, often with cakes or pastries. Lieutenant Colonel Kriebel, or "Papa Kriebel" as the younger prisoners called him, often spoke of his days in China during the Boxer Rebellion; others reminisced about their experiences during the First World War or in the Freikorps fighting the Communists. Hitler would sometimes give a speech. Sympathetic jailers and guards were said to listen in and soon, too, salute the prisoner with the words "Heil Hitler!"

Such a schedule afforded considerable amounts of free time. In Cell 11 on the ground floor, the twenty-four-year-old law student from Stettin, Hermann Fobke, turned the quarters into the "Thalia Tea Room." Fobke would arrange another service for the inmates: Cell 11 also became a publishing house of the "secret" prison newspaper, the *Landsberger Ehrenbürger*. The title was a pun on their type of imprisonment that could also mean both "Landsberg Honorary Citizen" as well as "Freeman."

The guards probably knew of this newspaper long before the censor supposedly discovered the venture in September 1924 by reading a letter in which an inmate, Emil Danneberg, had mentioned it. All copies of the paper were believed to have been destroyed, though at least one complete issue survives: No. 6, August 4, 1924, a special edition that commemorates the ten-year anniversary of the First World War. In this issue, Kriebel wrote about the mobilization of his company; Weber described a mountainous forest attack in the Vosges with his "snowshoe battalion." Rudolf Hess composed a poem on the slaughter at Verdun.

Generally, the style of the paper was said to have been informal, with jokes, riddles, reviews, and news items of the day. There were also caricatures of fellow prisoners and prison staff with attached verses. Hitler often wrote the lead article or added a drawing. One such copy survives: Hitler satirizing Dr. Weber's overzealous exercise instruction. His students stand up as best they can, with arms in slings, bandages around heads, and supporting themselves on crutches. The prisoners' newspaper aimed to appear in time for the Saturday-evening gatherings in the common room.

Lights went out at ten o'clock, though Hitler would soon receive an extension. The evening usually ended with a round of "Sieg Heil" and the singing of nationalist songs. They might also be accompanied by the prison band. One member of the Stosstrupp Hitler played the violin, another the lute, and others the harmonica, harp, and a raucous makeshift Stumpf fiddle with bells and tin cans attached onto the handle of a broom.

"You see," prisoner Hermann Fobke wrote to a friend in June 1924, "[life at Landsberg] is quite bearable."

52.

FACE-TO-FACE

A political stronghold for Nazi desperadoes.
—*Münchener Post*, ON LANDSBERG, NOVEMBER 5, 1924

Before the trial, Hitler had complained that he received very few visitors at Landsberg. This was certainly not the case afterward. A steady stream of guests beat down the path to the fortress, where, after verifying their identity, they stopped by the warden's office to fill out the *Sprechkarte*, listing their name, the prisoner they wished to see, and the date of visit. The warden, Otto Leybold, or his deputy, specified a length of time and signed the pass. The visitor was then escorted to one of the visitation rooms on the second floor.

Some of the first arrivals were, of course, old associates like Max Amann, or defendants at the trial, like Captain Röhm, Dr. Frick, and Wilhelm Brückner, all of whom had traveled together for a one-hour talk on the morning of April 10. Other veterans of the putsch and party came early and often: Alfred Rosenberg, Ulrich Graf, Julius Streicher, Hermann Esser, Anton Drexler, and Ernst "Putzi" Hanfstaengl, the latter appearing on April 11, the first of his five visits.

Putzi's little boy, Egon, who followed along on one of those outings, had imagined that Landsberg would be a dungeon with Hitler in chains, sleeping on the dirt and surrounded by rats. Instead, he found a clean and bright cell with a view of the garden. Other than that, what Egon remembered most was Hitler's voice, which, in one impassioned rant, had caused the table in the room to vibrate.

Visiting hours usually spanned from nine to noon, and from two to five in the afternoon. On some days, Hitler went from one person to the next. After Ludendorff left from his first visit on April 12, for instance, Hitler saw seven other people, including his lawyer, Lorenz Roder; fellow defendant Heinz Pernct; putsch veteran Max Sesselmann; and his photographer Heinrich Hoffmann, the latter bearing a basket of fruit as well as his trusty camera.

It was on this occasion that Hoffmann snapped a series of pictures about life behind the walls of Landsberg. One of these showed Hitler wearing lederhosen and posing with a newspaper. Another captured Hitler, Kriebel, Weber, and Emil Maurice, the latter with lute in hand, sitting around a small table adorned with a vase of flowers. These photographs—no doubt taken with the complicity of prison authorities—came to symbolize the leniency of Landsberg.

Although there is a great deal of truth to his image, it is important to remember that the primary reason for the prison's "indulgence" stemmed more from the type of sentence Hitler received at the trial (that is, fortress confinement) than any special treatment out of sympathy for Hitler himself. That is not to say that Landsberg warden Otto Leybold or his staff did not have extreme right-wing beliefs, as many of them did.

Indeed, the adulation that the prisoners, guests, and eventually the members of the prison staff came to show Hitler was no exaggeration. Ernst Röhm, who visited Hitler for the second time on May 1, left shaking his head in dismay at what Ludendorff called the "flatterers and Byzantines" who fawned upon the prisoner like a demigod. Kurt Lüdecke, who signed in three days later, however, imagined that the experience would prove a good one for Hitler. The inmate had retained the look of a "fire eater" in his eyes and yet, Lüdecke thought, unquestionably "appeared calmer and more certain of himself."

In all, 350 men, women, and children would visit Hitler at Landsberg, clocking in well over 450 visits. Prison guard Otto Lurker summed up the arrivals as representing "every class, every age, every condition." From the Alps to the sandy Baltic coasts, the visitors were said to have come by train, motorcar, and bicycle. Several came from Austria and Czechoslovakia. A young couple had even walked from northern Germany.

Landsberg records, however, show less regional diversity of the visitors than the guard remembered. No less than eight-tenths of the visitors came from Bavaria, with half of these from Munich. Only twenty-seven people were known to have come from Prussia, nine of these from Berlin. Many places did not have a single visitor. This included Schleswig-Holstein, a future bastion of Nazi support, as well as East Prussia, where its Junkers and landlords had long served as a stronghold for the German far right.

All of this highlights the fact that, despite the recent gains at the trial, the Nazi Party remained a predominantly regional organization. Still, this was changing. On October 23, 1924, the Leipzig publisher F. A. Brockhaus wrote to Landsberg to request information about Hitler for the upcoming, fifteenth edition of the renowned encyclopedia. Volume eight for the letter *H*, completed in 1931, would contain for the first time entries for both "Hitler, Adolf" and the "Hitlerputsch." The latter article described how Hitler had won back the party after his failed putsch.

The Landsberg warden was correct, however, about the wide range of occupations of the visitors to Hitler. There were professors, physicians, zoologists, engineers, architects, writers, reporters, and teachers, as well as bankers, bakers, bookkeepers, and students, in addition to military personnel and officers of the state police. In the first two months in confinement, Hitler also saw a composer, an organist, a singer, a piano technician, an antiquarian book dealer, a textile manufacturer, along with several mechanics and locksmiths. Business owners came who sold everything from hair products to hardware goods, typewriters to tombstones.

Hitler must have been particularly pleased with a visitor on the afternoon of Sunday, May 11. It was his fellow dispatch runner from the 16th Infantry Regiment, Ernst Schmidt, who had also served with him briefly after the war in everything from guard duty to testing gas masks. Hitler's wartime colleague was then working in interior design in the Bavarian village of Garching, east of Munich. The warden allotted only a ten-minute session, which was the most frequent time duration permitted for visitors during Hitler's confinement at Landsberg.

Another familiar face was Bruno Büchner, the former bicycle racer and pilot who owned one of Hitler's favorite inns in the Obersalzburg. Hitler had stayed there just a few months before the putsch, gushing about the beautiful mountainous landscape on rainy days. Other guests had remembered Hitler, under the pseudonym "Herr Wolff," cracking his ubiquitous dog whip and ranting about Berlin's "Jewish materialism." Büchner arrived for a visit on April 17 with his young wife, Elisabeth.

Many people, then and later, have commented on Hitler's effect on women, and anecdotal evidence has long suggested that women had flocked to Landsberg. So it is surprising how few women actually came to see him. The records show a total of fifty-seven female visitors, or less than one-sixth of the total. Yet even this figure is boosted by Hitler's sister, Angela; his niece Geli; his neighbor Marie Bechtold; and his landlady, Maria Reichert, who brought along her eleven-year-old daughter Antonie. Did Frau Reichert come to remind him of his rent? This was probably at least one reason for the visit of another woman to Landsberg, Babette Grau, the owner of the property on Corneliusstrasse where the Nazi Party rented its offices.

This relatively low number of women visitors also includes Kreszenzia Hechenberger, whose son Anton was killed on the march to the Odeonsplatz. The prison records, unfortunately, provide no details of their ten-minute visit on April 30, or whether she might contradict or support Hitler's boast at the trial that no mother had come forward to blame him for the loss of her child during the putsch.

Among the other female visitors, several of them had a closer connection to one of Hitler's men than they did Hitler: Scheubner-Richter's widow, Mathilde; Ludendorff's mistress and future wife, Mathilde von Kemnitz; Lorenz Roder's wife, Elisabeth; Hermann Esser's wife, Therese; and Hermann Göring's wife, Carin. The latter came on April 15, hoping to gain financial support for her and her husband. She left instead with a signed photograph of Hitler.

But despite this small number of women visitors to Hitler in Landsberg, some of them would play a significant role in Hitler's life. In addition to Geli, whom Hitler had supposedly given a full kiss on the mouth, if the prison governor is to be believed, one of the most influential of all the visitors would be Helene Bechstein, the wife of the prominent piano manufacturer who had nearly spirited him to Austria before his arrest.

On her first visit to Landsberg, May 15, Bechstein had thrown a tantrum when the gift she brought Hitler had to pass inspection. She tore open the package herself, sending the exquisite pralines cascading onto the prison floor. Perhaps the guards could find a machine gun hidden there, she screamed. Other visits would be less memorable for the staff, but there would be twelve in all, each one lasting at least one hour. Bechstein would clock in a total of eighteen hours and twenty-five minutes of face time, making her the visitor who spent the most time with Hitler. On two occasions, she brought her sixteen-year-old daughter, Lotte. That was enough to feed the rumor mills that she was grooming Hitler as her future son-in-law.

Bechstein's social rival, Elsa Bruckmann, a Romanian princess who married the publisher Hugo Bruckmann, was another Landsberg visitor who would later play a role in Hitler's life. She had hosted an iconic literary salon that, since the late nineteenth century, had attracted everyone from Nietzsche to Thomas Mann, Rainer Maria Rilke to Hugo von Hofmannsthal. It was at Landsberg that she would meet Hitler for the first time—and her eight-minute visit on May 22, 1924, would set her on a path to becoming one of Hitler's invaluable patrons as he made his climb to power.

Hitler was blunter about the importance of Bechstein and Bruckmann. Without women like these, Hitler was said to have stated, it would not have been possible to rebuild his party in the years after Landsberg.

HITLER's FAN MAIL was also accumulating in the office of the Landsberg censor. Three days after the verdict, a letter arrived from members of the "Aryan Bund" in Magdeburg. These men wanted to express the "pain and anger" that they felt at hearing the court's decision, which they compared to "a punch to the face." The extremists rhapsodized about

Hitler so much that prison authorities decided to withhold the letter. But there would be plenty of other communications expressing similar sentiments that made it through.

Someone gave Hitler a copy of the Swedish anti-Semitic paper *Vidi* so that he could read for himself the favorable reviews that his speeches at the trial had elicited. This paper particularly praised him for thundering at his Jewish enemies. His closing statement was, the paper concluded, "a masterpiece of power and logical astuteness." As for the rest of the proceedings, they had shown the "enormous villainy, deceit, and unscrupulousness of the dishonorable Judas-Iscariot trio of Kahr, Lossow, and Seisser."

Landsberg prisoners could, thanks to the privileges of fortress confinement, use their own money to buy supplies or arrange for services, like laundry. According to his expense reports, Hitler purchased mostly butter, eggs, potatoes, lemons, sugar, vanilla, coffee, spaghetti, macaroni, vermicelli, salad oil, vinegar essence, onions, and on at least one occasion, preserved meat (Rotti Suppenwürfel). Neighbor Emil Maurice in Cell 6 put his budding cooking skills to work for Hitler and the men in the "commander's wing."

Most surprising was perhaps one of Hitler's biggest purchases: It was beer. In July 1924, Hitler purchased no fewer than thirty bottles of beer and several bottles of spirits. The numbers did not drop off in the autumn either, with forty-eight bottles of beer charged to his account in August and sixty in September.

Packages arriving by mail or by guests would supplement these purchases, and in Hitler's case, they would range from fruit to flowers, books to brandy. Some visitors came with breads, pies, sausages, snacks, schnapps and liqueurs, and coffee beans from South America. There were the sourest pickles and sweetest cakes, as Hess put it. Other people brought fine art prints. Helene Bechstein gave them a gramophone player and probably also a number of records for the budding library: waltzes, military marches, Schubert's "Du bist die Ruh," and Richard Wagner's "Schmerzen."

On April 20, the day of Hitler's thirty-fifth birthday and Easter Sunday that year, the Landsberg prisoner entertained twenty-one people in twelve different visits. A veritable "flood of cards, letters, and telegrams" poured into the prison, as guard Otto Lurker recalled, along with a "forest of flowers" and a "mountain of packages." The letters alone were carted in with the help of laundry baskets, his colleague Franz Hemmrich said. All the cakes, cookies, chocolates, and other presents were said to have been stacked on tables and chairs, spilling over into another room. Hanfstaengl, visiting Landsberg two days later, compared Hitler's cell to a delicatessen. The prison guard Hemmrich was reminded of a flower shop, or a greenhouse.

The abundance of gifts, of course, allowed Hitler to shower them on fellow prisoners or prison guards, often on birthdays or anniversaries, which certainly did not hurt his relationship with the staff.

At first, Landsberg's Prisoner 21 relished this newfound celebrity. By the early summer, however, the visits had become so time-consuming and burdensome that Hitler let it be known that he wished them to be curtailed. He had, by this time, other matters on his mind.

53.

LIES, STUPIDITY, AND COWARDICE

The rulers of the day made a miscalculation in locking me up.
They would have been far wiser to let me make speeches all
the time, without giving me any respite!
—ADOLF HITLER, JULY 27–28, 1941

D espite the popularity from the trial and the victories for the radical
right-wing parties in recent elections, the National Socialists lan-
guished as a banned and suppressed party on the verge of unraveling.
Alfred Rosenberg, the designated leader of the party, communicated
with the loyal core by using the alias "Rolf Eidhalt." This was an anagram of the name Adolf Hitler and the last name meant roughly "Keep
the Oath."

The Nazis were operating clandestinely in the guise of various hunting, hiking, sporting, and singing clubs. Yet it was not the pursuit of
authorities that challenged the party the most. It was instead the tensions
and divisions within the underground organization itself.

There was a split between old party members who had remained in
Munich under Rosenberg and those who had fled abroad—many of them,
like Esser and Hanfstaengl, to Salzburg. There were those who wanted
to merge with other legal right-wing parties and those who wanted to
break away into splinter groups; those who wanted more nationalism,

those more socialism; those who pressed to achieve their goals with revolutionary violence and those who wanted to wage a campaign for parliamentary elections as a political party; those who wanted to destroy the republic and those who sought to preserve the social status quo against a threat from the left that, in their eyes, seemed more dangerous. And on it went.

As these disputes festered, Hitler remained vague and aloof, refusing to take sides. By the middle of June 1924, Hitler was telling his supporters that, until he could participate fully in the realm of politics, he was going to withdraw. He forbade the use of his name by any faction.

Nor, for that matter, were they to visit him in prison or forward along any political communications. He spread the news of this request in letters written by himself and his new "secretary," Hermann Fobke. "I have decided to withdraw from overt politics," Hitler wrote on June 16, 1924, until he could regain his freedom and become again what he called "a real leader." He stressed the word *real*.

Three weeks later, on July 7, Hitler confirmed this stance in public. He had, as the *Völkischer Kurier* reported, "resigned the leadership of the National Socialist movement." He was being overwhelmed, he said, and he was, frustratingly, limited by what he could accomplish as long as he remained behind prison walls. He also claimed to suffer from a "general overwork," and needed to concentrate on his latest project, which was going to be a "comprehensive book" outlining his autobiography and politics. He asked for privacy.

According to Landsberg records, Hitler had had at least one visitor every day in May and nearly every day in June. The number had slowed from April's nearly 200 visits (from 160 people) to only 92 visits (62 people) in June. By July, the number of visits had dwindled to 26, or less than one a day. Still, this was too many for Hitler. On July 29, he repeated his request to be left alone.

Hitler was also worried about fellow defendant Ernst Röhm, who, since his release at the trial, had been busy uniting the members of the banned Storm Troopers and their banned Kampfbund allies into a new organization called the Frontbann. He would soon have 30,000 members. Hitler opposed this development for many reasons, not least the leverage such a centralized and potentially powerful body would give to its leader, who was already showing more independence and even an unwillingness to affiliate with any single political party.

When Röhm visited Landsberg on June 17, 1924, Hitler told him to stop this work immediately. Röhm ignored him and went on building up his Frontbann. He also recruited a new leader: General Ludendorff.

By the early summer, Hitler had received access to a second room at Landsberg, which was strewn with stacks of books, magazines, newspapers, and papers, scattered helter-skelter. Most of these items had been gifts. Other works had been borrowed from fellow prisoner Hermann Fobke, who was using his time of incarceration to finish his law thesis. Hitler was taking the opportunity, as he wrote in a letter of May 1924, to "read and also learn."

By this time, Hitler was already deep in his writing project. On May 12, 1924, when a delegation of Nazis visited from Salzburg, Hitler was at work on his planned political manifesto. One of the visitors, Hans Prodinger, spoke of the project as offering "a thorough reckoning" against his opponents—the words "A Reckoning" would later serve as the book's subtitle. By the end of the month, Hitler had a title: *Four and a Half Years of Struggle Against Lies, Stupidity, and Cowardice*.

A promotional brochure appeared in June 1924 announcing Hitler's upcoming work of an estimated four hundred pages. Its contents were supposed to include an autobiographical discourse on his entrance into politics, the rise of the Nazi movement, and the inside account of the beer hall putsch. It also promised to treat various issues, such as "The Middle Class and the Social Question," "Judaism and Marxism," "Who started the Revolution?" "Crime or Stupidity?" "The Bolshevikization of Europe," and a plan for how this could be stopped. In time, as he worked on the draft, the ideological rants would come to overshadow the settling of accounts with his enemies of the putsch, which had probably most attracted the publisher.

Many people would later claim credit for suggesting that Hitler write what would eventually become the Nazi Party's canonical ideological treatise. Otto Strasser said that it was his brother Gregor, a veteran of the Landshut Storm Troopers, who first encouraged Hitler to put his thoughts on paper, because he was tired of being subjected to endless, repetitive speeches and he wanted to return to his card games. This is pure fiction. Strasser was not interned at Landsberg until February 4, 1924, and he remained there at the same time as Hitler for only twelve days, when the latter was transported to Munich for his trial. This short period was also two months *after* Hitler had already told the assistant state prosecutor, Hans Ehard, about his plans to write a memoir.

No more credible is the view that Hitler turned to the project as a way to avoid the squabbles among his subordinates and the necessity to take a stand. But Hitler had started writing well before he had withdrawn. The original plan for publication, after all, was July 1924.

A third view, however, has more plausibility. According to this theory, Hitler had turned to writing a book because he wanted to cash in on his newfound celebrity from the trial. Hitler could, no doubt, use any profits from the project to offset the court fines and legal fees, which were not small. (According to Lorenz Roder, the bill of 5,000 Reichsmarks would not be paid until 1934). But monetary compensation was clearly not the only, or even the main, reason.

As early as 1922, Hitler had thought of writing a book. The *Völkischer Beobachter* reported of such a plan, but at that time, Hitler had been too busy with his speeches and work with the party to make any progress. The confined space of the cell, by contrast, was ideal for focusing his energy, and the range of grievances from the putsch and trial left him with many grudges to settle.

"He occupies himself every day for many hours with the draft of his book," the warden of Landsberg, Otto Leybold, wrote in autumn 1924. The style of the manuscript resembled a speech—no surprise, perhaps, given that this was Hitler's preferred means of communication. His oratorical skills, however, did not transfer well from the beer hall onto the page.

Verbose, repetitive, and mired in long-winded digressions, filled with venomous hatred, Hitler's clumsy, bombastic text abounds in artificially constructed terms formed by piling nouns upon nouns and meanders through a thicket of dependent clauses. The journalist Dorothy Thompson described an overwrought style that read like "one long speech" bogged down with ghastly rants about people and races, and written in "inaccurate German and [with] unlimited self-satisfaction."

When Hitler discussed his hardships in Habsburg Vienna, for instance, he wrote: "He who has not himself been gripped in the clutches of this strangulating viper will never come to know its poisoned fangs." This single sentence, early biographer Rudolf Olden observed from exile in the 1930s, "contains more mistakes than one could correct in an entire essay. A viper has no clutches, and a snake which can coil itself around a human being has no poison fangs. Moreover, if a person is strangled by a snake, he never comes to know its fangs."

But there is another reason for the resemblance of Hitler's manuscript to a speech. Several key passages in *Mein Kampf*, or "My Struggle"—as the manuscript would be retitled in February 1925—were in fact derived from Hitler's speeches in Neithardt's courtroom. This was particularly the case for the autobiographical section. The three basic points Hitler made about his life in Vienna and the lessons he claimed to have learned there all appear in strikingly similar structure and style to his first speech at the trial.

This is also the case for some other comments about Marxism (chapter 7) as well as foreign policy in a closed session on February 28 and then again in his final speech. His rants on the British and French schemes for the "Balkanization" of Germany would anchor chapters 13 and 14 of the second volume of *Mein Kampf*.

For years, historians believed that Hitler had dictated the text to fellow inmates, first to Emil Maurice and then Rudolf Hess. Hess's then-fiancée and future wife, Ilse Pröhl, however, had long insisted that this was incorrect, and German historian Othmar Plöckinger has confirmed that in his pioneering studies of the text. After first writing out the manuscript by hand, Hitler switched, by early June 1924, to a typewriter, pecking it out himself with two fingers on a brand-new Remington portable, believed to have been a gift from Helene Bechstein.

The warden had provided a small varnished typewriter table and a large supply of paper. Winifred Wagner also sent Hitler paper, along with a package of pens, ink, erasers, and carbon paper. Someone else later brought him paper with the swastika—perhaps Nazi Party stationery that had survived the raid by the police. Additional privileges granted by the prison warden allowed Hitler, for a small fee, to keep his lights on for two extra hours. He was also up early in the morning, though this was not a habit for him, either before the putsch or later. Several prisoners recall hearing him type around five a.m.

After Hitler wrote a section of his manuscript, he sometimes took it to Rudolf Hess in Cell 5, and they discussed it over tea. On June 29, 1924, Hess wrote to his fiancée, Ilse, about Hitler's progress, which, by this point, had reached his accounts of the First World War, or chapter 5. Hitler, or "the tribune," as Hess called him, had read out the passage, slowing down and increasingly faltering, as he "made ever longer pauses" until finally dropping the page and sobbing.

By the end of the following month, Hitler had just finished writing his chapter on Vienna and his arrival to Munich. Hitler sat in the wicker chair in his corner of Hess's cell, reading what would become chapters 3 and 4 of *Mein Kampf*. Hess felt the blood rush through his veins—he felt enraptured and breathless, he said. Surprisingly, he thought the language was exquisite. He predicted that he was listening to Germany's "coming man."

With the stream of visitors slowing, Hitler progressed rapidly with his manuscript. By the first week of August, Hitler had asked Hess to proofread the expanding text. Then, after the private reading sessions, Hitler started repeating his performances on Saturday evenings to a larger group in the common room. These were the sessions that the prison guards remembered hearing from the staircase. The sounds of Hitler reading to his captive audience may have also inspired the legend that he dictated the text.

By August, Hitler believed he was only a week or two away from completing the manuscript. He had already asked Hess to help choose the most fitting color combinations for the cover and spine to adorn his planned luxury edition. August, however, came and went. Hitler then thought the book might be done in October, as did the Landsberg warden. Indeed the dedication at the front of the published book to the sixteen "martyrs of the putsch" is dated October 16, 1924.

But this autumn publication date would also prove to be premature. Worse than Hitler's underestimation of the amount of work ahead were the financial problems of the publisher, Franz Eher-Verlag, and the legal questions. As Hitler believed his release on parole was imminent, he did not want to jeopardize this fact. The hate-filled manuscript, outlining his plans for the future, contradicted on virtually every page his claim that he had withdrawn from politics.

Mein Kampf would not in fact be finished in the autumn of 1924, or even in prison at all. According to Emil Maurice, the manuscript was smuggled out of Landsberg hidden inside the wooden case of a gramophone player that had been donated by Helene Bechstein. For her services, Bechstein is believed to have received the original manuscript, or at least one of the typewritten versions. As for Maurice, he would receive the typewriter and one of the earliest printed luxury copies of the book, number 10, signed by the author, "To my loyal and brave shield bearer."

Hitler would finish writing the manuscript in April 1925 at Obersalzburg, where the 782-page tome was restructured and divided into two volumes. The music critic for *Völkischer Beobachter*, Josef Stolzing-Cerny, and Rudolf Hess's fiancée, Ilse Pröhl, did the lion's share of the editorial work. The first volume of *Mein Kampf* was published on July 18, 1925, by the party's Franz Eher-Verlag. The second volume appeared on December 11, 1926. By the end of the Second World War, the book had sold 12 million copies in eighteen languages.

54.

"A PERPETUAL DANGER"

*Germany against the entire world, and an entire world will
not force it down.*
                    —*Landsberger Ehrenbürger,*
                    PRISONER NEWSPAPER

Outside the prison walls, the republic seemed to be moving in the right direction. A new German currency had been introduced, finally ending the horror of hyperinflation. Foreign aid and investment had been pouring into the country. Unemployment dropped. The London Committee under American banker Charles G. Dawes hammered out a plan to reschedule Germany's reparations payments and reduce its short-term burdens. Weimar was on the verge of an explosion of cultural activity.

Hitler, in the meantime, hunkered down in his cell at Landsberg. Work on his book project and the confinements of prison were not the only reasons he remained outside the squabbling factions dividing his party. He was also on his best behavior. October 1, 1924—the earliest possible date for his parole—was nearing. Hitler believed that he would be freed on that date.

On September 13, Hitler wrote a letter to Jakob Werlin, a fellow Austrian and a car dealer at the Benz showroom on Schellingstrasse, adjacent to the offices where the Nazi newspaper *Völkischer Beobachter* had operated before its ban. Werlin had visited Hitler at Landsberg the previous day, arriving with Adolf Müller, the printer who would soon bring to press *Mein Kampf.* Now Hitler dashed out a follow-up letter to Werlin, which he planned to send with the help of one of the prison visitors, Lieutenant Colonel Kriebel's eighteen-year-old son, Wolfram. This was of course in clear violation of Landsberg regulations, which required mail to pass through the approval of the censor.

Hitler wanted a gray Benz touring car with a high-powered engine and wire wheels, preferably the model 11/40 or the 16/50. The only problem, Hitler added, was his finances. He did not expect to earn any royalties from his still-unpublished book until at least the middle of December (!), and his court costs and lawyer fees from the trial were enough, he said, to make his "hair stand on end." He asked the dealer for a discount on the automobile, and to keep one ready until he heard news of his fate, which he said would come soon.

As rumors of parole spread, the prisoners in the fortress fully expected the sentences to be reaching an end and began exchanging notes commemorating their time at Landsberg. "Nothing shall and will prevent us from collaborating on the deliverance of Germany from its inner and outer enemies," scrawled Wilhelm Briemann, a convicted member of the Stosstrupp Hitler on August 21, 1924, from his cell on the ground floor of B-Wing. Dr. Weber wrote to Captain Röhm, evading prison censors, about the hope for release "if only not in vain."

The main criteria for receiving parole would be "good conduct" in prison and an estimation of the courts that the internee had endeavored to make amends for the damages caused by his crimes. The warden of Landsberg, Otto Leybold, was supporting Hitler. Two weeks before the date, Leybold wrote a letter of recommendation, praising his famous prisoner for exemplary behavior:

> Hitler shows himself to be a man of order, of discipline, not only with regard to his own person, but also towards his fellow internees. He is contented, modest, and accommodating. He makes no demands, is quiet, reasonable, serious,

and without any abusiveness, scrupulously concerned to obey the confinements of the sentence. He is a man without personal vanity, is content with the catering of the institution, he does not smoke or drink, and, despite all comradeliness, knows how to command a certain authority with his fellow inmates.

Hitler was always polite toward guards and officials, Leybold added. He showed discretion with visitors, supposedly refraining from discussing politics and confining his correspondence mostly to thank-you notes.

Landsberg had, in short, helped rehabilitate Hitler, the warden argued, and the prisoner deserved to be released:

> During the ten months of his remand and sentence he has without doubt become more mature and quiet than he had been. He will not return to liberty with threats and thoughts of revenge against those in public office who oppose him and frustrated his plans in November 1923. He will be no agitator against the government, no enemy of other parties with a nationalist leaning. He emphasizes how convinced he is that a state cannot exist without firm internal order and firm government.

Ludwig Stenglein, however, disagreed. After a lackluster performance at the trial, Stenglein was working to keep Hitler behind bars. He never gave any indication of what caused the change, though he acted as if he had realized that he had made mistakes. Such a move may well have been prompted by his deputy, Hans Ehard, who had already shown himself to be a staunch opponent of Nazism. Ehard later called the verdict in the trial simply "a surrender of the constitutional government and . . . justice."

On September 23, 1924, the prosecutor filed the legal objection in hopes of preventing Hitler's release. The putsch had threatened both Bavaria and Germany with considerable dangers, Stenglein argued in the nine-page motion that had almost certainly been written by Ehard.

The prosecutors stressed the financial damages, the attacks on the police, the thefts at the printing press, the threat of a civil war, and, of course, the loss of life.

As evidenced by the long speeches at the trial, Hitler had clearly not changed his opinions. On the contrary, he had bragged about his crimes, promising to repeat them at the first opportunity. The implications were clear. If Hitler were released, Stenglein and Ehard warned, he would simply take up where he had left off in his plots against the state.

The prosecutors had the full support of the Munich police. On September 16, 1924, officers had searched the homes of former defendant Wilhelm Brückner and one of his colleagues. They found letters that had been smuggled out of Landsberg, and among them was the letter from Hitler that Wolfram Kriebel had been asked to mail.

The Landsberg prisoners had clearly been communicating with former fellow defendants at the trial, Ernst Röhm and Wilhelm Brückner, about the rebuilding of paramilitary societies under the umbrella organization of the Frontbann. All of this, in short, Stenglein and Ehard argued, confirmed what the Munich police now concluded: Hitler and the Landsberg prisoners posed "a perpetual danger to the internal and external security of the state."

This information was forwarded by special delivery to the criminal division of the Munich superior court. Its arrival was stamped at 12:10 p.m. on September 25, 1924. Earlier that morning, however, the court had already ruled in favor of parole. Hitler was going to be released on the first day of October, along with Kriebel and Weber. That is, unless the state prosecutor appealed, which was not likely, predicted *Allgemeine Zeitung.*

Yet that was exactly what Stenglein and Ehard did. Four days later, after a long weekend, Stenglein submitted another appeal, probably authored again by Ehard, to stave off the release of these prisoners.

To the surprise and great disappointment of Hitler's followers, this worked. The Bavarian court of appeals reversed the decision. Stenglein, Ehard, and the Munich police had managed to block Hitler's release, at least for the time being.

• • •

But the quest to free Hitler from prison was far from over. Supporters circulated a petition through Munich, Landsberg, and other parts of
Bavaria demanding his immediate release on parole. A couple thousand
people soon signed it. Page after page of signatories from almost every
occupation dramatically underscored the popularity Hitler had attained
in the aftermath of the trial.

By early October, the lawyers for Hitler, Kriebel, and Weber had each
appealed the court decision to deny parole for their clients. The three Landsberg prisoners had also signed a statement, attesting to Hitler's supposed
withdrawal from politics and citing his requests for privacy as evidence.
Further support for Hitler's case would come from an unexpected source.

Two of the lay judges at the trial, Philipp Herrmann and Leonhard
Beck, had admitted that they had only agreed to the "extraordinarily
difficult decision"—the guilty verdict!—because they believed that Hitler and his fellow defendants would be granted an early parole. What's
more, these lay judges, with their limited legal expertise (Herrmann was
an insurance salesman, Beck the owner of a stationery shop), had not
realized that the court's decision could be blocked upon appeal by the
prosecution. They wanted Hitler released, as they had assumed would
be the case.

Arguments raged from all sides until October 6, 1924, when the
Bavarian Supreme Court overturned the appeal and approved Hitler's
parole. This prompted Ludwig Stenglein and Hans Ehard, yet again, to
wage their own struggle against Hitler. Working day and night, Stenglein, or most likely Ehard, crafted another frantic, last-minute appeal
to prevent their release.

Clearly, the prosecution realized, even if it somehow succeeded in blocking Hitler's parole again, Stenglein and Ehard could not keep postponing
it indefinitely. Opting for a different strategy, they pressed for Hitler, in
the event of an early release, to be deported. By this time, both the Munich
police and the Bavarian state police had reached the same conclusion.

As early as March 26, 1924, on the eve of the verdict, the Munich
police had written to Austrian authorities to ask that, if a deportation

could be secured, would they be willing to receive Hitler. The state government of Linz had confirmed that it did in fact recognize the defendant's Austrian citizenship and his right of domicile in its city. Local Austrian authorities had been prepared to receive Hitler at Passau for the transfer across the border.

The problem was that, by the autumn, when the imminence of Hitler's parole drew closer, the Austrian government had changed its mind. Austrian chancellor Ignaz Seipel and the Christian Socialist cabinet now argued that the deportation of Adolf Hitler would pose "serious dangers for [Austria's] domestic and foreign policy." This was not least because Hitler advocated the union of Austria and Germany, which, if successful, would likely mean the overthrow of the government and the end of Austrian independence.

So on September 30, 1924, Seipel and his cabinet refused Hitler's return.

Austria had come up with a convenient rationale for this position—namely, that Hitler's military service raised questions about the validity of his Austrian citizenship. But that was immaterial, Bavaria countered, because Hitler had never formally renounced his Austrian citizenship. What's more, Hitler had volunteered to serve in the army of Germany, Austria's ally, and Austria had previously allowed such service to count as fulfilling the draft obligations of its citizens. Why was this case different?

Munich sent a representative to Vienna in early October to press its case for Hitler's deportation further, but Chancellor Seipel and the Austrian cabinet did not budge. That was how the matter stood in early December, when the Bavarian court was again scheduled to consider Hitler's parole.

On December 5, 1924, Stenglein and Ehard submitted what would become their final attempt to block Hitler's release. They retraced the many dangers the prisoner posed and the many rules he had violated at Landsberg. The warden, Otto Leybold, then, by request of the court, countered with another report praising Hitler's supposedly impeccable conduct.

Before submitting it, Leybold interviewed several guards and took down their observations. They were all overwhelmingly positive. Both Josef Pfeffer and Stefan Schuster praised Hitler for his open disposition, completely devoid of secrets. He was always polite, Franz Schön added, and correct in form. Hitler's only *proven* infraction, Leybold wrote in the official report, was the passing of a "rather innocuous" letter to a car dealer without the permission of the censor. Hitler was, in short, a "political idealist" and a model prisoner.

On December 19, 1924, the Bavarian Supreme Court announced that it had rejected the arguments against parole. It is striking that the original document for the court's decision does not appear to be extant. Legal critics have long suspected the influence of the minister of the interior, Franz Gürtner, no matter how fervently he denied it. Gürtner certainly covered his tracks, and bombing raids at the end of the Second World War destroyed many other archival holdings. Still, some hints of Gürtner's obstructionism survive.

One of them is from a confidential police report to the Ministry of the Interior in 1930, smuggled out of Germany by the great Weimar lawyer Robert M. W. Kempner, a former legal counsel to the Prussian police. This document recounts the history of Hitler's treasonous activities and concludes with a reference to the blocking of police objections to Hitler's parole by "the one-time Bavarian Minister of Justice, Franz Guertner." This is, of course, far from conclusive, but given the circumstances, the assertions are not farfetched. Hitler would later name Gürtner minister of justice in the Third Reich.

There is another factor that probably made Bavarian authorities more willing to consider Hitler's release on parole and, at the same time, abandon the pressure on Austria to receive him after deportation: the Reichstag elections, which had been called yet again for December 7, 1924.

With the reformed currency and the improving economy, extremists like the nationalist racist block had suffered a major defeat in the new polls. The upswing in their popularity in the immediate aftermath of the trial had passed, and the rightist block, with its squabbles and feuds, struggled to hold on to its post-trial gains. Its popular vote was cut in half: 1,918,300 to 907,300. In Bavaria, it was worse. The right-wing nationalists lost an estimated 70 percent of their supporters. Once again, for many observers, the far right seemed in steep decline. Not even Hitler, it was said, would be able to stop it.

Such reasoning may well have provided a convenient argument for members of the Ministry of Justice who pushed for Hitler's early parole—and, at the same time, weakened the resolve of their opponents.

News of Hitler's imminent release reached Landsberg on the morning of December 20. Word spread like wildfire through the prison, guard Hemmrich recalled. "Enormous jubilation broke out." Congratulations were exchanged. Hitler gathered his belongings, gave away other items as gifts, and thanked the staff for its support.

"When I left Landsberg," Hitler later said, "everybody wept. [The warden] and the other members of the prison staff . . . We'd won them all to our cause."

Hitler had served barely eight and a half months of a five-year sentence. As one official in the state prosecutor's office tabulated, Hitler was leaving prison 3 years, 333 days, 21 hours, and 50 minutes early. What might have happened had he remained behind bars until 1928, or if he had served a sentence more appropriate to his crimes?

At 12:15 p.m., December 20, 1924, Hitler stood outside Landsberg Prison as a free man. The photographer Heinrich Hoffmann and the future printer of his manuscript, Adolf Müller, had come to pick him up. They were, in fact, the second group to arrive. The first one, Anton Drexler and Gregor Strasser, who planned to take Hitler to Ludendorff, had been rebuffed. "The race for Hitler had begun sooner than I had expected," Hess later said of the rival factions vying for his attention.

Hoffmann, of course, wanted a photograph to commemorate the occasion. When Landsberg guards threatened to seize his camera if he set it up at the prison, they drove off to an old gate of the city and took the famous photograph there. "Get a move on, Hoffmann, or we'll have a crowd collecting," Hitler said impatiently as he waited, hat in hand and wearing his knee socks and trench coat, with presumably his lederhosen underneath. "Anyway, it's bloody cold!"

They made their way back to Munich, reaching his apartment on the Thierschstrasse, where several friends waited. Hitler stepped out of the backseat of the black automobile, now seeing himself much as his most fanatical supporters did—that is, not as the orchestrator of the failed putsch but as a leader, a *Führer*, destined to rule the nation.

Epilogue

O n November 8, 1923, a slight young man in an oversized trench coat had crashed a beer hall rally and declared the overthrow of the government. The night, he vowed, would end in victory or death. Seventeen hours later, however, it had ended in neither. Hitler had fled the scene of an ignominious defeat. Many astute observers, from the *New York Times* to *Frankfurter Zeitung*, believed that this fiasco meant the end of his career, and it might well have been too, had it not been for his trial in Munich.

Presiding judge Georg Neithardt had strained, twisted, and outright ignored the law, striving mainly to prevent the full extent of the actions of Bavaria's foremost authorities against the German republic and the Versailles Treaty from reaching the public. He sought above all to protect their reputation and that of the institutions they had commanded—and that is what gave Hitler his opportunity. He received wide latitude in what he could say and do—that is, as long as he did not reveal sensitive information that might harm Bavarian or German interests. Of course, it did not hurt that Neithardt agreed, on the whole, with Hitler's nationalistic agenda.

Had the proceedings taken place in the state court of Leipzig, where they were, by law, supposed to have been held, Hitler would almost certainly have been punished with more than the minimum sentence. Conviction of the death of four policemen alone might have warranted capital punishment. In Munich, however, Hitler faced charges for only a fraction of the crimes committed during the putsch.

In addition to the death of the policemen, there was the unlawful detention of government ministers, city council members, and Jewish citizens; the threats of violence against the people in the Bürgerbräu; the heists at the banknote-printing companies; the thefts and destruction of the rival newspaper; and the incitement to riot. But given the court's singular focus on high treason, these other crimes were soon forgotten.

Even so, Hitler was not prosecuted as the law demanded. The court slapped him with the absolute minimum penalty and then, instead of deporting him, ruled in favor of parole. Hitler was out of prison by the end of the year. He returned, just as the prosecutors Stenglein and Ehard had warned, to work where he had left off, though by that time he was much more dangerous to the republic. He had a clearer vision for the future, a more detailed plan on how to get there, and a much more confident perception of himself as a leader with the rarest of talents.

Hitler would later credit his experience in prison with giving him "that fearless faith, that optimism, that confidence in our destiny, which nothing could shake thereafter." Landsberg was clearly an important period in his life, but had Hitler paused a moment from his triumphalist and self-serving legend-building, he might have considered another factor that contributed to his renewed sense of mission.

He might have thanked presiding judge Georg Neithardt for his indulgence during the proceedings, the leniency of the verdict, and of course, the extraordinary decision to allow him to remain in Germany. Hitler would in fact have an opportunity to do so; in 1937, when Neithardt retired, Hitler sent him a note thanking him for his years of service. He might also have thanked Franz Gürtner and the Bavarian Ministry of Justice for their influence in the granting of his parole. So when the Great Depression struck, Hitler was neither locked up in prison nor deported from the country. He was a free man able to exploit the ruined economy and the republic already wrecked from within.

The trial of Adolf Hitler is not the story of his rise to power, but rather an episode that helped make that rise possible. It was this trial that catapulted this relatively minor local leader onto the national stage. Hitler's speeches and testimony in Neithardt's courtroom form his earliest major autobiography, defining himself before a public beyond the bccr halls of Munich that previously neither knew nor cared that much about him. Hitler quickly turned the dock into a platform for himself and his party while putting the young republic on trial.

For twenty-four days, Hitler had hammered the government and its leaders with verve, his shrill, guttural voice rising and falling, choking on emotion, clipping his syllables, sometimes spitting on his toothbrush mustache as he barked a relentless stream of attacks against his accusers. All his rhetorical and stagecraft talents were on full display. Hitler's performance in the former dining hall of the infantry academy included some of his most impressive and arguably most influential speeches of his career.

Reporters from Germany, the rest of Europe, and as far away as Argentina and Australia described his antics in detail. This was publicity that a local agitator could not have purchased, nor at this stage of his career even dreamed of achieving.

In the process, Hitler had transformed the beer hall fiasco into a personal and political triumph. He was no longer the buffoon who botched the putsch; he had become, in the eyes of his growing number of supporters, a patriot who had stood up for the German people against the treasonous oppression of Berlin, the cowardice of Bavaria, and the humiliations at the hands of the Allied powers. He was, in their view, a martyr taking the fall for his people, while his more distinguished allies sought cover, or, like Ludendorff, blamed everyone else for his own mistakes.

"How that man Hitler spoke!" said one war veteran who traced his infatuation with Hitler back to the Munich courtroom. "Those days of his trial became the first days of my faith in Hitler. From that time on I had no thought for anyone but Hitler." This view was echoed by many other people in the 1920s who sought out the Nazi Party and saw its leader as a "man of action" who promised the best hope for Germany in the future.

Another person drawn to Hitler given his performance at the trial was a young man with a newly minted PhD in German literature then working on a novel: Joseph Goebbels. From his home in Rheydt in the Ruhr, Goebbels had followed the proceedings, day by day, and found Hitler, as he recorded in his diary, an inspiring "idealist" if no intellectual. Goebbels felt, as he read the words in the newspaper, "carried to the stars."

He dashed out a letter to Hitler. "What you stated there is the catechism of a new political creed coming to birth in the midst of a collapsing, secularized world." He cited Goethe to express his enthusiasm: "To you a god has given the tongue with which to express our sufferings." This was the beginning of a frightful alliance that would last until their deaths together in the bunker in April 1945.

Hitler's life—from aspiring artist to genocidal mass murderer—is fraught with many tragic what-ifs and what-might-have-beens. His trial for high treason was yet another one of these. It was there in the Munich courtroom that Adolf Hitler could have been eliminated from the scene and perhaps forgotten. Instead, this haunting perversion of justice paved the way for the Third Reich and allowed Adolf Hitler to unleash the most unimaginable suffering upon humanity.

Acknowledgments

I t is a pleasure to thank the many people who helped me during the course of writing this book. First, I would like to thank my agent, Suzanne Gluck of William Morris Endeavor, for her overwhelming support of this project. Suzanne is the most spectacular agent on the planet! I am also extremely fortunate and grateful for having John A. Glusman at W. W. Norton as my editor. John is a brilliant editor and an absolute delight to work with. John and Suzanne are the dream team. This book could not have been written without them.

I want to thank the librarians and archivists at the Bayerisches Hauptstaatsarchiv, the Staatsarchiv München, the Institut für Zeitgeschichte München, the National Archives, the Hoover Institution of War and Peace, Franklin D. Roosevelt Presidential Library, Jessamine County Public Library, and many other libraries that provided interlibrary loans of rare books and microfilm. Special thanks to Dr. Christoph Bachmann, Lukas Herbeck, André Geister, Rita Williams, and the team at Staatsarchiv München for allowing me to have access to many valuable resources under their care, not least the prosecutor archives and the thrilling, newly discovered Adolf Hitler files from Landsberg Prison; thanks to Dr. Gerhard Hetzer and the archivists at the Bayerisches Hauptstaatsarchiv for making available a wealth of material, including the private papers of Deputy Prosecutor Hans Ehard, complete with an unpublished memoir from the trial, a collection of his interviews before his death in 1980, and many other surprises, such as Ehard's own entrance card to the trial; thanks to Jeannette Eggert at the Bayerisches Hauptstaatsarchiv for her help securing the parliamentary investigation material, which uncovered so many facts about the beer hall putsch; I am grateful, too, to the always professional and friendly staff at the Institut für Zeitgeschichte München, who likewise provided a welcoming environment in which to study their rich collections. The excitement of unwrapping a carton of papers to read an unpublished memoir of Hitler's bodyguard, Ulrich Graf, or the scribbles of the Landsberg Prison guard Franz Hemmrich, is unforgettable. Thanks, too, to the librarians and archivists at the Franklin Delano Roosevelt Presidential Library for their assistance, including providing me with a copy of Helen Niemeyer's handwritten memoir describing her experiences hiding Hitler in her attic while he was on the run from the police. I would also like to thank Susan Hormuth for her expert photographing of material from the National Archives and Library of Congress, and Ron Basich for his expertise shooting material in the Robert D. Murphy Collection to help shed light on his Munich dispatches as vice consul to the Department of State. Dr. Ron Critchfield and his talented team of librarians at the Jessamine County Public Library were tireless supporters of my research, securing a number of interlibrary loans of rare material and, in many cases, valuable microfilm that ranged from German files captured by the U.S. Army at the end of the Second World War at Passau and Neumarkt-St. Veit to diplomatic and consular reports from 1920s Munich. They kept the material coming, even throughout a monumental renovation project that has rendered the library even more of a beacon in the Bluegrass. All of the library directors, librarians, and archivists certainly went out of their way to open up a treasure trove of archival material and provided yet another reason why I love being a historian.

The Trial of Adolf Hitler began as a lecture in one of my European history classes that I used to teach at the University of Kentucky. I thought of those talks often as I walked all over Munich, tracking down sites related to the story of crime and punishment at heart of the book: retracing the path of the putschists from the Rosenheimerstrasse to the Odeonsplatz; the movements of the authorities, based on police reports and eyewitness accounts, as they faced the throngs of marchers approaching the Feldherrnhalle; walking the paths of Ernst Röhm's Reichskriegsflagge on the way to join Hitler and get some free beer. One of my favorite places was, no surprise, the district around the Blutenburgstrasse, where the Hitler trial took place, and where spectators, reporters, photographers, camera crews, and curiosity seekers milled about amid the armed guards, the barbed wire and other barricades. Exploring the sites of Munich 1923–1924 certainly has its surprises. The ground floor of the apartment building in which Hitler first lived when he moved to Munich in the spring of 1913, for instance, today hosts a bustling shop. The building in which Hitler lived during the putsch and the trial is now also a delightful boutique, this one selling Czech books, music, and art. Among many other unforgettable experiences in Munich and Bavaria, special thanks to retired Landsberg guard Josef Hagenbusch for his fascinating tales from his years at the prison and lore about wardens and staff during Hitler's stay, including Otto Leybold. I also want to thank many other people who helped and I often thought of in gratitude as I roamed the areas related to the putsch and the trial in Munich. At the top of the list are the late professors Raymond F. Betts and Jane Vance. I am deeply aware of how much I owe them, and I cherish their influence and memory. I also want to thank Professor David Olster, who not only taught me so much about the research process but also what it means to be a historian. Thanks, too, to my dear friend Matthew Slatkin for always being on the lookout for rare books to add to my Hitler library.

I want to thank Alexa Pugh and Lydia Brents at W. W. Norton in New York for all their help guiding this book on the journey from manuscript to publication. In London, I want to thank Georgina Morley at Macmillan for all her marvelous expertise and enthusiasm in editing the British edition of *The Trial of Adolf Hitler*. In Amsterdam, I would like to thank Job Lisman and the team at Uitgeverij Prometheus for the Dutch translation; in Barcelona, I want to thank Seix Barral for the Spanish-language edition; in São Paulo, Novo Seculo for the Portuguese translation; in Copenhagen, the team at Gyldendal for the Danish translation; in Oslo, Cappelen Damm for the Norwegian edition; and in Helsinki, Otavo for the Finnish translation. In addition to Suzanne Gluck, whom I cannot praise highly enough, I would like to express my deepest thanks to William Morris Endeavor's Simon Trewin in London, Anna

DeRoy in Beverly Hills, and Laura Bonner, Eve Atterbom, Clio Seraphim, and Samantha Frank in New York.

It is a joy to thank my family for putting up with my obsessive research all these years and rather frequent disappearances into 1920s Munich. As always, another big "I love you" goes to all of them: my daughter, Julia, now an academic star and animal lover extraordinaire; my son, Max, a fearless athlete and dazzling goal scorer, who has long counted the days until I finished the book so that we could play even more one-on-one soccer matches in the backyard; my mother, Cheryl King, for all her love and for instilling at the youngest age my first appreciation for the magic of storytelling and the power of the written word; Annika Levander, my mother-in-law. I still have the trillions of German marks (1923 currency, unfortunately) that she gave me and, even more important, all the good memories. She is deeply missed.

Above all, I would like to thank my wife, Sara, who helped this book in more ways than I count. She is, as always, the manuscript's first reader and critic, the first to hear my new ideas, however raw or half-baked, and never afraid to give her honest opinion. She improved the text tremendously with her exquisite editorial skills. I am fortunate to have such a wise and wonderful wife, who also happens to be a beautiful woman and an ideal companion to share my life.

Finally, I would like to thank my dad, Van King, for all his wisdom, kindness, and big-hearted generosity. He was an enthusiastic supporter of this project from the first day he heard about it. He died of cancer in 2013, but he lived long enough to see the book find a loving home at Norton in the United States, Macmillan in the United Kingdom, and several other excellent publishers around the world. Sharing this good news with him was one bright spot in a dark time. I am forever grateful for the time we had together. This book is dedicated to him with all my love and admiration.

Notes and Sources

There has never been a full, book-length account of the trial of Adolf Hitler in the English language, or, for that matter, any other language besides German. This is surprising, given the significance of the story as well as the wealth of archival material available for such a project: court documents, pretrial investigations, police files, the papers of lawyers for both the prosecution and the defense, and of course the verbatim trial transcript itself, which alone runs to almost three thousand pages.

Memoirs, diaries, correspondence, and other eyewitness accounts have been helpful for references to audience behavior or impressions of the judges, lawyers, defendants, witnesses, or other events in the courtroom that would not make the official transcript. I have also drawn on the extensive newspaper coverage of the proceedings in Germany, Austria, Switzerland, France, Scandinavia, Britain, Canada, the United States, and elsewhere, from Australia to Argentina. There were also news agencies, including the Wolffs Telegraphisches Bureau, Telegraphen-Union, Süddeutsches Korrespondenzbureau, Jewish Telegraphic Agency, Correspondance Internationale, Agence Havas, Agence Radio, Reuters, International News Service, Australian Press Association, Associated Press, United Press, and the British United Press.

It was very exciting that during the research of this project more than five hundred documents from the Landsberg record office dealing with Hitler's incarceration discovered in a Nuremberg flea market found their home at the Staatsarchiv München. These records—long presumed to have been lost or destroyed—have never appeared in English or any other language besides German. This is an important resource, dispelling some myths about Hitler's daily life at Landsberg, and join other valuable primary prison sources, which range from the reports of warden Otto Leybold on Hitler's behavior to a copy of the only known surviving issue of the prisoner newspaper, *Landsberger Ehrenbürger*, published in Cell 11.

There is an unpublished memoir of the prison guard Franz Hemmrich housed at the Institut für Zeitgeschichte München, along with a long interview he gave to a journalist in 1934; a memoir from another prison guard, Otto Lurker; a memoir from prisoner Hans Kallenbach; and correspondence from several prisoners such as Hermann Fobke, Rudolf Hess, and Adolf Hitler. There are accounts of people who visited him in prison, such as Ernst Hanfstaengl, Kurt G. W. Ludecke, Heinrich Hoffmann, Ludwig Ess, Ernst Hohenstatter, and Fritz Patzelt, who brought an early version of the new Storm Trooper "brown shirt" on his visit in June. Among the NSDAP Hauptarchiv, it was exciting to find a file from Landsberg mislabeled 1925—it was actually from 1924 and contains notes from several prisoners during Hitler's stay, including Rudolf Hess.

Among many other archival materials is the unpublished memoir of Helen Niemeyer, the woman at whose house Hitler hid during the police hunt. Her handwritten notes describe Hitler's stay in her attic while on the run from the police after the march to the Odeonsplatz. There are also many other unpublished memoirs, narratives, and other personal accounts of the period, including one by Hitler's bodyguard, Ulrich Graf; the valet of Max Erwin von Scheubner-Richter, the man who would march arm in arm with Hitler on November 9, 1923; a report and diary of the nominated finance minister Gottfried Feder; unpublished essays by Hitler's lawyer, Lorenz Roder, and files from other prominent defense lawyers, including Christoph Schramm. The private papers of the prosecutor Hans Ehard were also used, and these contain, among many other items, an unpublished memoir about his experiences at the trial.

The records of the Polizeidirektion München, Amtsgericht München, and the Bayerisches Staatsministerium des Innern pertaining to Hitler during this period were seized by the National Socialist Party for its NSDAP Hauptarchiv. These include the police and pretrial investigations of the putsch, along with a collection of unpublished interviews, questionnaires, memoirs and other first-person accounts of participants and eyewitnesses to the events of November 8–9, 1923. The police interrogated Alfred Rosenberg, Ernst Röhm, Heinrich Himmler, Heinrich Hoffmann, Hans Frank, Ulrich Graf, and many other suspects, both major and minor, arrested in the aftermath. The investigation launched by the parliamentary committee, with its 1,700 pages of findings, remains unpublished (MA 103476/1-4, BHStA), despite its wealth of information on the background of the putsch, including testimony of presiding judge Neithardt, prosecutor Stenglein, and Bavarian minister of justice Franz Gürtner. See also the holdings on this subject at PD 6718-6719, StAM and HA 69/1500A. (The published version of the study, Wilhelm Hoegner's anonymously appearing *Hitler und Kahr. Die bayerischen Napoleonsgrössen von 1923. Ein im Untersuchungsausschuss des Bayerischen Landtags aufgedeckter Justizskandal* [1928], covers only a fraction of the full investigation.) The files of the Stosstrupp Hitler trial were destroyed by a bombing raid, but a copy of the verdict survives (Proz.Reg.Nr. 187/1924, JVA 12436, StAM), along with some other relevant material preserved in the NSDAP-Hauptarchiv, particularly at HA 67/1493, 67/1494, 68/1494, 68/1498, and 80/1603. All of these police, court, and parliamentary investigative committee files help elucidate several crimes committed during the putsch that were largely omitted from the trial.

Some pamphlets from 1923 and 1924 were likewise helpful, particularly for understanding the volatile atmosphere, such as Albrecht Hoffmann's *Der 9. November 1923 im Lichte der völkischen Freiheitsbewegung* (Lorch Württemberg: K Rohm, 1923). The pamphlets ranged from those suppressed by Bavarian authorities for their critical treatment of the triumvirate, such as Karl Rothenbücher's *Der Fall Kahr* (Tübingen: Mohr, 1924), to those which were undoubtedly distributed to high-ranking military and civil-service circles and came to play a small role in the trial itself, such as the notorious so-called white-blue pamphlet, or Veni Vidi's *Ludendorff in Bayern oder Der Novemberputsch* (Leipzig: Veduka-Verlag,

1924). There is also *Nachdenkliches aus dem Hitler-Prozess*, published by Ludwig Ernst (München: Dr. Franz Pfeiffer & Co. 1924), and perceptive analyses in contemporary legal journals, particularly Alexander Graf zu Dohna's "Der Münchener Hochverratsprozess" in *Deutsche JuristenZeitung* 29 (1924), Heft 9/10. Among other primary sources, there are also reflections of Munich's diplomatic community, including the Vatican's Eugenio Pacelli; Britain's consul general, R. H. Clive; Württemberg's Carl Moser von Filseck; and US vice consul Robert Murphy, who wrote a memoir, *Diplomat Among Warriors*, and donated his papers to the Hoover Institution of War and Peace. Some of Murphy's political dispatches from Munich in 1924 (43.7, for instance) were removed in June 2005 "due to national security classification," but they are currently still available on microfilm in the Records of the Department of State at the National Archives relating to internal affairs of Germany, 1910–1929, RG 59, M336, file 862.00, No. 19 and No. 20.

It is a pleasure, too, to note the many scholarly works that have helped me understand Hitler and the trial. There is the excellent German edition of the transcript, published under the auspices of the Institut für Zeitgeschichte, with commentaries by Lothar Gruchmann, Reinhard Weber, and Otto Gritschneder, *Der Hitler-Prozess 1924. Wortlaut der Hauptverhandlung vor dem Volksgericht München I*, I–IV (1997–1999). These distinguished authorities have published prolifically on German legal history, and their contributions in this edition as well as in their other academic works have been invaluable to this project. Their work remains an indispensable resource for legal scholars and historians alike wishing to understand justice in the Weimar Republic.

For the life of Hitler, I have benefited from classic biographies by Ian Kershaw, Joachim C. Fest, John Toland, and Alan Bullock, and the new additions to the canon, Peter Longerich's *Hitler Biographie* (München: Siedler, 2015) and Volker Ullrich's *Adolf Hitler Biographie. Band 1: Die Jahre des Aufstiegs* (Frankfurt am Main: S. Fischer, 2013). I also went back to the early biographies, including the landmark publication by the former Munich correspondent for *Frankfurter Zeitung*, Konrad Heiden and the one by an editor at *Berliner Tageblatt*, Rudolf Olden, both published in exile abroad in the 1930s, the first in Zurich, the second in Amsterdam;

pioneering postwar work by Ernst Deuerlcin, *Hitler. Eine politische Biographie* (München: List, 1969), with more of his works cited below, and the biography by Walter Görlitz and Herbert A. Quint, *Adolf Hitler. Eine Biographie* (Stuttgart: Steingrüben-Verlag, 1952), the latter being pseudonyms for Otto Julius Frauendorf and Richard Freiherr v. Frankenberg. A number of fawning, pro-Hitler biographies of the 1930s were read too, with the hope of finding interviews by people who knew him, or other eyewitness accounts, as well as some international publications that emerged in the wake of the Nazi Party's early parliamentary successes. These ranged from Frédéric Hirth, *Hitler, ou le guerrier déchaîné* (Paris: éditions du tamourin, 1930) to Arne Melgård's "Vackre Adolf" published in the Swedish *Hemmets Journal* (1931). One pro-Nazi book published in 1934 by a British journalist under the pseudonym "Heinz A. Heinz," for instance, had interviews with Hitler's first Munich landlady, Frau Popp (Anna Popp) and the prison guard Franz Hemmrich. The latter's testimony complements, and in several ways enhances, his later handwritten notes at Munich's Institut für Zeitgeschichte, which were written decades later and contain some errors of memory.

For insightful, short studies, see especially Sebastian Haffner, *The Meaning of Hitler*, trans. Ewald Osers (Cambridge, MA: Harvard University Press, 1979); Eberhard Jäckel, *Hitler's World View: A Blueprint for Power*, trans. Herbert Arnold (Cambridge, MA: Harvard University Press, 1981); John Lukcas, *The Hitler of History* (New York: Vintage Books, 1998); Ron Rosenbaum, *Explaining Hitler: The Search for the Origins of His Evil* (New York: HarperPerennial, 1999); and William Carr, *Hitler: A Study in Personality and Politics* (London: Edward Arnold, 1978). Other valuable accounts of Hitler's life or a particular aspects of it, with relevance to this period were Laurence Rees, *Hitler's Charisma: Leading Millions into the Abyss* (New York: Pantheon Books, 2012); Andrew Nagorski, *Hitlerland: American Eyewitnesses to the Nazi Rise to Power* (New York: Simon & Schuster, 2012); Timothy W. Ryback, *Hitler's Private Library: The Books That Shaped His Life* (New York: Alfred A. Knopf, 2008); Yvonne Sherratt, *Hitler's Philosophers* (New Haven: Yale University Press, 2013); Stefan Ihrig, *Ataürk in the Nazi Imagination* (Cambridge, MA: Harvard University Press,

2014); and Detlev Clemens, *Herr Hitler in Germany. Wahrnehmung und Deutungen des Nationalsozialismus in Grossbritannien 1920 bis 1939* (Göttingen: Vandenhoeck & Ruprecht, 1996). Other helpful, provocative, and thought-provoking works include Lothar Machtan's *The Hidden Hitler*, trans. John Brownjohn (New York: Basic Books, 2001), as well as a diverse group of older portraits that, despite some shortcomings, still have merit beyond their role in the history of Hitler historiography, such as Werner Maser, William L. Shirer, Robert G. L. Waite, Robert Payne, and Walter C. Langer, the latter of whose work with the pre-CIA American espionage organization OSS led to the publication of *The Mind of Adolf Hitler: The Secret Wartime Report* (New York: Basic Books, 1972). I have also drawn upon the larger OSS files on Hitler at the National Archives that Langer helped declassify (the OSS Sourcebook), as well as the Soviet counterintelligence, the latter published as *The Hitler Book: The Secret Dossier Prepared for Stalin from the Interrogations of Hitler's Personal Aides*, eds. Henrik Eberle and Matthias Uhl, trans. Giles MacDonogh, with a foreword by Richard Overy (New York: Bristol Park Books, 2005). See also the work of former British MI6 agent turned Oxford historian Hugh R. Trevor-Roper, particularly his essay "The Mind of Adolf Hitler," which appeared as an introduction to *Hitler's Secret Conversations 1941–1944* (New York: Farrar, Straus and Young, Inc., 1953; Signet 1961).

For young Hitler, see especially Anton Joachimsthaler, *Hitlers Weg begann in München 1913–1923* (München: Herbig, 2000); Brigitte Hamann, *Hitler's Vienna: A Dictator's Apprenticeship*, trans. Thomas Thornton (Oxford: Oxford University Press, 1999); Franz Jetzinger, *Hitler's Youth*, trans. Lawrence Wilson (London: Hutchinson, 1958); Albrecht Tyrell *Vom 'Trommler' zum 'Führer.' Der Wandel von Hitlers Selbstverständnis zwischen 1919 und 1924 und die Entwicklung der NSDAP* (München: Wilhelm Fink Verlag, 1975); Thomas Weber, *Hitler's First War: Adolf Hitler, the Men of the List Regiment, and the First World War* (Oxford: Oxford University Press, 2010); Geoffrey Pridham, *Hitler's Rise to Power: The Nazi Movement in Bavaria, 1923–1933* (London: Hart-Davis, MacGibbon, 1973); Bradley F. Smith, *Adolf Hitler: His Family, Childhood, and Youth* (Stanford: Hoover Institution, 1967); Eugene Davidson, *The*

Making of Adolf Hitler (New York: Macmillan Publishing Co., 1977); Charles Bracelen Flood, *Hitler: The Path to Power* (Boston: Houghton Mifflin Company, 1989); and several works by Othmar Plöckinger, especially his studies on *Mein Kampf,* cited below. See also Ernst Deuerlein, ed., "Hitlers Eintritt in die Politik und die Reichswehr," *Vierteljahrshefte fur Zeitgeschichte* 7 (1959), 177–227; Reginald H. Phelps "Hitler als Parteiredner im Jahre 1920," *Vierteljahrshefte fur Zeitgeschichte* 11 (1963), 274–330; and Theodore Abel's Columbia University study of six hundred Storm Troopers, published as *Why Hitler Came into Power: An Answer Based on the Original Life Stories of Six Hundred of His Followers* (New York: Prentice-Hall, 1938).

For the putsch, see particularly Ernst Deuerlein's introduction and collection of documents he edited in *Der Hitler-Putsch. Bayerische Dokumente zum 8./9. November 1923* (Stuttgart: Deutsche Verlags-Anstalt, 1962), and Harold J. Gordon Jr., *Hitler and the Beer Hall Putsch* (Princeton: Princeton University Press, 1972). See also Richard Hanser's *Putsch!: How Hitler Made Revolution* (New York: Pyramid Books, 1971), and John Dornberg's *Munich 1923: The Story of Hitler's First Grab for Power* (New York: Harper & Row, 1982), as well as Hans Hubert Hofmann, *Der Hitlerputsch. Krisenjahre deutscher Geschichte 1920–1924* (München: Nymphenburger Verlagshandlung, 1961); Didier Chauvet's *Hitler et le putsch de la brasserie: Munich, 8/9 novembre 1923* (Paris: L'Harmattan, 2012); Georg Franz-Willing, *Putsch und Verbotszeit der Hitlerbewegung November 1923–Februar 1925* (Preussisch Oldendorf: Verlag K.W. Schütz, 1977); and Georges Bonnin, *Le putsch de Hitler: à Munich en 1923* (Les Sables-d'Olonne: Bonnin, 1966). For the aftermath, see the work by Lothar Gruchmann, Reinhard Weber, and Otto Gritschneder cited above; Otto Gritschneder's *Bewährungsfrist für den Terroristen Adolf H. Der Hitler-Putsch und die bayerische Justiz* (München: Verlag C. H. Beck, 1990); Otto Gritschneder's *Der Hitler-Prozess und sein Richter Georg Neithardt: Skandalurteil von 1924 ebnet Hitler den Weg* (München: Verlag C. H. Beck, 2001); Klaus Gietinger und Werner Reuss, eds., *Hitler vor Gericht. Der Prozess nach dem Putsch 1923—Fakten, Hintergründe, Analysen* (München: BR-Alpha, 2009), and David Jablonsky, *The Nazi Party in Dissolution: Hitler and the Verbotzeit, 1923–1925* (London:

F. Cass, 1989), which began as a doctoral dissertation at the University of Kansas. The trial was discussed briefly in chapters seven and eight of Peter Ross Range, *1924: The Year That Made Hitler* (New York: Little, Brown, 2016). Valuable collections of published documents from this period include Eberhard Jäckel und Axel Kuhn, eds., *Hitler. Sämtliche Aufzeichnungen 1905–1924* (Stuttgart: Deutsche Verlags-Anstalt, 1980); Ernst Deuerlein, ed., *Der Hitler-Putsch. Bayerische Dokumente zum 8./9. November 1923* (Stuttgart: Deutsche Verlags-Anstalt, 1962); Ernst Deuerlein, ed., *Der Aufstieg der NSDAP in Augenzeugenberichten* (Düsseldorf: Deutscher Taschenbuch Verlag, 1978); Peter Fleischmann, ed., *Hitler als Häftling in Landsberg am Lech 1923/1924* (Neustadt an der Aisch: Verlag Ph.C.W.Schmidt, 2015); Werner Jochmann, ed., *Adolf Hitlers Monologe im Führerhauptquartier 1941–1944* (München: Heyne, 1982); Werner Jochmann, ed., *Nationalsozialismus und Revolution. Ursprung und Geschichte der NSDAP in Hamburg 1922–1933. Dokumente* (Frankfurt am Main: Europäische Verlagsanstalt, 1963); Werner Maser, ed., *Hitler's Letters and Notes* (New York: Bantam, 1976); Jeremy Noakes and Geoffrey Pridham, *Nazism, 1919–1945: A Documentary Reader* (Exeter: University of Exeter, 1998); Othmar Plöckinger and Florian Beierl, eds., "Neue Dokumente zu Hitlers Buch Mein Kampf," in *Vierteljahrshefte fur Zeitgeschichte* 57, Heft 2 (2009), 261–318, along with documents published at the end of Georges Franz-Willing (1977) and Georges Bonnin (1966). Among other collections, there are a number of eyewitness accounts of Munich at this time that deserve more attention, such as the dispatches of *Vorwärts's* Joseph Roth; Correspondance Internationale's Victor Serge; *Argentinische Tag- und Wochenblatt's* Carl Christian Bry; the Catalan journalist Eugeni Xammar (who wrote for several papers in Madrid and Barcelona); the *Daily Herald's* Morgan Philips Price (formerly special correspondent for *Manchester Guardian*), who had been on the scene in Germany for five years before February 1924; and, for other non-journalists, the letters Hermann Göring's first wife, Carin, wrote at this time to her family in Stockholm, Sweden.

Quotations from the court proceedings, unless stated otherwise, come from one of the surviving verbatim records of the trial (Amtsgericht München transcript, NA T84 EAP 105/7), which was captured by the US Army in 1945, brought to Washington, DC, and, after being filmed, returned to Germany, where it is now kept at the Bundesarchiv. I have a copy of this transcript in my collection. I have likewise used the transcript of the trial published as *Der Hitler-Prozess vor dem Volksgericht in München* (München: Knorr & Hirth, 1924), a copy of which I also own, and *Der Hitler-Prozess. Auszüge aus den Verhandlungsberichten mit den Bildern der Angeklagten nach Zeichnungen von Otto von Kursell* (München: Deutscher Volksverlag, 1924), which was generously loaned to me. Unlike the Amtsgericht München transcript cited above, both of these two versions are heavily abridged and, of course, given their 1924 publication date, lack access to the trial's many closed sessions. Another version consulted is *The Hitler Trial Before the People's Court in Munich*, trans. H. Francis Freniere, Lucie Karcic, and Philip Fandek (Arlington, VA: University Publications of America, 1976), which is also abridged and comes without much commentary. For readers wanting to know more on this subject, see the German edition of the proceedings, published by the Institut für Zeitgeschichte and cited above, as well as the scholarship of its editors, Lothar Gruchmann, Reinhard Weber, and Otto Gritschneder. For more on law in the Weimar Republic, see, among other authorities, the scholarly work of Richard J. Evans, Heinrich Hannover and Elisabeth Hannover-Drück, Henning Grunwald, Benjamin Carter Hett, and Douglas G. Morris.

For the legal environment in Munich through the eyes of one of its brilliant lawyers, consult Reinhard Weber's edition of Max Hirschberg's *Jude und Demokrat. Erinnerungen eines Münchener Rechtsanwalts 1883 bis 1939* (München: R. Oldenbourg Verlag, 1998). Robert M. W. Kempner, a former legal counsel to the Prussian police in the 1920s, smuggled out some documents that show various efforts to deport Hitler and efforts to block his parole, which have helped for the chapters on Hitler's imprisonment (*Research Studies of the State College of Washington*, XIII, No. 2, June 1945). See also the unpublished manuscript in Ehard's papers, *Chronik der Bayerischen Justizverwaltung* (NL Ehard 90, BHStA), particularly folder 3 for the period of the putsch and the trial. Ehard's unpublished memoir of the trial, cited above, provides a fresh perspective on the proceedings, and Andreas Stenglein has written a short, valuable account in *Ludwig Stenglein, der Anklager im Hitler-Prozess 1924* (Bamberg-Gaustadt: Selbstverlag, 2000) with updates in later additions (website in German at andreas-stenglein.de), along with Stenglein discussions in the parliamentary committee investigation in the archives at BHStA cited below. Natalie Willsch has written on another lawyer at the trial in *Hellmuth Mayer (1895–1980). Vom Verteidiger im Hitler-Prozess 1924 zum liberal-konservativen Strafrechtswissenschaftler. Das vielgestaltige Leben und Werk des Kieler Strafrechtslehrers* (Baden-Baden: Nomos Verlagsgesellschaft, 2008). For more on the legal twists and turns in the fight for deportation and the Bavaria-Berlin disputes, see D. C. Watt, "Die bayerischen Bemühungen um Ausweisung Hitlers 1924," *Vierteljahrshefte für Zeitgeschichte* 6 (1958), 270–80, and Bernd Steger, "Der Hitlerprozess und Bayerns Verhältnis zum Reich 1923/1924," *Vierteljahrshefte für Zeitgeschichte* 23 (1977), 441–66.

For Munich's cultural life, see David Clay Large's *Where Ghosts Walked: Munich's Road to the Third Reich* (New York: W. W. Norton, 1997); Rainer Metzger, *Munich: Its Golden Age of Art and Culture 1890–1920* (London: Thames & Hudson 2009); and Christoph Stölzl, ed., *Die Zwanziger Jahre in München* (München: Münchner Stadtmuseum, 1979), a 750–page catalog to an exhibit at the Münchner Stadtmuseum, May to September 1979. I have also benefited from scholarly histories of the Weimar Republic, particularly the works by Richard J. Evans, Eric D. Weitz, Heinrich August Winkler, Eberhard Kolb, Hans Mommsen, Detlev J. K. Peukert, Peter Gay, Henry Ashby Turner Jr., Gordon A. Craig, James M. Diehl, John W. Wheeler-Bennett, Erich Eyck, Otto Friedrich, Pierre Broué, Frederick Taylor, F. L. Carsten, Paul Bookbinder, and Gerald D. Feldman—both his *The Great Disorder: Politics, Economics, and Society in the German Inflation, 1914–1924* (Oxford: Oxford University Press, 1997), and his *Hugo Stinnes. Biographie eines Industriellen 1870–1924* (München: Verlag C. H. Beck, 1998). Another excellent source is Wilhelm Hoegner's *Die Verratene Republik. Deutsche Geschichte 1919–1933* (München: Nymphenburger Verlagshandlung, 1979), which was begun in 1934 during his exile in Switzerland and completed in the late 1950s after his term of office as Bavaria's minister-president. Many other accounts of particular aspects of Weimar culture have helped as well, such as Brigitte Hamann's *Winifred Wagner oder Hitlers Bayreuth* (München: Piper, 2002); Wolfgang Martynkewicz's *Salon Deutschland. Geist und Macht 1900–1945* (Berlin: Aufbau, 2009); and Anna Maria Sigmund, *Des Führers bester Freund. Adolf Hitler, seine Nichte Geli Raubal und der "Ehrenarier" Emil Maurice—eine Dreiecksbeziehung* (München: Heyne, 2003). For *Mein Kampf*, see Othmar Plöckinger's *Geschichte eines Buches. Adolf Hitlers "Mein Kampf" 1922–1945* (München: Oldenbourg, 2006 and revised edition, 2011); Othmar Plöckinger's study with Florian Beierl "Neue Dokumente zu Hitlers Buch Mein Kampf," in *Vierteljahrshefte für Zeitgeschichte* 57, Heft 2 (2009), 261–318; Sven Felix Kellerhoff's *'Mein Kampf'. Die Karriere eines deutschen Buches* (Stuttgart: Klett-Cotta, 2015); Barbara Zehnpfennig, *Adolf Hitler. Mein Kampf. Studienkommentar* (Paderborn: Wilhelm Fink Verlag, 2011); Christian Zentner, *Adolf Hitlers Mein Kampf. Eine kommentierte Auswahl* (München: List, 1974); and the recent two-volume annotated edition, *Mein Kampf. Eine kritische Edition* (München: Institut für Zeitgeschichte, 2016), edited by Christian Hartmann, Thomas Vordermayer, Othmar Plöckinger, and Roman Töppel. As for the trial—and the period between the putsch and prison—this surprisingly under-studied period of Hitler's life has claims for being what US vice consul Robert Murphy wrote of his years in Munich: "Nowhere else in Europe in the 1920s was the past, present, and future of that turbulent continent more dramatically revealed."

Archives

BHStA   Bayerisches Hauptstaatsarchiv
FDR   Franklin D. Roosevelt Presidential Library
HA   NSDAP Hauptarchiv
HI   Hoover Institution, Stanford
IfZ   Institut für Zeitgeschichte, München
NA   National Archives, Washington, DC
StAM   Staatsarchiv München

Prologue

xix **pass and accompanying photo identification:** *Sicherungsmassnahmen anlässlich des Prozesses gegen Hitler u. Genossen*, February 23, 1924, HA 68/1498.

xix **in a small room:** *Sicherheitsvorkehrungen für das Kriegsschulgebäude während der Zeit des Hitler-Prozesses*, February 15, 1924, HA 68/1498.

xix **grenades in purses:** *New York Times*, February 27, 1924.

xix **anticipated high-treason trial:** *München-Augsburger Abendzeitung*, January 28, 1924; *Vorwärts,* February 24, 1924; *Prager Tagblatt* (Prague), February 26, 1924; and *Münchner Neueste Nachrichten*, February 27, 1924.

xix **According to tips:** Report, February 8, 1924, MA 104221, BHStA, and preparations, MINN 73699, BHStA.

xix **"a snot brake":** The German word is *"Rotzbremse."*

xix **He stood five-nine:** *Aufnahme-Buch für Schutzhaft, Untersuch. u. Festungshaft-Gefangene 1919*, JVA 17000, StAM.

xix **Still, he looked:** *Vossische Zeitung*, February 26, 1924, Abend Ausgabe, and *Le Petit Parisien*, February 27, 1924.

xix **Hitler stopped to kiss:** *L'Écho de Paris*, February 27, 1924.

xix **Austrian manners:** *Le Matin*, February 27, 1924.

xx **"proud and sneering":** United Press, February 26, 1924.

xx **"a tower":** Kurt G. W. Ludecke, *I Knew Hitler: The Story of a Nazi Who Escaped the Blood Purge* (New York: Charles Scribner's Sons, 1938), 65. This book Anglicized his last name, Lüdecke.

xx **"Bavarian Opera Bouffe":** *New York Times*, November 10, 1923.

xx **Hitler and Ludendorff shake hands:** Associated Press, February 27, 1924, and *Hamburger Anzeiger*, February 26, 1924.

xxi **the fate he feared the most:** Otto Gritschneder, *Der Hitler-Prozess und sein Richter Georg Neithardt. Skandalurteil von 1924 ebnet Hitler den Weg* (München: Verlag C. H. Beck, 2001), 52 and note 25, p.145.

Chapter 1: *BÜRGERBRÄUKELLER*

3 **"At the edge of large cities":** As quoted in David Clay Large, *Where Ghosts Walked: Munich's Road to the Third Reich* (New York: W. W. Norton, 1997), 32.

3 **a sharp pain:** Egon Hanfstaengl, unpublished memoir, 101, along with reflections from his days taking shooting lessons from Hitler's bodyguard, Ulrich Graf, Box 45, John Toland Papers, FDR.

3 **a small back bedroom:** Ernst Hanfstaengl, *Zwischen Weissem und Braunem Haus. Memoiren eines politischen Aussenseiters* (München: R. Piper, 1970), 52 and Kurt G. W. Ludecke, *I Knew Hitler: The Story of a Nazi Who Escaped the Blood Purge* (New York: Charles Scribner's Sons, 1938), 271–72, with the dimensions coming from an interview with his landlord in Heinz A. Heinz, *Germany's Hitler* (London: Hurst & Blackett, 1938), 240–41. According to the records of the Munich police, Hitler moved here on May 1, 1920. Antonie Reichert, daughter of his landlords, confirmed the date, September 9, 1952, ZS 287, IfZ.

4 **already thought of himself:** He saw his task as "theoretical deepening," Alfred Rosenberg, interrogation with Munich police, VIa 2500/23, June 6, 1924, HA 67/1493.

4 **deep in conversation:** Ian Kershaw, *Hitler 1889–1936: Hubris* (New York: W. W. Norton, 1999), 206.

4 **5 billion marks:** *Völkischer Beobachter*, November 8, 1923.

4 **3 billion marks cheaper:** *Münchener Post*, November 8, 1923.

4 **"Where is Captain Göring":** Hanfstaengl (1970), 129.

4 **suffering from pneumonia:** Björn Fontander, *Carin Göring skriver hem* (Stockholm: Carlssons, 1990), 107.

4 **special edition:** Alfred Rosenberg, interrogation, VIa 2500/23, June 6, 1924, HA 67/1493.

4 **"The moment for action":** Hanfstaengl (1970), 129.

5 **Around eight o'clock:** *Bericht an das Staatsministerium des Innern München*, December 5, 1923, HA 67/1491.

5 **starless night:** *Vorgänge beim Stab der 7.Division am 8.11. abends und 9.11. vom Verlassen des Bürgerbräukellers bis zur Wiederinbesitznahme des Kriegs-Ministeriums.* Ernst Deuerlein, ed., *Der Hitler-Putsch. Bayerische Dokumente zum 8./9. November 1923* (Stuttgart: Deutsche Verlags-Anstalt, 1962), Nr. 182, Anlage 4, 507.

5 **Benz:** This is often presented in historical accounts as a Mercedes, but that is incorrect. It was a Benz.

5 **popular venues:** Large (1997), xii–xiii.

5 **"mobbed by a huge crowd":** NA T84 EAP 105/7, 96.

5 **only a guest:** Police report, *Wahrnehmung im Bürgerbräukeller*, November 22, 1923, HA 67/1490.

5 **He walked straight ahead:** There is a tradition of Anton Drexler coming with

Hitler in the car, Hans Hubert Hofmann, *Der Hitlerputsch. Krisenjahre deutscher Geschichte 1920–1924* (München: Nymphenburger Verlagshandlung, 1961), 160. Hofmann cites Walter Görlitz and Herbert A. Quint, *Adolf Hitler: Eine Biographie* (Stuttgart: Steingrüben-Verlag, 1952), 201, but the latter do not cite any evidence. Drexler himself did not make this claim in his early interviews with the police or the press, nor do eyewitnesses whom police questioned note their arrival together either. He probably came, as he later said, with Max Amann.

5 **political and patriotic elite:** *Münchener Zeitung*, November 9, 1923.

6 **Both leaders managed:** *Bericht über meine Tätigkeit in der Zeit von 8.–9. November*, HA 67/1490.

6 **"contagion" and "quintessential evil":** Gustav von Kahr's speech, "Vom Volk zur Nation!" MA 104221, BHStA, and printed in *Münchner Neueste Nachrichten*, November 9, 1923.

6 **dry as straw:** undated confidential report, *Der Putsch vom 8.Nov.1923*, HA 67/1491.

6 **"Does anyone understand":** Johann Aigner, unpublished memoir, *Ein Beitrag zur Geschichte der nationalen Erhebung im November 1923*, 6, HA 5/114II.

6 **"In Munich," Hanfstaengl later said:** Ernst Hanfstaengl, *Hitler: The Memoir of a Nazi Insider Who Turned Against the Führer*, intro. John Willard Toland (New York: Arcade Publishing, 1957, repr. 2011), 96.

6 **cigar dealer:** Police report, Nr. 2673, *Persönliche Wahrnehmung vor dem Bürgerbräukeller in der Nacht v. 8./9.11.23*, November 20, 1923 HA 67/1490.

6 **passing out rifles:** Johann Georg Maurer, VI a F 413/24, November 21, 1923, HA 67/1494, Walter Hewel, VI a F 425/24, February 22, 1924, HA 67/1494, and MA 103476/3, 1217, BHStA.

6 **squad of about 125 men:** Harold J. Gordon Jr., *Hitler and the Beer Hall Putsch* (Princeton: Princeton University Press, 1972), 270.

6 **"specially dangerous work":** Josef Berchtold interview, Heinz (1938), 150.

7 **original core of the SS:** Richard J. Evans, *The Coming of the Third Reich* (New York: Penguin Books, 2003), 228. The SS developed over time into what Heinz Höhne called "the guillotine used by a gang of psychopaths obsessed with racial purity," Heinz Höhne, *The Order of the Death's Head: The Story of Hitler's SS* (New York: Penguin Books, 2000), 3.

7 **"madam of a brothel":** Rebecca West, "Greenhouse with Cyclamens I" (1946), in *A Train of Powder* (Chicago: Ivan R. Dee, 1955), 6.

7 **"hall protection":** or "Hall Defense" founded on or after February 24, 1920, Bruce Campbell, *The SA Generals and the Rise of Nazism* (Lexington: University Press of Kentucky, 1998), 20.

7 **The Storm Troopers wore gray:** Karl A. Kessler, *Der 9. November 1923 in München. Erlebnisse eines SA Mannes* (München: Walter, 1933), 8.

7 **officially adopted:** Kershaw (1999), 698, note 81. One of the first examples of the SA brown shirt is said to have been brought to Hitler at Landsberg by Fritz Patzelt

in June 1924. Landsberg records show that this man did visit on the alleged day, June 9, 143140, STA 14344, StAM. The brown caps came later, appearing at least by February 1927, Stabsführer der Oberstern SA-Führung, Akten-Vermerk, November 6, 1935, HA 5/129.

8 **"Death to the Jews!"** and **"toughest roughnecks"**: Truman Smith, *Berlin Alert: The Memoirs and Reports of Truman Smith*, ed. Robert Hessen (Stanford, CA: Hoover Institution Press, 1984), 57.

8 **"Cruelty impresses"**: Joachim C. Fest, *Hitler*, trans. Richard and Clara Winston (New York: Harcourt Brace Jovanovich, 1974), 144.

8 **"unless carried out dead"**: Eberhard Jäckel und Axel Kuhn, eds., *Hitler. Sämtliche Aufzeichnungen 1905–1924* (Stuttgart: Deutsche Verlags-Anstalt, 1980), Nr. 312, 513. See also the description as a "battering ram" in *Völkischer Beobachter*, August 14, 1921, Detlef Mühlberger, *Hitler's Voice: The Völkischer Beobachter, 1920–1933* (New York: Peter Lang, 2004), I, 55.

8 **finally dispersed the crowd:** Police report, *Wahrnehmung im Bürgerbräukeller*, November 22, 1923, HA 67/1490.

8 **glanced at his watch:** Berchtold interview in Heinz (1938), 154.

8 **glow of headlights:** Johann Aigner, unpublished memoir, *Ein Beitrag zur Geschichte der nationalen Erhebung im November 1923*, 6, HA 5/114II.

8 **"Out of the way"** and **"amazed and unprepared"**: Berchtold interview, Heinz (1938), 154.

8 **Several of the policemen:** see the description of the arrival by Max Beckerbauer, *Bericht über gemachte Wahrnehmungen anlässlich der Versammlung der vaterländischen Verbände am 8. November 1923*, November 22, 1923, HA 67/1490.

8 **Göring drew his sword:** Police report, Nr. 2364, *Bericht über meine gemachten Wahrnehmungen im Saale des Bürgerbräukellers am 8.11.23 abends*, November 22, 1923, HA 67/1490.

8 **He shouted something:** Police report, Nr. 1415, *Wahrnehmungen i[n] der Nacht vom 8./9.11.23 am Bürgerbräukeller*, November 20, 1923, HA 67/1490, and Nr. 1609, *Wahrnehmungen [ü]ber die Vorgänge im Bürgerbräukeller am 8. November 1923*, November 21, 1923.

9 **smashed it to the floor:** Marc Sesselmann, unpublished account, *Bericht*, November 1, 1935, HA 5/116, and incident reported by a detective, *Überwachung der Versammlung im Bürgerbräukeller am Donnerstag, den 8.11.1923*, November 20, 1923, HA 67/1490 and MA 103476/3, 1222, BHStA.

9 **Browning pistol:** NA T84/2 EAP 105/7, 1255.

9 **his bodyguard:** Ulrich Graf, unpublished memoir, 7, F14, IfZ.

9 **"Watch out":** NA T84 EAP 105/7, 98.

9 **"a kind of narrow path":** NA T84 EAP 105/7, 1344.

9 **thought it was Communist hecklers:** Kahr (NA T84/2 EAP 105/7, 1344); Lossow (NA T84/2 EAP 105/7, 1255), as well as Georg Stumpf, *Hitlerputsch im Bürgerbräukeller am 8.11.23*, November 23, 1923, HA 67/1490.

9 **"Halt!" "Get back!":** *Münchener Zeitung*, November 9, 1923, and the commotion also in the police report, *Teilnahme an der Versammlung im Bürgerbräukeller am 8.XI.1923*, November 21, 1923, HA 67/1490.

9 **pushed their way forward:** NA T84/2 EAP 105/7, 97 and Theodor Singer, *Versammlung der vaterl. Vereine im Münchener Bürgerbräukeller vom 8. November 1923*, November 21, 1923, HA 67/1490.

9 **confusion and panic:** Johann Aigner, unpublished memoir, *Ein Beitrag zur Geschichte der nationalen Erhebung im November 1923*, HA 5/114II.

9 **assembled the heavy machine gun:** NA T84 EAP 105/7, 125.

9 **a second shot:** Historical accounts often have only one shot, but many eyewitnesses report a second one: for instance, Friedrich Bernreuther, NA T84 EAP 105/7, 829, Georg Stumpf, *Hitlerputsch im Bürgerbräukeller am 8.11.23*, November 23, 1923, HA 67/1490, and an off-duty officer, Ludwig Weber, *Schilderung der Vorgänge in der Vaterländischen Versammlung am 8.11.23 im Bürgerbräukeller*, November 21, 1923, HA 67/1490. Some observers, such as Eugeni Xammar in the *La Veu de Catalunya* (November 17, 1923), claimed that Hitler fired both shots, but many other people present that night reported that a man near Hitler fired a gun, *Teilnahme an der Versammlung im Bürgerbräukeller am 8.XI.1923*, November 21, 1923, HA 67/1490, and a description of the second shooter is at NA T84/2 EAP 105/7, 961, 964. These examples could easily be multiplied by statements in both the police reports and in the press. Likewise some historians confuse the table and chair as one single incident, or choose one at the expense of others, but countless eyewitnesses near the front of the audience describe two separate instances.

10 **blocked his way:** Hitler later said that Hunglinger was the only officer he respected, NA T84 EAP 105/7, 806–7.

10 **"The national revolutions has broken out!":** Anz. Verz.XIX 421/23, *Antrag des I. Staatsanwalts beim Volksgericht München I auf Anberaumung der Hauptverhandlung*, January 8, 1924, Staatsanwaltschaften 3098, 3–4, StAM; *Münchner Neueste Nachrichten*, November 9, 1923, and police report, Johannes Müller, *Bericht über den Verlauf der Versammlung am 8. November 23*, November 21, 1923, HA 67/1490.

10 **booked earlier:** Rudolf Hess, *Briefe 1908–1933*, ed. Wolf Rüdiger Hess (München: Langen Müller, 1987), November 8, 1923, 311.

10 **It would take only:** NA T84 EAP 105/7, 977.

10 **The leaders hesitated:** NA T84/2 EAP 105/7, 1257.

Chapter 2: STARVING TRILLIONAIRES

11 **"It was quite a thrill":** Robert Murphy, *Diplomat Among Warriors* (Garden City, NY: Doubleday & Company, 1964), 25.

11 **population had soared:** David Clay Large, *Where Ghosts Walked: Munich's Road*

to the Third Reich (New York: W. W. Norton, 1997), xviii. By 1923, it was esti-mated at 630,711, *General Information Concerning District of American Consulate at Munich, Germany*, Box 6, Folder 11, HI.

11 **"Athens on the Isar":** Albrecht Hoffmann, *Der 9. November 1923 im Lichte der völkischen Freiheitsbewegung* (1923), 14. For more, see especially Large (1997); Rainer Metzger, *Munich: Its Golden Age of Art and Culture 1890–1920* (London: Thames & Hudson 2009); and Christoph Stölzl, ed., *Die Zwanziger Jahre in München: Katalog zur Ausstellung im Münchner Stadtmuseum Mai bis September 1979* (München: Münchner Stadtmuseum, 1979).

12 **"Prussian pig":** NA T84 EAP 105/7, 2361. For more on the resentment against Prussia, see, for instance, Volker Ullrich, *Adolf Hitler Biographie. Band 1: Die Jahre des Aufstiegs 1889–1939* (Frankfurt am Main: S. Fischer, 2013), 81.

12 **turnips:** *Kohlrübenwinter* or "Turnip winter" was a common description for the winter of 1916–1917.

12 **beer like dishwater:** Ernst Toller, *Eine Jugend in Deutschland* (Amsterdam: Querido Verlag; Hamburg, 1933: Rowohlt, 1998), 82.

12 **Some three-fourths of a million:** Frederick Taylor, *The Downfall of Money: Germany's Hyperinflation and the Destruction of the Middle Class* (New York: Bloomsbury Press, 2013), 18–19.

12 **a terrible price:** Richard Bessel, *Germany After the First World War* (Oxford: Clarendon Press, 1993), 6.

12 **Germany would be:** Margaret MacMillan, *Paris 1919: Six Months That Changed the World* (New York: Random House, 2002), 465–67, with the 33 billion figure following on 480.

13 **"peace of shame":** Erich Malitius, *Der 8. u. 9. November 1923. Die Geschichte von Treue und Verrat der deutschen Jugend* (Breslau: Handel, 1935), 4.

13 **"democracy without democrats":** Dietrich Orlow, *A History of Modern Germany 1871 to Present* (Upper Saddle River, NJ: Prentice Hall, 2002), 137.

14 **loss of many privileges:** David Jablonsky, *The Nazi Party in Dissolution: Hitler and the Verbotzeit, 1923–1925* (London: F. Cass, 1989), 1–2.

14 **"passive resistance":** Ian Kershaw, *Hitler 1889–1936: Hubris* (New York: W. W. Norton, 1999), 191.

14 **hyperinflation:** Gerald D. Feldman, *The Great Disorder: Politics, Economics, and Society in the German Inflation, 1914–1924* (Oxford: Oxford University Press, 1997), vii.

14 **The price of a single egg:** Hans Hubert Hofmann, *Der Hitlerputsch. Krisenjahre deutscher Geschichte 1920–1924* (München: Nymphenburger Verlagshandlung, 1961), 311, note 332.

15 **"biggest swindler and crook":** Taylor (2013), 249.

15 **Mussolini served as a model:** Kershaw (1999), 180. Within a week of Mussolini's *Marcia a Roma*, Hermann Esser was comparing Hitler to the Italian leader, speech November 3, 1922, St.R.V. 14/1922 ff, 23, HA 4/90.

15 **"If a German Mussolini":** *Daily Mail*, October 3, 1923. Selections from this article are printed in Eberhard Jäckel und Axel Kuhn, eds., *Hitler. Sämtliche Aufzeichnungen 1905–1924* (Stuttgart: Deutsche Verlags-Anstalt, 1980), Nr. 580, 1027.

15 **"hot-air merchant":** F. L. Carsten, *Britain and the Weimar Republic: The British Documents* (London: Batsford Academic and Educational Ltd, 1984), 116.

15 **The original plan:** MA 103476/3, 1207-1208, BHStA.

15 **By November 7:** Decision made at the meeting that day, Hitler said (NA T84/2 EAP 105/7, 93), as well did the host, Lieutenant Colonel Kriebel (NA T84/2 EAP 105/7, 402–3, 2621) and the indictment; Anz. Verz.XIX 421/23, *Antrag des I. Staatsanwalts beim Volksgericht München I auf Anberaumung der Hauptverhandlung,* January 8, 1924, Staatsanwaltschaften 3098, 15, StAM. Ulrich Graf remembered it this way as well, unpublished memoir, 60, F14, IfZ.

16 **Kahr's own plans:** For more on his politics, see *Die Politik des Bayerischen Volksparteï,* HA 5/114II, and the forthcoming scholarly edition of Kahr's *Lebenserinnerungen* (NL Kahr 51, BHStA), which is scheduled to be published by Ferdinand Kramer and Matthias Bischel.

16 **Hitler decided that:** *Erklärung des Herrn Oberstlandesgerichtsrats Ernst Pöhner über die Vorgänge vom 8./9. November 1923,* December 14, 1923, HA 5/120, and Lorenz Roder's unpublished *Herr Hitler hat kein Ehrenwort gebrochen,* HA 5/126.

Chapter 3: *FOUR BULLETS*

17 **"The National Socialist Storm Troopers":** NA T84 EAP 105/7, 429.

17 **stepping over the machine gun:** NA T84/2 EAP 105/7, 1346 and 1489.

17 **There were some 1,500 members:** Harold J. Gordon Jr., *Hitler and the Beer Hall Putsch* (Princeton: Princeton University Press, 1972), 271, note 7.

17 **This was Rudolph Hess:** Dietrich Orlow, "Rudolf Hess: Deputy Führer" in Ronald Smelser and Rainier Zitelmann's *The Nazi Elite,* trans. Mary Fischer (New York: New York University Press, 1993), 74–84.

17 **a list of names:** MA 103476/3, 1389, BHStA.

17 **Each one was to be arrested:** NA T84 EAP 105/7, 401–402. The timing of this hostage-taking is traditionally placed much later in the evening, even by authorities like Gordon (1972), 290. But this was not the case, as demonstrated by many police reports, press accounts, and the testimonies of other eyewitnesses including captor Rudolf Hess (letter to Klara and Fritz Hess, November 8, 1923, with continuations November 16 and December 4, 1923, in Rudolf Hess, *Briefe 1908–1933,* ed. Wolf Rüdiger Hess [München: Langen Müller, 1987], 311–12.) See also Johann Kress statement, VI a F 2601/23, December 7, 1923, HA 67/1493; Münchner Neueste Nachrichten, November 9, 1923; and *Bayerische Staatszeitung,* November 10, 1923.

18 **even looking anyone in the eyes:** See, for example, Kurt G. W. Ludecke, *I Knew Hitler: The Story of a Nazi Who Escaped the Blood Purge* (New York: Charles Scribner's Sons, 1938), 587.

18 **"An honorable and important":** Rudolf Hess to Klara and Fritz Hess, November 8, 1923, with continuation on November 16 and December 4, 1923, Nr. 322, in Hess (1987), 310.

18 **up a narrow staircase:** Police report, *Meldungen über die Vorkommnisse in der Nacht vom 8./9.11.1923*, HA 67/1490 and VI a F 168/24, January 30, 1924, HA 67/1494.

18 **Downstairs, meanwhile:** Scene in back room draws particularly on the indictment, the pretrial and trial testimony of eight men in the room as well as pamphlets, such as Friedrich Weber's *Die Wahrheit* (1923), press accounts such as *Bamberger Tagblatt*, November 13, 1923, and the memoir of Erich Ludendorff, *Auf dem Weg zur Feldherrnhalle. Lebenserinnerungen an die Zeit des 9.11.1923 mit Dokumenten in fünf Anlagen* (München: Ludendorff, 1937), 61.

18 **Ulrich Graf handed Hitler:** Graf testimony of November 25, 1924, Zur Pistolenkomödie HA 5/117. Graf passed over this scene very quickly in his unpublished memoir, 61–62, F14, IfZ.

18 **"No one leaves":** NA T84/2 EAP 105/7, 1346, and NA T84/2 EAP 105/7, 1489.

18 **Sweating:** NA T84/2 EAP 105/7, 1262.

19 **"I know that this is difficult . . ."** and **"Yes, I did":** Anz. Verz.XIX 421/23, *Antrag des I. Staatsanwalts beim Volksgericht München I auf Anberaumung der Hauptverhandlung*, January 8, 1924, Staatsanwaltschaften 3098, 4–5, StAM; NA T84/2 EAP 105/7, 1262, 1346, 1490.

19 **Kahr stood by the window:** NA T84 EAP 105/7, 163.

19 **"How incredible":** NA T84 EAP 105/7, 229. Hitler and his supporters claimed that there had not been any threats, Weber told his father-in-law in a letter, December 8, 1923, HA 5/114I.

20 **"There must be some disagreement":** John Dornberg, *Munich 1923: The Story of Hitler's First Grab for Power* (New York: Harper & Row, 1982), 92.

20 **"That's German loyalty?"** and **"That's German unity?":** NA T84/2 EAP 105/7, 972.

20 **"South America!"** and **"Theatre!":** NA T84 EAP/2 105/7, 978.

20 **black frock coat:** *Münchener Zeitung*, November 9, 1923, with headwaiter and comparisons, for instance, Ernst Hanfstaengl, *Zwischen Weissem und Braunem Haus. Memoiren eines politischen Aussenseiters* (München: R. Piper, 1970), 137, and Ludecke (1938), 185.

20 **"the friendliest intentions"** . . . **"What are you worrying about?":** NA T84/2 EAP 105/7, 956–57, with a slightly different wording, *Münchner Neueste Nachrichten*, November 9, 1923.

20 **"distorted with ecstasy":** NA T84/2 EAP 105/7, 1258.

Chapter 4: *GERMAN ULYSSES*

21 **"This is more":** Peter Gay, *Weimar Culture: The Outsider as Insider* (London: Penguin Books, 1992), 9.
21 **fetch Ludendorff:** Anz. Verz.XIX 421/23, *Antrag des I. Staatsanwalts beim Volksgericht München I auf Anberaumung der Hauptverhandlung*, January 8, 1924, Staatsanwaltschaften 3098, 7, StAM; see also NA T84/2 EAP 105/7, 98.
21 **He had come:** Mathilde Scheubner-Richter, August 18, 1952, ZS 292, IfZ.
21 **witness the genocide:** Paul Leverkuehn, *A German Officer During the Armenian Genocide: A Biography of Max von Scheubner-Richter*, trans. Alasdair Lean (London: Gomidas Institute, 2008), lxxxvi, 18–29. For more on Scheubner-Richter's outrage, see *The Armenian Genocide: Evidence from the German Foreign Office Archives, 1915–1916*, ed. Wolfgang Gust (New York: Berghahn Books, 2014).
22 **tactical and organizational level:** Harold J. Gordon Jr., *Hitler and the Beer Hall Putsch* (Princeton: Princeton University Press, 1972), 18.
23 **By one modern estimate:** Of a review of 1,672 NSDAP party members on November 9, 1923, or rather the 994 with available birth data, almost two-thirds were under the age of 31, Gordon (1972), 68–72.
23 **"All the others are replaceable":** Georg Franz-Willing, *Putsch und Verbotszeit der Hitlerbewegung November 1923–Februar 1925* (Preussisch Oldendorf: Verlag K. W. Schütz, 1977), 15. According to Mathilde Scheubner-Richter, Hitler said this in 1931 or 1932, August 18, 1952, ZS 292, IfZ. See also Hermann Esser, interview, March 5, 1964, Band II, 6, and March 6, 1964, Band I, 21, ED 561/4, IfZ.
23 **Drawing upon the lessons:** See Michael Kellogg, *The Russian Roots of Nazism: White Émigrés and the Making of National Socialism, 1917–1945* (Cambridge: Cambridge University Press, 2005), and Stefan Ihrig, *Atatürk in the Nazi Imagination* (Cambridge, MA: Harvard University Press, 2014).
23 **Three men joined:** Johann Aigner unpublished manuscript, *Ein Beitrag zur Geschichte der nationalen Erhebung im November 1923*, HA 5/114II.
24 **A trolley car:** observations by Johann Bruckmeier, police report Nr. 1609, *Wahrnehmungen [ü]ber die Vorgänge im Bürgerbräukeller am 8. November 1923*, November 21, 1923, HA 67/1490.
24 **pacing up and down:** Margarethe Ludendorff, *My Married Life with Ludendorff*, trans. Raglan Somerset (London: Hutchinson, c.1929), 248.
24 **"urgently desired":** November 9, 1923, NL Ehard 94, BHStA, and repeated, NA T84 EAP 105/7, 531.
24 **"ten Kaisers"** . . . **"the esoteric Ulysses":** *Atlantic Monthly*, June 1917.
25 **"cheerful and free"** . . . **"had been turned to ice":** Margarethe Ludendorff (1929), 19.
26 **"The Kaiser has sacked me"** . . . **"snatched the dictatorship":** Margarethe Ludendorff (1929), 172, 178, 180–81, 280. Ludendorff discusses it briefly in his

Auf dem Weg zur Feldherrnhalle. Lebenserinnerungen an die Zeit des 9.11.1923 mit Dokumenten in fünf Anlagen (München: Ludendorff, 1937), 4–5. For more, see Robert B. Asprey, *The German High Command at War: Hindenburg and Ludendorff Conduct World War I* (New York: Quill, 1991), 484, and Will Brownell and Denise Drace-Brownell, with Alex Rovt, *The First Nazi: Erich Ludendorff, the Man Who Made Hitler Possible* (New York: Counterpoint, 2016).

26 **boarded a train for Munich:** Ludendorff claimed, unconvincingly, that he had moved there to be near one of his sisters, Ludendorff (1937), 8; NA T84/2 EAP 105/7, 496.

27 **met Adolf Hitler:** Many historians claim that Hess introduced them, but Scheubner-Richter had brought them together four months earlier.

27 **"Germany's greatest commander":** He was later called "the greatest general of the war," *LIFE*, January 17, 1938. For more on Ludendorff's accolades and their shortcomings, see Brownell and Brownell with Rovt (2016).

27 **"driving determination"** and only political leader: NA T84/2 EAP 105/7, 525.

27 **"the continual coming and going":** Margarethe Ludendorff (1929), 245. Hermann Esser elaborated on Ludendorff's villa as a hub, interview, March 3, 1964, Band II, 30–32, ED 561/3, IfZ.

27 **went inside with Heinz Pernet:** He first denied he was in the car, but later admitted it, NA T84 EAP 105/7, 694. Another man in the car, Johann Aigner, acknowledged the fact as well, in his interrogation, VI a F 36/24, January 5, 1924, HA 68/1494. The rumor of Pöhner's son in the car was incorrect.

27 **tweed hunting jacket:** Historians often present Ludendorff wearing his military uniform, even eminent authorities Kershaw (1999), 207, and Gordon (1972), 288, but this was not the case, as many eyewitnesses that night make clear. Ludendorff's choice of attire is significant because it plays a role in the larger question of premeditation.

27 **foggy night:** Johann Aigner, *Ein Beitrag zur Geschichte der nationalen Erhebung im November 1923*, 8, HA 5/114II.

27 **"whirling speed":** NA T84 EAP 105/7, 531.

27 **Snow had begun:** Ernst Röhm, *The Memoirs of Ernst Röhm*, intro. Eleanor Hancock and trans. Geoffrey Brooks (London: Frontline Books, 2012), 142, *Völkischer Beobachter*, November 9, 1923.

Chapter 5: "LOUD, RAW, AND SCREECHING"

28 **"I have often had to make quick decisions":** NA T84 EAP 105/7, 532.

28 **"the November criminals"** and **"begin the advance against Berlin":** Anz. Verz. XIX 421/23, *Antrag des I. Staatsanwalts beim Volksgericht München I auf Anberaumung der Hauptverhandlung*, January 8, 1924, Staatsanwaltschaften 3098, 6, StAM.

28 **"Heil Hitler!":** *Münchner Neueste Nachrichten*, November 9, 1923.

29 **"struggling hard to reach a decision"** and **"May I say":** Karl Alexander von Müller, *Im Wandel einer Welt. Erinnerungen Band Drei, 1919–1932* (München: Süddeutscher, 1966), 162–63, and Harold J. Gordon Jr., *Hitler and the Beer Hall Putsch* (Princeton: Princeton University Press, 1972), 288.

29 **"loud, raw, and screeching":** *Neue Zürcher Zeitung*, November 10, 1923, Zweites Morgenblatt.

29 **the crowd roared its assent:** Karl Rothenbücher, *Der Fall Kahr* (Tübingen: Mohr, 1924), 6; *Salzburger Volksblatt*, November 9, 1923; and *Berchtesgadener Anzeiger*, November 12, 1923.

29 **"[turning] them inside out":** NA T84 EAP 105/7, 978.

29 **into the side room:** For the main eyewitness sources for the back room, see notes above to chapter 3.

29 **Sesselmann thought:** unpublished account by Marc Sesselmann (his real name was Max), *Bericht*, November 1, 1935, HA 5/116.

29 **"Attention!":** Anz. Verz.XIX 421/23, *Antrag des I. Staatsanwalts beim Volksgericht München I auf Anberaumung der Hauptverhandlung*, January 8, 1924, Staatsanwaltschaften 3098, 7, StAM.

29 **Ludendorff had arrived:** Erich Ludendorff, *Auf dem Weg zur Feldherrnhalle. Lebenserinnerungen an die Zeit des 9.11.1923 mit Dokumenten in fünf Anlagen* (München: Ludendorff, 1937), 61.

29 **Karl August Ritter von Kleinhenz:** NA T84 EAP 105/7, 1046.

29 **Hitler greeted Ludendorff:** Hitler probably confirmed what Scheubner-Richter had told the general on the way there. Ludendorff interrogation, November 9, 1923, NL Ehard 94, BHStA.

29 **"Gentlemen, I am"** … **"to cooperate with *us*":** NA T84/2 EAP 105/7, 1266, 1348, 1492.

30 **but many years later:** Ludendorff's son-in-law Heinz Pernet said that the general was informed of all the details, March 1967 communications with Georg Franz-Willing, *Putsch und Verbotszeit der Hitlerbewegung November 1923–Februar 1925* (Preussich Oldendorf: Verlag K.W. Schütz KG, 1977), 67, note 6.

30 **Kahr objected:** Lorenz Roder, *Herr Hitler hat kein Ehrenwort gebrochen*, HA 5/126.

30 **"Yes, yes, but far too":** Ernst Röhm, *The Memoirs of Ernst Röhm*, intro. Eleanor Hancock and trans. Geoffrey Brooks (London: Frontline Books, 2012), 46–47.

30 **"I can't take part"** and **"Your Excellency":** NA T84/2 EAP 105/7, 1362–63.

31 **"very distraught"** and **"painful silence":** *Erklärung des Herrn Oberstlandesgerichtsrats Ernst Pöhner über die Vorgänge vom 8./9. November 1923*, December 19, 1923, HA 5/120.

31 **"just a mistake":** John Dornberg, *Munich, 1923: The Story of Hitler's First Grab for Power* (New York: Harper & Row, 1982), 103.

31 **"a viceroy of the monarchy":** NA T84 EAP 105/7, 1348.

31 **"Put on an act"**: NA T84/2 EAP 105/7, 1260 and 1755. Lossow claimed to have said this both on the platform and on the way to the side room. Hitler, Weber, Pöhner, and Ludendorff, of course, doubted it. See debate at the trial.

31 **"There is no turning back"**: Anz. Verz.XIX 421/23, *Antrag des I. Staatsanwalts beim Volksgericht München I auf Anberaumung der Hauptverhandlung*, January 8, 1924, Staatsanwaltschaften 3098, 7, StAM, and NA T84/2 EAP 105/7, 101.

Chapter 6: *SPARKLING METROPOLIS*

32 **"Previously, the beautiful"**: Lion Feuchtwanger, *Erfolg. Drei Jahre Geschichte einer Provinz* (Berlin: Gustav Kiepenheuer Verlag, 1930; Berlin: Aufbau-Verlag, 1993), 31–32.

32 **a single black suitcase**: Karl Honisch letter, May 31, 1932 in folder HA 1/17.

32 **"furnished rooms"**: Anna Popp interview, Heinz A. Heinz, *Germany's Hitler* (London: Hurst & Blackett, 1938), 49.

32 **Rudolf Häusler**: One person, Karl Honisch, recalled seeing Hitler leave Vienna with a traveling companion, but said he could not remember that man's name, May 31, 1939, HA 1/17. Identification of this person was made in the 1990s by German historian Anton Joachimsthaler. See the revised edition of his work, *Hitlers Weg begann in München 1913–1923* (München: Herbig, 2000), 17, 80–81.

33 **more painters and sculptors**: David Clay Large, *Where Ghosts Walked: Munich's Road to the Third Reich* (New York: W. W. Norton, 1997), xvi. Peter Gay calls Munich the "capital of painters in the Empire," *Weimar Culture: The Outsider as Insider* (London: Penguin Books, 1992), 7.

33 **The word "kitsch"**: Rainer Metzger, *Munich: Its Golden Age of Art and Culture 1890–1920* (London: Thames & Hudson 2009), 195.

33 **fetched for him**: Josef Popp communication of May 1966, Werner Maser, *Hitler: Legend, Myth & Reality*, trans. Peter and Betty Ross (New York: Harper Torchbooks, 1974), 133.

33 **"the happiest"** . . . **"a Babylon of races"**: Adolf Hitler, *Mein Kampf*, trans. Ralph Manheim (Boston: Houghton Mifflin Company, 1943), 126.

33 **Karl Marx**: Marx was not known among the books Hitler owned at least by 1924: Timothy W. Ryback, *Hitler's Private Library: The Books That Shaped His Life* (New York: Alfred A. Knopf, 2008), 67–68. Hitler did, however, receive a five-volume set of Schopenhauer published in 1920 as a gift, December 1, 1923, Staatanswaltschaften 3099, StAM.

34 **Clausewitz's *On War***: Josef Popp in Maser (1974), 133.

34 **"Dear Frau Popp"**: Anna Popp interview in Heinz (1938), 52.

34 **"golden age"**: For more on Munich at this time, see the introduction to the notes.

34 **A *Doll's House***: The first draft of the opening and first three acts for this play, however, were written on vacation in Rome during late spring/early summer of

1878, Michael Meyer, *Ibsen: A Biography* (Garden City, NY: Doubleday & Company, 1971), 446–53.

34 **"pure painting"** . . . **"Blue Rider"**: Peg Weiss, *Kandinsky in Munich: The Formative Jugendstil Years* (Princeton: Princeton University Press, 1979), 3, and Frank Whitford, *Kandinsky* (London: Paul Hamlyn, 1971).

35 **"Painters, sculptors, writers"**: translation, Lothar Machtan, *The Hidden Hitler*, trans. John Brownjohn (New York: Basic Books, 2001), 60.

36 **Oswald Spengler:** Rainer Metzger, *Munich: Its Golden Age of Art and Culture 1890–1920* (London: Thames & Hudson 2009), 64–65, 191.

36 **Zurich:** Cabaret Voltaire opened across the street from the apartment of another former Munich resident, V. I. Lenin.

37 **a box of cigars:** Hans Hubert Hofmann, *Der Hitlerputsch. Krisenjahre deutscher Geschichte 1920–1924* (München: Nymphenburger Verlagshandlung, 1961), 38.

37 **"Isn't it wonderful"**: Volker Ullrich, *Adolf Hitler Biographie. Band 1: Die Jahre des Aufstiegs 1889–1939* (Frankfurt am Main: S. Fischer, 2013), 91.

37 **"like every philistine's idea"**: Richard Hanser, *Putsch!: How Hitler Made Revolution* (New York: Pyramid Books, 1971), 56. Additional description comes from Ernst Toller, *Eine Jugend in Deutschland* (Amsterdam: Querido Verlag, 1933; Hamburg: Rowohlt, 1998), 86. For more on Kurt Eisner, see Bernhard Grau, *Kurt Eisner 1867–1919. Eine Biographie* (München: Verlag C. H. Beck, 2001).

37 **"realm of light, beauty and reason"**: Joachim C. Fest, *Hitler*, trans. Richard and Clara Winston (New York: Harcourt Brace Jovanovich, 1974), 109.

37 **"the curtain will come down"** and **"must become a meadow"**: Hanser (1971), 141, 167.

38 **"coffeehouse anarchists"**: Richard M. Watt, *The Kings Depart: The Tragedy of Germany: Versailles and the German Revolution* (New York: Barnes & Noble Books, 2000), 326.

38 **bourgeois reform:** Pierre Broué, *The German Revolution, 1917-1923*, trans. John Archer and intro. Eric D. Weitz (Chicago: Haymarket Books, 2005), 280.

38 **Luitpold Gymnasium:** David Luhrssen, *Hammer of the Gods: The Thule Society and the Birth of Nazism* (Washington, DC: Potomac Books, 2012), 9.

39 **killing at least six hundred "Bolsheviks"**: Heinrich August Winkler, *Weimar 1918–1933. Die Geschichte der ersten Deutschen Demokratie* (München: Verlag C. H. Beck, 1998), 81.

39 **celebrated as liberators:** Toller (1933; 1998), 116.

39 **"cell of law and order"**: Wilhelm Hoegner, *Die verratene Republik. Deutsche Geschichte 1919–1933* (München: Nymphenburger Verlagshandlung, 1979), 109.

39 ***Einwohnerwehren:*** *Münchner Neueste Nachrichten* published Allied note, October 30, 1920, and Kahr's response the following day also in Carl Moser von Filseck, *Politik in Bayern 1919–1933. Berichte des württembergischen Gesandten*

Carl Moser von Filseck, ed. Wolfgang Benz. Schriftenreihe der Vierteljahrshefte für Zeitgeschichte Nummer 22/23 (Stuttgart: Deutsche Verlags-Anstalt, 1971), Nr. 211, 68. For more on the militia, see David Clay Large, *The Politics of Law and Order: A History of the Bavarian Einwohnerwehr 1918–1921* (Philadelphia: American Philosophical Society, 1980).

39 **Kahr had pledged to stand or fall:** *Der Oberbayer*, November 19–20, 1923.

40 **general state commissioner:** Generalstaatskommissar, *Niederschrift der Ministerrats-sitzung*, September 26, 1923, printed in Ernst Deuerlein, ed., *Der Hitler-Putsch. Bayerische Dokumente zum 8./9. November 1923* (Stuttgart: Deutsche Verlags-Anstalt, 1962), Nr. 12, 180–82, and *Chronik der Bayerischen Justizverwaltung*, 267–70, NL Ehard 90/3, BHStA.

40 **an umbrella:** *Zeitübersicht zur nationalen Erhebung und zu deren Missbrauch*, HA 5/127.

40 **"Danubian monarchy":** This term was in wide circulation, for example, *Gross-deutsche Zeitung*, March 25, 1924.

Chapter 7: HARVARD'S GIFT

41 **"It's a far cry":** Ernst Hanfstaengl, *The Memoir of a Nazi Insider Who Turned Against the Führer*, intro. John Willard Toland (New York: Arcade Publishing, 2011, first edition 1957), 31.

41 **"Putzi," or "Little Fellow":** this was given by his nurse, Kati, Peter Conradi, *Hitler's Piano Player: The Rise and Fall of Ernst Hanfstaengl, Confidant of Hitler, Ally of FDR* (New York: Carroll & Graf Publishers, 2004), 14.

42 **art-printing and reproduction business:** Rainer Metzger, *Munich: Its Golden Age of Art and Culture 1890–1920* (London: Thames & Hudson 2009), 198.

42 **"seven brass strings"** and **"a madhouse":** Hanfstaengl (2011, 1957), 27, 30.

42 **pledged a loan:** A copy of the contract was found by the police in a search of the *Völkischer Beobachter* offices after the putsch, Staatsanwaltschaften 3099, StAM. See also MA 103476/1, 114, BHStA. The importance of the loan to the party is in Detlef Mühlberger, *Hitler's Voice: The Völkischer Beobachter, 1920–1933* (New York: Peter Lang 2004), I, 21, and role of the paper for Hitler in Dietrich Orlow, *The History of the Nazi Party: 1919–1933* (Pittsburgh: University of Pittsburgh Press, 1969), 21.

42 **Hitler's paper expanded:** Horst J. Weber, *Die deutsche Presse, insbesondere die völkische, um den Hitlerprozess. Ein Beitrag zur Lehre von der Parteipresse*. Diss. (Universität Leipzig, 1930), 10.

42 **a cartoonist . . . "Work and Bread":** *Völkischer Beobachter*, August 29, 1923, Conradi (2004), 53.

42 **notorious sweet tooth:** Ernst Hanfstaengl, *Zwischen Weissem und Braunem Haus. Memoiren eines politischen Aussenseiters* (München: R. Piper, 1970), 44.

42 **dipping a piece of chocolate:** Helen Niemeyer, "Notes," 279, folder "Ernst Hanfstaengl (1)," John Toland Papers, FDR.

43 **"the upper crust":** Kurt G. W. Ludecke, *I Knew Hitler: The Story of a Nazi Who Escaped the Blood Purge* (New York: Charles Scribner's Sons, 1938), 95.

43 **"gangster hat":** Kershaw (1999), 188.

43 **"ridiculous little smudge":** Hanfstaengl (1957, 2011), 67.

43 **"I broke out laughing!":** H. R. Knickerbocker, *Is Tomorrow Hitler's?: 200 Questions on the Battle of Mankind* (New York: Reynal & Hitchcock, 1941), 1–2.

43 **caviar, pheasant, and raspberries:** Conradi (2004), 57.

43 **"journalistic delicacy":** Hanfstaengl (1970), 130.

43 **watched the events unfold:** Police report, November 19, 1923, HA, 67/1490; Fritz Stumpf, police report, *Putsch der Nat. Sozialisten in der Nacht v. 8./9. 23*, November 13, 1923, HA 67/1490, and MA 103476/3, 1223, BHStA; Sigmund Freiherr von Imhoff, November 15, 1923, Handakt der GSK, MA 104221, BHStA; Wilhelm Frick's testimony, NA T84/2 EAP 105/7, 714–19; *Bericht über den Verlauf der Nacht vom 8./9. November 1923*, HA 67/1490 and NA T84 EAP 105/7, 868–71.

44 **"completely powerless":** Police report, *Meldungen über die Vorkommnisse in der Nacht vom 8./9.11.1923*, HA 67/1490.

44 **"There is nothing":** NA T84/2 EAP 105/7, 871.

44 **Frick reminded:** Reports, Abteilung VIa, *Polizeiliche Massnahmen aus Anlass von Versammlungen*, November 19, 1923, and report by Fritz Stumpf, November 13, 1923, HA 67/1490.

45 **"to avoid bloodshed":** MA 103476/3, 1223, BHStA.

45 **"Wait for instructions":** John Dornberg, *Munich, 1923: The Story of Hitler's First Grab for Power* (New York: Harper & Row, 1982), 80.

45 **Frick had worked his way:** Reinhard Weber, " 'Ein tüchtiger Beamter von makelloser Vergangenheit.' Das Disziplinarverfahren gegen den Hochverräter Wilhelm Frick 1924," *Vierteljahrshefte für Zeitgeschichte* 42 (1994), Heft 1, 129–50; Frick's own account is at NA T84/2 EAP 105/7, 700–703, and his interrogation on November 10, 1923, Sonderakt Frick, HA 5/114I; and an assessment by Albert Krebs, *The Infancy of Nazism: The Memoirs of Ex-Gauleiter Albert Krebs 1923–1933*, ed. and trans. William Sheridan Allen (New York: New Viewpoints, 1976), 259–62.

Chapter 8: THE NEW REGIME

46 **"The rabble has to be scared":** Joachim C. Fest, *Hitler*, trans. Richard and Clara Winston (New York: Harcourt Brace Jovanovich, 1974), 133.

46 **out of Friedrich Schiller's play *Wilhelm Tell*:** Karl Alexander von Müller, NA T84/2 EAP 105/7, 981. See also NA T84/2 EAP 105/7, 1676–77 as well as the undated confidential report, *Der Putsch vom 8.Nov.1923*, HA 67/1491.

46 **"heavy heart" . . . "viceroy of the monarchy":** Anz. Verz.XIX 421/23, *Antrag des*

I. Staatsanwalts beim Volksgericht München I auf Anberaumung der Hauptverhandlung, January 8, 1924, Staatsanwaltschaften 3098, 9, StAM.

47 **"know neither rest nor peace"** . . . **"a Germany of power and greatness":** Anz. Verz.XIX 421/23, *Antrag des I. Staatsanwalts,* January 8, 1924, Staatsanwaltschaften 3098, 8, StAM.

47 **"Heil Hitler!":** *Münchner Neueste Nachrichten,* November 9, 1923.

47 **"mailed fist" style:** Associated Press, November 10, 1923.

47 **"the turning point of our history":** Anz. Verz.XIX 421/23, *Antrag des I. Staatsanwalts,* January 8, 1924, Staatsanwaltschaften 3098, 9, StAM; Erich Ludendorff, *Auf dem Weg zur Feldherrnhalle. Lebenserinnerungen an die Zeit des 9.11.1923 mit Dokumenten in fünf Anlagen* (München: Ludendorff, 1937), 61–62.

47 **Professor Müller watched:** NA T84/2 EAP 105/7, 980.

47 **rapturous applause:** *Berchtesgadener Anzeiger,* November 12, 1923.

47 **since the declaration:** *Erklärung des Herrn Oberlandesgerichtsrats Ernst Pöhner über die Vorgänge vom 8./9. November 1923,* December 19, 1923, HA 5/120.

47 **only thing missing:** undated confidential report, *Der Putsch vom 8.Nov.1923,* HA 67/1491.

47 **release the crowd:** Berchtold, April 17, 1924, MA 103476/3, 1216, BHStA, and search for alleged Socialists or Communists in crowd, police report, March 8, 1924, HA 68/1494, with detaining hostages, Anz. Verz.XIX 421/23, *Antrag des I. Staatsanwalts,* January 8, 1924, Staatsanwaltschaften 3098, 11, StAM.

48 **He apologized:** Eugen von Knilling told Carl Moser von Filseck, *Politik in Bayern 1919–1933. Berichte des württembergischen Gesandten Carl Moser von Filseck,* ed. Wolfgang Benz. Schriftenreihe der Vierteljahrshefte für Zeitgeschichte Nummer 22/23 (Stuttgart: Deutsche Verlags-Anstalt, 1971), November 14, 1923, Nr. 322, 144, and testimony of Alfred Rosenberg, VIa 2500/23, June 6, 1924, HA 67/1493.

48 **"unilateral, unscrupulous, and terroristic":** St.R.V. 14/1922 ff, 19, HA 4/90. See also Franz Schweyer, *Politische Geheimverbände. Blicke in die Vergangenheit und Gegenwart des Geheimburdwesens* (Freiburg: Herder, 1925).

48 **Hitler had given his word:** Later both Hitler and his lawyer, Lorenz Roder, argued that this promise had been conditional, for instance, Roder, *Herr Hitler hat kein Ehrenwort gebrochen,* HA 5/126.

48 **"like an angry schoolmaster":** Fest (1974), 778, note 48.

48 **he ordered Hess:** NA T84 EAP 105/7, 873.

Chapter 9: *"SAFELY DELIVERED"*

49 **"If active people could":** Ernst Toller, *Eine Jugend in Deutschland* (Amsterdam: Querido Verlag, 1933; Hamburg: Rowohlt, 1998), 153.

49 **Crowds:** *Ereignisse von der Nacht vom 8./9.11.23,* November 20, 1923, HA 67/1493.

49 **US vice consul:** He was soon promoted to consul of class 7, though still acting vice consul, Murphy to secretrary of state, December 21, 1923, Robert D. Murphy Papers, Box 6, HI.

50 **"a cold, bare office":** Robert Murphy interview, *People*, March 8, 1976.

50 **$50,50:** Murphy testimony, December 11, 1975, *US Intelligence Agencies and Activities: Intelligence costs and fiscal procedures*, US Congress House, Select Committee on Intelligence (1976), 1868.

50 **Milwaukee neighborhood:** *The News and Courier*, August 10, 1958.

50 **work typically consisted:** American Consular Service, *Summary of Business*, Form No.243, Robert D. Murphy Papers, Box 6, Folder 10, HI. See also Robert D. Murphy, *Diplomat Among Warriors* (Garden City, NY: Doubleday & Company, 1964), 15.

50 **"urgent," "confidential,"** and **"ACCORDING [TO] HITLER":** Murphy to Secretary of State, November 8, 1923, M336, 862.00/1338, No. 19, NA.

51 **"comradely festive evening":** *Völkischer Beobachter*, November 8, 1923.

51 **sick from jaundice:** Hermann Esser, interview, March 6, 1964, Band II, 11, ED 561/4, IfZ, with confirmations in police report, April 11, 1924, HA 67/1493 and Heinrich Hoffmann, who spoke with him that night, *Hitler Was My Friend*, trans. Lt-Col R.H. Stevens (London: Burke, 1955), 54.

51 **asked to stand in for Hitler:** NA T84 EAP 105/7, 575.

51 **"a demon speechmaker":** Joachim C. Fest, *Hitler*, trans. Richard and Clara Winston (New York: Harcourt Brace Jovanovich, 1974), 136.

51 **"Jewish big business":** Police report, VId/131, *Versammlung der "Reichskriegsflagge" im Löwenbräukeller am Donnerstag, den 8. November 1923 abends 8 Uhr*, November 27, 1923, HA 67/1490.

51 **"Safely Delivered":** Anz. Verz.XIX 421/23, *Antrag des I. Staatsanwalts*, January 8, 1924, Staatanswaltschaften 3098, 35, StAM.

51 **The call:** Albert Simmerding, January 19, 1924, and his statement in VI a F, February 22, 1924, HA 67/1494.

51 **The message:** NA T84 EAP 105/7, 576, with chauffer hurrying in, NA T84 EAP 105/7, 882–83.

51 **a former staff officer:** Röhm's resignation and its acceptance, November 17, 1923, HA 5/114I and Ernst Röhm, *The Memoirs of Ernst Röhm*, intro. Eleanor Hancock and trans. Geoffrey Brooks (London: Frontline Books, 2012), 112–15. For more on the twists and turns of this episode, see Eleanor Hancock, *Ernst Röhm: Hitler's SA Chief of Staff* (London: Palgrave Macmillan, 2008), 55–57.

52 **prominent scars:** Röhm (2012), 1–2, and Hancock (2008), 2.

52 **"the living image of war":** Kurt G. W. Ludecke, *I Knew Hitler: The Story of a Nazi Who Escaped the Blood Purge* (New York: Charles Scribner's Sons, 1938), 245.

52 **one of the few:** Franz Xaver Schwarz, July 21, 1945, ZS 1452, IfZ.

52 **"The Machine Gun King":** This nickname was especially popular with the

left-wing press, Hans Hubert Hofmann, *Der Hitlerputsch. Krisenjahre deutscher Geschichte 1920–1924* (München: Nymphenburger Verlagshandlung, 1961), 75.

52   **whispered something:** Friedrich Mayer, testimony in VI a F 404/24, February 13, 1924, HA 68/1494.

52   **Esser then announced:** Several historians present Röhm as making the annoucement to the crowd, but it was actually Esser: Police report, VId/131, November 27, 1923, HA 67/1490, along with numerous eyewitnesses and participants, including Esser himself, interview, March 6, 1964, Band II, 27, ED 561/4, IfZ.

52   **ripped off the republican:** IV a F 2671/23, December 6, 1923, HA 67/1493. See also Röhm's *Denkschrift über die Ereignisse des 8./9. November 1923*, November 17, 1923, HA 5/114I.

52   **a brass band:** NA T84 EAP 105/7, 576–77, with celebration in streets, NA T84/2 EAP 105/7, 716, and rushing out of cafés, NA T84/2 EAP 105/7, 609.

52   **At the front of the procession:** Heinrich Himmler interrogation, A.V.I.209/23, April 30, 1924, HA 68/1494. He was a member of Reichskriegflagge and did not join the National Socialists until August 2, 1925.

52   **carrying the fighting society's battle flag:** Peter Longerich, *Heinrich Himmler*, trans. Jeremy Noakes and Lesley Sharpe (Oxford: Oxford University Press, 2012), 68–69.

53   **the Franciscan Abbey Church:** Police reports in files at VIa 2500/23, Staatsanwaltschaften 3099, StAM; police reports, November 10, 1923 and November 13, 1923, HA 67/1493.

53   **Brückner led:** Police report, No.138, November 13, 1923, HA 67/1494, and Friedrich Mayer, VI a F 404/24, February 13, 1924, HA 68/1494.

53   **coffee:** A. Winderl, unpublished *Der Weg zur Feldherrnhalle*, HA 4/100.

53   **stored at the Corpshaus Palatia:** Karl Osswald testimony, February 3, 1924, HA 67/1493.

53   **bowling alley:** Andreas Mutz interrogations at VI a F 317/24, February 8, 1924, and Karl Hühnlein, VIa 2500/23, May 3, 1924, HA 67/1493.

53   **marched off:** Johann Sebastian Will testimony, IV a F 2671/23, December 5, 1923, HA 67/1493.

53   **to seize control:** Röhm, XIX 466/23, January 3, 1924, HA 67/1493; Röhm (2012), 145–46; NA T84/2 EAP 105/7, 2207; Ludendorff denied giving order, Ludendorff-Ehard interrogation, December 22, 1923, HA 5/114I.

54   **more than a hundred armed men:** Generalstaatskommissar Kahr an die Vorstandschaft der Bay. Offiziers-Regiments-Vereine, November 14, 1923, Ernst Deuerlein, ed. *Der Hitler-Putsch. Bayerische Dokumente zum 8./9. November 1923* (Stuttgart: Deutsche Verlags-Anstalt, 1962), Nr. 125, 385.

54   **one of the largest:** Wilhelm Hoegner, *Die Verratene Republik. Deutsche Geschichte 1919–1933* (München: Nymphenburger Verlagshandlung, 1979), 132. See also Friedrich Weber, November 16, 1923, MA 103476/3, 1123–24, BHStA, and Kameradschaft Freikorps und Bund Oberland, *Für das stolze Edelweiss.*

Bild- und Textband zur Geschichte von Freikorps Oberland und Bund Oberland (repr. München: Brienna-Verlag, 1999).

54 **already scheduled maneuvers:** Police report, *Bericht zur mündlichen Einvernahme durch Herrn Obereg.Rat Thenner*, November 13, 1923, HA 67/1490. Many members of Bund Oberland later confirmed this fact with the Munich police.

54 **"the rabble of racial alien Jews":** NA T84/2 EAP 105/7, 165.

54 **At the Army Engineer Barracks:** Anz. Verz.XIX 421/23, *Antrag des I. Staatsanwalts,* January 8, 1924, Staatsanwaltschaften 3098, 20–21, StAM, and VI a F 2500/23, Hans Oemler, December 18, 1923, HA 67/1493, Gordon (1972) 289, 296–98. See also the interrogation of Julius Schreck, VI a F 23/24, January 5, 1924, HA 67/1493.

55 **he then discovered:** Anz. Verz.XIX 421/23, *Antrag des I. Staatsanwalts,* January 8, 1924, Staatsanwaltschaften 3098, 25, StAM.

55 **General Ludendorff had decided:** Erich Ludendorff, *Auf dem Weg zur Feldherrnhalle. Lebenserinnerungen an die Zeit des 9.11.1923 mit Dokumenten in fünf Anlagen* (München: Ludendorff, 1937), 62.

55 **Hitler could not have imagined:** He was probably not at first as concerned as often portrayed by biographers and historians of the putsch, for instance, Werner Maser, *Der Sturm auf die Republik. Frühgeschichte der NSDAP* (Frankfurt am Main: Ullstein Sachbuch, 1981), 452, or Hans Hubert Hofmann, *Der Hitlerputsch. Krisenjahre deutscher Geschichte 1920–1924* (München: Nymphenburger Verlagshandlung, 1961), 169. Hitler did in fact want to give that impression in December 1923, but these statements seem to be an afterthought reflecting later disputes that were emerging between Hitler and Ludendorff. See also Ulrich Graf's testimony in his interrogation, VI a F 244/23–24, February 8, 1924, HA 67/1494. An earlier mistake, it was already said by his supporters, was to rely upon Kahr in the first place, *Salzburger Volksblatt,* November 9, 1923.

55 **forbade him:** Friedrich Weber testimony, NA T84/2 EAP 105/7, 168.

Chapter 10: COUNTER-PUTSCH

56 **"The leaders of the National Socialists":** VI a F 2500/23, December 18, 1923, HA 67/1493.

56 **"sheer madness"** and **"Who let":** Ernst Hanfstaengl, *Zwischen Weissem und Braunem Haus. Memoiren eines politischen Aussenseiters* (München: R. Piper, 1970), 138–39. See also Esser's interview, March 6, 1964, Band II, 33–35, ED 561/4, IfZ and Heinrich Hoffmann, who spoke with him not long afterward, *Hitler Was My Friend,* trans. Lt-Col R.H. Stevens (London: Burke, 1955), 55–56.

56 **also incredulous:** Hanfstaengl (1970), 138–39, and Helen Niemeyer, "Notes," 305, folder "Ernst Hanfstaengl (1)," John Toland Papers, FDR.

56 **shards of the beer mug:** Sesselmann, *Bericht,* November 1, 1935, HA 5/116.

57 **He chose instead:** Karl Rothenbücher, *Der Fall Kahr* (Tübingen: Mohr, 1924), 21–22.

57 **he greeted his daughter:** NA T84 EAP 105/7, 1351.

57 **Kahr appeared:** NA T84/2 EAP 105/7, 2052.

58 **he had already mobilized:** NA T84/2 EAP 105/7, 1404–5, with timing and additional details, including advice to abolish the Weimar Constitution at NA T84/2 EAP 105/7, 2050–53. See also *Die Drahtzieher in München*, HA 5/116. Kahr admitted this fact, NA T84/2 EAP 105/7, 1711.

58 **"What does Hitler actually" and "the famous march":** NA T84 EAP 105/7, 1352, with approximate timing, NA T84 EAP 105/7, 1440.

58 **Regensburg:** Telegramm aus Regensburg 9.11 2 Ur 40, HA 67/1491, and Rothenbücher (1924), 22–23.

58 **at about 9:15 p.m.:** NA T84/2 EAP 105/7, 1167–68; Fritz Stumpf, police report, *Putsch der Nat. Sozialisten in der Nacht v. 8./9. 23*, November 13, 1923, HA 67/1490, and Harold J. Gordon Jr., *Hitler and the Beer Hall Putsch* (Princeton: Princeton University Press, 1972), 277.

58 **"breathless":** Major Imhoff, November 15, 1923, MA 104221, BHStA. He repeated the statement at NA T84/2 EAP 105/7, 1167.

59 **Danner came at once:** NA T84/2 EAP 105/7, 1168–69. For more on the conversation, see the log at Kommandantur München, No. 4453/I, November 19, 1923, StAM, and Danner's report, *Ereignisse und Anordnungen am 8. November 1923*, Staatsanwaltschaften 3098, StAM.

59 **"a sad figure of a man":** Captain Hans Bergen testimony, NA T84/2 EAP 105/7, 1872, and Danner's version of the events at 1943–51.

60 **"a prisoner":** Kahr and Seisser were also believed to be prisoners, Jakob von Danner, *Ereignisse und Anordnungen am 8. November 1923*, Staatsanwaltschaften 3098, StAM and orders in his name, NA T84/2 EAP 105/7, 1941.

Chapter 11: INITIATIVE

61 **"We must seize":** Richard Hanser, *Putsch!: How Hitler Made Revolution* (New York: Pyramid Books, 1971), 338.

61 **Holzkirchnerstrasse 2:** Anz. Verz.XIX 421/23, *Antrag des I. Staatsanwalts beim Volksgericht München I auf Anberaumung der Hauptverhandlung*, January 8, 1924, Staatsanwaltschaften 3098, 11, StAM, and NA T84 EAP 105/7, 829–30.

61 **the recommendation:** Friedrich Weber, statement at Gefängnis Stadelheim, XIX 466/23, January 9, 1924, HA 67/1493.

61 **"Please regard yourselves":** John Dornberg's *Munich 1923: The Story of Hitler's First Grab for Power* (New York: Harper & Row, 1982), 156. For more, see MA 103476/3, 1367, BHStA.

61 **"This cuckoo's egg":** Harold J. Gordon Jr., *Hitler and the Beer Hall Putsch* (Princeton: Princeton University Press, 1972), 290, note 66.

62 **"conspiracy and intrigue":** Ernst Hanfstaengl, *Hitler: The Memoir of a Nazi Insider Who Turned Against the Führer*, intro. John Willard Toland (New York: Arcade Publishing, 1957, repr. 2011), 44.

62 **an early supper:** Elsa Gisler, November 19, 1923, HA 67/1493; Anna Schürz, November 20, 1923, HA 67/1493.

62 **Max Amann:** MA 103476/3, 1243–1246, BHStA, and work at the bank, interrogation, December 6, 1946, ZS-809, IfZ.

62 **still acted like one:** Albert Krebs, *The Infancy of Nazism: The Memoirs of Ex-Gauleiter Albert Krebs 1923–1933*, ed. and trans. William Sheridan Allen (New York: New Viewpoints, 1976), 246.

62 **"ruthless, hardheaded":** Helen Niemeyer, "Notes," 287, folder Ernst Hanfstaengl (1), John Toland Papers, FDR. Hermann Esser used similar terms in an interview, March 2, 1964, Band I, ED 561/3, IfZ. See also Ludwig Ess, letter to Adolf Hitler, March 6, 1925, HA 4/85.

62 **bear-hugged:** Gordon (1972), 60.

62 **"a commonplace man":** Thomas Weber, *Hitler's First War: Adolf Hitler, the Men of the List Regiment, and the First World War* (Oxford: Oxford University Press, 2010), 140.

63 **He lived on the fourth floor:** Police report, VId 1659 VId/131, HA 69/1500.

63 **It was Feder:** Hitler's praise of him, Adolf Hitler, *Mein Kampf*, trans. Ralph Manheim (Boston: Houghton Mifflin Company, 1943), 210, 215.

63 **the new finance committee:** Gottfried Feder, unpublished diary, *Tagebücher*, ED 874/5, 20, IfZ. Proclamation is in *Völkischer Beobachter*, November 9, 1923 and a copy in HA 5/119.

63 **withdrawing his own savings:** This was confirmed by employee at the bank, VI a F 161/24, January 21, 1924, HA 67/1494. See also *Münchner Neueste Nachrichten*, November 23, 1923, and *Völkischer Kurier*, May 14, 1924.

63 *Der Stürmer:* Horst J. Weber, *Die deutsche Presse, insbesondere die völkische, um den Hitlerprozess. Ein Beitrag zur Lehre von der Parteipresse*. Diss. (Universität Leipzig, 1930), 20.

63 **Streicher had arrived:** Police report, December 1, 1923, HA 67/1493.

63 **to craft a proclamation:** Philipp Bouhler, January 31, 1924, HA 67/1492.

63 **"the most shameful period":** *An die Münchner Bevölkerung!*, copy in HA 67/1492.

63 **the earliest known reference:** Ian Kershaw, *Hitler 1889–1936: Hubris* (New York: W. W. Norton, 1999), 208.

63 **Reich Chancellor:** *An alle Deutschen!*, copy in HA 67/1492.

63 **"open season" . . . "dead or alive":** Text of order relayed by a member of Stosstrupp Hitler and collected by parliamentary investigatory committee, with a copy filed at HA 69/1500A. See also *Völkischer Beobachter*, November 9, 1923.

64 **"weather vane":** NA T84 EAP 105/7, 209.

64 **"energetic, bold, and quick":** Ernst Röhm, *The Memoirs of Ernst Röhm*, intro. Eleanor Hancock and trans. Geoffrey Brooks (London: Frontline Books, 2012), 34.

65 **a midnight press conference:** NA T84/2 EAP 105/7, 721; police report, December 7, 1923, Ernst Deuerlein, ed., *Der Hitler-Putsch. Bayerische Dokumente zum 8./9. November 1923* (Stuttgart: Deutsche Verlags-Anstalt, 1962), Nr. 174, 475; *Erklärung des Herrn Oberstlandesgerichtsrats Ernst Pöhner über die Vorgänge vom 8./9. November 1923*, December 19, 1923, HA 5/120, along with interviews from participants Paul Egenter, Fritz Gerlich, and several other people in the files at HA 67/1493.

65 **"discipline":** NA T84/2 EAP 105/7, 348.

65 **opened the forum to questions:** Interrogation, January 30, 1924 and March 20, 1924, HA 67/1493, as well as Eugen Mündler, February 2, 1924, HA 67/1493.

65 **Wassermann had been detained:** Dr. Ludwig Wassermann statement, November 21, 1923, HA 5/114I, and police report, VI a F 566/24, March 21, 1924, HA 68/1494, and MA 103476/3, 1439, BHStA.

65 **completely indifferent:** MA 103476/3, 1231, BHStA.

Chapter 12: BARBARIAN HORDES

66 **"We do not have the right or authority":** David Clay Large, *Where Ghosts Walked: Munich's Road to the Third Reich* (New York: W. W. Norton, 1997), 179.

66 **"Without the Jews!":** Police report, *Hitlerputsch im Bürgerbräukeller*, November 22, 1923, HA 67/1490.

66 **"Ukrainian pogromists"... "What a pity":** Jewish Telegraphic Agency, November 14, 1923.

67 **"Ludendorff and Hitler declare war":** Jewish Telegraphic Agency, November 5, 1923.

67 **"Jewish paper":** Georg Fuchs, unpublished memoir, HA 5/114I, 71.

67 **Münchener Pest:** Berchtold interview in Heinz A. Heinz, *Germany's Hitler* (London: Hurst & Blackett, 1938), 157.

67 **"Poison Kitchen":** This was regularly used, for instance, Karl A. Kessler, *Der 9. November 1923 in München. Erlebnisse eines SA Mannes* (München: Walter, 1933), 15 and Erich Malitius, *Der 8. u. 9. November 1923. Die Geschichte von Treue und Verrat der deutschen Jugend* (Breslau: Handel, 1935), 12. For more on this image, see Ron Rosenbaum's excellent *Explaining Hitler: The Search for the Origins of His Evil* (New York: HarperPerennial, 1999) 38.

67 **Once inside the building:** *Münchener Post*, November 27, 1923, and *Münchner Neueste Nachrichten*, November 10, 1923.

67 **four large display windows:** *Münchener Zeitung*, November 9, 1923; *Vorwärts*, May 21, 1924; and *Münchener Post*, November 27, 1923, when it could finally be

published again. This delayed return was because of the destruction as well as the lifting of a ban placed on November 9, 1923. See also the treatment by a participant, Hans Kallenbach, *Mit Adolf Hitler auf Festung Landsberg* (München: Kress & Hornung, 1939), 26–27.

67 **Postcards were later:** Copies are in folders HA 5/125 and 67/1491.

67 **"We forced [open] the doors":** Berchtold interview in Heinz (1938), 157.

67 **any picture or bust:** *Salzburger Volksblatt*, November 10, 1923.

68 **The Stosstrupp Hitler hauled:** Ferdinand Mürriger gegen Berchtold, Maurice et al., A.V. XIX 466/29 December 24, 1923, Staatsanwaltschaften 3098, StAM.

68 **spare tires:** Proz.Reg.Nr. 187/1924 (Stosstrupp Hitler Trial), Gründe des Urteiles, May 3, 1924, HA 67/1493.

68 **this had probably:** MA 103476/3, 1217, BHStA.

68 **banner flew:** It was raised through a smashed window, report at VI a F 425/24, February 22, 1924, HA 67/1494.

68 **"smoking ruins":** *Der Zerstörung der 'Münchener Post.'* HA 5/116. For more, see MA 103476/3, 1232–34, BHStA.

68 **Emil Maurice:** Copy of his identity card, HA 4/94.

68 **the first leader:** Maurice led the Sports and Gymnastics Section, police report, September 27, 1921, HA 65/1483, as well as unpublished manuscript, *Regiment München, II Batallion, 6 Kompanie*, HA 4/100, and his interview with the International Military Tribunal, March 16, 1946, ZS 270, IfZ. For Maurice's work with the Hall Defense, see Bruce Campbell, *The SA Generals and the Rise of Nazism* (Lexington: University Press of Kentucky, 1998), 20, and his relationship with Hitler, Anna Maria Sigmund, *Des Führers bester Freund. Adolf Hitler, seine Nichte Geli Raubal und der "Ehrenarier" Emil Maurice—eine Dreiecksbeziehung* (München: Heyne, 2003).

68 **"Where is your husband?"** and **"We are the masters":** Sophie Auer testimony, Anz. Verz. XIX. 592/23, *Akt Hübner Ernst u. Gen. wegen Landfriedensbruch*, HA 67/1491.

69 **carrying off:** Proz.Reg.Nr. 187/1924 (Stosstrupp Hitler Trial), Gründe des Urteiles, May 3, 1924, HA 67/1493.

69 **substitute hostage:** NA T84 EAP 105/7, 1607.

69 **One group . . . "Jews and other":** MA 103476/3, 1447, 1234–35, 1056–57, 1070, BHStA.

69 **"All Jews out!":** Anz. Verz. XIX. 592/23, *Akt Hübner Ernst u. Gen. wegen Landfriedensbruch*, HA 67/1491.

69 **Police reports:** The arrest of Jews was not mentioned nearly as much in the press or reports as other crimes that night. See the police log, *Meldungen über die Vorkommnisse in der Nacht vom 8./9.11.1923*, HA 67/1490, and police report to Kahr, December 7, 1923, printed in Ernst Deuerlein, ed., *Der Hitler-Putsch. Bayerische Dokumente zum 8./9. November 1923* (Stuttgart: Deutsche Verlags-Anstalt, 1962), Nr. 174, 474–75.

70 **Jewish shop or delicatessen:** Richard J. Evans points out this error in his *Lying*

About Hitler: History, Holocaust, and the David Irving Trial (New York: Basic Books, 2002), 46–49. Hofmann's testimony is at NA T84 EAP 105/7, 886–87. For more on Hofmann's background, particularly as member of the Nazi Party, see the parliamentary investigation at MA 103476/2, 788, BHStA. Hofmann's visit at Landsberg is in the *Sprechkarte*, Folder No. 4, JVA 17.000, StAM.

70 **night of terror:** Account by a captive held there that night: report, November 18, 1923, HA 5/114I; Ludwig Wassermann statement, November 21, 1923, HA 5/114I; *Vorwärts*, November 26, 1923; Captain Johann Salbey's police report, November 22, 1923, printed in Deuerlein (1962), Nr. 136, Beilage C, 421. See also MA 103476/3, 1439, BHStA.

70 **Historian Erich Eyck suggested that twenty-four:** Erich Eyck, *A History of the Weimar Republic*, trans. Harlan P. Hanson and Robert G. L. Waite (Cambridge, MA: Harvard University Press, 1962), I, 276. Another figure is 20, Georg Franz-Willing, *Putsch und Verbotszeit der Hitlerbewegung November 1923–Februar 1925* (Preussisch Oldendorf: Verlag K.W. Schütz, 1977), 82–83. The number in the unpublished memoir and the words "protective custody" come from Johann Aigner, *Ein Beitrag zur Geschichte der nationalen Erhebung im November 1923*, 15, HA 5/114II. A similar figure (58) appears at MA 103476/3, 1236, BHStA.

Chapter 13: MIDNIGHT IN MUNICH

71 **"The peacocks need to be plucked":** Leonard Mosley, *The Reich Marshal: A Biography of Hermann Goering* (New York: Dell Publishing Co., 1975), 57–58.

71 **Hotel Continental:** Gustav von Stresemann, *Vermächtnis. Der Nachlass in Drei Bänden* (Berlin: Ullstein, 1932), I, 204.

71 **"a putsch in Munich":** *Akten der Reichskanzlei Weimarer Republik. Die Kabinette Stresemann I u. II.* Band II (1978), Nr. 231, 997–98. See also report, Nr. 264 November 11, 1923, HA 5/114II.

71 **emergency meeting:** Kabinettsitzung von 9. November 1923, 12 Uhr, R 43 I/1389 Bl 81–82 in *Akten der Reichskanzlei Weimarer Republik. Die Kabinette Stresemann I u. II.* Band II (1978), 998–1000.

71 **"more than a dash" . . . "might have been":** Viscount Edgar Vincent D'Abernon, *The Diary of an Ambassador* (Garden City, NY: Doubleday, Doran & Company, 1929–1931), III, 10.

72 **He had worked:** Carl Schorske, *German Social Democracy, 1905–1917: The Development of the Great Schism* (Cambridge, MA: Harvard University Press, 1955, 1983 edition), 123.

72 **"Mr. President":** Jonathan Wright, *Gustav Stresemann: Weimar's Greatest Statesman* (Oxford: Oxford University Press, 2002), 248.

72 **the monocle:** Friedrich von Rabenau, *Seeckt. Aus seinem Leben 1918–1936* (Leipzig: Hase & Koehler, 1940), 374.

72 **"The Sphinx":** Frédéric Hirth, *Hitler, ou le guerrier déchaîné* (Paris: éditions du Tambourin, 1930), 135, and F. L. Carsten, *The Reichswehr and Politics 1918–1933* (Berkeley: University of California Press, 1973), 104.

72 **"the public safety and order":** Article 48 of the Weimar Constitution.

73 **136 times:** Richard J. Evans, *The Coming of the Third Reich* (New York: Penguin Books, 2003), 80.

73 **replace it with a dictatorship:** Carsten (1973), 187.

73 **"welcome pretext"** and **"unforeseeable consequences":** Bayerische Gesandtschaft beim Hl. Stuhl an das Staatsministerium des Äussern, November 9, 1923, Ernst Deuerlein, ed., *Der Hitler-Putsch. Bayerische Dokumente zum 8./9. November 1923* (Stuttgart: Deutsche Verlags-Anstalt, 1962), Nr. 91, 317–18.

73 **"Prussian militarism"** and **"National dictatorship":** *New York Times*, November 9, 1923. See also *Münchner Neueste Nachrichten*, November 9, 1923, *Le Petit Parisien*, November 9, 1923, Reuters, November 8, 1923, and Deuerlein (1962), Nr. 267, 657.

74 **barking orders around the War Ministry:** Ernst Röhm, *The Memoirs of Ernst Röhm*, intro. Eleanor Hancock and trans. Geoffrey Brooks (London: Frontline Books, 2012), 147.

74 **Hitler was still not overly concerned:** Many historians assert the opposite, but this is not likely at this particular point in the evening. See, among many other eyewitness accounts, Ulrich Graf, VI a F 244/23–24, HA 67/1494.

74 **"[pace] up and down":** Ernst Hanfstaengl, *Hitler: The Memoir of a Nazi Insider Who Turned Against the Führer*, intro. John Willard Toland (New York: Arcade Publishing, 1957, repr. 2011), 102.

74 **"Your Excellency, surely":** NA T84/2 EAP 105/7, 1272 and 1942; See also Lossow's account, November 22, 1923 in Staatsanwaltschaften 3099, StAM.

74 **"vile raid":** NA T84/2 EAP 105/7, 1942.

74 **"extraordinarily excited and outraged":** NA T84/2 EAP 105/7, 1871.

75 **largest force currently available:** Harold J. Gordon Jr., *Hitler and the Beer Hall Putsch* (Princeton: Princeton University Press, 1972), 271–73.

Chapter 14: ORDINANCE NO. 264

76 **"I did not want to show":** NA T84/2 EAP 105/7, 2505.

76 **not too long after one a.m.:** This is most common view, though defense lawyer Alfred Holl placed the reunion at 1:15 a.m. at the latest: NA T84/2 EAP 105/7, 1747. See Kommandantur München, No. 4453/I, November 19, 1923, Staatsanwaltschaften 3098, StAM, and Ernst Deuerlein, ed. *Der Hitler-Putsch. Bayerische Dokumente zum 8./9. November 1923* (Stuttgart: Deutsche Verlags-Anstalt, 1962), 100.

76 **the Bavarian crown prince:** *Neue Zürcher Zeitung*, November 10, 1923, Erstes Morgenblatt. See also R. D. Murphy, Acting Vice Consul in Charge, Bavarian

political Analysis, November 23, 1923 (mailed), M336, 862.00, No. 19, NA and Graf von Soden's essay, *Münchner Neueste Nachrichten*, March 21, 1924.

76 **General von Seeckt:** Georges Bonnin, *Le putsch de Hitler: à Munich en 1923* (Les Sables-d'Olonne: Bonnin, 1966), 111. See also letter from Seeckt to Kahr on the eve of the putsch, November 5, 1923, excerpted in Didier Chauvet's *Hitler et le putsch de la brasserie: Munich, 8/9 novembre 1923* (Paris: L'Harmattan, 2012), 126–27.

76 **"this crazy mutiny":** *New York Times*, November 9, 1923.

76 **At 2:50 a.m.:** NA T84/2 EAP 105/7, 1275. Seisser dates the message incorrectly to 2:15 a.m., NA T84/2 EAP 105/7, 1499.

76 **"GENERAL STATE COMMISSIONER":** NA T84/2 EAP 105/7, 1276, 1356.

77 **"deceit and breach of promise":** *Aufruf*, November 9, 1923, copy in HA 67/1492.

77 **Ordinance No. 264:** A copy is in HA 68/1495. See also *Münchner Neueste Nachrichten*, November 10, 1923, and David Jablonsky, *The Nazi Party in Dissolution: Hitler and the Verbotzeit, 1923–1925* (London: F. Cass, 1989), 28–30.

77 **subsequent order:** Kommandantur München, No. 4453/I, November 19, 1923, Staatsanwaltschaften 3098, NA T84/2 EAP 105/7, 1092.

77 **"the immense danger":** NA T84/2 EAP 105/7, 930.

77 **"Publication of the morning newspapapers":** Deuerlein (1962), Nr. 182, Anlage 7, 513. See also Horst J. Weber, *Die deutsche Presse, insbesondere die völkische, um den Hitlerprozess. Ein Beitrag zur Lehre von der Parteipresse*. Diss. (Universitat Leipzig, 1930), 51.

78 **The editor then called:** NA T84/2 EAP 105/7, 242–43; *Erklärung des Herrn Oberstlandesgerichtsrats Ernst Pöhner über die Vorgänge vom 8./9. November 1923*, December 29, 1923, HA 5/120.

78 **Pöhner tried to call:** NA T84/2 EAP 105/7, 243.

78 **the doorbell rang:** Ibid., and Johann Aigner's unpublished memoir, *Ein Beitrag zur Geschichte der nationalen Erhebung im November 1923*, 12, HA 5/114II.

Chapter 15: "I AM NOT A COWARD"

79 **"I fear that your dream":** January 2, 1924, HA 5/114I.

79 **to arrest Wilhelm Frick:** Major Imhoff to I. Staatsanwalt beim Landgericht München I, November 15, 1923, MA 104221, BHStA.

79 **Their task:** The arrest of Frick draws on the testimony of Imhoff (NA T84/2 EAP 105/7, 1172–73), Frick (NA T84 EAP 105/7, 725–26), and Roder's notes, *Herr Hitler hat kein Ehrenwort gebrochen*, HA 5/126, along with NA T84 EAP 105/7, 2694 and the report, *Bericht an den Herrn Generalstaatskommissar München*, December 7, 1923, HA 67/1491.

79 **"Herr Frick, I'm awfully sorry":** NA T84/2 EAP 105/7, 1173.

79 **"On whose orders?" . . . "But which":** John Dornberg, *Munich 1923: The Story of Hitler's First Grab for Power* (New York: Harper & Row, 1982), 209.

80 **arrived at the War Ministry:** Around 4:30 or at least before 5:00 a.m., NA T84/2 EAP 105/7, 243.

80 **There would be speeches:** MA 103476/3, 1349, BHStA.

80 **"Propaganda, nothing but":** Hans Hubert Hofmann, *Der Hitlerputsch. Krisen-jahre deutscher Geschichte 1920–1924* (München: Nymphenburger Verlagshand-lung, 1961), 194.

80 **"The revolution of the November criminals"** . . . **"One would have":** *Völkischer Beobachter*, November 9, 1923.

81 **where Alfred Rosenberg was:** Alfred Rosenberg interrogation, VIa 2500/23, June 6, 1924, HA 67/1493.

81 **"It's all over":** Heinrich Hoffmann, *Hitler Was My Friend*, trans. Lt-Col R. H. Stevens (London: Burke, 1955), 55–56.

81 **Leupold had come over:** Scene draws upon the testimony of the men in the room, Col. Ludwig Leupold (NA T84 EAP 105/7, 195. 802–4); Adolf Hitler (NA T84/2 EAP 105/7, 110–11); Erich Ludendorff (NA T84/2 EAP 105/7, 538–40; as well as police report, November 22, 1923, HA 68/1494, and arguments of the prosecu-tion, Anz. Verz.XIX 421/23, *Antrag des I. Staatsanwalts beim Volksgericht München I auf Anberaumung der Hauptverhandlung*, January 8, 1924, Staatsanwaltschaften 3098, 28–29, StAM. Some people under Hitler and Ludendorff had, of course, realized the opposition of the triumvirate hours before: Richard Kolb, *Bericht über den 8. und 9. November 1923*, HA 5/116.

82 **"prepared to fight"** . . . **"right to exist":** NA T84 EAP 105/7, 804.

82 **They decided to move:** Walther Lembert, A.V. XIX 421/23, January 3, 1924, HA 67/1493.

Chapter 16: HOUR OF DECISION

83 **"If people gave him advice":** Margarethe Ludendorff, *My Married Life with Ludendorff*, trans. Raglan Somerset (London: Hutchinson, c.1929), 284.

83 **men lay about:** Hans Frank, *Im Angesicht des Galgens* (München-Gräfelfing: F. A. Beck, 1953), 61, and Walter Hewel interrogation, VI a F 425/24, February 22, 1924, HA 67/1494.

83 **wurst:** Julius Schaub, interrogation, April 25, 1924, HA 68/1494, with black coffee, Karl A. Kessler, *Der 9. November 1923 in München. Erlebnisse eines SA Mannes* (München: Walter, 1933), 18.

84 **"It's looking very serious":** Ulrich Graf, unpublished memoir, 63, F14, IfZ.

84 **"obviously overwrought and dead tired"** . . . **"future glory of new Germany":** *New York Times*, November 12, 1923.

84 **Firma Parcus:** Fritz Stahl, unpublished account, *Bericht*, January 18, 1938, HA 5/116 and *Münchener Post*, November 27, 1923, and Mühltaler: police report, *Meldungen über die Vorkommnisse in der Nacht vom 8./9.11.1923*, HA 67/1490.

85 **14,605 trillion marks:** Buchdruckerei und Verlagsanstalt Gebrüder Parcus an das Generalstaatskommissariat, November 19, 1923, printed in Ernst Deuerlein, ed., *Der Hitler-Putsch. Bayerische Dokumente zum 8./9. November 1923* (Stuttgart: Deutsche Verlags-Anstalt, 1962), Nr. 137, 423.

85 **He sent a personal emissary:** Max Neunzert, H.B.No.170/24, April 17, 1924, HA 67/1493, and *Das Bayerische Vaterland*, January 22, 1924.

85 **Outside, snow:** response of Karl Kessler, question 47, Fragebogen über Ereignisse an der Feldherrnhalle in München am 9. November 1923, January 1936 HA 5/115.

85 **Munich certainly did not seem:** *Münchener Zeitung*, November 9, 1923.

85 **"The Victory of the Swastika"** . . . **"the new National Socialist":** *Völkischer Beobachter*, November 9, 1923.

86 **a lively account:** *Münchner Neueste Nachrichten*, November 9, 1923.

86 **General Ludendorff had been:** *Le Matin*, November 9, 1923.

86 **a widespread fear:** *Le Petit Parisien*, November 9, 1923.

86 **warned of Germany:** London *Times*, November 9, 1923 and several others that picked up its story, such as Melbourne's *Weekly Times*, November 10, 1923, which followed the warnings in the *Manchester Guardian*.

86 **"Adolph [sic] Hitler's troops":** *New York Times*, November 9, 1923.

86 **"Ludendorff's aide":** John Dornberg, *Munich 1923: The Story of Hitler's First Grab for Power* (New York: Harper & Row, 1982), 195.

86 **"Hittler":** This would persist for some time, though it would be increasingly infrequent during the trial.

86 **Bavarian royalist:** *Time*, July 23, 1923. Another variant was "leader of Bavarian nationalists," *Illustrated London News*, November 17, 1923.

86 **"General Hitler":** *La Croix*, November 10, 1923.

87 **"alone, abandoned, and perplexed":** Dornberg (1982), 274; see also Ernst Röhm, *The Memoirs of Ernst Röhm*, intro. Eleanor Hancock and trans. Geoffrey Brooks (London: Frontline Books, 2012), 147–48.

87 **some 4,000 men:** Harold J. Gordon Jr., *Hitler and the Beer Hall Putsch* (Princeton: Princeton University Press, 1972), 273.

87 **"hopeless" and "orderly retreat":** NA T84 EAP 105/7, 435.

88 **Rosenheim:** Founded April 21, 1920, this was regarded the first branch of the party outside Munich.

88 **"dirt road":** NA T84 EAP 105/7, 542.

88 **news arrived:** Erich Ludendorff, *Auf dem Weg zur Feldherrnhalle. Lebenserinnerungen an die Zeit des 9.11.1923 mit Dokumenten in fünf Anlagen* (München: Ludendorff, 1937), 65.

88 **"The heavens will fall before":** Graf Helldorff statement, January 11, 1924, HA 5/114I.

88 **"We march":** NA T84/2 EAP 105/7, 114 and Ludendorff (1937), 65–66.

Chapter 17: IN THE COURTYARD

89 **"Since I am a wicked"**: Richard Hanser, *Putsch!: How Hitler Made Revolution* (New York: Pyramid Books, 1971), 210–11.

89 **"Red, Redder, and Reddest"**: NA T84 EAP 105/7, 435.

89 **the expedition**: *Die 6. Kompanie-ehemalige 4. Hundertschaft des Regiments München der S.A. der N.S.D.A.P. am 8. und 9. November 1923*, HA 4/93, and December 1, 1923, HA 67/1493.

89 **"hang Jewish profiteers"**: David Clay Large, *Where Ghosts Walked: Munich's Road to the Third Reich* (New York: W. W. Norton, 1997), 187.

89 **"time of shame is over"** and **"Heil Hitler!"**: *Münchner Neueste Nachrichten*, November 10, 1923.

90 **Stosstrupp Hitler detachment**: Proz.Reg.Nr. 187/1924 (Stosstrupp Hitler Trial), Gründe des Urteiles, May 3, 1924, HA 67/1493, and *Münchner Neueste Nachrichten*, November 10, 1923.

90 **barged into the building**: Berchtold interview, Heinz A. Heinz, *Germany's Hitler* (London: Hurst & Blackett, 1938), 159.

90 **What is your definition**: Julius Schaub, April 25, 1924, HA 68/1494.

90 **Councilman Albert Nussbaum**: NA T84/2 EAP 105/7, 1960–1961; *Meldungen über die Vorkommnisse in der Nacht vom 8./9.11.1923*, HA 67/1490.

90 **He snapped**: Heinrich Hoffmann, *Hitler Was My Friend*, trans. Lt-Col R. H. Stevens (London: Burke, 1955), 56.

90 **"blood brothers unto death"**: Ernst Röhm, *The Memoirs of Ernst Röhm*, intro. Eleanor Hancock and trans. Geoffrey Brooks (London: Frontline Books, 2012), 151.

91 **white flags**: Walther Lembert, A.V. XIX 421/23, January 3, 1924, HA 67/1493.

91 **previous commander and mentor**: Röhm (2012), 16–17, 29, with difficulties in relationship, 75. Epp's views of the putsch itself, particularly as benefit to France and enemies of Germany, *Berchtesgadener Anzeiger*, November 17–18, 1923. For more on this figure, see Katja-Maria Wächter, *Die Macht der Ohnmacht. Leben und Politik des Franz Xaver Ritter von Epp (1868–1946)* (Frankfurt am Main: P. Lang, 1999).

91 **He had also raised**: Albrecht Tyrell, "Exkurs. Zur Vorgeschichte der Erwebung des 'Völkischen Beobachters' durch die NSDAP" in his *Vom 'Trommler' zum 'Führer.' Der Wandel von Hitlers Selbstverständnis zwischen 1919 und 1924 und die Entwicklung der NSDAP* (München: Wilhelm Fink Verlag, 1975), 177.

91 **Resistance was futile**: Hildolf Freiherr von Thüngen, February 6, 1924, HA 67/1493.

91 **"totally outnumbered and outgunned"**: Translation in John Dornberg, *Munich 1923: The Story of Hitler's First Grab for Power* (New York: Harper & Row, 1982), 276. For more on the conversation: see the police report, *Umsturzversuch in der Nacht vom 8. auf 9.11.1923*, November 22, 1923, HA 68/1494.

91 **"an honorable surrender":** Röhm (2012), 153.

91 **shots were heard:** testimony of Alfred Andersch, Zum Akt Röhm, December 19, 1923, HA 5/114I.

91 **seventeen shots:** NA T84 EAP/2 105/7, 1076.

91 **Two Reichswehr soldiers:** Georg Träger was in the garage at the time, police report, December 17, 1923, HA 5/116. Helene Perutz also saw the wounded soldiers, police report, December 20, 1923, HA 5/116.

91 **In the eastern courtyard:** NA T84 EAP/2 105/7, 1067–68. For more, see the descriptions of the machine gun on the third floor of the garage, police report, December 17, 1923, HA 5/116; sketches of the courtyard in HA 5/114II, and report, *Leutnant Casellas und Fausts Tod im Wehrkreiskommando am 9 November 1923*, HA 5/114I. Röhm's admission is at Röhm (2012), 153–54.

91 **Martin Faust:** Zum Akt Röhm, December 19, 1923, HA 5/114I, and testimony of Wilhelm Greiner, PV19, December 29, 1923, HA 5/116.

92 **raised his right hand:** January 11, 1924, HA 5/114II, with rushing to aid, *Leutnant Casella's und Faust's Tod im Wehrkreiskommando am 9 November 1923*, HA 5/114, and police report, VI a F 2546/23, November 28, 1923, HA 67/1493.

Chapter 18: HITLER'S FOREIGN LEGION

93 **"Don't go along":** Alfred Rosenberg, *Memoirs of Alfred Rosenberg*, ed. Serge Lange and Ernst von Schenck and trans. Eric Posselt (Chicago: Ziff-Davis, 1949), 72.

93 **"flight of capital from Jews":** Marc (Max) Sesselmann, *Bericht*, November 1, 1935, HA 5/116.

93 **"You do not know then?"** ... **"Flee to safety":** Sesselmann, *Bericht*, November 1, 1935, HA 5/116. The police search of the apartment is in Abt VIa, *Betreff Pöhner, Ernst*, November 10, 1923, Staatsanwaltschaften 3099, StAM.

93 **Pöhner had been taken:** *Vernehmung Pöhner*, November 10, 1923, HA 5/120; Imhoff testimony, NA T84 EAP 105/7, 1173.

93 **"like a blow from a club":** NA T84/2 EAP 105/7, 244.

94 **in which building:** *Berliner Tageblatt*, November 9, 1923, Abend Ausgabe.

94 **some 2,000:** This figure seems more likely than the higher estimates given, for instance, by Hitler, who, from his position in the front of the procession, would have had more difficulty in gauging its size, NA T84/2 EAP 105/7, 2075. He also overestimated the crowd at the Bürgerbräu at 5,000, NA T84/2 EAP 105/7, 98.

94 **To his immediate left:** Many historians place Scheubner-Richter on the right, including John Dornberg, *Munich 1923: The Story of Hitler's First Grab for Power* (New York: Harper & Row, 1982), 283–84, but he was on the left. This was the view of both Scheubner-Richter's valet, in his unpublished memoir, Johann Aigner, *Ein Beitrag zur Geschichte der nationalen Erhebung im November 1923*, 14,

HA 5/114II, and Hitler's bodyguard, Ulrich Graf, unpublished memoir, F14, 67, IfZ, as well as in his answer to question 2, NSDAP questionnaire, filled out in February 1936 at HA 5/115. Many other people in the march agreed.

94 **"the most desperately daring decision":** This comes from a speech, November 11, 1935, translation, Richard Hanser, *Putsch!: How Hitler Made Revolution* (New York: Pyramid Books, 1971), 307.

94 **"Things look ugly":** Robert Cecil, *The Myth of the Master Race: Alfred Rosenberg and Nazi Ideology* (New York: Dodd Mead & Company, 1972), 41.

94 **might be their last walk:** NA T84/2 EAP 105/7, 113. Johann Prem also remembered hearing it, he wrote in his unpublished account, *Bericht über den 9. November 1923*, HA 5/115.

94 **faint sunshine:** Question 47, Karl Kessler and Lisbeth Kessler, Fragebogen HA 5/115.

94 **the rising sun of German freedom:** A. Rossmann, unpublished account, *Der neunte November 23*, HA 5/116.

94 **He wanted to march:** Proz.Reg.Nr. 187/1924 (Stosstrupp Hitler Trial), May 3, 1924, HA 67/1493.

94 **"to execute all the hostages":** XIX 466/23, February 15, 1924, HA 67/1494 and Ulrich Graf, unpublished memoir, F14, 64, IfZ.

95 **"worth a bullet":** Johann Georg Maurer doubted the phrase, VI a F 413/24, November 21, 1923, HA 67/1494. But the bulk of the evidence reflects the sense, if not also the words, for instance, at XIX 466/23, February 22, 1924, HA 67/1494, and Adalbert Stollwerck's testimony, VI a F 416/24, February 21, 1924, HA 68/1494. See also *Münchener Post*, October 30, 1925.

95 **back to captivity:** Heinrich von Knobloch, VI a F, February 20, 1924, HA 67/1494.

95 **He did not want:** NA T84/2 EAP 105/7, 115.

95 **"Hitlerputsch—the Rape of Kahr":** *Münchener Zeitung*, November 9, 1923. The editor of the paper, Adolf Schiedt, helped write Kahr's speeches, and so it is not a surprise to see phrase in the Kahr proclamation, November 9, 1923, MA 104221, BHStA.

95 **"like a swarm of bees":** NA T84 EAP 105/7, 438.

95 **"the deep joyful enthusiasm"** and **"We [were] workers":** Hans Hinkel, *Einer unter Hunderttausend* (München: Knorr & Hirth, 1938), translation in David Clay Large, *Where Ghosts Walked: Munich's Road to the Third Reich* (New York: W. W. Norton, 1997), 185.

95 **The young law student:** Hans Frank, *Im Angesicht des Galgens* (München-Gräfelfing: F. A. Beck, 1953), 61; See also Martyn Housden, *Hans Frank: Lebensraum and the Holocaust* (London: Palgrave Macmillan, 2003), 22.

96 **"Green Police":** The name derived from the green-and-black uniforms, Harold J. Gordon Jr., *Hitler and the Beer Hall Putsch* (Princeton: Princeton University Press, 1972), 124.

96 **the bridge:** NA T84/2 EAP 105/7, 115; Anz. Verz.XIX 421/23, *Antrag des I. Staatsanwalts beim Volksgericht München I auf Anberaumung der Hauptverhandlung,* January 8, 1924, Staatanswaltschaften 3098, 31–32, StAM; *Münchener Post,* November 27, 1923.

96 **"Don't shoot":** Georg Höfler, November 10, 1923, printed in Ernst Deuerlein, ed., *Der Hitler-Putsch. Bayerische Dokumente zum 8./9. November 1923* (Stuttgart: Deutsche Verlags-Anstalt, 1962), Nr. 98, 332.

96 **twenty-eight policemen:** Proz.Reg.Nr. 187/1924, May 3, 1924, HA 67/1493. The claim of saluting is in Karl A. Kessler, *Der 9. November 1923 in München. Erlebnisse eines SA Mannes* (München: Walter, 1933), 15.

96 **"The mood of the city":** Johann Aigner, unpublished memoir, *Ein Beitrag zur Geschichte der national Erhebung im November 1923,* 10, HA 5/114II.

96 **"one of the greatest generals":** Large (1997), 186.

96 **"a motley rabble":** Karl Alexander von Müller, *Im Wandel einer Welt* (München: Süddeutscher, 1966), 166; NA T84/2 EAP 105/7, 983.

97 **"a defeated army":** Otis C. Mitchell, *Hitler's Stormtroopers and the Attack on the German Republic, 1919–1933* (Jefferson, NC: McFarland, 2008), 78.

97 **a second Oktoberfest:** For more on his impressions, see Carl Zuckmayer, *A Part of Myself: Portrait of an Epoch,* trans. Richard and Clara Winston (New York: Harcourt, Brace, Jovanovich, 1970), 272–73.

Chapter 19: BLOOD LAND

98 **"If you cross the Rubicon":** *Vossische Zeitung,* February 27, 1924, Morgen Ausgabe.

98 **"prepare for a get-away":** Ernst Hanfstaengl, *Hitler: The Memoir of a Nazi Insider Who Turned Against the Führer,* intro. John Willard Toland (New York: Arcade Publishing, 1957, repr. 2011), 105.

98 **"It's terrible":** Ernst Hanfstaengl, *Zwischen Weissem und Braunem Haus. Memoiren eines politischen Aussenseiters* (München: R. Piper, 1970), 144. Rumors of the deaths circulated that morning, for instance, Anton Zahner, VI a F 405/24, February 14, 1924, HA 68/1494; Margarethe Ludendorff, *My Married Life with Ludendorff,* trans. Raglan Somerset (London: Hutchinson, c.1929), 251–52; NA T84/2 EAP 105/7, 1143; *Münchener Zeitung,* November 10–11, 1923; *Dalpilen* (Falun, Sweden), November 13, 1923.

99 **"At certain moments":** NA T84 EAP 105/7, 543.

99 **Ludendorff had been warned:** He changed directions, after receiving the information at corner of Theatinerstrasse and Perusastrasse, Richard Kolb, Fragebogen, 30, January 1936, HA 5/116. Kriebel, who walked farther away and did not hear warning, was surprised at the change in direction.

99 **presumably:** The procession as a military operation targeting rear and flanks, NA T84/2 EAP 105/7, 1281.

99 **Michael Freiherr von Godin:** Confidential file in Akt Freiherr v. Godin, Akt. Nr. 121, *Akten der Geheimen Staatspolizei*, Staatspolizeistelle Innsbruck, HA 5/117.

99 **His brother:** For more on Emmerich von Godin, see Thomas Weber, *Hitler's First War: Adolf Hitler, the Men of the List Regiment, and the First World War* (Oxford: Oxford University Press, 2010), 215. Godin wrote the recommendation on July 31, 1918.

99 **"Don't shoot":** NA T84/2 EAP 105/7, 172.

99 **Hitler locked arms with:** Mathilde Scheubner-Richter, unpublished account, citing Hitler as source, *Bericht*, April 4, 1936, HA 5/116.

100 **"rifle-butt and baton":** Michael von Godin, November 10, 1923, MA 104221, BHStA.

100 **One retired schoolteacher:** VIa, *Umsturzversuch 8./9. November 1923—hier Vorgänge am Odeonsplatz*, March 3, 1924, HA 68/1494.

100 **"perfectly horizontal":** Arno Schmidt, VI a F 489/24, March 1, 1924, HA 68/1494.

100 **while Hitler's men did not:** *Der Oberbayer*, November 19–20, 1923, and Anton Reithinger, *Umsturzversuch 8./9. November 1923—hier Vorgänge am Odeonsplatz*, March 3, 1924, HA 68/1494.

100 **Putsch veterans:** Many claimed that they had not fired, for instance, Erich Ludendorff, *Auf dem Weg zur Feldherrnhalle. Lebenserinnerungen an die Zeit des 9.11.1923 mit Dokumenten in fünf Anlagen* (München: Ludendorff, 1937), 68. One example admitting the opposite: Walter Hewel, MA 103476/3, 1347, BHStA.

100 **without hitting:** Lorenz Roder, unpublished account, *Herr Hitler hat kein Ehrenwort gebrochen*, HA 5/126.

100 **order to unload:** NA T84/2 EAP 105/7, 170. 2 SA-Company received order during the march, Karl Kessler, Fragebogen question 23, HA 5/115. Many guns, however, were found to be loaded, MA 103476/3, 1353–57, BHStA.

100 **"hideous racket" and "all was horror, agony, and confusion":** Berchtold interview in Heinz A. Heinz, *Germany's Hitler* (London: Hurst & Blackett, 1938), 160.

100 **in front and on the flank:** *Deutsches Tageblatt*, November 13, 1923.

101 **"lightning-fast":** NA T84 EAP 105/7, 544.

101 **Scheubner-Richter, who had been hit:** NA T84/2 EAP 105/7, 117, and location of shot, Johann Aigner, *Ein Beitrag zur Geschichte der nationalen Erhebung im November 1923*, 17, HA 5/114II.

101 **dislocated his shoulder:** NA T84/2 EAP 105/7, 117.

101 **he covered Hitler:** Adolf Hitler's letter from Landsberg, June 1924, Eberhard Jäckel und Axel Kuhn, eds., *Hitler. Sämtliche Aufzeichnungen 1905–1924* (Stuttgart: Deutsche Verlags-Anstalt, 1980), Nr. 640, 1235.

101 **Graf took bullets:** *Das geschah am 9. November 1923*, HA 5/116, and unpublished memoir, F14, 67–68, IfZ.

101 **Göring was shot:** Carin Göring, letter to her mother, Huldine, November 13, 1923, Björn Fontander, *Carin Göring skriver hem* (Stockholm: Carlssons, 1990), 108–9.

101 **"each shot jolted":** NA T84 EAP 105/7, 442.

101 **cursing:** Sesselmann also saw Kriebel yelling with fist in air, Sesselmann, *Bericht*, November 1, 1935, HA 5/116.

102 **a woman in a fur coat:** Hans Rickmers, letter from hospital, November 16, 1923, HA 5/116.

102 **"the most disgusting"** and **"completely crushed":** NA T84/2 EAP 105/7, 618.

102 **Bauerngirgl:** Otto Engelbrecht, questionnaire, answer to No. 36, HA 5/115.

102 **fled to the Ministry of the Interior:** Johann Prem, *Bericht über den 9. November 1923*, HA 5/115.

102 **a nearby café:** Karl A. Kessler, *Der 9. November 1923 in München. Erlebnisse eines SA Mannes* (München: Walter, 1933), 33.

102 **"This is madness!"** Richard Kolb, unpublished account, *Bericht über den 8. und 9. November 1923*, HA 5/116.

102 **"the last gesture":** John W. Wheeler-Bennett, *The Nemesis of Power: The German Army in Politics 1918–1945* (New York: St Martin's Press, 1954), 176.

102 **supposed bolt-upright stance:** This appears in many accounts, for instance, Richard Hanser, *Putsch!: How Hitler Made Revolution* (New York: Pyramid Books, 1971), 362, Hans Hubert Hofmann, *Der Hitlerputsch. Krisenjahre deutscher Geschichte 1920–1924* (München: Nymphenburger Verlagshandlung, 1961), 212, and many Hitler biographies, such as Ullrich (2013), 178. A number of eyewitnesses, however, report the contrary. See not only Robert Murphy's account cited below, but also the *New York Times*, November 11, 1923; *Le Petit Parisien*, November 13, 1923; *Le Matin*, November 13, 1923; *Boston Daily Globe*, November 11, 1923; *Vorwärts* added that he remained lying there, while his followers fled and *Münchener Post*, November 27, 1923. There were also criticisms of Ludendorff among those who believed that he had remained upright in a foolhardy manner.

102 **"fell flat to escape":** Robert Murphy, *Diplomat Among Warriors* (Garden City, NY: Doubleday & Company, 1964), 22.

103 **he apparently jumped:** information from Hermann Kriebel, July 12, 1938, HA 5/116.

103 **felt warmth:** Johann Aigner, *Ein Beitrag zur Geschichte der nationalen Erhebung im November 1923*, 16, HA 5/114II.

103 **bullets had ricocheted:** Chirugische Universitäts-Klinik, *Leichendiagnose des Schraut Otto*, November 13, 1923, HA 5/118.

103 **"Everywhere people were going down":** Berchtold interview in Heinz (1938), 161, and the bloodbath, as Gottfried Feder put it, in his unpublished diary, *Tagebücher*, ED 874/5, 20, IfZ.

103 **began to cry:** Friedrich Weber, NA T84/2 EAP 105/7, 173.

103 **The owner of a toy shop:** James Pool and Suzanne Pool, *Who Financed Hitler: The Secret Funding of Hitler's Rise to Power 1919–1933* (New York: Dial Press, 1979), 15, and Joachim C. Fest, *Hitler*, trans. Richard and Clara Winston (New York: Harcourt Brace Jovanovich, 1974), 166.

103 **to save the lives:** Dr. Ferdinand Sauerbruch, GStK.Nr. 15, BHStA, printed in
Ernst Deuerlein, ed., *Der Hitler-Putsch. Bayerische Dokumente zum 8./9. November 1923* (Stuttgart: Deutsche Verlags-Anstalt, 1962), Nr. 90, 316–17.

104 **shot in the head:** Johann Prem, *Bericht über den 9. November 1923*, HA 5/115.

104 **remained unidentified:** This was the waiter Karl Kuhn, *München-Augsburger
Abendzeitung*, November 12, 1923; *Münchener Zeitung*, November 12, 1923.

104 **"battlefield":** Suzanne St. Barbe Baker, *A Wayfarer in Bavaria* (Boston: Houghton
Mifflin, 1931), 36, in Charles Bracelen Flood, *Hitler: The Path to Power* (Boston:
Houghton Mifflin Company, 1989), 555.

104 **He refused to acknowledge:** A. Rossmann noted, in unpublished account, *Der
neunte November 23*, HA 5/116 and Ludendorff's restrained later account in his
memoir (1937), 68–69.

104 **mistaken for Ludendorff:** Ludendorff (1937), 69.

104 **"collection camps":** Theodor von der Pfordten, *Verfassungsentwurf*, Article 16,
MA 103476/3, 1174, BHStA, and printed in Hofmann (1961), Anhang, 288.

Chapter 20: FLIGHT

105 **"Ludendorff Arrested":** *Daily Mail* (Brisbane), November 11, 1923.

105 **scrambled for safety:** Dr. Walter Schultze, MA 103476/3, 1358–59, BHStA.

105 **An eyewitness:** *Münchner Neueste Nachrichten*, November 10, 1923.

105 **"Adolf the Swell-Head":** Robert G. L. Waite, *Vanguard of Nazism: The Free Corps
Movement in Postwar Germany 1918–1923* (New York: W. W. Norton, 1952), 259.

105 **He was said to have spotted:** Karl A. Kessler, *Der 9. November 1923 in München.
Erlebnisse eines SA Mannes* (München: Walter, 1933), 30, and *Die Vorgänge im
München am 8. und 9. November 1923*, HA 5/116. A boy was later brought forth as
evidence of Hitler's supposed rescue, though there is good reason to be skeptical,
Joachim C. Fest, *Hitler*, trans. Richard and Clara Winston (New York: Harcourt
Brace Jovanovich, 1974), 190.

106 **Two men in the building:** Tobias Mahl, "Die 'Arisierung' der Hofmöbelfabrik
Ballin in München," in Angelika Baumann und Andreas Heusler, eds., *München
arisiert. Entrechtung und Enteignung der Juden in der NS-Zeit* (München: C. H.
Beck, 2004).

106 **"partly covered in blood":** Dr. Emil Neustadt, April 24, 1934, HA 5/116.

106 **concealed weapons:** Kessler (1933), 33. See also Erich Malitius, *Der 8. u. 9.
November 1923. Die Geschichte von Treue und Verrat der deutschen Jugend* (Breslau: Handel, 1935), 13.

107 **arrested by the police:** Polizei Direktion an Generalstaatskommissar, November
13, 1923, MA 104221, BHStA.

107 **Röhm had surrendered:** Ernst Deuerlein, ed., *Der Hitler-Putsch. Bayerische Dokumente zum 8./9. November 1923* (Stuttgart: Deutsche Verlags-Anstalt, 1962), Nr.

182, Anlage 4, 511, and testimony of Lt. Col. Theodor Endres in Didier Chauvet's *Hitler et le putsch de la brasserie: Munich, 8/9 novembre 1923* (Paris: L'Harmattan, 2012), 153–54.

107 **"I was close to madness"** and **"I was sick":** Johann Aigner, *Ein Beitrag zur Geschichte der nationalen Erhebung im November 1923*, 18, HA 5/114II. Another description of the sight is the unpublished *Tatsachenbericht vom 9. November [23] bei der Feldherrnhalle München*, HA 5/116.

107 **Many newspapers:** *Vossische Zeitung*, November 9, 1923, Abend Ausgabe; *Le Figaro*, November 10, 1923; London *Times*, November 10, 1923; and *Newcastle Sun*, November 10, 1923, among others.

107 **Prince Arnulf Barracks:** *Le Petit Parisien*, November 10, 1923.

107 **fled to Rosenheim:** London's *Daily Mail* and Australian Cable Service, November 10, 1923; the Wolff Agency report in *La Croix*, November 11, 1923; *Chicago Daily Tribune*, November 12, 1923.

107 **Troenum:** *New York Times*, November 11, 1923, or Isar valley, *New York Times*, November 12, 1923.

107 **Monarchists gathering:** *Chicago Sunday Tribune*, November 11, 1923.

107 **"All's well":** *Le Petit Parisien*, November 11, 1923.

108 **"dangerous elements"** . . . **"go on fighting":** Helen Niemeyer, unpublished "Notes," 307–9, folder "Ernst Hanfstaengl (1)," John Toland Papers, FDR.

108 **like many other:** One putschist, Gerhard Rossbach, for instance, slipped into Austria, claiming to be a film director, Gerhard Rossbach, *Mein Weg durch die Zeit. Erinnerungen und Bekenntnisse* (Weilburg-Lahn: Vereinigte Weilburger Buchdruckereien, 1950), 82.

109 **The doctor and his first-aid man:** Dr. Walter Schultze, December 10, 1923, HA68/1497A, and MA 103476/3, 1357–59, BHStA.

109 **English traveling rugs:** Ernst Hanfstaengl, *Zwischen Weissem und Braunem Haus. Memoiren eines politischen Aussenseiters* (München: R. Piper, 1970), 149.

109 **they had renovated:** Helen Niemeyer, "Notes," 297, folder "Ernst Hanfstaengl (1)," John Toland Papers, FDR.

Chapter 21: *HOSTAGE ORDEAL*

110 **"Dear Rosenberg":** Alfred Rosenberg, *Memoirs of Alfred Rosenberg*, ed. Serge Lange and Ernst von Schenck, trans. Eric Posselt (Chicago: Ziff-Davis, 1949), 73. Drexler saw the note too, he told police, November 30, 1923, HA 68/1497A.

110 **Bella Ballin:** Later when the Nazis rose to power, Göring would help the Ballins leave the country, facilitating their emigration in October 1941 to Switzerland. The Ballins would later book passage to Argentina, but Bella, unfortunately, died en route. Robert, Martin, and Martin's wife, Thekla, would eventually settle in the United States. For more, see Tobias Mahl, "Die 'Arisierung' der Hofmöbelfabrik

Ballin in München," in Angelika Baumann und Andreas Heusler, eds., *München arisiert: Entrechtung und Enteignung der Juden in der NS-Zeit* (München: Beck, 2004).

110 **"furs and blankets":** Carin Göring, letter to her mother, Huldine, November 13, 1923, Björn Fontander, *Carin Göring skriver hem* (Stockholm: Carlssons, 1990), 109.

110 **list of the dead:** "Den toten Kameraden!," *Münchner Neueste Nachrichten*, November 15, 1923.

110 **"the twentieth casualty":** *München-Augsburger-Abendzeitung*, November 14, 1923.

111 **one man of the Stosstrupp Hitler:** Eduard Schmidt and Albert Nussbaum, XIX 466/23, February 15, 1924, HA 67/1494.

111 **"Another word":** Albert Nussbaum testimony, NA T84/2 EAP 105/7, 1964–1965. Heinrich von Knobloch confirmed the orders not to speak, VI a F, February 20, 1924, HA 67/1494.

111 **expected the worst:** NA T84/2 EAP 105/7, 1965.

111 **handing over:** Walter Hewel, VI a F 425/24, February 22, 1924, HA 67/1494, and NA T84/2 EAP 105/7, 1966.

111 **following the Storm Troopers' truck:** *Bayerische Staatszeitung*, November 10, 1923 and *Das Ende des Münchener Staatsstreichs*, Nr. 265, November 13, 1923, HA 5/114II.

111 **the next train:** *Meldungen über die Vorkommnisse in der Nacht vom 8./9.11.1923*, HA 67/1490, and the drive back, MA 103476/3, 1380–81, BHStA.

111 **"shot in the head":** NA T84 EAP 105/7, 830.

112 **ski lodge or hut:** Rudolf Hess to Klara and Fritz Hess, November 8, 1923, with continuations November 16 and December 4, 1923 in Rudolf Hess, *Briefe 1908–1933*, ed. Wolf Rüdiger Hess (München: Langen Müller, 1987), 312.

112 **At 4:10 p.m.:** MA 103476/3, 1368, BHStA.

112 **The government minister feared:** Franz Schweyer described it later in testimony in a different case before Amtsgericht München, *Zeugen-Vernehmung in der Privatklagesache Hitler gegen Dr. Strasse wegen Beleidigung*, January 5, 1929, HA 69/1507; The minister of Württemberg reported it too based on information from Eugen von Knilling, Carl Moser von Filseck, *Politik in Bayern 1919–1933. Berichte des württembergischen Gesandten Carl Moser von Filseck*, ed. Wolfgang Benz. Schriftenreihe der Vierteljahrshefte für Zeitgeschichte Nummer 22/23 (Stuttgart: Deutsche Verlags-Anstalt, 1971), November 14, 1923, Nr. 322, 144, and MA 103476/3, 1370–72, BHStA.

113 **had ended:** *Meldungen über die Vorkommnisse in der Nacht vom 8./9.11.1923*, HA 67/1490.

113 **at the publisher's villa:** police report, VI a F, January 16, 1924, HA 68/1494, *Münchner Neueste Nachrichten*, November 11, 1923, and MA 103476/3, 1368–69, BHStA.

Chapter 22: NEW NOVEMBER CRIMINALS

114 **November criminals:** This was a phrase that Hitler had used at least since his speech on September 18, 1922, printed in E. Jäckel und A. Kuhn, eds., *Hitler. Sämtliche Aufzeichnungen 1905–1924* (Stuttgart: Deutsche Verlags-Anstalt, 1980), Nr. 405, 692.

114 **"Without the applause":** Otto Strasser, *Hitler and I*, trans. Gwenda David and Eric Mosbacher (Boston: Houghton Mifflin Company, 1940), 42.

114 **weapons and ammunition:** Johann Salbey, November 10, 1923, MA 104221, BHStA.

114 **the Bürgerbräu manager:** Bürgerbräu an das Herrn Generalstaatskommissar Dr. v. Kahr, November 19, 1923, HA 68/1497.

114 **At around three p.m.:** Report, November 18, 1923, HA 5/114I.

114 **"Excellency, the Ludendorff-Hitler Putsch":** November 10, 1923, HA 5/114I.

114 **"Heil Hitler!" and "Down with Kahr!":** *München-Augsburger Abendzeitung*, November 10, 1923, and *Washington Post*, November 11, 1923, with the effects on the officials in Carl Moser von Filseck, *Politik in Bayern 1919–1933. Berichte des württembergischen Gesandten Carl Moser von Filseck*, ed. Wolfgang Benz. Schriftenreihe der Vierteljahrshefte für Zeitgeschichte Nummer 22/23 (Stuttgart: Deutsche Verlags-Anstalt, 1971), November 10–14, 1923, Nr. 122–24, 142–44.

115 **"traitors" . . . "Jew protectors":** Johann Salbey, November 10, 1923, MA 104221, BHStA. More on the insults in *Beschimpfung der Landespolizei*, November 13, 1923, HA 67/1491.

115 **"yelled, whistled, jeered":** Johann Salbey, November 10, 1923: MA 104221, BHStA.

115 **eighteen tankards:** *Tatsachenbericht vom 9. November [23] bei der Feldherrnhalle München*, HA 5/116.

115 **Police requested . . . "Hitler people":** Police report, *Meldungen über die Vorkommnisse in der Nacht vom 8./9.11.1923*, HA 67/1490.

115 **Kufstein:** *Neue Zürcher Zeitung*, November 12, 1923, Erstes Morgenblatt.

115 **rallying supporters:** For instance, Konrad Linder, *Familiengedenkblatt zum 9. November 1923*, HA 5/116.

115 **mounted police:** *Chicago Sunday Tribune*, November 11, 1923.

116 **"Danube Cossacks":** Ernst Röhm, *The Memoirs of Ernst Röhm*, intro. Eleanor Hancock and trans. Geoffrey Brooks (London: Frontline Books, 2012), 164.

116 **"sheer reactionary cowardice" and "the betrayal of the whole thing":** Josef Berchtold interview in Heinz A. Heinz, *Germany's Hitler* (London: Hurst & Blackett, 1938), 148. See also Berchtold's December 1923 letter to Stosstrupp Hitler members, which the police found in a search of Hans Wegelin's residence, January 14, 1924, HA 67/1493. Several observers contrasted Kahr's support and

then suppression of Hitler, such as *Illustrated London News*, November 17, 1923, report Nr. 265, *Das Ende des Münchener Staatsstreichs*, November 13, 1923, HA 5/114II, and Augsburg's *Sturmglocke*, November 24, 1923.

116 **No public gatherings:** This was not strictly enforced, *München-Augsburger Abendzeitung*, November 10, 1923.

116 **"General von Ludendorff"** . . . **"collapsed like a punctured balloon":** *New York World*, November 10, 1923.

116 **"the end of the buffoonery"** and **"second Ludendorff putsch":** *Berliner Tageblatt,* November 10, 1923, Morgen Ausgabe.

117 **"alien agitator"** and **"a German":** *New York Times*, November 10, 1923.

Chapter 23: TESTAMENT

118 **"Breach of promise here":** *München-Augsburger Abendzeitung*, November 12, 1923.

118 **"Gypsies":** See list in the folder HA 68/1495.

119 **One man in the party:** Ludwig Ess to Adolf Hitler, March 6, 1925, HA 4/85. Ess sent over the lists to NSDAP, November 10, 1925, Folders 215 and 1220, HA 4/85.

119 **authorities had discovered:** Ernst Deuerlein, ed., *Der Hitler-Putsch. Bayerische Dokumente zum 8./9. November 1923* (Stuttgart: Deutsche Verlags-Anstalt, 1962), Nr. 151, 445–47, Nr 181, 486–87; Nr. 188, 522, and Vienna's *Die Rote Fahne*, January 8, 1924.

119 **"preliminary agreement":** *The Nation*, December 19, 1923.

120 **"a hysteric":** *Berliner Tageblatt*, November 16, 1923.

120 **the most hated man:** *München-Augsburger Abendzeitung*, November 12, 1923 and *Münchner Neueste Nachrichten*, November 15, 1923.

120 **a cabinet meeting:** Deuerlein (1962), Nr. 92, 318–20.

120 **"Down with Kahr!":** Ibid., with quote, 320.

121 **at Uffing:** Helen Niemeyer, unpublished "Notes," 315–17, folder "Ernst Hanfstaengl (1)," John Toland Papers, FDR.

121 **Hitler had met:** MA 103476/1, 89, BHStA.

121 **Bechstein had become:** Max Amann, *Zeugen-Vernehmung in der Privatklagesache Hitler gegen Dr. Strausse wegen Beleidigung*, Amtsgericht München, January 5, 1929, HA 69/1507. For more on Bechstein, see Wolfgang Martynkewicz, *Salon Deutschland. Geist und Macht 1900–1945* (Berlin: Aufbau, 2009), 401–3.

122 **"someone who was staying"** . . . **"Now all is lost":** Helen Niemeyer, unpublished "Notes," 317–23, folder "Ernst Hanfstaengl (1)," John Toland Papers, FDR. For claim of a message from Ludendorff, see, for instance, *Salzburger Volksblatt*, November 13, 1923.

123 **"Today":** John Dornberg, *Munich 1923: The Story of Hitler's First Grab for Power* (New York: Harper & Row, 1982), 326.

123 **"ju-jitsu trick":** Ernst Hanfstaengl, *Hitler: The Memoir of a Nazi Insider Who Turned Against the Führer*, intro. John Willard Toland (New York: Arcade Publishing, 1957, repr. 2011), 108. Note too that her husband had told a slightly different version years before his memoir to the OSS that comes closer to Helen's and how Hitler "gave up the gun." There was no reference in this earlier version to a jiu jitsu trick, *Information obtained from Ernst Hanfstaengl*, OSS Sourcebook. Still, Hanfstaengl's improbable version often appears in biographies.

123 **Helen, by contrast … "while there was still time":** Helen Niemeyer, unpublished "Notes," 323–25, folder "Ernst Hanfstaengl (1)," John Toland Papers, FDR.

124 **"political testament":** Ernst Hanfstaengl, *Zwischen Weissem und Braunem Haus. Memoiren eines politischen Aussenseiters* (München: R. Piper, 1970), 149.

124 **"the entire organization":** Joachim C. Fest, *Hitler*, trans. Richard and Clara Winston (New York: Harcourt Brace Jovanovich, 1974), 187.

124 **"showed more shit":** HA 68/1497A.

124 **"Hitler had never taken me":** Alfred Rosenberg, *Memoirs of Alfred Rosenberg*, ed. Serge Lange and Ernst von Schenck, and trans. Eric Posselt (Chicago: Ziff-Davis, 1949), 73.

124 **a snap decision:** Ian Kershaw, *Hitler 1889–1936: Hubris* (New York: W. W. Norton, 1999), 225–26, and a reflection of his high standing, Georg Franz-Willing, *Putsch und Verbotszeit der Hitlerbewegung November 1923–Februar 1925* (Preussisch Oldendorf: Verlag K.W. Schütz, 1977), 193. It is also worth remembering that Hitler, at this time, could not have imagined such a trial and prison sentence as he would have. For a contrasting view, see Alan Bullock, who saw it as probably a deliberate attempt to prevent emergence of a rival, *Hitler: A Study in Tyranny* (New York: Harper & Row, 1971), 65, and his *Hitler and Stalin: Parallel Lives* (New York: Alfred A. Knopf, 1992), 150.

125 **"In the room stood":** Die Regierung von Oberbayern an das Generalstaatskommissariat, November 13, 1923, printed in Deuerlein (1962), Nr. 118, 372. It is possible that the police omitted reporting that Hitler threw a tantrum, shouting accusations at the government, as sometimes claimed.

125 **"bad, bad men"** and **"Uncle Dolf":** Helen Niemeyer, unpublished "Notes," 329, folder "Ernst Hanfstaengl (1)," John Toland Papers, FDR.

125 **the Bechstein car:** Ibid., and Volker Ullrich, *Adolf Hitler Biographie. Band 1: Die Jahre des Aufstiegs 1889–1939* (Frankfurt am Main: S. Fischer, 2013), 178.

Chapter 24: CURTAINS

126 **"We have to be careful":** *New York Times*, November 15, 1923.

126 **It had rained so hard:** Franz Hemmrich, unpublished memoir, *Erinnerungen eines Gefängnisbeamten*, ED 153-1, 6, IfZ, along with interview in Heinz A. Heinz, *Germany's Hitler* (London: Hurst & Blackett, 1938), 169.

126 **a telegram:** Die Regierung von Oberbayern an das Generalstaatskommissariat, November 12, 1923, Ernst Deuerlein, ed., *Der Hitler-Putsch. Bayerische Dokumente zum 8./9. November 1923* (Stuttgart: Deutsche Verlags-Anstalt, 1962), Nr. 107, 352.

126 **Arrangements had to be made:** Franz Hemmrich, unpublished memoir, *Erinnerungen eines Gefängnisbeamten*, ED 153-1, 6-8, IfZ; interview in Heinz (1938), 169–70. See also Otto Lurker, *Hitler hinter Festungsmauern. Ein Bild aus trüben Tagen* (Berlin: E. S. Mittler & Sohn, 1933), 4.

127 **"the loss of liberty":** Peter Fleischmann, ed., *Hitler als Häftling in Landsberg am Lech 1923/1924* (Neustadt an der Aisch: Verlag Ph.C.W.Schmidt, 2015), 24, citing Wilfried Otto's 1938 dissertation at Friedrich Schiller-Universität Jena, *Die Festungshaft: Ihre Vorläufer, Geschichte und Zukunft* (1938), 235. For more on Landsberg, see Fleischmann's excellent commentary.

127 **dark-blue uniform:** *Fränkischer Kurier*, April 27, 1924.

128 **"A dark hair"** and **"celebrity cell":** Hemmrich, ED 153-1, 9, IfZ. See also Hemmrich's interview in Heinz (1938), 170, and Lurker (1933), 5–6.

128 **"Catholic, 34 Years":** Schutzhaftanstalt Landsberg, Haftpapiere, Hitler, Adolf No.45, file 3/1, JVA 17.000, StAM, and Fleischmann (2015), 83.

128 **Cell 5:** Hemmrich, ED 153-1, 27, 113, IfZ.

128 **"a dislocation"** … **"result in a [permanent] partial rigidity":** Brinsteiner report, January 8, 1924, and Lurker (1933), 10–11.

128 **a discovery in store:** *Aufnahme-Buch für Schutzhaft, Untersuch. u. Festungshaft-Gefangene 1919*, JVA 15124, StAM. For more on the discovery of this file, see the opening of the Notes section.

128 **This claim:** Lev Bezymenski, *The Death of Adolf Hitler* (London, 1968), 46. According to the findings of the team under Soviet forensic pathologist Dr. Faust Shkaravski, Hitler's "left testicle could not be found either in the scrotum or on the spermatic cord inside the inguinal canal, nor in the small pelvis." The Russians had the wrong body, German historian Werner Maser argued. Even if they had found Hitler, could they really draw such a conclusion with so much soft tissue burned and the fact that they worked mostly with bone fragments? What's more, Hitler's many physicians had either somehow not noticed this condition or, when asked about the allegations, asserted unequivocally that his genitals were normal. Dr. Eduard Bloch, who treated Hitler in 1906 and 1907 in his Linz medical practice, told an interviewer with the American OSS that his patient had "no physical deformity" (March 5, 1943, OSS). Dr. Erwin Giesing, who examined Hitler in the fall of 1944, told American interrogators the same thing. But Giesing was an SS doctor specializing in ear, nose, and throat, and had, by his own admission elsewhere, given only a cursory look, which may not have sufficed to know. Bloch's comments too (*Colliers*, March 15, 1941) were almost forty years later, and contained many errors that made the OSS interviewer wonder if his memories had not been unduly influenced by reading Konrad Heiden's

biography. Hugh Trevor-Roper, formerly Oxford Regius Professor of Modern History and a British intelligence officer for MI6 who had been tasked in 1945 with finding proof of Hitler's death succinctly summed up the Soviet report as a medical as well as a political statement. Dr. Brinsteiner's report, therefore, comes as a surprise. Curiously, though, the Soviets identified the undescended testicle as the left and the Landsberg doctor the right. Perhaps this discrepancy was a simple error of perspective—i.e., the doctor's left or the patient's left—or even a result of note-keeping. In another one of Brinsteiner's notebooks, he had described the testicle as the left, but then scratched it out and marked it as the right one.

129 **"That is typical":** Carl Christian Bry, *Der Hitler-Putsch. Berichte und Kommentare eines Deutschland-Korrespondenten, 1922–1924 für das Argentinische Tag- und Wochenblatt,* ed. Martin Gregor-Dellin (Nördlingen: Greno, 1987), 145.

129 **"treasure trove" . . . "quick end":** Bry (1987), 150 and 157.

129 **"This Bürgerbräu coup d'état" . . . "comic opera stage":** *New York Times,* November 10, 1923.

129 **sheer vaudeville:** *Le Petit Parisien,* November 11, 1923. See also John Clayton's piece in *Chicago Daily Tribune,* November 10, 1923.

129 **"carnivalesque adventure":** *Le Matin,* November 10, 1923.

129 **"charlatan Hitler":** *Vossische Zeitung,* November 9, 1923, Abend Ausgabe.

129 **the party's obituary:** *Frankfurter Zeitung,* November 10, 1923.

129 **"the amateurish and abortive putsch":** *New York Times,* November 10, 1923.

130 **thanks largely:** Deuerlein (1962), 102.

130 **"supreme power":** *Niederschrift der Ministerratssitzung vom 12.11.1923,* printed in Deuerlein (1962), Nr. 105, 342.

130 **They banned right-wing papers:** Horst J. Weber, *Die deutsche Presse, insbesondere die völkische, um den Hitlerprozess. Ein Beitrag zur Lehre von der Parteipresse.* Diss. (Universität Leipzig, 1930), 12–13, 20.

131 **a rich Jewish rug merchant:** *Münchner Neueste Nachrichten,* November 13, 1923. The price was sometimes said to be 20 rugs, *Der Oberbayer,* November 19–20, 1923.

131 **"Helmets and rifles":** Franz Hemmrich interview, Heinz (1938), 170.

131 **the clang of weapons:** Lurker (1933), 6.

131 **Hitler claimed:** Die Regierung von Oberbayern an das Generalstaatskommissariat, November 13, 1924, Deuerlein (1962), Nr. 118, 373.

131 **a hunger strike . . . "sat there":** ED 153-1, 20, IfZ.

131 **Dr. Brinsteiner recorded:** January 8, 1924, OSS.

131 **"I've had enough":** This comes from a conversation in 1988 with the former Landsberg Prison psychologist Alois Maria Ott, then aged ninety-eight, Otto Gritschneder, *Bewährungsfrist für den Terroristen Adolf H. Der Hitler-Putsch und die bayerische Justiz* (München: Verlag C. H. Beck 1990), 35. In February 1924, Hitler would tell the court that he regretted not having died in the march like his colleagues: NA T84/2 EAP 105/7, 119.

131 **"thinner, and weaker"** and **"He was utterly":** Drexler interview in Heinz (1938), 164–65. Anton Drexler made the claim to end the hunger strike in 1934, though apparently not in 1933. For more, see Othmar Plöckinger, *Geschichte eines Buches. Adolf Hitlers 'Mein Kampf' 1922–1945* (München: Oldenbourg, 2011), 30–31, and Esser, interview, March 16, 1964, Band I, 2, ED 561/5, IfZ.

132 **"awfully depressed":** Knirsch in the Czech *Der Tag*, cited by Albrecht Tyrell, *Vom 'Trommler' zum 'Führer.' Der Wandel von Hitlers Selbstverständnis zwischen 1919 und 1924 und die Entwicklung der NSDAP* (München: Wilhelm Fink Verlag, 1975), 277, note 178.

132 **"timidly asked":** John Toland, *Adolf Hitler* (New York: Ballantine Books, 1976), 246.

132 **"no right to go on living"** and **"death by starvation":** Robert Payne, trans., *The Life and Death of Adolf Hitler* (New York: Popular Library, 1973), 184. His visit is mentioned in Deuerlein (1962), Nr. 168, 465. See also Brigitte Hamann, *Hitler's Vienna: A Dictator's Apprenticeship*, trans. Thomas Thornton (Oxford: Oxford University Press, 1999), 259–60.

132 **"now starve himself":** Ernst Hanfstaengl, *Zwischen Weissem und Braunem Haus. Memoiren eines politischen Aussenseiters* (München: R. Piper, 1970), 154.

132 **Wolf:** *Sprechkarte* December 3, 1923 in Lurker (1933), 18–20 with description of pleasure on p.8 and Franz Hemmrich, *Erinnerungen eines Gefängnisbeamten*, ED 153-1, 20, IfZ.

132 **a birthday present:** Ulrich Graf, unpublished memoir, 13, F14, IfZ.

Chapter 25: *TRIALS BEFORE THE TRIAL*

133 **"I must confess":** Hans Ehard, unpublished memoir, 37, NL Ehard 99, BHStA.

133 **Ludendorff worked hard:** Erich Ludendorff, *Auf dem Weg zur Feldherrnhalle. Lebenserinnerungen an die Zeit des 9.11.1923 mit Dokumenten in fünf Anlagen* (München: Ludendorff, 1937), 69–70, 73.

133 **coffee table:** *Eine halbe Stunde bei Ludendorff*, visit on December 2, 1923, HA 5/116.

133 **"He attached importance"** and **"parts of a mosaic":** Margarethe Ludendorff, *My Married Life with Ludendorff*, trans. Raglan Somerset (London: Hutchinson, c.1929), 260.

133 **"A good soldier wrecked":** Associated Press, November 11, 1923.

134 **perhaps from the grime:** This was what Carin Göring reported home in a letter from Innsbruck, November 13, 1923, Björn Fontander, *Carin Göring skriver hem* (Stockholm: Carlssons, 1990), 108–9.

134 **imagining he was:** Carin Göring, November 30, 1923 and December 8, 1923, to her sister Lily, ibid., 114, 116.

134 **his first morphine:** Carin Göring told this to her friend Helen Niemeyer,

unpublished "Notes," 291, folder "Ernst Hanfstaengl (1)," John Toland Papers, FDR. Carin described it too, December 20, 1923, Fontander (1990), 118. For his drug addiction, see Richard Overy, *Goering* (New York: Barnes & Noble Books, 2003), 7.

134 **"white as snow":** Carin Göring, December 28, 1923, to her father, Fontander (1990), 119.

134 **being watched:** Stenglein to police, November 12, 1923, 3099, StAM, and reported by Bezirksamt Garmisch, *Meldungen über die Vorkommnisse,* November 12, 1923, HA 67/1490.

134 **their bank accounts:** Paperwork in folder at HA 68/1497. See also police report, November 19, 1923, HA 68/1496.

134 **"like tramps":** Ernst Hanfstaengl, *Hitler: The Memoir of a Nazi Insider Who Turned Against the Führer,* intro. John Willard Toland (New York: Arcade Publishing, 1957, repr. 2011), 110.

134 **"Franz-Josef mutton-chop whiskers" . . . graceful:** Ernst Hanfstaengl, *Zwischen Weissem und Braunem Haus. Memoiren eines politischen Aussenseiters* (München: R. Piper, 1970), 153, 145.

135 **visited Hitler in prison:** Otto Lurker, *Hitler hinter Festungsmauern. Ein Bild aus trüben Tagen. Miterlebt und nach amtlichen Aktenstücken* (Berlin: E. S. Mittler & Sohn, 1933), 59.

135 **She found her half-brother:** Angela Raubal letter in John Toland, *Adolf Hitler* (New York: Ballantine Books, 1976), 248, with photograph of letter in insert following page 302. Other visitors would also find him improving, reported Linz's *Tages-Post,* January 3, 1924.

135 **His arm was healing:** Ehard noted the pain too on his visit, protocol, December 14, 1923, NL Ehard, 94, BHStA.

135 **five-volume edition:** December 1, 1923, Staatanswaltschaften 3099, StAM.

135 **a wool blanket:** Brigitte Hamann, *Winifred Wagner oder Hitlers Bayreuth* (München: Piper, 2002), 96–97.

135 **"[It] is by no means":** *New York Times,* November 15, 1923.

135 **supporters were urging the government:** there were many attempts circulating in Munich, see, for instance, Robert Murphy, *Confidential Political Report,* November 12, 1923, M336, 862.00/1371, No. 19, NA.

136 **An internal government:** *Aktenvermerk des Staatsministerium des Äusser: 'Die bayerischen staatspolitischen Notwendigkeiten, die sich aus den Ereignissen vom 8. und 9. Nov. 1923 ergeben,'* probably November 15, 1923, Ernst Deuerlein, ed., *Der Hitler-Putsch. Bayerische Dokumente zum 8./9. November 1923* (Stuttgart: Deutsche Verlags-Anstalt, 1962), Nr. 126, 386–90.

136 **tableau vivant:** Heinrich Hoffmann, *Hitler Was My Friend,* trans. Lt-Col R. H. Stevens (London: Burke, 1955), 57.

136 **"It is generally felt":** Richard Hanser's *Putsch!: How Hitler Made Revolution* (New York: Pyramid Books, 1971), 367.

136 **Murphy, predicted:** Robert Murphy, *Diplomat Among Warriors* (Garden City, NY: Doubleday & Company, 1964), 22, and page 17 of his *Confidential Political Report*, March 10, 1924 (Date of Mailing: April 3, 1924), M336, 862.00/1469, No. 20, NA.

137 **getting nowhere:** Franz Hemmrich, unpublished memoir, ED 153, IfZ.

137 **he had only:** Hans Ehard, unpublished memoir, 16, NL Ehard 99, BHStA.

137 **"Know yourself" and "recognize what is important":** *Dr. Hans Ehard 1887–1980. Eine Ausstellung des Bayerischen Hauptstaatsarchivs aus dem Nachlass des Bayerischen Ministerpräsidenten anlässlich seines 100. Geburtstages*, eds. Ludwig Morenz und Michael Stephan (München: Bayerisches Haupstaatsarchiv, 1987), 21.

137 **took the train to Landsberg:** Ehard interview with Guido Fuchs in *Abendzeitung*, February 25, 1974, NL Ehard 98, BHStA.

137 **"get something out of Hitler"** . . . **"hard and repellent":** Hans Ehard, unpublished memoir, 36–37, NL Ehard 99, BHStA.

137 **"was going to eat me":** John Dornberg, *Munich 1923: The Story of Hitler's First Grab for Power* (New York: Harper & Row, 1982), 328. The date is misprinted as November 12. It should be December 13, 1923.

138 **"a raw egg":** Ehard interview in *Abendzeitung*, February 25, 1974, copy in Ehard's papers, NL Ehard 98, BHStA.

138 **"I have nothing"** . . . **"like a charm":** translation, Dornberg (1982), 328–29.

138 **an umbrella:** *Hans Ehard über den Prozess gegen Adolf Hitler in Jahre 1924*, NL Ehard 98, BHStA.

138 **for five hours:** Some said ten hours (Dornberg, 1982, 329), or twelve hours [Charles Bracelen Flood, *Hitler: The Path to Power* (Boston: Houghton Mifflin Company, 1989), 571)]. I have followed the copy of protocol of December 14, 1923, which describes it as five hours, *Bericht des II.Staatsanwalts Dr. Ehard*, December 14, 1923, NL Ehard 94, BHStA.

138 **"the illuminating interview":** Dornberg (1982), 329.

138 **a document fifteen pages:** *Bericht des II.Staatsanwalts Dr. Ehard*, December 14, 1923, NL Ehard 94, BHStA.

139 **the trial of Adolf Hitler:** On eve of its opening, the proceedings were also called the "Ludendorff trial" or "Ludendorff-Pöhner trial," *Münchener Post*, January 29, 1924. This became rarer with time, though some, like *Miesbacher Anzeiger*, would continue with these designations.

139 **Staatsgerichtshof:** Leipzig had jurisdiction, despite the Bavarian attempt to deny it with its own law three days later, July 24, 1922. For more, see professor of law Alexander Graf zu Dohna's 1924 critique in "Der Münchener Hochverratsprozess," in *Deutsche Juristen-Zeitung* 29 (1924), Heft 9/10, 333ff, and Bavarian perceptions as a threat to sovereignty, Bernd Steger, "Der Hitlerprozess und Bayerns Verhältnis zum Reich 1923/1924," *Vierteljahrshefte für Zeitgeschichte* 23 (1977), 442, note 3. For more on the legal dispute, see Otto Gritschneder's landmark *Bewährungsfrist für den Terroristen Adolf H. Der Hitler-Putsch und die bayerische Justiz* (München: Verlag C. H. Beck 1990), 49–50.

140 **The People's Court:** *Chronik der Bayerischen Justizverwaltung*, 342–44, NL Ehard 90/3, BHStA, with more on the dispute with Berlin over jurisdiction, 291–95, 317–18. See also *Akten der Reichskanzlei Weimarer Republik. Die Kabinette Stresemann I u. II.* Band II (1978), Nr. 248, 1055–56, and Nr. 268, November 19, 1923, 1126, and Otto Gritschneder, "Das missbrauchte bayerische Volksgericht," in Lothar Gruchmann, Reinhard Weber, and Otto Gritschneder, eds., *Der Hitler-Prozess 1924. Wortlaut der Hauptverhandlung vor dem Volksgericht München I* (München: K. G. Saur, 1997), I, xvii–xli.

140 **"judicial kings":** This phrase comes from the lawyer Philipp Loewenfeld, Douglas G. Morris, *Justice Imperiled: The Anti-Nazi Lawyer Max Hirschberg in Weimar Germany* (Ann Arbor: University of Michigan Press, 2008), 45. See also Max Hirschberg's memoir, *Jude und Demokrat. Erinnerungen eines Münchener Rechtsanwalts 1883 bis 1939*, ed. Reinhard Weber (München: R. Oldenbourg Verlag, 1998).

140 **would probably have required:** Gritschneder (1990), 51. Berlin's lack of interest, particularly from Seeckt and Stresseman, and the government's instability, Bernd Steger, "Der Hitlerprozess und Bayerns Verhältnis zum Reich 1923/1924," *Vierteljahrshefte für Zeitgeschichte* 23 (1977), 444 and 447–48, 455.

141 **Straubing:** *Voralberger Tagblatt*, January 8, 1924, and other rumored venues, *Münchner Neueste Nachrichten*, January 9, 1924.

141 **even at Landsberg:** Franz Hemmrich, unpublished memoir, *Erinnerungen eines Gefängnisbeamten*, ED 153-1, 25–28, IfZ.

141 **had been shut down:** It was moved to Ohrdruf, Thuringia, where Seeckt scolded cadets in March 1924 as "mutineers," John W. Wheeler-Bennett, *The Nemesis of Power: The German Army in Politics 1918–1945* (New York: St Martin's Press, 1954), 178, note 1.

141 **Dr. Frankenstein:** *New York Times*, January 13, 1924.

141 **"What can they do to me?":** Hanfstaengl (1970), 156, with description of Egon in Hanfstaengl (1957, repr. 2011), 113. Hitler had earlier threatened to reveal what he knew about the clandestine training programs, Lothar Gruchmann, "Hitlers Denkschrift an die bayerische Justiz vom 16. Mai 1923," *Vierteljahrshefte für Zeitgeschichte* 39 (1991), 305–28.

141 **abruptly postponed:** Report, February 11, 1924, HA 5/114I; *Münchner Neueste Nachrichten*, February 11, 1924; *Regensburger Tagblatt*, February 12, 1924.

142 **resigned from office:** *Chronik der Bayerischen Justizverwaltung*, 328–29, NL Ehard 90/3, BHStA. Seisser remained, but some said he should retire as well, *Neue Freue Volkszeitung*, May 17, 1924.

142 **"mutinous":** R. D. Murphy, *Confidential Political Report*, mailed January 16, 1924 (incorrectly dated to 1923) M336, 862.00/1397, No. 20, NA; see also *Germania*, October 20, 1923.

142 **appealed to no less than:** *Münchener Zeitung*, February 25, 1924, and Hindenburg's refusal to intervene also in *Prager Tablatt*, February 24, 1924; *London Times*, February 25, 1924; and Report, Nr. 49, February 27, 1924, HA 5/114II.

142 **entirely behind closed doors:** *L'Écho de Paris*, February 25, 1924, or at least the most important parts in camera, *Tages-Post* (Linz, Austria), February 27, 1924.

142 **hired bodyguards:** Carl Christian Bry, *Der Hitler-Putsch. Berichte und Kommentare eines Deutschland-Korrespondenten, 1922–1924 für das Argentinische Tag- und Wochenblatt,* ed. Martin Gregor-Dellin (Nördlingen: Greno, 1987), 163, with threats, *Neue Zürcher Zeitung,* November 12, 1923, Erstes Mittagblatt.

142 **refused to appear:** *New York Times,* February 10, 1924.

142 **One story said:** Associated Press, February 26, 1924.

142 **Several defendants:** *Münchner Neueste Nachrichten,* February 24, 1924. In Pöhner's case, this went back for some time, most recently January 1924, according to his medical history, Der Vorstand der II. med. Klinik, Anz. Verz. Nr. Ib 235/24, October 7, 1924, HA 69/1503. This ailment was reported, for instance, by *München-Augsburger Abendzeitung,* January 28, 1924, and *Völkischer Kurier,* February 6, 1924. The sickness had allegedly spread to witnesses, *Chicago Daily Tribune,* February 26, 1924.

142 **needed mental help:** *Le Petit Parisien,* November 27, 1923, with his depression noted and yet assessed as capable of standing trial: Dr. Brinsteiner, *Gutachten über den Geisteszustand des Untersuchungsgefangenen Adolf Hitler,* January 8, 1924, 19–20, OSS.

142 **insomnia:** Reinhard Weber, "'Ein tüchtiger Beamter von makelloser Vergangenheit.' Das Disziplinarverfahren gegen den Hochverräter Wilhelm Frick 1924," *Vierteljahrshefte für Zeitgeschichte* 42 (1994), Heft 1, 131.

142 **poisoned:** *The Daily Mail* (Brisbane), February 8, 1924.

143 **another hunger strike:** Kriebel was also in the hospital on eve of trial, VI a F 406/24, February 20, 1924, HA 67/1494.

143 **thugs and hooligans:** *Neue Freie Presse,* February 24, 1924; one example of planned interruption, intercepted by police, February 8, 1924, MA 104221, BHStA, and preparations in MINN 73699, BHStA.

Chapter 26: *"WE WILL NOT HURT GERMANY!"*

147 **"Let justice be done":** Anz. Verz. XIX 421/1923, Proz.Reg.Nr. 20, 68, 97/1924, Staatsanwaltschaften 3098, 23, StAM. Neithardt's Latin citation, however, omitted the word "et" ("and"). For more, see Lothar Gruchmann, Reinhard Weber, and Otto Gritschneder, *Der Hitler-Prozess 1924. Wortlaut der Hauptverhandlung vor dem Volksgericht München I,* I–IV (1997–1999), I, 353, note 9.

147 **authorized passes:** *Sicherungsmassnahmen anlässlich des Prozesses gegen Hitler u. Genossen,* February 23, 1924, HA 68/1498. A copy of Ehard's pass is in his papers, NL Ehard 97, BHStA.

147 **cold, snowy morning:** *Berliner Tageblatt,* February 26, 1924.

147 **security lines:** *Sicherheitsvorkehrungen für das Kriegsschulegebäude während der Zeit des Hitler-Prozesses,* February 15, 1924, HA 68/1498.

147 **"Never in my long career":** *Le Gaulois*, February 27, 1924. Many other papers commented on the security measures, such as *Die Welt am Samtag*, February 24, 1924; *Nordre Bergenhus Amtstidende* February 27, 1924; and *Prager Tagblatt*, February 28, 1924.

147 **almost reddish glow:** *Vossische Zeitung*, February 26, 1924, Abend Ausgabe, and *Münchner Neueste Nachrichten*, February 24, 1924.

148 **too many women:** *Das Bayerische Vaterland*, February 27, 1924.

148 **too many foreigners:** *Markt Grafinger Wochenblatt*, February 29, 1924. A lot of English was heard, *Münchner Neueste Nachrichten*, February 27, 1924 and *Völkischer Kurier,* February 27, 1924.

148 **The room:** *Skizze des Sitzungssaales für der Infanterieschule Blutenburgerstr. 3/I,* MINN 73699, BHStA.

148 **Acoustics:** *Berliner Tageblatt*, February 26, 1924, Morgen Ausgabe.

148 **Only sixty:** No.292/24, February 19, 1924, NL Ehard 97, BHStA. The demand was much higher, noted, for instance, in *Arbeiter-Zeitung* (Vienna), February 26, 1924.

148 **middle of the gallery:** *Le Petit Parisien*, February 27, 1924.

148 **elegantly dressed:** *L'Écho de Paris*, February 27, 1924. This is no surprise, given the requests for passes in files at HA 68/1498.

148 **one originally intended:** *Münchener Post*, February 27, 1924.

148 **At the front of the procession:** *Miesbacher Anzeiger*, February 26, 1924, and *Deutsche Allgemeine Zeitung*, February 26, 1924.

148 **a dark-blue suit:** Ludendorff is often depicted as wearing his uniform this day, but he did not: *Vossische Zeitung*, February 26, 1924, Abend Ausgabe; *Le Matin*, February 27, 1924; and Reuters, February 26, 1924, among many others.

148 **looked new:** *L'Ouest-Éclair*, February 27, 1924.

149 **"Was this provincial dandy":** Edgar Ansel Mowrer, *Germany Puts the Clock Back* (New York: William Morrow, 1933), 252. See also OSS Sourcebook, 642, and Lilian T. Mowrer describing his impressions in her *Journalist's Wife* (New York: William Morrow, 1937), 186.

149 **"swarm of bees":** *Vossische Zeitung*, February 26, 1924, Abend Ausgabe.

149 **The presiding judge:** Neithardt had held the rank of superior court director since 1920. Otto Gritschneder*, Bewährungsfrist für den Terroristen Adolf H. Der Hitler-Putsch und die bayerische Justiz* (München: Verlag C. H. Beck 1990), 63.

150 **Not in the courtroom:** *L'Humanité*, February 25, 1924, and Linz's *Tages-Post*, February 23, 1924.

150 **three lay judges:** Some historians confuse the alternates, but this was the correct composition of the tribunal.

150 **326 of 354 cases:** E. J. Gumbel, *Vier Jahre politischer Mord* (Berlin-Fichtenau: Verlag der Neuen Gesellschaft, 1922), 73–78, with the left-wing defendants, 79–80.

150 **At 8:52 a.m.:** NA T84 EAP 105/7, 3.

150 **a Munich writer:** Hitler had called himself a writer already on his move August 22, 1909, to Sechshauserstrasse 58 in Vienna. Volker Ullrich, *Adolf Hitler*

Biographie. Band 1: Die Jahre des Aufstiegs 1889–1939 (Frankfurt am Main: S. Fischer, 2013), 52.

150 **rumors circulated:** NA T84 EAP 105/7, 204; *Vossische Zeitung*, February 28, 1924, Morgen Ausgabe. See also the one overheard by Hans von Hülsen, Ernst Deuerlein, ed., *Der Aufstieg der NSDAP in Augenzeugenberichten* (Düsseldorf: Deutscher Tashenbuch Verlag, 1978), 205.

150 **some members:** *Le Petit Parisien*, February 28, 1924. See also *L'Ouest-Eclair*, February 28, 1924.

150 **In January 1922:** MA 103476/1, 74, BHStA. Hitler's actions at the demonstration of May 1, 1923 should have led to the revocation of his probation, Gritschneder (1990), 58.

151 **a rival:** The man Hitler assaulted was Otto Ballerstedt, the leader of the Bayernbund. Ballerstedt was murdered on the "Night of the Long Knives" attacks of June 30, 1934.

151 **a single month's incarceration:** Ullrich (2013), 134.

151 **"On November 8, 1923":** Anz. Verz.XIX 421/23, *Antrag des I. Staatsanwalts beim Volksgericht München I auf Anberaumung der Hauptverhandlung*, January 8, 1924, Staatanswaltschaften 3098, 2, StAM, and read out at this point, *Der Hitler-Prozess vor dem Volksgericht in München* (München: Knorr & Hirth, 1924), I, 2. This document does not have the charges against the last two defendants added to list, Lieutenant Colonel Kriebel and Heinz Pernet. For those, see Stenglein's *Nachtragsanklage*, January 24, 1924, and February 7, 1924, Staatanswaltschaften 3099, StAM.

151 **Ehard would open:** *Münchner Neueste Nachrichten*, February 27, 1924.

151 **had almost certainly:** Ehard unpublished memoir, 41–42, NL Ehard 99, BHStA.

151 **finest mind:** *Bayerischer Kurier*, March 17, 1924.

151 **"the springboard"** . . . **"It is our supposition":** Anz. Verz.XIX 421/23, *Antrag des I. Staatsanwalts,* 4, 6, 32, 33, Staatsanwaltschaften 3098 StAM.

152 **more than one hour:** Associated Press, February 27, 1924; or slightly longer, *Miesbacher Anzeiger*, February 26, 1924, or slightly less, Report Nr. 50, February 28, 1924, HA 5/114II.

152 **"a threat to national":** NA T84 EAP 105/7, 3, and surprise, such as Prague's *Prager Tagblatt*, February 28, 1924 and Vienna's *Reichspost*, February 28, 1924.

153 **"trying the case":** NA T84 EAP 105/7, 10.

153 **"There is no harm":** NA T84 EAP 105/7, 13. Holl's background is in Nr. 72, March 25, 1924, HA 5/114II.

153 **"monstrous":** NA T84 EAP 105/7, 16.

153 **"deeply shaken":** NA T84 EAP 105/7, 24.

153 **"If I were a prosecutor"** . . . **"That's going a little":** NA T84 EAP 105/7, 24.

153 **"We do not want"** . . . **"We will not hurt Germany!":** NA T84 EAP 105/7, 25. Hitler had previously threatened to reveal the training his men received from the state, thereby avoiding prosecution after the May Day celebration, Lothar

Gruchmann, "Hitlers Denkschrift an die bayerische Justiz vom 16. Mai 1923," VfZ, 39 (1991), 305–28.

153 "public interest": NA T84 EAP 105/7, 26.

154 "the prosecution will of course" and "The prosecution does not intend": NA T84 EAP 105/7, 31.

154 the din: Ibid.

154 "The trial is to be public" and "The court will decide": NA T84 EAP 105/7, 32.

Chapter 27: DEFENDANT HITLER

155 "I made the decision": NA T84/2 EAP 105/7, 120.

155 tapering fingers: G. Ward Price, 17, in OSS Sourcebook OSS, and G. Ward Price, *I Know These Dictators* (London: George G. Harrap, 1937), 18.

155 "a rather dashing": *Allgemeine Rundschau*, March 20, 1924.

155 "When I came to Munich": NA T84 EAP 105/7, 33–34.

156 a full year later: A few newspapers did in fact date Hitler's arrival in Munich in the correct year of 1913, for example, *Salzburger Volksblatt*, November 10, 1923, but this was before Hitler could spin his tale in the courtroom. Other people had noted this too, for instance, Kurt G. W. Ludecke, *I Knew Hitler: The Story of a Nazi Who Escaped the Blood Purge* (New York: Charles Scribner's Sons, 1938), 47, but the correct year was shown by the Austrian Social Democrat and fellow Braunau-born, Franz Jetzinger, *Hitler's Youth*, trans. Lawrence Wilson (London: Hutchinson, 1958), particularly 156–59, and how he preserved the documents from the Gestapo, 175–82.

156 registering for military service: Conscription Act of 1889. For more, see Jetzinger (1958), 145.

156 "unfit for combatant": Jetzinger (1958), 155, with conclusion of motive on 157 and 158. Kershaw agrees that the military served as primary reason for his departure, Ian Kershaw, *Hitler 1889–1936: Hubris* (New York: W. W. Norton, 1999), 81, as does Thomas Weber, *Hitler's First War: Adolf Hitler, the Men of the List Regiment, and the First World War* (Oxford: Oxford University Press, 2010), 13.

156 The impression: As Hitler gained prominence, some reporters began to challenge his account of his military service. See, for instance, a number of articles from January 1931 in *Münchener Post* and then *Echo der Woche*. For a discussion of this dispute, along with Hitler's lawsuit, see Lothar Machtan, *The Hidden Hitler*, trans. John Brownjohn (New York: Basic Books, 2001), 65–88, and Weber (2010), 282–87.

157 "Rear Area Pig": Weber (2010), 91, and, discussion of Hitler's experience of the war, particularly 91–105.

157 "fighting for the Germans": Hitler of course saw action, particularly at Ypres on

October 29, 1914, when 349 men of the List Regiment were killed. On November 3, 1914, he was promoted to *Gefreiter* and six days later became a dispatch runner for regimental headquarters.

157 **"For war injuries"** and **"completely blinded":** NA T84 EAP 105/7, 34.

157 **October 5:** Hitler did not date the first wound at the trial and used October 7 in *Mein Kampf.* But October 5 is more accurate, Anton Joachimsthaler, *Hitlers Weg begann in München 1913–1923* (München: Herbig, 2000), 163–64; Weber (2010), 154; and Peter Longerich, *Hitler. Biographie* (München: Siedler, 2015), 48. A copy of his hospital record in HA 4/96.

157 **police escorted:** *Wache anlässlich des Hitler-Prozesses,* February 20, 1924, HA 68/1498.

157 **Eight rooms:** *Sicherheitsvorkehrungen für das Kriegsschulegebäude während der Zeit des Hitler-Prozesses,* February 15, 1924, HA 68/1498. A preview of the arrangement appeared in brief in *Die Welt am Samtag,* February 24, 1924, and with more detail in *Fränkischer Kurier,* March 4, 1924.

157 **not required to remain:** *Sicherungsmassnahmen anlässlich des Hitlerprozesses,* February 21, 1924, HA 68/1498.

158 **"Your Honor":** NA T84 EAP 105/7, 36.

158 **"a genius":** *Vossische Zeitung,* February 27, 1924, Morgen Ausgabe.

158 **in a courteous:** *Berliner Tageblatt,* February 26, 1924, Abend Ausgabe, and *Prager Tageblatt,* February 28, 1924.

158 **almost nervous:** London *Times,* February 27, 1924 and *Völkischer Kurier,* February 27, 1924.

158 **a dazzling performance:** *Markt Grafinger Wochenblatt,* February 29, 1924.

158 **tribune of the people:** *La Croix,* February 28, 1924.

158 **a charlatan:** *L'Écho de Paris,* February 28, 1924.

158 **It was not difficult:** *Le Petit Parisien,* February 27, 1924.

158 **Hitler would talk:** For higher estimates of four hours, see for instance, *Hamburger Anzeiger,* February 27, 1924; *Der Landsmann,* February 27, 1924; *Das Bayerische Vaterland,* February 28, 1924; or slightly longer than that, Vienna's *Die Rote Fahne,* February 27, 1924.

159 **"Very Good"** . . . **"an absolute anti-Semite":** NA T84 EAP 105/7, 36-37 and *Vorwärts,* February 27, 1924.

159 **"Lieutenant Colonel Hitler":** *Auckland Star,* February 28, 1924.

159 **"Herr Von Hitler":** United Press (British), February 29, 1924, and Reuters, February 26, 1924.

159 **self-taught:** *Hamburger Illustrierte Zeitung,* Nr. 9, 1924.

159 **"granite foundation":** Adolf Hitler, *Mein Kampf,* trans. Ralph Manheim (Boston: Houghton Mifflin Company, 1943), 22.

159 **not a single verifiable:** Brigitte Hamann, *Hitler's Vienna: A Dictator's Apprenticeship,* trans. Thomas Thornton (Oxford: Oxford University Press, 1999), 347–57,

and Joachimsthaler (2000), 10 and 96. His comments in the fall at Lechberg, August 1919, Volker Ullrich, *Adolf Hitler Biographie. Band 1: Die Jahre des Aufstiegs 1889–1939* (Frankfurt am Main: S. Fischer, 2013), 100. Hitler's first famous essay on the "Jewish Question," prompted by Karl Mayr, was finished September 16, 1919. See also Ernst Deuerlein, ed., "Hitlers Eintritt in die Politik und die Reichswehr," *Vierteljahrshefte für Zeitgeschichte* 7 (1959), 177–227.

159 **September 1907:** Kershaw (1999), 37, and Hamann (1999), 30. A February 1908 date is also sometimes given for his return, after he rented the apartment at Stumpergasse 31.

160 **Hitler had not returned:** Anton Joachimsthaler discovered this fact. See his discussion of the election in his revised study, Joachimsthaler (2000), 190–216.

160 *Vertrauensmann:* Vertrauensmann der sozialistischen Propaganda-Abteilung des 2.Inf. Rgt., Joachimsthaler (2000), 83, 198–202, 210–12.

160 **Many of Hitler's colleagues:** Esser was, for instance, a Social Democrat until he joined NSDAP on March 8, 1920, as member Nr. 881 (He became Nr. 2 in the refounded NSDAP in March 1925). Heinrich Hoffmann admitted wearing a red armband, *Hitler Was My Friend*, trans. Lt-Col R. H. Stevens (London: Burke, 1955), 35–37. For more on the left wing near Hitler, see Hellmuth Auerbach, "Hitlers politische Lehrjahre und die Münchner Gesellschaft 1919–1923," *Vierteljahrshefte für Zeitgeschichte* 25 (1977), 1–45.

160 **Hitler never admitted:** There were earlier hints: Ernst Toller noted hearing the rumors, *Eine Jugend in Deutschland* (Amsterdam: Querido Verlag, 1933; Hamburg: Rowohlt, 1998), 148. In 1953, Werner Maser secured an admission from Hermann Esser that it was possible that Hitler wore a red armband in the spring of 1919, Maser, *Hitler: Legend, Myth & Reality*, trans. Peter and Betty Ross (New York: Harper Torchbooks, 1974), 367, note 153. Historian Ernst Deuerlein had also come to believe that Hitler wanted to join the Independent Social Democrats, he told Werner Maser, *Hitler's Mein Kampf: An Analysis*, trans. R. H. Barry (London: Faber and Faber, 1970), 203, note 2. Some historians point to recently rediscovered grainy film of "Hitler" in a funeral procession for Kurt Eisner as evidence, though this is by no means accepted as Hitler by everyone, and there are some reasons to doubt it. Whether Hitler did or did not join the procession does not, of course, confirm or refute the basic point that he had taken on this responsibility at this time.

161 **"Germany will only be saved":** NA T84 EAP 105/7, 41.

161 **"socialism for dummies"** and **"despair and confusion":** Horst J. Weber, *Die deutsche Presse, insbesondere die völkische, um den Hitlerprozess. Ein Beitrag zur Lehre von der Parteipresse.* Diss. (Universität Leipzig, 1930), 48.

161 **Nazi propaganda:** *Bozner Nachrichten*, March 7, 1924.

161 **the crowd:** London *Times*, February 27, 1924; *The Independent*, March 1, 1924; and *Le Petit Journal,* February 26, 1924.

161 **"to gain seats in parliament"** . . . **"from hour to hour":** NA T84 EAP 105/7, 52–53.

162 **his swagger:** *L'Impartial*, February 29, 1924.

162 **a group of six men:** NA T84 EAP 105/7, 39, 43–44, with evidence contradicting his claim to have been the seventh member in the membership lists of the National Socialist Party, *Mitglieder Liste*, HA 8/171. There were six other members of the steering committee, but that was not what Hitler said or implied in the courtroom.

162 **"I must categorically":** *The Hitler Trial Before the People's Court in Munich*, trans. H. Francis Freniere, Lucie Karcic, and Philip Fandek (Arlington, VA: University Publications of America, 1976), I, 58.

163 **"If someone":** NA T84 EAP 105/7, 73.

163 **"the will to make":** NA T84 EAP 105/7, 86–87.

163 **"For all these months":** NA T84 EAP 105/7, 82.

163 **"I did not come":** NA T84 EAP 105/7, 120.

163 **"There is no"** . . . **"wanted the best":** NA T84 EAP 105/7, 122.

163 **"exhaustive"** and **"Examination":** NA T84 EAP 105/7, 127.

Chapter 28: *CONFESSIONS AND DISTORTIONS*

164 **"I had already":** NA T84 EAP 105/7, 218.

164 **Photographers and camera crews:** *Sicherheitsmassnahmen anlässlich des Hitlerprozesses*, February 21, 1924, and *Sicherungsmassnahmen anlässlich des Prozesses gegen Hitler u. Genossen*, February 23, 1924, HA 68/1498.

164 **A motorcycle dealer:** Staatsministerium des Innern, Nr. 2004 k a a 539, November 21, 1924, HA 68/1498.

164 **passes that granted:** Der Präsident des Landgerichts München I an den Herrn Präsidenten der Polizeidirektion München, February 19, 1924, Nr. 292/24, HA 68/1498. Examples of cards are in HA 5/114I and Ehard's pass is preserved in his papers, NL Ehard 97, BHStA.

165 **"the scum of the Hitler crowd":** *Allgemeine Zeitung*, March 7, 1924.

165 **The police presence:** *Berliner Tageblatt*, February 27, 1924, Abend Ausgabe.

165 **"state of siege":** NA T84 EAP 105/7, 908.

165 **"beer patriots":** United Press, February 25, 1924.

165 **"beer hall revolution":** *Ingolstädter Anzeiger*, March 1, 1924.

165 **"Putsch Trial Called Joke":** *Vancouver Sun*, February 27, 1924.

165 **"ludicrous beer cellar putsch":** United Press, printed in *Berkeley Daily Gazette*, February 25, 1924.

165 **"Czechoslovakian":** *Le Petit Journal*, February 26, 1924.

165 **"It was either do or die":** *Das Bayerische Vaterland*, February 27, 1924.

165 **"the old Hitler":** *Das Bayerische Vaterland*, February 27, 1924. Jews were attacked

in almost every speech in these days, Ian Kershaw, *Hitler 1889–1936: Hubris* (New York: W. W. Norton, 1999), 151.

166 **"a farce" and "the Whitewashing of Ludendorff":** Charges picked up in many papers, via Australian Press Association, including Brisbane's *The Telegraph*; Melbourne's *The Argus*; Newcastle's *Morning Herald*; and both *The Mercury* and the *The Advocate* in Hobart and Burnie, Tasmania, all published on February 27, 1924.

166 **"Why was Kahr":** *Vossische Zeitung*, February 27, 1924, Morgen Ausgabe. See also *Hamburger Illustrierte Zeitung*, Nr. 9, 1924.

166 **ran a photo:** *L'Humanité*, February 27, 1924.

166 **one of the most financially solvent:** MA 103476/3, 1124, BHStA. For more on Weber's life, see Svantje Insenhöfer, *Dr. Friedrich Weber. Reichstierärzteführer von 1934 bis 1945* (Hannover dissertation, 2008).

166 **The Truth:** Dr. Weber, *Die Wahrheit* (1923).

166 **hard to counter:** *Der Oberbayer*, November 14–15, 1923.

166 **He seemed like:** *Allgemeine Rundschau*, March 20, 1924.

167 **"big speech":** *Vossische Zeitung*, February 27, 1924, Abend Ausgabe.

167 **The audience:** *Le Petit Parisien*, February 28, 1924.

167 **"break the fetters":** NA T84 EAP 105/7, 138–39.

167 **"Marxism, Jews" . . . "launch a crusade":** NA T84 EAP 105/7, 139–40.

167 **"nothing left to do":** NA T84 EAP 105/7, 151.

168 **"When did you first" and "We never received":** NA T84 EAP 105/7, 169.

168 **"broken their word":** NA T84 EAP 105/7, 175.

168 **"your own objectives?" . . . "My, you seem":** NA T84 EAP 105/7, 193.

168 **"Haven't you ever heard":** NA T84 EAP 105/7, 194.

168 **"Outrageous!":** *Das Bayerische Vaterland*, February 28, 1924.

168 **watched Ludendorff stand up:** *Le Matin*, February 28, 1924.

169 **"Good, that's what" and "Actually you wanted":** NA T84 EAP 105/7, 195.

169 **jumping to his feet:** Nr. 51, Report, February 29, 1924, HA 5/114II.

169 **The audience cheered:** This was noted in the transcript at NA T84 EAP 105/7, 195. The disposition of the audience in the scene appears in many accounts, for instance, *Vossische Zeitung*, February 27, 1924; *Le Petit Parisien*, February 28, 1924; and a 1924 published transcript of the trial, *Der Hitler-Prozess. Auszüge aus den Verhandlungsberichten mit den Bildern der Angeklagten nach Zeichnungen von Otto von Kursell* (München: Deutscher Volksverlag, 1924), 33.

169 **But wasn't . . . "So that the":** NA T84 EAP 105/7, 198. Weber's response was recorded in *Der Hitler-Prozess vor dem Volksgericht in München* (München: Knorr & Hirth, 1924), I, 35.

169 **more Bohemian:** *Vossische Zeitung*, February 26, 1924, Abend Ausgabe.

170 **Pöhner made no attempt to deny:** His arguments on the stand were no surprise, given his pretrial statement, *Erklärung des Herrn Oberlandesgerichtsrats Ernst Pöhner über die Vorgänge vom 8./9. November 1923*, December 9, 1923, HA 5/120.

Three years before that, Pöhner had espoused these themes, as related by Würt-temberg delegate, Carl Moser von Filseck, *Politik in Bayern 1919–1933. Berichte des württembergischen Gesandten Carl Moser von Filseck*, ed. Wolfgang Benz. Schriftenreihe der Vierteljahrshefte für Zeitgeschichte Nummer 22/23 (Stutt-gart: Deutsche Verlags-Anstalt, 1971), July 8, 1920, Nr. 149, 64.

170 **on the eve:** This occurred on the morning of November 8, not November 7, as stated in the indictment.

170 **Pöhner spoke:** *Vossische Zeitung*, February 28, Morgen Ausgabe and *Hamburger Illustrierte Zeitung* 1924, Nr. 9.

170 **"putting on an act":** NA T84 EAP 105/7, 235.

170 **"simply unfathomable":** NA T84 EAP 105/7, 257.

170 **"I do not think":** NA T84 EAP 105/7, 258.

171 **a smirk:** *Berliner Tageblatt*, February 28, 1924, Morgen Ausgabe.

171 **"We have been":** NA T84 EAP 105/7, 273. The transcript also notes merriment in the audience.

Chapter 29: BEHIND CLOSED DOORS

172 **"I have tried":** NA T84 EAP 105/7, 379.

172 **Snow blanketed:** *L'Ouest-Éclair*, February 28, 1924, British United Press, Febru-ary 28, 1924.

172 **Ludendorff's car:** NA T84 EAP 105/7, 278; *Münchner Neueste Nachrichten*, Feb-ruary 29, 1924; *Prager Tagblatt*, February 29, 1924; and *Daily Mail*, February 29, 1924. London *Times*, for one, was skeptical of the general's excuse, February 29, 1924.

172 **someone had misplaced:** Agence Havas, February 29, 1924.

172 **Room 130:** VId, *Sicherungsmassnahmen anlässlich des Prozesses gegen Hitler und Genossen*, February 19, 1924, HA 68/1498.

172 **"Bavarian colossus":** *Le Petit Parisien*, February 29, 1924.

173 **"a ruthless, merciless"** . . . **"November criminals":** NA T84 EAP 105/7, 281–82.

173 **"Hittler":** *L'Action Française*, February 29, 1924.

173 **incorrectly spelling:** *Le Gaulois*, United Press, and Telegraphen-Union were still calling him "Hittler."

173 **"See you in"** . . . **"not to rest":** NA T84 EAP 105/7, 282.

173 **"a convinced Bavarian"** and **"German Austria":** NA T84 EAP 105/7, 286.

174 *Le Petit Parisien* **guessed:** *Le Petit Parisien*, February 29, 1924. *Argentinische Tag- und Wochenblatt* agreed that the most important facts were disclosed only in closed session, March 12, 1924, Carl Christian Bry, *Der Hitler-Putsch. Berichte und Kommentare eines Deutschland-Korrespondenten, 1922–1924 für das Argen-tinische Tag- und Wochenblatt*, ed. Martin Gregor-Dellin (Nördlingen: Greno, 1987), 186.

174 **"great war of liberation"**: NA T84 EAP 105/7, 288.

174 **"criminal government"**: NA T84 EAP 105/7, 290.

174 **"Lieutenant Colonel!"**: NA T84 EAP 105/7, 291.

175 **"tremendous power"**: NA T84 EAP 105/7, 296.

175 **"We can wage"**: NA T84 EAP 105/7, 295.

175 **"border police"**: NA T84 EAP 105/7, 305.

175 **"no doubt that"**: NA T84 EAP 105/7, 306.

175 **the exact order**: *Befehl des Deutschen Kampfbundes* ("Grenzschutzbefehl"), October 16, 1923, printed in Ernst Deuerlein, ed., *Der Hitler-Putsch. Bayerische Dokumente zum 8./9. November 1923* (Stuttgart: Deutsche Verlags-Anstalt, 1962), Nr. 42, 221–23.

175 **"Now?" . . . "That is not striking"**: NA T84 EAP 105/7, 307–8.

176 **One of the judges**: NA T84 EAP 105/7, 312. Pöhner also agreed, though the transcript identifies the speaker as Frick [NA T84 EAP 105/7, 310–12]. Given the references made to his talk the previous day and the use of favorite phrases, such as "Ich mache keinen Hehl," this is clearly Pöhner.

176 **"They were trained" . . . "By officers of the Reichswehr"**: NA T84 EAP 105/7, 313.

176 **"everyone would then"**: NA T84 EAP 105/7, 347–48.

177 **"moment of mobilization"**: NA T84 EAP 105/7, 363.

177 **"I considered it"**: NA T84 EAP 105/7, 366.

177 **"the Balkanization of Germany"**: NA T84 EAP 105/7, 369.

177 **"Once it was Spain"**: NA T84 EAP 105/7, 370.

178 **"a tremendous, unprecedented" . . . "High treason is"**: NA T84 EAP 105/7, 373–75.

178 **"Do not believe"**: NA T84 EAP 105/7, 377.

Chapter 30: THE DEFENSE ATTACKS

179 **"Ludendorff towers over"**: NA T84 EAP 105/7, 418.

179 **"a party" and "Tragedy at Munich"**: *Rosenheimer Anzeiger*, March 1/2, 1924, and imagery repeated, *Bayerischer Kurier*, March 11, 1924, and elsewhere, such as *Der Hitler-Prozess. Auszüge aus den Verhandlungsberichten mit den Bildern der Angeklagten nach Zeichnungen von Otto von Kursell* (München: Deutscher Volksverlag, 1924), 3, 5–6.

179 **Many people were expecting**: *Münchener Zeitung*, February 29, 1924.

179 **"If the public sessions"**: London *Times*, February 29, 1924.

180 **"apparently a Bulgarian" and "such men"**: NA T84 EAP 105/7, 384–85.

180 **unremitting smirk**: The article was not identified, but it was probably *Berliner Lokal-Anzeiger*, February 27, 1924.

181 **"springboard" and "a little nudge"**: NA T84 EAP 105/7, 402.

181 **"Safely Delivered":** NA T84 EAP 105/7, 408. For its finding, see XIX 466/23, December 28, 1923, HA 67/1494.

181 **"First report to Frick"** . . . **"I mean, if that":** NA T84 EAP 105/7, 409.

182 **"That was the best":** NA T84 EAP 105/7, 419.

182 **"Outrageous!":** The heckling was noted in transcript, NA T84 EAP 105/7, 419–20.

182 **"Shame" and "That is no officer!":** Nr. 53, March 2, 1924, HA 5/114II.

182 **"I would like"** . . . **"I do not believe":** NA T84 EAP 105/7, 420.

182 **"very harsh":** *Berliner Tageblatt*, February 29, 1924, Abend Ausgabe.

182 **"That is going":** NA T84 EAP 105/7, 421.

183 **"I would not have taken":** NA T84 EAP 105/7, 460.

183 **"According to the sentiments":** NA T84 EAP 105/7, 472.

183 **like a bomb:** *Völkischer Kurier*, March 4, 1924.

Chapter 31: *A MASTERPIECE OF IGNORANCE*

184 **"Is Ludendorff a super-patriot?":** *Calgary Daily Herald*, February 27, 1924.

184 **The general:** *Vossische Zeitung*, March 1, 1924, Abend Ausgabe; *L'Écho de Paris*, March 1, 1924; *Le Petit Parisien*, March 1, 1924; *Chicago Daily Tribune*, March 1, 1924; *Le Figaro*, March 1, 1924; Nr. 53, March 2, 1924, HA 5/114II; Erich Ludendorff, *Auf dem Weg zur Feldherrnhalle. Lebenserinnerungen an die Zeit des 9.11.1923 mit Dokumenten in fünf Anlagen* (München: Ludendorff, 1937), 80.

184 **blue suit:** *Washington Post*, March 1, 1924. Other people noted that he seemed old and tired, *Bozner Nachrichten*, March 4, 1924.

184 **horn-rimmed eyeglasses:** *Cairns Post*, March 3, 1924 and Reuter, March 3, 1924.

185 **"I cannot express myself"** . . . **"detrimental to the interests":** NA T84 EAP 105/7, 482.

185 **He attacked:** A pro-Hitler transcript published in 1924 highlighted the passage on "The Jewish Question," while printing Ludendorff's attacks on Catholics with smaller headlines. It also put the general's praise of brave Catholic and Protestants in bold, *Der Hitler-Prozess. Auszüge aus den Verhandlungsberichten mit den Bildern der Angeklagten nach Zeichnungen von Otto von Kursell* (München: Deutscher Volksverlag, 1924), 52.

185 **in complete silence:** *Le Canada*, March 1, 1924 and Ludendorff (1937), 82.

185 **"a new high point":** *Rosenheimer Anzeiger*, March 1/2, 1924.

185 **"a masterpiece of political ignorance":** *New York Times*, March 2, 1924.

185 **"great confidence":** NA T84 EAP 105/7, 514–15.

185 **"a procession of enlightenment":** NA T84 EAP 105/7, 543.

186 **"betrayal, treason, and attempted"** . . . **"We want":** NA T84 EAP 105/7, 545.

186 **"That was only":** NA T84 EAP 105/7, 547. The word *nur* ["only"] was handwritten into place in the transcript.

186 **the staff at the Löwenbräu beer hall:** *Volksblatt*, March 8, 1924, and cheering him outside building too, London *Times*, March 1, 1924.

186 **few complaints:** Ernst Röhm, *The Memoirs of Ernst Röhm*, intro. Eleanor Hancock and trans. Geoffrey Brooks (London: Frontline Books, 2012), 201–2.

186 **former dorm room:** *Sicherheitsvorkehrungen für das Kriegsschulegebäude während der Zeit des Hitler-Prozesses*, February 15, 1924, HA 68/1498.

186 **launching another hunger strike:** Or even ending one said to have begun, Associated Press, February 27, 1924.

187 **"the road of humiliation and penance":** Röhm (2012), 202. This was also the hope of Hitler and Brückner, he said, and credited Kohl with noting how this road could have been avoided by more effective cooperation among the defence lawyers.

187 **"Your Honor":** NA T84 EAP 105/7, 551.

187 **Röhm spoke:** *Le Gaulois*, March 2, 1924.

187 **"rather uninteresting":** *Berliner Tageblatt*, March 1, 1924, Abend Ausgabe. He was also compared to a stereotypical Prussian officer: *La Justice*, March 1–2, 1924.

187 **"I am an officer and a soldier":** NA T84 EAP 105/7, 551.

187 **"peculiar snort-like sound":** For more on the wound to his nose and rudimentary plastic surgery, see Eleanor Hancock, Ernst *Röhm: Hitler's SA Chief of Staff* (New York: Palgrave Macmillan, 2008), 2, 18.

188 **"very disheartening":** NA T84 EAP 105/7, 556.

188 **blindly obedient:** *Allgemeine Rundschau*, March 20, 1924.

188 **"Comrade Ebert":** NA T84 EAP 105/7, 566.

188 **"Dismal weather":** *L'Écho de Paris*, March 2, 1924.

188 **"It is understandable"** . . . **"Our enthusiasm was extraordinary":** NA T84 EAP 105/7, 589.

189 **A list of missing property:** Br.B.Nr.11223, November 24, 1923, HA 67/1493.

189 **"a rather confused":** *Vossische Zeitung* March 1, 1924, Abend Ausgabe.

189 **"ruthless combat"** . . . **"greatest faith":** NA T84 EAP 105/7, 605–7.

190 **"I must really":** NA T84 EAP 105/7, 619.

190 **several reporters:** *Berliner Tageblatt*, March 1, 1924, Abend Ausgabe; London *Times*, March 1, 1924; *L'Action Française*, March 2, 1924; and *Le Temps,* March 3, 1924, among others, though crowd still favored defendants, *La Siècle*, March 2, 1924.

Chapter 32: CUP OF BITTERNESS

191 **"He got us":** NA T84 EAP 105/7, 655.

191 **"register of the dead":** *Vorwärts*, February 29, 1924.

192 **"most superfluous"** and **"pomposity and personal ambition":** NA T84 EAP 105/7, 627.

192 **"There can be"**: NA T84 EAP 105/7, 631.

192 **"Fiery"**: London *Times*, March 7, 1924.

192 **whenever he spoke**: *Völkischer Kurier*, March 4, 1924.

192 **"A preliminary inquiry"**: NA T84 EAP 105/7, 633.

193 **"Staff Sergeant Ebert"**: NA T84 EAP 105/7, 638. For debunking, see *Vorwärts*, March 9, 1924.

194 **"conferences and negotiations"**: NA T84 EAP 105/7, 639.

194 **several officers**: *Vossische Zeitung*, March 3, 1924, Abend Ausgabe.

194 **"no longer existed"**: NA T84 EAP 105/7, 668. Neithardt was referring to Wagner's claim at NA T84 EAP 105/7, 668, 643.

195 **"Was that a question"** and **"the difference in age"**: NA T84 EAP 105/7, 670.

195 **"from the commander"**: NA T84 EAP 105/7, 673.

196 **ranked as among**: Agence Havas, March 4, 1924.

196 **best suited him**: *Bayerischer Kurier*, March 4, 1924.

Chapter 33: DR. FRICK

197 **"I dismissed all"**: NA T84/2 EAP 105/7, 724.

197 **"Comedy, comedy"**: *La Presse*, March 2, 1924.

197 **"words, words"** and **"a black eye"**: *New York Times*, March 2, 1924.

197 **"phantasmagoria"**: *Neue Zürcher Zeitung*, April 2, 1924, Erstes Morgenblatt.

198 **"vulgar and violent"**: Eugenio Pacelli to Pietro Gasparri, Dokument Nr. 1091, November 14, 1923, "Kritische Online-Edition der Nuntiaturberichte Eugenio Pacellis (1917–1929)" at www.pacelli-edition.de.

198 **"battle against Rome"**: See also the coverage of the controversy in *Berliner Börsen-Zeitung*, March 4, 1924, Morgen Ausgabe; *La Croix*, March 11, 1924 and March 13, 1924; *Hennefer Volks-Zeitung*, March 6, 1924; and *Meraner Zeitung*, March 14, 1924. See also *Der Landsmann*, March 5, 1924.

198 **"ineloquently written"**: *Time*, March 10, 1924.

198 **"revealing his own true nature"**: *Germania*, March 1, 1924.

198 **"an impulsive and ambitious"**: *L'Écho de Paris*, February 26, 1924.

199 **"the Hitler-Ludendorff mess"**: *Vorwärts*, March 3, 1924.

199 **already a rumor**: United Press, March 5, 1924, and his decision not to run reported after the trial, for instance, *Meraner Zeitung*, April 4, 1924.

199 **rising popularity**: Munich favoring Hitler and Ludendorff, *La Siècle*, March 2, 1924.

199 **"dereliction of duty"**: Anz. Verz.XIX 421/23, *Antrag des I. Staatsanwalts beim Volksgericht München I auf Anberaumung der Hauptverhandlung*, January 8, 1924, Staatsanwaltschaften 3098, 35–36, StAM. For more on Frick, see Reinhard Weber, "'Ein tüchtiger Beamter von makelloser Vergangenheit.' Das

Disziplinarverfahren gegen den Hochverräter Wilhelm Frick 1924," *Vierteljahrshefte für Zeitgeschichte* 42 (1994), Heft 1, 129–50.

200   **elegant:** *Le Petit Parisien*, February 27, 1924.

200   **"tall and thin":** *Berliner Tageblatt*, February 26, 1924.

200   **"Without [it], a state" . . . "a game ball":** NA T84 EAP 105/7, 700.

200   **"still small":** NA T84 EAP 105/7, 704.

200   **"Marxist-infected workers"** and **"the germ of Germany's":** NA T84 EAP 105/7, 704. Georg Fuchs would later elaborate on the "Germ cell" in an unpublished essay on early history of Nazi Party, drawing on insights of Pöhner and Frick, *Zur Vorgeschichte der nationalsozialistischen Erhebung*, HA 4/113.

200   **"I had already heard":** NA T84 EAP 105/7, 714.

201   **"He admits nothing" . . . He spoke like:** *Vossische Zeitung*, March 4, 1924, Morgen Ausgabe.

Chapter 34: FIRST WITNESSES

202   **"I think it was":** NA T84 EAP 105/7, 961.

202   **cheerful and confident:** *Münchener Zeitung*, March 1–2, 1924.

202   **The police had been complaining . . . "The defendants were not":** Cabinet meeting minutes, March 4, 1924, Ernst Deuerlein, ed., *Der Aufstieg der NSDAP in Augenzeugenberichten* (Düsseldorf: Deutscher Taschenbuch Verlag, 1978), 215–17. Neithardt's sympathy was widely noted, for instance, *Vorwärts*, March 6, 1924, and Carl Moser von Filseck, *Politik in Bayern 1919–1933. Berichte des württembergischen Gesandten Carl Moser von Filseck*, ed. Wolfgang Benz. Schriftenreihe der Vierteljahrshefte für Zeitgeschichte Nummer 22/23 (Stuttgart: Deutsche Verlags-Anstalt, 1971), March 2, 1924, Nr. 75, 153.

203   **If he were the presiding judge:** *Das Bayerische Vaterland*, March 7, 1924.

204   **the so-called white-blue:** this was a pamphlet by "Veni Vidi" entitled *Ludendorff in Bayern, oder Der Novemberputsch* (Leipzig: Veduka-Verlag, 1924).

204   **the memorandum:** "Der Putsch am 8.November 1923. Vorgeschichte und Verlauf," printed in Ernst Deuerlein, ed., *Der Hitler-Putsch. Bayerische Dokumente zum 8./9. November 1923* (Stuttgart: Deutsche Verlags-Anstalt, 1962), Nr. 182, 487–515, with additional points in Anlage 4a and 4b, 530–35.

204   **"Secret!"** and **"Confidential!":** NA T84 EAP 105/7, 750.

204   **"I found that":** NA T84 EAP 105/7, 750.

205   **"striking agreement":** NA T84 EAP 105/7, 760.

205   **the defendants were allowed:** *Le Gaulois*, March 5, 1924.

205   **"foppish manner":** *Allgemeine Zeitung*, March 7, 1924.

205   **he wore a field-gray:** *Time*, March 17, 1924, and talking with Hitler, Associated Press, March 5, 1924.

206 **Ensconced in closed session:** NA T84 EAP 105/7, 774.

207 **At 2:52 that afternoon:** NA T84 EAP 105/7, 817.

207 **"The Day of the Police":** *Vossische Zeitung*, March 5, 1924, Morgen Ausgabe.

207 **"What specifically happened":** NA T84 EAP 105/7, 828.

207 **"assume the political leadership":** NA T84 EAP 105/7, 861. Hitler is often said to have gained this sense in prison, but the development from so-called drummer to leader was much more complicated than that, beginning well before the legend which places it solely at Landsberg.

207 **He pulled out a copy:** The article he cites was published in *Münchner Neueste Nachrichten*, November 9, 1923.

208 **turned to the prosecutor:** Nr. 57, March 7, 1924, HA 5/114II; and *Vorwärts*, March 5, 1924.

208 **"My quarrel and reckoning":** NA T84 EAP 105/7, 862.

Chapter 35: *THE PROSECUTOR'S MISFORTUNES*

209 **" 'I cannot elaborate' ":** NA T84 EAP 105/7, 2133.

209 **the most fantastic:** *Vossische Zeitung*, March 6, 1924, Abend Ausgabe.

209 **"a parody of justice":** *L'Écho de Paris*, March 4, 1924.

209 **"Your Excellency":** *Le Canada* (Montreal), March 1, 1924, and March 6, 1924.

210 **"Monsieur Hitler":** *Le Petit Parisien*, February 27, 1924.

210 **he did not dare:** *La Presse*, March 6, 1924.

210 **his white goatee:** H. R. Knickerbocker, *Is Tomorrow Hitler's?: 200 Questions on the Battle of Mankind* (New York: Reynal & Hitchcock, 1941), 11.

210 **"His Majesty the king":** *Berliner Tageblatt*, March 1, 1924, Abend Ausgabe.

210 **the sight of a young officer:** *Wiener Zeitung*, March 6, 1924.

210 **"scrawlings":** NA T84 EAP 105/7, 908. These were probably the drawings published in *Le Matin*, March 2, 1924.

211 **"The Leader of the Beer Revolution":** NA T84 EAP 105/7, 908.

211 **had been arrested on suspicion:** Telegraphen-Union, March 4, 1924; *Berliner Börsen-Zeitung*, March 5, 1924. See also VIa H.B.123/24, February 28, 1924, HA 68/1494.

211 **"arrest craze":** NA T84 EAP 105/7, 911.

211 **"We are not dealing":** Ibid.

211 **Some members of the audience:** *Le Matin*, March 7, 1924.

211 **Stenglein stood up:** *Prager Tagblatt*, March 7, 1924.

211 **something unintelligible:** *L'Écho de Paris*, March 7, 1924.

211 **the prosecutor's voice:** *Vossische Zeitung*, March 6, 1924, Abend Ausgabe; *Berliner Tageblatt*, March 6, Abend Ausgabe; *Le Petit Parisien*, March 7, 1924.

211 **"During these proceedings":** NA T84 EAP 105/7, 912.

212 **slamming the door:** *Vossische Zeitung*, March 6, 1924, Abend Ausgabe.

212 **"expressions of an insulting"**: NA T84 EAP 105/7, 912.

212 **"There will always"**: NA T84 EAP 105/7, 913.

212 **Several people applauded:** It took some time for the presiding judge to make himself heard in the commotion, London *Times*, March 7, 1924.

212 **"Bravo!"**: This is noted in one of the abridged transcripts published in 1924, *Der Hitler-Prozess. Auszüge aus den Verhandlungsberichten mit den Bildern der Angeklagten nach Zeichnungen von Otto von Kursell* (München: Deutscher Volksverlag, 1924), 85.

212 **"Prosecutor Humiliated"**: *Evening Post* (Auckland New Zealand), March 7, 1924.

212 **"an uproar"** and **"the most scandalous"**: *New York Times*, March 7, 1924.

212 **"extraordinary display"**: *Völkischer Kurier*, March 8, 1924.

212 **"patience of an angel"**: *Bayerischer Kurier*, March 7, 1924.

212 **"German heroes"**: *Vossische Zeitung*, March 6, 1924, Abend Ausgabe.

213 **"scandal of justice"**: *Berliner Tageblatt*, March 6, Abend Ausgabe, with other accounts of prosecutor's dignity, for instance, *Vancouver Sun*, March 9, 1924, and critiques of Kohl's attack, *Münchner Neueste Nachrichten*, March 8, 1924, and *Münchener Post*, March 7, 1924.

213 **"unprecedented vaudeville-esque"**: *Le Petit Parisien*, March 7, 1924. Many other newspapers raised the question of the trial continuing, such as *L'Humanité*, March 7, 1924, with the uncertainty of the prosecutor's return, Reuters, March 8, 1924, or the difficulty of finding a replacement, Vienna's *Arbeiter-Zeitung*, March 7, 1924.

Chapter 36: PRIORITIES

214 **"A far more serious scheme"**: London *Times*, March 13, 1924.

214 **"more than 2,000"**: Agence Havas, March 6, 1924.

214 **probably more than a little:** This was hinted at in Ehard's depiction of the meeting at the Ministry of Justice in his unpublished memoir, 41, NL Ehard 99, BHStA. Gürtner admitted that he had met with the lawyers at this time of the trial, *Chronik der Bayerischen Justizverwaltung*, 384, copy in NL Ehard 90/3, BHStA.

214 **"incompatible with the dignity"**: NA T84/2 EAP 105/7, 917.

214 **All was soon calm:** *L'Écho de Paris*, March 8, 1924.

215 **closing ranks:** *L'Humanité*, March 8, 1924.

215 **walk of repentance:** *Münchener Post*, March 8–9, 1924.

215 **"sheer hypocrisy"** and **"serious collaboration"**: NA T84/2 EAP 105/7, 918.

215 **Schiedt was one:** *Berliner Tageblatt*, March 7, 1924, Abend Ausgabe, *Le Matin*, March 8, 1924.

216 **"useful, indeed necessary"** and **"battle against Marxism"**: NA T84/2 EAP 105/7, 920.

216 **No, he did not:** The fact that Kahr's speechwriter knew so little of Kahr's supposed game was itself revealing. Was it really impossible not to use the same winks and gestures with his staff as he claimed to have done with Lossow and Seisser?, asked the foreign correspondent, Carl Christian Bry, *Der Hitler-Putsch. Berichte und Kommentare eines Deutschland-Korrespondenten, 1922–1924 für das Argentinische Tag- und Wochenblatt*, ed. Martin Gregor-Dellin (Nördlingen: Greno, 1987), 195.

216 **"That will not do!":** NA T84/2 EAP 105/7, 945.

216 **"harassed by rather":** *Le Petit Journal*, March 8, 1924.

216 **without hesitation:** *L'Humanité*, March 8, 1924. The witness had appealed to his right as a civil servant to refuse to answer a question on the basis of an official duty of confidentiality [Paragraph 53 of the Criminal Procedural Code]. But was he, as a speechmaker, really an employee of the state or of Kahr personally? The judge was reluctant to press the witness. For more, see Gruchmann, Weber, and Gritschneder (1998), II, 576, note 4.

217 **"My impression":** *The Hitler Trial Before the People's Court in Munich*, trans. H. Francis Freniere, Lucie Karcic, and Philip Fandek (Arlington, VA: University Publications of America, 1976), II, 24.

217 **the defense did not:** *Le Gaulois*, March 8, 1924.

217 **"The senior councilor" ... "I am not reading":** NA T84/2 EAP 105/7, 990. On his reading, see *Berliner Tageblatt*, March 8, 1924, Morgen Ausgabe.

217 **The white-blue pamphlet:** This was "Veni Vidi," *Ludendorff in Bayern, oder Der Novemberputsch* (Leipzig: Veduka-Verlag, 1924).

218 **without much interest:** *Le Temps*, March 9, 1924, and no major revelations, report, Nr. 57, March 7, 1924, HA 5/114II.

Chapter 37: "PECULIAR GENTLEMEN"

219 **"Hitler is not":** *Arbeiterwille*, February 28, 1924.

219 **"We are not taking part":** NA T84/2 EAP 105/7, 1111.

220 **"With Hitler" and "Evidence that":** NA T84/2 EAP 105/7, 1113–14.

220 **"We see the Reichswehr" and "In our love of":** NA T84/2 EAP 105/7, 1130.

220 **"mountains, lakes":** NA T84/2 EAP 105/7, 1146.

221 **he told the court:** NA T84/2 EAP 105/7, 1148. See also Eberhard Jäckel und Axel Kuhn, eds., *Hitler. Sämtliche Aufzeichnungen 1905–1924* (Stuttgart: Deutsche Verlags-Anstalt, 1980), Nr. 602, 1059. Hitler would in the next months continue to separate himself from Ludendorff with regard to the general's insults on Catholics.

221 **the first high-ranking:** Interest waned with many of the military witnesses, *Journal des débats politiques et littéraires*, March 10, 1924.

221 **"I believe that":** NA T84/2 EAP 105/7, 1154.

221 "And neither could": NA T84/2 EAP 105/7, 1158.

221 "peculiar gentlemen": *Berliner Tageblatt*, March 9, Morgen Ausgabe.

222 "judicial comedy": *Le Matin*, March 22, 1924. There were of course many variants of this description, such as the "Bürgerbräu comedy," *Vorwärts*, March 9, 1924; or "terrible comedy," *Münchener Post*, March 6, 1924.

222 "secret orders": NA T84 EAP 105/7, 1180.

223 "I want to be careful": NA T84 EAP 105/7, 1185.

223 "I actually do not know": Ibid.

Chapter 38: *A DANGEROUS GAME*

224 "I attached no significance": NA T84 EAP 105/7, 1239.

224 "the occupied territory": *New York Times*, March 11, 1924. One photo of a recent morning showing armed guards and camera crews is in *Der Welt Spiegel*, March 9, 1924, and the cover of *Hamburger Illustrierte Zeitung*, Nr. 9.

225 "manipulators of the entire": NA T84 EAP 105/7, 1215–16.

225 "unbiased and impartial": NA T84 EAP 105/7, 1217.

225 "dead silence": *Berliner Tageblatt*, March 10, 1924, Abend Ausgabe. The crowd was even larger than usual, Reuters, March 10, 1924.

225 General von Lossow entered: *Münchener Post*, March 11, 1924; *Le Petit Parisien*, March 11, 1924; *Le Figaro*, March 11, 1924.

225 it could have: *Daily Telegraph*, March 11, 1924.

226 "cross swords": *L'Écho de Paris*, March 11, 1924.

226 "increasingly impossible" and "dictatorial authority": NA T84/2 EAP 105/7, 1221.

226 136 times: Richard J. Evans, *The Coming of the Third Reich* (New York: Penguin Books, 2003), 80.

226 "These were people": NA T84/2 EAP 105/7, 1225.

226 "a bit childish": NA T84/2 EAP 105/7, 1226.

226 "In the beginning" . . . "healthy core": NA T84/2 EAP 105/7, 1234–37.

227 "a swashbuckling little": *New York Times*, March 11, 1924.

228 "I would have to talk": NA T84/2 EAP 105/7, 1240.

228 "pure invention": NA T84/2 EAP 105/7, 1252.

228 "a plethora of" . . . "quick glances": NA T84/2 EAP 105/7, 1257–60.

229 "contempt . . . [as] pitiful creatures": *The Hitler Trial Before the People's Court in Munich*, trans. H. Francis Freniere, Lucie Karcic, and Philip Fandek (Arlington, VA: University Publications of America, 1976), II, 159.

229 "to assign": NA T84/2 EAP 105/7, 1270.

229 "hugely important questions": NA T84/2 EAP 105/7, 1286.

229 "Herr Lossow's statement": NA T84/2 EAP 105/7, 1287.

Chapter 39: *AVOIDING THE RUBBLE*

230 **"In short, everywhere"**: NA T84/2 EAP 105/7, 1329.

230 **high expectations**: *Münchener Zeitung*, March 11, 1924, and *Le Gaulois*, March 12, 1924.

230 **Kahr walked in**: *Berliner Tageblatt*, March 11, 1924, Abend Ausgabe; and *Münchener Zeitung*, March 11, 1924.

230 **His hair was oiled**: Carl Christian Bry, March 11, 1924, *Der Hitler-Putsch. Berichte und Kommentare eines Deutschland-Korrespondenten, 1922–1924 für das Argentinische Tag- und Wochenblatt*, ed. Martin Gregor-Dellin (Nördlingen: Greno, 1987), 181.

230 **"a true peasant"**: *L'Ouest-Éclair*, March 12, 1924.

231 **he was inscrutable**: *Bayerischer Kurier*, March 12, 1924.

231 **Kahr's voice was hesitant**: *L'Écho de Paris*, March 12, 1924 and March 13, 1924; *Münchener Post*, March 12, 1924.

231 **"political pressure"**: NA T84/2 EAP 105/7, 1327, and not a military attack against Berlin, NA T84/2 EAP 105/7, 1339.

231 **"abysmal"**: NA T84/2 EAP 105/7, 1327.

231 **"clothing, footgear, equipment"**: NA T84/2 EAP 105/7, 1329.

231 **"My first reaction" … "unspeakable misfortune"**: NA T84/2 EAP 105/7, 1344–45.

232 **again asked the witness to stop reading**: Kahr was widely described as reading, *Grossdeutsche Zeitung*, March 12, 1924, and *Allgemeine Zeitung*, March 12, 1924.

232 **The foreign correspondent**: *Le Matin*, March 12, 1924.

232 **"Aren't you privy"**: NA T84/2 EAP 105/7, 1372.

232 **"No"**: Ibid.

232 **Reichswehr order**: Ia Nr. 800/23, MA 103476/2, 989, BHStA and printed in Ernst Deuerlein, ed., *Der Aufstieg der NSDAP in Augenzeugenberichten* (Düsseldorf: Deutscher Taschenbuch Verlag, 1978), 189.

233 **"It may have passed"**: NA T84/2 EAP 105/7, 1373.

233 **tripled in size**: Minutes of meeting, November 6, 1923, report, *Zur Vorgeschichte des 8. Novembers 1923*, HA 5/127. See also F. L. Carsten, *The Reichswehr and Politics 1918–1933* (Berkeley: University of California Press, 1973), 179.

233 **"I don't know" and "I don't remember"** and other evasions in this session: NA T84/2 EAP 105/7, 1372–87.

233 **"This is indeed"**: NA T84/2 EAP 105/7, 1387.

233 **"I was dealing"**: NA T84/2 EAP 105/7, 1393.

234 **"to check if"**: NA T84/2 EAP 105/7, 1414.

234 **"The authority of the general state commissioner"**: NA T84/2 EAP 105/7, 1423. For more on this ploy, see the memo of defense counsel Hellmuth Mayer, February 19, 1924, HA 5/114I, and his "Münchner Hochverratsprozess," *Der Gerichtssaal* 91 (1925), 93–124. For more on this lawyer, see Natalie Willsch,

Hellmuth Mayer (1895–1980). Vom Verteidiger im Hitler-Prozess 1924 zum liberal-konservativen Strafrechtswissenschaftler. Das vielgestaltige Leben und Werk des Kieler Strafrechtslehrers (Baden-Baden: Nomos Verlagsgesellschaft, 2008), based on her dissertation at Christian-Albrechts-Universität zu Kiel.

235　**"the crucial point":** NA T84/2 EAP 105/7, 1431.

235　**"That was not so simple":** NA T84/2 EAP 105/7, 1441.

Chapter 40: *DAY THIRTEEN*

236　**"I assume that the court":** NA T84/2 EAP 105/7, 1508.

236　**"high treason"** and **"We do not give":** *Völkischer Kurier*, February 23–24, 1924; February 29, 1924, Erste Beilage; and March 14, 1924, Erste Beilage.

237　**"Nervous tension":** *New York Times*, March 13, 1924.

237　**charged atmosphere:** *Le Figaro*, March 13, 1924.

237　**"the drummer":** NA T84/2 EAP 105/7, 1463.

237　**"only a means":** NA T84/2 EAP 105/7, 1464.

237　**impressed many reporters:** *Das Bayerische Vaterland*, March 13, 1924; *Münchener Post*, March 13, 1924. See also *Le Matin*, March 13, 1924, and *L'Humanité*, March 13, 1924.

237　**"[Hitler] repeatedly promised":** NA T84/2 EAP 105/7, 1473.

238　**"That is an easy":** NA T84/2 EAP 105/7, 1481.

238　**"It is my opinion":** Ibid.

238　**"ill-starred, senseless"** . . . **"in its darkest hour":** NA T84/2 EAP 105/7, 1482–83.

239　**"What insolence!":** NA T84/2 EAP 105/7, 1490. Some accounts attributed the quote to Stenglein, or Ehard, but the transcript and context make it clear that the source was Hitler.

239　**"reddened with anger":** *Le Gaulois*, March 13, 1924.

239　**A shouting match:** Agence Havas, March 13, 1924.

239　**A reporter for:** *Berliner Tageblatt*, March 12, Abend Ausgabe.

239　**"It would have been":** NA T84/2 EAP 105/7, 1501.

240　**"unchallenged throughout":** NA T84/2 EAP 105/7, 1503.

240　**"misrepresentation of the"** . . . **"The high treason":** NA T84/2 EAP 105/7, 1506–9.

241　**"Scandalous!"** NA T84/2 EAP 105/7, 1510. There was some question at first if Ehard said it, but he admitted it at 1510 and again at 1512.

Chapter 41: *A PUTSCH, NOT A PUTSCH*

242　**"Defendants, witnesses, judges,":** *L'Écho de Paris*, March 13, 1924.

242　**"Hitler adventure":** *Le Petit Parisien*, November 10, 1923.

242 **Bavaria, it was predicted:** *New York Times*, March 14, 1924. See also the earlier
   testimony of Bavarian authorities, December 8, 1923, HA 5/114I.

242 **"Germany is arming":** the *Chicago Daily News* verdict was picked up in Europe,
   for instance, by *Le Matin*, March 15, 1924.

243 **"on to Berlin":** NA T84/2 EAP 105/7, 1624.

243 **"If the gentlemen today":** NA T84/2 EAP 105/7, 1637.

244 **"Bavarian Bismarck":** R. D. Murphy, *Confidential Political Report*, mailed January 16, 1924 (incorrectly dated to 1923) M336, 862.00/1397, No. 20, NA.

244 **"Whether you can":** NA T84/2 EAP 105/7, 1640.

244 **"Am I now a liar":** NA T84/2 EAP 105/7, 1678 and 1679.

244 **"I will remember":** NA T84/2 EAP 105/7, 1679.

244 **The courtroom erupted:** *Berliner Tageblatt*, March 14, Morgen Ausgabe. The
   transcript notes the clamor as well (NA T84/2 EAP 105/7, 1679).

244 **"dignity of the court":** NA T84/2 EAP 105/7, 1695.

244 **Hitler was again shouting:** *Vorwärts*, March 14, 1924.

245 **"eye to eye":** NA T84/2 EAP 105/7, 1697.

245 **"by sheer lung power":** *The Outlook*, March 26, 1924.

245 **a series of devious traps:** This had already been said earlier, too, when Kahr first
   took the stand, *Bayerischer Kurier*, March 12, 1924.

245 **Inquisition or a medieval torture chamber:** *Vossische Zeitung*, March 14, Morgen
   Ausgabe, and *Le Matin*, March 14, 1924.

Chapter 42: BLOW-UP

247 **"German Versus German":** *Auckland Star*, March 12, 1924.

247 **"not pretty":** *Berliner Tageblatt*, March 11, 1924, Morgen Ausgabe.

248 **"Our soldiers are not":** NA T84/2 EAP 105/7, 1734.

248 **"The defendants did not conceive":** NA T84/2 EAP 105/7, 1735.

248 **"Brooches, necklaces":** *Washington Post*, citing the *New York Herald*, March 15,
   1924. See also *The Sentinel*, April 18, 1924.

248 **"How do you know":** NA T84/2 EAP 105/7, 1737.

248 **"No, never!":** NA T84/2 EAP 105/7, 1740.

248 **"only eunuchs and castrati":** NA T84/2 EAP 105/7, 1751. For more on Lossow's
   words, see Graf Helldorff statement, January 11, 1924, HA 5/114I.

249 **"I would be grateful":** NA T84/2 EAP 105/7, 1757.

249 **"a tough opponent":** Agence Havas, March 16, 1924, with more on his sarcasm,
   Münchener Post, March 11 and 13, 1924. The questioning gave the impression of
   a duel, *Vossische Zeitung*, March 15, 1924.

249 **"confidential talks":** NA T84/2 EAP 105/7, 1768.

249 **"We are obliged":** NA T84/2 EAP 105/7, 1769. Hitler's excitement was noted by,
   for instance, *Le Temps*, March 16, 1924.

249 **army barracks:** NA T84/2 EAP 105/7, 1769. *Völkischer Kurier* reported it as well, March 15, 1924.

249 **"The witness has already" . . . "I know that":** NA T84/2 EAP 105/7, 1769.

250 **"Far be it":** NA T84/2 EAP 105/7, 1773.

250 **There was stirring:** This is noted in an abridged transcript published in 1924, *Der Hitler-Prozess. Auszüge aus den Verhandlungsberichten mit den Bildern der Angeklagten nach Zeichnungen von Otto von Kursell* (München: Deutscher Volksverlag, 1924), 182.

250 **"You have no right":** NA T84/2 EAP 105/7, 1773.

250 **"as if he had":** H. R. Knickerbocker, *Is Tomorrow Hitler's?: 200 Questions on the Battle of Mankind* (New York: Reynal & Hitchcock, 1941), 12.

250 **"lively confrontation":** *Le Figaro*, March 15, 1924.

251 **"a little more calmly":** NA T84/2 EAP 105/7, 1805.

251 **impossible to silence Hitler:** Ernst Deuerlein, ed., *Der Aufstieg der NSDAP in Augenzeugenberichten* (Düsseldorf: Deutscher Taschenbuch Verlag, 1978), 216.

251 **"Lieutenant General!":** NA T84/2 EAP 105/7, 1806.

251 **The witness:** *Völkischer Kurier*, March 15, 1924, and *The Sun* (Sydney), March 16, 1924.

251 **"gross impropriety":** NA T84/2 EAP 105/7, 1806.

251 **Hitler seemed yet again:** Audience cheers and cries of "Bravo!" continued for Hitler and the defense counsel, *Münchner Neueste Nachrichten*, March 15, 1924.

Chapter 43: HINTS

252 **"The witnesses for the prosecution":** NA T84/2 EAP 105/7, 1609.

252 **The first question:** *Bayerischer Kurier*, March 17, 1924.

252 **"clear to anyone":** NA T84/2 EAP 105/7, 1853.

253 **People's Court:** *Chronik der Bayerischen Justizverwaltung*, 342–44, NL Ehard 90/3, BHStA. For more on the institution, see Otto Gritschneder, "Das missbrauchte bayerische Volksgericht," in Lothar Gruchmann, Reinhard Weber, and Otto Gritschneder, eds., *Der Hitler-Prozess 1924* (München: K. G. Saur, 1997), xxxvii–xl.

253 **hairdressers, for one:** NA T84/2 EAP 105/7, 1610–11.

253 **what facts actually:** For instance, *Argentinische Tag- und Wochenblatt*, March 11, 1924, criticized the lack of revelations, particularly in public sessions, Carl Christian Bry, *Der Hitler-Putsch. Berichte und Kommentare eines Deutschland-Korrespondenten, 1922–1924 für das Argentinische Tag- und Wochenblatt*, ed. Martin Gregor-Dellin (Nördlingen: Greno, 1987), 183.

253 **legal fables:** *L'Écho de Paris*, March 7, 1924.

253 **charade would end:** *L'Humanité*, March 18, 1924.

254 **"The volunteers reported" . . . "Because the events":** NA T84/2 EAP 105/7, 1914–15.

254 **"precise reports"** and **"obviously convinced"**: NA T84/2 EAP 105/7, 1923.

254 **"political leadership"**: NA T84/2 EAP 105/7, 1930.

254 **Shouts:** Ibid. This is recorded in the protocol as coming from Ehard.

254 **"[Kahr's] weakness"**: *The Hitler Trial Before the People's Court in Munich*, trans. H. Francis Freniere, Lucie Karcic, and Philip Fandek (Arlington, VA: University Publications of America, 1976), III, 37.

255 **At 1:20:** NA T84/2 EAP 105/7, 1974.

Chapter 44: HITLER'S BODYGUARD TAKES THE STAND

256 **"This is not the type of trial"**: NA T84/2 EAP 105/7, 2161.

256 **"revelations"** . . . **"not less subversive"**: Edgar Vincent, Viscount D'Abernon, *The Diary of an Ambassador* (Garden City, NY: Doubleday, Doran & Company, 1929–1931), III, 56.

257 **when the defendants entered the courtroom:** Carl Moser von Filseck, *Politik in Bayern 1919–1933. Berichte des württembergischen Gesandten Carl Moser von Filseck*, ed. Wolfgang Benz. Schriftenreihe der Vierteljahrshefte für Zeitgeschichte Nummer 22/23 (Stuttgart: Deutsche Verlags-Anstalt, 1971), March 13, 1924, Nr. 86, 155-156.

257 **"insolent bravado"**: R. D. Murphy, *Confidential Political Report*, March 10, 1924 (Date of Mailing: April 3, 1924), M336, 862.00/1469, No. 20, NA, and he repeated this phrase in his later memoir, *Diplomat Among Warriors* (Garden City, NY: Doubleday & Company, 1964), 22.

257 **on the cover:** "The Hitler Trial Or How Kahr Saved the Fatherland," *Simplicissimus*, March 17, 1924.

258 **Not a word:** NA T84/2 EAP 105/7, 1978, and again, with information on contract, at 2039–40. See also *Münchener Post*, March 1–2, 1924.

258 **They no longer dared:** *Le Temps*, March 15, 1924.

258 **Rumors circulated that:** United Press, March 6, 1924.

258 **one of the challengers:** *Time*, March 17, 1924.

258 **but several journalists:** *Berliner Börsen-Zeitung*, March 17, 1924, Abend Ausgabe, and *Le Matin*, March 18, 1924, among others.

258 **"the gag on the will"**: NA T84/2 EAP 105/7, 2047.

258 **"smashed"** and **"Difficult days"**: Ulrich Graf, unpublished memoir, 68, F14, IfZ.

259 **"quite interesting"**: *Berliner Volks-Zeitung*, March 18, 1924, Morgen Ausgabe.

259 **"Was the meeting"**: NA T84/2 EAP 105/7, 2070.

259 **"This is Ludendorff!"**: NA T84/2 EAP 105/7, 2080.

259 **"I did not just shout"**: NA T84/2 EAP 105/7, 2081.

Chapter 45: *VOLTE-FACE*

261 **"I already foresee that this trial"**: NA T84/2 EAP 105/7, 2136.

261 **"guttural thunder"**: This was the phrase used by biographer Konrad Heiden, who heard Hitler speak in 1923, when he was a Munich student and correspondent for *Frankfurter Zeitung.*

261 **"thickhead politician"** and **"a moral coward"**: United Press, March 21, 1924.

261 **"Ludendorff the Clueless"**: *Augsburger Postzeitung*, February 17, 1924, and February 21, 1924.

262 **"a military march"** and **"moral coercion"**: NA T84/2 EAP 105/7, 2108–9.

262 **"I have heard so many"**: NA T84/2 EAP 105/7, 2111.

262 **"Ludendorff denies what"**: *Le Petit Journal*, March 19, 1924. Indeed, compare Ludendorff's statements, particularly at 2108–14 with his remarks in his first interrogation by Hans Ehard, November 9, 1923, NL Ehard 94, BHStA.

262 **"The brave general"**: *L'Humanité,* March 19, 1924. See also the critiques of Ludendorff's "retreat" in *Berliner Tageblatt*, March 18, 1924, Abend Ausgabe, and *Frankfurter Zeitung*, March 19 and 20, 1924.

262 **"I am now the political leader"**: NA T84/2 EAP 105/7, 2120.

263 **"an immense wave"** . . . **"In the final"**: NA T84/2 EAP 105/7, 2123.

263 **"international, Marxist, defeatist"**: NA T84/2 EAP 105/7, 2131. A pro-Hitler transcript inserted the word "Jewish" in this statement, *Der Hitler-Prozess. Auszüge aus den Verhandlungsberichten mit den Bildern der Angeklagten nach Zeichnungen von Otto von Kursell* (München: Deutscher Volksverlag, 1924), 218. This was not in the Amtsgericht Münchens transcript.

263 **"Munich's great treason trial"** . . . **"amazingly paradoxical"**: *New York Times*, March 19, 1924. Nine years later, the reporter, Thomas R. Ybarra, would see Hitler again, interviewing him in his office, *Colliers*, July 1, 1933; a copy (extracted) also appears in the OSS Sourcebook, NA.

263 **"young Germany"**: *Vossische Zeitung*, March 19, 1924, Morgen Ausgabe.

264 **announced his decision**: This came as a surprise, *Berliner Volks-Zeitung*, March 18, 1924, Morgen Ausgabe.

264 **"a higher interest"**: NA T84/2 EAP 105/7, 2137.

264 **"the whole world"**: NA T84/2 EAP 105/7, 2135.

265 **"vindicate themselves"**: NA T84/2 EAP 105/7, 2151.

265 **"committed crimes"** . . . **"forces him"**: NA T84/2 EAP 105/7, 2153–55.

Chapter 46: "GOOD TIMES FOR TRAITORS"

266 **"My good gentlemen":** NA T84/2 EAP 105/7, 2291.

266 **a powerful person:** NA T84/2 EAP 105/7, 2167. Neithardt was probably referring to the article published in *Frankfurter Zeitung*, March 1, 1924.

267 **"accessories which have"** . . . **"a hard, tough":** NA T84/2 EAP 105/7, 2169.

267 **"decay of state authority"** . . . **"should never be allowed":** NA T84/2 EAP 105/7, 2170–72.

267 **"stupefying":** *Le Petit Parisien*, March 22, 1924.

267 **"responsibility for the events":** NA T84/2 EAP 105/7, 2175.

267 **"Arisen from humble"** . . . **"oppressed and disarmed":** NA T84/2 EAP 105/7, 2185–86.

268 **The prosecutor's statement:** *Le Temps*, March 23, 1924, *Berliner Lokal-Anzeiger*, March 21, 1924.

268 **eulogy:** *Le Petit Parisien*, March 22, 1924, or glorification, July 22, 1924, HA 68/1498. See also the critique in *Nordhäuser Volkszeitung*, March 24, 1924.

268 **the defense lawyers later thanked:** NA T84/2 EAP 105/7, 2312.

268 **"As human beings":** NA T84/2 EAP 105/7, 2189.

268 **"a real man" and "a model of the stern":** NA T84/2 EAP 105/7, 2189, 2193.

268 **proposed the milder option:** NA T84/2 EAP 105/7, 2216–17.

269 **"Class justice":** *L'Humanité*, March 25, 1924.

269 **"as little convincing":** *L'Humanité*, March 22, 1924.

269 **"as many compliments":** The *Daily Telegraph*, March 22, 1924, and Reuters, March 22, 1924.

269 **token and a mere formality:** *Le Matin*, March 22, 1924.

269 **"good times for traitors":** *Berliner Volks-Zeitung*, March 22, 1924.

270 **"Six years ago"** . . . **"for their own personal":** NA T84/2 EAP 105/7, 2219.

270 **"Gentlemen of the court"** . . . **"admitted his guilt":** NA T84/2 EAP 105/7, 2228–32.

271 **"immeasurable bitterness":** NA T84/2 EAP 105/7, 2235.

271 **"What happened here":** NA T84/2 EAP 105/7, 2232.

271 **"principal offenders":** NA T84/2 EAP 105/7, 2262.

272 **"provocative and rabble-rousing":** NA T84/2 EAP 105/7, 2287.

272 **"Here was a man"** . . . **"My good gentlemen":** NA T84/2 EAP 105/7, 2289–91.

Chapter 47: FROM MUNICH TO VALHALLA

273 **"When Geman Republicans":** *New York Times*, March 25, 1924.

273 **"so-called Treaty"** . . . **"sadistic malice":** NA T84/2 EAP 105/7, 2293.

273 "cowardice and corruption" . . . "I am at a loss": NA T84/2 EAP 105/7, 2294, 2333–34.

274 "treason and perjury": NA T84/2 EAP 105/7, 2369.

274 "What kind of a Fatherland": NA T84/2 EAP 105/7, 2382.

274 "Bavaria is": *New York Times*, March 25, 1924.

274 several empty seats: *Journal des débats politiques et littéraires*, March 27, 1924.

274 The Meistersinger: *Münchener Post*, March 28, 1924.

275 "Or the pleadings": NA T84/2 EAP 105/7, 2570.

275 "If legislation no longer": NA T84/2 EAP 105/7, 2607.

275 "For the majority": NA T84/2 EAP 105/7, 2805.

276 "second Siegfried": NA T84/2 EAP 105/7, 2838. This image appeared earlier in the press, for instance, *Deutsches Tageblatt*, November 13, 1923.

276 "Jews, deserters" and "alien race": NA T84/2 EAP 105/7, 2849.

277 "Fritz": NA T84/2 EAP 105/7, 2850, twice at 2853, and again at 2855. The laughter is noted in one of 1924's published abridged transcripts, *Der Hitler-Prozess. Auszüge aus den Verhandlungsberichten mit den Bildern der Angeklagten nach Zeichnungen von Otto von Kursell* (München: Deutscher Volksverlag, 1924), 258.

277 "its struggle for existence": NA T84/2 EAP 105/7, 2865.

277 "grand battles": NA T84/2 EAP 105/7, 2867.

277 "We will be lost": NA T84/2 EAP 105/7, 2870.

277 "hear the cry": NA T84/2 EAP 105/7, 2871.

277 "World history will not send": NA T84/2 EAP 105/7, 2869. Ludendorff appeared as "Mars in the flesh": *Evening Post*, March 29, 1924, and his speech pompous, *Le Temps*, March 29, 1924.

277 "Ludendorff Exalts Himself" . . . "a tremendous ovation": *New York Times*, March 28, 1924.

Chapter 48: FINAL WORDS

279 "It goes without saying": NA T84/2 EAP 105/7, 2144.

279 the audience had reacted: *Le Figaro*, March 28, 1924.

279 "poured out a torrent": *New York Times*, March 28, 1924.

279 "a crime of high treason": NA T84/2 EAP 105/7, 2871.

280 "a stab in the back" . . . "immorality in 440 articles": NA T84/2 EAP 105/7, 2876–87.

281 thumping the table: Hitler hit the table several times that session, including at this point in his speech, noted in one of the 1924 abridged transcripts, *Der Hitler-Prozess. Auszüge aus den Verhandlungsberichten mit den Bildern der Angeklagten nach Zeichnungen von Otto von Kursell* (München: Deutscher Volksverlag, 1924), 265.

281 "high treason and" . . . "at odds with himself": NA T84/2 EAP 105/7, 2888–89.

282 **"the racial tubercuosis"** . . . **"Believe me":** NA T84/2 EAP 105/7, 2895.
282 **"only wanted to be"** . . . **"The trial is concluded":** NA T84/2 EAP 105/7, 2897–916.
285 **the audience cheered:** Reuters, March 27, 1924.
285 **unabashed triumph:** *Le Matin*, March 28, 1924.
285 **drink a good beer:** *Das Bayerische Vaterland*, March 20, 1924.

Chapter 49: ENDINGS AND BEGINNINGS

286 **"If Germany cages":** letter, March 22, 1924, Staatsanwaltschaften 3099, StAM.
286 **discussions raged:** *Neue Freie Presse*, March 29, 1924, among many others.
286 **the most significant:** *Miesbacher Anzeiger*, February 26, 1924. This was often claimed, both in anticipation of the proceedings, *Der Landsmann*, February 26, 1924, as well as during the trial itself, *Vossische Zeitung*, March 6, 1924, Abend Ausgabe.
286 **"courageously":** David Clay Large *Where Ghosts Walked: Munich's Road to the Third Reich* (New York: W. W. Norton, 1997), 193. For more, see also Robert Eben Sackett, *Popular Entertainment, Class and Politics in Munich, 1900–1923* (Cambridge, MA: Harvard University Press, 1982), and Jeffrey S. Gaab, *Munich: Hofbräuhaus & History—Beer, Culture, & Politics* (New York: Peter Lang, 2006), 67. Gaab's book began as part of his economic history seminar at University of Munich in the summer of 1997.
286 **"measureless hubris":** *Vorwärts*, March 28, 1924.
287 **"virtuoso of rhetoric"** and **"moved thousands":** *Frankfurter Zeitung*, March 28, 1924.
287 **"the struggle of everyone"** and **"apotheosis":** *L'Écho de Paris*, March 8, 1924.
287 **"Alice in Wonderland"** . . . **"collapsible when not":** *Public Ledger*, March 21, 1924.
287 **"Austrian scene painter"** and **"must carry":** *Vancouver Sun*, March 9, 1924.
287 **Only Hitler would be punished:** *Le Petit Parisien*, March 22, 1924. This was the conclusion of many legal experts as well, for instance, Munich professor of law Karl Rothenbücher, *Der Fall Kahr* (Tübingen: Mohr, 1924), 30. Ludendorff, at least, would be acquitted, or given only a token punishment, predicted many French papers, *L'Écho de Paris*, March 22, 1924; *La Croix*, March 26, 1924; and *L'Action Française*, March 26, 1924.
288 **Hitler would not be making:** Robert Murphy, *Diplomat Among Warriors* (Garden City, NY: Doubleday & Company, 1964), 22.
288 **authorities feared the outbreak:** Kommando der Landspolizei München, Abtlg. A/Nr.678, Kommandobefehl für Dienstag, 1.4.24, March 31, 1924, HA 69/1499, and repeated in "Letzte Warnung!," April 1, 1924. See also, among others, *New York Times*, March 25, 1924; *Le Gaulois*, March 25, 1924; *Vorwärts*, March 29,

1924; *Le Temps*, March 30, 1924; *Münchener Zeitung*, March 31, 1924; and United Press Association (British), April 1, 1924. Police measures are also in MINN 73699, BHStA.

288 **over the weekend:** *Sicherung des Hitler-Prozesses*, March 12, 1924, HA 68/1498.

288 **a riot being plotted:** VId, *Überwachung,* March 29, 1924, HA 68/1498. Other rumors of disturbances reached the public, *Berliner Tageblatt*, March 28, 1924, Abend Ausgabe, with more on the pressures, *Frankfurter Zeitung*, March 28, 1924, and *Bayerischer Kurier*, March 29, 1924, with threats to free defendants, *L'Écho de Paris*, April 2, 1924.

288 **a telegram arrived:** Telegramm aus Augsburg 2658. 33/31.W, March 31, 1924, police report, VIa 1010/24, same day, HA 68/1498.

288 **"a pathetic bastard":** This and many others in the collection, StAnW 3099, StAM.

288 **death threats:** Hans Ehard, unpublished memoir, 30, NL Ehard 99, BHStA.

288 **several leaders of the police:** *Zusammenfassung der Ergebnisse der Besprechung am 31.März 1924 vormittags 9 ¼ Uhr in die Bücherei der Polizeidirektion*, HA 68/1498.

289 **the French consulate:** Kommando der Landspolizei München, Abtlg. A/Nr.678, *Kommandobefehl für Dienstag, 1.4.24*, March 31, 1924, HA 69/1499. For more on the security arrangements before the verdict, see *Sicherung des Urteilsverkundigung*, March 31, 1924, MINN 73699, BHStA.

289 **the homes of:** Ibid., and Ehard unpublished memoir, 30, NL Ehard 99, BHStA.

289 **"they should not be decapitated"** and **"They say in effect":** *Time*, March 24, 1924.

289 **The number of people compromised:** *L'Intransigeant*, March 21, 1924.

289 **Italy:** Telegraphen-Union, March 29, 1924; *Allgemeine Zeitung*, March 29, 1924; *Dalpilen* (Falun, Sweden), April 1, 1924; and adamantly so, in *Berliner Börsen-Zeitung*, March 29, 1924, Abend Ausgabe.

289 **Corfu:** NA T84 EAP 105/7, 2825–26, and reported widely, for instance, *Das Bayerische Vaterland*, April 1, 1924; *Le Figaro*, April 2, 1924; and Ernst Röhm, *The Memoirs of Ernst Röhm*, intro. Eleanor Hancock and trans. Geoffrey Brooks (London: Frontline Books, 2012), 202.

289 **Greece:** Carl Moser von Filseck, *Politik in Bayern 1919–1933. Berichte des württembergischen Gesandten Carl Moser von Filseck*, ed. Wolfgang Benz. Schriftenreihe der Vierteljahrshefte für Zeitgeschichte Nummer 22/23 (Stuttgart: Deutsche Verlags-Anstalt, 1971), March 26, 1924, Nr. 101, 157.

289 **Switzerland:** *Northern Standard* (Darwin, Northern Territory, Australia), April 1, 1924.

289 **small men:** *Allgemeine Rundschau*, March 20, 1924.

289 **their flight from Munich:** *Frankfurter Zeitung*, March 31, 1924, and *Völkischer Kurier*, April 9, 1924.

290 **No trial in recent memory:** *Bayerischer Kurier*, March 15, 1924.

290 **"a man possessed"** and **"cause a world to collapse":** *Vorwärts*, March 7, 1924.

Chapter 50: NOMEN EST OMEN

291 **"If I had to conduct":** Georg Neithardt, *Einige Bemerkungen des Vorsitzenden im Hitler-Prozess über die Prozessleitung*, April 1924, Nachlass Hans Ehard 97, BHStA.

291 **Journalists, likewise:** *Deutsche Allgemeine Zeitung*, April 2, 1924, and Telegraphen-Union, April 1, 1924.

291 **"breathless excitement":** *Berliner Tageblatt*, April 1, 1924, Abend Ausgabe, and similar expressions in other papers, for instance, *Grossdeutsche Zeitung*, April 2, 1924.

291 **The atmosphere:** *L'Écho de Paris*, April 2, 1924.

291 **flower bouquets:** *Quebec Daily Telegraph*, April 1, 1924; *Münchner Neueste Nachrichten*, April 2, 1924; *Volksblatt*, April 5, 1924; and Hans Ehard, unpublished memoir, 29, NL Ehard 99, BHStA.

291 **they had assembled:** Even some distinguished authorities mistakenly place this photograph afterward, but it clearly took place before the session, Hans Ehard, unpublished memoir, 28–29, NL Ehard 99, BHStA, and the account by the defendant Robert Wagner, September 12, 1924 HA 69/1501. Also many historians forget that this photograph was not complete. Pöhner was missing.

292 **He sported:** Weber's cap was, of course, not worn in the courtroom, Landgericht München I, Report, September 2, 1924, HA 69/1501. The scandal of the uniforms, however, paled in comparison to the last weeks of the proceedings, rightly concluded the *Münchener Post*, April 19–20, 1924.

292 **the verdict was read:** Anz. Verz. XIX 421/1923, Proz.Reg.Nr. 20, 68, 97/1924, Staatsanwaltschaften 3098, StAM.

292 **"Unacceptable!" and "Scandalous!":** *L'Écho de Paris*, April 2, 1924.

292 **shout and curse:** *Der Landsmann*, April 2, 1924, and scenes of hysteria, *The Sentinel*, April 4, 1924.

292 **reporters rushing out:** *Münchner Neueste Nachrichten*, April 2, 1924, and *Grossdeutsche Zeitung*, April 2, 1924.

293 **"Bravo!":** *L'Écho de Paris*, April 2, 1924; *Neue Zürcher Zeitung*, April 2, 1924, Erstes Morgenblatt.

293 **the justification for the verdict:** This was a shoddy patchwork, with spelling mistakes, grammatical errors, internal contradictions, clumsy legal expressions, and many omissions. For more, see Otto Gritschneder, *Bewährungsfrist für den Terroristen Adolf H. Der Hitler-Putsch und die bayerische Justiz* (München: Verlag C. H. Beck 1990), 61.

293 **"The only question":** Anz. Verz. XIX 421/1923, Proz.Reg.Nr. 20, 68, 97/1924, Staatsanwaltschaften 3098, 13, StAM, and more on the reasoning, 28–30.

294 **"A whole range of eyewitnesses":** Anz. Verz. XIX 421/1923, Proz.Reg.Nr. 20, 68, 97/1924, Staatsanwaltschaften 3098, 40, StAM.

294 **"purely patriotic spirit"**: Anz. Verz. XIX 421/1923, Proz.Reg.Nr. 20, 68, 97/1924, Staatsanwaltschaften 3098, 42, StAM.

294 **seemed to him**: Anz. Verz. XIX 421/1923, Proz.Reg.Nr. 20, 68, 97/1924, Staatsanwaltschaften 3098, 43–44, StAM. For more on the verdict itself, see Otto Gritschneder, *Der Hitler-Prozess und sein Richter Georg Neithardt. Skandalurteil von 1924 ebnet Hitler den Weg* (München: Verlag C. H. Beck, 2001), 93–95.

294 **"the wellspring of"**: Henning Grunwald, *Courtroom to Revolutionary Stage: Performance and Ideology in Weimar Political Trials* (Oxford: Oxford University Press, 2012), 2.

295 **"black day"**: *Berliner Volks-Zeitung*, April 1, 1923, Abend Ausgabe, and *Bayerischer Kurier*, April 3, 1924.

295 ***Nomen est omen!***: *Münchener Post*, March 28, 1924.

295 **April Fool's**: *Neue Zürcher Zeitung*, April 2, 1924, Erstes Morgenblatt.

295 **"The verdict"**: *Frankfurter Zeitung*, April 2, 1924.

295 **"Munich justice"**: *Neue Zürcher Zeitung*, April 2, 1924, Erstes Morgenblatt.

295 **"comedy of justice"**: *Le Petit Parisien*, April 2, 1924.

295 **praised their actions**: *Berliner Tageblatt*, April 1, 1924, Abend Ausgabe.

295 **"shame and sorrow"**: *Das Bild*, April 1, 1924 and *Berliner Volks-Zeitung*, April 2, 1924, Morgen Ausgabe.

296 **"political mess of Bavaria"**: *Vossische Zeitung* April 2, 1924, Morgen Ausgabe. This seemed a political, not a legal verdict, agreed *The Spectator*, April 5, 1924.

296 **"miscarriage of justice"**: *Vorwärts,* April 2, 1924.

297 **"reasonable reserve"**: Ernst Röhm, *The Memoirs of Ernst Röhm*, intro. Eleanor Hancock and trans. Geoffrey Brooks (London: Frontline Books, 2012), 200.

297 **"Never before had"**: Max Hirschberg, *Jude und Demokrat. Erinnerungen eines Münchener Rechtsanwalts 1883 bis 1939*, ed. Reinhard Weber (München: R. Oldenbourg Verlag, 1998), 242.

297 **But the perversion**: Alexander Graf von Dohna, "Der Münchener Hochverratsprozess," in *Deutsche Juristen-Zeitung* 29 (1924) Heft 9/10, 335.

297 **"Hitler is a German-Austrian"**: Anz. Verz. XIX 421/1923, Proz.Reg.Nr. 20, 68, 97/1924, Staatsanwaltschaften 3098, 44, StAM.

297 **Loud bravos**: *Neue Zürcher Zeitung*, April 2, 1924, Erstes Morgenblatt.

298 **"a disgrace, which this uniform"**: Lothar Gruchmann, Reinhard Weber, and Otto Gritschneder, eds., *Der Hitler-Prozess 1924. Wortlaut der Hauptverhandlung vor dem Volksgericht München I* (München: K. G. Saur, 1997), IV, 1593.

298 **"Heil Ludendorff!"**: *Berliner Volks-Zeitung*, April 1, 1924, Abend Ausgabe.

298 **"storm of applause"**: Agence Havas, April 2, 1924, and *Meraner Zeitung*, April 2, 1924.

298 **looked genuinely confused**: *New York Times*, April 2, 1924.

298 **apparently not exerting**: Another eyewitness said the police refused, *Der Hitler-Prozess. Auszüge aus den Verhandlungsberichten mit den Bildern der Angeklagten*

nach Zeichnungen von Otto von Kursell (München: Deutscher Volksverlag, 1924), 272.

298 **singing nationalist anthems:** *Bericht über die Vorfälle an der Pappenheimstrasse anlässlich der Urteilsverkündung im Hitler-Prozess*, am 1. April 1924, April 2, 1924, HA 69/1499.

298 **"blood red":** *Berliner Volks-Zeitung*, April 1, 1924, Abend Ausgabe.

298 **"I am a free man":** *Berliner Tageblatt*, April 1, 1924, Abend Ausgabe.

298 **"a wild ovation"** and **"the throngs":** *New York Times*. April 2, 1924. Ludendorff at main entrance, police report, Kommando der Schutzmannschaft, Nr. 1306, April 16, 1924, HA 69/1499.

298 **The crowds outside:** *Münchner Neueste Nachrichten*, April 2, 1924, and *Grossdeutsche Zeitung*, April 4, 1924.

298 **On the hood:** *Le Petit Parisien*, April 2, 1924.

299 **"Down with the republic!":** *Quebec Daily Telegraph*, April 1, 1924.

299 **mounted police charged:** See the police files, particularly HA 69/1499, and the coverage in the press, for instance, *Grossdeutsche Zeitung*, April 5–6, 1924.

299 **He walked up to the window:** Some biographers depict Hitler hurrying outside to a waiting car at the end, or even during the reading of the verdict, John Toland, *Adolf Hitler* (New York: Ballantine Books, 1977), 261, but this was not the case. Hitler remained in the room until the end, and then afterward came to the window: *Münchner Neueste Nachrichten*, April 2, 1924; *New York Times*, April 2, 1924; *Frankfurter Zeitung*, April 3, 1924; *Le Gaulois*, April 2, 1924; and Hans Ehard, unpublished memoir, 28, NL Ehard 99, BHStA, to cite only a few observers.

Chapter 51: CAESAR IN CELL 7

303 **"In the welter of":** *The Saturday Review*, March 22, 1924.

303 **A laurel wreath:** Otto Gritschneder, *Bewährungsfrist für den Terroristen Adolf H. Der Hitler-Putsch und die bayerische Justiz* (München: Verlag C. H. Beck 1990), 47. Flowers were also arriving, *Berliner Tageblatt*, April 3, 1924, Abend Ausgabe.

303 **Georg Schott's *Das Volksbuch*:** *Völkischer Kurier*, December 17, 1924, recommended his book for Christmas reading that year.

304 **"We marvel and honor"** . . . **"man of the people":** *Grossdeutsche Zeitung*, May 8, 1924.

304 **spring elections:** David Jablonsky, *The Nazi Party in Dissolution: Hitler and the Verbotzeit, 1923–1925* (London: F. Cass, 1989), 81–86.

304 **"only increased by":** David Clay Large, *Where Ghosts Walked: Munich's Road to the Third Reich* (New York: W. W. Norton, 1997), 194.

305 **Cell 7:** Otto Lurker, *Hitler hinter Festungsmauern. Ein Bild aus trüben Tagen*

(Berlin: E. S. Mittler & Sohn, 1933), 16, and Franz Hemmrich, *Erinnerungen eines Gefängnisbeamten*, ED 153-1, 27, 113, IfZ.

305 **"the commander's wing":** This is the view of both prisoner and prison guard, for instance, Hans Kallenbach, *Mit Adolf Hitler auf Festung Landsberg* (München: Kress & Hornung, 1939), 56, and Franz Hemmrich, unpublished memoir, ED 153-1, 28, IfZ. This has also been rendered as "commander's hill," probably from a misreading of the German Gothic script, in the case of Kallenbach, or the handwriting, in case of Hemmrich.

305 **The first was:** Stosstrupp Hitler trial: Proz.Reg.Nr. 187/1924, May 3, 1924, HA 67/1493.

305 **after hearing:** Rudolf Hess to Klara Hess, May 11, 1924, in Rudolf Hess, *Briefe 1908–1933*, ed. Wolf Rüdiger Hess (München: Langen Müller, 1987), 322.

305 **The People's Court:** This institution did not end with the Hitler trial, as often said, for instance, by Hans Hubert Hofmann, *Der Hitlerputsch. Krisenjahre deutscher Geschichte 1920–1924* (München: Nymphenburger Verlagshandlung, 1961), 245. It was instead the Hess trial. For more, see *Chronik der Bayerischen Justizverwaltung*, 342–45, 356, NL Ehard 90/3, BHStA.

305 **a routine:** Rudolf Hess to Fritz Hess, August 17, 1924 in Hess (1987), 349; Kallenbach (1939), 73–74, 78–79, 101 and 104; Lurker (1933), 17–19, 51–53, and 55; Hermann Fobke to Ludolf Haase, June 23, 1924, printed in Werner Jochmann, *Nationalsozialismus und Revolution. Ursprung und Geschichte der NSDAP in Hamburg 1922–1933. Dokumente* (Frankfurt am Main: Europäische Verlagsanstalt, 1963), 91–92.

305 **breakfast at seven:** Franz Hemmrich, unpublished memoir, ED 153-1, 110, IfZ.

305 **Kalfaktoren:** ED 153-1, 27, 31, 40, 59–60, 113, IfZ.

305 **practice jiu jitsu:** Kallenbach (1939), 80, and Hemmrich, ED 153-1, 34, IfZ. Both use the older spelling of "jiu jitsu," which lives on today in the Brazilian form [Brazilian jiu jitsu] as it developed from the 1920s in Rio de Janeiro.

306 **one of the better athletes:** Lurker (1933), 32, and Heinz (1938), 177.

306 **rarely, if ever:** Kallenbach (1939) 79.

306 **Hitler usually refrained:** Ibid. A leader could not play and risk losing, Ernst Hanfstaengl, *Zwischen Weissem und Braunem Haus. Memoiren eines politischen Aussenseiters* (München: R. Piper, 1970), 157.

306 **a referee of the matches:** Hemmrich in Heinz (1938), 174 and 183.

306 **"a Brazilian coffee planter":** Lurker (1933), 24.

306 **"a worker of the brain" and "a worker of the fist":** Rudolf Hess to Fritz Hess, August 17, 1924, Hess (1987), 349.

306 **"the Hitler Path":** Kallenbach (1939), 95, and Hemmrich, ED 153-1, 36–37, IfZ.

307 **"every blessed knot":** Hemmrich interview in Heinz (1938), 175.

307 **the prisoners of the main penitentiary:** The *Kalfaktoren*, ED 153-1, 27, 31, 40, 59–60, 113, IfZ.

307 **He sketched imaginary museums:** Rudolf Hess to Ilse Pröhl, May 18, 1924, in Hess (1987), 326–27.

308 **Tantalus-like tortures:** Kallenbach (1939), 95.

308 **"Papa Kriebel":** Kallenbach (1939), 65. Another nickname was "China," ED 153-1, 31, IfZ.

308 **"Thalia":** Kallenbach (1939), 71. Fobke was in Cell 11, not Cell 1, as sometimes claimed, John Toland, *Adolf Hitler* (New York: Ballantine Books, 1976), 267.

308 **"snowshoe battalion":** *Landsberger Ehrenbürger*, August 4, 1924, copy is found filed in HA 4/92.

309 **the prison band:** Lurker (1933), 34.

309 **"You see":** Hermann Fobke letter to Ludolf Haase, June 23, 1924, printed in Jochmann (1963), 92.

Chapter 52: *FACE-TO-FACE*

310 **"A political stronghold":** *Münchener Post*, November 5, 1924.

310 **after verifying:** *Fränkischer Kurier*, April 27, 1924 and ED 153-1, 47–48, IfZ.

310 **Sprechkarte:** Folder No. 4, JVA 17.000, StAM.

310 **Some of the first arrivals:** The list of visitors is at 143140, STA 14344, StAM.

311 **bearing a basket:** Heinrich Hoffmann, *Hitler Was My Friend*, trans. Lt-Col R. H. Stevens (London: Burke, 1955), 58–59.

311 **"flatterers and Byzantines":** *General Ludendorff über die Vorgänge in München*, HA 5/116.

311 **"fire eater" and "appeared calmer":** Kurt G. W. Ludecke, *I Knew Hitler: The Story of a Nazi Who Escaped the Blood Purge* (New York: Charles Scribner's Sons, 1938), 233.

311 **In all:** The list is at 143140, STA 14344, StAM. The list ends in October 1924, though Hitler probably did not receive many visitors in November and December, given his hope for parole and his work on his manuscript.

311 **"every class, every age":** Otto Lurker, *Hitler hinter Festungsmauern. Ein Bild aus trüben Tagen* (Berlin: E. S. Mittler & Sohn, 1933), 57. See also the Landsberg report to Ministry of Justice, September 18, 1924, HA 69/1501.

312 **less regional diversity:** For more on this subject, see Fleischmann (2015), 50–51.

312 **F. A. Brockhaus:** October 23, 1924, JVA 17.000, StAM.

312 **Ernst Schmidt:** *Sprechkarte*, May 11, 1924, folder 4, JVA 17.000, StAM. According to Lothar Machtan, this was Hitler's "special pal" and male lover, *The Hidden Hitler*, trans. John Brownjohn (New York: Basic Books, 2001), 67–69, 71, 88–100. Thomas Weber finds the assertions "tantalizing," but concludes that there is no evidence of such intimacy, *Hitler's First War: Adolf Hitler, the Men of the List Regiment, and the First World War* (Oxford: Oxford University Press, 2010), 138. There

is nothing in Landsberg files or the prison memoirs to confirm, refute, or otherwise shed light on the matter.

313 **his landlady, Maria:** Request for bill made for November and December 1923, Ernst Deuerlein, ed., *Der Hitler-Putsch. Bayerische Dokumente zum 8./9. November 1923* (Stuttgart: Deutsche Verlags-Anstalt, 1962), No.258, 628.

313 **April 15:** Björn Fontander, *Carin Göring skriver hem* (Stockholm: Carlssons, 1990), 154, and April 15, 1924, 143140, STA 14344, StAM.

314 **a full kiss:** ED 153-1, 48, IfZ.

314 **She tore open:** ED 153-1, 48–49, IfZ.

314 **Lotte:** May 15, 1924 and August 5, 1924, *Sprechkarte*, Folder No. 4, JVA 17.000, StAM, and 143140 STA 14344 StAM.

314 **feed the rumor mills:** A few years later, Bechstein was said to be pushing her daughter on Hitler in the tea room of the Vier Jahreszeiten, according to one hotel employee, Josef Lampersberger, February 1960, P.II.c. No. 1176, ZS 3146, IfZ.

314 **eight-minute visit:** *Sprechkarte*, May 22, 1924, Folder No. 4, JVA 17.000, StAM.

314 **Without women:** OSS Sourcebook, 47, NA, based upon Otto Dietrich, *Mit Hitler in die Macht. Persönliche Erlebnisse mit meinem Führer* (München: F. Eher, 1934), 142–43.

314 **"Aryan Bund" . . . "punch to the face":** Aryan Bund, letter to Hitler, April 4, 1924, printed in Lurker (1933), 25–26.

315 **Jewish enemies . . . "enormous villainy":** Lurker (1933), 29–30.

315 **According to his expense reports:** JVA 15162/17, StAM.

315 **"commander's wing":** This is sometimes translated as "commander's hill," probably due to a misreading of the Gothic script or the German handwriting of sources from Landsberg Prison. See note above on page 429.

315 **pies:** Hitler letter to Frau Deutschenbauer, October 1, 1924, Eberhard Jäckel und Axel Kuhn, eds., *Hitler. Sämtliche Aufzeichnungen 1905–1924* (Stuttgart: Deutsche Verlags-Anstalt, 1980), Nr. 661, 1245.

315 **coffee beans:** ED 153-1, 115, IfZ.

315 **a gramophone player:** Rudolf Hess to Ilse Pröhl, October 14, 1924, in Rudolf Hess, *Briefe 1908–1933*, ed. Wolf Rüdiger Hess (München: Langen Müller, 1987), 353.

316 **"flood of cards" . . . "mountain of packages":** Lurker (1933), 20. A description of the mail also appears in *Fränkischer Kurier*, April 27, 1924.

316 **laundry baskets:** ED 153-1, 46, IfZ.

316 **a delicatessen:** Ernst Hanfstaengl, *Zwischen Weissem und Braunem Haus. Memoiren eines politischen Aussenseiters* (München: R. Piper, 1970), 157.

316 **a flower shop:** Hemmrich interview in Heinz A. Heinz, *Germany's Hitler* (London: Hurst & Blackett, 1938), 172, and greenhouse in his memoir, ED 153-1, 47, IfZ.

316 **Hitler let it be known:** *Völkischer Kurier*, July 15, 1924.

Chapter 53: *LIES, STUPIDITY, AND COWARDICE*

317 **"The rulers of the day":** *Hitler's Secret Conversations 1941–1944,* intro. H. R. Trevor-Roper (New York: Signet Books, 1961), 46.

317 **"Rolf Eidhalt":** December 5, 1923, HA 4/90 and January 15, 1924, HA 68/1497A.

317 **anagram of the name:** Alfred Rosenberg, *Memoirs of Alfred Rosenberg,* ed. Serge Lange and Ernst von Schenck, and trans. Eric Posselt (Chicago: Ziff-Davis, 1949), 77.

317 **in the guise:** Police report, *Illegale Fortführung des verbotene Organisationen,* HA 68/1497, and David Jablonsky, *The Nazi Party in Dissolution: Hitler and the Verbotzeit, 1923–1925* (London: F. Cass, 1989), 48.

317 **a split between old party members:** Rosenberg led the party now called Grossdeutsche Volksgemeinschaft, or Greater German National Community (GVG). Esser, Streicher, and their allies usurped Rosenberg. Ludendorff branched out into the Deutschvölkische Freiheitspartei, or National Socialist Freedom Party (DVFP).

318 **"I have decided to withdraw":** Hitler to Ludolf Haase, June 16, 1924, letter printed in Werner Jochmann, *Nationalsozialismus und Revolution. Ursprung und Geschichte der NSDAP in Hamburg 1922–1933. Dokumente* (Frankfurt am Main: Europäische Verlagsanstalt, 1963), 78. Hitler's decision was only for the duration of his fortress confinement, Hermann Fobke wrote in a letter to Dr. Adalbert Volck, July 18, 1924, copy in HA 15A/1632 and printed in Jochmann (1963), 94. See also Hitler's words on the episode in *Völkischer Beobachter,* February 26, 1925.

318 **"a real leader":** Hitler to Ludolf Haase, June 16, 1924 in Jochmann (1963), 78.

318 **"resigned the leadership"** . . . **"comprehensive book":** *Völkischer Kurier,* July 7, 1924.

318 **Landsberg records:** 143140, STA 14344, StAM.

318 **a new organization called the Frontbann:** Rudolf Hess, *Erklärung,* October 9, 1924, and another outline of differences, XIX 734/24, December 1, 1924, HA 69/1501. For more on this organization, see files at HA 15A and 16A/1627–37, and treatment by Eleanor Hancock, *Ernst Röhm: Hitler's SA Chief of Staff* (New York: Palgrave Macmillan, 2008), 71–81, as well as Ernst Röhm, *The Memoirs of Ernst Röhm,* intro. Eleanor Hancock and trans. Geoffrey Brooks (London: Frontline Books, 2012), 221–22.

319 **stacks of books, magazines:** Wilhelm Laforce, *Leipziger Neueste Nachrichten,* August 9, 1933, cited in Othmar Plöckinger, *Geschichte eines Buches. Adolf Hitlers 'Mein Kampf' 1922–1945* (München: Oldenbourg, 2011), 61.

319 **"a thorough reckoning":** *Volksruf,* May 17, 1924, cited in Plöckinger (2011), 34.

319 ***Four and a Half Years of Struggle:*** A copy of the brochure is in Folder No. 3/1, JVA 17.000, StAM.

319 **"The Middle Class"** . . . **"The Bolshevikization of Europe":** Ibid.

320 **it was his brother Gregor:** Otto Strasser, *Hitler and I*, trans. Gwenda David and Eric Mosbacher (Boston: Houghton Mifflin Company, 1940), 53.

320 **Strasser was not interned:** Strafgefängnis Landsberg a. Lech, February 4 to February 26, HA 3/66.

320 **Hitler had turned to writing:** Julius Schaub, July 27, 1951, ZS 137-1, IfZ..

320 **As early as 1922:** For more, see Plöckinger (2011), 11–15.

320 **"He occupies himself every day":** Ian Kershaw, *Hitler 1889–1936: Hubris* (New York: W. W. Norton, 1999), 235, and Ernst Deuerlein, ed., *Der Aufstieg der NSDAP in Augenzeugenberichten* (Düsseldorf: Deutscher Taschenbuch Verlag, 1978), 238,

321 **"one long speech"** and **"inaccurate German":** Peter Kurth, *American Cassandra: The Life of Dorothy Thompson* (Boston: Little, Brown and Company, 1990), 159.

321 **"He who has not himself"** and **"contains more mistakes":** Joachim C. Fest, *Hitler*, trans. Richard and Clara Winston (New York: Harcourt Brace Jovanovich, 1974), 203.

321 **the resemblance of Hitler's manuscript:** For more, see Plöckinger (2011), 22.

321 **Ilse Pröhl, however:** Ilse Hess letter to Werner Maser, dated June 29, 1965, Werner Maser, *Hitler's Mein Kampf: An Analysis*, trans. R. H. Barry (London: Faber and Faber, 1970), 23. She claimed that Hitler had typed it himself using two fingers, at least for the first volume. Emil Maurice had long said that as well, for instance, June 23, 1951, ZS 270, IfZ, and Max Amann said he had written it first in longhand, August 13, 1945, G.N.S., ZS-809, IfZ. Most Hitler biographies, by contrast, have presented Hitler as dictating the text. One exception was John Toland, who also knew that Hitler had typed it, *Adolf Hitler* (New York: Ballantine Books, 1976), 266, though he, too, had Hess taking dictation at times. Another exception was the biography by Otto Julius Frauendorf and Richard Freiherr von Frankenberg, writing under the names Walter Görlitz und Herbert A. Quint, *Adolf Hitler. Eine Biographie* (Stuttgart: Steingrüben-Verlag, 1952), 236. See also Dr. Ha/Ku, August 14, 1940, HA 3/63.

321 **typewriter table:** Hemmrich, ED 153-1, 39, IfZ.

321 **Winifred Wagner also sent:** Brigitte Hamann, *Winifred Wagner oder Hitlers Bayreuth* (München: Piper, 2002), 99.

322 **"the tribune":** Hitler must have liked this nickname for another reason: This was the title used by the hero of his beloved Wagner opera *Rienzi*.

322 **"made ever longer":** Rudolf Hess to Ilse Pröhl, June 29, 1924, in Rudolf Hess, *Briefe 1908–1933*, ed. Wolf Rüdiger Hess (München: Langen Müller, 1987), 342.

322 **"coming man":** Rudolf Hess to Ilse Pröhl, July 23, 1924, in Hess (1987), 347.

322 **may have also inspired the legend:** Plöckinger (2011), 122–25. Dictation figured prominently in the accounts of the Landsberg Prison guards, Otto Lurker, *Hitler hinter Festungsmauern. Ein Bild aus trüben Tagen* (Berlin: E. S. Mittler & Sohn, 1933), 56, and Franz Hemmrich, though, significantly, not those of the prisoners.

323 **dated October 16, 1924:** Adolf Hitler, *Mein Kampf*, trans. Ralph Manheim (Boston: Houghton Mifflin Company, 1943), dedication.

323 **this autumn publication date:** Manuscript estimated at 400 pages in length in early November, *Fränkischer Kurier*, November 6, 1924.

323 **Bechstein is believed to have received:** The head of the NSDAP Hauptarchiv attempted in vain to obtain the manuscript, or at least a few sheets, or even a photograph, for an upcoming exhibition. NSDAP Hauptarchiv, file HA 3/63. The view that Bechstein possesed a copy is found before, too, for instance, G. Ward Price, *I Know These Dictators* (London: George G. Harrap & Co. ltd, 1937), 83–84, and not long afterward, too, such as Max Amann, August 13, 1945, ZS-809, IfZ.

323 **he would receive the typewriter:** Anna Maria Sigmund, *Des Führers bester Freund. Adolf Hitler, seine Nichte Geli Raubal und der "Ehrenarier" Emil Maurice— eine Dreiecksbeziehung* (München: Heyne, 2003), 81.

323 **"To my loyal and brave":** Image of inscription in Sigismund (2003), 73.

Chapter 54: "A PERPETUAL DANGER"

324 **"Germany against the":** *Landsberger Ehrenbürger*, August 4, 1924.

324 **Hitler believed that he would be freed:** Hermann Fobke to Dr. Adalbert Volck, July 29, 1924, printed in Werner Jochmann, *Nationalsozialismus und Revolution. Ursprung und Geschichte der NSDAP in Hamburg 1922–1933. Dokumente* (Frankfurt am Main: Europäische Verlagsanstalt, 1963), 124. Belief in early parole persisted, Fobke to Ludolf Haase, August 21, 1924, 134.

325 **"hair stand on end":** Hitler to Jakob Werlin, September 13, 1924, STA 14344, StAM.

325 **"Nothing shall and will":** Wilhelm Briemann, August 21, 1924, HA 4/92.

325 **"if only not in vain":** Friedrich Weber, note, HA 4/92.

325 **"good conduct":** Otto Gritschneder, *Bewährungsfrist für den Terroristen Adolf H. Der Hitler-Putsch und die bayerische Justiz* (München: Verlag C. H. Beck 1990), 97–98.

325 **"Hitler shows himself"** and **"During the ten months":** Ian Kershaw, *Hitler 1889–1936: Hubris* (New York: W. W. Norton, 1999), 235. The German text was published by Otto Lurker, *Hitler hinter Festungsmauern. Ein Bild aus trüben Tagen* (Berlin: E. S. Mittler & Sohn, 1933), 60–62.

326 **"a surrender of the constitutional":** Ehard unpublished memoir, 41, NL Ehard 99, BHStA.

327 **The implications were clear:** Jewish Telegraphic Agency, September 19, 1924.

327 **the full support of the Munich police:** police report (VIa), September 16, 1924, HA 68/1497A, and September 27, 1924, STA 14344, StAM.

327 **They found letters:** Copies of letters Kriebel to Röhm, Friedrich Weber to Mathilde Weber, and others confiscated are located at STA 14344 StAM and HA 69/1501.

327 **"a perpetual danger":** Polizeidirektion München, VIa 2427, September 23, 1924, STA 14344, StAM.

327 **already ruled in favor of parole:** Beschluss Anz.Verz. XIX 421/1923, September 25, 1924, STA 14344, StAM.

327 **not likely:** *Allgemeine Zeitung*, September 26, 1924.

327 **Stenglein submitted:** Anz.Verz.XIX 421/23, September 29, 1924, STA 14344, StAM, and Kershaw (1999), 237.

328 **Supporters circulated a petition:** HA 14A/1500 and the press campaign, for instance, *Völkischer Kurier*, November 23–24, 1924.

328 **"extraordinarily difficult decision":** Nr. 26899, July 6, 1924, Staatsanwaltschaften 3099, StAM. Hitler later credited these lay judges, or particularly Philipp Herrmann, "a scowling, supercilious man," Hitler said, according to the table talk, February 3–4, 1942, *Hitler's Secret Conversations 1941–1944*, intro. H. R. Trevor-Roper (New York: Signet Books, 1961), 282

329 **Austrian authorities had been prepared:** D. C. Watt, "Die Bayerischen Bemühungen um Ausweisung Hitlers 1924," *Vierteljahrshefte für Zeitgeschichte* 6 (1958), 272.

329 **the Austrian government had changed:** Jewish Telegraphic Agency, October 15, 1924.

329 **"serious dangers":** Austrian efforts to block deportation are in Franz Jetzinger, *Hitler's Youth*, trans. Lawrence Wilson (London: Hutchinson, 1958), 163–64. A Social Democratic deputy in the assembly of Upper Austria until 1934, when Dolfuss suppressed the party, Jetzinger also served as librarian at Upper Austrian Provincial Archives in Linz. For more on this issue, see also D. C. Watt, "Die Bayerischen Bemühungen um Ausweisung Hitlers 1924," *Vierteljahrshefte für Zeitgeschichte* 6 (1958), 270–80.

329 **their final attempt to block:** Der erste Staatsanwalt, December 5, 1924, 154151, STA 14344, StAM.

329 **Leybold interviewed several guards:** Folder No. 3/1, JVA 17.000, StAM.

330 **"rather innocuous"** and **"political idealist":** Leybold, December 14, 1924, 152149, STA 14344, StAM.

330 **"one-time Bavarian Minister of Justice":** Robert M. W. Kempner, "Blueprint of the Nazi Underground—Past and Future Subversive Activities," *Research Studies of the State College of Washington*, XIII, No. 2, June 1945, Document B. Weimar lawyer Max Hirschberg noted the minister's influence in this affair too, in his memoir, *Jude und Demokrat. Erinnerungen eines Münchener Rechtsanwalts 1883 bis 1939*, ed. Reinhard Weber (München: R. Oldenbourg Verlag, 1998), 242. For more hints on Gürtner's influence, see Ehard's continuation to his unpublished memoir in his papers, NL Ehard 99, 6, BHStA. This claim is also made by Wilhelm Hoegner, *Die Verratene Republik. Deutsche Geschichte 1919–1933* (München: Nymphenburger Verlagshandlung, 1979), 190, and Otto Gritschneder *Bewährungsfrist für den Terroristen Adolf H. Der Hitler-Putsch und die bayerische Justiz* (München: Verlag C. H. Beck 1990), 107, who concluded that the decision could only have been political. Gürtner's unconvincing denial of any influence on

the proceedings was published before the trial, for instance, Telegraphen-Union, February 25, 1924.

330 **the Reichstag elections:** Bernd Steger, "Der Hitlerprozess und Bayerns Verhältnis zum Reich 1923/1924," *Vierteljahrshefte für Zeitgeschichte* 23 (1977), note 66, 463.

331 **News of Hitler's imminent release:** Dringendes Telegramm, XIX 421/23, December 20, 1924, STA 14344, StAM.

331 **"Enormous jubiliation":** Hemmrich interview in Heinz A. Heinz, *Germany's Hitler* (London: Hurst & Blackett, 1938), 193.

331 **"When I left Landsberg":** February 3–4, 1942, *Hitler's Secret Conversations 1941– 1944*, intro. H. R. Trevor-Roper (New York: Signet Books, 1961), 282

331 **3 years, 333 days:** A.V.XIX 421/1923, March 18, 1926, HA 69/1501.

331 **"The race for Hitler":** Rudolf Hess to Ilse Pröhl, December 20, 1924, in Rudolf Hess, *Briefe 1908–1933*, ed. Wolf Rüdiger Hess (München: Langen Müller, 1987), 359.

331 **they drove off:** ED 153-1, 63, IfZ.

331 **"Get a move" and "Anyway":** Heinrich Hoffmann, *Hitler Was My Friend*, trans. Lt-Col R. H. Stevens (London: Burke, 1955), 61.

Epilogue

333 **Many astute observers:** *New York Times*, November 10, 1923, and *Frankfurter Zeitung*, November 10, 1923.

333 **Conviction of the death:** Otto Gritschneder, *Der Hitler-Prozess und sein Richter Georg Neithardt. Skandalurteil von 1924 ebnet Hitler den Weg* (München: Verlag C. H. Beck, 2001), 51. See also Alexander Graf zu Dohna, "Der Münchener Hochverratsprozess," *Deutsche Juristen-Zeitung* 29 (1924), 333ff, and Neithardt's own response, April 1924, Nachlass Hans Ehard 97, BHStA.

334 **"that fearless faith":** John Toland, *Adolf Hitler* (New York: Ballantine Books, 1976), 274. See also H. R. Trevor-Roper, "The Mind of Adolf Hitler," *Hitler's Secret Conversations 1941–1944*, intro. H. R. Trevor-Roper (New York: Signet Books, 1961), xxviii.

335 **"How that man" and "Those days of his trial":** Interview published in Theodore Abel, *Why Hitler Came into Power: An Answer Based on the Original Life Stories of Six Hundred of His Followers* (New York: Prentice-Hall, 1938), 70.

335 **"idealist" and "carried to the stars":** Toby Thacker, *Joseph Goebbels: Life and Death* (New York: Palgrave Macmillan, 2010), 33. Thacker calls the Hitler trial "a turning point" in Goebbels's life, 34, and Peter Longerich dates this "turn to politics" to April 4, 1924, *Goebbels: A Biography*, trans. Alan Bance, Jeremy Noakes, and Lesley Sharpe (New York: Random House, 2015), 36–39.

336 **"What you stated" and "To you a god":** Joachim C. Fest, *Hitler*, trans. Richard and Clara Winston (New York: Harcourt Brace Jovanovich, 1974), 200.

Illustration Credits

Frontispiece The Bürgerbräukeller in Munich, 1923 (b/w photo) / © SZ Photo / Bridgeman Images

INSERT

1. NSDAP Hauptarchiv
2. Armed Nazis prepare to enter Munich following the Hitler Putsch or Beer-Hall Putsch (November 8, 1923) / Photo © PVDE / Bridgeman Images
3. Hitler Putsch, 1923 (b/w photo) / © SZ Photo / Scherl / Bridgeman Images
4. Munich Putsch, 1923 (b/w photo) / German Photographer (20th Century) / Private Collection / Peter Newark Historical Pictures / Bridgeman Images
5. Mounted police after the defeat of the Hitler Putsch, 1923 (b/w photo) / © SZ Photo / Knorr & Hirth / Bridgeman Images
6. National Archives
7. Library of Congress, Prints & Photographs Division
8. Library of Congress, Prints & Photographs Division
9. Library of Congress, Prints & Photographs Division
10. Library of Congress, Prints & Photographs Division
11. akg-images / Interfoto
12. The trial of Adolf Hitler, 1924 / © SZ Photo / Bridgeman Images
13. Trial against Hitler and Ludendorff on February 26, 1924 (b/w photo) / © SZ Photo / Scherl / Bridgeman Images
14. Erich Ludendorff and Adolf Hitler (b/w photo) / © SZ Photo / Scherl / Bridgeman Images
15. National Archives
16. Munich Putsch trial (b/w photo), German Photographer (20th Century) / Private Collection / Peter Newark Military Pictures / Bridgeman Images
17. Hitler's prison cell during his detention in the fortress of Landsberg (b/w photo) / © SZ Photo / Scherl / Bridgeman Images
18. Adolf Hitler in Landsberg Prison, 1924 (b/w photo), German Photographer (20th Century) / Private Collection / Peter Newark Historical Pictures / Bridgeman Images
19. Adolf Hitler in prison in Landsberg (b/w photo) / © SZ Photo / Bridgeman Images
20. Library of Congress, Prints & Photographs Division
21. National Archives
22. Adolf Hitler on December 20, 1924 / Photo © Tallandier / Bridgeman Images

Index